Schriften zum europäischen, internationalen und vergleichenden Unternehmens- und Wirtschaftsrecht

Edited by

Prof. Dr. Ulrich Ehricke, Universität zu Köln
Prof. Dr. Ingo Saenger, Universität Münster
Prof. Dr. Christoph H. Seibt, LL.M.,
Freshfields Bruckhaus Deringer LLP

Volume 16

Fabian Hertel

Effective Internal Control and Corporate Compliance

A Law and Economics Impact Analysis of the Mysteries of a German Aktiengesellschaft Listed on the NYSE

Nomos

The Deutsche Nationalbibliothek lists this publication in the Deutsche Nationalbibliografie; detailed bibliographic data are available on the Internet at http://dnb.d-nb.de

a.t.: Berlin, HU, Diss., 2018

original title: Effective Internal Control and Corporate Compliance – Mandates of SOX, SEC Rules, FCPA, USSG, NYSE Listing Standards and German Law, Including Best Practice and Enforcement, and a Law and Economics Impact Analysis of the Mysteries of a German Listed Aktiengesellschaft being Listed on the NYSE.

ISBN 978-3-8487-5743-5 (Print)
978-3-8452-9906-8 (ePDF)

British Library Cataloguing-in-Publication Data
A catalogue record for this book is available from the British Library.

ISBN 978-3-8487-5743-5 (Print)
978-3-8452-9906-8 (ePDF)

Library of Congress Cataloging-in-Publication Data
Hertel, Fabian
Effective Internal Control and Corporate Compliance
A Law and Economics Impact Analysis of the Mysteries of a German Aktiengesellschaft Listed on the NYSE
Fabian Hertel
651 pp.
Includes bibliographic references.

ISBN 978-3-8487-5743-5 (Print)
978-3-8452-9906-8 (ePDF)

1st Edition 2019

Dedicated to my family.

"If men were angels, no government would be necessary.
If angels were to govern men, neither external nor
internal controls on government would be necessary."
James Madison, The Federalist Papers, No. 51, 1788

Preliminary Remarks

The Faculty of Law of Humboldt-Universität zu Berlin accepted this dissertation in the summer semester 2018. The major part of the thesis was finalized at the end of 2015. Legislative changes and important updates have been incorporated until June 2017.

I owe my deepest thank to Prof. Dr. iur. Dr. rer. nat. Dr. h.c. Christian Kirchner, LL.M. (Harvard) (†) who accepted my proposal for this research and encouraged me in my pursuit to go "beyond" the law and to include rules and related incentives of non-statutory provisions.

Also, I owe my greatest thank to Prof. a.D. Dr. Christine Windbichler, LL.M. (Berkeley) who took on the task of the supervision of my thesis at a well-advanced stage of drafting and who provided invaluable and detailed comments, and helped me, in every respect, to finish my research. I am very grateful.

Equally, I express my gratitude to Prof. Richard W. Painter, S. Walter Richey Professor of Corporate Law, University of Minnesota Law School who took on the task as second reader showing the bond between the Faculty of Law of Humboldt-Universität zu Berlin and University of Minnesota Law School. Further, I thank Prof. em. Dr. Thomas Raiser and Prof. Dr. Gregor Bachmann, LL.M. (Michigan) for forming the commission of my disputation.

The preliminary basis of my thesis was laid by my research, supervised by Prof. Painter, conducted at the University of Minnesota Law School during my Master of Laws-studies (2008/09). During these studies, Prof. Francesco Parisi, Oppenheimer Wolff and Donnelly Professor of Law, shaped my understanding of Law and Economics. I gained deeper insight into U.S. law during my stay as *Visiting Researcher* at the University of California Berkeley School of Law (Boalt Hall) sponsored by Prof. em. Richard Buxbaum.

This thesis was supported by a stipend of the Land Berlin - *Elsa-Neumann-Stipendium* (formerly NaföG-Stipendium) and the German Academic Exchange Service (*DAAD*) in respect to my stay at the University of California Berkeley School of Law (Boalt Hall).

I owe special thanks to Dr. phil. Sebastian Schweinfurth who made the numerous hours at the library more bearable and to my wife, Nicola Iburg, who commented on my 'work-in-progress' and endured my student life longer than expected.

Berlin, November 2018

Short Table of Contents

Table of Contents

Abbreviations

AAA	American Accounting Association
ABA	American Bar Association
Academy of Management Rev.	Academy of Management Review
ACCA	Association of Chartered Certified Accountants
Acct. Horizons	Accounting Horizons (*Journal*)
Acct. Mgmt. Rev.	Accounting Management Review
Acct. Rev.	Accounting Review
ACFE	Association of Certified Fraud Examiners
Admin. L. Rev.	Administrative Law Review
AeA	American Electronics Association
AG	(German) stock corporation (*Aktiengesellschaft*)
AG	Die Aktiengesellschaft (*Journal*)
AICP	American Institute of Certified Public Accountants
AIM	Alternative Investment Market (in London)
AktG	(German) Stock Corporation Act
Ala. L. Rev.	Alabama Law Review
alt.	alternative
Am. Crim. L. Rev.	American Criminal Law Review
Am. J. Comp. L.	American Journal of Comparative Law
approx.	approximately
AReG	Abschlussprüfungsreformgesetz
AS	Auditing Standard (PCAPB)
B.U. L. Rev.	Boston University Law Review
B.Y.U.L. Rev.	Brigham Young University Law Review
BaFin	(German) Federal Financial Supervisory Authority (*Bundesanstalt für Finanzdienstleistungsaufsicht*)
BAG	(German) Federal Labor Court (*Bundesarbeitsgericht*)
BB	Betriebs-Berater (*Journal*)

BDI	Bundesverband der Deutschen Industrie
BDSG	(German) Federal Data Protection Act (*Bundesdatenschutzgesetz*)
Begr RegE	Reasoning of draft bill by the Federal Government (*Begründung Regierungsentwurf*)
BetrVG	(German) Works Constitution Act (*Betriebsverfassungsgesetz*)
BGB	(German) Civil Code (*Bürgerliches Gesetzbuch*)
BGBl.	Bundesgesetzblatt
BGH	(German) Federal Court of Justice (*Bundesgerichtshof*)
BGHZ	Decisions of the BGH in civil cases (*Entscheidungen des Bundesgerichtshofes in Zivilsachen*) (*Journal*)
BilMoG	Bilanzrechtsmodernisierungsgesetz
BKA	(German) Federal Criminal Police Office (*Bundeskriminalamt*)
BKR	Zeitschrift für Bank- und Kapitalmarktrecht
BMI	(German) Federal Ministry of the Interior
Boston College L. Rev.	Boston College Law Review
BT-Drucks.	Official Records of Bundestag (*Bundestagsdrucksachen*)
Buffalo Crim. L. Rev.	Buffalo Criminal Law Review
Bus. Law.	The Business Lawyer (*Journal*)
Business and Society Rev.	Business and Society Review
BVerfG	German) Constitutional Court (*Bundesverfassungsgericht*)
Cardozo L. Rev.	Cardozo Law Review
Case W. Res. L. Rev.	Case Western Reserve Law Review
Cath. U. L. Rev.	Catholic University Law Review
CB	Compliance Berater (*Journal*)
CCO	Chief Compliance Officer
CCZ	Corporate Compliance Zeitschrift
CEO	Chief Executive Officer
cf.	(*confer*) compare with
CFO	Chief Financial Officer
CFR	(U.S.) Code of Federal Regulations
Colum. Bus. L. Rev.	Columbia Business Law Review

Colum. L. Rev.	Columbia Law Review
COM	Commission
COO	Chief Operating Officer
Cornell L. Rev.	Cornell Law Review
COSO	Committee of Sponsoring Organizations of the Treadway Commission
CPA	Certified Public Accountant
CSR	Corporate Social Responsibility
D&O insurance	Directors' and Officers' insurance
DB	Der Betrieb (*Journal*)
Del. Ch.	Delaware Court of Chancery
Del. J. Corp. L.	Delaware Journal of Corporate Law
DGCL	Delaware General Corporate Law
DIIR	Deutsche Institut für interne Revision
DLF	Deutschlandfunk
DOJ	(U.S.) Department of Justice
Drucks.	Printed Matter (*Drucksache*)
DStR	Deutsches Steuerrecht (*Journal*)
e.g.	(*exempli gratia*) for example
EBOR	European Business Organization Law Review
EC	European Community
ECFR	European Company and Financial Law Review
ECtHR	European Court of Human Rights
ed.	editor
EIOPA	European Insurance and Occupational Pensions Authority
Emory L. J.	Emory Law Journal
EPA	Environmental Protection Agency
ERC	Ethics Resource Center
ERM	Enterprise Risk Management
et seq.	(*et sequentes*) and those (pages or sections) that follow
EU	European Union
EuZW	Europäische Zeitschrift für Wirtschaftsrecht
EWiR	Entscheidungen zum Wirtschaftrecht (*Journal*)
Exchange Act	The Securities Exchange Act of 1934

F.A.Z.	Frankfurter Allgemeine Zeitung
FAQ	Frequently Asked Questions
FASB	Financial Accounting Standards Board
FCPA	Foreign Corrupt Practices Act of 1977
FEI	Financial Executives International
FINRA	Financial Industry Regulatory Authority
Fla. St. U. L. Rev.	Florida State University Law Review
fn.	footnote
Fordham J. Corp. & Fin. L.	Fordham Journal of Corporate & Financial Law
Ga. J. Int'l & Comp. L.	Georgia Journal of International & Comparative Law
Ga. St. U. L. Rev.	Georgia State University Law Review
GAO	(U.S.) Government Accountability Office
GC	General Counsel
GCGC	German Corporate Governance Code
Geo. L. J.	Georgetown Law Review
GG	(German) Basic Law (*Grundgesetz*)
GmbHG	(German) Limited Liability Companies Act
GWB	(German) Antitrust Act (*Gesetz gegen Wettbewerbsbeschränkungen*)
GWR	Gesellschafts- und Wirtschaftsrecht (*Journal*)
Harvard Bus. Rev.	Harvard Business Review
Harvard J. Law & Public Policy	Harvard Journal Law & Public Policy
Harvard L. Rev.	Harvard Law Review
HFR	Humboldt Forum Recht
HGB	(German) Commercial Code (*Handelsgesetzbuch*)
HHS	(U.S.) Department of Health and Human Services
Hous. L. Rev.	Houston Law Review
i.e.	(*id est*) that is
IAS	International Accounting Standards
ICC	International Chamber of Commerce
ICFR	Internal Control over Financial Reporting

id.	(*idem*) in the same work
IDW	Institut der Wirtschaftsprüfer
IFRS	International Financial Reporting Standards
IIA	Institute of Internal Auditors
InstitutsVergV	(German) Remuneration Ordinance for Institutions (*Instituts-Vergütungsverordnung*)
IMA	Institute of Management Accountants
Inc.	Incorporated
Int. J. Disclosure and Governance	International Journal of Disclosure and Governance
Iowa J. Corp. L.	Iowa Journal of Corporate Law
Iowa L. Rev.	Iowa Law Review
IPO	Initial Public Offering
ISA	International Standard on Auditing
IT	Information technology
ITRB	Der IT-Rechts-Berater (*Journal*)
J. Legal Stud.	Journal of Legal Studies
J. Acct. and Econ.	Journal Accounting and Economics
J. Bus. & Tech.	Journal of Business and Technical Communication
J. Corp. Law	Journal of Corporate Law
J. Econ. Perspectives	Journal of Economic Perspectives
J.L. & Econ.	Journal of Law & Economics
Journal of Bus. Ethics	Journal of Business Ethics
JuS	Juristische Schulung (*Journal*)
KGaA	(German) Limited Joint-Stock Partnership (*Kommanditgesellschaft auf Aktien*)
KonTraG	(German) Law on Control and Transparency in Business (*Gesetz zur Kontrolle und Transparenz im Unternehmensbereich*)
KoR	Zeitschrift für internationale und kapitalmarktorientierte Rechnungslegung
LAG	(German) Labor Court (*Landesarbeitsgericht*)
LCM	Listed Company Manual
LG	(German) District Court (*Landgericht*)
Loy. U. Chi. L. J.	Loyola University Chicago Law Journal
LTO	Legal Tribune Online

MaComp	Minimum Requirements for the Compliance Function and Additional Requirements Governing Rules of Conduct, Organization and Transparency pursuant to Sections 31 et seq. of the Securities Trading Act (Wertpapierhandelsgesetz - WpHG) for Investment Services Enterprises - MaComp
MaGo	Minimum Requirements for the Governance System of Insurance Undertakings - Circular 2/2017 (VA)
mar.	margin
MaRisk (BA)	Minimum Requirements for Risk Management - MaRisk, Circulation 10/2012 (BA)
Marq. L. Rev.	Marquette Law Review
MBA	Master of Business Administration
Memo	Memorandum
Mercer L. Rev.	Mercer Law Review
Mich. L. Rev.	Michigan Law Review
Mich. St. L. Rev.	Michigan State Law Review
MiFID	Markets in Financial Instruments Directive
MMR	MultiMedia und Recht (*Journal*)
MschrKrim	Monatschrift Kriminologie und Strafrechtsreform (*Journal*)
N.Y.L. Sch. L. Rev.	New York Law School Law Review
N.Y.U.L. Rev.	New York University Law Review
NACD	National Association of Corporate Directors
NASD	National Association of Securities Dealers
NJOZ	Neue Juristische Online Zeitschrift
NJW	Neue Juristische Wochenschrift (*Journal*)
Notre Dame L. Rev.	Notre Dame Law Review
NRW	North Rhine-Westphalia
NStZ	Neue Zeitschrift für Strafrecht
NYSE	New York Stock Exchange
NYSE Commission	NYSE Commission on Corporate Governance
NYSE-LCM	NYSE Listed Company Manual
NZ L. Rev.	New Zealand Law Review
NZA	Neue Zeitschrift für Arbeitsrecht

NZG	Neue Zeitschrift für Gesellschaftsrecht
NZWiSt	Neue Zeitschrift für Wirtschafts-, Steuer- und Unternehmensstrafrecht
OECD	Organization for Economic Co-operation and Development
OJEU	Official Journal of the European Union
OLG	(German) Higher Regional Court (*Oberlandesgericht*)
OWiG	(German) Law on Administrative Offences
p. / pp.	page(s)
par.	paragraph
PCAOB	Public Company Accounting Oversight Board
PS	Prüfstandard
Pub. L.	Public Law
PwC	PricewaterhouseCoopers
Q.J. Econ.	Quarterly Journal of Economic
RabelsZ	Rabels Zeitschrift für ausländisches und internationales Privatrecht
RegE	Draft bill by the Federal Government (*Regierungsentwurf*)
Rev. Finac. Stud.	Review of Financial Studies
RICO	Racketeer Influenced and Corrupt Organizations Act
S. C. L. Rev.	South Carolina Law Review
San Diego Int'l L. J.	San Diego International Law Journal
SAS	Statement on Auditing Standards issued by the Auditing Standards Board of the American Institute of Certified Public Accountants
SEC	Securities and Exchange Commission
sec.	Section
Securities Act	The Securities Act of 1933
Seton Hall L. Rev.	Seton Hall Law Review
SOX	Sarbanes Oxley Act of 2002
SPD	(German) Social Democratic Party

SRO	Self-Regulatory Organization
SSRN	Social Science Research Network
Stan. L. Rev.	Stanford Law Review
Stetson L. Rev.	Stetson Law Review
StGB	(German) Criminal Code (*Strafgesetzbuch*)
StPO	(German) Criminal Procedural Code (*Strafprozessordnung*)
Supreme Court Econ. Rev.	Supreme Court Economic Review
TKG	(German) Telecommunications Act (*Telekommunikationsgesetz*)
TransPuG	Transparenz- und Publizitätsgesetz
U. Chi. L. Rev.	University of Chicago Law Review
U. Pa. L. Rev.	University of Pennsylvania Law Review
U. Rich. L. Rev.	University of Richmond Law Review
U.C. Davis Bus. L. J.	University of California Davis Business Law Journal
U.S.	United States
U.S. GAAP	United States Generally Accepted Accounting Principles
U.S.F. L. Rev.	University of San Francisco Law Review
UK	United Kingdom
USAM	United States Attorney Manual
USC	United States Code
USSC	United States Sentencing Commission
USSG	United States Sentencing Guidelines
Va. J. Soc. Pol'y & L.	Virginia Journal of Social Policy and the Law
Va. L. Rev.	Virginia Law Review
VAG	(German) Insurance Supervision Act (*Versicherungsaufsichtsgesetz*)
Vand. L. Rev.	Vanderbilt Law Review
VGR	Gesellschaftsrechtliche Vereinigung - Wissenschaftliche Vereinigung für Unternehmens- und Gesellschaftsrecht
VorstAG	(German) Act on the Appropriateness of Management Board Compensation (*Gesetz zur Angemessenheit der Vorstandsvergütung*)
vs.	versus

Wake Forest L. Rev.	Wake Forest Law Review
Wall St. J.	Wall Street Journal
Wash. U. L. Quarterly	Washington University Law Quarterly
WDR	Westdeutscher Rundfunk
Willamette L. Rev.	Willamette Law Review
wistra	Zeitschrift für Wirtschafts- und Steuerstrafrecht
WM	Wertpapier Mitteilungen IV (*Journal*)
Wm. Mitchell L. Rev.	William Mitchell Law Review
WpHG	(German) Securities Trading Act (*Wertpapierhandelsgesetz*)
WPK	(German) Chamber of Public Accountants (*Wirtschaftsprüferkammer*)
WuW	Wirtschaft und Wettbewerb (*Journal*)
Yale J. on Reg.	Yale Journal on Regulation
Yale L. J.	Yale Law Journal
ZCG	Zeitschrift für Corporate Governance
ZfSozW	Zeitschrift für Sozialwissenschaft
ZHR	Zeitschrift für das Gesamte Handels- und Wirtschaftsrecht
ZIP	Zeitschrift für Wirtschaftsrecht
ZIR	Zeitschrift Interne Revision
ZIS	Zeitschrift für Internationale Strafrechtsdogmatik
ZRFC	Risk, Fraud & Compliance (*Journal*)
ZRFG	Risk, Fraud & Governance (*Journal*)
ZRP	Zeitschrift für Rechtspolitik
ZStW	Zeitschrift für die gesamte Strafrechtswissenschaft

Introduction

In Germany, internal control and especially corporate compliance became a major issue after the corruption scandal at Siemens revealed in 2006.[1] Due to its then-cross-listing on the NYSE and the extraterritorial application of U.S. anti-corruption law, U.S. law enforcement agencies, the Department of Justice (DOJ) and the Securities and Exchange Commission (SEC), investigated Siemens and the subsequent U.S. fines of about one billion dollars dramatically revealed the magnitude of the outreach of U.S. law and the potential consequences for its violation. The analysis of the thesis seizes on the example of Siemens but is by far broader and detached from any specifics of the Siemens case including the delisting of Siemens from the NYSE in 2014. Within the field of corporate governance which includes corporate compliance[2], the Siemens case unveiled two major questions: What are effective internal control and compliance systems and what is the impact of being listed on the NYSE in this regard? These two questions are embedded in the overarching corporate governance issue of how to govern and control a stock corporation. In the thesis, the focus is set to analyze the internal systems of corporations which shall ensure the compliance of the corporation with the applicable statutory law, rules, and regulations.

From a legal standpoint, a German stock corporation listed on the NYSE is subject to certain U.S. regulation since conflict of law rules for capital markets law draw on the location of the capital market.[3] Moreover, the extraterritorial application of U.S. law renders German corporations subject to U.S. law. Therefore, German corporations listed on the NYSE have to follow U.S. regulations with regard to internal control and corporate compliance. In the U.S., the concept of internal control including corporate compliance and especially compliance programs to address corporate misconduct has a long history with a major step in 1991 when compliance programs were introduced into the United States Sentencing Guidelines (USSG) as a measure to reduce corporate sanctions.[4] In 2001, the discus-

---

1 See *infra* at chapter 14.

2 Cf. *Kremer/Klahold*, ZGR 2010, 113.

3 *Lehmann*, in: Münch Komm BGB, Int. Capital Markets Law, Basics, mar. 122.

4 See *infra* at chapter 5, C.

sion in the U.S. to enhance corporate governance had a tremendous peak after the accounting scandals of Enron and Worldcom which alarmed the legislator and led to far reaching legislation since the corporate governance system had to be reformed[5]. The scandals of the 2000s were attributed to a gatekeeper failure including "senior executives, independent directors, large auditing firms, outside lawyers, securities analysts, the financial media, and debt rating agencies".[6] The most prominent legislation is the Sarbanes-Oxley Act of 2002 (SOX). SOX and especially sec. 404 SOX caused considerable concern for U.S. and non-U.S. corporations.[7] It is somehow devastating to see the effect of mainly one single provision of SOX on academia, public interest groups, and governmental agencies. The dimension of the resonance clearly demonstrates that Congress and the SEC[8] underestimated the effects.

Within the legal field in Germany, the research on corporate compliance has drawn more and more academic attention in the recent years.[9] Before this change, general corporate governance issues such as the audit committee were *en vogue*. The focus of academic debate were mostly on singular issues related to top management and supervising bodies such as independent members of the board of directors, the establishment of the audit committee, management compensation, and company loans to management. In contrast to these measures of corporate governance, internal control and compliance systems provide measures to mitigate risk, to foster compliance with law, and to provide accurate financial data. Also in Germany, numerous scandals, revealed after the Siemens case, demonstrate that compliance issues needed to be addressed more firmly. These cases included corruption at Ferrostal, MAN, Daimler or other violations of law at Volkswagen and Telekom to name some of the prominent cases.[10] Numer-

5 See e.g. *Ribstein*, 3 NZ L. Rev. 365 (2005), p. 366; *Coates*, 21 J. Econ. Perspectives 91 (2007), p. 92.

6 *Ribstein*, 2006, p. 367; cf. *Coffee*, 2002, p. 4 et seq.

7 *Stoltenberg/Lacey/George/Cuthbert*, 53 Am. J. Comp. L. 457 (2005), p. 457.

8 See SEC Release No. 8238, at VII, E.

9 Cf. Hauschka, Corporate Compliance; *Dreher/Hoffmann*, ZGR 2016, 445; *Kort*, FS Roth, 407; *id.*, ZGR 2010, 440; *Köhler/Marten/Schlereth*, DB 2009, 1477, 1481; *AKEIÜ Schmalenbach-Ges.*, DB 2010, 1509.

10 *Vetter*, FS v. Westphalen, 719, 720: naming *Deutsche Bahn*, *Deutsche Telekom*, *Lidl*, *Siemens*. See *Schneider*, NZG 2009, 1321; *Hauschka*, ZIP 2004, 877; *Campos Nave/Bonenberger*, BB 2008, 734; *Hauschka/Greeve*, BB 2007, 165; *Berg*, AG 2007, 271; on the details of Siemens AG: *Kindler*, FS Roth, 2011, 367, 368 et seq.

ous antitrust violations add to the picture of corporate misconduct in Germany.[11] Non-compliance has become an operational risk.[12]

11 See *Lampert*, BB 2002, 2237.
12 *Schneider*, ZIP 2003, 645; cf. *Bürkle*, ZIP 2004, 877, 879.

Chapter 1: Topic

In both legal systems, the challenge of corporate governance is to provide sophisticated supervision of the corporation and especially management. Internal control and corporate compliance play a vital role within corporate governance. In general, corporate governance, compliance, and risk management interrelate.[13] The governance of the corporation encompasses compliance and risk management throughout the corporation involving the relationships of all stakeholders especially the management board and the supervisory board. Compliance and risk management apply particularly to management in order to control its behavior. In this regard, internal control provides a management tool to ensure appropriate compliance and risk taking throughout the corporation. Internal control provides a control framework within the corporation which enables management and supervisors to control the corporation and helps to prevent criminal acts, such as fraud and corruption, and ensures accurate transparency for the financial markets. It uses preventive and detective controls for this purpose.[14] The main task of internal control is to provide information to the audit committee on two aspects: first, on the internal control system itself to ensure an effective system providing measures to prevent and detect misconduct and, second, on misconduct especially from management to enable the audit committee to address such misconduct. In the context of compliance, ethical conduct may be addressed through guidelines[15] providing a gateway to implement ethics into corporations. Ethical guidance is essential to achieve corporate compliance.[16]

---

13 Cf. *Kort*, NZG 2008, 81, 82; *Menzies*, in: Menzies, Sarbanes-Oxley, p. 3 et seq.

14 Cf. SEC Release No. 8810, at fn. 30; *Green*, SOX Guide, p. 65.

15 *Kort*, NZG 2008, 81, 86; cf. *Bergmoser/Theusinger/Gushurst*, BB 2008, Beilage 5, 1, 10; cf. *AKEIÜ Schmalenbach-Ges.*, DB 2010, 1509.

16 *Bussmann*, FS Achenbach, 57, 73 et seq.; *Bussmann/Salvenmoser*, CCZ 2008, 192, 194; *Bussmann*, 2007 MschrKrim 260, 270 et seq. See *Deiseroth/Derleder*, ZRP 2008, 248, 249: after an ethics seminar, a Bayer AG employee reported massive medical fraud.

A. Corporate Governance: Internal Control and Agency Costs

One important issue corporate governance has to deal with is agency costs.[17] These costs occur due to the separation of ownership and control in publicly held corporations.[18] For the purpose of controlling these costs, monitoring is an important factor in the governance structure. It has been claimed that the shareholders as owners of the corporation might be good monitors.[19] But this notion disregards the impact of the free rider problem[20] especially in widely held public corporations. Due to the free rider problem, each individual shareholder would be better off not engaging in monitoring since an active shareholder will only be rewarded proportionally for her efforts but will bear all the costs. Hence, out of a perspective of a rational shareholder engaging in monitoring does not make any economic sense.[21] Therefore, the board of directors, accountable to the shareholders, is the "focal point" of the corporate governance system.[22] Within the U.S. corporate governance structure, the board of directors "serves a key role in [...] monitoring management".[23] The same holds for German corporations. Obviously, this cannot solve the problem in total since directors are still agents for the owners with an implied agency cost problem. Moreover, independent directors cannot solve the problem of information asymmetry.[24] With regard to the agency problem and information asymmetry, internal control strengthens monitoring of management, which is conflicted by the self-serving bias and do not wish to be monitored, in order to reduce agency costs.[25] Thus, effective oversight by the board of directors is essential. Internal control provides directors with a monitoring tool which includes the upstream communication of information. One good

17 See *Jensen/Meckling*, Theory of the Firm.

18 *Berle/Means*, Corporation.

19 *Adams*, 34 Iowa J. Corp. L. 409 (2009), p. 422.

20 *Ribstein*, 3 NZ L. Rev. 365 (2005), p. 367; *Adams*, 34 Iowa J. Corp. L. 409 (2009), p. 422.

21 See in general: *Albanese/van Fleet*, 10 Acct. Mgmt. Rev. 244 (1985).

22 SEC Release No. 8220, at I.

23 *Prentice/Spence*, 95 Geo. L. J. 1843 (2007), p. 1864.

24 *Cosenza*, 2007 B.Y.U.L. Rev. 1, p. 23; in general on asymmetric information *Greenwald/Stiglitz*, 1990; *Akerlof*, 84 Q.J. Econ. 488 (1970).

25 *Prentice*, 29 Cardozo L. Rev. 703 (2007), p. 708; cf. *Langevoort*, 31 J. Corp. L. 949 (2006), p. 960; *Langevoort*, 105 Mich. L. Rev. 1817 (2007), p. 1834; *Ribstein*, 2004 Mich. St. L. Rev. 279, p. 283; cf. *Jensen/Meckling*, Theory of the Firm, p. 167.

indicator to determine where to allocate internal control resources are incentives for management resulting in agency costs.[26]

B. Choice of the Topic and Aims of the Analysis

Several aspects led to the choice of the topic. At first, the impact of the most important capital market and U.S. law on German law and corporations, since it has been noted that U.S. legal concepts increasingly impact European and German corporation law[27] including corporate compliance[28], and the magnitude of this impact in the field of internal control and corporate compliance. Second, the impact of serving two masters, i.e. a corporation being subject to two potentially different sets of rules. This is a problem which almost every multi-national corporation faces. In this regard, legislators and rule setting agencies will get insight into the issues which foreign corporations may face for being subject to their regulation. In this regard, the scope has to include more than only SOX to capture the impact of the legal environment in which SOX is part of. Also, the incentive structure of the legal system is important since people are affected not only by one statute. The findings of the thesis will show that such broad analysis is necessary to reveal the impact and friction of SOX and the all other regulation affecting internal control and compliance. Research has been conducted on the impact of SOX on German corporate governance mainly finding that SOX requirements do not contradict German corporate law and may be implemented due to the discretion of the management board.[29] While the finding is generally merited, a broader scope provides in depth results revealing further aspects of impact and friction. Third, with regard to the research on legal transplants, a law and economics impact analysis with the chosen setup provides an example of how the impact and, in particular, unintended consequences may be revealed prior to transplanting a foreign legal rule into the home jurisdiction. Forth, using law and economics to conduct an impact analysis provides the opportunity to demonstrate the advantages of law and economics to reveal the importance of incentive structures to achieve legislative goals. Thereby,

26 *Langevoort*, 2006, p. 973.
27 *Fleischer*, ECFR 2005, 378, 379; *id.*, NZG 2004, 1129 et seq.
28 *Fleischer*, NZG 2004, 1129, 1131; *v. Rosen*, AG 2008, 537; *Bürkle*, BB 2005, 565.
29 See *Nicklisch*, Auswirkungen SOX.

it is important to set the incentive level accurately.[30] As it will be shown, enforcement is import for inducing corporations to implement effective internal controls. Fifth, the research on effective internal control including corporate compliance will provide insight to better address corporate misconduct. This is important against the background of numerous corporate scandals in the U.S. and Germany.

The aims of this analysis are manifold. First of all, the impact of U.S. securities law on German internal control systems especially corporate compliance will be shown. Therefore, the main focus of the thesis will be set to large German *Aktiengesellschaften* listed on the NYSE. As part of the impact analysis, the U.S. and German conditions and requirements for internal control systems of listed corporations will be compiled. Thus, corporations will be able to gain insight into the various options of modeling internal control systems. As the case may be, advantageous U.S. corporate compliance concepts may be adopted in Germany. Due to the impact analysis of this thesis, each corporation will be enabled to consider the occurring friction and the general costs and benefits of being cross-listed or otherwise subject to U.S. law. Moreover, listed corporations may assess the rules and requirements which are applicable to them and which further rules and requirements they have to fulfill with regard to a potential listing on the NYSE. Moreover, it is the goal of the thesis to show the incentives for corporate leaders to comply with internal control requirements and how to comply.

Many corporations including foreign private issuers have complained about the lack of guidance for corporations on how to comply with sec. 404 SOX especially regarding the identification of internal control deficiencies, measuring the significance of such deficiencies, and what comprises a material weakness.[31] Such guidance is necessary as the recent examples of corporations, especially German foreign private issuers, with difficulties in complying with SOX mandates show.[32] In Germany, rather widespread uncertainty exists of how to deal with compliance.[33] One important aspect of the thesis is to provide corporations, especially German *Aktiengesellschaften*, with the needed guidance. Furthermore, *Aktiengesellschaften* currently listed on the NYSE will be better equipped to evaluate the pros and cons of being listed on the NYSE. Likewise, corporations

30 Cf. *Arlen/Kraakman*, 72 N.Y.U.L. Rev. 687 (1997), p. 711.

31 Cf. *Agami*, CPA Journal 2006.

32 See for Daimler AG: *Spiegel Online*, Daimler.

33 *Kremer/Klahold*, ZGR 2010, 113, 116.

which consider a listing on the NYSE will be able to evaluate the pros and cons more accurately.

A further aim of the thesis is to provide the NYSE and other exchanges with a better understanding of the impact and friction which may occur due to the listing of foreign corporations on the respective exchange. Moreover, the legislators and the exchanges may use findings of the impact analysis to revise their rules in order to reduce friction and increase efficiency. With these measures, the attractiveness of the specific capital market for foreign corporations may be enhanced. In general, the results will provide scholars, executives, lawmakers, and regulators with a clearer picture on the impact of U.S. internal control and compliance requirements on German corporations.

A further aspect of the thesis is to advance the research on legal transplants. With regard to the conventional comparative law approach, it has been suggested to extend the conventional method of comparative law for analyzing the expected impact of legal transplants within the receiving jurisdiction *ex ante* by using law and economics to conduct an impact analysis with the assumptions of new institutional economics.[34] The setup of the thesis provides an example for how to structure and conduct such a law and economics impact analysis for analyzing the impact of legal transplants within the receiving jurisdiction, for the complexity of such analysis, and for the results which may be achieved.

In light of the notion that it is the genuine duty of jurisprudence to maintain the functionality of the corporate law regime in the aftermath of scandals[35], it is the aim of the thesis to further the research on effective of internal control and corporate compliance and to address reforms. In this regard, the pros and cons of criminal vs. civil liability will be considered including whether corporate criminal liability is necessary to tackle corporate misconduct.

34 Cf. *Kirchner*, in: New Frontiers of Law and Economics, p. 202 et seq. See for the law and economics approach on the comparative impact analysis more generally: *id.*, in: Riesenhuber, sec. 5, mar. 32 et seq. See for an *ex post* econometric impact analysis of the 'transplant effect' of legal transplants: *Berkowitz/Pistor/Richard*, 47 European Economic Review 165 (2003). See on legal transplants *infra* at chapter 2, D.

35 *Windbichler*, FS HU-Juristische Fakultät, 1079, 1081.

C. U.S. Understanding and the Meaning of the Term "Internal Control" and Further Terminology

The term "internal control" is used differently in the U.S. and Germany. In the U.S., it is used in the sense of an internal monitoring or surveillance system as in the "COSO – Internal Control – Integrated Framework" (COSO I) which is a private-sector framework for designing, implementing, and conducting internal control and assessing the effectiveness of internal control[36].[37] In Germany, internal controls are often referred to as a part of the internal monitoring system of sec. 91(2) AktG and is, therefore, narrower than the U.S. term. It has been noted that the U.S. concept of internal control would be equivalent to the German concept of internal monitoring system and, thus, could not be translated into German with 'internal controls'.[38] Throughout the thesis, the term will be used in the wider U.S.-sense of COSO I. Depending on specific wording of legislation or regulation, the terms compliance system, compliance program, internal control and compliance system or internal control including compliance measures will be used indicating that only partial aspects of COSO I internal control are addressed.

Moreover with regard to internal control related to financial reporting, the term 'internal control over financial reporting' has been defined in Exchange Act Rule 13a-15(f). Therefore in order to allow for a differentiation, the term 'internal control regarding financial reporting' will be used within the German/EU context. In light of deficiencies of internal controls, the term 'material weakness' and also the term 'significant deficiency' are used in sec. 302(a)(5)(A) SOX. While the COSO I-version of 1992 and the Directive 2006/43/EC in art. 41(4) used the term 'material weakness', the current COSO I uses the term 'major deficiency' and in art. 11(2)(j) Regulation (EU) No 537/2014 the term 'significant deficiency' is used. Throughout the thesis, terminology will be used as used in the laws, standards, and regulations. German terms are mostly translated according to EU terminology.

---

36 COSO I, Executive Summary, foreword. See for details on the Committee of Sponsoring Organizations of the Treadway Commission (COSO) and on COSO I *infra* at chapter 4, C. I.

37 Cf. *Glage/Grötzner*, in: Hauschka, Corporate Compliance, sec. 14, mar. 39 et seq.; *Bussmann/Matschke*, Crime, Law and Social Change 2008, 349, 353; *Schoberth/Servatius/Thees*, BB 2006, 2571, 2572.

38 Cf. *Lück*, DB 1998, 8, 9; *Amling/Bantleon*, WPg 2014, 343, at fn. 16 'unfortunate' translation of the English "internal control" into German as "*Internes Kontrollsystem*".

D. Scope and Limitations of the Analysis

The analysis is purely functional as it takes the U.S. understanding of "internal control" as its focal point. Due to the COSO I definition of internal control, internal control aims to achieve preset goals in three categories: effectiveness and efficiency of operations, reliability of reporting, and compliance with laws and regulations.[39] In two of the three categories, corporations have to adhere to laws, regulations, and standards in order to design and operate their internal controls. The main focus of the thesis will be set to financial reporting and compliance with law. The thesis will only touch on risk management systems when appropriate. All relevant U.S. and German rules addressing or influencing internal control will be considered. Especially in the field of corporate governance, it is important to include corporate law and capital markets law.[40] In order to obtain meaningful insights from the impact analysis, all regulatory aspects affecting internal control and compliance especially the social environment of the respective legal rules have to be included in the analysis to analyze the interaction of the different incentive structures within the United States and Germany.[41] This includes best practices and enforcement. The setup of the thesis seizes on the linkage between corporate law and capital markets law as well as of U.S. law and European/German law and combines this starting point with the linkage of law and economics in order to achieve a complex interdisciplinarity necessary to acquire meaningful insight to advance the research on effective and efficient internal control relevant for functional capital markets and compliance with law. In general, capital markets and investors operate on the principle that corporations issue reliable and complete financial data and good internal controls are perceived to be an important factor in achieving accurate financial reporting.[42]

The analysis considers the rules and best practice regarding internal control and compliance applicable for a general, large German *Aktiengesellschaft* listed in Germany[43] and on the NYSE. In the U.S., two major regulatory regimes address internal control and corporate compliance.

---

39 COSO I, mar. 19.

40 Cf. *Windbichler*, FS HU-Juristische Fakultät, 1079, 1080; *id.*, FS Rokas 1389, 1390; *Fleischer*, ZIP 2006, 451 et seq.; *Fleischer*, ZGR 2007, 500 et seq.

41 Cf. *Kirchner*, FS HU-Juristische Fakultät, 937, 950 et seq.; *id.*, in: New Frontiers of Law and Economics, p. 203. See also *Windbichler*, FS Rokas 1389, 1390 on the scope of corporate governance being "more than corporate law".

42 *Zhang/Pany*, CPA Journal 2008.

43 Cf. regarding the specifics of listed corporations: *Fleischer*, ZIP 2006, 451, 454.

One regime addresses internal control with regard to corporate governance and particularly financial reporting. The other one addresses corporate compliance mostly from a standpoint of criminal law. Internal control with emphasis on financial reporting is addressed by SOX, SEC rules and regulation, auditing standards of the Public Company Accounting Oversight Board (PCAOB), NYSE listing standards, and U.S. GAAP, as well as the Foreign Corrupt Practices Act of 1977 (FCPA) and the General Corporate Law of Delaware (DGCL). Likewise, compliance with laws and regulation is addressed by the common law principle of 'corporate criminal liability,' the USSG, the DOJ enforcement policy, and the SEC enforcement policy. The FCPA and the DGCL address both aspects. While internal control systems are generally attributed to financial reporting and compliance programs to compliance with laws and regulation, both are part of internal control in light of COSO I. In the U.S., financial reporting mandates draw heavily on COSO I as their underlying basis in contrast to the requirements for compliance programs. Nevertheless, the requirements for compliance programs have a similar scope than COSO I addressing mostly identical elements such as ethics, board of directors' involvement, and monitoring.

In the context of U.S. corporate criminal liability, effective internal control and compliance systems are an important element to deter corporate crime but other *ex post* policing measures such as investigation, self-reporting, and cooperation will also be addressed to provide for the context of how to effectively deter corporate crime. In Germany, aspects of internal control are addressed by EU law and regulated within corporate law, commercial law, criminal law, the law on administrative offences, and more specific law such as capital markets law, data protection law, labor and employment law, and the specific law of regulated industries influencing internal control of general, listed corporations.

The scope of the thesis is limited to U.S. mandates and best practice applicable to foreign corporations listed on the NYSE including further mandates regarded as best practice. With regard to U.S. state corporate law, only the impact of the General Corporate Law of Delaware will be considered since it is widely regarded as the most important corporate law in the U.S.[44] Also, as it is the aim of this thesis to analyze the impact of U.S. law and best practice following the enactment of SOX in 2002, any U.S. rules and best practice which impacted German law and best practice before

44 Cf. *Thompson*, 40 Hous. L. Rev. 99 (2003), p. 108; *Bebchuk/Cohen*, 46 J. L. & Econ. 383 (2003), p. 391.

2002 will be disregarded and any U.S. rules and best practice which impacted German law and best practice need to be carved out of the current German law and best practice in order to evaluate their impact. Moreover, compliance with law and compliance programs may also be relevant in the context of U.S. civil corporate liability especially in the environmental sector and the health care sector.[45] The Environmental Protection Agency[46] and the Department of Health and Human Services[47] published guidelines on compliance programs. Corporations may receive leniency if their compliance program complies with the stated requirements providing incentives for corporations to fulfill these requirements. Since these guidelines are sector-specific and not all corporations listed on the NYSE are necessarily subject to these guidelines, civil corporate liability and the sector-specific guidelines will be excluded from the research at hand.

With regard to German law, the aspects regarding the audit committee will be excluded from the thesis as far as they concern its implementation in a two-tier board system and the impact of the audit committee itself originating from a one-tier board system. These issues have been dealt with elsewhere[48] and the focus of this thesis is on internal control and not on the committee receiving parts of the information provided by internal controls. The audit committee will only be addressed as far as it is a necessary player within internal control. Also, group law issues will only be excluded since U.S. corporate law does not have specific group law and since group law is a specific field of research by itself. Furthermore, the issue whether corporate criminal liability fits into the German concept of individual guilt as an element of justifying punishment within German criminal law will be excluded from the thesis.

45 Also in the context of federal procurement, Federal Acquisition Rule 52.203-13 mandates to implement internal control and a compliance program similar to the USSG mandates (*Biegelman*, FCPA Guidebook, p. 68 et seq.). See for more detail on corporate civil liability *Oded*, Corporate Compliance, p. 128 et seq.

46 EPA, Incentives for Self-Policing.

47 HHS, Compliance Program Guidance.

48 See e.g. *Hopt/Roth*, in: Großkomm AktG, sec. 107, mar. 298 et seq.

Chapter 2: Method

The analysis will be conducted as an impact analysis using the analytical tools of law and economics. It does not follow the traditional path of a functional comparison of law even though the setup of the analysis may suggest this at first glance. While the functional comparison of law focuses in general on the similarities and differences of the compared statutory rules and compares the different approaches[49], the impact analysis focuses on the impact which foreign rules, i.e. legal transplants, will have within the receiving jurisdiction. The setup used for the impact analysis serves as a general setup to analyze the impact of legal transplants.

A. *Law and Economics*

The analysis will be conducted using a social science approach. The analytical methods of economics used within law and economics provide a valuable set of tools. The economic analysis of law, with its emphasis on incentive effects and on costs and benefits, provides an important tool for the analysis of corporate law and policy.[50] The law regarding listed corporations is exceptionally suitable to conduct a law and economics analysis.[51]

Law and economics applies the concepts and empirical methods of economics to the analysis of law.[52] It has its main focus on the analysis of the incentives set by exogenous rules.[53] The rules in this context are the law which provides the framework for the analysis. The law has an impact on the individuals of society by providing incentives either as a penalty or as a reward.[54] The impact cannot be reasonably measured or predicted by analyzing the real world due to its manifold diversity. Thus, models are used in social science to simplify the real world in order to make the analysis man-

---

49 Cf. *Zweigert/Kötz*, Rechtsvergleichung, p. 6 et seq. and p. 42 et seq.

50 *Marks*, in: Encyclopedia of Law and Economics, p. 710.

51 *Windbichler*, FS HU-Juristische Fakultät, 1079, 1093; *Fleischer*, ZGR 2007, 500, 503. See with regard to the reception of law and economics in Germany: *Grechenig/Gelter*, RabelsZ 2008, 513.

52 *Parisi*, 2004, p. 2.

53 *Voigt*, 2002, p. 45.

54 Cf. *Kirchner*, in: Riesenhuber, sec. 5, mar. 36 et seq.

ageable and the results meaningful.[55] Within each model, assumptions are used to reduce the complexity of the real world in order to achieve simplicity. In law and economics, this is especially helpful in order to analyze how individuals will react to the incentives provided by law. Being able to predict the behavior of individuals in responds to incentives allows to formulate proposals for changes in law leading to socially favorable changes in behavior. In this regard, sanctions or liability provide individuals with incentives to act or refrain to act. The relevant measure for the incentive level is the expected liability, i.e. sanction times the probability of detection.

The analytical tools of economics will be used for the analysis since the legal method does not provide a sufficient set of tools for a social science analysis.[56] The use of models and assumptions is not within the scope of the legal method. Law and economics, however, provides the opportunity to formulate testable hypotheses.[57] Thus, the real impact of legal rules can only be analyzed with a social science approach which allows the introduction of assumptions into the analysis.[58] The use of testable hypotheses and assumptions reduces the influence of guesswork and general experience on the results of an impact analysis and allows for the proposal of changes in law leading to a more efficient and effective law. The impact analysis has not yet become a tool within the legal analysis in Germany[59] but provides valuable insight to predict how individuals will react to changes of incentives[60].

Moreover, the traditional legal analysis does not consider the overall incentives structures influencing the addressees of legal statutes. For example, reasoning that auditing standards are not law and are, therefore, irrelevant for the legal analysis of auditing statutes neglects the actual impact of auditing standards on corporate leaders. In order to obtain an unqualified attestation of the external auditor, corporate leaders will take the auditing standards applicable for the auditors into account. Legal advice on the au-

---

55 *Felderer/Homburg*, Makroökonomik, p. 10.

56 Cf. *Kirchner*, FS HU-Juristische Fakultät, 937, 937; *id.*, in: New Frontiers of Law and Economics, p. 204; *Kirchner/Koch*, ZfSozW 1989, 111 et seq. See also *Zweigert/Kötz*, Rechtsvergleichung, p. 11 et seq.

57 *Kirchner*, 11 International Review of Law and Economics 277 (1991), p. 287; *id.*, BB 2000, 105, 108.

58 Cf. *Kirchner*, in: New Frontiers of Law and Economics, p. 204; *id.*, in: Ökonomische Analyse des Rechts, p. 66.

59 *Weber-Rey*, ZGR 2010, 543, 565; *Dreher*, ZGR 2010, 496, 501.

60 Cf. *Kirchner*, FS HU-Juristische Fakultät, 937, 942 et seq.; *id.*, in: Riesenhuber, sec. 5, mar. 3.

diting statutes indicating that the auditing standards are not mandatory does not help the corporate leader with her task to structure and execute the auditing process. Since the law does not provide for isolated regulation, all relevant factors influencing corporate leaders have to be considered for an impact analysis in order to achieve comprehensive results.

With regard to considerations of efficiency, the *Kaldor-Hicks* criterion will be used. The *Kaldor-Hicks* criterion for efficiency suggests that a change of rules is more efficient and thus should be made if the increase in utility of the gainers is greater than the loss in utility of the losers in regard to the change.[61] The gainers were therefore able to compensate the losers for loss while no actual transfer between gainers and losers will be conducted. Society as a whole will gain from the change of rules.

B. Private Ordering vs. Regulation

With regard to the issue of private ordering or regulation, it is generally assumed that law and especially corporate law should be designed to foster the efficient use of assets.[62] To achieve this, contractarians – scholars viewing the corporation as a nexus of contracts – believe in private ordering and the power of free bargaining, i.e. the market.[63] In contrast to contractarians, anti-contractarians believe in categorical rules and, therefore, favor regulatory solutions.[64] The contractarian view leads to efficient results only under the assumptions of the neoclassical economic theory.[65] Thus, it does not account for "[m]arket failure, disparities in bargaining, imperfect and asymmetrical information, moral hazards, satisficing", and requires rational actors.[66] Due to the underlying assumptions of the new institutional economics for this thesis, only a regulatory approach will lead to towards efficient results.

---

61 See *Kaldor*, The Economic Journal 49, 549 (1939) and *Hicks*, The Economic Journal 49, 696 (1939).
62 *Brown*, 90 Marq. L. Rev. 309 (2006), p. 310.
63 *Brown*, 90 Marq. L. Rev. 309 (2006), p. 310 et seq.; *Ribstein*, 3 NZ L. Rev. 365 (2005), p. 365. See also *Ribstein*, 28 Iowa J. Corp. L. 1 (2002).
64 *Ribstein*, 3 NZ L. Rev. 365 (2005), p. 365.
65 Cf. *Brown*, 90 Marq. L. Rev. 309 (2006), p. 311.
66 *Brown*, 90 Marq. L. Rev. 309 (2006), p. 311.

C. *Setup of the Impact Analysis*

In order to analyze the impact, a model will be used by defining a stable basis for each part of the thesis, by introducing into such stable bases several variables, and by using the assumptions of the new institutional economics.[67] The occurring impact and friction of these variables and the changes to the incentive structure will be analyzed.[68] For the analysis, a positive approach will be used.[69] This is necessary in order to conduct an impact analysis.[70] Thus, the current status will be described and the real impact depicted.[71] In contrast to a normative analysis, a specific goal or policy is preset.[72] Based on efficiency considerations, proposals will be made regarding alternative rules which are more efficient with regard to the goals and polices of the current rules. The main focus of the impact analysis will be the modifications of the incentive structure of the affected individuals due to the variables inserted into the stable basis. Due to the change of the rules regarding internal control systems, the incentive structure also changes. This leads to a change of behavior of the individuals which, then, results in an economic change. The economic change is, thus, the impact of the modifications.[73]

For the model, the assumptions of the new institutional economics will be used. Due to the evolved skepticism of the neoclassical theory, new institutional economics is a valuable approach towards such analysis.[74] Thus, scarce recourses, constant preferences, self-interest of individual actors with bounded rationality, transaction costs, and asymmetrical information will be assumed. The assumptions of the new institutional economics deviate from the assumptions of the neoclassical economics mainly in regard to obtaining information which is priceless and effortless in the latter case.[75] Due to perfect and costless information, individuals are able to act completely rational on a fully informed basis.[76] Consequently, neoclassical eco-

---

67 Cf. *Kirchner*, in: New Frontiers of Law and Economics, p. 205.
68 Cf. *Kirchner*, in: Riesenhuber, sec. 5, mar. 36.
69 Usually, the *Chicago School* of law and economics is in favor of a positive analysis. (*Posner*, in: Economic Foundations of Private Law, p. 8).
70 Cf. *Kirchner*, in: Riesenhuber, sec. 5, mar. 3.
71 Cf. *Posner*, Economic Analysis of Law, p. 25.
72 Cf. *Parisi*, 2004, p. 9.
73 Cf. *Mercuro/Medema*, Economics and the Law, p. 22; *Kirchner*, BB 2000, 105, 108.
74 *Windbichler*, FS HU-Juristische Fakultät, 1079, 1094.
75 Cf. *Kirchner*, in: Riesenhuber, sec. 5 mar. 46 et seq.
76 Cf. *Lieth*, Ökonomische Analyse des Rechts, p. 35.

nomics assume *inter alia* perfect rationality and symmetrical information of individuals. By assuming symmetrical information, the principal-agent problem vanishes.[77]

By introducing positive transaction costs into the model, the neoclassical view of perfect individual rationality is no longer feasible for the analysis.[78] In new institutional economics, the term bounded rationality has been mainly introduced to characterize how individuals attempt to maximize their utility in a world with positive transaction costs[79] and cognitive limits of decision makers[80]. Due to transaction costs, individuals are not able to foresee all contingencies[81] and, thus, their maximization of utility remains imperfect. Nevertheless, the concept of bounded rationality implies that individuals are maximizers responding to incentives.[82] Together with the assumption of constant preferences, changes of the incentive structure leads to changes of the behavior of individuals.[83]

A further effect of positive transaction costs is asymmetrical information since obtaining information is not costless. Due to asymmetrical information, opportunistic behavior occurs prior to the conclusion of a contract as adverse selection and during the execution of a contract as moral hazard.[84] In particular within principal-agent relationships, opportunistic behavior is an issue due to asymmetrical information.

Based on the assumptions of the new institutional economics, the incentive structure of the individuals and their behavior can be predicted within the model. The assumptions of the new institutional economics have been chosen for this analysis because friction occurs due to positive transaction costs, the principal-agent problem, *ex post* opportunism, and informational asymmetry.[85] Since the main focus of the thesis is to analyze this friction which does occur due to the impact of U.S. internal control and corporate

---

77 Cf. *Kirchner*, FS HU-Juristische Fakultät, 937, 951 et seq.

78 Complete rationality implies zero transaction costs. See *Kreps*, Microeconomic, p. 745: "A completely rational individual has the ability to foresee everything that might happen and to evaluate and optimally choose among available courses of action, all in the blink of an eye and at no cost"; cf. *Furubotn/Richter*, New Institutional Economics, p. 23.

79 Cf. *Furubotn/Richter*, New Institutional Economics, p. 3 et seq. and p. 171.

80 Cf. *Furubotn/Richter*, New Institutional Economics, p. 447.

81 *Kreps*, Microeconomic, p. 745; cf. *Furubotn/Richter*, New Institutional Economics, p. 10.

82 Cf. *Posner*, Economic Analysis of Law, p. 4 and p. 15.

83 *Lieth*, Ökonomische Analyse des Rechts, p. 56.

84 *Furubotn/Richter*, New Institutional Economics, p. 139.

85 Cf. *Furubotn/Richter*, New Institutional Economics, pp. 12, 49, and 62.

compliance on German internal control systems, the use of frictionless neoclassical economics was precluded.[86]

In order to conduct an impact analysis using the analytical tools of economics, data needs to be accumulated. Within law and economics, the law represents this data. As a prerequisite for the impact analysis, the status quo of the law needs to be compiled and depicted. Thus, the current legal mandates and best practice in the U.S. and Germany have to be determined using classical legal methods.[87] Then, the incentive structure of these mandates will be determined using the assumptions of the new institutional economics.

As a subpart of the impact analysis, a cost-benefit analysis will be conducted to evaluate the costs and benefits of German *Aktiengesellschaften* for being listed on the NYSE in regard to the occurring friction. Since each corporation has its specific costs and benefits, no detailed calculation will be possible. Instead, the general or average costs will be used for the cost-benefit analysis as far as possible.

D. *Legal Transplants and De Facto Legal Transplants: Extraterritorial Application of Foreign Law and Voluntary Submission under a Foreign Jurisdiction*

The setup of the impact analysis fulfills the attributes of a legal transplant. In its famous monograph, *Alan Watson* describes legal transplant as "the moving of a rule or a system of law from one country to another, or from one people to another".[88] The setup anticipates the implementation of the U.S. rules regarding internal control and compliance into the German legal system. In reality, the transplantation does not explicitly occur on the legislative level but on the corporation level. Due to the listing of German corporations on the NYSE, these corporations have to comply with the German rules and the applicable U.S. rules. In case one corporation is subject to the rules of two jurisdictions without a legal hierarchy between these jurisdictions, this situation leads to *de facto* legal transplants of the rules foreign to the law governing the corporation but only on the corpo-

86 See on neoclassical economics and new institutional economics: *Furubotn/Richter*, New Institutional Economics, p. 246 et seq.

87 See on the steps to make use of law and economics: *Kirchner/Koch*, ZfSozW 1989, 111, 121 et seq.

88 *Watson*, Legal Transplants, p. 21 et seq.; cf. *Fleischer*, ECFR 2005, 378.

ration level. Even though national legislators may not be the driving force for legal transplants[89], *de facto* legal transplants exist for all instances when a natural person or a legal entity are subject to two jurisdictions without a legal hierarchy between these jurisdictions. Being cross-listed is an example of *de facto* legal transplants as the analysis in this thesis shows. *De facto* legal transplants occur in case of extraterritorial application of foreign law and voluntary submission under a foreign jurisdiction.

It has been noted that legal transplants have not received the necessary scholarly attention.[90] But legal transplants bear the danger of a "transplant shock" within the receiving jurisdiction.[91] Legal transplants will have an impact on the receiving jurisdiction and may cause friction. In this regard, it has been noted that the elements of a corporate governance system are complementary and that transplanting an element of one system into another system may lead to an inefficient result especially in case these systems differ.[92] In order to eliminate or reduce the impact and potential friction, the magnitude of a transplant shock including the expected impact and friction should be measured in advance. After analyzing the impact and friction of a proposed legal transplant, the transplant shock needs to be cushioned by adjusting the new rules or the receiving jurisdiction in order to achieve efficient results. Cushioning the transplant shock is important to ensure the success of a legal transplant. The impact of these adjustments, however, will also need to be considered. Similar to legal transplants, also the extraterritorial application of law may lead to friction due to the path dependence of legal norms and enforcement actions of foreign agencies.[93] For the success of legal transplants, it is important for the receiving jurisdiction to focus on the reform strategy by understanding the meaning and purpose of a foreign legal rule considering the acceptance of such rule by its addressees.[94] It is hypothesized that legal transplants will receive greater acceptance if the implemented foreign legal rule leads to no, or little, impact and friction within the receiving jurisdiction. In order to ensure that the impact and friction of the legal transplants are low, lawmakers should conduct an impact analysis prior to transplanting foreign

89 *Fleischer*, ECFR 2005, 378, 388.
90 *Fleischer*, ECFR 2005, 378, 385.
91 Cf. *Fleischer*, ECFR 2005, 378, 386; *Berkowitz/Pistor/Richard*, 47 European Economic Review 165 (2003).
92 *Schmidt/Spindler*, in: Convergence and Persistence, p. 121 et seq.
93 *Painter*, FS Kirchner, 1247, 1251 et seq. and 1260.
94 *Berkowitz/Pistor/Richard*, 47 European Economic Review 165 (2003), p. 192; cf. *Fleischer*, ECFR 2005, 378, 392 et seq.

rules using the methodical model used for this thesis. With the results of such analysis, lawmakers are able to adjust the legal transplants. With such adjustments, the potential impact and friction will be reduced increasing the prospects that the addressees will accept the new rule ensuring its success. Without an adjustment, the unreflecting adoption of, e.g. U.S. law in Germany, is prone to failure.[95] Moreover, by analyzing the impact of legal transplants on the incentive regime of the addressees, unexpected consequences will be reviled reducing the probability of unintended consequences of legal transplants. Hence, the modeled impact analysis provides a useful tool for legislators to analyze the impact of a legal transplant in advance, i.e. *ex ante*, in order to reduce the impact, friction, and unintended consequences increasing the success of a legal transplant.[96] Also, corporations may be able to determine the impact and potential friction of *de facto* legal transplants prior to decide on a cross-listing or other decision leading to comply with two or more different legal regimes.

Lawmakers and corporations should consider that transplanting flexible rules leads to greater success of the legal transplant within a receiving jurisdiction.[97] Likewise, as the impact analysis will show[98], implementing rules into a flexible legal framework, which leaves the addressee ample discretion on how to comply with the mandates, leads to less friction and, thus, to greater acceptance and success of the transplanted rules.[99]

An impact analysis of *de facto* legal transplants, however, is different to an impact analysis of legal transplants. That is because *de facto* legal transplants are different to legal transplants since corporations listed on the NYSE are directly subject to the U.S. legal system with all enforcement and best practice considerations and, at the same time, they are subject to the German legal system. Corporations have to serve two masters at the same time. An impact analysis of a legal transplant does not have to take into account that corporations are directly subject to the U.S. legal system including best practice and enforcement impacting the corporation. Rather, an impact analysis of a legal transplant has to take the functioning of the transplanted legal rule within the environment of its originating jurisdiction including best practice and enforcement into account but does not have to consider the direct impact on the incentive structure of corpora-

95 *Kremer/Klahold*, ZGR 2010, 113, 117.
96 Cf. *Kirchner*, in: New Frontiers of Law and Economics, p. 203.
97 *Fleischer*, ECFR 2005, 378, 393.
98 See *infra* at chapter 12, B. I. 1. c) (1) and II. 1.
99 Cf. *Fleischer*, ECFR 2005, 378, 393.

tions for serving two masters. It follows, that the setup of an impact analysis of legal transplants has to account for such difference. While it is necessary to analyze the impact on the incentive structure in case of serving two masters within the setup of analyzing *de facto* legal transplants, it is necessary to analyze how foreign rules function without the incentive regime of the environment of their originating jurisdiction and instead within the incentive regime of the receiving jurisdiction.

Chapter 3: Course of the Thesis

The method of the impact analysis leads to the following course of the thesis. In part I, the requirements and the incentive structure of U.S. law and best practice regarding internal control and compliance systems applicable for German corporations listed on the NYSE will be depicted representing the *de facto* legal transplants and the variables for the impact analysis. The requirements and the incentive structure reflect the status quo. In part II, the requirements and incentive structure of German law and best practice regarding internal control and compliance systems will be depicted representing the receiving jurisdiction and the stable basis for the impact analysis. The requirements and the incentive structure also reflect the status quo. In part III, the impact analysis will be conducted considering the legal and social environment of both jurisdictions. Also, the cost-benefit analysis will be conducted before concisely addressing the Siemens case as an example of the impact. In part IV, the thesis focuses on how to achieve effective and efficient internal control and corporate compliance systems, how to induce corporations to implement effective systems, and how to evaluate the effectiveness. In this regard, the weaknesses and shortcomings of the current status quo will be considered to further the research on these topics. Also, with regard to legal transplants, these considerations show that a legal transplant may need to be modified prior to its implementation within the receiving jurisdiction. Before concluding, reform suggestions for the USSG as well as German law to enhance corporate compliance through effective internal control and compliance systems will be presented in part V considering the current academic debate in Germany.

Part One U.S. Requirements for Internal Control and Compliance Systems

The following analysis encompasses relevant U.S. laws, regulations, and best practice, as well as incentive structures for corporations listed on the NYSE to engage in internal controls related to financial reporting and compliance with laws. The concise analysis aims to extract the mandates, requirements, and best practice of internal control and corporate compliance as well as the incentive structures to comply with such mandates, requirements, and best practice. In chapter 4, the mandates for internal control systems especially with regard to financial reporting will be analyzed followed by chapter 5 dealing with compliance with laws and regulations including compliance programs. Before concluding, chapter 6 summarizes key aspects of internal control systems and incentives to engage in internal control.

Chapter 4: Internal Control Especially Regarding Financial Reporting

With regard to internal control with emphasis on financial reporting, the mandates for internal control of sec. 302 and 404 SOX including related SEC rules and regulations as well as best practice will be analyzed. SOX aims to enhance financial reporting through effective internal controls since the quality of financial reporting depends essentially on their effectiveness.[100] SOX mainly requires corporations to implement effective 'disclosure controls and procedures' as well as effective 'internal control over financial reporting.' While neither SOX nor the SEC prescribe specific mandates for internal control, the guidance provided for the assessment of the effectiveness of disclosure controls and procedures and internal control over financial reporting has to be used in an inverted process to obtain guidance for the designing and operation of internal control. The analysis includes the incentives for officers to comply with the SOX mandates which affect internal control and gatekeepers.

Besides the legal mandates and the SEC guidance, the requirements of the PCAOB Auditing Standard no. 5 (PCAOB AS 5) will be depicted since the external auditor has to comply with this professional standard in order to attest to and report on management's assessment of the internal control over financial reporting pursuant to sec. 404(b) SOX. PCAOB AS 5 provides guidance with regard to internal control systems addressing financial reporting. In addition, the COSO frameworks and guidelines will be portrayed in order to provide further insight into internal control and its relation to enterprise risk management. Especially COSO I is important as it is the theoretical basis and the *de facto* standard of U.S. internal control. Also the SEC refers *inter alia* to COSO I for corporations to design and operate their internal controls. In order to render the impact analysis of being listed on the NYSE more complete, the mandates and best practices of the NYSE listing standards will be analyzed regarding internal control including incentives provided by NYSE enforcement. Similarly, remarks on the professional standards for internal and external auditors and the implications of financial reporting in accordance with U.S. GAAP and IFRS im-

100 *Shakespeare*, 3 J. Bus. & Tech. 333 (2008), p. 348.

pacting the corporation aim to consider the impact on the incentive structure of corporate leaders beyond legal mandates. At last, risk considerations after the financial crisis of 2008 will be depicted as best practice.

A. Sarbanes Oxley Act

SOX is regarded as the most important legislation in securities law since the 1930s[101] and fostered the worldwide acceptance of COSO I as a standard for internal controls systems[102]. The main purpose of SOX, as it can be observed in its full title 'Public Company Accounting Reform and Investor Protection Act of 2002', was to restore investor confidence in the capital markets especially in regard to financial reporting by reorganizing the auditing process and improving disclosure.[103] The main purpose has the objective to improve corporate disclosure subject to the reporting requirements of the Exchange Act[104] by increasing the gatekeeper function of the external auditors and heightening the oversight duties of the board of directors and senior officers.[105] While not without criticism[106], it is believed that SOX is successful in fostering its main purpose.[107]

With the enactment of SOX, the federal legislator used its legislative power regarding securities law to influence corporate governance. With the triad of sec. 302, 404, and 906 SOX, Congress intended to send a message to CEOs and CFOs of public corporations to take their responsibilities

101 *Shakespeare*, 3 J. Bus. & Tech. 333 (2008), p. 355.

102 *Dierks/Sandmann/Herre*, CCZ 2013, 164, 165; cf. *Gehringer/Fröhler*, in: Bürkle, Compliance in Versicherungsunternehmen, sec. 9, mar. 8 et seq. With regard to the importance of SOX: *Moeller*, SOX Internal Controls, p. 14; *Mengel*, Compliance und Arbeitsrecht, at Introduction, B; *Hillebrand*, Früherkennungs- und Überwachungssystem, p. 42 et seq. and p. 154 et seq. See *infra* at chapter 12, A. IV.

103 SEC Release No. 8238, at V, A; *Donaldson*, 2003, at III; *Shakespeare*, 3 J. Bus. & Tech. 333 (2008), p. 333; cf. *Coates*, 21 J. Econ. Perspectives 91 (2007), p. 91.

104 15 USC 78a et seq.

105 *Brown*, 90 Marq. L. Rev. 309 (2006), p. 309; cf. *Moeller*, SOX Internal Controls, p. 14; *Waxman*, CPA Journal 2004; *Seligman*, 80 Notre Dame L. Rev. 1159 (2005), p. 1184 et seq.

106 E.g. *Romano*, 114 Yale L. J. 1521 (2005); *Ribstein*, 28 Iowa J. Corp. L. 1 (2002). See for details regarding the critique on SOX *infra* at chapter 16, A. I. 1.

107 E.g. *Shakespeare*, 3 J. Bus. & Tech. 333 (2008), p. 355; *Brown*, 90 Marq. L. Rev. 309 (2006), p. 326; *Prentice/Spence*, 95 Geo. L. J. 1843 (2007), p. 1887; *Coates*, 21 J. Econ. Perspectives 91 (2007), p. 107.

for reporting systems more serious.[108] SOX focused U.S. law back on the personal liability of management besides criminal liability of the corporation.[109] In this regard, sec. 302 and 404 SOX enhance the already existing liability of management for financial reporting.[110] Besides the existing requirement to sign the financial statements, Congress intended to substantiate the requirements to highlight their responsibility. The pre-existing system of internal control and anti-fraud rules was not strong enough in light of the scandals of the 2000s.[111]

The main change with regard to the certification requirement for CEO and CFO due to SOX is that the requirements have been clarified and heightened and that the external auditors have to attest to specific disclosures regarding internal controls.[112] With regard to sec. 302 and 404 SOX, it is inevitable to assign the CEO and CFO with the authority to carry out the mandated duties.[113] Thereby, the internal control requirements of sec. 302 and 404 SOX pursue two separate but related objectives.[114] On the one hand, material inside and outside information has to come to the attention of management.[115] On the other hand, monitors such as the board of directors or external auditors are to be permitted to assess the quality of information flow and processing by management.[116] The main aspect of sec. 404 SOX is to reemphasize the central relationship between the maintenance of effective internal control over financial reporting and the preparation of reliable financial statements.[117]

The mandates of SOX address various constituencies within the corporation. The directors and officers face higher responsibilities regarding corporate governance and especially internal controls issues. Also external auditors face challenges due to increased responsibilities and new tasks. This is consistent with the goal of SOX to regulate auditors to better perform as gatekeepers.[118] In a typical U.S. way of legislation, SOX provides for the broad direction through statue leaving the details to independent agencies,

---

108 *Prentice*, 29 Cardozo L. Rev. 703 (2007), p. 706.
109 *Schünemann*, FS Tiedemann, 429, 444.
110 Cf. *Nelson*, 31 Academy of Management Rev. 30 (2006), p. 33.
111 *Coates*, 21 J. Econ. Perspectives 91 (2007), p. 94.
112 *Coates*, 21 J. Econ. Perspectives 91 (2007), p. 111.
113 Cf. *Quall*, CPA Journal 2004.
114 *Langevoort*, 31 J. Corp. L. 949 (2006), p. 957 et seq.
115 *Langevoort*, 31 J. Corp. L. 949 (2006), p. 958.
116 *Langevoort*, 31 J. Corp. L. 949 (2006), p. 958.
117 Cf. SEC Release No. 8762, at I.
118 *Coates*, 21 J. Econ. Perspectives 91 (2007), p. 96.

here the SEC. The idea is to leave the details up to better-informed regulators.[119] This approach allows for faster corrections if rules prove to be ineffective or inefficient and closer participation of private actors.

With regard to internal control systems, SOX required the SEC to implement rules on corporate responsibility for financial reports (sec. 302 SOX) and management assessment of internal controls (sec. 404 SOX). In order to implement sec. 302 and 404 SOX, the SEC promulgated Exchange Act Rule 13a-15 building on COSO I[120]. They require corporations to implement two separate but overlapping internal control systems.[121] The first system – disclosure controls and procedures required by sec. 302 SOX – is designed to provide non-financial information to management for any type of disclosure requirements mandated by the securities laws.[122] The second system – the internal control over financial reporting – is required by sec. 404 SOX with the emphasis on financial information. With regard to sec. 404 SOX, Item 308 of Regulation S-K mandates a report of management on internal control over financial reporting. Due to the audit requirement of the external auditors pursuant to sec. 404(b) SOX together with Rule 2-02(f) Regulation S-X, corporations focus especially on internal control over financial reporting.[123] So far, the main attention of commentators has been on sec. 404 SOX presumably due to the required auditor attestation and the more detailed instructions of Item 308 Regulation S-K.[124] On first glance, the mandates of SOX and related SEC rules for management to implement internal controls seem straight forward. On closer examination, management faces contradicting incentives to implement effective and efficient internal controls.

An important aspect of SOX is that it does not specifically address foreign corporations. Since SOX is part of the federal securities laws, their general applicability for foreign corporations determines the applicability of SOX. The securities laws do not differentiate between domestic and foreign corporations subject to sec. 13(a) Exchange Act.[125] Thus, as long as foreign corporations are listed on a U.S. exchange, they are subject to SOX equally to their domestic counterparts.[126] In order to accommodate the

119 Cf. *McDonnell*, 2004 Mich. St. L. Rev. 505, p. 506.
120 *Dodwell*, CPA Journal 2008.
121 Cf. *Langevoort*, 31 J. Corp. L. 949 (2006), p. 955.
122 Cf. *Langevoort*, 31 J. Corp. L. 949 (2006), p. 955.
123 *Langevoort*, 31 J. Corp. L. 949 (2006), p. 955.
124 Cf. *Langevoort*, 31 J. Corp. L. 949 (2006), p. 955.
125 SEC Release No. 8238, at II, H, 1.
126 *Fried Frank*, 2006, p. 2.

harsh consequences for foreign corporations subject to SOX, the SEC tried to ease the burdens for foreign corporations as far as possible under the clear wording of SOX. As far as foreign corporations are not subject to identical mandates than U.S. corporations, the differences will be addressed within the context.

The following analysis of SOX's internal control requirements will proceed by illustrating the mandates of sec. 302 SOX and related SEC rules and regulation followed by the mandates of sec. 404 SOX and related SEC rules and regulation. For both parts, special emphasis will be put on the requirements to fulfill the internal control mandates in order to provide guidance for corporations. After depicting the requirements of sec. 302 and 404 SOX, the incentives for officers to comply with these mandates will be analyzed. As a last step, further sections of SOX peripherally affecting internal controls will be addressed.

I. Disclosure Controls and Procedures: Corporate Responsibility for Financial Reports (Section 302 SOX) together with related SEC Rules and Regulations

In sec. 302 SOX Congress established corporate officer responsibility for financial reports to address the widely shared perception that officers lacked focus on financial and disclosure matters.[127] The SEC was required to promulgate rules which mandate that the principal executive officer and the principal financial officer of each corporation filing reports under sec. 13(a) Exchange Act make the mandated certifications. The officers are required to certify that they are personally responsible for establishing, maintaining, and regularly evaluating the effectiveness of the internal controls.[128] This personal responsibility has been described as being among "the most draconian sections of [SOX]".[129] Such liability reminds the CEO and CFO of their responsibility for being "personally" involved in the internal control and compliance system.[130] The personal involvement aims to ensure that the CEO and CFO are actually involved in the process of financial reporting.[131] Furthermore, the officers are required to disclose facts

127 *Johnson/Sides*, 30 Wm. Mitchell L. Rev. 1149 (2004), p. 1178.
128 Cf. SEC Release No. 8124, at Summary.
129 *Seligman*, 80 Notre Dame L. Rev. 1159 (2005), p. 1181.
130 *Seligman*, 80 Notre Dame L. Rev. 1159 (2005), p. 1181.
131 Cf. *Prentice/Spence*, 95 Geo. L. J. 1843 (2007), p. 1899.

to the corporation's auditors[132] and the audit committee of the board of directors about the internal controls. Moreover, the quarterly and annual reports have to include management's evaluation of the effectiveness of the internal controls including information on any significant changes within internal controls.

The certification of sec. 302 SOX does not only address internal control. The CEO and CFO also have to certify their personal responsibility for the accuracy of the financial statements by certifying that they reviewed the annual or quarterly report (sec. 302(a)(1) SOX), that, based on their knowledge, such report does not contain any untrue statement of a material fact or omit to state a material fact necessary in order to make the statements, in light of the circumstances under which such statements were made, not misleading (sec. 302(a)(2) SOX), and that, based on their knowledge, the financial statements, and other financial information included in such reports, fairly present in all material aspects the financial condition and results of operations as of, and for, the periods presented in the report (sec. 302(a)(3) SOX). With regard to internal controls, sec. 302 SOX requires that the CEO and CFO certify that they are responsible for establishing and maintaining internal controls (sec. 302(a)(4)(A) SOX), have designed the internal controls so that material information reaches them (sec. 302(a)(4)(B) SOX), evaluated the effectiveness of the internal controls (sec. 302(a)(4)(C) SOX), and have presented their conclusion about the effectiveness in each quarterly and annual report (sec. 302(a)(4)(D) SOX). Moreover, the CEO and CFO have to certify that they disclosed to the external auditor and the audit committee all significant deficiencies in the design or operation of internal controls which could adversely affect the corporation's ability to record, process, summarize, and report financial data and have identified for the corporation's auditors any material weaknesses in internal control (sec. 302(a)(5)(A) SOX), and any fraud that involves manage-

132 In the context of sec. 302 SOX, it has been stressed that the term auditor would refer both to external and internal auditors (*Moeller*, SOX Internal Controls, p. 33). In sec. 302 SOX, however, the term "auditor" is only used within the disclosure requirement of the signing officers regarding all significant deficiencies and any material weaknesses which have to be disclosed to the corporation's auditors and the audit committee. Since the audit committee is comprised of independent directors, the term auditor is more like to refer to outsiders like the external auditors. Also, the line of reporting and hierarchy within the corporation ranks the internal auditors under the CEO and CFO. Hence, it is highly unlikely to require a superior to disclose information to a subordinate. Thus, sec. 302 SOX is more likely to refer only to the external auditors.

ment or other employees with a significant role in the corporation's internal controls (sec. 302(a)(5)(B) SOX). They also have to certify that they disclosed in the respective report any significant changes in internal controls or other factors that could significantly affect internal controls including any corrective actions with regard to significant deficiencies and material weaknesses (sec. 302(a)(6) SOX).

In order to accommodate the certification requirements of sec. 302 SOX, the SEC adopted Exchange Act Rule 13a-14(a). Also, the SEC promulgated Exchange Act Rule 13a-15(a) requiring the corporation to maintain disclosure controls and procedures which are defined in Exchange Act Rule 13a-15(e). Furthermore, Exchange Act Rule 13a-15(b) requires the corporation to evaluate the effectiveness of disclosure controls and procedures. In Item 307[133] Regulation S-K, the SEC requires the corporation to disclose the conclusions of the CEO and CFO regarding the effectiveness of the disclosure controls and procedures. Thereby, the SEC ensures that interested parties will receive the information.

The rules regarding disclosure controls and procedures are necessary to address inconsistent legislation of SOX. In sec. 302 SOX, the signing officers are required to certify on the corporation's "internal controls".[134] The main problem of SOX leading to the complicated and confusing rule making of the SEC is that SOX itself does not clearly distinguish between "internal controls" for the certification required by sec. 302 SOX and the "internal control structure and procedures for financial reporting" in sec. 404 SOX. In sec. 302(a)(4)(A) SOX, the CEO and CFO have to state their responsibility for establishing and maintaining internal controls including the evaluation of such controls (sec. 302(a)(4)(C) SOX) and in sec. 404(a)(1) SOX management has to state their responsibility for establishing and maintaining an adequate internal control structure and procedures for financial reporting including the assessment of the effectiveness of such controls (sec. 404(a)(2) SOX). In order to accommodate for both certification requirements, the SEC draws on the fact that internal controls may address financial and non-financial information. The solution of the SEC includes the differentiation between non-financial internal controls of sec. 302(a)(4) SOX and financial internal controls of sec. 302(a)(5) and 302(a)(6) SOX to-

133 17 CFR 229.307.

134 The SEC notes that sec. 302 SOX includes more detailed statements on internal controls than proposed by the SEC in SEC Release No. 46079 "June Proposals" (cf. SEC Release No. 8124, at II, B, 3).

gether with sec. 404 SOX.[135] While non-financial internal controls are defined in Exchange Act Rule 13a-15(e) as disclosure controls and procedures, financial internal controls are defined in Exchange Act Rule 13a-15(f) as internal control over financial reporting. Both forms of internal controls may substantially overlap.[136] The non-financial internal controls contemplated by sec. 302(a)(4) SOX are regarded to embody controls and procedures addressing the quality and timeliness of disclosures[137] pursuant to the Exchange Act and are designed to ensure that the information for such disclosure is "recorded, processed, summarized and reported, within the time periods specified in the [SEC]'s rules and forms".[138] Whereas, the pre-existing concept of internal controls pertains to the corporation's financial reporting which has been embodied in sec. 13(b)(2) Exchange Act prior to the enactment of sec. 302(a)(5) and 302(a)(6) and sec. 404 SOX.[139] The SEC states its belief that it has been Congress's intent to have the CEO and CFO certify non-financial information as well as financial information within the quarterly and annual report.[140] By introducing the concept of disclosure controls and procedures for non-financial internal controls, the SEC tries to maintain the pre-existing concept of internal controls regarding financial information without expanding it to non-financial information.[141] Therefore, in addition to the mandates of sec. 302 SOX, the SEC adopted rules to require the corporation to maintain non-financial internal controls in order to distinguish non-financial internal controls from financial internal controls. These mandates are only indirectly inherent in sec. 302 SOX as the CEO and CFO have to certify that they have the responsibility to maintain internal controls and that they evaluated their effectiveness. The complicated and confusing solution of the SEC to use Exchange Act Rule 13a-15 and for separating and defining internal controls for non-financial and financial information is the result of the inexact legislation of SOX. With the mandate of Exchange Act Rule 13a-15(a) to require disclosure controls and procedures, the SEC acquires the prerogative of interpretation over the content of the certification requirements of sec. 302(a)(4)(A) and 302(a)(4)(C) SOX, i.e. over non-fi-

135 Cf. SEC Release No. 8124, at II, B, 3; SEC Release No. 8238, at II, D.
136 SEC Release No. 8238, at II, D.
137 SEC Release No. 8124, at II, B, 3.
138 SEC Release No. 8238, at II, D; also SEC Release No. 8124, at II, B, 3.
139 Cf. SEC Release No. 8124, at II, B, 3.
140 SEC Release No. 8124, at II, B, 3.
141 Cf. SEC Release No. 8124, at II, B, 3.

nancial internal controls. Due to the clear wording, foreign corporations are subject to the certification requirements of sec. 302 SOX.[142]

1. Certification Requirements for CEO and CFO – Exchange Act Rule 13a-14(a)

The certification requirements are laid out in Exchange Act Rule 13a-14(a) implementing the certification requirements of sec. 302(a) SOX. Each report filed on Form 10-Q, Form 10-K, or Form 20-F must include certifications specified in the applicable exhibit filing requirements of such report.[143] In order to accommodate the differentiation of the SEC between disclosure controls and procedures and internal control over financial reporting, the certification requirement of Exchange Act Rule 13a-14(a) deviates from sec. 302 SOX. The certification requirement adds to sec. 302(a)(3) SOX that, to the officer's knowledge, cash flows are also fairly presented in all material aspects in the financial statements. The certification requirement also adds to the certification that the signing officer is responsible for designing, establishing, and maintaining disclosure controls and procedures (sec. 302(a)(4)(A) SOX) and for internal control over financial reporting which has to be designed to provide reasonable assurance regarding the reliability of financial reporting and the preparation of financial statements for external purposes in accordance with U.S. GAAP. Likewise, the signing officer has evaluated the effectiveness of the disclosure controls and procedures (sec. 302(a)(4)(C) SOX) and has presented in the report their conclusions about the effectiveness of their disclosure controls and

142 Cf. SEC Release No. 8124, at II, B, 1, (a); in SEC Release No. 46079 "June Proposals" the SEC excluded foreign corporations form any mandatory requirements regarding internal controls because these are regarded to raise issues due to possible inconsistencies with the laws or practices of the foreign corporations' home jurisdiction and stock exchange requirements (at II, D).

143 Pursuant to Item 6 of Form 10-Q and Item 15(b) of Form 10-K, reports filed on these forms have to comply with Item 601 of Regulation S K. Pursuant to Item 601(a)(3) Regulation S-K, Item 601 only applies to the forms specified in the Exhibit Table. For Forms 10-Q and 10-K, No. 31 of the Instructions to the Exhibit Table of Item 601 requires for the certifications of the CEO and CFO the exact wording set out in No. 31 of the description of exhibits of Item 601. With regard to Form 20-F, the certifying officers have to use the exact wording set out in No. 12 of the Instructions as to Exhibits of Form 20-F. Both Item 601 Regulation S-K and No. 12 of the Instructions as to Exhibits of Form 20-F resemble similarly the requirements set out in sec. 302(a) SOX.

procedures (sec. 302(a)(4)(D) SOX). Furthermore, the respective officer has to certify that she has disclosed to the corporation's auditors and the audit committee of the board of directors (A) all significant deficiencies in the design or operation of internal control over financial reporting which could adversely affect the corporation's ability to record, process, summarize, and report financial data and have identified for the corporation's auditors any material weaknesses in internal control over financial reporting (sec. 302(a)(5)(A) SOX); and (B) any fraud, whether or not material, that involves management or other employees who have a significant role in the corporation's internal control over financial reporting (sec. 302(a)(5)(B) SOX). The certifying officer also has to certify that she discloses in the respective report any occurred change in the corporation's internal control over financial reporting.

In order to render the signing officers confident to sign the required certification, effective disclosure controls and procedures provide such confidence with regard to non-financial information. For confidence in certifying the financial statements with regard to financial information, sec. 404 SOX has been set in place by Congress.[144] A good documentation of the financial calculations is needed to make the officers comfortable to sign the financial reports with regard to the received information from reporting subordinates.[145] Each subordinate should be required to certify the information they provide in the same way as the CFO and the CEO are required to certify.[146] Moreover, open discussions of internal control issues between the CFO and financial staff should be encouraged to bring up and solve all issues endangering the corporation not to file complete and accurate financial statements.[147] Foreign corporations are not required to file quarterly reports due to sec. 13(a)(2) Exchange Act combined with Exchange Act Rule 13a-13(b)(2) combined with Exchange Act Rule 13a-16 eliminating the necessity for the sec. 302 SOX certification in quarterly reports. Also current reports of foreign corporations, e.g. reports on Form 6-K, are not subject to this certification requirement.[148]

---

144 *Prentice/Spence*, 95 Geo. L. J. 1843 (2007), p. 1901 et seq.

145 *Moeller*, SOX Internal Controls, p. 33.

146 Cf. *Kuntz*, in: The Metropolitan Corporate Counsel 2005; *Ferrara/Rust*, PLI Corporate Governance, p. 246; *Moeller*, SOX Internal Controls, p. 33.

147 Cf. *Kuntz*, in: The Metropolitan Corporate Counsel 2005.

148 Foreign corporations have to file any information on Form 6-K which they have to file pursuant to home laws and regulations. Since these home filings are not mandated by the SEC, the SEC believes that a Form 6-K report does not consti-

2. Mandates and Requirements of Disclosure Controls and Procedures – Exchange Act Rule 13a-15(a)

With regard to non-financial internal control, Exchange Act Rule 13a-15(a) mandates the corporation to maintain disclosure controls and procedures. The term "disclosure controls and procedures" is defined in Exchange Act Rule 13a-15(e) as controls and other procedures of a corporation that are designed to ensure that information required to be disclosed by the corporation in the reports that it files or submits under the Exchange Act is recorded, processed, summarized and reported, within the time periods specified in the SEC rules and forms. Disclosure controls and procedures include, without limitation, controls and procedures designed to ensure that information required to be disclosed by a corporation in the reports that it files or submits under the Exchange Act is accumulated and communicated to management, including its CEO and CFO, as appropriate to allow timely decisions regarding required disclosure as well as controls and procedures to address all issues the CEO and CFO have to certify in light of sec. 302 SOX. Disclosure controls and procedures also have to ensure full and timely disclosure in current reports, definitive proxy materials, and definitive information statements, even though these reporting forms are not subject to the certification requirement of Exchange Act Rule 13a-14(a).[149] That is because disclosure controls and procedures are intended to capture all information required to be disclosed in the Exchange Act reports.[150] All information includes financial and non-financial information. Therefore, all non-financial disclosures on a Form 10-K, 10-Q, or 20-F are covered by disclosure controls and procedures, e.g. the MD&A section, legal proceedings, disclosure of market risk, the business, properties, and executive compensation.[151] The SEC does not provide any further guidance on the requirements of disclosure controls and procedures. An information system is obligatory to process all the information which has to be disclosed by the Exchange Act. The signing officers are only required to ensure that material information is made known to them. Disclosure controls and procedures do not encompass the broad concept of COSO I internal controls which is particularly not limited to secure compliance with

tutes a periodic report. Therefore, the SEC reasons that the Form 6-K filings are not subject to sec. 302 SOX (cf. SEC Release No. 8124, at fn. 50).

149 SEC Release No. 8124, at II, B, 2.

150 *Waxman*, CPA Journal 2004.

151 *Waxman*, CPA Journal 2004.

federal securities laws.[152] The SEC notes that it does not require any particular procedures for conducting the required review and evaluation.[153] Nevertheless, the SEC recommends to create a committee with responsibility for considering the materiality of information and determining disclosures obligations on a timely basis which could include the principal accounting officer, the GC, and the principal risk management officer.[154] Also, the corporation should develop a review and evaluation process consistent with its business and internal management and oversight practices.[155]

3. Management's Evaluation of the Effectiveness of Disclosure Controls and Procedures

Pursuant to Exchange Act Rule 13a-15(b), management, including the CEO and CFO, has to evaluate the effectiveness of the disclosure controls and procedures at the end of each fiscal quarter. Due to Exchange Act Rule 13a-15(b)(1), foreign corporations have to evaluate their disclosure controls and procedures only at the end of each fiscal year. The SEC notes that it does not require any particular procedures for the evaluation.[156] Nevertheless, the SEC expects the disclosure controls and procedures to provide at least reasonable assurance regarding their objectives for management's determination that disclosure controls and procedures are effective.[157] With regard to the sec. 302 SOX requirements, it is has been suggested to apply the same risk-based approach of PCAOB AS 5.[158]

II. Internal Control over Financial Reporting: Management Assessment of Internal Controls (Section 404 SOX) together with related SEC Rules and Regulations

In sec. 404 SOX, Congress did not impose direct obligations on corporations. Rather, sec. 404 SOX requires the SEC to promulgate rules requiring

152 SEC Release No, 8238, at II, D.
153 SEC Release No. 8124, at II, B, 3.
154 SEC Release No. 8124, at II, B, 3 and at fn. 60.
155 SEC Release No. 8124, at II, B, 3.
156 SEC Release No. 8124, at II, B, 3.
157 SEC Release No. 8238, at II, F, 4.
158 *Moeller*, SOX Internal Controls, p. 187 et seq.

each annual report of a corporation pursuant to sec. 13(a) Exchange Act[159] to contain an internal control report. The rules have to require that the internal control report contains a statement of management's responsibility to establish and maintain an adequate internal control structure and procedures for financial reporting (sec. 404(a)(1) SOX). Also, the internal control report has to contain management's assessment of the effectiveness of the internal control structure and procedures for financial reporting as of the end of the most recent fiscal year of the issuer (sec. 404(a)(2) SOX). As a third mandate, sec. 404(b) SOX requires the registered public accounting firm preparing or issuing the annual report of a corporation to attest to, and report on, management's assessment regarding sec. 404(a)(2) SOX. The attestation must be made in accordance with PCAOB AS 5.[160] A separate engagement of a public accounting firm for the sec. 404(b) SOX attestation is not allowed (sec. 404(b)(s. 2) SOX). Sec. 404(c) SOX is only relevant for small corporations.[161] In contrast to sec. 404(a) SOX, sec. 404(b) SOX places an obligation on the public accounting firm that prepares and issues the audit report. This obligation also affects management. Since the auditing firm has to comply with the standards of the PCAOB, the assessment of management will be influences by these standards.[162]

The two mandates of sec. 404(a) SOX represent the goals that each corporation has implemented adequate and effective internal control over financial reporting. Management has to assess each of the two goals within the evaluation process of sec. 404(a)(2) SOX. First, management has to ensure and assess whether the design of the system of internal control over financial reporting is adequate to address financial reporting risks, i.e. if it prevents or detects material misstatements of financial statements. Second, management has to ensure and assess whether the system of internal control over financial reporting actually operates effectively as planned. Management's evaluation also has to include any change in internal control over financial reporting. As a measure to provide assurance for investors of management's assessment, the external auditor has to attest to the assessment of management as required by sec. 404(b) SOX. The disclosure requirements of sec. 404 SOX ensure that investors and enforcement agencies will be provided with important information.

159 15 USC 78m(a) or 78o(d).

160 See for a detailed analysis *infra* at chapter 4, B.

161 See *infra* at chapter 20, B. I. 2. c) (3).

162 See *infra* at chapter 4, B.

In order to fulfill its assignments of sec. 404 SOX, the SEC promulgated Exchange Act Rule 13a-15 and Item 308 of Regulation S-K. Exchange Act Rule 13a-15(a) seizes on the assumption of sec. 404(a)(1) SOX that every corporation must have internal control over financial reporting since management must state its responsibility to establish and maintain "an adequate internal control structure and procedures for financial reporting". Exchange Act Rule 13a-15(c) implements sec. 404(a)(2) SOX by requiring management to evaluate the effectiveness of the internal control over financial reporting. With regard to the new disclosure obligations of sec. 404 SOX, the SEC issued Item 308 Regulation S-K requiring a report of management containing management's statement on responsibility for internal controls over financial reporting, management's assessment of the effectiveness of the internal control over financial reporting, and the attestation report of the external auditors.

1. Mandates and Requirements of Internal Control over Financial Reporting – Exchange Act Rules 13a-15(a)

Exchange Act Rule 13a-15(a) requires every corporation that either had been required to file an annual report pursuant to sec. 13(a) of the Exchange Act for the prior fiscal year, or had filed an annual report with the SEC for the prior fiscal year to maintain internal control over financial reporting as defined in Exchange Act Rule 13a-15(f). In order to provide insight into the mandates and requirements of internal control over financial reporting, the SEC definition and elements for internal control over financial reporting, factors influencing the design of internal control over financial reporting, fraud prevention and detection through internal control over financial reporting, and the implementation process will be depicted.

a) Elements of Internal Control over Financial Reporting – Exchange Act Rules 13a-15(f)

In Exchange Act Rule 13a-15(f), the SEC defines internal control over financial reporting for purposes of sec. 404 SOX-related internal controls. In general, the term internal control is used to refer to the mandates of sec. 404 SOX. But the SEC noticed that there has been some confusion about the exact meaning and scope of the term internal control because the term has been mainly used by accountants prior to SOX.[163] By diverging from the exact wording of sec. 404(a)(1) SOX "internal control structures and procedures for financial reporting", the SEC defines in Exchange Act Rule 13a-15(f) the term "internal control over financial reporting". While using this term, the SEC accommodates the specific language used by corporations and auditors with regard to the objectives of SOX.[164] The SEC refers to the definition of internal control used by the American Institute of Certified Public Accountants (AICPA) in SAS No. 78[165] to derive a definition for sec. 404 SOX purposes. The AICPA incorporated into SAS No. 78 the definition of internal control by COSO I.[166] Therefore, the definition of internal control over financial reporting reflects the part of COSO I regarding financial reporting.[167] The use of the AICPA standard shows the intent of the SEC to build on the existing mandates and practices for internal controls and the reliance on the CPAs right after the enactment of SOX.[168]

In Exchange Act Rule 13a-15(f), the SEC defines the term "internal control over financial reporting" as: [...] [a] process designed by, or under the supervision of, the [corporation]'s principal executive and principal financial officers, or persons performing similar functions, and effected by the [corporation]'s board of directors, management and other personnel, to provide reasonable assurance regarding the reliability of financial reporting and the preparation of financial statements for external purposes in accordance with generally accepted accounting principles and includes those policies and procedures that: (1) Pertain to the maintenance of records that in reasonable detail accurately and fairly reflect the transactions and dispositions of the assets of the [corporation]; (2) Provide reasonable assurance that transactions are recorded as necessary to permit preparation of financial statements in accordance with generally accepted accounting principles, and that receipts and expenditures of the [corporation] are being made only in accordance with authorizations of management and directors of the [corporation]; and (3) Provide reasonable assurance regarding prevention or timely detection of unauthorized acquisition, use or disposition of the [corporation]'s assets that could have a material effect on the finan-

163 SEC Release No. 8238, at II, A, 1 and 3. For more details on the history of the term see: *Root*, Beyond COSO.

164 Cf. SEC Release No. 8238, at II, A, 3.

165 Codified by AU § 319; superseded by SAS 109, AU § 314 and SAS 110, AU § 318.

166 SEC Release No. 8238, at II, A, 1.

167 SEC Release No. 8238, at II, A, 3.

168 In subsequent releases, the SEC explicitly refrains from further relying on the standards of the AICPA successor PCAOB (see SEC Release No. 8810, at fn. 47).

cial statements. In light of the definition, the CEO and CFO have to design and, together with the board of directors, management and other personnel, effect internal control over financial reporting which reasonably ensure the reliability of financial reporting and the preparation of financial statements in accordance with U.S. GAAP. The corporation has to maintain records reasonably reflecting accurately and fairly the transactions and dispositions of assets necessary to prepare the financial statements. Also, internal control over financial reporting has to ensure that receipts and expenditures are only made when authorized and that unauthorized acquisition, use, or disposition of assets potentially leading to material misstatements of financial statements is prevented or timely detected. While the definition is based on the COSO I definition of internal control, it is limited to the second of the three COSO I categories "reliability of financial reporting", therefore eliminating categories one and three "effectiveness and efficiency of operations" and "compliance with applicable laws and regulations" of the COSO I definition for sec. 404 SOX purposes. The SEC definition of internal control further incorporates in clauses (1) and (2) the matters of sec. 103(2)(A)(iii)(II) and 404(b) SOX regarding the annual auditor's evaluation of internal control. By incorporating these two clauses, the SEC wants to ensure that the assessment of management (sec. 404(a)(2) SOX) covers the matters which the auditors are required to attest to and report on in the audit report.[169] In clause (3), the SEC highlights the purpose of internal control to safeguard the assets of the corporation.[170]

Within the definition of internal control over financial reporting, the term "reasonable assurance" is critical.[171] Prior to SOX, courts interpreted "reasonable assurance" to require only cost-justified controls.[172] The term "reasonable assurance" conforms with sec. 13(b)(2) Exchange Act[173] and, therefore, relates to similar language in the FCPA, implemented in sec. 13(b)(7) Exchange Act, defining "reasonable assurance" and "reasonable detail" as "such level of detail and degree of assurance as would satisfy prudent officials in the conduct of their own affairs"[174]. In this regard, the

169 Cf. SEC Release No. 8238, at II, A, 3.

170 Cf. SEC Release No. 8238, at II, A, 3; Clause (3) encompasses the 1994 addendum to COSO I which dealt with concerns that the then-current definition of internal control within COSO I did not adequately address controls relating to safeguarding the corporation's assets required by the FCPA.

171 *Waxman*, CPA Journal 2004.

172 *SEC v. World-Wide Coin Investment Ltd.*, 567 F. Supp. 724 (N.D. Ga. 1983) at 751.

173 SEC Release No. 8238, at II, F, 4.

174 SEC Release No. 8810, at I.

SEC has long held that reasonableness is not an "absolute standard" for perfect financial records.[175] Internal control over financial reporting has inherent limitations since it involves human diligence and compliance, and is subject to human failures. These controls can also be circumvented by collusion or improper management override.[176] Therefore, internal control over financial reporting cannot prevent or detect all misstatements including unintentional errors or intentional behavior such as fraud.[177] By fulfilling the level of reasonable assurance, the internal control over financial reporting of a corporation will only have a remote likelihood that material misstatements will not be prevented or not be detected on a timely basis.[178] The difference between reasonable assurance and absolute assurance is a recognizable margin[179] which has been named to be less than 10% likelihood that the cumulative risk of known internal control weaknesses results in a material misstatement[180]. A factor to provide reasonable assurance is that all identified control weaknesses are promptly corrected.[181] In general, it depends on the corporation's facts and circumstances what constitutes reasonableness.[182] If the corporation reaches the level of reasonable assurance, internal control over financial reporting is adequate. The same conclusion regarding adequacy can be reached if no material weaknesses exist in internal control over financial reporting.[183] The definition of internal control over financial reporting is in line with the mandates for internal accounting controls of sec. 13(b)(2)(B) Exchange Act which has been implemented by the Foreign Corrupt Practices Act of 1977.[184] Therefore, the internal controls of a corporation which fulfill the SOX requirements also fulfill in general the FCPA requirements[185] for internal accounting controls. In contrast to the FCPA, SOX mandates in conjunction with related SEC and PCAOB rules address corporate governance issues in greater detail[186] providing more guidance for management. Thus,

175 SEC Release No. 8810, at I.
176 SEC Release No. 8810, at I.
177 SEC Release No. 8810, at I.
178 *Waxman*, CPA Journal 2004.
179 *Waxman*, CPA Journal 2004.
180 Cf. IIA Guide 2008, p. 14.
181 IIA Guide 2008, p. 14.
182 *Waxman*, CPA Journal 2004.
183 Cf. *infra* at chapter 4, A. II. 2. b) (3).
184 Cf. SEC Release No. 8238, at II, A, 3; *Waxman*, CPA Journal 2004.
185 See *infra* at chapter 5, A. I.
186 *Seligman*, 80 Notre Dame L. Rev. 1159 (2005), p. 1184.

one of the major criticisms of the FCPA, failing to provide guidance, has been avoided by the SEC.

Besides the definition of internal control over financial reporting, the SEC does not require any specifics with regard to the design of these controls and does not provide further guidance on what constitutes internal controls over financial reporting. Nevertheless, the SEC describes a control to consist of policies, procedures, and activities which may be integrated into a process to foster an objective.[187] The scope of a control may be entity-wide, or specific for an account balance, class of transactions or application. Controls usually have ample characteristics such as being "automated or manual", "reconciliations", "segregation of duties", "review and approval authorizations", "safeguarding and accountability of assets", or "preventing or detecting error or fraud".[188] Controls within a process may consist of financial reporting controls and operational controls.[189] Some guidance can be drawn from SEC enforcement proceedings used in special circumstances to reform parts of the corporate governance structure of corporations affecting internal controls[190] providing insight into measures the SEC determines appropriate to improve internal controls. These measures include direct reporting of the GC to the audit committee on the corporation's financial reporting obligations[191], requiring the appointment of an internal auditor reporting directly to the audit committee[192], and requiring training of the board of directors[193]. It can be concluded that a direct reporting line of the officers responsible for internal controls to the audit committee is essential for effective internal controls. Qualified directors are also important for adequately fulfilling their task within the internal control system. In general, internal controls have to be scalable to quickly adjust to an increase of demand.[194] Thereby, the corporation cannot easily outgrow its internal control.[195]

Following from best practice, controls over spreadsheets are essential to comply with sec. 404 SOX.[196] Corporations commonly use spreadsheets to

187 SEC Release No. 8810, at fn. 27.
188 SEC Release No. 8810, at fn. 27.
189 SEC Release No. 8810, at fn. 27.
190 Cf. *Brown*, 57 Cath. U. L. Rev. 45 (2007), p. 59 et seq.
191 SEC Release No. 49675, III, E, 2, a.
192 SEC Release No. 19986.
193 SEC Release No. 8651, III, E, 1.
194 *Moeller*, SOX Internal Controls, p. 164.
195 *Moeller*, SOX Internal Controls, p. 164.
196 *PwC*, 2004, p. 4.

organize their operational, financial, and management information.[197] After identifying all spreadsheets and assessing their complexity and involved risks, various controls may be used to mitigate the risks.[198]

b) Factors Influencing the Design of Internal Control over Financial Reporting

The SEC refrains from providing more guidance on the substance of internal control over financial reporting to avoid limiting corporations in their efforts to design suitable internal control over financial reporting specifically addressing the needs and particularities of each corporation.[199] Therefore, corporations do not have to follow any particular guidance for designing its internal control over financial reporting. Nevertheless, corporations have to consider the following factors for their design. First, due to sec. 13(l) Exchange Act implemented by sec. 409 SOX, the SEC requires real time reports on Form 8-K being filed within four business days after the triggering events.[200] Therefore, the internal control system has to ensure the timeliness and appropriateness of such reporting. Second, designing

197 *PwC*, 2004, p. 2.

198 *PwC*, 2004, p. 4 et seq. These controls include change control requiring testing and sign-off of changes, version control ensuring that only current and approved spreadsheet versions will be used by creating name conventions and directory structures, access control by assigning limited assess e.g. read only and password protection, input control assuring complete and accurate input through reconciliations, data has to be secured and integrity ensured by protecting cells to be changed, documentation is necessary to understand the business objective and specific function of the spreadsheets, a process to back up spreadsheets on a regular basis, archiving historical files in segregated storage as read only, inspecting the logic within critical spreadsheets by an outsider which should be documented, and monitoring by implementing analytics to find errors in spreadsheets.

199 Cf. SEC Release No. 8810, at III, B.

200 See SEC Release No. 8400; prior to SOX, the SEC granted a period of 14 days to file a Form 8-K report (*Moeller*, SOX Internal Controls, p. 191). The triggering events are listed in Items 1-6 and 9 of Form 8-K: entry and termination into a material definitive agreement, bankruptcy or receivership, completion of acquisition or disposition of assets, results of operations and financial conditions, creation of a direct financial obligation or an obligation under an off-balance sheet arrangement, triggering events that accelerate or increase a direct financial obligation or an obligation under an off-balance sheet arrangement, costs associated with exit or disposal activities, material impairments, notice of delisting or fail-

the internal controls considering best practice will be more efficient since the external auditors and the SEC will be familiar with such kind of design. External auditors have their own standards for their sec. 404(b) attestation and the SEC has its own standard for considering if the reporting obligations of the corporations in regard to internal control over financial reporting have been met. In case a corporation does not align its internal control over financial reporting to these standards, it will face considerable more effort to convince the external auditor and the SEC that its internal control over financial reporting fulfills the regulatory requirements. Hence, corporations have an incentive to consider these standards for designing their internal control over financial reporting. Third, the audit committee is responsible for overseeing management with regard to internal control over financial reporting and has to review management's reports. Since the audit committee is totally comprised of independent directors due to sec. 10A(m)(3)(A) Exchange Act, implemented by sec. 301 SOX, the independent directors are likely knowledgeable of the best practice regarding internal control over financial reporting including the standards of the external auditors and the SEC rendering these directors probably more comfortable to deal with known internal control over financial reporting structures, either due to their own knowledge or the advice of consultants likely to favor known internal control structures. Forth, since sec. 407 SOX encourages the audit committee to be comprised of at least one financial expert who has *inter alia* experience with internal accounting controls (sec. 407(b)(3) SOX), this audit committee member will be familiar with the standards of the external auditors and the SEC. Due to these factors, management should consider the triggering events of Form 8-K and the best practice of internal control over financial reporting including the standards of the external auditors and the SEC for designing their internal control over financial reporting. At the end, internal control over fi-

---

ure to satisfy a continued listing rule or standard as well as transfer of listing, unregistered sales of equity securities, material modifications to rights of security holders, changes in the certifying accountant, non-reliance of previously issued financial statements or a related audit report or completed interim review, changes in control, departure of directors or principal officers as well as election of directors and appointment of principal officers, amendments to articles of incorporation or by-laws as well as change in fiscal year, temporary suspension of trading under the employee benefit plans, amendments to the code of ethics or waiver of a provision of the code of ethics, and financial statements and exhibits for any business acquisition.

nancial reporting has to be adequate and effective so that the external auditors attest to management's assessment of the effectiveness.

In contrast to the design of internal control over financial reporting, the evaluation process of these controls has received more attention from the SEC and PCAOB so that their specifications impact the designing process of internal control over financial reporting. The requirements for management's assessment of the effectiveness of internal control over financial reporting have by far the greatest impact. The SEC requires management to use an appropriate framework for the assessment. Currently, the COSO I framework serves as the *de facto* standard but other frameworks may be used. While sec. 404 SOX and related rules do not prescribe any specific design of internal controls over financial reporting, the performance goals and objectives are set by the framework such as COSO I. Thus, no matter how each corporation designs its internal control over financial reporting, it has to achieve the requirements set by the chosen framework.[201] The framework has to be used to define the aims of each individual design of internal control over financial reporting. Thereby, management has to use an inverted process to design internal control over financial reporting by starting with the performance goals of the internal control system set by the framework to design the specific controls of the internal control system. Despite the impact of COSO I as the *de facto* standard for the evaluation process, COSO I has an even greater standard setting effect for internal control over financial reporting since most of the definition of Exchange Act Rule 13a-15(f) resembles COSO I. It follows that the requirements for management's assessment of internal control over financial reporting have twofold importance for management. First, for conducting the evaluation process itself, and, second, for designing internal control over financial reporting. From the SEC release adopting the sec. 404 SOX mandates and particularly from the guidance for the evaluation process, it can be extracted that the internal control over financial reporting should at least contain the following internal controls: "controls over initiating, recording and reconciling account balances, classes of transactions and disclosure and related assertions included in the financial statements; controls related to the initiation and processing of non-routine and non-systematic transactions; controls related to the selection and application of appropriate accounting policies; and controls related to the prevention, identification, and detection of fraud".[202] The requirements of internal control over

201 Cf. SEC Release No. 8810, at II, A. See further *infra* at chapter 4, A. II. 2. b) (1).
202 SEC Release No. 8238, at II, B, 3, d.

financial reporting following from COSO I and the PCAOB will be dealt with below.[203]

c) Fraud Prevention and Detection through Internal Control over Financial Reporting

In light of SOX mandates for internal controls, the prevention and detection of fraud has become a pointed issue as it has been noted that "after SOX [internal controls] increasingly are intended to prevent fraud".[204] Nevertheless, fraud is not expressly mentioned in the definition of internal control over financial reporting of Exchange Act Rule 13a-15(f). Due to sec. 302(a)(5)(B) SOX which the SEC interprets to relate to internal control over financial reporting, the CEO and CFO have to disclose to the audit committee and the external auditors any fraud that involves management or employees with a significant role in internal controls. In relation to the scope of internal control over financial reporting, the disclosing duty is limited to fraud in the context of financial reporting. While the disclosing requirement as such does not require any controls to prevent or detect fraud, the SEC expects corporations to maintain within internal control over financial reporting "controls related to the prevention, identification, and detection of fraud"[205] since fraud, especially securities fraud, may affect the reliability of the financial statements. These controls are thought to prevent or at least detect financial fraud such as Ponzi schemes illustrated by the *Madoff* case. While neither sec. 302(a)(5)(B) SOX nor Exchange Act Rule 13a-15(f) expressly require corporations to implement controls related to fraud, SOX's internal controls have been criticized for being ineffective to address high-level fraud.[206] The critique is merited with regard to the observation that internal control over financial reporting is ineffective to address high-level fraud[207] but misses the point by criticizing SOX for such ineffectiveness. The main focus of internal control over financial reporting in SOX is accurate financial reporting. As most inaccuracies in financial reporting do not result from fraud[208], the main focus of internal

203 See *infra* at chapter 4, C. I. for COSO I and at chapter 4, B. for the PCAOB.
204 *Cunningham*, 29 J. Corp. L. 267 (2004), p. 277.
205 SEC Release No. 8238, at II, B, d.
206 Cf. *Carney*, 55 Emory L. J. 141 (2006), p. 142.
207 Cf. *Oversightsystems*, 2005, p. 1.
208 *Brown*, 2006, p. 327.

control over financial reporting should not be fraud. More importantly, internal control over financial reporting has inherent limitations[209] which are especially pointed with regard to intentional behavior such as fraud. Unintentional behavior such as negligent entering of financial data as well as low level intentional behavior can be addressed by financial internal controls e.g. automated software controls requiring the entry of financial data in a specific format or restrictions on authority to modify financial data. Even with regard to intentional behavior such as fraud, internal control over financial reporting is important within the overall compliance system as it makes violations of law more difficult to carry out. It serves as an important underlying factor to prevent and detect fraud as corporations detect fraudulent financial reporting earlier and may deter financial fraud or minimize its adverse effects through improved disclosure.[210] Internal control over financial reporting, however, is not by itself effective to prevent and detect all intentional and unintentional behavior leading to inaccurate financial statements. Financial controls may be circumvented or overridden especially from high-level executives in order to intentionally violate accounting provisions.[211] Without further elements to prevent circumvention and overrides of financial controls, especially from high-level managers, such controls will be ineffective. Further elements are also needed to offset the inherent limitations of financial controls. This finding is supported by research indicating that internal controls are in general an important factor to prevent and detect fraud as more than 35% of global occupational fraud cases in 2008 to 2011 lacked internal controls all together.[212] The other control weaknesses contributing to fraud: "lack of management review, override of existing internal controls, poor tone at the top, lack of independent audits, lack of competent personnel in oversight roles, lack of clear lines of authority, lack of employee fraud education, lack of reporting mechanisms"[213] show that other than strictly financial related control elements are necessary to prevent and detect fraud. Corporations need to implement controls addressing fraud as a general mean to comply with the law and to fulfill SEC expectations. The finding demonstrates the aspect that the elements of COSO I internal controls overlap.[214]

---

209 See *infra* at chapter 4, C. I. 1. b).
210 SEC Release No. 8238, at V, A. See also *infra* at chapter 13, B. III.
211 See *infra* at chapter 4, C. I. 1. b).
212 ACFE Report 2010, p. 45; ACFE Report 2012, p. 38.
213 ACFE Report 2010, p. 45; ACFE Report 2012, p. 38.
214 See *infra* at chapter 4, C. I. 1. a).

A comprehensive approach to internal controls such as COSO I provides for such elements through a general compliance program. These elements are more important to address intentional violations such as fraud so that financial controls will not be circumvented or overridden. Such elements are e.g. control environment, reporting hotlines, internal audit and management reviews tone at the top, and a culture of compliance. In order to render the compliance program effective with regard to fraud, a specific fraud risk management program is advisable. The elements of the fraud risk management program should be part of the general compliance program and have to focus on the main reasons for executive fraud: "pressures to do 'whatever it takes' to meet goals", "seek personal gain", "think 'I won't get caught", and "they do not consider their actions fraudulent".[215] A comprehensive fraud risk management program should include: a policy statement including a definition of fraud and the commitment of management for a zero tolerance policy regarding fraud; assigning the responsibility for the fraud risk management program to a fraud control officer; conducting fraud risk assessments; measures to increase fraud awareness through communication and training including the evaluation of the effectiveness of training; implementation of fraud reporting lines including hotlines; implementation of fraud prevention and detection controls; review of such controls; reduction of unnecessary entities within the organizational structure to prevent misuse; integration of anti-fraud policy in contracts with vendors, contractors, and business partners; investigations of prospective employees, contractors, vendors, and business partners assuring that no fraud history exists; communication that fraud detection controls exist but refraining from communicating details; and mandatory vacation periods or job rotation assignments for employees in key finance and accounting control positions.[216] Thereby, a fraud risk management program facilitates reporting of suspicious behavior fostering vigilant reviews of internal audit and management and increases the likelihood that tips by employees will reach appropriate departments within the corporation so that fraud will be detected.[217]

While the named elements of a general compliance program are also recommended by COSO I for the second internal control category reliability

215 *Oversightsystems*, 2007, p. 2.

216 IIA/AICPA/ACFE, 2008, p. 6 et seq.

217 Cf. for detection methods for occupational fraud: ACFE Report 2010, p. 16; ACFE Report 2012, p. 14.

of financial reporting[218], they are more pointed in the third internal control category compliance with applicable laws and regulations. It follows that SOX mandated internal control over financial reporting prevents and detects fraud but a general compliance program including elements to address fraud is needed. The same issue exists with regard to the ability of the FCPA internal accounting controls to address corruption.[219] As no compliance program is able to prevent and detect all fraudulent behavior, the level of accuracy of the compliance program to be considered effective is important. With regard to internal control over financial reporting, the definition sets the level of accuracy to reasonable assurance. For the general compliance program, the effectiveness requirements for such programs are set out in the USSG, which will be discussed further below[220], and also in the DOJ Principles of Federal Prosecution of Business Organizations, the so-called "Filip memorandum", which will be discussed below.[221]

Apart from high-level intentional violations of law, internal controls are equipped to some point to address intentional violations of mid and low level employees as restricted authority and appropriate reviews by management serve to protect financial controls from overriding and circumvention. Since high-level management ultimately controls internal control over financial reporting and the compliance program, these systems are insufficient to address high-level fraud. At this point, corporate governance and ethics play a vital role to address high-level intentional violations of laws in order to achieve the goal of accurate financial reporting and compliance with laws and regulations in general. To some part, corporate governance addresses the issue of intentional violations of laws by high-level management through general means of oversight by the board of directors and especially the audit committee. SOX also addresses insufficient oversight within the corporate governance setting which will be dealt with below.[222] Nevertheless, for all levels within the corporation but especially in regard to high-level management, controls and oversight do have their limits. Therefore, fostering ethical behavior is crucial to achieve compliance with laws and regulations as the single best way to prevent intentional violations of law is to eliminate the intent to violate the law.

---

218 See *infra* at chapter 4, C. I. 1. a).
219 See *infra* at chapter 5, A.
220 See *infra* at chapter 5, C. II. 1.
221 See *infra* at chapter 5, D. I.
222 See *infra* at chapter 4, A. IV.

d) Implementation of Internal Control over Financial Reporting and Documentation

In most large corporations, internal control over financial reporting are already implemented. Nevertheless, new controls will be added or existing controls will be revised. In case of a major overhaul of the existing controls, the guidance for implementing controls should be considered for the process. For the implementation of internal control over financial reporting, an implementation team has to be formed with sufficient authority, resources and access to management which develops an implementation plan subject to approval by a supervising committee which corresponds with the CEO, CFO, GC, and the board of directors, especially with the audit committee, regarding the requirements of the implementation project.[223] The implementation team is responsible for executing the implementation plan. It should consist of representatives of all critical disciplines of the corporation such as accounting, internal audit, IT, foreign divisions, key business units, and treasury.[224] An important issue of the implementation process is the documentation of the implemented internal controls. Prior to SOX, the documentation of internal control was often provided by the external auditors.[225] While the external auditors may still provide help for the documentation, they are no longer allowed to do the whole documentation according to sec. 10A(g)(2) Exchange Act. The detailed documentation can be built on an already existing internal control structure. The documentation of internal controls is a prerequisite for the evaluation process of internal control over financial reporting. Therefore, the documentation should include the internal control objectives and any known internal control deficiencies.[226] While it would also be feasible to document the internal controls as part of the evaluation process, corporations should execute this step during the implementation process in order to reduce the workload of the evaluation process.

In general, three common methods of documentation exist: narratives, flowcharts, and internal control questionnaires which may be used separately or in combination.[227] The documentation should start at the policy

223 *Quall*, CPA Journal 2004.
224 *Quall*, CPA Journal 2004.
225 *Moeller*, SOX Internal Controls, p. 85.
226 *Quall*, CPA Journal 2004.
227 *Quall*, CPA Journal 2004.

and procedure manual or similar documentation.[228] System descriptions are also a good starting point. Narratives are a written description of corporation's internal controls and financial cycles and should include "[d]escriptions of every document and record used in the accounting system", "[d]escriptions of every process that occurs, whether manual or computer-generated, drilled down to the lowest level possible (e.g., preparation of purchase orders with the applicable sign offs)", "[d]escriptions of the disposition of every document and record in the system", and "[i]ndications of the identified control related to the document or procedure[: e.g.] authorizations and approvals, preparer and reviewer sign-offs, verification, and separation of duties".[229] Flowcharts are a symbolic representation of the corporation's flow of documents and processes and better represent document workflow and separation of duties.[230] They have the advantage of being easily updated. The documentation is usually best done by using flowcharts showing inputs, outputs, process steps, and key decision points for each process.[231] The documentation should include key transaction flows and control points.[232] In most cases, software will be used for the documentation process requiring well-trained users who "must be able to correctly understand the computer-generated documentation and evaluate its findings and conclusions".[233] Moreover, reliable storage of the documentation including back-ups is essential.

2. Management's Evaluation of the Effectiveness of Internal Control over Financial Reporting – Exchange Act Rule 13a-15(c)

With the enactment of Exchange Act Rule 13a-15(c), the SEC fulfilled Congress's assignment to require corporations subject to sec. 13(a) Exchange Act to assess the effectiveness of internal control over financial reporting. The first implementing release did not contain substantive guidance on the evaluation process[234] despite comments to the SEC's proposed rules raising the issue that the SEC definition of internal controls does neither include any guidelines for management to determine the effectiveness

228 *Quall*, CPA Journal 2004.
229 *Quall*, CPA Journal 2004.
230 *Quall*, CPA Journal 2004.
231 *Moeller*, SOX Internal Controls, p. 164.
232 *Moeller*, SOX Internal Controls, p. 161.
233 *Quall*, CPA Journal 2004.
234 Cf. *Langevoort*, 31 J. Corp. L. 949 (2006), p. 955.

of internal control nor any definition what constitutes effective internal controls.[235] Due to ongoing criticism[236], the SEC published further guidance for corporations in 2005[237] initiating the comprehensive amendments to the guidance on management's report on internal control over financial reporting, known as the "2007 reforms", allowing management to conduct a top-down, risk-based evaluation.[238] This guidance is widely used by corporations.[239] The responsibility for the review, documentation, and assessment of internal controls over financial reporting rests with management, internal audit, and consultants. In this regard, sec. 404 SOX and related SEC rules "strengthen the burden placed upon the board of directors and the [CEO] and [CFO]".[240] The external auditors have to attest to and rely on the sufficiency of the internal controls reviews made by management.[241] Exchange Act Rule 13a-15(c) requires that management including the principal executive and principal financial officers[242] evaluate the effectiveness of the internal control over financial reporting as of the end of each fiscal year. Management's assessment has to use procedures to sufficiently evaluate the design and the operating effectiveness of internal control over financial reporting.[243] It is one of the primary obligations of management to determine whether internal controls have material weaknesses.[244] The SEC notes that the method for the evaluation will vary from corporation to corporation.[245]

The following requirements for the evaluation of the effectiveness of internal control over financial reporting are fundamental for every evaluation especially if management decides to refrain from using the optional guidance of the SEC for the evaluation process introduced as part of the

---

235 SEC Release No. 8238, at II, A, 2.

236 See e.g. *Committee Capital Markets Reg.*, 2006, p. 19; *Grundfest/Bochner*, 105 Mich. L. Rev. 1643 (2007); *Gupta/Leech*, 3 Int. J. Disclosure and Governance 27 (2006).

237 See SEC, Staff Statement; SEC, ICFR-FAQ. This guidance of 2005 remains relevant (SEC Release No. 8810, at III, H).

238 See SEC Release No. 8809 and SEC Release No. 8810.

239 SEC Study Sec. 404, p. 2.

240 *Seligman*, 80 Notre Dame L. Rev. 1159 (2005), p. 1183.

241 *Moeller*, SOX Internal Controls, p. 40.

242 Exchange Act Rule 13a-15(c) further notes that, alternatively to the CEO and CFO, persons performing similar functions have to participate in management's evaluation.

243 SEC Release No. 8238, at II, B, 3, d.

244 Cf. *Waxman*, CPA Journal 2004.

245 SEC Release No. 8238, at II, B, 3, d.

2007 reforms. Management's evaluation of internal control over financial reporting has to be based on a suitable, recognized control framework that is established by a body or group that has followed due-process procedures including the broad distribution of the framework for public comment.[246] So far, the SEC considers COSO I to fulfill the requirements of Exchange Act Rule 13a-15(c).[247] Nevertheless, the SEC does not mandate COSO I and will accept other frameworks which satisfy the intent of SOX without diminishing the benefits to investors.[248] Thus, while foreign corporations have the obligation to evaluate their internal control over financial reporting, they may draw on a home country framework for the evaluation[249] as long as it fulfills the SEC requirements for a suitable framework. Management has to disclose the used framework pursuant Item 308(a)(2) Regulation S-K. Due to the SEC's emphasis on COSO I, it became the "*de facto* standard" for sec. 404 SOX purposes.[250]

Corporations have to maintain evidential matter including documentation to provide reasonable support of management's assessment regarding the conducted evaluation and development of the assessment of the effectiveness.[251] Such evidential matter is inherent in internal control and required by sec. 13(b)(2)(A) Exchange Act so that each corporation has to "make and keep books, records, and accounts, which, in reasonable detail, accurately and fairly reflect the transactions and dispositions of the assets of the [corporation]".[252] Management's assessment has to be documented with regard to the design of internal controls and testing processes.[253] The documentation has to provide reasonable support "for the evaluation of

246 SEC Release No. 8238, at II, B, 3, a. A suitable framework has to be "free from bias; permit reasonably consistent qualitative and quantitative measurements of a [corporation]'s internal control; be sufficiently complete so that those relevant factors that would alter a conclusion about the effectiveness of a [corporation]'s internal controls are not omitted; and be relevant to an evaluation of internal control over financial reporting" (*Id.*).

247 SEC Release No. 8238, at II, B, 2; cf. *Langevoort*, 31 J. Corp. L. 949 (2006), p. 955.

248 SEC Release No. 8238, at II, B, 2. The Guidance on Assessing Control of the Canadian Institute of Chartered Accountants and the Turnbull Report of the Institute of Charted Accountants in England & Wales are other suitable frameworks (SEC Release No. 8238, at fn. 67).

249 SEC Release No. 8238, at fn. 68.

250 *Langevoort*, 31 J. Corp. L. 949 (2006), p. 955.

251 Introduction to Item 308 No. 2 Regulation S-K; cf. SEC Release No. 8238, at II, B, 3, d.

252 SEC Release No. 8238, at II, B, 3, d and fn. 76.

253 SEC Release No. 8238, at II, B, 3, d.

whether the control is designed to prevent or detect material misstatements or omissions; for the conclusion that the tests were appropriately planned and performed; and that the results of the tests were appropriately considered".[254] The external auditor will also use this documentation for its sec. 404(b) SOX assessment.[255]

Following the SEC release adopting the Exchange Act Rule 13a-15, internal controls which have to be included in the assessment are: "controls over initiating, recording and reconciling account balances, classes of transactions and disclosure and related assertions included in the financial statements; controls related to the initiation and processing of non-routine and non-systematic transactions; controls related to the selection and application of appropriate accounting policies; and controls related to the prevention, identification, and detection of fraud".[256] Further SEC requirements forbid that management delegates the assessment of internal control over financial reporting to the external auditor.[257] For the location of the management's internal control report within the annual report, the SEC recommends to locate the report near the corporation's MD&A disclosure or within the document immediately preceding corporation's financial statements.[258]

a) SEC Reforms of 2007

In 2007, the SEC implemented the guidance of 2005 into the SEC rules fostering a top-down, risk-based approach for the evaluation process. Since the SEC did not provide any further guidance on management's evaluation prior to 2005, the then-current auditing standard no. 2[259] of the PCAOB (PCAOB AS 2) became the *de facto* standard for management's evaluation.[260] This has been named as one of the reasons which led to excessive documentation and testing of internal controls by management.[261] In order to ease the high burden of sec. 404 SOX which corporations experienced and to reduce the pressure on management to align the evaluation

254 SEC Release No. 8238, at II, B, 3, d.
255 SEC Release No. 8238, at II, B, 3, d; SEC Release No. 8810, at I.
256 SEC Release No. 8238, at II, B, 3, d.
257 SEC Release No. 8238, at II, B, 3, b.
258 SEC Release No. 8238, at II, B, 3, e.
259 Superseded by PCAOB AS 5.
260 SEC Release No. 8809, at VI; cf. *Moeller*, SOX Internal Controls, p. 13.
261 SEC Release No. 8809, at VI.

with the auditing standards[262], the SEC amended its rules to facilitate more effective and efficient evaluations of internal control over financial reporting by management and external auditors. The SEC allows especially that management and the external auditors have different testing approaches.[263] In connection to the SEC rules amendments, the SEC issued an interpretive release to provide guidance for management regarding its evaluation and assessment.[264] The SEC guidance enables management to "adopt a more efficient and independent evaluation of the effectiveness of internal controls" instead of imitating an external auditor evaluation pursuant to PCAOB AS 5 in order to ensure satisfying the external auditors.[265] It remains advisable, however, to use PCAOB AS 5 as guidance for management's evaluation procedures in order to consider the mandates for the external auditors. Since the SEC and the PCAOB aligned their reforms of the evaluation process, the main ideas are at least similar minimizing potential friction between both standards. Furthermore, due to the 2007 reforms, efficiency is enhanced since management is only required to evaluate changes in risks and internal controls in an updated evaluation rather than recreating the entire process.[266]

The top-down, risk-based approach provides sufficient flexibility to address each corporation's internal control specifically and is more flexible with regard to documentation and testing standards reducing redundant reviews. It follows, however, that the guidance for the evaluation can only be standardized to a certain point. The risk-based approach enables management to focus its evaluation on areas of financial reporting that pose the highest risk to reliable financial reporting.[267] The approach includes a holistic view of risk that identifies corporate-wide vulnerabilities and allows greater consideration of fraud controls.[268] The top-down approach allows management to focus more on entity-level controls for evaluating whether internal control over financial reporting is effective. Nevertheless, in most circumstances, entity-level controls will not by themselves be adequate to address financial reporting risks.[269] In general, the SEC believes that the top-down, risk-based approach together with the broad guidelines

262 SEC Release No. 8809, at IV, A.
263 SEC Release No. 8810, at I.
264 See SEC Release No. 8810.
265 *Dodwell*, CPA Journal 2008.
266 Cf. *Dodwell*, CPA Journal 2008.
267 SEC Release No. 8810, at I.
268 Cf. *Dodwell*, CPA Journal 2008.
269 SEC Release No. 8810, at III, B.

of the interpretive guidelines will prevent a one-size-fits-all approach.[270] In any case, management has to design and evaluate internal control over financial reporting considering the specific circumstances of its corporation.

Due to Exchange Act Rule 13a-15(c), an evaluation of internal control over financial reporting conducted in accordance with the interpretive guidance issued by the SEC in SEC Release No. 8810[271] will satisfy the evaluation requirement of Exchange Act Rule 13a-15(c). The evaluation does not have to be conducted pursuant to the interpretive guidance since other ways to conduct the evaluation are accepted by the SEC (Exchange Act Rule 13a-15(c)). Since the interpretive guidance is not mandatory, corporations which have established an internal control over financial reporting evaluation process different from the interpretive guidance do not have to alter their procedures.[272] The interpretive guidance is intended to provide greater clarity and transparency about the sec. 404 SOX obligations.[273] Consistent with the initial SEC policy, however, the interpretive guidance does not provide any guidance on how to design internal control over financial reporting to comply with the chosen control framework.[274]

b) SEC Guidance Regarding Management's Report on Internal Control over Financial Reporting

The interpretive guidance (SEC Release No. 8809 and SEC Release No. 8810) is based on two principles. The first principle encompasses management's duty to evaluate whether the implemented internal control over financial reporting adequately addresses the risk that a material misstatement of the financial statements would not be prevented or detected in a timely manner.[275] The guidance describes a top-down, risk-based approach including the role of entity-level controls in assessing financial reporting risks and the adequacy of internal control over financial reporting. It is the belief of the SEC that such approach will provide sufficient flexibility for corporations, and will result in both effective and efficient evaluations of

270 SEC Release No. 8810, at III, B; also *Coates*, 21 J. Econ. Perspectives 91 (2007), p. 103.

271 SEC Release No. 8810 is also SEC Release No. 34-55929 cited in Exchange Act Rule 13a-15(c).

272 SEC Release No. 8809, at II, A, 3.

273 SEC Release No. 8809, at VI, A.

274 Cf. SEC Release No. 8810, at I.

275 SEC Release No. 8810, at I.

the effectiveness of internal control over financial reporting.[276] Since the approach is risk-based, management does not have to identify every control in a business process or document such processes impacting internal control over financial reporting. Rather, management can focus its evaluation and documentation for the overall assessment of internal controls on such processes it determines to adequately address the risks of a material misstatement of the financial statements. Since the approach is top-down, management may conclude an entity-level control to be sufficient to adequately address a risk of a material misstatement and is not required to evaluate any other control regarding the particular risk. The second principle states that management's evaluation of evidence regarding the operation of the corporation's controls should be based on its assessment of risk.[277] The risk-based judgment allows management to choose the evaluation procedures in light of the risk magnitude that areas of financial reporting pose on the reliability of financial reporting. Thus, management may use more efficient approaches for gathering evidence in low-risk areas and perform more extensive testing in high-risk areas.[278] The interpretive guidance addresses: the evaluation process including *inter alia* identifying financial reporting risks and controls and evaluating evidence on the operating effectiveness of internal control over financial reporting, and reporting considerations including *inter alia* the evaluation of control deficiencies, and disclosures about material weaknesses.[279] The interpretive guidance places emphasis on identified areas of concern: variation of evaluation approaches for gathering evidence based on risk assessment, explanation of ongoing monitoring activities as evidence in the evaluation, explanation of the purpose of documentation and management's flexibility regarding documentation for its assessment, and flexibility for management in making judgments regarding adequate evidence in low-risk areas.

The interpretive guidance starts with the evaluation process followed by reporting considerations. While the evaluation process's main purpose is to unveil deficiencies in internal control over financial reporting, the reporting considerations address the classification of such deficiencies as material weaknesses, significant deficiencies, or other deficiencies. Management has to evaluate if the implemented internal control over financial reporting will achieve its objective. From the definition of internal control

---

276 SEC Release No. 8809, at II, A, 3; SEC Release No. 8810, at I.
277 SEC Release No. 8810, at I.
278 SEC Release No. 8810, at I.
279 SEC Release No. 8810, at II.

over financial reporting in Exchange Act Rule 13a-15(f) if follows that it is the objective of internal control over financial reporting to provide reasonable assurance regarding the reliability of financial reporting and the preparation of financial statements for external purposes in accordance with U.S. GAAP. Since management is not permitted to conclude the internal control over financial reporting to be effective if there are one or more material weaknesses (Item 308(a)(3) Regulation S-K), management has to assess whether any material weaknesses exist as of the end of the fiscal year[280]. In order to determine if material weaknesses exist, management has to identify the risks to reliable financial reporting, evaluate whether controls exist to adequately address these risks, and evaluate the operational evidence of the controls included in the evaluation based on its assessment of risk.[281] The evaluation process has two major steps. In the first step, management has to evaluate whether the design of internal control over financial reporting is adequate, i.e. if the basis is theoretically given for effective internal control over financial reporting. If management determines material weaknesses in the design of internal control over financial reporting, management is prevented to determine internal control over financial reporting to be effective. In the second step, management evaluates the actual performance of such controls. If management determines material weaknesses in the performance, it is prevented to determine internal control over financial reporting to be effective.

(1) Evaluation of Adequate Design of Internal Control over Financial Reporting

For the first step of the evaluation, management has to identify financial reporting risks and has to evaluate if the controls adequately address these risks. Management has to make the evaluation in accordance with a SEC-suitable control framework. The frameworks define elements of internal control rendering internal control effective.[282] Thus, management has to assess if the corporation's internal control over financial reporting includes policies, procedures, and activities the chosen control framework requires for an internal control system to be effective. Since the control framework may not be limited to controls for financial reporting, as it is the case of

280 Cf. SEC Release No. 8810, at II, A.
281 SEC Release No. 8810, at II, A.
282 SEC Release No. 8810, at II, A.

COSO I, the SEC expects management to follow an evaluation process in all material aspects of the control framework even beyond financial reporting areas.[283] The evaluation has to include entity-wide and other pervasive elements of internal control[284] which may address internal control elements not specifically addressing financial reporting. In light of COSO I, the expectation of the SEC reflects the aspect that internal control categories may overlap.[285] This is best shown by the example of fraud prevention and detection which falls in the two COSO I categories 'financial reporting' and 'compliance with law'. Hence the evaluation needs to include controls addressing compliance with law regarding fraud and other crimes leading to material misstatements of the financial statements.

At first, the interpretive guidance addresses the identification of financial reporting risks, including changes to those risks, and of controls that adequately address those risks. The identification of financial reporting risks, i.e. risks resulting in a material misstatement of the financial statements, begins with determining how U.S. GAAP applies to the corporation.[286] Under U.S. GAAP, the financial statements must fairly present to investors the corporation's financial position.[287] Fair representation is not given in case of material misstatements or omissions. It is management's duty to consider sources and the potential likelihood of misstatements in financial statements. Risks of misstatements may arise due to internal or external factors impacting the business or from sources such as "the initiation, authorization, processing and recording of transactions and other adjustments that are reflected in financial [statements]".[288] Also, the vulnerability of the corporation to fraudulent financial reporting, misappropriation of assets and corruption, and the likelihood of such activities leading to material misstatements of the financial statements should be part of management's considerations for identifying financial reporting risks.

After identifying financial reporting risks, management has to identify controls that adequately address such risks.[289] Management has to evaluate if the implemented controls would in theory, i.e. if operating properly, adequately address the corporation's financial reporting risks. The evaluation involves judgment if the controls can effectively prevent or detect misstate-

283 Cf. SEC Release No. 8810, at II, A.
284 Cf. SEC Release No. 8810, at II, A.
285 See *infra* at chapter 4, C. I. 1. a).
286 SEC Release No. 8810, at II, A, 1, a.
287 SEC Release No. 8810, at II, A, 1, a.
288 SEC Release No. 8810, at II, A, 1, a.
289 SEC Release No. 8810, at II, A, 1, b.

ments.[290] The SEC only suggests using predefined control objectives to assess whether the controls are designed to operate effectively.[291] With such objectives, management sets a benchmark against which it determines the controls to meet these benchmarks. If the design of internal controls fulfills the benchmarks, management will determine internal controls to be effective. As will be discussed below[292], such control objectives are a requisite for a more objective judgment on the effectiveness of controls and allows external auditors to better evaluate the conclusion of management by determining if the set control objectives are reasonable. In case management concludes that a financial reporting risk is not adequately addressed by a control, i.e. a deficiency in internal control over financial reporting exists, it has to determine if such deficiency constitutes a material weakness.

In the process of identifying controls adequately addressing financial reporting risks, management is not required to identify all controls addressing those risks.[293] Due to the top-down, risk-based approach, management may stop identifying controls that may exist for addressing a financial reporting risk or identifying redundant controls, unless redundancy is required to address the financial reporting risk, as long as management determines the financial reporting risk to be adequately addressed by the identified control.[294] Since identifying one control addressing adequately a financial reporting risk is sufficient, management may choose an entity-level control or the control for which management can most efficiently evaluate the evidence of operation. In case adequate IT general controls exist and management has determined such controls to operate effectively, management may determine the automated controls to be more efficient to evaluate than manual controls.[295] The SEC uses the term "entity-level control" to describe aspects and controls of a system of internal control that affect the whole system of internal controls such as "controls related to the control environment" encompassing "management's philosophy and operating style, integrity and ethical values; board or audit committee oversight; and assignment of authority and responsibility", "controls over management override", "the [corporation]'s risk assessment process", "central-

290 SEC Release No. 8810, at II, A, 1, b.
291 SEC Release No. 8810, at fn. 28.
292 See *infra* at chapter 16, B. IV.
293 SEC Release No. 8810, at II, A, 1, b.
294 Cf. SEC Release No. 8810, at II, A, 1, b.
295 SEC Release No. 8810, at II, A, 1, b.

ized processing and controls, including shared service environments"; "controls to monitor results of operations"; "controls to monitor other controls, including activities of the internal audit function, the audit committee, and self-assessment programs"; "controls over the period-end financial reporting process"; and "policies that address significant business control and risk management practices".[296] In addition to identifying controls addressing finance reporting risks, management has to evaluate if controls exist which address the entity-level and other elements of internal control over financial reporting that the chosen control framework requires for an effective internal control system.[297] Such elements are e.g. control environment, management override, entity-level risk assessment process, and monitoring activities including monitoring results of operations and other controls by internal audit, the audit committee, and self-assessment programs.[298] Moreover, management has to evaluate controls over the period-end financial reporting process including matters such as: "procedures to enter transaction totals into the general ledger; the initiation, authorization, recording and processing of journal entries in the general ledger; procedures for the selection and application of accounting policies; procedures used to record recurring and non-recurring adjustments to the annual and quarterly financial statements; and procedures for preparing annual and quarterly financial statements and related disclosures"[299], and policies addressing significant business control and risk management practices.[300] While considering entity-level controls as a control to adequately addressing a financial reporting risk, management has to consider that such controls may be more indirect and, therefore, less effective than controls directly designed to address a specific financial reporting risk which may render the entity-level control not adequate to address a financial risk.[301] The SEC suggests that entity-level controls are sufficient if they are designed to operate at the process, application, transaction, or account-level with a level of precision leading to adequately address the risk of a material misstatement of the financial statements.[302] In such a case, management would not need to identify or evaluate additional controls.

---

296 SEC Release No. 8810, at fn. 21.
297 SEC Release No. 8810, at II, A, 1, b.
298 SEC Release No. 8810, at II, A, 1, b and fn. 31.
299 SEC Release No. 8810, at fn. 32.
300 SEC Release No. 8810, at II, A, 1, b.
301 SEC Release No. 8810, at II, A, 1, c.
302 SEC Release No. 8810, at II, A, 1, c.

Considering the risks and controls within the IT general controls is an integral part of the evaluation of internal control over financial reporting which the SEC recommends not to be part of a separate evaluation.[303] Nevertheless, IT general controls should only be evaluated as far as those controls are necessary for the proper and consistent operation of other controls designed to adequately address financial reporting risks such as "program development, program changes, computer operations, and access to programs and data".[304] While IT general controls are in general not sufficient to address financial reporting risks, they are important for the controls addressing financial reporting risks which are automated or dependent on IT functionality.[305] Therefore, management's evaluation process of internal control over financial reporting has to include for the automated or IT dependent controls the relevant IT general controls providing IT functionality.

An important and cost intensive part of the evaluation process is documentation of the design of the controls in operation to adequately address the financial reporting risks including the entity-level controls and other elements necessary for effective internal control over financial reporting.[306] In order to reduce costs and promote efficiency, only those controls, and not all, have to be documented which management considered adequate and sufficient to address financial reporting risks.[307] A number of ways for documentation such as "policy manuals, process models, flowcharts, job descriptions, documents, internal memorandums, [and] forms" may be used by management.[308]

(2) Evaluation of Effective Operation of Internal Control over Financial Reporting

After addressing the issue of identifying financial reporting risks and related controls, the interpretive guidance addresses the issue of evaluating the evidence regarding the effective operation of internal control over financial reporting.[309] This second step of management's evaluation requires man-

303 SEC Release No. 8810, at II, A, 1, d.
304 SEC Release No. 8810, at II, A, 1, d.
305 SEC Release No. 8810, at II, A, 1, d.
306 Cf. SEC Release No. 8810, at II, A, 1, e.
307 Cf. SEC Release No. 8810, at II, A, 1, e.
308 SEC Release No. 8810, at II, A, 1, e. See *supra* at chapter 4, A. II. 1. d).
309 SEC Release No. 8810, at II, A, 2.

agement to test whether the implemented internal control over financial reporting actually operate effectively, i.e. operate as designed, and whether the person performing the control possess the sufficient authority and competence to perform the control effectively.[310] Only the controls management identified as adequate to address the financial reporting risks have to be tested.[311] As part of the evaluation process regarding the effective operation of the identified adequate controls, management has to tailor its assessment of risk associated with the financial statements to the risk associated with the related controls. Since the overall evaluation approach is risk-based, management should focus on the highest cumulated risk of both financial statements and related controls. The assessment of the cumulated risk should also include the impact of entity-level controls on the risk of failure of particular controls.[312] Testing methods include direct testing of particular controls and ongoing monitoring activities.[313] The scope and amount of testing necessary for management to obtain sufficient evidence on the effective operation of a control depends on the assessed cumulated risk. Sufficient evidence encompasses the quantity of evidence and qualitative characteristics of the evidence. As qualitative characteristics have been named: "nature of the evaluation procedures performed, the period of time to which the evidence relates, the objectivity of those evaluating the controls, and, in case of ongoing monitoring activities, the extent of validation through direct testing of underlying controls".[314] The SEC takes the view that no one within the corporation will have absolute objectivity, but personnel will have varying degrees of objectivity based on their job function, their relationship to the control being evaluated, and their level of authority and responsibility within the organization.[315] The most objective are usually personnel whose core function involves testing or compliance authority within the corporation such as internal audit.[316]

The level of evidence needed for management's assessment of the effective operation of the identified adequate controls depends on the correlation between the risk of misstatement of financial statements and the risk

310 SEC Release No. 8810, at II, A, 2.
311 Cf. SEC Release No. 8810, at II, A, 2.
312 SEC Release No. 8810, at II, A, 2.
313 SEC Release No. 8810, at II, A, 2.
314 SEC Release No. 8810, at II, A, 2.
315 SEC Release No. 8810, at fn. 40.
316 SEC Release No. 8810, at fn. 40. See for the role of internal audit within the evaluation process *infra* at chapter 4, A. II. 2. c).

of control failure.[317] In order to determine the risk of misstating financial statements, management should consider materiality and susceptibility of the underlying account balances, transactions, or other supporting information to a misstatement leading to a material misstatement in the financial statements. The SEC names the following circumstances affecting management's consideration whether the risk of a misstatement in the financial statements is higher or lower: involvement of judgment in determining the recorded amounts, susceptibility to fraud, complexity of accounting requirements, sensitivity to changes in the nature or volume of the underlying transactions, sensitivity to "changes in environmental factors, such as technological and/or economic developments".[318] Likewise, with regard to the risk of control failure, the SEC names examples management has to consider for the likelihood that a control might fail to operate effectively: "type of control, [automated or manual], and the frequency with which it operates", "complexity of the control", "risk of management override", "judgment required to operate the control", "competence of the personnel who perform the control or monitor its performance", "[w]hether there have been changes in key personnel who either perform the control or monitor its performance", "nature and materiality of misstatements that the control is intended to prevent or detect", "degree to which the control relies on the effectiveness of other controls (for example, IT general controls)", and "evidence of the operation of the control for prior year(s)".[319] In the process of determining the evidence needed for the assessment, management may consider entity-level controls such as a highly effective control environment which may lead to a lower level of needed evidence regarding e.g. the likelihood of a control failure. It has to be noted, however, that an entity-level control such as a strong control environment will not eliminate the need to evaluate the operation of the control at least to some degree.[320]

Management has to decide on the appropriate evaluation methods and procedures to obtain sufficient evidence. For the determination, management uses its assessment of the cumulated risk comprised of the risk of financial misstatements and related controls. The evaluation methods and procedures may be integrated into the daily responsibility of personnel or implemented specifically for the evaluation of internal control over finan-

317 SEC Release No. 8810, at II, A, 2, a.
318 SEC Release No. 8810, at II, A, 2, a.
319 SEC Release No. 8810, at II, A, 2, a.
320 SEC Release No. 8810, at II, A, 2, a.

cial reporting providing the needed evidence through direct tests of controls, ongoing monitoring, or a combination of both.[321] Evidence of direct testing is only of a specific point in time and may be used for providing information about the reliability of ongoing monitoring activities. Ongoing monitoring includes self-assessment procedures and procedures to analyze predefined key performance indicators.[322] The quality of evidence from self-assessment depends on the objectivity of the performing personnel.[323] Depending on the magnitude of the cumulated risk of financial reporting, management has to increase the reliability of the evidence.[324] Hence, ongoing monitoring controls may be executed by more objective personnel and validated through periodic direct testing of the underlying controls.[325] In case of low cumulated risk of financial reporting, management may determine the evidence from ongoing monitoring to be sufficient and that no direct tests are necessary. With the gathered evidence, management evaluates whether the controls operate effectively by considering matters such as whether the control operated as designed, "how the control was applied, the consistency with which it was applied, and whether the person performing the control possesses the necessary authority and competence to perform the control effectively".[326] If management determines a control to operate non-effective, a deficiency exists which management has to evaluate whether it constitutes a material weakness.[327] Management's evaluation has to be supported by evidential matter providing reasonable support for the assessment.[328] Therefore, management has to document the methods and procedures utilized to gather and evaluate the evidence such as documenting the overall strategy for the evaluation approach, evaluation procedures, and the basis for management concluding controls to be effective.[329] The documentation regarding the evaluation basis includes evidential matter regarding the conclusion about the effectiveness of the corporation's entity-level and other elements of internal

321 SEC Release No. 8810, at II, A, 2, b.
322 SEC Release No. 8810, at II, A, 2, b and fn. 44.
323 Cf. SEC Release No. 8810, at II, A, 2, b.
324 Cf. SEC Release No. 8810, at II, A, 2, b.
325 SEC Release No. 8810, at II, A, 2, b.
326 SEC Release No. 8810, at II, A, 2, b.
327 SEC Release No. 8810, at II, A, 2, b.
328 SEC Release No. 8810, at II, A, 2, c.
329 SEC Release No. 8810, at II, A, 2, c.

control over financial reporting the chosen framework considers as necessary for an effective system of internal control.[330]

For the evaluation of effective operation of internal control over financial reporting with regard to multiple locations or business units, management has to determine whether centrally operating controls will adequately address financial reporting risk.[331] Otherwise, management has to evaluate in general the evidence of the operation of the controls at the individual location or business unit considering location-specific risks. The thoroughness of the process to gather evidence depends *inter alia* on the complexity or the judgment level of the operation at the individual location, and the magnitude of risk that controls will fail.[332]

(3) Determination of Material Weaknesses or Significant Deficiencies in Design or Operation of Internal Control over Financial Reporting

The signing officers have to certify that they have disclosed material weaknesses and significant deficiencies of internal control over financial reporting to the external auditors and the audit committee pursuant to Exchange Act Rule 13a-14(a) which requires the CEO and CFO to certify the requirements set out in sec. 302(a)(5) SOX.[333] Due to the reporting obligations of management, management has to determine whether a control deficiency is a material weakness which also has to be reported pursuant to Item 308(a)(3) Regulation S-K, or whether a control deficiency is a significant deficiency. Within this process, management has to consider in particular the implications of combined deficiencies and the severity of a control deficiency regarding quantitative and qualitative factors.[334] Prior to the definitions of the terms "material weakness" and "significant deficiency", the

---

330 SEC Release No. 8810, at II, A, 2, c.

331 SEC Release No. 8810, at II, A, 3.

332 SEC Release No. 8810, at II, A, 3.

333 The reporting requirement of significant deficiencies to the audit committee and the external auditors pursuant to Exchange Rule 13a-14(a) is not straight forward. The rules only address that each report must include certifications in the form of the applicable exhibit filing requirements. By interpreting the mandates of sec. 302(a)(5)(A) and (B) SOX to relate to sec. 404 SOX internal control over financial reporting, the SEC mandates in Item 601 Instruction to Exhibit Table No. 31 Regulation S-K applicable for forms 10-Q and 10-K that the certifying officers have to certify sec. 302(a)(5)(A) and (B) SOX mandates with regard to internal control over financial reporting.

334 SEC Release No. 8810, at II, B, 1.

SEC assumed the terms material weakness and significant deficiency to represent deficiencies in the design or operation of internal control that could adversely affect a corporation's ability to record, process, summarize and report financial data consistent with the assertions of management in the corporation's financial statements, with a material weakness constituting a greater deficiency than a significant deficiency.[335] This general idea of material weakness and significant deficiency resembles sec. 302(a)(5)(A) SOX and is still valid but has been clarified by the subsequent definitions of the two terms. In Exchange Act Rule 12b-2[336], the SEC defined a material weakness to be "a deficiency, or a combination of deficiencies, in internal control over financial reporting such that there is a reasonable possibility that a material misstatement of the [corporation]'s annual or interim financial statements will not be prevented or detected on a timely basis". With regard to the definition of material weakness, management has to evaluate whether there is a reasonable possibility that the deficient internal control system will fail to prevent or detect a material misstatement of a financial statement. The SEC refers to PCAOB AS 5 which states that a reasonable possibility of an event is when the likelihood of an event is either "reasonably possible" or "probable".[337] The SEC also suggests to include the magnitude of the potential misstatement resulting from deficiencies in the evaluation of the severity of a deficiency.[338] The SEC names various risk factors leading to a reasonable possibility that a deficiency will result in a misstatement of financial statements: "[t]he nature of the financial reporting elements involved", "[t]he susceptibility of the related asset or liability to loss or fraud", "[t]he subjectivity, complexity, or extent of judgment required to determine the amount involved", "[t]he interaction or relationship of the control with other controls, including whether they are interdependent or redundant", "[t]he interaction of the deficiencies", and "[t]he possible future consequences of the deficiency".[339] With regard to the magnitude of a misstatements, factors affecting the magnitude are e.g. "[t]he financial statement amounts or total of transactions exposed to the deficiency", and "[t]he volume of activity in the account balance or class of transactions exposed to the deficiency that has occurred in the current period or

335 SEC Release No. 8238, at fn. 73.
336 Amended by SEC Release No. 8809, at II, C.
337 SEC Release No. 8810, at fn. 47.
338 SEC Release No. 8810, at II, B, 1.
339 SEC Release No. 8810, at II, B, 1.

that is expected in future periods."[340] Moreover, management should consider the effect of "compensating" controls designed to back up other controls to reduce the risk of failure.[341]

The SEC previously addressed indicators for the existence of material weaknesses. In the Proposing Release[342] to the interpretive guidance, the SEC listed "strong indicators that a material weakness in [internal control over financial reporting] exists".[343] In the interpretive guidance, however, these strong indicators have been eliminated. But some of the situational background within the Proposing Release has been integrated into guidance for management to evaluate situations which indicate deficiencies in the internal control over financial reporting which may also constitute a material weakness.[344] The SEC justifies this removal from the interpretive guidance by stating that "an overly detailed list may create a list of *de facto* material weaknesses" which would improperly eliminate managerial judgment.[345] Nevertheless, the SEC highlights the indicative effect of certain circumstances now integrated into the guidance for evaluating if a deficiency is present within internal control over financial reporting and if such deficiency constitutes a material weakness.[346] The discarded scenarios, however, may still be used by management to get an idea of what may constitute a material weakness, even though, the implications of these examples are not straight forward in regard to complying with Exchange Act Rule 13a-15(c). The following situations have been included in the interpretive guidance as indicators for a deficiency in internal control over financial reporting which management has to evaluate if they are in effect a

340 SEC Release No. 8810, at II, B, 1.

341 SEC Release No. 8810, at II, B, 1 and fn. 49.

342 SEC Release No. 8762.

343 SEC Release No. 8762, at III, B, 1: The indicators are an ineffective control environment including identification of fraud of any magnitude on the part of senior management, significant deficiencies that have been identified and remain unaddressed after some reasonable period of time, and ineffective oversight of the corporation's external financial reporting and internal control over financial reporting by the corporation's audit committee; restatement of previously issued financial statements to reflect the correction of a material misstatement; identification by the auditor of a material misstatement in financial statements in the current period under circumstances that indicate the misstatement would not have been discovered by the corporation's internal control over financial reporting; and for complex entities in highly regulated industries an ineffective regulatory compliance function.

344 See SEC Release No. 8810, at II, B, 1.

345 SEC Release No. 8810, at III, F, 2.

346 SEC Release No. 8810, at III, F, 2.

deficiency and, if so, whether they constitute a material weakness.[347] The situations are: "[i]dentification of fraud, whether or not material, on the part of senior management", "[r]estatement of previously issued finical statements to reflect the correction of a material misstatement", "[i]dentification of a material misstatement of the financial statements in the current period in circumstances that indicate the misstatement would not have been detected by the [corporation]'s [internal control over financial reporting]", and "[i]neffective oversight of the [corporation]'s external financial reporting and internal control over financial reporting by the [corporation]'s audit committee".[348] The reporting of management's assessment of the effectiveness of internal control over financial reporting has to use clear language in a way that internal control over financial reporting is either effective without qualification or non-effective.[349] With regard to the definition of material weaknesses, scenarios of deficiencies representing no material weakness will be depicted further below.[350]

The following detailed analysis of the definition of material weakness will provide further guidance on what constitutes a material weakness for management's evaluation of the effectiveness of internal control over financial reporting. As stated in the interpretive guidance, the determination if an individual control, or a combination of controls, adequately addresses a financial reporting risk depends on the judgment of management whether the controls are designed, and, therefore, able to effectively prevent or detect, at least in theory, misstatements that could result in a material misstatements in the financial statements.[351] If management determines that, besides one or more controls for a specific financial reporting risk, there is a reasonable possibility that a material misstatement of the financial statements will not be prevented or detected on a timely basis, this deficiency constitutes a material weakness pursuant to Exchange Act Rule 12b-2. Thus, internal control over financial reporting is not adequate as long as there is a material weakness in the design of internal control over financial reporting. Likewise, if management determines that none of the controls addressing a specific financial reporting risk operates so that there is a reasonable possibility that a material misstatement of the financial statements will be prevented or detected on a timely basis, this deficiency

347 SEC Release No. 8810, at II, B, 1.
348 SEC Release No. 8810, at II, B, 1.
349 Cf. SEC Release No. 8810, at II, B, 2.
350 See *infra* at chapter 4, A. II. 2. e).
351 SEC Release No. 8810, at II, A, 1, b.

constitutes a material weakness. Further elements of the definition of material weakness have to be considered for determining if a deficiency constitutes a material weakness. A deficiency in internal control over financial reporting is not material and, therefore, not a material weakness, if there is only a remote, i.e. not reasonable, possibility that a material misstatement of the financial statements will not be prevented or detect on a timely basis. A deficiency is likewise not material if the misstatement of the financial statements itself is not material. Usually, materiality is defined as a substantial likelihood that a reasonable investor would attach to the information importance in determining whether to buy or sell securities of a corporation.[352] If follows that if the misstatement of financial statements is so minimal that a reasonable investor would probably not consider the misstatement in her decision to buy or sell the security, the deficiency in internal control over financial reporting is not a material weakness.

A significantly more important scenario that a deficiency, or a combination of deficiencies, of a control does not lead to a material misstatement is that one or more other controls adequately address the specific financial reporting risk, in case of a design deficiency, or one or more other controls operating effectively, in case of a operating deficiency. If other controls adequately address a specific financial reporting risk or operate effectively, the deficiency of the first control will not be causal for a material misstatement in the financial statements because such material misstatement will be prevented or detected by the other controls. Thus, while the deficiency of the first control sets the basis for a material weakness, another control interrupts the causation between cause and result by eliminating the result of a material misstatement of financial statements. This finding is consistent with the interpretive guidance which states that management only has to identify one control for each financial reporting risk as long as this control is adequate and operates effectively.[353] It follows that the system of internal controls over financial reporting may have multiple deficiencies in its design without having even one material weakness as long as management determines that each financial reporting risk is addressed by at least one adequate control. Therefore, the identification of financial reporting risks is of crucial importance. If management misses one financial reporting risk, which is not addressed by one adequate control, management will determine the system of internal control over financial reporting to be adequate and will not be prevented to find it effective. Likewise, manage-

352 See e.g. Exchange Act Rule 12-b on "Material".
353 SEC Release No. 8810, at II, A, 1, b.

ment's evaluation of the adequacy of the controls is of similar importance. If management misses a deficiency of a control constituting a material weakness or falsely determines a deficiency not be a material weakness, management will also determine the system of internal control over financial reporting to be adequate and will not be prevented to find it effective.

In contrast, identifying controls is not as important. If management misses an adequate control for a specific financial reporting risk, it will be forced to implement an adequate control or fix a deficient control addressing such risk. If management misses deficient controls while all financial reporting risks are addressed by at least one adequate control, such kind of scenario is an issue of efficiency rather than of effectiveness. Thus, in order to increase efficiency in the system of internal control over financial reporting, management has to keep on identifying controls even beyond the point when each financial reporting risk is addressed by at least one adequate control. Then, management will be able to discontinue redundant adequate controls to improve efficiency, unless redundancy itself is required to address a financial reporting risk, and non-adequate controls, unless managements believes that such controls, rendered adequate or not, are important as back up controls for the overall dependability of internal control over financial reporting. Management should continue identifying controls as long as marginal benefits of increased efficiency will exceed marginal costs of the identification process.

With regard to operating deficiencies, the false determination of the operating effectiveness of a control will lead to a false evaluation of internal control over financial reporting as long as no other control secures effectiveness. Thus, the positive evaluation that a control operates effectively has to have more evidential standing than a negative evaluation to prevent management to falsely determine internal control over financial reporting to be effective. If management falsely determines a control to operate non-effective while it actually is effective management has to remedy the operating deficiency if it constitutes a material weakness, i.e. if no other control addressing the same financial reporting risk operates effectively. Such kind of scenario constitutes an efficiency issue rather than an effectiveness issue. In common with design deficiencies, management has to take the same efficiency considerations into account if an operating deficiency does not constitute a material weakness. It follows from the forgoing that the evaluation process has to start with the identification of the financial reporting risk and the changes to such risks in order to minimize the risk of a false evaluation. Moreover, a system of internal controls may have multiple design and operating deficiencies as long as they do not constitute a material weakness. That is when every financial reporting risk of a corporation is adequately addressed by one internal control which operates effectively.

Shortly after issuing the interpretive guidance, the SEC also promulgate a definition of the term "significant deficiency" to provide management with additional guidance regarding the evaluation in light of sec. 302 and 404 SOX.[354] Pursuant to Exchange Act Rule 12b-2 "[t]he term significant deficiency is a deficiency, or a combination of deficiencies, in internal control over financial reporting that is less severe than a material weakness, yet important enough to merit attention by those responsible for oversight of the registrant's financial reporting". This definition is likewise in line with PCAOB AS 5.[355] Following the definition, management has to consider whether the remaining deficiencies are significant after determining which deficiencies in internal control over financial reporting constitute a material weakness, if any. Management has to report these significant deficiencies to the audit committee and the external auditors. Management may also report other deficiencies if it determines these deficiencies to be relevant for the audit committee or the external auditors.[356]

c) The Role of Internal Audit in Management's Evaluation

In many corporations, internal audit executes the assessment of internal control over financial reporting.[357] Even though SOX does not refer to the internal auditors to perform this function, it is within managerial discretion to delegate the assessment function under the supervision of management to internal audit. Due to this assessment function, internal audit has a much greater set of responsibilities and importance within the corporation.[358] Due to independence concerns, some voices within the profession opposed the new responsibility.[359] But due to changes within the internal audit standards, internal audit is allowed to perform the sec. 404 SOX assessment.[360] IIA standard no. 1110 requires the internal audit to be independent in general and especially when reporting to the board of direc-

354 SEC Release No. 8829, at I.
355 Cf. SEC Release No. 8829, at II, Comments on the Proposal.
356 Cf. SEC Release No. 8829, at II, Comments on the Proposal.
357 *Moeller*, SOX Internal Controls, p. 155.
358 *Moeller*, SOX Internal Controls, p. 156.
359 *Moeller*, SOX Internal Controls, p. 156.
360 *Moeller*, SOX Internal Controls, p. 156.

tors.[361] Within the sec. 404 SOX assessment, internal audit may have three different roles.

The first option assigns internal audit a lead function for the assessment. Thus, internal audit identifies key processes, document their internal controls, and performs appropriate test on those controls.[362] Internal audit would follow a documentation format which has been coordinated with the external auditors but would perform the assessment independently. As mandated by sec. 404(b) SOX, the external auditors would then attest to and report on the assessment performed by internal audit. This option uses best the knowledge and skills of internal auditors which is generally qualified to perform the assessment of the effectiveness of internal control over financial reporting due to their understanding of internal controls combined with good documentation skills[363] and objectivity.

A second option for the assessment of internal control over financial reporting is to use an internal source different from internal audit or an external source to perform the sec. 404 SOX assessment.[364] The external auditor is not allowed to perform this task.[365] Internal audit may then assist the external auditors in their independent sec. 404(b) SOX review. This may reduce external audit costs[366] since internal audit can provide extensive assistance to the external auditors without jeopardizing the independence of the external auditors' review. In case internal audit implemented the internal controls over financial reporting but is not involved in the process to assess the effectiveness of internal control over financial reporting, the external auditors may still accept the assistance of internal audit for the review process. This can be concluded since internal audit may provide assistance to the external auditors even if internal audit assessed the effectiveness of internal control over financial reporting as stipulated by PCAOB AS 5.[367] Hence, the less internal audit is involved in internal control over financial reporting the more the external auditors can accept assistance from internal audit to review management's assessment of internal control over financial reporting. A drawback of the second option is that internal audit is not available to perform the assessment of the effectiveness. This may lead to an ineffective assessment process in case the team performing

361 Cf. *Moeller*, SOX Internal Controls, p. 326.
362 *Moeller*, SOX Internal Controls, p. 157.
363 *Moeller*, SOX Internal Controls, p. 157.
364 *Moeller*, SOX Internal Controls, p. 157.
365 See sec. 404(b)(s. 2) SOX.
366 *Moeller*, SOX Internal Controls, p. 157.
367 See *infra* at chapter 4, B.

the assessment lacks time, resources, or process knowledge to perform the assessment.[368] If a corporation has a different unit similarly strong in control and audit functions as internal audit such as quality assurance or risk assessment, this option might work best.[369]

The third option assigns less responsibility to internal audit. It may either provide help to an internal source executing the assessment process or to the external auditors for their review without actually being involved in one of the other processes.[370] The third option may mainly be used in a setup in which the internal audit should not be deeply involved in the sec. 404 SOX review processes. One setup may be that internal audit has been assigned the responsibility for setting up internal controls over financial reporting and to keep them current. If management chooses to separate the implementation process from any review process in order to foster separation of duties to a very strict standard, the third option might be chosen which enables a high separation of duties standard while still using the knowledge and resources of internal audit. Such separation is consistent with the IIA internal audit standards which recommend that internal audit should not be directly responsible for implementing the internal control testing and documentation process if they will be requested to review such processes.[371] Another setup may be that internal audit lacks the resources to perform any sec. 404 SOX process. Moreover, a setup may occur in which the resources of internal audit are needed for other tasks and management decides to assign only a small fraction of internal audit resources to the sec. 404 SOX processes.[372] In any case, the CFO, or the officer responsible for accounting, finance and control processes within the corporation, should work with the external auditor to decide on the appropriate option for the corporation on how to best use internal audit within management's evaluation of internal control over financial reporting.[373]

368 *Moeller*, SOX Internal Controls, p. 157.
369 *Moeller*, SOX Internal Controls, p. 157.
370 *Moeller*, SOX Internal Controls, p. 157.
371 *Moeller*, SOX Internal Controls, p. 158 et seq.
372 Cf. *Moeller*, SOX Internal Controls, p. 157.
373 *Moeller*, SOX Internal Controls, p. 157.

d) Characteristics of U.S. Corporations Reporting Material Weaknesses

The characteristics of corporations reporting material weaknesses will provide insight regarding the circumstances under which corporations will be prone to material weaknesses. This insight will provide guidance for corporations, regulators, and enforcement divisions on the sensitive aspects of internal control over financial reporting on which they have to focus. Various studies analyzed the characteristics of corporations reporting material weaknesses. Corporations disclosing material weaknesses tend to be "smaller, younger, financially weaker, more complex, growing rapidly, or undergoing restructuring".[374] Corporations having entity-wide internal control weaknesses are "smaller, younger and weaker financially" while corporations with account-specific weaknesses are "healthy financially but have complex, diversified, and rapidly changing operations".[375] Account-specific weaknesses are most common in current accrual accounts such as accounts receivable and inventory accounts[376] as well as complex accounts such as derivative and tax accounts[377] which are prone to material weaknesses.[378] In general, all corporations have to assess and enhance their efforts, if indicated, especially with regard to staffing and complexity to avoid material weaknesses. Internal control weaknesses mostly relate to insufficient resources for internal control over financial reporting[379], lack of competent staff[380], and audit committees with less financial expertise[381]. Common material weaknesses are "deficient revenue-recognition policies, lack of segregation of duties, deficiencies in the period-end reporting process and accounting policies, and inappropriate account reconciliation".[382]

---

374 *Doyle/Ge/McVay*, 2006. For smaller and for financially weaker corporations also *Bryan/Lilien*, 2005. For small corporations *Grothe*, 2007a, p. 2; cf. *Zhang/Pany*, CPA Journal 2008; *Bedard/Graham/Hoitash/Hoitash*, CPA Journal 2007. For financially weaker cf. *Zhang/Pany*, CPA Journal 2008.

375 *Doyle/Ge/McVay*, 2006; also *Ashbaugh-Skaife/Collins/Kinney*, 2006.

376 *Ge/McVay*, 19 Acct. Horizons 137 (2005), p. 137.

377 *Grothe*, 2007a, p. 2.

378 *Ge/McVay*, 19 Acct. Horizons 137 (2005), p. 137.

379 *Ge/McVay*, 19 Acct. Horizons 137 (2005), p. 137.

380 *Grothe*, 2007a, p. 2.

381 *Hoitash/Hoitash/Bedard*, 2008; *Zhang/Zhou/Zhou*, 2006.

382 *Ge/McVay*, 19 Acct. Horizons 137 (2005), p. 137.

e) Essence of Management's Evaluation of Internal Control over Financial Reporting

In short, management has to focus its evaluation of internal control over financial reporting on material weaknesses in the design and operation of controls addressing risks of misstatements in the financial statements. Inherent in this process and required by securities law, management has to set a second focus on significant deficiencies. The evaluation of the design effectiveness largely depends on management's judgment, while the evaluation of the operation effectiveness depends on comparing predefined benchmarks and key performance indicators with the evidence obtained through monitoring regarding the operation of the controls. For the evaluation, management has to identify the risks of financial misstatements including controls addressing these risks, and has to evaluate the design and operation of such controls. Due to Item 308(a)(3) Regulation S-K, management is not permitted to consider internal control over financial reporting effective if one or more material weaknesses exist.

There are two different parts of internal control over financial reporting in which a deficiency may constitute a material weakness: in the design and in the operation of internal control over financial reporting. The rationale is that a perfectly designed internal control system will not be effective if the controls will not operate effectively. Equally, controls operating effectively will be of limited use if the design is not adequate. It follows that management's evaluation of only one of the two parts of internal control over financial reporting is insufficient for determining its effectiveness. In light of the definition of material weakness and reflecting the interpretive guidance of the SEC, a material weakness in the design exists in essence if a financial reporting risk leading to a material misstatement in the financial statements is not addressed by at least one adequate control. With regard to the operation, a material weakness exists in essence if no control addressing a financial reporting risk leading to a material misstatement in the financial statements operates effectively.

After the determination whether a deficiency constitutes a material weakness, management has to consider if a deficiency which is not a material weakness is a significant deficiency. In light of the definition of significant deficiency in Exchange Act Rule 12b-2, all deficiencies, which are less severe than a material weakness, may be important enough to be reported to the audit committee and the external auditors. These are especially those deficiencies which would by themselves constitute a material weakness if no other control would either adequately address the financial reporting risk or operate effectively. With regard to all other deficiencies, management has to consider qualitative and quantitative parameters. If a deficiency is not a material weakness e.g. due to a remote likelihood but will lead to an exponential misstatement if it occurs, management should consider such deficiency as a significant deficiency. In general, all deficiencies which have been considered not to be a material weakness in a close or controversial process should be considered as significant deficiencies. For example, a close majority vote of the evaluators on the issue whether a deficiency constitutes a material weakness is such a controversial process. Similar to the determination of a material weakness, a deficiency should rather be considered significant than not.

3. Management's Evaluation of Any Change in the Corporation's Internal Control over Financial Reporting – Exchange Rule 13a-15(d)

Pursuant to Exchange Rule 13a-15(d) implementing sec. 302(a)(6) SOX, management has to evaluate, with the participation of the CEO and CFO, any change in the corporation's internal control over financial reporting that occurred during each of the corporation's fiscal quarters that has materially affected, or is reasonably likely to materially affect, the corporation's internal control over financial reporting. Materiality is usually defined as matters to which there is a substantial likelihood that a reasonable investor would attach importance in determining whether to buy or sell a security.[383] Management faces the challenge to decide which changes in the corporation's internal control over financial reporting are material.[384] Thereby, the safest way is to disclose every change which is not clearly immaterial.[385] In case a material weakness occurred which has not been corrected prior to the next financial report, Item 308 Regulation S-K requires management to disclose the deficiency or weakness, and the corporation must report the change as being corrected in a later financial report.[386] The SEC does not require corporations to disclose any reason for the change.[387] Management has to decide, however, whether the reason for the change in

383 Cf. Exchange Act Rule 12b-2.
384 *Waxman*, CPA Journal 2004.
385 *Waxman*, CPA Journal 2004.
386 Cf. *Waxman*, CPA Journal 2004.
387 *Waxman*, CPA Journal 2004.

internal control over financial reporting, or any other information about the change, is material information due to Exchange Act Rule 12b-20.

Current Exchange Rule 13a-15(d) is a concession by the SEC to concerns raised by affected circles with regard to proposed quarterly evaluations.[388] Also, rules requiring quarterly evaluation would have gone beyond the mandates of sec. 404 SOX. Due to these concerns, the SEC did not implement rules requiring a quarterly evaluation. But still, the SEC requires more than what has been mandated by sec. 404 SOX in order to provide investors with information if a significant change to internal control over financial reporting occurred during the financial quarter. Foreign corporations are only required to evaluate their internal control over financial reporting every fiscal year due to the fact that foreign corporations are only required to file an annual report on Form 20-F. Therefore, the evaluation of foreign corporations' internal control over financial reporting is only required every fiscal year.

4. Management's Report on Internal Control over Financial Reporting – Item 308 Regulation S-K

By implementing Item 308[389] of Regulation S-K[390] and Item 15 of Form 20-F[391] in case of foreign corporations respectively, the SEC requires that management provides a report on the corporation's internal control over financial reporting together with the annual report ensuring disclosure of all relevant information mandated by sec. 404 SOX. The Item 308 report has to include a statement of management's responsibility to establish and maintain adequate internal control over financial reporting for the corpo-

388 Cf. SEC Release No. 8238, at II, C. The rules formerly proposed by the SEC required quarterly evaluations of internal control over financial reporting in order to align these evaluation requirements with the evaluation requirements for the corporation's disclosure controls and procedures of Exchange Act Rule 13a-15(a). The adoption of such a rule was strongly opposed due to concerns regarding high costs, on the one hand, and marginal benefit to investors, on the other hand. Some of the internal control over financial reporting measures are only used at the end of the fiscal year, thus, reducing the meaningfulness of a quarterly evaluation.

389 17 CFR 229.308.

390 Regulation S-K is applicable to the content of the non-financial statement portions of the annual report under sec. 13 and 15(d) Exchange Act (Item 10(a)(2) Regulation S-K).

391 17 CFR 249.220f.

ration (Item 308(a)(1) Regulation S-K). Item 308(a)(3) Regulation S-K mandates to publish management's assessment of the effectiveness of internal control over financial reporting. The assessment has to state whether or not internal control over financial reporting is effective as of the end of the most recent fiscal year, and disclose any material weakness in internal control over financial reporting identified by management. Thereby, management is not permitted to conclude that internal control over financial reporting is effective in case one or more material weaknesses were identified. If management identifies material weaknesses and will remedy all these weaknesses by the end of the fiscal year, it may conclude that internal control over financial reporting is effective as of the end of the fiscal year.[392] The identified material weaknesses may still have to be reported by management pursuant to Item 308 of Regulation S-K if appropriate or required.[393] Due to Item 308(c) Regulation S-K, management has to disclose any changes in internal control over financial reporting identified in connection with the evaluation required by Exchange Act Rule 13a-15(d). Moreover, management has to state the used framework for the evaluation pursuant to Item 308(a)(2) Regulation S-K. Furthermore, a statement that the corporation's registered public accounting firm that audited the financial statements included in the annual report containing the disclosure required by Item 308 has issued an attestation report on the corporation's internal control over financial reporting is required by Item 308(a)(4) Regulation S-K. The attestation report has to be provided within the annual report (Item 308(b) Regulation S-K). Thereby, providing public notice in regard to sec. 404(b) SOX.

Beyond the reporting requirements of Item 308(a) Regulation S-K, the SEC encourages corporations to disclose surrounding information regarding the disclosed material weaknesses such as the nature and impact of any material weakness, and remediating actions planned or executed.[394] Such information may be required by Exchange Act Rule 12b-20.

---

392 SEC Release No. 8810, at fn. 20.
393 SEC Release No. 8810, at fn. 20.
394 SEC Release No. 8810, at II, B, 3.

5. External Auditors' Attestation to Management's Assessment within the Internal Control Report – Section 404(b) SOX

In Regulation S-X, the SEC prescribes the form and content of the financial statements. With the revision of Rules 1-02 and 2-02 Regulation S-X, the SEC integrates the attestation requirements for the external auditors of sec. 404(b) SOX.[395] In Rule 1-02(a)(2) Regulation S-X, the SEC defines an attestation report on internal control over financial reporting to include the external auditors' opinion as to whether the corporation maintained, in all material respects, effective internal control over financial reporting. Due to Rule 2-02(f)(2) Regulation S-X, the external auditor has to state the opinion whether, in all material respect, the corporation maintained effective internal control over financial reporting.[396] Requiring the external auditor to attest directly on the effectiveness of internal control over financial reporting would convey whether the disclosure of management's assessment is fairly stated.[397] Concerns have been raised that, in contrast to the Rules 2-02(f) Regulation S-X, sec. 404(b) SOX requires the external auditor to attest to the assessment of management regarding the effectiveness of internal control over financial reporting.[398] The SEC justifies the external auditor to attest directly on the effectiveness of internal control over financial reporting by stating that "it more effectively communicates the auditor's responsibility in relation to management's process and necessarily conveys whether management's assessment is fairly stated".[399] The SEC believes Rule 2-02(f) Regulation S-X to be "fully consistent with […] the objectives of Section 404(b) of Sarbanes-Oxley" and seems to view the direct attestation on the effectiveness merely as a pre-step for the auditor to opine on management's assessment on the effectiveness of internal control over financial reporting since PCAOB AS 5 still requires the auditor to attest to the assessment of management.[400] The specific requirements of the PCAOB for external auditors regarding the attestation report on internal control over financial reporting and the implications for management will be discussed below.[401]

---

395 Cf. SEC Release No. 8238, at II, G.
396 Cf. SEC Release No. 8809, at II, B, 3.
397 Cf. SEC Release No. 8809, at II, B, 1.
398 See SEC Release No. 8809, at II, B, 2.
399 SEC Release No. 8809, at II, B, 3.
400 See SEC Release No. 8809, at II, B, 3.
401 See *infra* at chapter 4, B.

III. Incentives to Comply with SOX Internal Control Mandates Including Sec. 906 SOX

The signing officers face various and partially contradicting incentives to comply with the SOX mandates for internal controls. An ostensible incentive for officers to comply with SOX's internal control mandates is liability. In general, any person is liable under sec. 18(a) Exchange Act for providing any statement in a report filed pursuant to the Exchange Act or any Exchange Act Rule or Regulation which is false or misleading with respect to any material fact. The quarterly and annual reports as well as the internal control report of sec. 404 SOX as part of each annual report fall under sec. 18(a) Exchange Act.[402] In light of sec. 18(a) Exchange Act liability, the certification requirement of sec. 302(a)(1) to (3) SOX specifies the responsibility of the CEO and CFO for the accuracy of the financial statements ensuring the involvement of the signing officers in the process of compiling the statements. Sec. 302 SOX does not change the liability standard of sec. 18(a) Exchange Act which provides the sued officer with the opportunity to prove that she acted in good faith and had no knowledge that the statements were false or misleading. Rather, sec. 302 SOX makes it more difficult for the signing officers to prove that they acted in good faith and had no knowledge of the false or misleading financial statements. In addition, an officer providing a false certification could be subject to SEC enforcement action for violating sec. 13(a) Exchange Act pursuant to sec. 21, 21C and 21D Exchange Act and to both SEC and private actions for material misstatements or omissions violating sec. 10(b) Exchange Act and Exchange Act Rule 10b-5.[403] Since officers have been responsible for corporate disclosures prior to SOX, a false certification may also result in liability under Sections 11 and 12(a)(2) Securities Act when an annual or quarterly report is incorporated by reference into a registration statement on Form S-3 of F-3 or into a prospectus filed pursuant to Securities Act Rule 424(b).[404] Besides the existing liability, sec. 302 and 404 SOX enhanced the already existing liability with regard to disclosure controls and procedures and internal control over financial reporting.

A further layer of deterrence is provided by sec. 906 SOX. In sec. 906 SOX, Congress established a criminal penalty for the CEO and CFO for a knowingly false certification. The certification has to include that the peri-

402 Cf. *Waxman*, CPA Journal 2004.
403 Cf. SEC Release No. 8124, at II, B, 6.
404 SEC Release No. 8124, at fn. 70.

odic report fully complies with the requirements of sec. 13(a) Exchange Act and the information of the report fairly represents, in all material aspects, the financial conditions and results of operations of the issuer. In Exchange Act Rule 13a-14(b), the SEC adverts to the certification requirement of sec. 1350 of Chapter 63 of Title 18 of the USC for each periodic report. Sec. 1350 USC has been implemented by sec. 906 SOX. There is no form specified to be used. While a violation of sec. 906 is a federal crime, the sec. 906 certification is not subject to liability under sec. 18 Exchange Act.[405]

In sec. 304 SOX, the CEO and CFO face an additional monetary penalty if the corporation is required to prepare an accounting restatement due to the material non-compliance of the corporation with any financial reporting requirement under federal securities law as a result of misconduct (sec. 304(a) SOX). Then, the CEO and CFO have to reimburse the corporation for any bonus or other incentive-based or equity-based compensation they received within the last 12-month period following the filing of the incorrect financial document (sec. 304(a)(1) SOX), and any profits realized from the sale of securities of the corporation during that 12-month period (sec. 304(a)(2) SOX). Thus, sec. 304 SOX adds a further layer to the incentives regime for the CEO and CFO to fulfill their responsibilities for accurate internal controls regarding financial reporting. Similar to sec. 304 SOX, sec. 305(a) SOX provides further incentives for officers and directors to refrain from committing securities fraud and violating sec. 10(b) Exchange Act by easing the standard for courts to bar persons to serve as officers and directors. In sec. 1105 SOX, the SEC has been granted the same authority to prohibit persons from serving as officers or directors.

An important factor to effectuate the personal liability for the signing officers is enforcement especially by the SEC to increase the expected liability since non-optimal law enforcement generally provides incentives for less than optimal internal controls[406]. In this regard, it has been noted that the enforcement level of SOX, to predict expected liability, would still be open but likely be high due to the priority SOX has received by regulators.[407] Otherwise, it has been indicated that the SEC will only engage in moderate enforcement of SOX.[408] One major obstacle for the failure of the FCPA to lead corporations to implement effective internal controls has

405 Cf. SEC Release No. 8238, at III, B.
406 Cf. *Langevoort*, 2002 Colum. Bus. L. Rev. 71, p. 80.
407 Cf. *Langevoort*, 31 J. Corp. L. 949 (2006), p. 967 et seq.
408 *Langevoort*, 105 Mich. L. Rev. 1817 (2007), p. 1853.

been the narrow interpretation of the internal control mandates within the FCPA by the SEC and a subsequent lack of enforcement for violations.[409] After the enactment of SOX, the SEC increased its enforcement actions especially with regard to financial fraud.[410] Also, to deter executive fraud, the probability of being caught and tried is important. For executives, the individual sanction depends *inter alia* on the willingness of the board of directors to start legal action to recoup payments to executives triggered by fraudulent behavior.[411]

Besides the incentives for officers to implement effective internal controls due to personal liability, various reasons may seduce management to implement less than perfect internal controls. The main obvious reason is costs.[412] Costs and benefits of SOX's internal control mandates will be discussed below.[413] If costs were the only issue with regard to the implementation of effective internal controls, management might just be trusted to strike for the optimal balance between costs and benefits.[414] Other issues than costs, however, undermine management's incentives to implement optimal internal controls. First and foremost, the agency problem exist which is one of the main reasons for the need of internal controls.[415] If management leaves internal controls less than optimal this may provide for sufficient leeway to conceal self-interested or even fraudulent behavior which is of particular interest for management since internal control provides the opportunity for monitors to assess management's actions and performance.[416] Thus, the implementation of effective internal controls should not be left entirely to management but should be executed under the guidance and oversight of the board of directors.[417] In order to ensure that the board of directors engages in oversight, the law has to prescribe such oversight with the goal of optimally balance costs and benefits.[418] Besides the agency problem, the oversight of outside directors is also impor-

409 See *infra* at chapter 5, A.

410 *Brown*, 57 Cath. U. L. Rev. 45 (2007), p. 77; cf. *Ruder/Sun/Sycz*, 80 Notre Dame L. Rev. 1103 (2005), p. 1106 et seq. See *Cutler*, 2004.

411 *Langevoort*, 42 Wake Forest L. Rev. 627 (2007), p. 628.

412 Cf. *Langevoort*, 31 J. Corp. L. 949 (2006), p. 958.

413 See *infra* at chapter 13, B.

414 *Langevoort*, 31 J. Corp. L. 949 (2006), p. 958.

415 Cf. *Langevoort*, 31 J. Corp. L. 949 (2006), pp. 958 and 972; *Langevoort*, 2002 Colum. Bus. L. Rev. 71, p. 80; *Coates*, 21 J. Econ. Perspectives 91 (2007), p. 104. See for more details on agency costs *supra* at chapter 1, A.

416 Cf. *Langevoort*, 31 J. Corp. L. 949 (2006), p. 958.

417 *Langevoort*, 31 J. Corp. L. 949 (2006), p. 959.

418 Cf. *Langevoort*, 31 J. Corp. L. 949 (2006), p. 959.

tant due to the fact that a further factor interfering with the objective of optimal internal controls is related to the growth of a corporation. For example, internal controls which were suitable for a start-up corporation will not be suitable anymore once the corporation turns into a large corporation.[419] Even within an already large corporation, changes within the corporation may render the internal controls ineffective. The major challenge for management in this regard is to notice even gradual changes before such gradual changes result in ineffective internal controls.[420] Outside directors not involved in the day-to-day business are more likely to notice inappropriate internal controls as they will have a fresh view on the corporation.

Following the argument that management would have non-optimal incentives to implement internal controls, it has been indicated that corporations might only comply with SOX, "in letter while changing little in spirit".[421] As will be shown below, corporate leaders have similar incentives to "mimic" compliance programs in order to receive leniency based on the USSG.[422] In this regard, some authors stress that courts and regulatory agencies may not have sufficient expertise or resources to unveil such mimicked compliance programs.[423] In difference to the USSG-context, however, the external auditors will be better equipped to identify mimicked internal control including compliance measures as part of their sec. 404(b) SOX review than courts and agencies are. Thus, while a possibility remains that officers will only mimic internal control with regard to SOX, there is a much reduced likelihood that officers will actually do so. Moreover, the attestation requirement of sec. 404(b) SOX is a further factor to achieve compliance with the internal control mandates rendering violations of the internal control mandates by management significantly more difficult. Also, in case of a qualified attestation report of the external auditors, the SEC has a starting point to pursue investigations. Due to SEC enforcement and external auditor attestation, the incentive scheme for management to implement the SOX mandated internal controls is effective which is indicated by the attention dedicated to comply with SOX's internal control man-

419 Cf. *Langevoort*, 31 J. Corp. L. 949 (2006), p. 958.
420 Cf. *Langevoort*, 31 J. Corp. L. 949 (2006), p. 958.
421 *McDonnell*, 2004 Mich. St. L. Rev. 505, p. 529.
422 See *infra* at chapter 5, C. III.
423 See *Krawiec*, 81 Wash. U. L. Quarterly 487 (2003), p. 491 et seq.; cf. *Pape*, Corporate Compliance, p. 216 and *infra* at chapter 16, A. I. 2. a) (2).

dates represented by the substantial SOX-related implementation costs depicted below.[424]

Furthermore, due to the personal certification requirement of the CEO and CFO, that they evaluated the internal controls, their defense of claiming to have been unaware of control deficiencies is "weakened".[425] These officers are threatened with even more severe consequences due to private lawsuits or SEC sanctions if a disclosed material weakness has not been fixed resulting in a material financial misstatement since they positively knew about the weakness.[426] Thus, the incentives to fix any material weakness, and even those weaknesses which are arguably not material, are strong for the signing officers since they bear full personal liability for failing to fix deficiencies but only share a fraction of the fixing costs equal to their stake in the corporation.[427] Also independent directors including the members of the audit committee have increased incentives to invest in internal controls due to their enhanced oversight role.[428] Likewise, lower level employees entrusted with internal control related tasks such as the internal audit and the compliance and ethics department have incentives to call for investing in their departments. Moreover, officers will engage in internal controls as they will provide confidence for the signing officers to sign the required certifications. Taken all incentives of corporate agents including those for external auditor[429], lawyers and other consultants[430] together, it is very likely that corporations overspend on SOX-related internal controls. In addition to the incentives for management to implement effective internal controls due to liability, the benefits of effective internal controls such as lower costs of capital provide further incentives to implement effective internal controls.[431]

In summarizing the incentives scheme for management to implement SOX mandated internal control, the personal liability of the CEO and CFO together with the increased enforcement actions of the SEC provide strong incentives for management to comply with the SOX mandates.

---

424 See *infra* at chapter 13, B. I.

425 *Coates*, 21 J. Econ. Perspectives 91 (2007), p. 103; cf. *Moeller*, SOX Internal Controls, p. 184.

426 *Coates*, 21 J. Econ. Perspectives 91 (2007), p. 103.

427 *Coates*, 21 J. Econ. Perspectives 91 (2007), p. 103; cf. *Gupta/Leech*, 3 Int. J. Disclosure and Governance 27 (2006), p. 31.

428 *Coates*, 21 J. Econ. Perspectives 91 (2007), p. 104.

429 See *infra* at chapter 13, B. II.

430 See *infra* at chapter 13, B. II.

431 See *infra* at chapter 13, B. III.

While non-optimal incentives to implement effective internal controls may be attributed to the agency problem, the attestation of the external auditors (sec. 404(b) SOX) and the tendency of management to overspend on internal control as well as the benefits of lower costs of capital provide generally for sufficient incentives for management to engage in effective internal control as required by SOX. Nevertheless, the implementation of internal controls is also subject to the principal-agent problem so that all internal control related processes have to be overseen by the board of directors[432]. Besides the named incentives, SOX-related internal controls are overall beneficial for corporations providing incentives to implement effective internal control. In general, the benefits such as improved financial reporting, deterrence of fraud, more effective internal control, reduction of agency costs, and lower costs of capital outweigh the costs such as implementation and maintenance costs related to sec. 302 and 404 SOX internal controls, opportunity costs, and rent-seeking of interested parties.[433]

IV. Further SOX Mandates Affecting Internal Control and Gatekeepers

Besides the preeminent relevance of sec. 302 and 404 SOX to internal controls, further sections of SOX peripheral affect internal controls by addressing gatekeepers including whistleblowers. Sec. 301 SOX addresses the constitution of the audit committee, a part of the board of directors, with the purpose to strengthen its effectiveness. In sec. 406 SOX, a code of ethics for senior financial officers is required affecting the internal control environment. The role of lawyers as gatekeepers is addressed in sec. 307 SOX. Whistleblower protection against retaliation is addressed in sec. 806, 1107 SOX. Since some authors claim that too much emphasis would be on outside gatekeepers e.g. accountants, outside legal counsel[434] and rating agencies, outside gatekeepers should be regarded as additional checks on management since insiders will always be better informed than outside gatekeepers. Therefore, the main emphasis has to be on internal gatekeepers.

---

432 See regarding ineffective director oversight: *Prentice*, 91 Cornell L. Rev. 775 (2006), p. 828.

433 See *infra* at chapter 13, B.

434 Cf. *Ide*, 54 Mercer L. Rev. 829 (2003), p. 842 et seq.

1. Audit Committee – Sections 301, 407 SOX

In sec. 301 SOX, the main focus is on the audit committee. Within the internal control system, the audit committee has an important responsibility to oversee management's duty to implement effective and efficient internal controls. The main impact of sec. 301 SOX is to require the audit committee to be comprised of solely independent members of the board of directors. Besides the independence requirement for the audit committee, sec. 301 SOX addresses an internal control related issue by requiring the audit committee to establish procedures within the corporation to handle complaints related to accounting, internal accounting controls, or auditing matters (sec. 10A(m)(4)(A) Exchange Act) and procedures for the confidential, anonymous submission by employees of concerns regarding questionable accounting or auditing matters (sec. 10A(m)(4)(A) Exchange Act). In light of the disclosure requirement of Item 407(f) Regulation S-K to indicate whether the corporation has a process for shareholders to communicate with the board of directors, such communication should be integrated into the communication process required by sec. 10A(m)(4) Exchange Act.

Sec. 301 SOX amended sec. 10A Exchange Act requiring the SEC to promulgate a rule to direct the U.S. exchanges to prohibit the listing of any securities of a corporation that is not in compliance with sec. 301 SOX. Thus, the SEC promulgated Exchange Act Rule 10A-3. Due to Exchange Act Rule 10A-3(a)(1), the NYSE is obligated to require listed corporations to comply with the requirements of Exchange Act Rule 10A-3 in order to be listed. The listing requirements of the NYSE are dealt with below.[435] With regard to the independence requirement of sec. 301 SOX, the same critique as for sec. 404 SOX has been raised for sec. 301 SOX. Therefore, it has been argued that mandating an entirely independent audit committee imposes too high costs on corporations, especially on smaller corporations, compared to the benefits.[436] Studies have shown, however, that institutional investors are willing to pay a premium for good corporate governance.[437] Hence, corporations are able to attract investors despite higher costs for independent directors. In addition, various studies found that more independent directors on the audit committee improve financial reporting.[438] Furthermore, several studies found that an audit committee

435 See *infra* at chapter 4, D. I.
436 E.g. *Romano*, 114 Yale L. J. 1521 (2005), p. 1530.
437 See *infra* at chapter 13, A.
438 *Prentice/Spence*, 95 Geo. L. J. 1843 (2007), at fn. 147-157 (citations omitted).

solely comprised of independent directors is more likely to be active and to take their responsibility towards financial reporting more seriously.[439] In addition, corporations with entirely independent audit committee are less likely to be a subject of SEC enforcement or restating of earnings.[440] It has also been shown that those corporations which voluntarily adopted provisions of SOX, such as the audit committee requirements, were rewarded by the markets.[441] In general, empirical evidence suggests that SOX's requirement that the audit committee has to be entirely independent is beneficial to the market.[442]

A further issue of sec. 301 SOX is that it does not differentiate between foreign and domestic corporations.[443] In order to comply with SOX, foreign corporations face difficulties with regard to the audit committee and independent directors, since the provisions of SOX are drafted with regard to the U.S. corporate governance structure. The main characteristic of this structure is that a one-tier board of directors is responsible to run the corporation. Also, other constituencies than the shareholders are usually not part of the consideration of the board while running the corporation. These characteristics are not unilateral throughout the world. National law may mandate foreign corporations to have a two-tier board structure or to have employee representatives on either a one-tier board (Sweden) or a two-tier board (Germany).[444] As far as employee representatives are employees of the corporation or its subsidiaries, these directors are by definition not independent since they receive wages from the corporation or its subsidiaries pursuant to sec. 10A(m)(3)(B)(i) and Exchange Act Rule 10A-3(b)(1)(ii)(A). The different structures of corporate governance make it impossible for several foreign corporations to comply with the Exchange Act and their national law at the same time. The SEC realized this intractable conflict and promulgated within Exchange Act Rule 10A-3 several modifications form the mandates of SOX for foreign corporations. With regard to a two-tier board system, Exchange Act Rule 10A-3(e)(3) defines that the term "board of directors" means the supervisory board or non-management board to ensure that the audit committee is not part of the governing authority of a corporation similar to the officers. Exchange Act

439 *Prentice/Spence*, 95 Geo. L. J. 1843 (2007), at fn. 161 (citations omitted).
440 *Prentice/Spence*, 95 Geo. L. J. 1843 (2007), p. 1874 (citations omitted).
441 *Aggarwal/Williamson*, 2006.
442 *Aggarwal/Williamson*, 2006.
443 *Fried Frank*, 2006, p. 2.
444 Cf. *Kraakman*, Anatomy of Corporate Law, p. 62.

Rule 10A-3(b)(1)(iv)(C) exempts an employee of a foreign corporation from the independence's requirements of section 10A(m)(3) Exchange Act as long, as she is not a CEO, if the employee serves on the board or the audit committee due to the corporation's governing law or documents, an employee collective bargaining or similar agreement, or other home country legal or listing requirements. Moreover, in order to clarify the position of the SEC, the instructions to Exchange Act Rule 10A-3 state that several requirements of the rule do not conflict or affect any national requirements and are only related to the assignment of responsibility between the audit committee and management. Moreover, in order to preserve the exception made by Exchange Act Rule 10A-3, U.S. exchanges address foreign corporations differently than domestic corporations.[445]

With regard to sec. 407(a) SOX, corporations are required to disclose whether the audit committee is comprised of at least one member who is a financial expert or to explain why not.[446] Thus, corporations have an incentive to have at least one financial expert on the audit committee as defined by the SEC. With the financial expertise, the audit committee shall be equipped to appropriately fulfill its oversight role regarding financial reporting. The SEC has been required in sec. 407(a) SOX to define the term financial expert considering the requirements of sec. 407(b) SOX. The SEC defined the term financial expert as a person who has an understanding of U.S. GAAP and financial statements; the ability to assess the general application of such principles in connection with the accounting for estimates, accruals and reserves; experience preparing, auditing, analyzing or evaluating financial statements that present a breadth and level of complexity of accounting issues that are generally comparable to the breadth and complexity of issues that can reasonably be expected to be raised by the registrant's financial statements, or experience actively supervising one or more persons engaged in such activities; an understanding of internal controls and procedures for financial reporting; and an understanding of audit committee functions.[447] The person must have acquired such attributes through at least one of the following: (1) education and experience as a principal financial officer, principal accounting officer, controller, public accountant or auditor or experience in one or more positions that involve the performance of similar functions; (2) experience actively supervising a principal financial officer, principal accounting officer, controller, public

445 See *infra* at chapter 4, D. I.
446 Cf. SEC Release No. 8177.
447 SEC Release No. 8177, at II, 4, c.

accountant, auditor or person performing similar functions; (3) experience overseeing or assessing the performance of companies or public accountants with respect to the preparation, auditing, or evaluation of financial statements; or (4) other relevant experience.[448]

2. Rules of Professional Responsibility for Attorneys – Section 307 SOX

Due to sec. 307 SOX, the SEC promulgated standard of professional conduct for attorneys requiring an attorney to report evidence of a material violation of securities laws or breach of fiduciary duty or similar violation by the corporation to the GC or CEO, and to the board of directors if the initial report did not result in an appropriate response.[449] Besides outside counsel, also in-house lawyers "appearing and practicing before the [SEC]" are subject to the sec. 307 SOX reporting obligation.[450] With regard to foreign attorneys (outside counsel and in-house lawyers), they may opt out of the reporting obligation essentially by always appearing before the SEC "in consultation with" a U.S. lawyer.[451] The reporting requirements should be actively incorporated and used for the design of internal control structures. Especially in-house lawyers are able to serve as a control measure and to convey to the board of directors.[452] In order to serve this function more effectively, the possible influence of management on in-house lawyers should be minimized by transferring the selection and compensation decision in regard to in-house lawyers from the CEO to the board of directors.[453] Similar to sec. 301 SOX which requires the audit committee to deal with the outside auditors, who also serve a gatekeeper function, the directors should deal with the issues regarding their in-house gatekeepers, i.e. in-house lawyers. If in-house lawyers are required to serve a gatekeeper function, then, all the measures to protect gatekeepers form undue influence should be applied to them including a direct reporting opportunity to the audit committee or the board of directors, and protection against retaliation.

448 SEC Release No. 8177, at II, 4, c.

449 See SEC Release No. 8185.

450 Cf. 17 CFR 205.2(g); *Koniak/Cohen/Cramton*, 2010, p. 83; *Kim*, 74 Fordham L. Rev. 983 (2005).

451 Cf. 17 CFR 205.2(j); *Koniak/Cohen/Cramton*, 2010, p. 19.

452 Cf. *Kostant*, 52 N. Y. L. Sch. L. Rev. 535 (2007/2008), p. 550 et seq.

453 *Kostant*, 52 N. Y. L. Sch. L. Rev. 535 (2007/2008), p. 551.

3. Code of Ethics for Senior Financial Officers – Section 406 SOX

In sec. 406 SOX, the SEC has been mandated to issue rules requiring each corporation subject to the Exchange Act to disclose whether the corporation has adopted a code of ethics for senior financial officers, applicable to its principal financial officer and comptroller or principal accounting officer, and, if not, to explain why. The SEC issued Item 406 Regulation S-K requiring the sec. 406 SOX disclosure.[454] In Item 406(b) Regulation S-K, the code of ethics is described as written standards that are reasonably designed to deter wrongdoing and to promote honest and ethical conduct, including the ethical handling of actual or apparent conflicts of interest between personal and professional relationships (Item 406(b)(1) Regulation S-K), full, fair, accurate, timely, and understandable disclosure in reports and documents that a corporation files with the SEC and in other public communications (Item 406(b)(2) Regulation S-K), compliance with applicable governmental laws, rules and regulations (Item 406(b)(3) Regulation S-K), the prompt internal reporting of violations of the code to an appropriate person or persons identified in the code (Item 406(b)(4) Regulation S-K), and accountability for adherence to the code (Item 406(b)(5) Regulation S-K). In contrast to sec. 406 SOX, the NYSE code of business conduct and ethics[455] has a wider scope than sec. 406 SOX which focuses only on senior financial officers.[456] The sec. 406 SOX code of ethics may be a portion of a broader document enabling corporations to include the sec. 406 SOX code of ethics into the NYSE code of business conduct and ethics.[457] While corporations have to adhere to Item 406 Regulation S-K, it has been observed that the required code of ethics would not provide "much value".[458] Codes of ethics, however, are believed to provide value by promoting a good tone at the top and a culture of compliance which are the focal elements of an effective internal control system as recommended by COSO I.[459]

---

454 See SEC Release No. 8177.

455 See *infra* at chapter 4, D. I. 2.

456 Cf. *Johnson/Sides*, 30 Wm. Mitchell L. Rev. 1149 (2004), p. 1186.

457 Cf. Instruction No. 1 to Item 406 Regulation S-K.

458 *Langevoort*, 96 Va. L. Rev. 9 (2010), p. 9; cf. *Rodrigues/Stegemoller*, 96 Va. L. Rev. 1 (2010), p. 10.

459 See on elements of the internal control system recommended by COSO I *infra* at chapter 4, C. I. 2.

4. Whistleblowing: Protection Against Retaliation and Program to Reward Whistleblowers – Sections 806, 1107 SOX and Section 922 Dodd-Frank Act

In sec. 806 and 1107 SOX, retaliation against whistleblowers is prohibited to encourage whistleblowing. Whistleblowing is extraordinarily important to detect fraud[460], especially with regard to fraud committed by management[461]. Since whistleblowing is important to detect fraud, potential whistleblowers have to have incentives to blow the whistle. Until recently, whistleblower had weak incentives to blow the whistle.[462] In light of sec. 21F Exchange Act implemented by sec. 922 Dodd-Frank Act, the SEC launched a program to reward whistleblowers[463] providing for demanded monetary incentives[464]. Similarly to sec. 806 and 1107 SOX, sec. 21F(h) Exchange Act prohibits retaliation against whistleblowers.

V. Conclusion

The enactment of SOX including the internal control mandates has become a far greater issue as predicted by Congress and the SEC. The seemingly short and simple mandates of sec. 302 and 404 SOX have turned out to require massive preparatory work by corporations as sec. 302 and 404 SOX only state the desirable result of effective internal controls without any guidance on how to achieve the result. In order to achieve the result, however, comprehensive guidance is necessary which has been totally missed by Congress and in particular by the SEC. The gap of guidance had been filled by the accounting standards of the PCAOB which led to costly inefficiencies. With the 2007 reforms, the SEC regained control over the SOX's internal control process and the implementation of the risk-based, top-down approach fostering efficiency. In general, SOX's internal controls lead to improved disclosure of non-financial and especially financial information of corporations and, thus, achieved a premier goal of SOX to restore investor confidence. As a result of the heightened effectiveness of in-

---

460 ACFE Report 2010, p. 16; ACFE Report 2012, p. 14.

461 ACFE Report 2006, p. 29.

462 *Dyck/Morse/Zingales*, 2008; *Rapp*, 87 B.U. L. Rev. 91 (2007), p. 154.

463 See SEC Release No. 64545; SEC Release No. 2011-116. See also *Fleischer*, ZGR 2011, 155, 179.

464 *Dyck/Morse/Zingales*, 2008; *Rapp*, 87 B.U. L. Rev. 91 (2007), p. 154.

ternal controls, managers will have more difficulties in engaging in questionable accounting practices or outright securities fraud.

Due to SOX, the officers face several challenges and increased responsibilities. A major challenge is to establish effective internal controls pursuant to sec. 302 and 404 SOX. The SEC requires corporations to establish non-financial internal controls and financial internal controls, i.e. disclosure controls and procedures, and internal control over financial reporting. The effectiveness of the controls systems has to be evaluated and material weaknesses have to be disclosed. The signing officers have to certify their responsibility with regard to these duties as well as the accuracy of the financial statements and face personal civil liability pursuant to sec. 302 SOX combined with sec. 18 Exchange Act and criminal liability pursuant to sec. 906 SOX. The incentive regime for management of SOX to implement effective internal controls is effective but subject to inefficiencies attributed to over caution of management and rent-seeking of lawyers, external auditors, and other consultants.

Due to sec. 302 SOX, the SEC requires the CEO and CFO of each corporation filing reports under sec. 13(a) Exchange Act to certify their responsibility for the accuracy of financial reports, for establishing and maintaining internal controls so that material information reaches such officers, for evaluating the effectiveness of the internal controls, and for disclosing their conclusion about the effectiveness in each quarterly and annual report. In order to differentiate between internal controls in regard to sec. 302 and sec. 404 SOX, the SEC decided that sec. 302 SOX internal controls address non-financial information through disclosure controls and procedures. In addition to the certification requirements of sec. 302 SOX, each corporation has to maintain disclosure controls and procedures which have to be designed to ensure that information required to be disclosed by the federal securities laws is recorded, processed, summarized and reported within the time periods specified by the SEC. An information system capturing and processing the relevant information including good documentation is necessary to render the certifying officers confident with regard to non-financial internal controls. Management, including the CEO and CFO, has to evaluate the effectiveness of the disclosure controls and procedures at the end of each fiscal quarter. Since foreign corporations are not required to file a quarterly report, the sec. 302 SOX certification and evaluation of the effectiveness of disclosure controls and procedures are only due once per year for foreign corporations. The SEC expects management to follow an evaluation process in all material aspects of the chosen control framework even beyond financial reporting areas which the control framework requires for an internal control system to be effective.

Due to sec. 404(a)(1) SOX, corporations are required to implement adequately designed and effectively operated internal control over financial reporting. Such controls are adequately designed if they provide for only a remote likelihood that material misstatements will not be prevented or detected on a timely basis, i.e. if no material weakness exists within the design. Internal control over financial reporting operates effectively if no material weakness exits. The required evaluation of management regarding the effectiveness of internal control over financial reporting has to account for both requirements. The two requirements are interdependent as neither poorly designed nor ineffective internal controls will achieve the goal of reliable financial reporting even though they might operate effectively in the former case or are adequately designed in latter case. The most important aspect of sec. 404 SOX are material weaknesses. In order to avoid material weaknesses, all financial reporting risks potentially leading to a material misstatement in the financial statements have to be addressed by at least one adequate control which operates effectively. Since one adequate control operating effectively is sufficient for addressing a financial reporting risk, a system of internal controls may have multiple design and operating deficiencies as long as they do not constitute a material weakness. The core issue of management's efforts to achieve adequate and effective internal control over financial reporting as required by sec. 404(a) SOX is to accurately determine all financial reporting risks potentially leading to a material misstatement in the financial statements. In order to accurately address such financial reporting risks, management has to implement internal control over financial reporting using the comprehensive approach of the COSO I framework. In contrast to identifying financial reporting risks, the identification of controls poses only an issue of efficiency rather than effectiveness as long as each financial reporting risk is addressed by at least one adequate control operating effectively. Following from sec. 404(a)(2) SOX, management has to evaluate the effectiveness of internal control over financial reporting. In order to effectuate the requirements of sec. 404(a) SOX and to provide more confidence for investors in the work of management, sec. 404(b) SOX requires the attestation of the external auditor with regard to management's evaluation of the effectiveness of internal control over financial reporting. Management has to file the internal control report required by sec. 404 SOX each fiscal year and it has to report on any material changes in the corporation's internal control over financial reporting each quarter except for foreign corporations which are only required to report on material changes every fiscal year.

With regard to financial controls addressing fraud, SOX itself does not require corporations to implement controls related to fraud. Due to SEC expectations and as part of the general necessity to foster compliance with laws, corporations have to implement into internal control over financial reporting controls related to the prevention, identification, and detection of fraud. Corporations have to implement specific fraud risk management elements into the general compliance program to address fraudulent behavior. Since internal control over financial reporting and the compliance program are insufficient to address high-level management fraud, corporate governance and ethical behavior play a vital role to address such fraud. While corporate governance issues are addressed in sec. 301 SOX, ethical behavior is addressed in sec. 406 SOX and generally in COSO I.

B. PCAOB Auditing Standard No. 5

In order to attest to, and report on management's assessment of the internal control over financial reporting pursuant to sec. 404(b) SOX, the corporation's public accounting firm has to state the opinion whether, in all material aspect, the corporation maintained effective internal control over financial reporting (Rule 2-02-(f)(2) Regulation S-X). Thus, external auditors have to attest directly on the effectiveness of internal control over financial reporting which conveys whether management's assessment is fairly stated.[465] For the evaluation of the effectiveness of internal control over financial reporting, the PCAOB issued AS 5 "An Audit of Internal Control Over Financial Reporting That Is Integrated with An Audit of Financial Statements"[466] in its capacity to issue auditing standards which public ac-

465 See for more details *supra* at chapter 4, A. 5.

466 See PCAOB, AS 5. Prior to PCAOB AS 2, the PCAOB referred to the statement on auditing standards no. 78 of the AICPA for the report on management's assessment of the effectiveness of internal control over financial reporting conducted by the external auditors. Before SOX, external auditors were governed by peer-related rules established by the American Institute of Certified Accountants and auditing standards issued by the AICPA's Auditing Standards Board (*Moeller*, SOX Internal Controls, p. 53).

counting firms have to adhere to (sec. 103(1) SOX). The PCAOB[467] auditing standards are foremost mandatory for external auditor. In light of the requirement to attest to and report on management's assessment of the effectiveness of internal control over financial reporting required by sec. 404(b) SOX, the auditing standards influence management's assessment of the effectiveness of internal control over financial reporting and the design of internal control over financial reporting. While PCAOB AS 5 is not mandatory for management and internal auditors, it serves as guideline towards efficient and effective internal controls over financial reporting.[468] In general, management has incentives to align the design and evaluation of internal control over financial reporting to PCAOB AS 5 in order to increase the likelihood that external auditors will issue an unqualified attestation. In order to accommodate the needs of the external auditors to comply with PCAOB AS 5 and to facilitate the external auditor's evaluation process, it is highly advisable for management and internal auditors to align internal control over financial reporting with PCAOB AS 5.

Prior to the issuing of PCAOB AS 5 and the 2007 reforms[469], superseded PCAOB AS 2[470] has been the *de facto* standard for management's evaluation of internal control over financial reporting.[471] Since no other guidance existed for management's assessment, PCAOB AS 2 provided the scope for internal control testing.[472] PCAOB AS 2 required the external auditors to focus even on minor internal control issues leading to an unnecessarily inflated auditing process.[473] The external auditors of mainly large corporations applied PCAOB AS 2 overly conservative and detailed.[474] Due to the non-risk-based approach of PCAOB AS 2, senior management and the audit committee of the board of directors received unfiltered reports for each and every minor weakness of internal control over financial re-

467 The PCAOB has been established by sec. 101 SOX and is *inter alia* responsible to establish and adopt rules regarding the audit, quality report, ethics, independence, and other standards relating to the preparation of audit reports for issuers (sec. 101(c)(2) SOX). The PCAOB is administered through five board members appointed by the SEC with the requirement that three members have to be non-CPA members (sec. 101(e)(1) and (2) SOX).

468 Cf. *Moeller*, SOX Internal Controls, p. 79.

469 See *supra* at chapter 4, A. II. 2. a).

470 See PCAOB, AS 2.

471 *Langevoort*, 31 J. Corp. L. 949 (2006), p. 955. See *supra* at chapter 4, A. II. 2. a).

472 *Moeller*, SOX Internal Controls, p. 20.

473 *Moeller*, SOX Internal Controls, p. 21.

474 *Moeller*, SOX Internal Controls, p. 53.

porting significant or not.[475] This process required enormous resources and blocked management and the audit committee from concentrating on significant weaknesses of internal controls.[476] PCAOB AS 2 has been heavily criticized due to its inflexible and cumbersome approach towards the assessment of internal controls. The high costs for sec. 404 SOX internal controls were in part attributed to such overly detailed documentation requirements. In order to reduce costs[477], the PCAOB issued AS 5 implementing a top-down, risk-based approach.[478] Being top-down, the external auditors start testing at the top, i.e. company level controls and financial statements.[479] A risk-based approach includes not only to neglect low-risk areas but also to increase attention on higher-risk areas of internal controls.[480] PCAOB AS 5 allows to consider the risk potential of a specific accounting error but requires clear documentation regarding the process of classifying risk.[481] Moreover, PCAOB AS 5 allows to refer to previous sec. 404 SOX work instead of starting the whole review process all over again each year.[482] This leads to reduced costs once a profound sec. 404 SOX review has been carried out on which subsequent assessments can be based on. The new risk-based approach provides further relief for corporations by allowing to use previous assessments of automated controls which have not been changed during the current reporting period.[483] In essence, PCAOB AS 5 directs to an innovative risk-assessment methodology to ensure efficiency.[484] The top-down approach promises to be both effective and efficient.[485]

---

475 *Moeller*, SOX Internal Controls, p. 175.
476 *Moeller*, SOX Internal Controls, p. 175.
477 *Zhang/Pany*, CPA Journal 2008.
478 Prior to the issuing of PCAOB AS 5 and similar to the SEC (see SEC, Staff Statement; SEC, ICFR-FAQ), the PCAOB published additional guidance in 2006 to provide external auditors with technical guidance for how to conduct an effective and cost-efficient PCAOB AS 2 audit of internal control over financial reporting (see PCAOB, Release No. 2005-009 and PCAOB, Release No. 2005-023).
479 *Zhang/Pany*, CPA Journal 2008.
480 Cf. *O'Brien*, CPA Journal 2006b.
481 *Moeller*, SOX Internal Controls, p. 20.
482 *Moeller*, SOX Internal Controls, p. 168.
483 *Moeller*, SOX Internal Controls, p. 168.
484 Cf. *Dodwell*, CPA Journal 2008.
485 *O'Brien*, CPA Journal 2006b.

I. Requirements of Auditing Standard No. 5

The following description depicts the elements of PCAOB AS 5 which corporations have to consider for designing, operating, and evaluating internal control over financial reporting in order to render internal control over financial reporting more effective and the audit of internal control over financial reporting more efficient. Before analyzing the auditing process itself, three important aspects have to be considered. First, with regard to the issue of choosing a suitable control framework, PCAOB AS 5 requires the external auditors to use the same suitable control framework as management uses for its evaluation.[486] Nevertheless, management should confer with the external auditors with regard to choosing a suitable control framework. Since COSO I is by far the predominant framework, coordinating the choice of the control framework will not become a great issue between management and external auditors in most cases.

Second, in order to address the risk of fraud, the external auditors have to take their results of their SAS No. 99, AU § 316 fraud risk audit into account for evaluating whether the corporation's internal controls sufficiently address risks of material misstatements due to fraud and management override of other controls. Management should have such controls in place to prevent and detect fraud and management override to satisfy the external auditors. Such controls addressing fraud and management override are: "controls over significant, unusual transaction, particularly those that result in late or unusual journal entries", "controls over journal entries and adjustments made in the period-end financial reporting process", "controls over related party transactions", "controls related to significant management estimates", and "controls that mitigate incentives for, and pressures on, management to falsify or inappropriately manage financial results".[487]

Third, the external auditors may use the evidence about the effectiveness of financial reporting provided by internal auditors or other corporate personnel or any other directly assisting corporate employee.[488] While using the work of others, the external auditors have to assess the competence and objectivity of corporate personnel. The higher the competence of corporate personnel, the greater use the external auditors may make of the work.[489] In this regard, it is important for each corporation to ensure that

486 PCAOB, AS 5, par. 5.
487 PCAOB, AS 5, par. 14.
488 PCAOB, AS 5, par. 17.
489 PCAOB, AS 5, par. 18.

corporate personnel is trained to provide accurate work to the external auditors, in order to facilitate the overall auditing process of management's assessment resulting in reduced audit costs and higher quality of the audit. The degree to which the external auditor will use internal work depends also on the risk associated with the control being tested.[490] The internal auditors meeting the standards of the IIA are in general considered to have the competence and objectivity necessary for PCAOB AS 5 purposes.[491] With regard to the use of the work of others, it has to be understood by all parties that the external auditor's work has to be independent of the audited corporation.[492] Otherwise, a conflict of duties may occur.[493] Since external auditors are allowed to use the work of internal personnel under the named restrictions, management should provide for such personnel necessary to conduct such pre-auditing work in order to increase the efficiency with regard to management's assessment of the effectiveness[494] and the external auditor's attestation to the assessment. Since the external auditors have to perform their own work in high-risk areas, internal personnel may still provide their work conducted with regard to such areas. With regard to less risk areas, internal personnel faces a dilemma. One the one hand, the top-down, risk-based approach of the SEC guidance for management's assessment leads internal personnel to focus on high-risk areas. On the other hand, external auditors may use the work of internal personnel especially with regard to lower risk areas. Thus, management has to consider increasing the efforts of internal personnel with regard to lower risk areas despite the top-down, risk-based approach in order to reduce the efforts of the external auditors regarding such areas. Similarly, conducting management's assessment with more objective personnel will also increase the likelihood that external auditors will use the work of such personnel. Thus, management should consider to use more objective personnel for its assessment.

The top-down, risk-based approach requires the external auditors to first assess internal control over financial reporting from an overview perspective prior to assess any detailed levels.[495] According to PCAOB AS 5[496], the external auditors will use the top-down approach to select the controls

490 PCAOB, AS 5, par. 19.
491 *Moeller*, SOX Internal Controls, p. 66. See *infra* at chapter 4, E.
492 *Moeller*, SOX Internal Controls, p. 66.
493 *Moeller*, SOX Internal Controls, p. 66.
494 See *supra* at chapter 4, A. II. 2. b) (2).
495 *Moeller*, SOX Internal Controls, p. 66.
496 PCAOB, AS 5, par. 21 et seq.

which will be tested. A top-down approach begins at the financial statement level with the external auditor's understanding of the overall risks to internal control over financial reporting. Then, the external auditors will consider entity-level controls before working on to significant accounts and disclosures and their relevant assertions. For selecting controls for testing, the external auditors will consider the risks of misstatements in the corporation's process and will select those controls which sufficiently address such risks. Similar to the SEC guidance, external auditors have to test entity-level controls which are important for the overall effectiveness of internal control over financial reporting. If an entity-level control sufficiently addressed a risk of misstatement, external auditors are not required to test additional controls addressing such particular risk. Entity-level controls the external auditors should consider are: "controls related to the control environment", "control over management override", "the risk assessment process", "centralized processing and controls, including shared service environments", "controls to monitor results of operations", "controls to monitor other controls, including activities of the internal audit function, the audit committee, and self-assessment programs", "controls over the period-end financial reporting process", and "policies that address significant business control and risk management practices".[497] Due to the importance for the control environment, external auditors have to evaluate whether management's philosophy and operating style foster effective internal control over financial reporting, whether the corporation developed and promotes sound integrity and ethical values especially on the officers' level, and whether the board of directors or the audit committee understands and executes oversight over internal controls. The oversight over internal controls of the audit committee should include the financial reporting process. With regard to the period-end financial reporting process, the external auditors are required to evaluate the process due to its importance including "procedures used to enter transaction totals into the general ledger", "procedures related to the selection and application of accounting policies", "procedures used to initiate, authorize, record, and process journal entries in the general ledger", "procedures used to record recurring and nonrecurring adjustments to the annual and quarterly financial statements", and "procedures for preparing annual and quarterly financial statements and related disclosures".[498] In order to facilitate the work of the external auditors and to increase the likelihood of an unqualified attestation, manage-

497 PCAOB, AS 5, par. 24.
498 PCAOB, AS 5, par. 26.

ment has to provide for a control environment which satisfies the named factors and has to provide for a period-end financial reporting process which includes the named procedures.

After considering entity-level controls, the external auditors have to identify significant accounts, disclosures, and relevant assertions including the assessment of risk.[499] Due to their importance, significant accounts have to have controls in place which address the risks of material misstatements. In case such risks are significantly different, different controls might be necessary to adequately address those risks.[500] PCAOB AS 5 states risk factors relevant for the identification of significant accounts and disclosures and their relevant assertions.[501] These risk factors, however, are indicators for the significance of the account but not primarily for the risk of material misstatements. As part of identifying significant accounts, external auditors should determine the likely sources leading to material misstatements in financial statements.[502] With regard to the likely sources of misstatement, the external auditors have to further understand such sources in order to select the controls to be tested. Thus, management has to have controls in place addressing such sources which will be achieved when adhering to the SEC guidance requiring that each financial reporting risk has to be addressed by at least one adequate control. For implementing internal controls addressing financial reporting risks, management may consider the objectives the external auditors should achieve to understand the likely sources of potential misstatements.[503] Therefore, management should "understand the flow of transactions related to the relevant assertions, including how these transactions are imitated, authorized, processed, and recorded", has to have controls in place which address the points in the corporation's processes which potentially lead to material misstatements including misstatements due to fraud, and has to have con-

499 PCAOB, AS 5, par. 28 et seq.

500 PCAOB, AS 5, par. 32.

501 PCAOB, AS 5, par. 29: "size and compositing of the account", "susceptibility to misstatement due to errors or fraud", "volume of activity, complexity, and homogeneity of the individual transactions processed through account or reflected in the disclosure", "nature of the account or disclosure", "accounting and reporting complexities associated with the account or disclosure", "exposure to losses in the account", "possibility of significant contingent liabilities arising from the activities reflected in the account or disclosure", "existence of related party transactions in the account", and "changes from the prior period in account or disclosure characteristics".

502 PCAOB, AS 5, par. 30.

503 PCAOB, AS 5, par. 34.

trols in place which prevent or timely detect unauthorized acquisition, use, or disposition of the corporation's assets that could result in a material misstatement of financial statements.[504] Management's considerations and implementation of internal controls have to include IT affecting the corporation's flow of transactions.[505] The documentation of internal control over financial reporting has to be sufficient to enable the external auditors to understand the likely sources of misstatements including the performance of walkthroughs by which the external auditor will follow a transaction form origination through the corporation's processes using the same documents and IT as internal personnel[506]. These walkthroughs are also usually performed by internal auditors during their work within the corporation.[507] The documentation of such internal walkthroughs may assist the external auditors with their audit.[508]

External auditors have to select controls for testing which are important for the conclusion that the internal controls sufficiently address the assess risk of misstatement to each relevant assertion.[509] Since PCAOB AS 5 does neither require the external auditors to test all controls addressing a specific risk of misstatement nor redundant controls, unless redundancy is itself a control objective, PCAOB AS 5 is in line with the SEC guidance which only requires that at least one adequate control addresses each financial reporting risk. The testing conducted by the external auditors has to include the design and operation effectiveness of internal control over financial reporting. For testing the design effectiveness of internal control over financial reporting, the external auditors have to determine whether the internal controls satisfy the corporation's control objectives and whether they can effectively prevent and detect errors or fraud that could result in material misstatements in the financial statements if such controls operate as prescribed by personnel possessing the necessary authority and competence to effectively carry out such controls.[510] For PCAOB AS 5 purposes, a control objective has been defined as providing "a specific target against which to evaluate the effectiveness of a control. A control objective for internal control over financial reporting generally relates to a relevant assertion and states a criterion for evaluating whether the [corporation's] control proce-

504 Cf. PCAOB, AS 5, par. 34.
505 PCAOB, AS 5, par. 36.
506 PCAOB, AS 5, par. 37.
507 *Moeller*, SOX Internal Controls, p. 71.
508 *Moeller*, SOX Internal Controls, p. 71.
509 PCAOB, AS 5, par. 39.
510 PCAOB, AS 5, par. 42.

dures in a specific area provide reasonable assurance that a misstatement or omission in that relevant assertion is prevented or detected by controls on a timely basis".[511] Management should confer with the external auditors and other counsel for establishing control objectives which ensure that the internal controls will be able to effectively prevent and detect errors or fraud potentially leading to material misstatements in the financial statements. With regard to the operating effectiveness of internal control over financial reporting, the external auditors have to determine whether the controls are operating as designed and whether the personnel performing the controls possess the necessary authority and competence.[512] Thus, management has to ensure that all controls operate as designed and are operated by personnel equipped with the necessary authority and competence. The evidence needed for testing the operating effectiveness depends on the risk that a control might not be effective and the risk of a material weakness absent such specific control.[513] Generally, a conclusion that a control is not operating effectively can be supported by less evidence than is necessary to support a conclusion that a control is operation effectively.[514] Thus, internal personnel conducting the assessment of the effectiveness of internal control over financial reporting has to consider the risk factors provided in PCAOB AS 5[515] for determining the level of evidence needed for testing in order to render external auditors confident to use their work as part of the external auditors' audit. Management may also

---

511 PCAOB, AS 5, par. A2.
512 PCAOB, AS 5, par. 44.
513 PCAOB, AS 5, par. 46.
514 PCAOB, AS 5, par. 47.
515 See PCAOB, AS 5, par. 47: "the nature and materiality of misstatements that the control is intended to prevent or detect", "the inherent risk associated with the related account(s) and assertion(s)", "whether there have been changes in the volume or nature of transactions that might adversely affect control design or operating effectiveness", "whether the account has a history of errors", "the effectiveness of entity-level controls, especially controls that monitor other controls", "the nature of the control and the frequency with which it operates", "the degree to which the control relies on the effectiveness of other controls (e.g. the control environment or information technology general controls)", "the competence of the personnel who perform the control or monitor its performance and whether there have been changes in key personnel who perform the control or monitor its performance", "whether the control relies on performance by an individual or is automated (i.e., an automated control would generally be expected to be lower risk if relevant information technology general controls are effective)", and "the complexity of the controls and the significance of the judgments that must be made in connection with its operation".

consider such risk factors when designing internal control over financial reporting in order to reduce the risk that a control might not be effective. Testing methods providing evidence from least to most are: "inquiry, observation, inspection of relevant documentation, re-performance of a control".[516] The external auditors may take audit results of internal control over financial reporting of previous years into account.[517] Once an effective internal control over financial reporting has been implemented auditing costs will be less in the future.

The external auditors have to search only for deficiencies which are individually or in combination material weaknesses.[518] In planning and performing the audit, the external auditors are not required to search for deficiencies that are individually or in combination less severe than a material weakness. The severity of a deficiency depends on the likelihood, i.e. whether there is a reasonable possibility[519], that internal controls will fail to prevent or detect a misstatement and the magnitude of the potential misstatement.[520] In line with the SEC[521], PCAOB AS 5 acknowledges that internal control over financial reporting has inherent limitations which do not expressly include relative costs and benefits.[522] Risk factors indicate that there is a reasonable possibility that a deficiency, or a combination of deficiencies, will result in a misstatement of an account balance or disclosure such as "the nature of the financial statement accounts, disclosures, and assertions involved", "the susceptibility of the related asset or liability to loss or fraud", "the subjectivity, complexity, or extent of judgment required to determine the amount involved", "the interaction or relationship of the control with other controls, including whether they are interdependent or redundant", "the interaction of the deficiencies", and "the possible future consequences of the deficiency".[523] These risk factors have to be dealt with by management for the design of the internal control over financial reporting at least to the point in which the risk factors might result in a material weakness. Indicators of material weaknesses in internal control over financial reporting are: "identification of fraud, whether or not material, on the part of senior management", "restatement of previously is-

516 PCAOB, AS 5, par. 50.
517 PCAOB, AS 5, par. 58 et seq.
518 PCAOB, AS 5, par. 62.
519 PCAOB, AS 5, par. 64.
520 PCAOB, AS 5, par. 63.
521 SEC Release No. 8810, I.
522 PCAOB, AS 5, par. A5.
523 PCAOB, AS 5, par. 65.

sued financial statements to reflect the correction of a material misstatement", "identification by the auditor of a material misstatement of financial statements in the current period in circumstances that indicate that the misstatement would not have been detected by the company's internal control over financial reporting", and "ineffective oversight of the company's external financial reporting and internal control over financial reporting by the company's audit committee".[524] Management has to address these indicators, if present in the corporation, in order to render internal control over financial reporting effective.

The external auditors are only required to report significant deficiencies to the audit committee while lesser deficiencies will only be reported to management.[525] Thus, the audit committee can focus on the important deficiencies while management will still be enabled to improve internal control over financial reporting to avoid lesser deficiencies to become significant deficiencies or material weaknesses in the future. The external auditors should inform the audit committee in an overview about the lesser deficiencies reported to management to enable the audit committee to inquire on improvements made by management or to request more details from management regarding these deficiencies. The audit committee has to have good documentation in case of a disputed accounting treatment by e.g. the external auditors.[526]

II. Differences and Similarities Between SEC Guidance on Management's Assessment of the Effectiveness of Internal Control over Financial Reporting and PCAOB AS No. 5

The influence of PCAOB AS 5 on management including recommendations for designing and operating internal control over financial reporting is strong and diverse. Therefore, it is important to understand the differences and similarities between PCAOB AS 5 and the SEC guidance on management's assessment of the effectiveness of internal control over financial reporting in order assess to which degree management has to adhere to the influence of PCAOB AS 5. In general, since the external auditors have to directly evaluate the effectiveness of internal control over fi-

524 PCAOB, AS 5, par. 69.
525 *Moeller*, SOX Internal Controls, p. 78.
526 *Moeller*, SOX Internal Controls, p. 28.

nancial reporting[527], management's assessment of the effectiveness and external auditors' evaluation seem to be similar. It is important to note, however, that management and external auditors have different roles within internal control over financial reporting[528] leading to different approaches towards the evaluation process. It is management's primary aim to establish effective internal control over financial reporting while the external auditors only evaluate whether management successfully achieved this aim.

The SEC guidance on the evaluation of the effectiveness of internal control over financial reporting and PCAOB AS 5 are in general similar but different in detail, i.e. they are overlapping but not congruent. In contrast to the SEC guidance, PCAOB AS 5 highlights the identification of key controls as important. The SEC guidance, however, achieves a similar result while focusing on weighted financial risks for material misstatements and related controls.[529] Moreover, PCAOB AS 5 has a stronger emphasis on internal audit, auditing issues such as basic accounting cycles, and some less used techniques such as narratives for documentation and audit testing. A salient difference is that PCAOB AS 5 does not specifically separate the evaluation process between the design and the operation of internal control over financial reporting but seems to include all relevant testing methods for both evaluation steps. In general, the SEC guidance is the more detailed approach and separates the evaluation process in two steps in line with the two sec. 404 SOX mandates to provide for adequate and effective internal control over financial reporting. PCAOB AS 5 is more prone to lead to unnecessary documentation and testing with its emphasis of business cycles and key controls. With regard to the evaluation process, the most important factor for both approaches is the absence of material weaknesses since Item 308(a)(3) Regulation S-K bars management to conclude internal control over financial reporting to be effective if there are one or more material weaknesses in the controls. Likewise, external auditors cannot consider internal control over financial reporting effective if one or more material weaknesses exist.[530] Since the definitions of material weakness and significant deficiency in PCAOB AS 5 and in Exchange Act Rule 12b-2 are the same[531], management and the external auditors base their

527 Cf. SEC Release No. 8809, at fn. 61.
528 Cf. SEC Release No. 8810, at, III, A.
529 See IIA Guide 2008, p. 31 on the definition on "key control".
530 PCAOB, AS 5, par. 2.
531 Cf. PCAOB, AS 5, par. A7 and A 11.

conclusion about the effectiveness of internal control over financial reporting on the same footage.

An important difference becomes apparent with regard to the consideration of financial reporting risks. The SEC guidance focuses generally on all financial reporting risks potentially leading to material misstatements regardless of any accounts. In contrast to the SEC guidance, the external auditors focus predominantly on significant accounts and consider likely sources of potential material misstatements only as part of identifying significant accounts.[532] While entity-level controls will be considered in general, PCAOB AS 5 focuses on significant accounts below the level of entity-level controls. Hence, PCAOB AS 5 neglects financial reporting risks outside significant accounts which may, nevertheless, lead to material misstatements. It follows that management has incentives to focus on significant accounts and entity-level controls for determining financial reporting risks in order to satisfy the external auditors. But, in order to comply with the SOX mandates for internal control over financial reporting including the SEC guidance, management has to consider financial reporting risk potentially leading to material misstatements beyond entity-level controls and significant accounts in order to design adequate and effective internal control over financial reporting.

For auditing purposes, obtaining a general conclusion about the effectiveness of internal control over financial reporting including the use of sample controls of entity-level controls and significant accounts to test the effectiveness may be sufficient. But, as shown by the SEC guidance, truly adequate and effective internal control over financial reporting requires that each financial reporting risk potentially leading to a material misstatement is addressed at least by one adequate control. Especially with regard to entity-level controls, the SEC guidance indicates that such controls are important for the overall internal control system but are less likely to adequately address a specific financial reporting risk.[533] Thus, it may not be sufficient to focus on entity-level controls for designing and operating effective internal control over financial reporting. Hence, focusing on entity-level controls and significant accounts is conclusive for auditing purposes but designing and operating truly adequate and effective internal control over financial reporting requires more than duplicating auditing patterns.

532 Cf. PCAOB, AS 5, par. 30.
533 See *supra* at chapter 4, A. II. 2. a).

III. Conclusion

In general, as the external auditors have to attest to the effectiveness of internal control over financial reporting, management has to consider PCAOB AS 5 for designing, operating, and evaluating effective internal control over financial reporting and should consider to provide all emphasized controls and procedures as well as for accurate work of mostly objective internal personnel including good documentation to render the external auditors confident to use such work. Nevertheless, management has to consider both implications deriving from PCAOB AS 5 and SEC guidance. While following PCAOB AS 5 may result in the desired unqualified attestation on management's assessment of the effectiveness of internal control over financial reporting, officers still need to considering more than auditing patterns for implement adequate and effective internal control over financial reporting in order to avoid liability.

C. The Frameworks of the Committee of Sponsoring Organizations of the Treadway Commission (COSO)

The Committee of Sponsoring Organizations of the Treadway Commission (COSO) is a voluntary private-sector organization sponsored by five U.S. associations of accountants: American Accounting Association (AAA), American Institute of Certified Public Accountants (AICPA), Financial Executives International (FEI), Institute of Internal Auditors (IIA), and Institute of Management Accountants (IMA).[534] It is dedicated to establish more effective, efficient, and ethical business operations on a global basis.[535] COSO has its roots in 1985 when the major objective of the National Commission on Fraudulent Financial Reporting 1985, known as the Treadway Commission, was to identify the causes of fraudulent financial reporting.[536] The Treadway Commission created a framework addressing compliance[537] and made several recommendations directly addressing internal control. Prior to COSO I, various internal control concepts and definitions existed in the U.S. In 1977, the FCPA was enacted including a provision concerning internal controls. One of the major obstacles was that no co-

534 Cf. *Dierks/Sandmann/Herre*, CCZ 2013, 164, 165.
535 COSO Homepage.
536 Cf. *National Commission on Fraudulent Financial Reporting*, 1987.
537 *Biegelman/Bartow*, Culture of Compliance, p. 42.

herent definition of internal controls existed at that point in time.[538] Each constituency defined internal controls differently. Based on the recommendations of the Treadway Commission, COSO developed the COSO Internal Control – Integrated Framework of 1992 (COSO I).[539] Since 1992, COSO I provides for an overall basis for all groups concerned to formulate guidelines for their specific fields. COSO I serves as the underlying framework for all internal control related mandates and requirements in the U.S.[540] In 2004, COSO issued COSO Enterprise Risk Management – Integrated Framework (COSO II) which "expands on internal control, providing a more robust and extensive focus on the broader subject of enterprise risk management" incorporating COSO I without the intent to replace COSO I.[541] In 2009, COSO issued the COSO Internal Control – Integrated Framework – Guidance on Monitoring Internal Control Systems (COSO Monitoring)[542], guidance will be provided for corporations to clarify the monitoring component of COSO I.[543]

In 2013, COSO I has been subject to a major update in order to accommodate increased complexity of businesses due to globalization and IT-related developments as well as to enhance and specify the framework and to broaden its scope especially with regard to non-financial reporting.[544] The update of COSO I in 2013 did not change fundamental aspects such as the definition of internal control or the main five interrelated components.[545] As of December 2014, the 2013 version of COSO I superseded the version of 1992.[546]

In the following, an analysis of COSO I will provide insight on the requirements of COSO I. The analysis will include the guidance provided by COSO Monitoring with regard to the monitoring component of COSO I. Subsequently, the interrelation between COSO I and COSO II will be depicted to show how internal controls are integrated into enterprise risk management and to provide insight into the opportunities of enterprise risk management. It has to be understood, however, that all COSO publi-

---

538 *Moeller*, SOX Internal Controls, p. 90; cf. *Seligman*, 80 Notre Dame L. Rev. 1159 (2005), p. 1182.

539 Cf. COSO I, p. 97.

540 See *infra* at chapter 6, A.

541 COSO II, p. V.

542 See COSO Monitoring.

543 COSO Monitoring Introduction, p. 1.

544 COSO I, mar. 5; cf. *Dierks/Sandmann*, CCZ 2013, 164, 167.

545 COSO I, mar. 4 et seq.

546 COSO, 2013 FAQ, no. 6.

cations, especially COSO I, are frameworks to provide general elements and concepts for internal control but are not intended to provide specific guidance for single corporations for how to design and operate their specific internal control.[547]

I. COSO Internal Control – Integrated Framework of 2013

The COSO I framework is the first attempt to provide a common basis for all parties involved in internal controls. COSO I internal control consists of five interrelated components: "the control environment, risk assessment, control activities, information and communication, and monitoring".[548] All five components are relevant for each objectives' category: effectiveness and efficiency of operations, reliability of financial reporting, and compliance with laws and regulations.[549] Each of the components is associated with principles and related points of focus which need to be considered for designing and operating internal control. In total, COSO I consists of 17 principles and 77 points of focus.[550] The components are an integral part of the management process.[551] They have a direct relationship with the objectives a corporation tries to achieve.[552] All components and objectives are relevant for the whole corporation and each of its units[553], so that internal control is not a serial process.[554] Especially for large corporations, internal controls have to be formal and structured.[555]

1. COSO I Definition of Internal Control

COSO I defines internal control as: "a process, effected by a [corporation]'s board of directors, management and other personnel, designed to provide reasonable assurance regarding the achievement of objectives relating to

547 Cf. *Gupta*, 2009, p. 70; *Gupta/Leech*, 3 Int. J. Disclosure and Governance 27 (2006), p. 32.
548 COSO I, mar. 34.
549 COSO I, mar. 19.
550 See for an overview in German *Amling/Bantleon*, WPg 2014, 343, 351 et seq.
551 COSO I, mar. 34 et seq.
552 COSO I, mar. 36 et seq.
553 COSO I, mar. 36.
554 COSO I, mar. 40.
555 Cf. COSO I, Executive Summary, p. 2.

operations, reporting, and compliance".[556] The broad definition of internal controls within COSO I provides for sufficient leeway to ensure that each corporation is enabled to adjust their internal control to fit its specific needs. Therefore, COSO I is aimed not to lead to a one-size-fits-all proposition.[557]

The main characteristic of internal control defined by COSO I is that it is a process reflecting that an internal control does not stand alone as a means of itself.[558] Rather, it is a series of actions that permeate the corporation's activities inherent in the way management runs the business.[559] Internal controls should be integrated into the business processes rendering internal control a part of each business process since internal control is viewed as being most effective when integrated into the business processes rather than "built on".[560]

As indicated by the COSO I definition of internal control, the people of the corporation play an important role within internal control. While internal control should be of everyone's responsibility within the corporation, the board of directors and management establish the corporation's objectives and put control mechanisms in place.[561] In this regard, the effectiveness of the internal control system depends especially on the board of directors, management, and internal auditors.[562] The functions and responsibilities within internal control systems will be depicted below.[563]

a) Objectives to Achieve with Internal Control

The achievement of objectives is the central goal of internal control. The COSO I definition categorizes the objectives into three categories. The categorization is intended to enable the management to focus on separate aspects of internal control while responsibilities and categories may overlap.[564] With regard to the objectives financial reporting and compliance with law, these two objectives are mainly based on standards imposed by

---

556 COSO I, mar. 14.
557 Cf. COSO I, mar. 16 and 18.
558 Cf. COSO I, mar. 15.
559 COSO I, mar. 23.
560 COSO I, mar. 24.
561 COSO I, mar. 25.
562 COSO I, mar. 487.
563 See *infra* at chapter 6, A. II.
564 COSO I, mar. 19 et seq.

external institutions such as the SEC reporting requirements for listed corporations and, thus set from outside of the corporation.[565] In large corporations, it is crucial to have a well structured process to set objectives. It is likely that objectives will overlap different categories of objectives. With regard to overlapping objectives, management has to consider whether objectives have to meet external benchmarks which do not relate to the predominant category of the respective objective. In general, all objectives have to be measurable[566] in order to enable unambiguous verification of their accomplishment. Objectives have to be revised periodically in order to ensure consistency and appropriateness. In order to allocate resources efficiently, activity objectives that are critical to achieve corporation-wide objectives have to be identified to prioritize objectives.[567]

b) Limitations of Internal Control

The definition of internal control requires only to provide for reasonable assurance to achieve the objectives. In this regard, it has to be understood that even the best designed, implemented, and monitored internal control system can only provide for reasonable assurance to management and the board of directors regarding the achievement of the corporation's objectives.[568] Internal controls are "not a panacea".[569]

Reasonable assurance can only be provided due to the inherent limitations of all internal control systems.[570] The "human factor" within the control system leads to the limitations due to bad decision-making, errors, mistakes, circumvention of controls, and the ability to override controls. Bad decision-making may be caused by constraints such as limited time, information, procure, or lack of experience. Breakdowns even of well designed internal controls may occur due to errors, judgment mistakes, misunderstanding of instructions, or lack of experience. One of the main reasons limiting the effectiveness of the internal control system is linked to the managers who are responsible for the functioning of the internal control system. Prescribed internal control procedures may be overridden by

565 COSO I, mar. 21.
566 COSO I, mar. 43.
567 Cf. COSO I, mar. 46.
568 COSO I, mar. 84.
569 COSO I, mar. 476.
570 COSO I, mar. 475 et seq.

managers with sufficient authority for illegitimate purposes. Override practices include also deliberate misrepresentations to external parties and the issuing of false documents. Management override as a limitation of internal controls is only related to illegitimate purposes since management override for legitimate purposes is important to deal with non-standard events and gaps within the internal control system. Legitimate override has to be well communicated and documented. The internal control system may also fail due to collusion.[571] In case two or more individuals work together to conceal or circumvent internal controls e.g. when two individuals with segregated authority work together, the internal control system may not detect the action.

At last, corporations also have to consider costs and benefits of establishing internal controls.[572] In this regard, management should develop and maintain an internal control system balancing the allocation of human resources considering the areas of greatest risk, complexity, or other factors relevant for the corporation.[573] Costs alone, however, are not an acceptable reason to avoid the implementation of internal controls.

2. COSO I Components

COSO I internal control consists of five interrelated components: "the control environment, risk assessment, control activities, information and communication, and monitoring".[574] The requirements for each component will be depicted in the following focusing on mandates for the design and operation of internal control in order to fulfill the COSO I requirements.

a) Control Environment

The control environment, as the first component, is of critical importance for an effective internal control system as it provides the foundation for all other components of internal control[575] since all five COSO I components are interrelated so that all other components are influenced by the control

571 COSO I, mar. 486.
572 COSO I, mar. 130 et seq.
573 COSO I, mar. 137.
574 COSO I, mar. 34.
575 COSO I, mar. 143.

environment.[576] The control environment sets the tone of a corporation. It is usually referred to as "tone at the top". The tone at the top is most important for internal control and must be impacted by management's and the board of directors' individual values of integrity and ethical values as well as their operating style and personal conduct.[577] The board of directors and the audit committee have a vital role the control environment. The directors have to use their influence on management in order to establish integrity and ethical values within the internal control system. In order to fulfill the required tasks within the internal control, the board of directors needs to have the expertise, resources, and willingness to provide for the necessary independent governance, guidance, and oversight.[578] Also management has to communicate what is wrong and what is right to its employees through mission and values statements, code of conducts and further formally expressed expectations.[579] This is especially important in large corporations since informal communication has a limited outreach.[580] With regard to autonomous operating divisions and foreign and domestic subsidiaries, their control environment may vary due to differences in local management's preferences, value judgments and management styles.[581]

With regard to the component 'control environment', COSO I sets out the following principles: (no. 1) demonstration of commitment to integrity and ethical values, (no. 2) demonstration by the board of director's independence from management and exercise of oversight of the development and performance of internal control, (no. 3) establishment by the management of structures, reporting lines, and appropriate authorities and responsibilities in the pursuit of objectives, (no. 4) demonstration of a commitment to attract, develop and retain competent individuals in alignment with objectives, and (no. 5) holding individuals accountable for their internal control responsibilities in the pursuit of objectives.[582]

With regard to the principle no. 1, management should determine the points of focus: (1) setting the tone at the top, (2) establishing standards for conduct, (3) evaluating the adherence to the standards of conduct, and

576 COSO I, mar. 146.
577 COSO I, mar. 148 et seq. See also *Langevoort*, 2016.
578 Cf. COSO I, mar. 166.
579 COSO I, mar. 148.
580 Cf. COSO I, mar. 150; *Ramos*, SOX 404, p. 26.
581 COSO I, mar. 180 et seq.
582 COSO I, mar. 143.

(4) addressing deviations in a timely manner.[583] With regard to the principle no. 2, management should determine the points of focus: (1) establishing oversight responsibilities, (2) applying relevant expertise, (3) operating independently, and (4) providing oversight for the system of internal control.[584] With regard to the principle no. 3, management should determine the points of focus: (1) considering all structures of the corporation, (2) establishing reporting lines, and (3) defining, assigning and limiting authorities and responsibilities.[585] With regard to the principle no. 4, management should determine the points of focus: (1) establishing policies and practices, (2) evaluating competence and addressing shortcomings, (3) attracting, developing, and retaining individuals, and (4) planning and preparing for succession.[586] With regard to the principle no. 5, management should determine the points of focus: (1) enforcing accountability through structures, authorities, and responsibilities, (2) establishing performance measures, incentives, and rewards, (3) evaluating performance measures, incentives, and rewords for ongoing relevance, (4) considering excessive pressures, and (5) evaluating performance and rewarding or disciplining individuals.[587]

b) Risk Assessment

The second component is risk assessment. Each corporation faces risks from external and internal sources.[588] These risks challenge the business success which is defined by management as business targets, i.e. objectives. Risk is an inherent and essential part in doing business. Management has the duty to determine "how much risk is to be prudently accepted, and strive to maintain risk within these levels".[589] Prior to assess these risks, management has to set objectives as they are a prerequisite for the risk assessment.[590] Setting objectives is essential for internal control even though not itself a COSO I component of internal control. The process of assessing risk is the identification and analysis of relevant risks concerning the

583 COSO I, mar. 147.
584 COSO I, mar. 166.
585 COSO I, mar. 178.
586 COSO I, mar. 192.
587 COSO I, mar. 204.
588 COSO I, mar. 226.
589 COSO I, mar. 230.
590 COSO I, mar. 236.

achievement of the formulated objectives which form the basis for determining how the risks should be managed.[591] This has to include changes of the risk environment. Identifying and analyzing risk has to be an ongoing process within a corporation.[592]

For assessing risk, the risk identification process is important. It is crucial to effective risk assessment.[593] For identifying risks, management has to consider the entity-level and the activity level. A specific focus will need to be set on the potential of fraud and corruption.[594] Even though risk identification is the crucial process within risk assessment, it is not effective to identify and consider all risks. Limitations are necessary.[595] Otherwise, management might lose the focus on the essential risks. It is not easy to determine where to draw the line.[596] In general, it has more adverse effects for a corporation that an adverse event occurs which has not been identified as a risk before, than dealing with some more risk factors which prove, in hindsight, to be insignificant for the corporation. The risk analysis process follows the risk identification. Generally, management should classify the identified risks.[597] In order to manage the risk, certain techniques can be used such as risk avoidance by simply not pursuing the risky activity, risk sharing with e.g. an insurer or by hedging the risk at the exchanges. Furthermore, the risk might be reduced by designing and implementing internal control procedures. At last, the risk can be accepted, if appropriate.[598] The risk managing process involves judgment based on assumptions about the risks, and the analysis of the costs to reduce the level of risk.[599] It is fundamental for the risk assessment process to identify changing conditions in the economic, industry, and regulatory environments of the corporation and take necessary actions since the internal control system may not function with the same effectiveness under new circumstances.[600] Also, management has to be aware of potential internal control issues if key activities of the business are changed. An essential part

591 COSO I, Executive Summary, p. 4.
592 COSO I, mar. 268.
593 COSO I, mar. 278.
594 Cf. COSO I, mar. 302 et seq.
595 COSO I, mar. 282.
596 COSO I, mar. 282.
597 COSO I, mar. 283 et seq.
598 COSO I, mar. 294.
599 COSO I, mar. 293.
600 COSO I, mar. 325.

of that process is an information system which captures, processes, and reports changing conditions.[601]

With regard to the component 'risk assessment', COSO I sets out the principles: (no. 6) specification of objectives with sufficient clarity to enable the identification and assessment of risks relating to objectives, (no. 7) identification of risks to the achievement of its objectives across the corporation and analysis of risks as a basis for determining how the risks should be managed, (no. 8) consideration of the potential for fraud in assessing risks to the achievement of objectives, and (no. 9) identification and assessment of changes that could significantly impact the system of control.[602]

With regard to the principle no. 6, management should determine five subgroups of points of focus: (1) focus points relating to operations objectives: (a) reflecting management's choices, (b) considering the tolerance for risk, (c) including operations and financial performance goals, and (d) forming a basis for committing of resources; (2) focus points relating to external financial reporting objectives: (a) complying with applicable accounting standards, (b) considering materiality, and (c) reflecting corporation activities; (3) focus points relating to external non-financial reporting objectives: (a) complying with externally established standards and frameworks, (b) considering the required level of precision, and (c) reflecting entity activities; and (4) focus points relating to internal reporting objectives: (a) reflecting management's choices, (b) considering the required level of precision, and (c) reflecting corporation activities; (5) relating to compliance objectives: (a) reflecting external laws and regulations, and (b) considering tolerance for risk.[603] With regard to the principle no. 7, management should determine the points of focus: (1) including corporation, subsidiary, division, operating unit, and functional levels, (2) analyzing internal and external factors, (3) involving appropriate levels of management, (4) estimating significance of risks identified, and (5) determining how to respond to risks.[604] With regard to the principle no. 8, management should determine the points of focus: (1) considering various types of fraud, (2) assessing incentive and pressures, (3) assessing opportunities, and (4) assessing attitudes and rationalizations.[605] With regard to the principle no. 9, management should determine the focus points: (1) assessing changes in

601 COSO I, mar. 328. See *infra* at chapter 4, C. I. 2. d).
602 COSO I, mar. 226.
603 COSO I, mar. 239 et seq.
604 COSO I, mar. 267.
605 COSO I, mar. 302.

the external environment, (2) assessing changes in the business model, and (3) assessing changes in leadership.[606]

c) Control Activities

The third component of COSO I is control activities. The risk assessment has identified actions which address the risk endangering the achievement of the objectives.[607] The control activities are put in place to ensure that the identified actions are carried out properly and in a timely manner.[608] Control activities include approvals, authorizations, verifications, physical controls, controls over standing data, reconciliations, supervisory controls, and segregation of duties.[609] In general, control activities consist of two elements: a policy and procedures to affect the policy.[610] Since corporations widely rely on information systems, they have to have controls in place for all information systems, i.e. financial, compliance, and operational.[611] Two broad categories of control activities exist to control information systems with manual and automated elements.[612] The first category encompasses general controls which are part of all application systems and provide for continuous and proper operation.[613] The second category, application controls, serves as a control of various transactions through means within the application software and related manual procedures.[614] By means of these controls, the information system is enabled to provide for complete, accurate, and valid information.[615]

With regard to the component 'control activities,' COSO I sets out the principles: (no. 10) selection and development of control activities that contribute to the mitigation of risks to the achievement of objectives to acceptable levels, (no. 11) selection and development of general control activities over technology to support the achievement of objectives, and (no. 12)

606 COSO I, mar. 324.
607 COSO I, mar. 334.
608 COSO I, mar. 335.
609 COSO I, mar. 349.
610 Cf. COSO I, mar. 382.
611 COSO I, mar. 341 et seq.
612 Cf. COSO I, mar. 354.
613 COSO I, mar. 355.
614 Cf. COSO I, mar. 339.
615 COSO I, mar. 341.

development of control activities through policies that establish what is expected and in procedures that put policies into action.[616]

With regard to the principle no. 10, management should determine the points of focus: (1) integrating with risk assessment, (2) considering corporation-specific factors, (3) determining relevant business processes, and (4) evaluating a mix of control activity types.[617] With regard to the principle no. 11, management should determine the points of focus: (1) determining dependency between the use of technology in business processes and technology in general controls, (2) establishing relevant technology infrastructure control activities, (3) establishing relevant security management process control activities, and (4) establishing relevant technology acquisition, development, and maintenance process control activities.[618] With regard to the principle no. 12, management should determine the points of focus: (1) establishing policies and procedures to support deployment of management's directives, (2) establishing responsibility and accountability for executing policies and procedures, (3) performing in a timely manner, (4) taking corrective action, (5) performing using competent personnel, and (6) reassessing policies and procedures.[619]

d) Information and Communication

Information and communication are the fourth component of COSO I. This component supports the functioning of all components of internal control.[620] An information system has to process relevant, timely and quality information from internal and external sources.[621] Also, effective communication is a necessary prerequisite for effective internal controls and has to flow down, across and up in the corporation.[622] Upstream communication is particularly import.[623] In order to fulfill the communication requirements, each employee has to understand her own role within the in-

616 COSO I, mar. 330.
617 COSO I, mar. 333.
618 COSO I, mar. 365.
619 COSO I, mar. 381.
620 COSO I, mar. 391.
621 COSO I, mar. 392.
622 Cf. COSO I, mar. 393.
623 COSO I, mar. 423 et seq.

ternal control system.[624] The communication process has to include external parties such as customers, suppliers, regulators, and shareholders.[625]

With regard to the component 'information and communication,' COSO I sets out the principles: (no. 13) obtaining or generating and using relevant, quality information to support the functioning of other components of internal control, (no. 14) internal communication of information, including objectives and responsibilities for internal control, necessary to support the functioning of other components of internal control, and (no. 15) communication with external parties regarding matters affecting the functioning of other components of internal control.[626]

With regard to the principle no. 13, management should determine the points of focus: (1) identifying information requirements, (2) capturing internal and external sources of data, (3) processing relevant data into information, (4) maintaining quality throughout processing, and (5) considering costs and benefits.[627] With regard to the principle no. 14, management should determine the points of focus: (1) communicating internal control information, (2) communicating with the board of directors, (3) providing separate communication lines, and (4) selecting relevant method of communication.[628] With regard to the principle no. 15, management should determine the points of focus: (1) communicating to external parties, (2) enabling inbound communication, (3) communicating with the board of directors, (4) providing separate communication lines, and (5) selecting relevant method of communication.[629]

e) Monitoring

The final component of COSO I is monitoring of the internal control system. Since monitoring is more specifically addressed in the COSO Guidance on monitoring of 2009 which remains in force despite the 2013 update of COSO I[630], the following will only provide for a basic overview of the COSO I component. The monitoring process has to include mechanisms to address necessary modifications within the internal control sys-

---

624 COSO I, mar. 420.
625 COSO I, mar. 433.
626 COSO I, mar. 390.
627 COSO I, mar. 397.
628 COSO I, mar. 418.
629 COSO I, mar. 432.
630 COSO, 2013 FAQ, no. 15.

tem.[631] Thereby, the system can react dynamically as conditions change. The monitoring process consists of two parts an ongoing monitoring activity and a separate evaluation.[632] A further part of the monitoring component is to report internal control deficiencies upstream.[633] Monitoring is important for management to determine if changes to the internal control system are indicated.[634] The ongoing development of the internal control system is necessary to ensure the same level of effectiveness. Due to its real time monitoring activities, ongoing monitoring tends to be more effective than separate evaluations.[635] In general, internal auditors can be particularly effective in monitoring the corporation's activities.[636]

With regard to the component 'monitoring', COSO I sets out the principles: (no. 16) selection, development, and performing ongoing and/or separate evaluations to ascertain whether the components of internal control are present and functioning, and (no. 17) evaluation and communication of internal control deficiencies in a timely manner to those parties responsible for taking corrective action, including senior management and the board of directors, as appropriate.[637]

With regard to the principle no. 16, management should determine the points of focus: (1) considering a mix of ongoing and separate evaluations, (2) considering rate of change, (3) establishing baseline understanding, (4) using knowledgeable personnel, (5) integrating with business processes, (6) adjusting scope and frequency, and (7) evaluating objectively.[638] With regard to principle no. 17, management should determine the points of focus: (1) assessing results, (2) communicating deficiencies, and (3) monitoring corrective actions.[639]

3. Effectiveness of Internal Control

The effectiveness of internal control is important since non-effective internal control will not provide reasonable assurance that the corporation will

631 Cf. COSO I, mar. 445.
632 COSO I, mar. 449.
633 COSO I, mar. 464.
634 COSO I, mar. 468.
635 COSO I, mar. 451.
636 COSO I, mar. 515.
637 COSO I, mar. 443.
638 COSO I, mar. 449.
639 COSO I, mar. 467.

achieve its objectives. Since each internal control system is unique, there is no one-size-fits-all standard to determine the effectiveness of the internal control system. Nevertheless, COSO I suggests that internal controls are effective if management determines that the board of directors and management "have reasonable assurance" that each of the three categories work and that they work in an integrated manner.[640] COSO I states that a particular internal control system is effective if the subjective judgment of the management determines through an assessment that "the five components are present and functioning effectively". Therefore, each of the five components is a criterion to determine the overall effectiveness of internal control system.[641]

The effectiveness of the internal control system is questioned if deficiencies exist within the system.[642] In this regard, an internal control system is not considered to be effective if a major deficiency exists.[643] A major deficiency has been described by COSO I to exist if an internal control deficiency or a combination of deficiencies is severe enough to adversely affect the likelihood that the corporation can achieve its objectives.[644] In general, management uses judgment to determine the severity of a deficiency.[645]

II. COSO Internal Control – Integrated Framework – Guidance on Monitoring Internal Control Systems of 2009

The COSO Internal Control – Integrated Framework – Guidance on Monitoring Internal Control Systems (COSO Monitoring) has been developed to clarify the monitoring component of COSO I.[646] Two aspects of COSO Monitoring are, first, sensitizing management of the importance of the monitoring component of COSO I including its function "as a unifying component of [COSO I]", and, second, to improve internal control "while reducing the costs of gaining continued assurance that internal control operates effectively", thus, fostering effectiveness and efficiency of internal control.[647] COSO Monitoring is not intended replace COSO I but ex-

640 COSO I, mar. 86 et seq.
641 COSO I, mar. 92.
642 Cf. COSO I, mar. 102 et seq.
643 COSO I, mar. 87.
644 COSO I, mar. 102.
645 COSO I, mar. 103.
646 COSO Monitoring Introduction, p. 1.
647 COSO Monitoring, "From the Chairman" and p. 1.

pounds on the principles of COSO I to guide corporations in implementing effective and efficient monitoring.[648] In contrast to COSO I, COSO Monitoring puts a stronger emphasis on efficiency. Effective monitoring can reduce the amount of time management spends for assessing the effectiveness of internal controls.[649] Continuous monitoring will also prevent management to engage in more and reactive considerations to address issues related to ineffective internal control since internal controls may deteriorate over time if they are not monitored effectively.[650] Appropriately designed and implemented monitoring will foster efficiency by identifying and correcting internal control issues on a timely basis, by producing more accurate and reliable information for decision making, by preparing financial statements more accurately and timely, and by putting management in the position to provide periodic certifications on the effectiveness of internal control.[651] Especially the requirements of SOX to evaluate the effectiveness of internal control have placed a heavy burden on management. In this regard, effective monitoring can provide the signing officers with the confidence that the internal control system is and remains effective.[652]

The basis of monitoring should be "a fundamental analysis of risks and an understanding of how controls may or may not manage or mitigate those risks".[653] In this regard, management has to understand that it is not sufficient to implement internal control once with huge effort without realizing that internal control is an ongoing issue of managing the corporation. In fact, internal control is an ongoing process which includes the execution, monitoring, and re-adjustment of internal control. Adequately designed and executed monitoring provides information to the appropriate management level to determine the effectiveness of the internal control system, and identifies and communicates internal control deficiencies in a timely manner to those management levels responsible for taking corrective actions as well as to management and the board of directors as appropriate.[654]

648 COSO Monitoring Introduction, p. 1 et seq.
649 Cf. COSO Monitoring Introduction, p. 1.
650 Cf. COSO Monitoring Introduction, p. 2.
651 COSO Monitoring Introduction, p. 2.
652 Cf. COSO Monitoring Introduction, p. 1 et seq.
653 COSO Monitoring, p. 3.
654 COSO Monitoring, p. 14.

III. COSO Enterprise Risk Management – Integrated Framework of 2004

In 2004, COSO issued COSO Enterprise Risk Management – Integrated Framework (COSO II) which "expands on internal control, providing a more robust and extensive focus on the broader subject of enterprise risk management".[655] Enterprise risk management provides management with an opportunity to effectively handle uncertainty together with associated risk and opportunity, thereby, enhancing the capacity to build value.[656] COSO II aims to provide key principles and guidance on enhanced risk management and corporate governance in light of the corporate scandals of the 2000s.[657] Thereby, COSO II incorporates COSO I without the intent to replace COSO I which remains the predominant framework regarding SOX's internal control requirements.[658] Thus, COSO II provides also insight into the design of internal controls in the sense of SOX.[659] Effective internal control is also essential for effective enterprise risk management[660] so that internal control is an integral part of COSO II[661]. In general, COSO II combines risk culture and control culture and strengthens the link between internal control, risks, and achievement of objectives.[662] COSO II serves as a tool to better design and evaluate risk management with special emphasis on internal controls.[663]

The major strength of COSO II is to provide for a comprehensive approach towards risk considering risks between units avoiding isolated risk assessment of individual units.[664] Within COSO II, it is important to notice that each business unit faces its own specific risks which have to be addressed on a local level due to the specifics of local risks and the detailed knowledge of local management with regard to local risks.[665] While only risk affecting the whole enterprise will find their way into the overall risk management system, management has to ensure that local management addresses the local risks appropriately. In addition to this local risk man-

---

655 COSO II, p. V.
656 COSO II, p. 1.
657 COSO II, p. V.
658 COSO II, p. V.
659 *Moeller*, SOX Internal Controls, p. 243.
660 *Bressac*, 2005, p. 12.
661 *protivit*, 2006, p. 20.
662 *Bressac*, 2005, p. 17.
663 *Moeller*, SOX Internal Controls, p. 243.
664 *Moeller*, SOX Internal Controls, p. 243 et seq.
665 *Moeller*, SOX Internal Controls, p. 270 et seq.

agement, each business unit is infiltrated by the overall risk management net. In multinational corporations, a specific need exists to get local management involved into the risk management on the local level especially with regard to compliance with laws and regulations. Different levels of the corporation may be affected by laws and regulation depending on the outreach. On a worldwide level, international law and national laws with an exterritorial application[666], e.g. the FCPA, may be considered within the risk management on the top level. Different implications regarding enforcement and understanding of the international law, however, may lead to a different risk assessment on national levels of the corporation.

1. COSO II Definition and Components of Enterprise Risk Management

COSO II defines enterprise risk management as "a process, effected by a [corporation]'s board of directors, management and other personnel, applied in strategy setting and across the enterprise, designed to identify potential events that may affect the entity, and manage risk to be within its risk appetite, to provide reasonable assurance regarding the achievement of entity objectives."[667] COSO II encompasses four objectives categories: (1) strategic – high-level goals, (2) operations – effective and efficient use of resources, (3) reporting – reliability of reporting, and (4) compliance – with applicable laws and regulations, as well as eight risk components: internal environment, objective setting, event identification, risk assessment, risk response, control activities, information and communication, and monitoring.[668]

2. Comparison of COSO II to COSO I

As mentioned above, COSO II incorporates COSO I. With regard to the objectives, the four categories – strategic, operations, reporting, and compliance – of COSO II are geared to achieve the corporation's objectives similarly to the three categories – effectiveness and efficiency of operations, reliability of financial reporting, and compliance with laws and regulations – of COSO I. The new COSO II category 'strategy' aims to provide for

666 See *Painter/Kaal*, 2010.
667 COSO II, p. 2.
668 COSO II, p. 3 et seq.

overarching principles used to align all three remaining categories. In contrast to COSO I which focuses on internal control to address the risks of achieving the objectives, COSO II provides for a comprehensive approach towards risk and includes internal control as a tool to manage risk within the enterprise.

With regard to the COSO II components, COSO II expands and elaborates on the COSO I's components.[669] The main difference between both frameworks is that COSO II incorporates as components the elements of the designing and implementation process of COSO I internal control which COSO I only mentions as necessary prerequisites for internal control. These elements are the COSO II components objective setting and event identification. The COSO II component 'risk response' is inherent in the COSO I component risk assessment. In essence, COSO II provides a framework for enterprise risk management to comprehensively address all relevant risks to achieve the corporation's objectives. It incorporates all factors of COSO I. While the SEC has not expressively stated that COSO II represents a suitable control framework, COSO II is believed to fulfill the requirements[670].

IV. Conclusion

The COSO frameworks provide a comprehensive basis for internal control and, through COSO II, guidance on how to integrate internal control into comprehensive enterprise risk management. It is important to understand that all COSO publications are only frameworks providing guidance and have to be applied to the specifics of each corporation in order to achieve efficient and effective internal control. Also, internal control has inherent limitations.

For internal control in the U.S., COSO I together with COSO Monitoring is still the predominant framework despite the publication of COSO II. COSO II may be considered by corporations wishing to engage in comprehensive risk management with integrated internal control. In order to fulfill the COSO I requirements for internal control, corporations have to define objectives in the categories operations, financial reporting, and compliance with laws and regulations in order to achieve the overall business goals. Internal control has to be comprised of the five compo-

669 *Bressac*, 2005, p. 12.
670 Cf. *protiviti*, 2006, p. 21.

nents: control environment, risk assessment, control deficiencies, information and communication, and monitoring. Ensuring effectiveness particularly in an efficient manner, it the task of monitoring which has to be strongly emphasized by management. In case material weaknesses exist, internal control may not be considered effective.

The people of the corporation have the most important role within internal controls. As they execute internal controls, their ethical values and integrity are important for the effectiveness of internal control. For this reason, the control environment sets the basis for effective internal controls as it defines the environment and the way people execute internal controls. While monitoring and other control means will provide for mechanisms to foster compliance with the predefined ethical values, controlling the actions of people will become more difficult the further up the corporate hierarchy. Therefore, establishing ethical values and integrity is most important within executive level management.

D. NYSE Listed Company Manual Regarding Internal Control Systems

The NYSE Listed Company Manual (NYSE-LCM) is the rulebook for corporations listed on the NYSE – also called listing standards. Every corporation listed on the NYSE is subject to the NYSE listing standards. The listing standards constitute a private contract between the NYSE and the listed corporation. The content of the listing standards is not limited by securities laws and regulations. Hence, the NYSE can require stricter mandates for corporate governance and internal control than required e.g. by SOX and SEC rules. As a U.S. national exchange, the NYSE is a self-regulatory organization (sec. 3(a)(26) Exchange Act), a form of public-private hybrid[671], which regulates the market under the oversight of the SEC. Therefore, the listing rules of the NYSE are subject to the approval of the SEC which will be granted if the SEC finds that the listing standards are consistent with the federal securities laws and regulations (sec. 19(b)(1) Exchange Act and related Rule 19b-4 Exchange Act). The governance of the market through stock exchanges is a long recognized substitute for governmental regulation of listed corporations.[672] While the NYSE remains free in adopt-

671 *Thompson*, 38 Wake Forest L. Rev. 961 (2003), p. 970.

672 *Thompson*, 38 Wake Forest L. Rev. 961 (2003), p. 972 et seq.: Several potential advantages are incentives to adopt rules that investors have confidence in the market, flexibility of regulation by exchanges to respond more flexible than govern-

ing changes to its listing standards, the SEC has "considerable" influence on the exchanges.[673] In light of self-regulation, the NYSE proclaims to require "the highest standards of accountability and transparency, including enhanced governance requirements" and, thereby, to have taken a leadership role in setting standards for corporate governance.[674] Undisputed, the NYSE listing standards constitute "best practices" for corporate governance[675] strongly influencing U.S. corporate governance.[676]

I. Mandates and Best Practice for Corporate Governance and Internal Control

In section 3, the rulebook deals with corporate responsibility and matters of corporate governance. In the wake of the corporate scandals of the 2000s, the NYSE was encouraged to adopt new listing standards with strong emphasis on corporate governance.[677] Already before the scandals of the 2000s, the NYSE had considered changes to the listing standards reflecting new developments with regard to corporate governance.[678] With the implementation of Rule 303A NYSE-LCM into the listing standards, the NYSE underscored its strong commitment to corporate governance and compliance.[679] Rule 303A NYSE-LCM has been introduced with even further reaching requirements for listed corporations than mandated by SOX or the SEC,[680] especially with regard to director independence.[681] In general, the requirements of Rule 303A NYSE-LCM fully apply to U.S. domestic corporations listing common equity securities (Rule 303A.00

---

mental regulation to changes in the market, expertise of exchanges regarding the needs of investors and listed corporations, and shifting governance and enforcement costs away from government.

673 Cf. *Bainbridge*, 2002, p. 25 et seq. See for an example of SEC influence on the NYSE: NYSE Report, p. 1.

674 See NYSE Financial Compliance.

675 *Thompson*, 38 Wake Forest L. Rev. 961 (2003), p. 977; *Bainbridge*, 2002, p. 24.

676 *Johnson/Sides*, 30 Wm. Mitchell L. Rev. 1149 (2004), p. 1214.

677 Cf. NYSE Report, p. 1. The NYSE Report provides the basis of the changes to its corporate governance listing standards resulting in the introduction of Rule 303A approved by the SEC (SEC Release No. 48745).

678 Cf. *Bainbridge*, 2002, p. 7; *Coates*, 21 J. Econ. Perspectives 91 (2007), p. 111.

679 Cf. *New York City Bar*, Report 2006, p. H-20.

680 Cf. *Ide*, 54 Mercer L. Rev. 829 (2003), p. 850 et seq.

681 NYSE The Exchange, p. 2. The NYSE listing rules require a majority of directors to be independent (Rule 303A.01 NYSE-LCM).

NYSE-LCM). Exceptions to this rule are likewise listed in Rule 303A.00 NYSE-LCM. Due to Rule 303A.00 NYSE-LCM listed foreign corporations are not subject to Rule 303A NYSE-LCM except for Rules 303A.06, 303A.11, and 303A.12(b) and (c) NYSE-LCM. Therefore, listed foreign corporations can follow home country corporate governance standards except for the aforementioned rules. Listed foreign corporations are free, however, to choose to follow NYSE domestic corporate governance standards to the extent permitted by the foreign corporation's home jurisdiction.[682] As a result of the exception, most corporate governance provisions of Rule 303A NYSE-LCM are not mandatory for listed foreign corporations. Nevertheless, the non-mandatory parts of Rule 303A NYSE-LCM constitute the best practice standard for corporate governance in the U.S. with regard to listed foreign corporations and will, therefore, be considered as best practice.

1. Mandates for the Internal Control System of Listed Foreign Corporations

Foreign listed corporations have to comply with the following mandates. Due to Rule 303A.06 NYSE-LCM, listed corporations, including listed foreign corporations, must have an audit committee which satisfies the requirements of Exchange Act Rule 10A-3 in order to be listed on the NYSE. Exchange Act Rule 10A-3 roots from sec. 301 SOX implementing standards relating to audit committees into sec. 10A(m) Exchange Act.[683] Since the mandates of sec. 301 SOX and Exchange Act Rule 10A-3 do not distinguish between domestic and listed foreign corporations, each corporation including listed foreign corporations is subject to Rule 303A.06 NYSE-LCM leaving the NYSE no room for further exceptions regarding listed foreign corporations.[684] In essence, Exchange Act Rule 10A-3(b)(3)(i) requires the

---

682 Cf. NYSE-LCM FAQ, p. 14.

683 Sec. 301 SOX requires the SEC to promulgate a rule to direct the U.S. securities exchanges to prohibit the listing of any securities of an issuer that is not in compliance with sec. 301 SOX. Thus, the SEC promulgated Exchange Act Rule 10A-3. Due to Exchange Act Rule 10A-3(a)(1), the NYSE is obligated to require listed corporations to comply with the requirements of Exchange Act Rule 10A-3 in order to be listed at the NYSE.

684 Exchange Act Rule 10A-3 considers exemptions for foreign corporations but they are not of relevance in this context. The independence requirement of directors is subject to certain exemptions (Exchange Act Rule 10A-3 (b)(1)(iv)(C), (b)(1)(iv)(D), and (b)(1)(iv)(E)). A further exemption is not relevant for German

audit committee of a listed corporation to establish direct communication lines to receive complaints, "regardless of source"[685], regarding accounting, internal accounting controls, or auditing matters. Pursuant to Exchange Act Rule 10A-3(b)(3)(ii), the audit committee has to establish communication lines to receive concerns of employees regarding questionable accounting or auditing matters confidentially and anonymously. No mandates exist for the design of the communication procedures.[686] The communication systems should be integrated into the internal control system. Moreover, the audit committee is *inter alia* directly responsible for the registered public accounting firm's audit report of sec. 404(b) SOX (Exchange Act Rule 10A-3(b)(2)).

Pursuant to Rule 303A.11 NYSE-LCM, listed foreign corporations must disclose any significant differences between the actual followed corporate governance practice and those followed by U.S. domestic corporations under NYSE listing standards. The disclosure has to be a brief, general summary of the significant differences and does not have to be an item-by-item analysis.[687] If the foreign corporation decides to follow in part or totally U.S. domestic corporate governance standards it has to indicate to which point differences still exist or has to state that no such differences exist.[688] The statement of the differences has to be included in the annual report which must be filed on Form 20-F[689].[690] With regard to the NYSE listing standards, the foreign corporation may follow home country corporate standards if the listing standards do not represent mandates of the federal securities laws and SEC rules. The purpose of Rule 303A.11 NYSE-LCM is to address the issue of listed foreign corporations to be subject to two corporate governance regimes – the home country regime and the U.S. corporate governance regime and to make U.S. shareholders aware of any differ-

issuers and, furthermore, provides relatively no change to the internal control requirements of Exchange Act Rule 10A-3 (Exchange Act Rule 10A-3 (c)(3)). Due to the Instruction No. 2 of Exchange Act Rule 10A-3, home legal or listing requirements have priority over Exchange Act Rule 10A-3(b)(2) through (b)(5), (c)(3)(v) and (c)(3)(vi) in case the board of directors is not allowed to delegate the required responsibilities to the audit committee.

685 SEC Release No. 8220.

686 SEC Release No. 8220.

687 Cf. NYSE-LCM, Commentary to Rule 303A.11.

688 Cf. NYSE-LCM FAQ, p. 14.

689 On Form 20-F, the significant differences have to be depicted in Item 16G: Corporate Governance.

690 Cf. NYSE-LCM, Disclosure Requirement to Rule 303A.11.

ences[691], if any. In most cases, a foreign corporation will not be able to fully comply with all the requirements of Rule 303A NYSE-LCM due to home country law. With regard to German corporations (previously) listed on the NYSE, corporations consider(-ed) the NYSE listing standards for their corporate governance following voluntarily the NYSE listing standards as far as permitted by German law.[692] In most cases, the various committees, mandated by the NYSE listing standards only for U.S. corporations, have not been implemented by German corporations listed on the NYSE beside the mandatory audit committee.[693]

With regard to the certification requirement of Rule 303.12 NYSE-LCM, listed foreign corporations are only required to comply with the certification requirements of Rule 303A.12(b) and (c) NYSE-LCM. Therefore, the CEO must promptly notify the NYSE in case an executive officer becomes aware of any non-compliance with any applicable provision of Rule 303A NYSE-LCM[694] (Rule 303A.12(b) NYSE-LCM), and the corporation must submit an executed written affirmation annually to the NYSE and an interim written affirmation as and when required to on the form specified by the NYSE (Rule 303A.12(c) NYSE-LCM). The written affirmation and the interim written affirmation for listed foreign corporations contain NYSE forms on which the corporation or the CEO notifies the NYSE of the compliance status with regard to Rule 303A.06 NYSE-LCM. The certification and reporting mandates of Rule 303A.12(b) and (c) NYSE-LCM provide an extra layer to ensure that listed foreign corporations comply in particular with Rule 303A.06 NYSE-LCM since the NYSE has to prohibit any issuer form being listed if the issuer is not in compliance with Rule 10A-3 Exchange Act. Thus, Rule 303A.12(b) and (c) NYSE-LCM provide that the CEO periodically deals with the issue of being compliant with Rule 10A-3 Exchange Act.

---

691 Cf. NYSE-LCM, Commentary to Rule 303A.11.

692 Cf. *Siemens*, 20-F 2010, Item 16G, p. 184 et seq.; also *Deutsche Bank*, 20-F, Item 16G, p. 199 et seq.; *Fresenius*, 20-F, Item 16G, p. 111 et seq.; *SAP*, 20-F, Item 16G, p. 140 et seq.; *Schäfer*, ZGR 2004, 416, 419.

693 Cf. in particular *Siemens*, 20-F 2010, Item 16G, p. 184 et seq.; also *Deutsche Bank*, 20-F, Item 16G, p. 199 et seq.; *Fresenius*, 20-F, Item 16G, p. 111 et seq.; *SAP*, 20-F, Item 16G, p. 140 et seq.

694 For listed foreign corporations, only Rules 303A.06, 303A.11, and 303.12(b) and (c) NYSE-LCM apply.

2. Best Practice for the Internal Control System of Listed Foreign Corporations

The best practice for listed foreign corporations includes the following with regard to internal control. Rule 303A.03 NYSE-LCM requires the corporation to provide *inter alia* a method for all interested parties to communicate directly with the presiding director or with the non-management or independent directors as a group which exceeds the procedures regarding complaints to the independent directors of the audit committee as required by Exchange Act Rule 10A-3(b)(3) and set out as a minimum requirement in Rule 303A.07(b)(iii) NYSE-LCM. The same procedures to comply with the requirements of Exchange Act Rule 10A-3(b)(3) regarding complaints to the audit committee may be used for such method.[695]

Rule 303A.05 NYSE-LCM requires listed corporations to have a compensation committee composed entirely of independent directors. It is responsible to review and approve the CEO compensation and to make recommendations to the board of directors regarding non-CEO executive officer compensation (Rule 303A.05(b)(i)(A) and (b)(i)(B) NYSE-LCM). The NYSE considers compensation to be an important factor of corporate governance which has to be dealt with by the compensation committee or another committee responsible for compensation.[696] As part of the compensation package, the committee has to consider incentive based compensation.[697] In this context, the committee should note that U.S. best practice suggests incentives regarding internal controls to be part of the compensation package. [698] Thus, the best practice of the NYSE listing standards includes for listed foreign corporations to establish a compensation committee or to assign the responsibilities regarding compensation to another committee which should consider incentives with regard to internal controls as a part of the incentive based compensation of management.

With regard to internal control, Rule 303A.07(b) NYSE-LCM assigns additional responsibilities to the audit committee. The mandates of the listing standards reach further than SOX and SEC rules. It has to be noted that the audit committee's functions specified in Rule 303A.07 NYSE-LCM

695 Cf. NYSE-LCM, Disclosure Requirements to Rule 303A.03.

696 U.S. listed corporations are not required to have a formal compensation committee but requires to allocate its responsibilities to committees of their own denomination (cf. NYSE-LCM, Commentary to Rule 303A.05).

697 Cf. NYSE-LCM, Commentary to Rule 303A.05.

698 Cf. NYSE Commission on Corporate Governance, p. 3.

should not be allocated to a different committee.[699] Due to Rule 303A.07(b)(i)(A) NYSE-LCM, the audit committee's purpose is to assist the board of directors' oversight of the integrity of the financial statements, the corporation's compliance with legal and regulatory requirements, and the performance of the internal audit function. Thus, the audit committee is in particular responsible for the COSO I categories 'reliability of financial reporting' and 'compliance with laws and regulations'. The audit committee's duties and responsibilities include to obtain and review at least annually the report by the external auditor regarding internal quality-control procedures and any material issues raised by the internal quality-control review (Rule 303A.07(b)(iii)(A) NYSE-LCM). The internal quality-controls relate to the COSO I category 'effective and efficient operations' requiring the audit committee to deal at least in part with all three COSO I categories. Moreover, the audit committee's duty and responsibility encompass to discuss policies with respect to risk assessment and risk management (Rule 303A.07(b)(iii)(D) NYSE-LCM). The assessment and management of the corporation's exposure to risk remains, nevertheless, the duty of the CEO and senior management.[700] The audit committee has to discuss the guidelines and policies to govern the risk assessment and risk management process of management, and the major financial risk exposures of the corporation including the steps taken by management to monitor and control such exposures.[701] An indication of the importance of the internal control function is the audit committee's duty to meet with the internal auditors (Rule 303A.07(b)(iii)(E) NYSE-LCM). Due to Rule 303A.07(b)(iii)(F) NYSE-LCM, the audit committee should review with the external auditor any audit problems or difficulties and management's response which includes the items of internal control letters issued or to be issued, and the internal audit function with regard to responsibilities, budget, and staffing.[702]

In light of the aforementioned requirements of Rule 303A.07(b) NYSE-LCM which represent elements of internal control, the NYSE points out that it is the audit committee's duty to review major issues as to the adequacy of the internal controls and any special steps adopted in light of material control deficiencies.[703] Through the assignment of duties and respon-

---

699 Cf. NYSE-LCM, General Commentary to Rule 303A.07.
700 Cf. NYSE-LCM, Commentary to Rule 303A.07(b)(iii)(D).
701 Cf. NYSE-LCM, Commentary to Rule 303A.07(b)(iii)(D).
702 Cf. NYSE-LCM, Commentary to Rule 303A.07(b)(iii)(F).
703 Cf. NYSE-LCM, General Commentary to Rule 303A.07(b).

sibilities to the audit committee regarding internal control and risk management, the NYSE elevates the audit committee to represent the ultimate oversight function with regard to internal control and risk management. The NYSE tries to ensure that the audit committee will receive accurate information regarding internal control and risk management from an internal source which is independent from senior management to supplement any information received from the external auditors. Moreover, the information should reach the audit committee directly from the independent source without the involvement of senior management. The accuracy and completeness of information is crucial to ensure that deficiencies or circumventions of the internal controls are reported to the audit committee including those instances concerning senior management. This is important to deal with one of the most important shortcomings of internal control systems: the prevalent difficulty to prevent fraud and misconduct of senior management.[704] The NYSE assigns the duty to provide accurate and independent information to the audit committee to an internal audit function. In order to safeguard its information source, the audit committee has the responsibility to provide for an internal audit function capable to perform its duty. If the audit committee determines that the internal audit function is not appropriately equipped to perform its duty, the board of directors has to direct management to sufficiently equip the internal audit function. Thus, the NYSE listing standards require the audit committee to ensure the adequacy of internal control and to ensure that the internal audit function, as its information source, is sufficiently equipped to perform its duty.

Due to Rule 303A.07(c) NYSE-LCM, every listed corporation has to have an internal audit function.[705] Internal audit has to provide for an ongoing assessment of the risk management process and internal control system which can be outsourced to a third party other than the external auditor.[706] The NYSE underscores the importance of the internal audit function by assigning the audit committee the detailed oversight of the performance and equipment of the internal audit function. The NYSE does not further prescribe how the internal audit function has to be designed. The IIA provides professional standards and rules of conduct for internal auditors.[707] These

704 See *supra* at chapter 4, A. II. 1. c).

705 Requiring an internal audit function within the listing standards has been recommended to the NYSE by the IIA (NYSE Report, p. A-82).

706 Cf. NYSE-LCM, Commentary to Rule 303A.07(c).

707 See *infra* at chapter 4, E.

standards and rules are regarded as best practice concerning the internal audit function.[708] According to the IIA, internal audit is an independent, objective assurance and consulting activity designed to add value and improve and organization's operation.[709] It provides for a systematic approach to evaluate and improve the effectiveness of risk management, control, and governance processes.[710]

Rule 303A.10 NYSE-LCM prescribes that a listed corporation has to have a code of business conduct and ethics which may help to focus the board of directors and management on areas of ethical risk, to provide guidance to personnel to help them recognize and deal with ethical issues, to provide mechanisms to report unethical conduct, and to foster a culture of honesty and accountability.[711] The requirements of Rule 303A.10 NYSE-LCM are consistent with the COSO I component 'control environment'. The code must also contain compliance standards and procedures that will facilitate the effective operation of the code.[712] It should further address the following topic with regard to internal controls: protection and proper use of listed corporation assets; proactive promotion of compliance with laws, rules, and regulations; proactive encouragement of the reporting of any illegal or unethical behavior including the encouragement of employees to consult appropriate corporate sources when in doubt about the best course of action, to report violations of laws, rules, regulations, or the code of business conduct; and safeguarding that employees know that the corporation will not allow retaliation for reports made in good faith.[713] Therefore, the code of conduct required by the NYSE addresses issues of the FCPA to protect the corporation's assets and the COSO I category of 'compliance with laws and regulations'.

With regard to the certification requirements, best practice suggests that the CEO of a listed foreign corporation certifies that she is unaware of any violation of the NYSE corporate governance listing standards (Rule 303A.12(a) NYSE-LCM). The annual certification will focus management on the requirements and best practices of the listing standards.[714]

708 *Deloitte*, Internal Audit, p. 1.
709 IIA Definition of Internal Audit.
710 Deloitte, Internal Audit, p. 1.
711 Cf. NYSE-LCM, Commentary to Rule 303A.10.
712 Cf. NYSE-LCM, Commentary to Rule 303A.10.
713 Cf. NYSE-LCM, Commentary to Rule 303A.10.
714 Cf. NYSE-LCM, Commentary to Rule 303A.12(a).

3. Summary of the Mandates and Best Practice of the NYSE Listing Standards

The NYSE listing standards require listed foreign corporations only to comply with Rule 303A.06, 303A.11 and 303A.12(b) and (c) NYSE-LCM. All other requirements constitute the best practice for listed foreign corporations. With regard to internal control, the NYSE requires listed foreign corporations to comply with Rule 10A-3 Exchange Act, to state the significant differences between the foreign corporation's corporate governance and the NYSE corporate governance standards, and to notify the NYSE of the compliance status with regard to Rule 303A.06 NYSE-LCM and in case the CEO becomes aware of any non-compliance with any applicable provision of Rule 303A NYSE-LCM. The NYSE best practice suggests for listed foreign corporations to extend the communication procedures of Rule 10A-3 Exchange Act, and to include incentives regarding internal control into the incentive based compensation of management. Moreover, the audit committee of the foreign corporation should have the responsibility to oversee the financial statements, the compliance with legal and regulatory requirements and the performance of the internal audit function, and to review the internal quality-control, the risk management and risk assessment, any audit problems or difficulties, and the internal audit function. Furthermore, the audit committee should have the important responsibility to review the adequacy of the internal controls and any steps adopted in light of material control deficiencies. The most important best practice for listed foreign corporations is to implement an internal audit function. In addition, best practice also suggests to adopt a code of business conduct and ethics, and to require the CEO to certify that she is not aware of any violation of the NYSE corporate governance listing standards.

II. NYSE Enforcement Policy: Sanctions and Cooperation

Under the oversight of the NYSE Regulation, Inc., the enforcement of the NYSE regarding market oversight functions is conducted by the Financial Industry Regulatory Authority (FINRA). Prior to June 2010, the NYSE enforcement has been conducted by the NYSE Regulation, Inc., an independent subsidiary of the NYSE, as the NYSE enforcement division.[715] Since June 2010, FINRA conducts the enforcement of NYSE rules while NYSE

715 See NYSE Disciplinary Actions.

Regulation, Inc. will remain ultimately responsible for overseeing FINRA's performance of regulatory service.[716] FINRA is a Self-Regulatory Organization (SRO) originating from the merger of the National Association of Securities Dealers (NASD) and the NYSE Regulation, Inc.[717]

The enforcement function includes to enforce compliance with the federal securities laws and regulations, and the policies and rules of the NYSE.[718] The enforcement policies of the NYSE provides for incentives for the listed corporations to comply with the NYSE listing standards and federal securities laws and regulations, and for further insight into the best practice with regard to the listing standards. In 2005, the NYSE Regulation, Inc. issued two information memoranda regarding the determination of sanctions by the NYSE[719], and cooperation of NYSE members in light of investigations[720]. The NYSE information memoranda cover in essence the same topics as the SEC's Seaboard Report.[721] The memoranda can still be used as guidance since the FINRA Sanction Guidelines reflect, with fewer details, the position of the NYSE information memoranda.[722]

The sanctions memorandum provides guidance regarding the factors considered by the NYSE in determining sanctions.[723] The catalogue of factors is only a framework for evaluating the individual facts of each case.[724] Although the sanctions memorandum does not provide for binding rules, it does provide for incentives for the board of directors and management to implement an effective internal control system in order to benefit from lower sanctions in case of a violation, and to prevent circumstances which would lead to an increase of a sanction. In the following, all factors related to internal control will be depicted constituting NYSE best practice for internal controls. The NYSE will consider various factors which an effective internal control system addresses. One of the main factors with regard to

716 See FINRA/NYSE News Release.

717 See SEC Release No. 56145.

718 All U.S. exchange's rules have to provide that violations by its members of the Exchange Act, related rules and regulations, and rules of the exchange are appropriately disciplined (sec. 15A(b)(7) Exchange Act). NYSE Rule 476 provides for this requirement. Also, each exchange has to provide for enforcement of its rules (sec. 19(g)(1)(A) Exchange Act). The NYSE complies with this provision through FINRA in light of FINRA Rule 8310.

719 NYSE Sanctions Memo.

720 NYSE Cooperation Memo.

721 *Baker & Hostetler*, Executive Alert, p. 2. See also *infra* at chapter 5, E.

722 Cf. FINRA Sanction Guidelines, p. 6.

723 NYSE Sanctions Memo, p. 1.

724 NYSE Sanctions Memo, p. 2.

internal control is the factor effectiveness of operational, supervisory, and compliance controls.[725] It deals, in essence, with the important elements constituting an internal control system. Besides "the effectiveness of [...] the operational, supervisory, and compliance policies and procedures", the NYSE will consider if "adequate resources have been devoted" to and "periodic reviews" have been conducted by the corporation of its "internal controls".[726] The risk management processes will also be considered under this factor.[727] Thus, the factor effectiveness of operational, supervisory, and compliance controls provides, in general, for an incentive for the board of directors and management to implement an effective internal control system including the devotion of adequate resources, periodic reviews, and an appropriate risk management. The other factors considered by the NYSE to determine sanctions deal with circumstances which are addressed by elements of an effective internal control system. Therefore, the sanctions memorandum provides for incentives to implement an effective internal control system with emphasis on specific elements which address the circumstances. The NYSE considers harm caused by a violation as a factor to determine the sanction.[728] An effective internal control system aims to prevent or minimize harm caused by a violation through timely detecting violations. While an internal control system will not always prevent violations or harm[729], it enables management to timely address violations and harm caused in order to reduce harm compared to the situation without an effective internal control system. Since less harm leads to a more positive consideration by the NYSE of the factor "harm caused by a violation", the sanction will be less. Therefore, the corporation's board of directors and management have an incentive to implement an effective internal control system fostering timely detection of violations. In the same way, an effective internal control system with emphasis on timely detection of violations can positively influence the considerations of the NYSE of the factor "extent of misconduct" which includes "the length of time which the misconduct occurred" as well as "the number, size and impact of the violations".[730] A timely detection of misconduct will reduce the length of its occurrence as well as the number, size, and impact of the violations leading to reduced

725 NYSE Sanctions Memo, p. 3.
726 NYSE Sanctions Memo, p. 3.
727 Cf. NYSE Sanctions Memo, p. 3.
728 NYSE Sanctions Memo, p. 2.
729 See *supra* at chapter 4, C. I. 1. b).
730 NYSE Sanctions Memo, p. 2.

sanctions. A further factor to determine sanctions is neglecting or disregarding "red flags" as warning signs.[731] The failure of a corporation to act in light of warning signs of the existence of a violation will be considered to determine the sanction. The NYSE expects the listed corporation to increase supervision, to take all necessary actions in case of warning signs to cease the conduct which may result in a violation, and to take corrective measures to prevent further wrongful conduct.[732] The most important features of an effective internal control system are to detect violations by analyzing warning signs, to increase supervision, and to immediately act to stop wrongdoing. Therefore, the corporation has an incentive to implement an effective internal control system which ensures that "red flags" are not neglected or disregarded in order to reduce a potential sanction by the NYSE. As an additional factor to determine sanctions, the NYSE considers the effectiveness of training and education programs addressing misconduct. Thus, the internal control system has to provide for effective training and education programs in order to profit from lower sanctions. The NYSE will also consider the prior disciplinary record of the corporation as a factor to determine the sanction.[733] In case the member of the NYSE shows a record of accepting repeated sanctions as a cost of business[734], the NYSE will increase the sanction.[735] An effective internal control system including a corporate culture of integrity and ethical behavior[736] can help to outlaw the acceptance of repeated sanctions as a cost of business preventing the employees to engage in such a practice. Hence, the NYSE would have no indication in case of a violation to increase the sentence to deter a practice of accepting sanctions as a cost of business. Thus, the internal control system of the listed corporation has to outlaw the acceptance of repeated sanctions as a cost of business within its corporate culture of integrity and ethical behavior in order to reduce the likelihood of increased sanctions. Furthermore, the NYSE will consider the factor "acceptance of responsibility".[737] Thus, the corporation has an incentive to implement the acceptance of responsibility as a part of the corporate culture in order to foster ethical behavior and to reduce potential sanctions.

---

731 NYSE Sanctions Memo, p. 3.

732 NYSE Sanctions Memo, p. 3.

733 NYSE Sanctions Memo, p. 3.

734 Economists tend to view law as a set of official prices (*Cooter*, 84 Colum. L. Rev. 1523 (1984), p. 1523).

735 NYSE Sanctions Memo, p. 3.

736 See *supra* at chapter 4, C. I. 2. a).

737 NYSE Sanctions Memo, p. 3.

Moreover, cooperation is considered as a factor by the NYSE.[738] The sanction memorandum points out that only "proactive and exceptional" cooperation may be rewarded and refers to the cooperation memorandum for more details.[739] The cooperation memorandum provides guidance on the obligation of NYSE members to cooperate with reviews, examinations and investigations of violations of federal securities laws and regulations and NYSE rules and policies, and to provide disclosure to the NYSE of violations of the NYSE rules or the federal securities laws.[740] Besides the enumeration of the disclosure and cooperation obligations of the NYSE members, the memorandum – in the same way as the sanctions memorandum – provides an incentive for NYSE members to implement internal controls including a culture of compliance. The NYSE considers the culture of compliance as a factor to determine if the corporation can demonstrate proactive and exceptional cooperation, i.e. "extraordinary cooperation".[741] For extraordinary cooperation, the NYSE may exercise leniency for violations of the NYSE rules or federal securities laws.[742] The NYSE considers culture of compliance to be "usually demonstrated by a sparse disciplinary history, through self-policing, informative and complete self-reporting, prompt customer remediation, and consistent cooperation with the [NYSE] and other regulatory bodies".[743] Thus, in order to provide the basis for receiving leniency, the listed corporation has to put strong emphasis on an internal control system which prevents violations of the federal securities laws and NYSE rules, which detects such violations in a timely and comprehensive manner in order to enable management to disclose to and cooperate with the NYSE and other regulatory bodies, and which includes a corporate culture of integrity and ethical behavior fostering disciplinary measures, acceptance of responsibility and candid cooperation with the NYSE and other regulatory bodies. The policy of the NYSE to reward cooperation of violators is in line with the policy of the SEC and DOJ.[744] Similar to these policies, the NYSE needs to provide sufficient sanction mitigation for optimal incentives for corporations to engage in internal control systems and cooperation.[745]

---

738 NYSE Sanctions Memo, p. 4.
739 NYSE Sanctions Memo, p. 4.
740 NYSE Cooperation Memo, p. 1.
741 NYSE Cooperation Memo, p. 3 et seq.
742 NYSE Cooperation Memo, p. 5.
743 NYSE Cooperation Memo, p. 4 et seq.
744 New York City Bar, Report 2006, p. H-16. See also *infra* at chapter 5, D. and E.
745 See *infra* at chapter 5, B. II.

In summary, the board of directors and management of a listed corporation have incentives to implement an effective internal control system reflecting the best practice of the two NYSE information memoranda. Such an internal control system includes effective operational, supervisory, and compliance policies and procedures. It is equipped with adequate resources and will be reviewed periodically. Also, appropriate risk management has to be part of the internal control system. The internal control system aims to prevent violations of federal securities laws and NYSE rules, and to provide for timely detection and information of misconduct and violations, as well as to process "red flags". After the detection of misconduct or violations, the internal control systems has to provide for measures to ensure that management takes immediate action to cease the wrongful conduct and corrective measures to prevent further wrongful conduct. As part of the internal controls system, a corporate culture of integrity and ethical behavior has to be implemented by management which outlaws to accept sanctions as a cost of business and which fosters the acceptance of responsibility. Proactive and exceptional cooperation with enforcement agencies has to be part of the corporate culture as well. Further measures of internal controls are effective training and education programs.

III. NYSE Commission on Corporate Governance

In 2009 – in light of the financial crisis of 2008 –, the NYSE sponsored a Commission on Corporate Governance (NYSE Commission) in order to strengthen U.S. best practices for corporate governance.[746] The NYSE aimed with the formation of the NYSE Commission to "create a constructive dialog in the financial community regarding corporate governance that will benefit issuers, investors and the overall market".[747] The NYSE Commission's intent was to evaluate and make recommendations of the "roles of, and relationships, accountability and communication among, board of directors, management, stockholders and other corporate stakeholders", and corporate governance structures and corporate mechanisms impacting the governance of the corporation.[748] In its final report[749], the

---

746 See NYSE News Release Sept. 1, 2009; Report of NYSE Commission on Corporate Governance, p. 1.

747 NYSE News Release Sept. 1, 2009.

748 NYSE News Release Nov. 12, 2009.

749 Report of NYSE Commission on Corporate Governance, p. 1.

NYSE Commission concludes that "the governance system generally works well".[750] The NYSE Commission developed ten core principles of corporate governance.[751] These principles represent fundamental concepts of corporate governance even though ever changing definitions of best practices, "often […] on an annual basis", brought "dramatic changes" to corporate governance within the first decade of the 21st century confusing stakeholders about the content of '"good governance"'.[752] In the following, the principles relating to internal controls will be depicted.

In principle two, the NYSE Commission finds that the board of directors and management are responsible for corporate governance due to their legal obligation.[753] The director's obligations include to ensure appropriate risk management to avoid excessive risk taking, and to work with management to build an environment of high integrity, including adherence to the rule of law and ethical standards.[754] One step the board can take to create an environment of integrity and ethical behavior within the corporation is to hire promising officers who have a record of living ethical values. The directors should also provide for incentives for appropriate risk taking.[755] It is management's primary responsibility to create an environment for a culture of integrity.[756] The corporate environment encompasses an ethical tone at the top.[757] Furthermore, monitoring processes, risk management, and internal controls have to be implemented as well as internal communication systems.[758] Management has to prevent retaliation against personnel reporting problems.[759] Risk taking has to be disciplined through incentive compensation.[760] Moreover, management has to provide accurate information to the board of directors and has to develop the corporate strategy.[761] Also with regard to SEC regulations, management has to disclose adequately information regarding its risk management and internal

750 Report of NYSE Commission on Corporate Governance, p. 32.
751 Cf. NYSE Commission on Corporate Governance, Overview of Principles and Summary.
752 Report of NYSE Commission on Corporate Governance, p. 10.
753 Report of NYSE Commission on Corporate Governance, p. 3.
754 Report of NYSE Commission on Corporate Governance, p. 27.
755 Report of NYSE Commission on Corporate Governance, p. 27.
756 Report of NYSE Commission on Corporate Governance, p. 3.
757 Report of NYSE Commission on Corporate Governance, p. 28.
758 Report of NYSE Commission on Corporate Governance, p. 3.
759 Report of NYSE Commission on Corporate Governance, p. 3.
760 Report of NYSE Commission on Corporate Governance, p. 3.
761 Report of NYSE Commission on Corporate Governance, p. 3.

controls.[762] Due to principle four, corporate governance has to be integrated into the business strategy and objectives including prudent risk management and a culture of integrity.[763]

In essence, the NYSE Commission highlights with regard to internal control the responsibility of the board of directors and management to implement appropriate corporate governance including an environment and culture of integrity, rule of law, and ethical behavior. Excessive risk taking has to be prevented through an appropriate risk assessment and incentives to take only reasonable risk. It is the responsibility of management to ensure good communication throughout the corporation and external recipients, especially the board of directors has to be informed in an honest and candid manner. The findings of the NYSE Commission mainly support the corporate governance requirements of the NYSE listing standards. While the report does not represent directly the views of the NYSE on corporate governance and internal control issues, it represents best practice with regard to NYSE corporate governance standards and can be used as guidance on the NYSE listing standards.

IV. Conclusion

The listing standards of the NYSE, especially Rule 303A NYSE-LCM, have a considerable influence on U.S. corporate governance. With regard to listed foreign corporations, the NYSE listing standards do not have a strong impact on internal control based on mandates but together with related NYSE enforcement, representing best practice, they have a considerable influence on listed foreign corporations.

Under the oversight of the SEC, the NYSE expands the corporate governance requirements for listed U.S. corporations far beyond the requirements of the federal securities laws and SEC regulation.[764] The impact of the NYSE listing standards on the mandates and requirements for internal control systems of listed corporations, however, is limited. The listing standards focus primarily on the role of independent directors.[765] Nevertheless, the listing standards underscore the importance of internal control by enhancing the responsibilities of the audit committee to deal with all three

762 Report of NYSE Commission on Corporate Governance, p. 27.
763 Report of NYSE Commission on Corporate Governance, p. 4.
764 Cf. *Johnson/Sides*, 30 Wm. Mitchell L. Rev. 1149 (2004), p. 1167.
765 Cf. *Ide*, 54 Mercer L. Rev. 829 (2003), p. 850.

COSO I categories and requiring an internal audit function. The requirement of an internal audit function is one of the most important additions by the NYSE to the mandates of SOX and the SEC providing further guidelines on the structure of internal controls. The internal audit function assists the audit committee in its task to oversee the internal control system. Also, the internal audit function helps to ensure that the internal controls operate effectively and that management is prevented from circumventing internal controls by directly providing independent information to the audit committee.

With regard to foreign corporation, the NYSE listing standards do not add any significant layer of mandates to the requirements of the federal securities laws and SEC rules for foreign corporation. Nevertheless, the NYSE listing standards constitute best practice with regard to corporate governance and internal control. Therefore, the enhanced duties of the audit committee and the implementation of an internal audit function will constitute significant additions to the SOX and SEC mandates for the internal controls of listed foreign corporations if a corporation opts to comply with the NYSE best practice. In this regard, two NYSE information memoranda and NYSE listing rules provide significant incentives for the board of directors and management to implement an effective internal control system reflecting the best practice of the two memoranda. The NYSE Commission's report on corporate governance will guide corporations with regard to U.S. best practice of corporate governance and the NYSE listing standards. One important aspect is that incentive based compensation for managers should include incentives with regard to internal control.

E. Professional Standards for Internal and External Auditors

For internal and external auditors the national professional organizations, the IIA and the AICPA, publish professional standards which their members have to adhere to during an audit. While these standards do not directly apply to corporations, they are affected since their employees, in case of internal auditors, or their external auditors will perform their audit in accordance with such standards. With regard to external auditors, they have to follow the AICPA auditing standards for conducting their audit. In light of internal control, SAS No. 109, AU § 314 essentially resembles COSO I and SAS No. 110, AU § 318 provides guidance on testing and evaluating the obtained evidence of the audit. After the scandals and prior to any rules of the PCAOB, the AICPA issued SAS No. 99, AU § 316 to mandate the external auditors to perform reviews to detect and correct financial statement fraud.[766] SAS No. 99 provides in exhibit 86 guidance on anti-fraud programs and controls similar to COSO I.

The private IIA standards do not have the same authority than the PCAOB auditing standards since the PCAOB auditing standards are mandatory regulation[767]. The IIA standards mandate internal audit to "evaluate and contribute to the improvement of governance, risk management, and control processes".[768] With regard to the governance process, internal audit has to promote ethics and values and must evaluate "the design, implementation, and effectiveness of the [corporation]'s ethics-related objectives, programs, and activities".[769] Internal audit has a similar role with regard to risk management with a special emphasis on evaluating the potential of fraud and how the corporation addresses such fraud risk.[770] With regard to control, internal audit has to evaluate the adequacy, effectiveness, and efficiency of controls including the promotion of continuous improvements regarding "the reliability and integrity of financial and operating information, effectiveness and efficiency of operations and programs, safeguarding of assets, and compliance with laws, regulations, policies, procedures, and contracts".[771]

F. *Financial Reporting in Accordance with U.S. GAAP and IFRS*

The SEC generally requires corporations to prepare their financial reporting in accordance with U.S. GAAP. Since 2008, pursuant to Rule 4-01(a)(2) Regulation S-X, listed foreign corporations may prepare their financial reporting in accordance with IFRS without reconciliation to U.S. GAAP.[772] It follows that listed foreign corporations may align their financial reporting objectives of internal control to ensure financial reporting in accordance with IFRS by evaluating how IFRS applies to the corporation as part of the identification of financial reporting risks. The differences of U.S. GAAP

766 *Moeller*, SOX Internal Controls, p. 64.
767 See *supra* at chapter 4, B.
768 IIA Standard No. 2100.
769 IIA Standard No. 2110.
770 IIA Standard No. 2120.
771 IIA Standard No. 2130.
772 SEC Release No. 8879.

and IFRS have to be taken into account when using U.S. best practice for designing and operating internal control regarding financial reporting.[773]

G. Risk Considerations After the Financial Crisis of 2008

Towards the end of the 2000s, the focus in the U.S. moved beyond internal control to the broader concept of governance, risk, and compliance.[774] After the scandals of the 2000s, the emphasis has been on internal control without requiring a broader concept of enterprise risk management. While SOX led to less risk-taking of corporate leaders[775], it did not to require an effective risk management system. Only the NYSE implemented the duty of the audit committee to discuss policies of risk assessment, risk management, and the major financial risk exposures of the corporation including the steps taken by management to monitor and control such exposures. The OECD also recommends in its corporate governance principles that an appropriate systems of control has to encompass risk management, financial and operational control, and compliance with the law.[776] The financial crisis in 2008 shows the danger inherent in managerial decisions ignoring or neglecting risks associated with financial products. In 2008, risk management has been underdeveloped and lacked a comprehensive approach by addressing risk only at various units of the corporation.[777] In addition, boards of directors failed in their role to exercise risk oversight.[778] Thus, the financial crisis of 2008 has also been attributed to failures in corporate governance, mostly with regard to the risk management system.[779] As a result of the financial crisis, the SEC increased the disclosure requirements regarding compensation, risk, and corporate governance by requiring the proxy and information statements to include information on practices to

773 See SEC Comparison of U.S. GAAP and IFRS for differences and similarities.

774 Cf. *KPMG*, 2010, p. 1.

775 *Cohen/Dey/Lys*, 2007; *Bargeron/Lehn/Zutter*, 2008.

776 OECD Corporate Governance, p. 62.

777 *Bainbridge*, 34 J. Corp. L. 967 (2009), p. 971.

778 *Oxley*, 2011, at 01:01:45: replying to the author's question (at 01:01:16) if the financial crisis could partially be attributed to a gatekeepers' failure similar to the events leading to SOX. Also *Kaal/Painter*, 40 Seton Hall L. Rev. 1433 (2010), p. 1457.

779 See *Kirkpatrick*, OECD, 2009; *Kirchner*, FS Hopt, 2095. *Cheffis*, 2009 argues against a failure.

risk management, the board of directors' role in risk oversight[780], and compensation policies to determine whether corporations induce excessive or inappropriate risk-taking.[781] These disclosure requirements provide incentives for corporations to engage in risk management, compensation policies, and board risk oversight which investors will credit. Hence, corporate boards become more "risk-savvy" and require enhanced risk intelligence and reporting.[782] Enterprise risk management has become a priority for management.[783] In order to establish an effective enterprise risk management, a framework such as COSO II has to be used. Important aspects for an effective enterprise risk management are using a holistic approach towards risk including coherent communication between employees in order to capture all relevant risks, determining appropriate risk appetite and risk tolerance of the corporation, building risk management into the business by aligning governance and control infrastructure, and assigning responsibilities for risk management.[784] Enterprise risk management has the potential to be migrated from a compliance obligation to a competitive tool[785] since effective enterprise risk management will reduce costs, improve financial reporting, and improve decision-making.[786] While the current mandates of SOX and the other regulations only require corporations to implement effective internal control, comprehensive enterprise risk management has become the best practice indicating the road for improvements towards more effective corporate governance.

---

780 See for the board of directors' role in risk oversight: *NACD*, 2009.
781 SEC Release No. 9089, SEC Release No. 2009-268.
782 *KPMG*, 2011a, p. 1.
783 *KPMG*, 2011a, p. 1.
784 *KPMG*, 2011b, p. 3 et seq.
785 *KPMG*, 2011a, p. 2.
786 *KPMG*, 2009, p. 2.

Chapter 5: Compliance with Law Including Compliance Programs

Compliance with law including compliance programs is not expressly mandated as compared to the mandates regarding internal controls systems. The FCPA addresses corruption together with internal controls regarding accurate book keeping and internal accounting controls. While SOX incorporated all financial reporting mandates of the FCPA, the elements of an effective anti-bribery compliance programs are only induced through the FCPA-related DOJ enforcement policy. With regard to compliance and in particular compliance programs, non-mandatory rules, guidelines, and business practices provide strong incentives for corporations to follow their specific requirements regarding compliance related internal control. Due to corporate criminal liability, corporations have incentives to engage in internal control without mandating any specific corporate behavior. Similarly, as part of the current U.S. corporate criminal liability regime, the U.S. Sentencing Guidelines (USSG) do not mandate specific corporate behavior regarding internal control but provide incentives for corporations to follow the guidelines through sanction mitigation. In addition, the enforcement policies of the DOJ and the SEC provide further incentives for corporations to engage in effective compliance measures.

In the following, the requirements for anti-bribery compliance programs of the FCPA will be analyzed followed by the corporate criminal liability regime and the USSG. The analysis is followed by the analysis of the DOJ enforcement policy and the SEC enforcement policy. The requirements of the DGCL including the relevant case law will be depicted as they represent best practice for German corporations listed on the NYSE. The NYSE enforcement policy has already dealt with above.[787]

787 See *supra* at chapter 4, D. II.

A. Foreign Corrupt Practices Act of 1977

The Foreign Corrupt Practices Act[788], enacted in 1977, was a congressional attempt to curtail bribes paid to foreign government officials to obtain business in their countries.[789] Bribery is of major concern since it weakens economic development, undermines confidence in the market, and distorts competition.[790] The FCPA aims to reduce bribery in bribery-prone countries leading to more open markets in those countries in the long run which will benefit U.S. corporations[791]. The birth of the FCPA was due to the Watergate scandal of the early 1970s in the U.S.[792] In this context, the SEC investigated into so-called slush funds[793] and revealed that the slush fund money had not only been given to political parties but also to bribe officials in foreign countries possibly violating securities laws.[794] In order to tackle corporate bribery, the FCPA was enacted including anti-bribery provisions and the requirement for corporations subject to the Exchange Act to keep accurate books and records, and adequate internal controls because most bribes were not accounted correctly, if at all.[795] The FCPA implemented sec. 30A(a) and (g) Exchange Act which prohibits for corporations subject to the Exchange Act to make payments, or even an offer for payments, of "anything of value" to foreign officials, foreign political parties, or intermediates of foreign officials or foreign parties to obtain or retain business. Affirmative defenses are the lawfulness of a prohibited action under the foreign written laws and regulations, or reasonable and *bona fide* expenditure directly related to the promotion, demonstration, or explanation of products or services, or the execution or performance of a contract (sec. 30A(c) Exchange Act). Moreover, so-called "grease payments" are not covered by the FCPA due to sec. 30A(b) Exchange Act.[796] In sec. 78dd-2 of title 15 USC, the FCPA expands the prohibition of bribery to "domestic concerns" which includes U.S. citizens, nationals or residents, and busi-

---

788 Title I of Pub. Law No. 95-213 (1977), current through Pub Law No. 105-366 (1998).

789 *Leary/Dooley/Stryker*, in: The Metropolitan Corporate Counsel 2007.

790 *Breuer*, 2010; cf. Transparency International, Schäden durch Korruption.

791 *Posner*, Economic Analysis of Law, p. 456.

792 *Biegelman*, in: FCPA Guidebook, p. 8.

793 Slush funds are unaudited, secret funds within an organization to be used e.g. for bribes.

794 *Biegelman*, in: FCPA Guidebook, p. 9.

795 *Biegelman*, in: FCPA Guidebook, p. 14 et seq.

796 Routine governmental actions are defined in sec. 30A(f)(3) Exchange Act.

nesses with their principal place of business in the U.S. or businesses organized under State law.[797] Furthermore, any person while in the territory of the U.S. is subject the bribery prohibition (sec. 78dd-3(a) of title 15 USC). Corporations listed on the NYSE are subject to sec. 30A Exchange Act and, therefore, to the FCPA anti-bribery provisions.

The FCPA implemented sec. 13(a)(2) Exchange Act requiring corporations subject to the Exchange Act to make and keep books, records, and accounts, which reflect the transactions and dispositions of the corporation's assets (sec. 13(a)(2)(A) Exchange Act). The FCPA also mandates in sec. 13(a)(2)(B) Exchange Act that such corporations have to devise and maintain a system of internal accounting controls to improve the accuracy of financial reporting and to provide investors assurance of the integrity of corporate management[798]. The internal control system has to be sufficient to provide reasonable assurances that (i) transactions are executed in accordance with management's general or specific authorization; (ii) transactions are recorded as necessary (I) to permit preparation of financial statements in conformity with generally accepted accounting principles or any other criteria applicable to such statements, and (II) to maintain accountability for assets; (iii) access to assets is permitted only in accordance with management's general or specific authorization; and (iv) the recorded accountability for assets is compared with the existing assets at reasonable intervals and appropriate action is taken with respect to any differences. The FCPA internal control system has the goal to foster the preparation of accurate financial statements, and to prevent and detect fraud including theft of assets.[799] The requirements to limit the access to the corporation's assets aim to prevent the use of slush funds and off-the-books accounts.[800] The provision is further intended to foster accurate book keeping.[801] Therefore, each corporation has to truthfully account for all its payments. The book keeping requirement of all transactions including any transactions related to bribery or corruption aims to deter such violations in the first place. Since bribes are almost always on the books disguised as some other business expense to conceal their true nature, the government's evidentiary burden is reduced.[802] While corporations will face legal action in case they

797 "Domestic concern" is defined in sec. 78dd-2(h) USC.
798 *Prentice*, 29 Cardozo L. Rev. 703 (2007), p. 709.
799 *Coates*, 21 J. Econ. Perspectives 91 (2007), p. 101.
800 *Biegelman*, in: FCPA Guidebook, p. 34.
801 *Biegelman*, in: FCPA Guidebook, p. 34.
802 *Biegelman*, in: FCPA Guidebook, p. 24.

book any bribery or corruption related transactions, they will also face legal action if they omit to book these transactions due to the record keeping requirement of the FCPA.[803] The evidence that government needs for prosecuting bribes, however, can more easily found in the books and records.[804] Governmental prosecution does not have to prove an actual bribe, rather, that a payment was made and not recorded properly on the corporation's books.[805] Sec. 13(a)(2) Exchange Act overlaps with sec. 302 and 404 SOX which have been described as an extension of the FCPA mandates for internal controls.[806] Through the enhanced attention on internal controls by SOX, corporations were able to detect payments violating FCPA's anti-bribery mandates.[807] One of the major obstacles of the FCPA prior to SOX was that sec. 13(b)(2) Exchange Act does neither provide for precise and detailed requirements of internal controls nor for officer certification leading to its ineffectiveness.[808] An underlying framework such as COSO I has also not been available for corporate leaders. While the ineffectiveness can be attributed to some part to a lack of details and precise requirements[809], it is largely a result of a lack of consequent enforcement of the FCPA's provisions.[810] Since 2007 in line with heightened scrutiny on officers through SOX[811], enforcement has been sharply increased especially on foreign corporations.[812]

I. Requirements for FCPA Internal Controls (Section 13(b)(2) Exchange Act) and Anti-Bribery Compliance Program Including DOJ Guidance and Decisions

The FCPA requires corporations in sec. 13(b)(2) Exchange Act to engage in book keeping and to implement internal accounting controls. The anti-

---

803 Cf. *Biegelman*, in: FCPA Guidebook, p. 35.
804 *Biegelman*, in: FCPA Guidebook, p. 24.
805 *Biegelman*, in: FCPA Guidebook, p. 24.
806 Cf. *Prentice/Spence*, 95 Geo. L. J. 1843 (2007), p. 1903.
807 *Prentice*, 29 Cardozo L. Rev. 703 (2007), p. 725; cf. *Bixby*, 2010, p. 115.
808 *Seligman*, 80 Notre Dame L. Rev. 1159 (2005), p. 1182.
809 GAO, 1981, p. 1.
810 Cf. *Langevoort*, 31 J. Corp. L. 949 (2006), p. 953; *Langevoort*, 105 Mich. L. Rev. 1817 (2007), p. 1841; cf. *Seligman*, 80 Notre Dame L. Rev. 1159 (2005), p. 1184.
811 *Searcey*, Wall St. J.
812 Cf. FCPA Blog, 2011; *Weinstein/Meyer/Clark*, 2010; *Friedman/Smithline/Kleine*, 2011.

bribery provision of sec. 30A Exchange Act necessitate corporations to implement an anti-bribery compliance system to ensure compliance with sec. 30A Exchange Act, even though such system is not legally mandated. In order to comply with the internal control mandates of sec. 13(b)(2) Exchange Act, corporations have to keep books and have to implement an internal accounting system. The system has the objectives: "appropriate reflection of corporate transactions and the disposition of assets, effective administration of other facets of the corporation's internal accounting control, preparation of the financial statements in accordance with U.S. GAAP, and accurate auditing".[813] The internal accounting controls have to provide for how gifts, travel and entertainment, rebates, refunds, commissions, charitable donations, and other high-risk expenses have to be booked in order to be effective.[814] In general, an effective internal control system fulfilling the requirements of SOX also fulfills the FCPA requirements of sec. 13(b)(2) Exchange Act.[815] The internal accounting controls are important within the overall compliance system as such controls make violations of laws more difficult to carry out. Sec. 13(a)(2) SOX internal accounting controls, however, are not by themselves effective to prevent and detect all intentional and unintentional FCPA violations. Accounting controls may be circumvented or overridden especially from high-level executives in order to intentionally violate the FCPA, and they may also fail to detect unintentional FCPA violations due to inherent limitations.[816] Without further elements to prevent circumvention and overrides of accounting controls especially from high-level managers, such controls will be ineffective. A comprehensive approach to internal controls such as COSO I provides for such elements through a compliance program which provides a basis that accounting controls will not be circumvented or overridden and for elements to offset the limitations of accounting controls. Such elements are e.g. the tone at the top and a culture of compliance. In order to render the compliance program effective to address FCPA violations, corporations have to implement an anti-bribery compliance system. The anti-bribery compliance system has to be part of the general compliance system[817], as recommended by COSO I. Within COSO I[818], anti-bribery violations are

---

813 SEC Release No. 8238, at fn. 76.
814 *Biegelman*, in: FCPA Guidebook, p. 257.
815 See *supra* at chapter 4, A. II. 1. a).
816 See *supra* at chapter 4, C. I. 1. b).
817 *Biegelman*, in: FCPA Guidebook, p. 219.
818 See *supra* at chapter 4, C. I.

more accurately addressed by the third internal control objective "compliance with laws and regulations" even though related internal accounting controls belong to the second internal control category "reliability of financial reporting" demonstrating the overlap of COSO I control objectives. In essence, an anti-bribery compliance system resembles a general compliance system with the particular focus on corruption. Therefore, the general elements of a compliance program, such as tone at the top and culture of compliance, are necessary for the anti-bribery compliance program. Each corporation should have an individual anti-bribery compliance program which incorporates industry standard[819], and which has to address all applicable anti-bribery laws the corporation has to comply with.[820] An anti-corruption program is only comprehensive if it does not focus only on FCPA mandates but on laws and policies of other countries.[821]

With regard to the elements for effective anti-bribery compliance, the FCPA does not mandate any specifics. The DOJ opinion procedure releases and non-prosecution agreements provide valuable insight. The DOJ provides upon request of corporations an opinion regarding possible FCPA violations. The DOJ opinion procedures releases provide a valuable source of how to design and revise an anti-corruption compliance program.[822] Based on DOJ Opinion Procedure Release 04-02[823], the following elements are advisable for the anti-bribery components of the compliance program: a clearly articulated corporate policy against violations of the FCPA and foreign anti-bribery laws in a compliance code; compliance standards and procedures that reasonably reduce the prospect of a FCPA or foreign anti-bribery law violation by directors, officers, employees and all business partners; implementation of a CCO with a direct reporting line to the audit committee and the responsibility for the implementation and oversight of compliance with policies, standards and procedures of the compliance program; effective communication of the anti-bribery components of the compliance program to all affected stakeholders[824] by regular training concerning the requirements of the FCPA and foreign anti-bribery laws and annual certifications by all affected stakeholders certifying the compliance with

---

819 *O'Melveny & Myers*, 2006, p. 74.
820 *Biegelman*, in: FCPA Guidebook, p. 219.
821 *Biegelman*, in: FCPA Guidebook, p. 211.
822 *Biegelman*, in: FCPA Guidebook, p. 217.
823 DOJ, Opinion Release 04-02.
824 The DOJ Opinion Release 04-02 includes as stakeholders: shareholders' representatives directly involved in oversight, directors, officers, employees, agents, consultants, representatives, and joint venture partners.

the FCPA and foreign anti-bribery laws; a reporting system including a hotline to report violations of the compliance code and suspicious conduct; appropriate disciplinary procedures for violations of the FCPA, foreign anti-bribery laws, and the compliance code; procedures to ensure business relations with reputable business partners; documentation of due diligence records; procedures to ensure that substantial discretionary authority is not delegated to individuals with a propensity to engage in illegal or improper activities; a policy to include in all contracts with business partners provisions setting forth anti-bribery representations and undertakings, relating to compliance with the FCPA and foreign anti-bribery laws as well as other relevant laws, allowing for internal and independent audits of the books and records of the business partner to ensure compliance with the named provisions, and providing for termination of the contracts with a business partner failing to comply with the anti-bribery laws and regulations; and independent audits by outside counsel and auditors at least every three years to ensure that the compliance code and anti-corruption provisions are effective. In addition to these elements, the DOJ set out, in the year 2005, in the deferred prosecution agreement between the DOJ v. Monsanto Company[825] further elements of a compliance and ethics program to detect and prevent violations of the FCPA such as: a reporting system designed to ensure reporting without the fear of retaliation or going through the chain of command or reporting to the immediate superior[826]; establishing and maintain a committee to supervise the review of the retention of any agent, consultant, or other representative for purposes of business development or lobbying in a foreign jurisdiction, the retention of any contractor or sub-contractor for a project in which a foreign government or public international organization, or instrumentalities thereof is the ultimate customer or beneficiary, and all related contracts, as well as to supervise the review of the suitability of all prospective joint venture partners for purposes of complying with the FCPA, the adequacy of the due diligence performed with regard to such partners, and any due diligence in connection with approvals of the retention of sub-agents, sub-contractors, and consultants by the joint venture for purposes of business development outside the U.S.[827]; periodic reviews by independent legal and audit firms at least every five years[828]; and procedures to objectively determine regions

825 DOJ, Deferred Prosecution Agreement Monsanto.
826 DOJ, Deferred Prosecution Agreement Monsanto, Appendix B, p. 4.
827 DOJ, Deferred Prosecution Agreement Monsanto, Appendix B, p. 2.
828 DOJ, Deferred Prosecution Agreement Monsanto, Appendix B, p. 5.

and countries which pose higher risks of corruption so that rigorous FCPA audits of the corporation's operations have to include detailed audits of the books and records with specific attention to FCPA red flags, audits of selected business partners authorized by governing contract or retention agreement, and interviews with relevant employees, consultants, and business partners[829].

The following elements have also been named to be important for an effective anti-corruption compliance program: clear policy defining bribery and prohibiting it in any shape, manner, or form including public and commercial bribery; definition of foreign government officials, third parties, and associated corruption risks; description of the FCPA and other relevant anti-corruption laws; identification of red flags and associated risks; holding employees accountable for disregarding or not reporting a red flag; business partner and third party due diligence; transparency in business dealings with government officials; guidance on anti-money laundering, lobbyists, charitable donations, influence of government officials in hiring decisions, and related risks; mechanisms for requesting guidance; and a non-retaliation policy.[830] Furthermore, an important aspect of an effective anti-bribery compliance program is to implement controls on the methods of payment.[831] In general, building a strong partnership between internal audit, and the compliance and legal divisions is essential for an effective compliance program[832] which requires also clear assignments of responsibilities for the different divisions. In this regard, effective communication and training is a further key feature of an effective compliance program.[833] With regard to communication between regional divisions, the CFO has the responsibility to establish good communication between regional financial officers.[834] Through such system, a regional officer has the opportunity to investigate whether an accounting issue which might be materially significant to the regional corporation is also significant for the whole corporation.[835] In addition, the OECD Practice Guidance on Internal Controls, Ethics, and Compliance provide guidance on internal accounting controls and anti-bribery compliance systems.[836] The OECD rec-

829 DOJ, Deferred Prosecution Agreement Monsanto, Appendix B, p. 6.
830 *Biegelman*, in: FCPA Guidebook, p. 220.
831 *O'Melveny & Myers*, 2006, p. 77.
832 *Biegelman*, in: FCPA Guidebook, p. 257.
833 *Langevoort*, 2002 Colum. Bus. L. Rev. 71, p. 81.
834 Cf. *Moeller*, SOX Internal Controls, p. 34.
835 Cf. *Moeller*, SOX Internal Controls, p. 34.
836 OECD Good Practice Guidance.

ommendations resemble the depicted elements of the anti-bribery component of the compliance program and further highlight the importance of a "strong, explicit and visible support and commitment from senior management" to such anti-bribery elements[837], the duty of individuals at all levels of the corporation to comply with the anti-bribery provisions[838], the need of measures to encourage and provide positive support for the observance of such duty[839], and the need for effective measures for providing guidance and advice for how to comply with such duty to all individuals[840].

In a corporate acquisition process, the buyer has to have FCPA due diligence as part of the standard due diligence since corporations may be liable for previous bribery of the target corporation.[841] Based on the DOJ Opinion Procedure Release 08-02, corporations are required to implement a risk-based approach to compliance for a period of 180 days after closing of a transaction for which the requestor was not able to carry out a comprehensive anti-corruption FCPA due diligence before closure.[842] Immediately after closure, the buyer has to implement its own code of conduct and a specific anti-corruption program within the new subsidiary.[843] The implementation process had to include effective communication of the new code of conduct to all target employees and anti-corruption training for all officers and other employees in positions endangered to corruption.[844] After the 180 days period, the DOJ requires that the standard anti-corruption program is implemented into the new subsidiary.

In order to effectively prevent and detect corruption, the compliance program has to be focus on red flags indicating the possibility for corruption. The program has to be able to capture, process, and evaluate red flags. As red flags have been named: unusual payment patterns or financial arrangements; a history of corruption in the country; a refusal by the foreign joint venture partner or representative to provide a certification that it will not take any action in furtherance of an unlawful offer, promise, or payment to a foreign public official and not take any act that would cause the U.S. corporation to be in violation of the FCPA; unusually high commissions; lack of transparency in expenses and accounting records; apparent

837 OECD Good Practice Guidance, at A, 1.
838 OECD Good Practice Guidance, at A, 3.
839 OECD Good Practice Guidance, at A, 9.
840 OECD Good Practice Guidance, at A, 11, i.
841 *O'Melveny & Myers*, 2006, p. 57.
842 DOJ, Opinion Release 08-02.
843 DOJ, Opinion Release 08-02.
844 DOJ, Opinion Release 08-02.

lack of qualifications or resources on the part of the joint venture partner or representative to perform the services offered; and whether the joint venture partner or representative has been recommended by an official of the potential governmental customer;[845] even dollar amounts; expense reimbursement just under the receipt submission requirement amount; one-time payments to vendors and third parties; duplicate names, payments, or invoice numbers; sequential invoice numbers; payments in countries where the corporation does not do business; business addresses that are also home addresses of corporation employees; businesses using mail drop addresses; advances to employees where no reimbursement is requested;[846] questionable integrity; reputation for paying or receiving bribes; subject of media scrutiny for misconduct, litigation, or other potentially problematic issues; prior legal issues including criminal charges for improper business practices; no adequate number or appropriately skilled staff to operate the business and carry out the contract; reluctance to disclose the true owner of the operation; lack of truthfulness or cooperation in the due diligence phase; lack of experience or expertise in the particular business or industry; third party's business is not listed in standard industry directories and is unknown to others already established in that industry; no one will provide references or references are questionable; use of shell companies; questionable business associates and subcontractors; unrealistic, exaggerated, or false representation of business results; claim of having close relationships with government officials for special favors; requests fees that are much larger than the normal market rate for comparable work without providing a reasonable explanation; expenses for which there is no accounting; off-the-books transactions; business conducted mostly in cash; influence and contacts are primary deliverables; family members and close friends who are government officials; third party was a former government official; third party was recommended by government official; business relationships with government officials; reluctance to provide written agreements or updates of work to be performed; unexpected requests for additional money; refusing to include an audit clause or is uncooperative during such an audit; providing or requesting phony invoices or documentation;[847] payments to or by offshore holding corporations in jurisdictions known for corruption and money laundering; payments from foreign

845 DOJ, Lay Person's Guide.
846 *Biegelman*, in: FCPA Guidebook, p. 258 et seq.
847 *Biegelman*, in: FCPA Guidebook, p. 222.

banks enabling for concealing the purchaser's identity; and payments appearing to large for the cause of the transaction[848].

Corporations also have to use red flags of corruption as guidance to evaluate risk potentials for the occurrence of FCPA violations. In order to assess corruption risks, management has to evaluate the detection and prevention controls with regard to corruption; has to use surveys of employees and management; and has to conduct interviews with employees in management, finance, legal, and sales and marketing who interact with government officials, review internal corruption reports.[849] Moreover, the evaluation of corruption risk includes to review: the documentation of risks including their magnitude and likelihood; whether operating in high-risk geographies regarding corruption; analysis of the specific risk for the corporation by taking into account contact with foreign officials, state-owned enterprises, business partners, and third parties, sales and marketing employees, supply channels, joint ventures, mergers and acquisitions, lobbyists, and charitable donations.[850] The available information on worldwide corruption risks such as provided by Transparency International[851] has to be used for evaluating the risk of corruption in different countries. In this regard, low to zero enforcement actions against corruption are an indicator for endemic corruption especially in the judiciary, police and government in a country.[852] In order to process the different risk factors, it has been suggested to make use of sophisticated information technology which is used e.g. by large financial institutions to deal with the anti-money laundering requirements of the U.S. PATRIOT Act.[853] The system requires three main elements: (1) risk scoring, identifying ranking the risks of customers, products, and services; (2) enhanced due diligence for high-risk customers; and (3) individual ongoing monitoring of these customers according to their risk profile.[854] The use of technology may provide an effective tool to organize, review, and analyze corruption risks.[855]

As a general aspect indicated in DOJ v. Monsanto Company and DOJ Opinion Procedure Release 08-02, the compliance program has to account for the risk magnitude of corruption in different regions and countries us-

---

848 *O'Melveny & Myers*, 2006, p. 77 et seq.
849 *Biegelman*, in: FCPA Guidebook, p. 255.
850 *Biegelman*, in: FCPA Guidebook, p. 256.
851 See http://www.transparency.org/whatwedo/publications visited: May 19, 2012.
852 *PwC*, 2009, p. 25.
853 *Spinelli/Moritz/Perlman*, in: FCPA Guidebook, p. 230, 233.
854 *Spinelli/Moritz/Perlman*, in: FCPA Guidebook, p. 230, 233.
855 *Spinelli/Moritz/Perlman*, in: FCPA Guidebook, p. 230, 233.

ing a risk-based approach to corruption which allows for efficiency considerations. The DOJ divides total corruption risk into three different levels low, medium, and high.[856] While most effort and resources have to be devoted to high and medium level risk regions and countries, low level risks may not be neglected as the FCPA has no materiality standard for violations so that even insignificant inaccuracies or sloppy accounting in small dollar transactions can be violations of the accounting provisions.[857] Nevertheless, general constraints on resources as well as efficiency considerations require within a risk-based approach to focus on high risks and to devote fewer resources to low risks.[858] As no compliance program is able to prevent and detect all FCPA violations, the level of accuracy of the compliance program to be considered effective is important. Since the anti-bribery elements are a part of the general compliance program, the effectiveness requirements for such programs are decisive set out in the USSG, discussed below[859], and in the DOJ Principles of Federal Prosecution of Business Organizations, discussed below.[860]

The effectiveness of the anti-bribery compliance program depends on monitoring, auditing, and evaluating the program's effectiveness. An important element of direct monitoring is to detect red flags of agents' wrongdoing.[861] The review of red flags may be carried out by internal audit.[862] The auditing of the compliance program has to focus on internal accounting controls and anti-corruption program elements.[863] Internal audit would be appropriate to take suitable steps to work with the responsible officers to expand and improve internal controls.[864] Thereby, internal audit has to place a strong emphasis on performing reviews surrounding significant internal controls areas.[865] One part of the task can be done through detailed risk assessment of internal control environments, discussions of these assessments with the responsible officers, and a detailed plan docu-

---

856 DOJ, Opinion Release 08-02.

857 *Leary/Dooley/Stryker*, in: The Metropolitan Corporate Counsel 2007.

858 The different importance the DOJ attributes to the different risk levels of corruption can be seen based on the reporting requirements with regard to high risk due diligence elements being due 90 days, medium risk elements 120 days, and low-risk elements 180 days after closing (DOJ, Opinion Release 08-02).

859 See *infra* at chapter 5, C. II. 1.

860 See *infra* at chapter 5, D. I.

861 *Langevoort*, 2002 Colum. Bus. L. Rev. 71, p. 86.

862 *Biegelman*, in: FCPA Guidebook, p. 255.

863 *Biegelman*, in: FCPA Guidebook, p. 256.

864 Cf. *Moeller*, SOX Internal Controls, p. 33.

865 *Moeller*, SOX Internal Controls, p. 33.

menting how these internal controls will be reviewed.[866] In order to effectuate the compliance program especially with regard to the anti-bribery components, internal audit has to have the authority to inspect all the books and records within the corporation and has to report its findings to the responsible officers such as the GC, CCO, or CFO and the audit committee.[867] As part of the monitoring and evaluation process of the anti-bribery components of the compliance program, internal audit should review[868]: employee expense reports of employees doing business in high-risk roles and areas such as working with lobbyists, public sector, government officials; employee expense reports of employees having excessive travel and entertainment expenses; gifts; employee reports indicating if payments were made to government officials; audits of third parties to determine that due diligence took place; audits if third party contracts have been prepared and approved by in-house attorneys; audits that third party contacts are in writing and contain anti-corruption language and clauses, termination rights in case of non-compliance, and contractual required audits; any anti-corruption finding has to reach the responsible officers such as CFO, GC, CCO and audit committee; anti-corruption onside audits in subsidiaries in high-risk countries; and audits of business relationships with government officials where the government official selects the contractor.

Further crucial factors to effectuate the anti-bribery components of the compliance program are effective and efficient training and its evaluation. The training has to address all relevant aspects of the compliance program. Efficient training has to account for the probability that an employee is involved in or encounters FCPA violations within the corporation. As a minimum requirement for training, all persons within the corporation who have government touch points as well as the corporation's governing authority and overseeing managers have to receive comprehensive training. A more effective approach to training is to train all employees and anyone who acts on the corporation's behalf including third parties who interact with government employees.[869] More detailed training is required for salespersons, senior management, finance employees, and controls and compli-

---

866 *Moeller*, SOX Internal Controls, p. 33.
867 *O'Melveny & Myers*, 2006, at fn. 204.
868 *Biegelman*, in: FCPA Guidebook, p. 259 et seq.
869 *Biegelman*, in: FCPA Guidebook, p. 242.

ance managers.[870] The best practice for training methods include[871]: onsite training in addition to online training for all employees; continuous training for trainers; online available frequently-asked-questions; usage of real-world scenarios and examples/role-plays; training in native language; attendance has to be mandatory; and track, document and refresh training for both in-person and online training. Training has to include details on red flags of corruption.[872] Training should also include quiz for testing training participation, training on whistleblower hotlines, information on non-retaliation, and should be held at least every year.[873] Evaluating training success is important for the corporation to show the training is effective.[874] The evaluation has to include the efforts the corporation puts into the anti-corruption program such as time, money, and other resources.[875] The employee awareness and knowledge of the FCPA compliance program, laws, regulations, corporation policy requirements have to be evaluated by using employee surveys.[876] A decrease in violations and non-compliance may be an indicator that the training is successful especially with regard to create a culture of compliance.[877]

II. Incentives to Comply with the FCPA Including Increased Enforcement Actions

The incentives to comply with the FCPA mandates and to implement an effective anti-corruption program and internal accounting controls are fines, disgorgement of gains[878], and a drop in market capitalization due to

---

870 *Biegelman*, in: FCPA Guidebook, p. 242.
871 *Biegelman*, in: FCPA Guidebook, p. 244.
872 *Biegelman*, in: FCPA Guidebook, p. 243.
873 *Biegelman*, in: FCPA Guidebook, p. 246.
874 *Biegelman*, in: FCPA Guidebook, p. 248.
875 *Biegelman*, in: FCPA Guidebook, p. 248.
876 Such surveys may include questions such as: What does FCPA stand for? Do you know what a facilitation payment is and whether it is allowed by the company? Do you know how to report FCPA misconduct and/or ask for guidance? Can you provide examples of improper conduct with respect to anti-corruption that would require reporting? Do you know the name of the corporation's compliance officer? (*Biegelman*, in: FCPA Guidebook, p. 249) A further question may be: How do you rate the senior management commitment to compliance?
877 *Biegelman*, in: FCPA Guidebook, p. 248.
878 Cf. e.g. sec. 8C2.9 USSG.

FCPA enforcement actions[879].[880] In addition, a corporation which violated the FCPA may be subject under closer scrutiny by the government including the implementation of a monitor.[881] As the FCPA has no materiality standard for violations, even insignificant inaccuracies or sloppy accounting in small dollar transactions can be violations of the accounting provisions.[882] Thus, management cannot plead ignorance of a transaction to avoid liability as they can be held accountable for what they should reasonably have known, particularly when adequate internal controls are lacking.[883] The FCPA provides for both criminal and civil penalties.[884] For violating the anti-bribery provision of sec. 30A(a) Exchange Act, criminal fines can be as high as $2 million for corporations and $100,000 for individuals, and civil fines can be as high as $10,000 for either corporations or individuals for each furtherance of the offense[885] while prison sentences for individuals may reach five years (sec. 32(c) Exchange Act). More severe are the fines for violating the accounting mandates of sec. 13(b) Exchange Act by knowingly circumventing or knowingly fail to implement internal accounting controls or knowingly falsify books and records (sec. 13(b)(5) Exchange Act) which can be as high as $5 million or an imprisonment of up to 20 years for individuals and $25 million for corporations (sec. 32(a) Exchange Act). Due to the Alternative Fines Act, the actual fine may be up to twice the benefit the individual sought to obtain by making the corrupt payment (sec. 3571(d) of title 18 USC). Moreover, a FCPA violation may result in civil or criminal forfeiture of assets due to the Civil Asset Forfeiture Reform Act of 2000 (sec. 981 of title 18 USC). As a harsh consequence of a FCPA violation, corporations may be barred from governmental contracts.[886] The U.S. government may also deny export licenses for corpora-

879 *O'Melveny & Myers*, 2006, p. 28.
880 *Spinelli/Moritz/Perlman*, in: FCPA Guidebook, p. 230, 234.
881 *Spinelli/Moritz/Perlman*, in: FCPA Guidebook, p. 230, 234.
882 *Leary/Dooley/Stryker*, in: The Metropolitan Corporate Counsel 2007.
883 *Leary/Dooley/Stryker*, in: The Metropolitan Corporate Counsel 2007.
884 Cf. *Leary/Dooley/Stryker*, in: The Metropolitan Corporate Counsel 2007; *Biegelman*, in: FCPA Guidebook, p. 24 et seq.
885 Office of the U.S. Attorneys, USAM, Criminal Resource Manual, 1019 Sanctions Against Bribery; *O'Melveny & Myers*, 2006, p. 26.
886 *Office of Management and Budget*, Guidelines on Nonprocurement, sec. 180.800(a)(3); cf. Office of the U.S. Attorneys, USAM, Criminal Resource Manual, 1019 Sanctions Against Bribery. Also *Garrett*, 97 Va. L. Rev. 1775 (2011), p. 1778.

tions.[887] Furthermore, private lawsuits under Racketeer Influenced and Corrupt Organizations Act (RICO) or other federal or state laws could be additional consequences of failure to prevent violations by implementing a compliance program.[888] Further incentives to comply with the FCPA are the high fines for systematic bribery mostly imposed by settlements with the DOJ[889], loss of "goodwill", and internal investigations[890]. In this regard, a study found that the costs for bribery are predominantly attributed to the imposed fines than to loss of reputation.[891] A compliance program also provides benefits to the corporation by reducing the fraud and corruption risk[892] which is an incentive for corporations to implement such program.[893]

The DOJ is responsible for the criminal prosecution of violations of the anti-bribery provisions, while the SEC has civil enforcement jurisdiction over corporations subject to the Exchange Act, and over those acting on their behalf.[894] In addition to its criminal jurisdiction, the DOJ also has civil jurisdiction with respect to those who are subject to the FCPA, but are not subject to SEC jurisdiction. Where public corporations are involved, the DOJ and the SEC will usually exercise their respective jurisdictions and conduct parallel, coordinated investigations and enforcement actions. Violations of sec. 13(a)(2) Exchange Act may be enforced civilly by the SEC and criminally by the DOJ. The SEC implemented a special FCPA unit for a proactive approach to identify FCPA violations.[895] Since 2007, the FCPA enforcement increased tremendously confirming a "new era of FCPA en-

887 Office of the U.S. Attorneys, USAM, Criminal Resource Manual, 1019 Sanctions Against Bribery; DOJ, Lay Person's Guide.

888 DOJ, Lay Person's Guide.

889 FCPA Blog, 2011: FCPA Settlements Siemens $800 million (2008), Halliburton $579 million (2009), BAE $400 million (2010), Snamprogetti/Eni $365 million (2010), Technip $338 million (2010), Daimler $185 million (2010), Alcatel-Lucent $137 million (2010), Panalpina $81.8 million (2010), ABB $58.3 million (2010), and Pride $56.1 million (2010).

890 *O'Melveny & Myers*, 2006, p. 28.

891 *Karpoff/Lee/Martin*, 2012.

892 *Biegelman*, in: FCPA Guidebook, p. 212.

893 See also *infra* at chapter 13, B. III.

894 DOJ, Lay Person's Guide; *Biegelman*, in: FCPA Guidebook, p. 24. See also on DOJ and SEC enforcement: DOJ/SEC, FCPA Resource Guide.

895 *Khuzami*, 2009.

forcement".[896] The enforcement actions predominantly include disgorgement of profits acquired due to FCPA violations.[897] Besides actions brought against corporations, the DOJ increasingly focuses on persecuting individuals.[898] The heightened enforcement actions lead to closer attention of management towards anti-corruption.[899] In general, it is part of the DOJ enforcement policy to hit hard on large corporations in order to send a message to the market that certain behavior is not tolerated. In case of the FCPA, it is remarkable that eight from the largest ten DOJ settlements have been with foreign corporations.[900] As reasons for the high penalties imposed on foreign corporations have been named the seriousness of the matters indicating that prosecutors only investigate the most serious matters, the goal to protect U.S. consumers and U.S. corporations form unfair foreign competition, the limited ability of U.S. prosecutors to effectively detect and investigate misconduct in foreign countries leading to the need of higher fines to achieve similar deterrence, and less lobbing power of foreign corporations.[901]

While corporations have strong incentives to comply with the FCPA provisions, they have not sufficient incentives to implement effective anti-corruption compliance programs. The incentive structure to implement effective anti-corruption compliance programs is linked to the general DOJ enforcement policy of non- and deferred prosecution agreements.[902] Based on the USAM Principles of Federal Prosecution of Business Organizations (Filip Memorandum), prosecutors will consider for their decision whether to indict a corporation *inter alia* if the corporation had implemented an effective compliance program. With regard to FCPA violations, the compliance program has to be effective to prevent and detect corruption. As it will be shown below, corporations may receive the benefits of an imple-

896 *Breuer*, 2010; cf. *Friedman/Smithline/Kleine*, 2011; *Weinstein/Meyer/Clark*, 2010. In 2007, the DOJ brought 18 and the SEC 17 FCPA enforcement actions; in 2008, the DOJ brought 20 and the SEC 13 actions; in 2009, the DOJ brought 26 and the SEC 14 actions; in 2010, the DOJ brought 48 and the SEC 26 actions; and in 2011, the DOJ brought 23 and the SEC 25 actions (cf. *Gibson Dunn*, 2012).

897 *Bixby*, 12 San Diego Int'l L. J. 89 (2010), p. 109.

898 *Weinstein/Meyer/Clark*, 2010; *Bixby*, 2010, p. 111.

899 Cf. *PwC*, 2009, p. 2 et seq.

900 Cf. FCPA Blog, 2011. As a reaction to the increased harsh penalties for foreign corporations, the U.S. have been criticized for inappropriate prosecution and have been questioned for their criminal law and enforcement (Cf. *Garrett*, 97 Va. L. Rev. 1775 (2011), pp. 1776 and 1780).

901 *Garrett*, 97 Va. L. Rev. 1775 (2011), pp. 1813 and 1849 et seq.

902 See *infra* at chapter 5, D.

mented compliance program for non- or deferred prosecution agreements merely by implementing "paper-tiger" compliance program which mimic effective programs but are non-effective. Moreover, the DOJ enforcement policy to grant non- and deferred prosecution agreements does not provide for reliable means to offset the detriment associated with the litigation dilemma.[903] Similarly, corporations would not have sufficient incentives to implement internal accounting controls since the FCPA does not require an external audit similar to sec. 404(b) SOX. But since sec. 404 SOX internal control over financial reporting fulfills the requirements of the FCPA, corporations engage in effective internal accounting controls. In essence, corporations will engage in compliance programs with a focus on anti-corruption measures due to the increased enforcement but they do not have sufficient incentives to engage in truly effective anti-corruption compliance programs.

III. Conclusion

The FCPA requires in sec. 13(b)(2) Exchange Act to implement internal accounting controls and prohibits in sec. 30A Exchange Act to bribe foreign government officials. In order to fulfill the mandates regarding the internal accounting controls, an internal control system fulfilling the mandates of sec. 302 and 404 SOX is sufficient. While such controls by themselves are not sufficient to effectively prevent and detect intentional and unintentional violations of the FCPA, anti-bribery elements have to be implemented into the general compliance system. The new era of enforcement startled corporations to increase their efforts to fight corruption in light of the harsh consequences of FCPA violations especially the possibility of disgorgement of gains, seizure of assets, and debarment from governmental contracts. But corporations lack incentives to engage in truly effective anti-corruption compliance programs.

B. Corporate Criminal Liability

Under common law, corporations are criminally liable for the crimes of their agents. Federal corporate criminal liability is grounded on the theory of *respondeat superior* established by *New York Central and Hudson River*

903 See *infra* at chapter 5, B. II.

Railroad Co. vs. United States[904]. Corporations are liable for the wrongdoing of their agents committed within the scope of their authority in order to benefit the corporation.[905] Corporate criminal liability requires proof of a crime of a corporate agent. The knowledge of the identity of the culpable agent, however, is not strictly necessary.[906] In case multiple agents may have committed the crime alternatively, such finding of the jury may suffice to convict the corporation leading to so-called "patchwork verdicts".[907] While no case law specifically addresses the issue[908], there is a good likelihood that a criminal act of a specific individual perpetrator does not have to be proven rendering the conviction especially of corporations with a large number of employees more likely.[909] Thus, the mere possibility that no proof of a specific criminal act of an individual agent may be required under common law increases the expected liability.

I. Corporate Measures to Deter Corporate Crime Including Compliance Program

Corporate criminal liability has the purpose to deter corporate crime. Corporations can deter crime through prevention and policing measures by affecting the wrongdoer's benefits, the *ex ante* direct costs of committing the crime, the likelihood of detecting crime and sanctioning of the wrongdoer[910], and the magnitude of the imposed sanction[911].[912] In this regard, an

---

904 212 U.S. 481 (1909).

905 *Id.* See also *Beale*, 2013; *Beale*, ZStW 2014, 27 et seq.

906 *United States v. Gen. Motors Corp.*, 121 F.2d 376, 411 (7th Cir. 1941); *President Coolidge (Dollar S.S. Co.) v. United States*, 101 F2d 638 (9th Cir. 1939); *United States v. Austin-Bagley Corp.*, 31 F.2d 229, 233 (2nd Cir. 1929); *Cassuto*, 13 Va. J. Soc. Pol'y & L., 179 (2005-2006), p. 206 and fn. 116.

907 *Arthur Andersen LLP v. United States*, 374 F.3d 281, 291 n.8 (5th Cir. 2004); *United States v. Bank of New Eng., N.A.*, 821 F.2d 844, 856 (1st Cir. 1987); *United States v. Shortt Accountancy Group Corp.*, 785 F.2d 1448, 1454 (9th Cir. 1986); *Weissmann*, 2007, p. 1320 and fn. 9; cf. *Beale*, 2013, p. 9; *Beale*, ZStW 2014, 27, 34; *Eichenwald*, NYTimes 2002. See in general: *Neumann Vu*, 104 Colum. L. Rev 459 (2004).

908 *Cassuto*, 13 Va. J. Soc. Pol'y & L., 179 (2005-2006), fn. 116.

909 See on the difficulties to prove the criminal act of a specific corporate agent *infra* at chapter 8, E. III. 3.

910 *Arlen* 1994, p. 835.

911 *Arlen/Kraakman*, 1997, p. 699; cf. *Arlen*, 2011a, p. 26.

912 See also *Oded*, Corporate Compliance, p. 176 et seq.

effective compliance program is an element to deter corporate crime. By implementing prevention measures corporations can deter corporate crime *ex ante*.[913] These measures may reduce benefits for wrongdoers, increase the direct cost of wrongdoing, or make the wrongdoing more difficult to carry out.[914] Especially in large corporations with separate ownership and control, preventing crime is particularly important.[915] Since managers do not directly benefit from corporate crime, the corporation determines through incentives such as promotion or compensation policies if managers benefit indirectly from corporate crime.[916] The indirect benefit is mostly attributed to an increase of compensation and job security.[917] As a prevention measure, corporations have to structure their promotion and compensation policies on long-run returns instead of short-term results in order to avoid short-run benefits for the employee and the corporation which may result in a detriment for the corporation in the long-run.[918] Also, parts of the compliance program, such as the code of conduct, foster crime prevention. Through policing measures, corporations can increase the effectiveness of government's efforts to deter crime by engaging in: *ex ante* monitoring as part of an ongoing compliance program, and *ex post* investigation, cooperation, reporting and auditing.[919] Policing measures increase the probability for individual wrongdoers to be sanctioned since investigating, detecting, and reporting criminal conduct to government, as well as cooperation, increase the likelihood that wrongdoers will be sanctioned.[920] In this regard, an effective culture of compliance can help to deter criminal conduct by increasing psychological costs of wrongdoers and by making it harder to obtain accomplices or to conceal wrongdoing.[921] Generally, the purpose of compliance programs is to deter violations directly by training employees and shifting corporate culture, and to deter crime indirectly by increasing the probability that wrongdoing will be detected and, thereby, increasing the expected sanction.[922]

---

913 *Arlen*, 2011b, p. 12; *Arlen/Kraakman*, 1997, p. 701; *Arlen*, 2011a, p. 2.
914 *Arlen*, 2011b, p. 12.
915 *Arlen*, 2011b, p. 12.
916 *Arlen*, 2011b, p. 12; cf. *id.*, 2011a, p. 19.
917 *Arlen*, 2011b, p. 12.
918 *Arlen*, 2011b, p. 12; *id.*, 2011a, p. 27; cf. *Arlen/Kraakman*, 1997, p. 704.
919 *Arlen*, 2011a, p. 28; *Arlen/Kraakman*, 1997, p. 706 et seq.; cf. *Arlen*, 2011b, p. 11 et seq.; cf. *Oded*, Corporate Compliance, p. 185.
920 *Arlen*, 2011b, p. 10; *id.*, 2011a, p. 2.
921 *Arlen*, 2011b, p. 10; *id.*, 2011a, p. 26.
922 *Arlen*, 2011b, p. 28; cf. *Baer*, 50 Boston College L. Rev. 949 (2009), p. 959.

II. Incentive Structure of Corporate Criminal Liability

Through corporate criminal liability corporations are induced to engage in prevention and policing measures to deter misconduct of corporate agents. Under the principle of *respondeat superior*, corporations are strictly, i.e. vicariously, liable for criminal acts of their agents.[923] Due to vicarious liability, corporations, as the principle of their agents, face the full expected costs of damages, regardless of any effort by the corporation to avoid the harm.[924] Thus, corporations have an incentive to control their agents through optimal prevention measures.[925] Vicarious liability does not, however, induce corporations to optimally invest in *ex ante* and *ex post* policing.[926] Rather, policing measures are different to prevention measures since policing measures have two contrary effects on the expected liability[927] of corporations.[928] First, they can deter some wrongdoing of corporate agents and, thereby, reduce the expected liability of corporations.[929] Second, they impose costs on corporations, besides their direct costs of implementation[930], by increasing the expected liability of the corporation since they increase the probability that government detects and sanctions corporate crime.[931] Through *ex ante* and *ex post* policing measures, the corporation produces information on misconduct which reaches government through *ex post* policing measures leading to a higher probability that government will sanction corporations.[932] Since policing measures increase the probability of sanctioning criminal agents, corporations will not optimally engage in policing measures.[933] If the increase in liability exceeds the increase in deterrence, corporations will not engage in any policing measures re-

923 *Respondeat superior* includes crimes committed by all employees not only by senior management (*Arlen*, 2011a, p. 5 with further insight).

924 Cf. *Arlen/Kraakman*, 1997, p. 718 et seq.; *Krawiec*, 32 Fla. St. U. L. Rev. 571 (2005), p. 575.

925 *Kraakman*, in: Encyclopedia of Law and Economics, p. 135 et seq.; *Krawiec*, 32 Fla. St. U. L. Rev. 571 (2005), p. 576 (defined as: internal compliance structures).

926 *Arlen*, 2011a, p. 37 et seq.; *id.*, 2011b, p. 13; *Arlen/Kraakman*, 1997, p. 707; *Arlen*, 23 J. Legal Stud. 833 (1994), p. 847.

927 Expected liability given by the probability of sanction multiplied by the penalty (*Arlen*, 2011b, p. 15).

928 *Arlen*, 2011a, p. 42 et seq.; *id.*, 2011b, p. 13; *Arlen/Kraakman*, 1997, p. 708.

929 *Arlen*, 2011b, p. 13; *Arlen/Kraakman*, 1997, p. 708.

930 *Arlen*, 2011b, p. 13 et seq.; cf. *Goldsmith/King*, 50 Vand. L. Rev. 1 (1997), p. 16.

931 *Arlen/Kraakman*, 1997, p. 708; cf. *Arlen*, 2011b, p. 14; *id.*, 2011a, p. 38.

932 Cf. *Arlen*, 2011b, p. 28; *Oded*, Corporate Compliance, p. 191.

933 *Arlen/Kraakman*, 1997, p. 706 et seq.; *id.*, 2011b, p. 14.

gardless of the amount of the imposed sanction.[934] That is because corporations face a higher expected sanction when engaging in corporate policing measures than when refraining from such measures.[935] The increase of expected liability represents the fact that effective policing measures will identify and disclose information that could be used in governmental proceedings or civil lawsuits imposing "significant" costs on corporations.[936] This fact is known as the litigation dilemma[937] which has "very direct consequences on the incentive to create or administer" policing measures[938]. Hence, effective policing measures increase the probability of being subject to sanctions such as the criminal fine, criminal restitution, government-imposed civil penalties, and private civil sanctions.[939] Moreover, corporations may suffer from reputational and market penalties, as well as other collateral consequences especially when indicted or convicted of fraud.[940] These sanctions are significant as they often exceed the criminal fine by far.[941] The main threats to corporations result from governmental proceedings using the produced information to sanction the corporation, or from civil proceedings using the U.S. doctrine of discovery[942] to obtain information. In this regard, the scope and limitations of evidentiary privileges is important in order to define the scale of the litigation dilemma.[943] Due to the litigation dilemma, the effectiveness of the policing measures training, monitoring, and auditing are affected.[944]

934 *Arlen/Kraakman*, 1997, p. 708.
935 *Arlen*, 2011b, pp. 2 and 4; cf. *Arlen/Kraakman*, 1997, p. 707; *Arlen*, 23 J. Legal Stud. 833 (1994), p. 836.
936 USSC, Ad Hoc Report, p. 106; cf. *Webb/Molo*, 71 Wash. U. L. Q. 375 (1993), p. 381.
937 USSC, Ad Hoc Report, p. 106.
938 USSC, Ad Hoc Report, p. 116; cf. *Murphy*, 13 ETHIKOS 4 (2000).
939 *Arlen*, 2011b, p. 30 et seq.; *id.*, 2011a, p. 7; *Posner*, Economic Analysis of Law, p. 458; *Arlen/Kraakman*, 1997, p. 750.
940 Cf. *Arlen*, 2011a, p. 8 et seq.
941 Cf. *Arlen*, 2011a, at fn. 13; *Alexander/Arlen/Cohen*, 42 Journal of Law and Economics 393 (1999), p. 409 et seq.
942 Under the U.S. doctrine of discovery, parties in a lawsuit may seek evidence from the other party *inter alia* through requests for answers to interrogatories and requests for production of documents. Discovery may be limited by the common law privilege of protected self-evaluation (cf. USSC, Ad Hoc Report, p. 114 et seq.). See for an overview: *Imberg/Geissl*, CCZ 2009, 190.
943 Cf. USSC, Ad Hoc Report, p. 109.
944 USSC, Ad Hoc Report, p. 116 et seq.

It follows that policing measures impose direct and indirect costs on corporations but they also provide for benefits.[945] The benefits of compliance programs may outweigh the detriments of the litigation dilemma. As part of the business decision to implement an effective compliance program, corporations have to take its advantages into consideration. The advantages of policing measures are: enabling the corporation to assess more accurately the criminal or civil liability[946] and "[providing] a [corporation with] more control over the direction and scope of the investigation"[947]; allowing the corporation to take more informed business decisions[948] since the *ex ante* policing measures provide the corporation with important information regarding potential legal issues within the corporation[949]; meeting reporting obligations of statutes and regulations[950]; disseminating law-abiding corporate ethos, addressing problems more quickly minimizing their impact, helping to demonstrate a crime to be the act of a rouge employee, and diminishing the corporation's exposure to sentencing[951]. Despite these advantages, corporations tend to implement policing measures reflecting a tradeoff of effectiveness and safety with regard to the litigation dilemma. This finding is consistent with the notion of the Ad Hoc Advisory Group of 2003[952] that, in the end, it would remain a business decision balancing the pros and cons of how to implement *ex ante* policing measures and engage in reporting.[953] In consequence, corporations generally do not consider the advantages of policing measures to outweigh the detriments of the litigation dilemma. In essence, strict vicarious liability is able to optimally induce prevention measures but is unable to induce optimal policing measures at the same time.[954]

---

945 Cf. *Goldsmith/King*, 50 Vand. L. Rev. 1 (1997), p. 13 et seq.

946 USSC, Ad Hoc Report, p. 107; *Goldsmith/King*, 50 Vand. L. Rev. 1 (1997), p. 14.

947 *Goldsmith/King*, 50 Vand. L. Rev. 1 (1997), p. 13.

948 USSC, Ad Hoc Report, p. 107.

949 Cf. *Hopson/Koehler*, CCZ 2008, 208, 213; *Goldsmith/King*, 50 Vand. L. Rev. 1 (1997), p. 13.

950 USSC, Ad Hoc Report, p. 107.

951 *Webb/Molo*, 71 Wash. U. L. Q. 375 (1993), p. 376.

952 The Ad Hoc Advisory Group has been formed by the USSC to review the general effectiveness of the USSG (cf. USSC, Ad Hoc Report, p. 1).

953 Cf. USSC, Ad Hoc Report, p. 120. The report refers to "compliance programs". But since *ex ante* policing measures are an important part of compliance programs, the statement still holds.

954 *Arlen/Kraakman*, 72 N.Y.U.L. Rev. 687 (1997), p. 709 et seq.

III. Conclusion

Corporate criminal liability has the main purpose to deter corporate crime. Corporations can deter crime *ex ante* by implementing prevention measures which may reduce benefits for wrongdoers, increase the direct cost of wrongdoing, or make wrongdoing more difficult to carry out. In addition to prevention measures, corporations can increase the effectiveness of government's efforts to deter corporate crime by intervening *ex ante* and *ex post* through policing measures such as *ex ante* monitoring as part of an ongoing compliance program, *ex post* investigation, cooperation, reporting, and auditing. Strict criminal liability provides for optimal incentives for corporations to engage in prevention measures but lacks optimal incentives for policing measures since policing measures increase the expected liability of corporations by increasing the probability that government detects and sanctions corporate crime. In the same way, policing measures identify and disclose information that could be used in governmental proceedings or civil lawsuits. This litigation dilemma further diminishes the effectiveness of policing measures.

C. United States Sentencing Guidelines (USSG) – Sentencing of Organizations

The United States Sentencing Guidelines[955] (USSG) were introduced by the U.S. Sentencing Commission (USSC) based on the Sentencing Reform Act in 1991 to structure "previously unfettered sentencing discretion", make administration of punishment more certain, and to target specific offenders for more serious penalties.[956] The general purpose of the USSG is to harmonize criminal sentencing of U.S. federal courts. The USSG provide non-binding guidance[957] for federal judges to determine the sanctions for criminal conduct.[958] The two key purposes of sentencing fostered by the USSG are just punishment and deterrence.[959] In chapter eight, 'Sentencing of Organizations', the USSG address criminal conduct of corporations.[960] Due to corporate criminal liability, a corporation can be held vi-

955 Also referred to as Federal Sentencing Guidelines (FSG).
956 *Desio*, 39 Wake Forest L. Rev. 559 (2004), p. 563.
957 Cf. *United States v. Booker*, 543 U.S. 220 (2005); *Arlen*, 2011b, at fn. 5.
958 Cf. USSG, Introductory Commentary to chapter 8.
959 *Desio*, 39 Wake Forest L. Rev. 559 (2004), p. 559.
960 *Desio*, 39 Wake Forest L. Rev. 559 (2004), p. 559.

cariously liable for criminal acts of its agents.[961] In order to induce corporations to further the goals of the Sentencing Reform Act, prevention and deterrence of criminal conduct[962], the USSG provide incentives for corporations to detect and prevent criminal conduct. These incentives should lead corporations "to reduce and ultimately eliminate criminal conduct by providing a structural foundation from which [it] may self-police its own conduct through an effective compliance and ethics program".[963] Therefore, the "ultimate" purpose of the USSG is to promote "good corporate citizenship" by encouraging to implement effective compliance programs.[964] The USSG resemble a "duty-based composite regime" in which the corporations are strictly liable for the acts of their agents, but sanctions may be substantially reduced if the corporation satisfies the USSG self-policing duties: effective compliance program, reporting, and cooperation.[965] In light of the corporate scandals of the 2000s, sec. 805(a)(5) SOX ordered the USSC to review if chapter eight of the USSG is sufficient to deter and punish criminal conduct. In 2004, the USSC implemented the revised version of chapter eight instituting "more rigorous criteria for compliance programs" and placing "greater responsibility on directors and management to oversee these programs".[966] The USSC revised and strengthened the criteria for an effective compliance and ethics program harmonizing the USSG with the best practices as reflected *inter alia* by SOX.[967]

The USSG represent a novel approach to provide incentives for corporations to deter crime in conjunction with the incentives provided by crimi-

---

961 See *supra* at chapter 5, B.

962 *Murphy*, 87 Iowa L. Rev. 697 (2002), p. 699.

963 USSG, Introductory Commentary to chapter 8.

964 *Murphy*, 87 Iowa L. Rev. 697 (2002), p. 706. See also *New York City Bar*, Report 2006, p. H-5.

965 *Arlen*, 2011b, p. 4; *Krawiec*, 32 Fla. St. U. L. Rev. 571 (2005), p. 572; *Arlen/Kraakman*, 72 N.Y.U.L. Rev. 687 (1997), p. 689 et seq. See *Arlen*, 23 J. Legal Stud. 833 (1994), p. 861 et seq. for the potential to eliminate the perverse effects of *respondeat superior* through duty-based corporate liability. See also *infra* at chapter 16, B. I. 2. d).

966 *New York City Bar*, Report 2006, p. H-5; *Hess/McWhorter/Fort*, 11 Fordham J. Corp & Fin. L. 725 (2006), p. 725.

967 *Desio*, 39 Wake Forest L. Rev. 559 (2004), p. 561. As part of the revision, the USSC emphasized the importance of an effective compliance and ethics program by establishing a separate section of the USSG (cf. *Desio*, 39 Wake Forest L. Rev. 559 (2004), p. 561).

nal law.[968] General restraints on resources result in an inability of U.S. law enforcement to effectively detect and prosecute offenses such as fraud.[969] Likewise, federal authorities cannot effectively deter corporate crime without the help of corporations.[970] The USSG-approach further acknowledges the difference between individual and corporate offenders focusing on deterrence and incentives to prevent and detect criminal conduct.[971] In the following, the procedure of the USSG to determine corporate sanctions and the requirements of the mitigating factors "effective compliance and ethics program" and "reporting, cooperation and acceptance of responsibility" will be depicted.

I. Applicability of Mitigating Factors

In USSG chapter eight part C 'fines,' the USSG define the method to determine sanctions for corporations. The method includes the mitigating factors of the USSG representing the requirements for corporations to receive leniency in light of criminal conduct. The mitigating factors are 'Effective Compliance and Ethics Program' (sec. 8C2.5 (f) USSG) and 'Self-Reporting, Cooperation, and Acceptance of Responsibility' (sec. 8C2.5 (g) USSG). The applicability of the mitigating factor 'effective compliance and ethics program' is limited due to sec. 8C2.5 (f)(2) USSG if the corporation, after becoming aware of an offense, unreasonably delayed reporting of the offense. Yet, the corporation is allowed a reasonable period of time to conduct an internal investigation, and is not required to report in case the corporation concluded, based on the information then available, that no offense has been committed.[972] The factor does also not apply in case high-level personnel, including directors, the CEO, or other managers in charge of major business or functional units[973], or specific individuals responsible

---

968 Cf. *Steer*, 2001, p. 2.

969 Cf. *Driscoll/Hoffman/Murphy*, 99 Business and Society Rev. 35 (1998), p. 49. See *supra* at chapter 4, A. II. 1. c).

970 *Arlen*, 2011b, p. 1; *id.*, 23 J. Legal Stud. 833 (1994), p. 835. See *infra* at chapter 16, B. I. 1.

971 Cf. *Murphy*, 87 Iowa L. Rev. 697 (2002), p. 702 et seq. See *infra* at chapter 16, B. I. 1.

972 Cf. USSG, Commentary to sec. 8C2.5 no. 10.

973 Cf. definition of "high-level personnel" in USSG, Commentary to sec. 8A1.2 no. 3 (B) to which the USSG, Commentary to sec. 8C2.5 no. 3 and sec. 8C2.5 (f) (3)(A) combined with the USSG, Commentary to sec. 8B2.1 no. 1 refer to.

for the compliance and ethics program[974] participated in, condoned, or were willfully ignorant of the offense (sec. 8C2.5 (f)(3)(A) USSG). Despite the involvement of high-level personnel or specific individuals responsible for the compliance and ethics program, the mitigating factor of sec. 8C2.5 (f)(1) USSG may still apply due to sec. 8C2.5 (f)(3)(C) USSG. This provision was implemented in 2010 by the USSC in order to eliminate the former restrictions allowing the mitigation of fines for corporations with effective compliance programs in place, despite the involvement of such personnel in the criminal conduct.[975] The provision requires that (i) such specific individuals have direct reporting obligations to the board of directors or the audit committee[976], (ii) the compliance and ethics program detected the offense before discovery outside the corporation or before such discovery was reasonably likely, (iii) the corporation promptly reported the offense to appropriate governmental authorities, (iv) and no individual with operational responsibility for the compliance and ethics program participated in, condoned, or was willfully ignorant of the offense. In addition, the reporting authority must be assigned to individuals with operational responsibility.[977] Thus, implementing a CCO with direct reporting obligations to the board of directors or the audit committee is advisable.

In case courts impose probation on a corporation (sec. 8D1.1 USSG), it may require the corporation to develop an effective compliance and ethics program consistent with sec. 8B2.1 USSG (sec. 8D1.4 (b)(1) USSG) if the corporation lacks such program or if an existing program has not been determined to be effective. In order to evaluate the effectiveness of the program submitted under the terms of probation, the court may employ appropriate experts and should approve any program consistent with sec. 8B2.1 USSG that appears reasonably to prevent and detect criminal conduct.[978] In order to deter any corporate policy accepting repeated sanctions

974 Sec. 8C2.5 (f)(3)(A) referring to sec. 8B2.1 (b)(2)(C) USSG.

975 *Arlen*, 2011b, at fn. 24.

976 In order to fulfill the requirement of "direct reporting obligations", an individual has to have express authority to communicate personally to the board of directors or the audit committee promptly on matters involving criminal conduct, and on the implementation and effectiveness of the compliance and ethics program (cf. Commentary to sec. 8C2.5 no. 11). For proving express authority, corporations should document the reporting authority. Personally reporting excludes indirect reports through superiors or paper reports (*McGreal*, 66 Bus. Law. 125 (2010), p. 128).

977 Cf. *McGreal*, 66 Bus. Law. 125 (2010), p. 128.

978 Cf. USSG, Commentary to sec. 8D1.4 no. 1.

as a cost of business, courts shall deprive the corporation of all gain to the corporation form the offense that has not been paid as restitution or by way of other remedial measures (sec. 8C2.9 USSG).

II. Requirements of Mitigating Factors

The USSG provide requirements for how to design compliance and ethics programs but in a rather functional manner.[979] They serve more as a model of "structured flexibility" providing benchmarks[980] which allows all corporations to follow the USSG[981] preventing a one-size-fits-all approach.

1. Effective Compliance and Ethics Program – Section 8B2.1 USSG

In sec. 8B2.1 USSG, the USSG set out the requirements for an effective compliance and ethics program which is intended "to achieve reasonable prevention and detection of criminal conduct for which the corporation would be vicariously liable" and which "has a direct bearing on the appropriate penalties and probation terms [...] if the corporation is convicted and sentenced for a criminal offense".[982] The effective compliance and ethics program's main purpose is to prevent and detect criminal conduct (sec. 8B2.1 (a)(1) USSG). Thereby, the corporation has to exercise due diligence to achieve this purpose. Requiring due diligence has been described as the "keystone" of the USSG providing for a flexible setting to prevent static application of the USSG's standards as "a series of formal steps".[983] Moreover, due diligence requires ongoing efforts with regard to the compliance and ethics program.[984] A further main purpose of the compliance and ethics program is to promote a corporate culture that encourages ethical conduct and a commitment to compliance with the law (sec. 8B2.1 (a) (2) USSG). The compliance and ethics program has to be reasonably designed, implemented, and enforced so that the program is generally effective in preventing and detecting criminal conduct (sec. 8B2.1 (a) USSG).

979 *Desio*, 39 Wake Forest L. Rev. 559 (2004), p. 561.
980 *Swenson/Clark*, 1 Corporate Conduct Quarterly 1 (1991).
981 Cf. *Steer*, 2001, p. 7.
982 Cf. USSG, Background of Commentary to sec. 8B2.1.
983 *Driscoll/Hoffman/Murphy*, 99 Business and Society Rev. 35 (1998), p. 41 et seq.
984 *Driscoll/Hoffman/Murphy*, 99 Business and Society Rev. 35 (1998), p. 41 et seq. and p. 50.

The USSG recognize that even the best ethics and compliance program cannot assure that the program will never fail[985] addressing the impact of the hindsight bias. Therefore, the USSG state that it cannot necessarily be concluded that a program is not generally effective in preventing and detecting criminal conduct if an offense occurs (sec. 8B2.1 (a) USSG). This is consistent with the concept of due diligence since due diligence requires only all reasonable effort to achieve a goal but not certainty.

While sec. 8B2.1 (a) USSG formulates the two main purposes of the effective compliance and ethics program, sec. 8B2.1 (b) USSG lists the seven minimal requirements a corporation has to adhere to in order to show that the corporation exercised "due diligence" to prevent and detect criminal conduct and the "promotion of a corporate culture that encourages ethical conduct and a commitment to compliance with the law". First, the corporation has to establish standards and procedures to prevent and detect criminal conduct (sec. 8B2.1 (b)(1) USSG). The USSG define standards and procedures as "standards of conduct and internal controls that are reasonable capable of reducing the likelihood of criminal conduct".[986] Second, the board of directors[987] has to be knowledgeable about the content and operation of the compliance and ethics program and has to exercise oversight with regard to the implementation and effectiveness of the compliance and ethics program (sec. 8B2.1 (b)(2)(A) USSG[988]). The board of directors and management[989] have the responsibility to ensure that the corporation has an effective compliance and ethics program[990], and the overall responsibility for the compliance and ethics program has to be assigned to specific individual(s) of the board of directors and management (sec. 8B2.1 (b)(2)(B) USSG). Moreover, the board of directors and management have to exercise their duties consistent with the due diligence requirement to prevent and detect criminal conduct and they have to promote a corporate

985 Cf. *Driscoll/Hoffman/Murphy*, 99 Business and Society Rev. 35 (1998), p. 40.

986 Cf. USSG, Commentary to sec. 8B2.1 no. 1.

987 The USSG address the "governing authority" which is defined as the board of directors or the highest level of governing body of the organization if the organization does not have a board of directors (cf. USSG, Commentary to sec. 8B2.1 no. 1).

988 This subsection has been implemented into the USSG as part of the sec. 805(a)(5) SOX review.

989 The USSG use the term "high-level personnel" defined by Commentary to sec. 8B2.1 no. 1 referring to USSG, Commentary to sec. 8A1.2 which may also encompasses also managers below the officer's level.

990 This element has been implemented into the USSG as part of the sec. 805(a)(5) SOX review.

culture that encourages ethical conduct and a commitment to compliance with the law.[991] The day-to-day operational responsibility for the compliance and ethics program has to be delegated to specific individual(s) within the corporation who report to management and, as appropriate, to the board of directors or the audit committee on the effectiveness of the compliance and ethics program (sec. 8B2.1 (b)(2)(C) USSG)[992]. In order to fulfill such responsibility, the responsible individual(s) have to be given "adequate resources, appropriate authority, and direct access" to the board of directors or the audit committee (sec. 8B2.1 (b)(2)(C) USSG). At least annually, the individual(s) responsible for the day-to-day operations should give the board of directors or the audit committee information regarding the implementation and effectiveness of the compliance program.[993] The USSG do not specify how to assign the responsibility for the compliance and ethics program within the corporation. Consistent with the USSG-mandates, the following recommendation for assigning responsibility is directed to large listed corporations. With regard to the overall responsibility, at least one independent director should take on the overall responsibility as well as one officer. On the board of director's level, a member of the audit committee could assume this responsibility. On the management level, a CCO should be implemented assuming the responsibility of the compliance and ethics program including the day-to-day operations. If the CCO is not part of officer's level, the officer, to whom the CCO reports to, should assume the responsibility for the compliance and ethics program while the responsibility for the day-to-day operations should rest with the CCO. In order to fulfill her day-to-day duties, the CCO should use the internal audit in particular to assess compliance risks and the effectiveness of the compliance system. Third, the corporation should devote reasonable efforts not to assign substantial authority, with regard to the compliance and ethics program, to personnel with known illegal activities or other conduct inconsistent with such program (sec. 8B2.1 (b)(3) USSG). Thus, the corporation has to screen its personnel prior to assigning authority regarding the compliance and ethics program.[994] In order to comply with sec. 8B2.1 (b)(3) USSG, the corporation has to ensure that only individuals are hired or promoted to the board of directors, management, or substantial authority

991 Cf. USSG, Commentary to sec. 8B2.1 no. 3.

992 This subsection has been implemented into the USSG as part of the sec. 805(a)(5) SOX review.

993 Cf. USSG, Commentary to sec. 8B2.1 no. 3.

994 *Desio*, 39 Wake Forest L. Rev. 559 (2004), p. 561.

personnel who will perform their assigned duties in a manner consistent with the compliance and ethics program.[995] With respect to the hiring or promotion, the corporation should consider the "relatedness of the individual's illegal activities and other misconduct to the specific responsibilities […]" of the individual, the recency of such acts, and whether the individual has engaged in other such acts.[996] Fourth, the corporation has to communicate periodically its standards and procedures, and other aspects of the compliance and ethics program, to the board of directors, management, substantial authority personnel, and the employees, through effective training and by disseminating information appropriate to such individuals' respective roles and responsibilities (sec. 8B2.1 (b)(4)(A) and (B) USSG). Fifth, the corporation has to ensure that the compliance and ethics program is followed, including monitoring and auditing, in order to detect criminal conduct (sec. 8B2.1 (b)(5)(A) USSG). Moreover, the corporation has to evaluate periodically the effectiveness of the compliance and ethics program (sec. 8B2.1 (b)(5)(B) USSG[997]). Furthermore, the corporation has to have and publicize a system by which the employees may report or seek guidance regarding potential or actual criminal conduct without fear of retaliation (sec. 8B2.1 (b)(5)(C) USSG). The system may include mechanisms that allow for anonymity or confidentiality[998] but these mechanisms are not mandatory. Sixth, the corporation has to promote and enforce the compliance and ethics program consistently throughout the corporation by providing appropriate incentives to perform in accordance with such program, and disciplinary measures for engaging in criminal conduct and for failing to take reasonable steps to prevent or detect such conduct (sec. 8B2.1 (b)(6)(A) and (B) USSG). With regard to punishment for failure to detect wrongdoing, the corporation has to have standards and procedures to ensure that all personnel is punished in the same way to avoid double standards. Such double standards may arise by ignoring wrongdoing of senior executives in contrast to discipline a low-level employee for the same conduct.[999] Such double standards constitute real threats to the effectiveness of compliance and ethics programs.[1000] Therefore, corporations

995 Cf. USSG, Commentary to sec. 8B2.1 no. 4 (B).

996 Cf. USSG, Commentary to sec. 8B2.1 no. 4 (B).

997 This subsection has been implemented into the USSG as part of the sec. 805(a)(5) SOX review.

998 This element has been implemented into the USSG as part of the sec. 805(a)(5) SOX review.

999 *Driscoll/Hoffman/Murphy*, 99 Business and Society Rev. 35 (1998), p. 47.

1000 *Driscoll/Hoffman/Murphy*, 99 Business and Society Rev. 35 (1998), p. 47.

should implement a disciplinary manual to provide guidance on disciplinary measures, and should require the compliance officer or the compliance committee to conduct routine reviews of disciplinary cases involving the compliance program in order to avoid the development of double standards and to assess the effectiveness of the disciplinary measures.[1001] Seventh, the corporation has to address any occurring criminal conduct and has to take corrective measures as appropriate. Therefore, after the detection of criminal conduct, the corporation has take reasonable steps to respond appropriately to the criminal conduct by remedying the occurred harm, reporting and cooperation[1002], and, in order to prevent further similar criminal conduct, by assessing[1003] the compliance and ethics program and making any necessary modifications to such program (sec. 8B2.1 (b)(7) USSG). As one important step to prevent further similar criminal conduct, the corporation has to determine the root of the criminal conduct.[1004] Management has to ensure that corrective measures of the compliance and ethics program are effective since the recurrence of similar misconduct raises doubts that the corporation has implemented an effective compliance and ethics program.[1005]

With regard to all seven minimal requirements, the USSG state further factors to consider in meeting the requirements of the ethics and compliance program.[1006] As one factor, the corporation has to incorporate and follow applicable industry practice[1007] or any standards called for by any applicable governmental regulation, since the failure to do so counteracts a conclusion that the corporation has an effective compliance and ethics program.[1008] Thus, with regard to listed corporations, the compliance standards called for by the SEC regulation have to be followed. These include *inter alia* and not exclusively the standards of COSO I.[1009] An additional factor to consider is the size of the corporation since the necessary features of the corporation's standards and procedures depend on its size.[1010] In or-

1001 Cf. *Driscoll/Hoffman/Murphy*, 99 Business and Society Rev. 35 (1998), p. 47.
1002 Cf. USSG, Commentary to sec. 8B2.1 no. 6.
1003 Cf. USSG, Commentary to sec. 8B2.1 no. 6.
1004 Cf. *Driscoll/Hoffman/Murphy*, 99 Business and Society Rev. 35 (1998), p. 47.
1005 Cf. USSG, Commentary to sec. 8B2.1 no. 2 (D).
1006 Cf. USSG, Commentary to sec. 8B2.1 no. 2.
1007 An example of such industry standards is: the Defense Industry Initiative (cf. *Krawiec*, 81 Wash. U. L. Quarterly 487 (2003), p. 497).
1008 Cf. USSG, Commentary to sec. 8B2.1 no. 2 (B).
1009 See *supra* at chapter 4, A. II. 2. b) (1).
1010 Cf. USSG, Commentary to sec. 8B2.1 no. 2 (C)(i).

der to meet the requirements of sec. 8B2.1 USSG, large corporations have to meet a high standard of formalization of their compliance and ethics program's operations and have to devote appropriate resources to the operations consistent with the corporation's size.[1011] Also, large corporations should encourage small corporations, especially their trade partners, to implement effective compliance and ethics programs.[1012] Formality of a compliance and ethics program includes to have a formal line of authority and business organization in which the board of directors is responsible for the oversight of the compliance and ethics program and is not directly involved in managing such program.[1013] Moreover, the corporation should provide for formal staff training sessions and formal monitoring procedures[1014] including separate evaluations. A formal program also includes hiring separate staff to carry out the compliance and ethics program instead of only using available personnel.[1015] Furthermore, the corporation has to develop a compliance and ethics program which is specifically designed for its unique needs.[1016] In general, formality demonstrates the commitment of the corporation to the compliance and ethics program.[1017] As part of implementing and successfully maintaining[1018] the seven minimal requirements, the corporation has to assess periodically the risk of criminal conduct and has to take appropriate actions to design, implement, or modify each requirement to reduce the risk of criminal conduct identified through such process (sec. 8B2.1 (c) USSG[1019]). Therefore, a corporation has to assess the nature and seriousness of criminal conduct, the likelihood that such conduct may occur, and the prior history of the corporation.[1020] Moreover, the corporation has to prioritize periodically, as appropriate, the actions taken with regard to the seven requirements in order to focus on preventing and detecting criminal conduct, identified in the assessment process, as most serious, and most likely to occur.[1021] Then, the

1011 Cf. USSG, Commentary to sec. 8B2.1 no. 2 (C)(ii).
1012 Cf. USSG, Commentary to sec. 8B2.1 no. 2 (C)(ii).
1013 Cf. USSG, Commentary to sec. 8B2.1 no. 2 (C)(iii).
1014 Cf. USSG, Commentary to sec. 8B2.1 no. 2 (C)(iii).
1015 Cf. USSG, Commentary to sec. 8B2.1 no. 2 (C)(iii).
1016 Cf. USSG, Commentary to sec. 8B2.1 no. 2 (C)(iii).
1017 Cf. USSG, Commentary to sec. 8B2.1 no. 2 (C)(iii).
1018 *Desio*, 39 Wake Forest L. Rev. 559 (2004), p. 561.
1019 This subsection has been implemented into the USSG as part of the sec. 805(a)(5) SOX review.
1020 Cf. USSG, Commentary to sec. 8B2.1 no. 7 (A)(i) through (iii).
1021 Cf. USSG, Commentary to sec. 8B2.1 no. 7 (B).

corporation has to modify, as appropriate, the actions taken pursuant to any of the seven requirements to reduce the risk of criminal conduct identified in the assessment process as most serious and most likely to occur.[1022] In addition, even though not addressed by the USSG, documenting the compliance program and compliance activities of the corporation is essential to provide proof that the corporation exercised due diligence.[1023] Moreover, the seven minimal requirements have to include anti-corruption elements in order to establish an effective compliance program.[1024]

2. Self-Reporting, Cooperation, and Acceptance of Responsibility – Section 8C2.5 (g) USSG

'Self-reporting, cooperation, and acceptance of responsibility' is the second mitigating factor with regard to the culpability score. A corporation will receive the greatest mitigating effect if it reported the offense to appropriate governmental authorities – prior to an imminent threat of disclosure or government investigation and within a reasonably prompt time after becoming aware of the offense –, fully cooperated in the investigation, and clearly demonstrated recognition and affirmative acceptance of responsibility for its criminal conduct (sec. 8C2.5 (g)(1) USSG). The cooperation must be timely and thorough, thus, the cooperation must begin essentially at the same time as the criminal investigation, and should include the disclosure of all pertinent information known by the corporation.[1025] With regard to affirmative acceptance of responsibility, an entry of a guilty plea prior to the commencement of trial combined with truthful evidence of the involvement in the offense and related conduct usually constitutes significant evidence of affirmative acceptance of responsibility.[1026] Nevertheless, corporations can only be sure to receive leniency for affirmative acceptance of responsibility in case of a plea guilty. Thus, the USSG do not provide for strong incentives to report detected suspicious activities unless the

1022 Cf. USSG, Commentary to sec. 8B2.1 no. 7 (C).

1023 *Driscoll/Hoffman/Murphy*, 99 Business and Society Rev. 35 (1998), p. 48.

1024 *Biegelman*, in: FCPA Guidebook, p. 217.

1025 Cf. USSG, Commentary to sec. 8C2.5 no. 13. "[P]ertinent information" is information which is sufficient for law enforcement personnel to identify the nature and extent of the offense and the individuals responsible for the criminal conduct (cf. USSG, Commentary to sec. 8C2.5 no. 13).

1026 Cf. USSG, Commentary to sec. 8C2.5 no. 14 and *id.* for further details on the issue.

corporation is prepared to plead guilty.[1027] The corporation will only receive significantly reduced credit as compared to sec. 8C2.5 (g)(1) USSG if it fully cooperated and clearly demonstrated recognition and affirmative acceptance of responsibility for criminal conduct (sec. 8C2.5 (g)(2) USSG), but did not report the offense. For only accepting responsibility, it will receive even further reduced credit (sec. 8C2.5 (g)(3) USSG).

III. Incentive Structure to Comply with the USSG

Especially in the beginning of the USSG, corporate leaders feared that courts would not determine compliance programs to be effective, and, therefore, would deny the mitigating factor of such program. These fears were attributed to the hindsight argument that a truly effective program would have prevented the criminal act in the first place.[1028] Even today corporations cannot be sure if and how judges will apply the USSG, because the USSG are only advisory and provide considerable discretion with regard to the actually imposed fine.[1029] Nevertheless, a study found that corporations have expended "vigorous efforts" in the recent years to enhance "ethical performance and reduce organizational misconduct" since the enactment of the USSG-carrot-and-stick-approach.[1030]

One of the main purposes of the USSG is to induce corporations to engage in policing measures[1031] by providing for lower sanctions if corporations adopted effective policing measures and to "punish those that fail to do so"[1032]. On first glance, the corporation has an incentive to implement an effective compliance and ethics program which fulfills the requirements of sec. 8C2.1 USSG[1033] and to provide for measures enabling the corporation to fulfill the requirements of reporting, cooperation, and acceptance of responsibility. The USSG, however, do not provide for sufficient mitigation to induce optimal policing.[1034] Unlike provided by the USSG, the "mitigation amount should be larger [...] the greater the impact of opti-

1027 *Arlen*, 2011b, p. 21; *Arlen/Kraakman*, 72 N.Y.U.L. Rev. 687 (1997), p. 748.

1028 *Webb/Molo*, 71 Wash. U. L. Q. 375 (1993), p. 396; cf. *Guthrie/Rachlinski/Wistrich*, 86 Cornell L. Rev. 777 (2001), p. 799.

1029 *Arlen*, 2011b, at fn. 16.

1030 Ethics Resource Center, 2011, p. 29.

1031 Cf. USSG, Introductory Commentary to chapter 8.

1032 USSC, Ad Hoc Report, p. 8.

1033 Cf. *Murphy*, 87 Iowa L. Rev. 697 (2002), p. 703.

1034 *Arlen/Kraakman*, 72 N.Y.U.L. Rev. 687 (1997), p. 746; *Arlen*, 2011b, pp. 21-32.

mal policing measures on the probability of detection" in order to induce optimal policing.[1035] The mitigated sanction of the USSG, however, does not necessarily equal the social cost of the crime divided by the probability of detection when the corporation engages optimally in policing.[1036] Under the USSG, the mitigated sanction is "not necessarily based on the harm caused", but if so, it is limited to "pecuniary losses" and does not include "all the social costs of the harm".[1037] In addition, "to induce optimal deterrence, the total sanction (civil, criminal, and market-based) must equal the social cost of wrongdoing multiplied by one over the probability of detection".[1038] The USSG, in contrast, encompass only the criminal sanction and, therefore, will not induce corporations to engage in optimal prevention and policing measures.[1039] Under the current regime, every regulator with sanctioning authority would need to provide sanction mitigation to induce optimal policing measures.

The main issue of the limited scope of the USSG is that effective policing measures will identify and disclose information besides the information leading to criminal sanctions that could be used in other governmental proceedings or civil lawsuits.[1040] Hence, effective policing measures increase the probability of being subject to further sanctions beyond the criminal fine such as criminal restitution, government-imposed civil penalties, and private civil sanctions.[1041] Moreover, corporations may suffer from reputational and market penalties, as well as other collateral consequences especially when indicted or convicted of fraud.[1042] These further sanctions are significant as they often exceed the criminal fine by far.[1043] Thus, while based on the USSG, the actual criminal sanction may be reduced if the corporation adopts effective policing measures, the overall expected liability increases due to such measures[1044] leading to "significant" indirect costs for

1035 *Arlen/Kraakman*, 72 N.Y.U.L. Rev. 687 (1997), p. 746.
1036 *Arlen/Kraakman*, 72 N.Y.U.L. Rev. 687 (1997), p. 749.
1037 *Arlen/Kraakman*, 72 N.Y.U.L. Rev. 687 (1997), p. 749.
1038 *Arlen/Kraakman*, 72 N.Y.U.L. Rev. 687 (1997), p. 750. See for further details: *Arlen*, 2011a, p. 5 et seq.
1039 *Arlen/Kraakman*, 72 N.Y.U.L. Rev. 687 (1997), p. 750 et seq.
1040 USSC, Ad Hoc Report, p. 106; *Webb/Molo*, 71 Wash. U. L. Q. 375 (1993), p. 381.
1041 *Arlen*, 2011b, p. 30 et seq.; *id.*, 2011a, p. 7; *Arlen/Kraakman*, 72 N.Y.U.L. Rev. 687 (1997), p. 750.
1042 Cf. *Arlen*, 2011a, p. 8 et seq.
1043 Cf. *Arlen*, 2011a, at fn. 13; *Alexander/Arlen/Cohen*, 42 Journal of Law and Economics 393 (1999), p. 409 et seq.
1044 *Arlen*, 2011b, p. 31.

corporations[1045]. The increase of expected liability is known as the litigation dilemma[1046] which has an undermining effect on the incentives for corporations to implement policing measures first hand[1047], since the USSG do neither mitigate the direct costs for policing measures[1048] nor the full indirect costs[1049]. Corporations tend to implement policing measures reflecting a tradeoff of effectiveness and safety with regard to the litigation dilemma. This finding is consistent with the notion of the Ad Hoc Advisory Group of 2003 that, at the end, it would remain a business decision balancing the pros and cons of how to implement and engage in policing measures.[1050] The Ad Hoc Advisory Group of 2003 also recognized that the USSG provide for non-optimal incentives for corporations to engage in policing measures due to the litigation dilemma.[1051] Consistent with this finding is the criticism of the USSG-approach to be ineffective and to induce corporations to implement "cosmetic" compliance programs complying with the USSG only *prima facie* resulting in "paper tiger" compliance programs.[1052]

Furthermore, the USSG most intensely undermine the incentives to implement effective policing measures "when effective sanction mitigation is most needed".[1053] That is when managers of large firms are involved in wrongdoings.[1054] The USSC-reasoning to impose higher sanctions on large corporations is based on three principles.[1055] According to the USSC, corporations are more culpable if high-level management is involved in crime, especially with regard to large corporations, since the involvement or tolerance of criminal conduct of such management "is increasingly a breach of trust or abuse of position".[1056] The USSG increase the culpability score

1045 USSC, Ad Hoc Report, p. 106; cf. *Webb/Molo*, 71 Wash. U. L. Q. 375 (1993), p. 381.

1046 USSC, Ad Hoc Report, p. 106. See *supra* at chapter 5, B. II.

1047 *Arlen*, 2011b, p. 14; USSC, Ad Hoc Report, p. 116; cf. *Murphy*, 13 ETHIKOS 4 (2000).

1048 USSC, Ad Hoc Report, p. 108.

1049 Cf. *Arlen/Kraakman*, 72 N.Y.U.L. Rev. 687 (1997), p. 749 et seq.

1050 Cf. USSC, Ad Hoc Report, p. 120.

1051 Cf. USSC, Ad Hoc Report, p. 120.

1052 Cf. *Krawiec*, 81 Wash. U. L. Quarterly 487 (2003), p. 487 et seq. See on the critique on the USSG *infra* at chapter 16, A. I. 2. a) (2).

1053 *Arlen*, 2011b, p. 5.

1054 *Arlen*, 2011b, p. 5, p. 22 et seq., and p. 25 et seq.; cf. *Kraakman*, in: Encyclopedia of Law and Economics, p. 137.

1055 Cf. USSG, Background to sec. 8C2.5.

1056 Cf. USSG, Background to sec. 8C2.5.

gradually based upon the size of the corporation if high-level personnel is involved in criminal conduct or if criminal conduct has been tolerated throughout the corporation by substantial authority personnel (sec. 8C2.5 (b) USSG). Due to the increased culpability score, the mitigating effect of the USSG-mitigation factors is more reduced for large corporations compared to smaller corporations leading to a higher sanction for large corporations. Therefore, the expected sanction of large corporations is higher which further reduces the already insufficient incentives to engage in policing measures demonstrating the finding that higher sanctions do not solve the issue of insufficient incentives for engaging in policing measures.[1057] Thus, the USSG provide for even less optimal incentives to implement optimal policing measures in case of large corporations.

The incentives of the USSG are not undermined by the DOJ-policy of granting deferred and non-prosecution agreements.[1058] The USSG are still important for those corporations which are convicted by prosecutors despite the DOJ-policy[1059] or which are not confident to benefit from the policy[1060]. Due to general prevention of crime or other policy reasons, corporations may still be indicted even though they have an effective compliance program in place. Especially FCPA violations appear to be prosecuted despite full cooperation.[1061] Since corporations do not have a guarantee of never being indicted, the USSG still provide incentives.

In essence, the USSG do not provide for optimal incentives for corporations to engage in effective policing measures. As the law and economics analysis reveals, they do not provide for sufficient sanction mitigation to offset the increase of expected liability due to the litigation dilemma. Therefore, corporations only have non-optimal incentives to engage in effective policing measures inducing corporations to engage in "cosmetic" compliance measures which are not effective to deter corporate crime. Overall, it can only be concluded that corporations are aware of the need for compliance programs but fail to implement effective programs.

1057 Cf. *infra* at chapter 16, B. I. 2. a).
1058 See *infra* at chapter 5, D.
1059 *Arlen*, 2011b, p. 7.
1060 *Arlen*, 2011b, p. 18.
1061 *Arlen*, 2011b, at fn. 22.

IV. Conclusion

The USSG aim to provide just punishment and deterrence. In the context of internal control, the USSG provide incentives for corporations to engage in *ex ante* and *ex post* policing measures. Thereby, the USSG provide guidance on how to structure a compliance and ethics program by adhering to seven elements. Despite its aim to induce corporations to engage in effective policing measures, the USSG only provide corporations with non-optimal incentives to engage in policing measures which are not effective to deter corporate crime.

D. Department of Justice Enforcement Policy: Non- and Deferred Prosecution Agreements

The enforcement policy of the DOJ regarding corporations aims to encourage corporations to engage in self-policing, self-reporting, remediation, and cooperation by providing leniency in light of corporate crime. The prosecutors possess wide discretion to investigate and charge corporations reaching from granting amnesty or immunity from prosecution, via leniency and non- and deferred prosecution agreements, to indictment and conviction mostly through plea bargain rather than trial.[1062] In the process of reaching an agreement between the DOJ and the corporations, the sanctions are often negotiated.[1063]

The United States Attorney Manual (USAM) is designed to provide prosecutors internal DOJ guidance for the prosecution of violations of federal law (USAM 1-1.000). In the USAM Principles of Federal Prosecution of Business Organizations, prosecutors are provided with factors to determine whether to indict a corporation for misconduct of its employees. The USAM Principles of Federal Prosecution of Business Organizations are similar to the USSG with the important difference that the USSG only apply after indicting a corporation while the DOJ enforcement policy intervenes prior to indictment. As the USSG aim to provide incentives for corporation to engage in self-policing, self-reporting, remediation, and coopera-

1062 *Garrett*, 97 Va. L. Rev. 1775 (2011), p. 1788 et seq.
1063 *Henning*, 116 Yale L. J. Pocket Part 312 (2007), p. 314 et seq.

tion[1064], the severe adverse effects of indicting a corporation[1065] contradict these incentives. Due to necessary indictment and conviction of corporations for the USSG to be applicable, corporations face collateral penalties or reputational sanctions not imposed on corporations only subject to civil penalties.[1066] The evolvement of the DOJ enforcement policy is only due to the limitations of the USSG so that in a perfect corporate criminal liability environment the DOJ enforcement policy would be obsolete.[1067] Under the current USSG-regime, the magnitude of sanction mitigation available for federal prosecutors based on the DOJ enforcement policy is "significantly greater" than the amount available under the USSG.[1068]

Due to corporate criminal liability[1069] including a strong *respondeat superior* concept[1070] and since no corporation can ensure that no employee will violate the law, corporations have incentives to adhere to the reduced sentencing mechanisms provided by the DOJ.[1071] To establish liability of the corporation for illegal acts of its directors, officers, employees, and agents, the prosecutors have to show that the action of the individual were within the scope of her duties and were at least partially intended to benefit the corporation (9-28.200). The DOJ enforcement policy provides for a quasi duty-based corporate liability regime[1072] and is similar to the USSG-approach but has been named to be "superior" to the USSG when prosecutors provide leniency for corporations that fully cooperate and self-report without exceptions.[1073] Due to the superiority of the DOJ enforcement policy, the DOJ does not primarily rely on the USSG to induce corporate policing.[1074] Rather, the DOJ established an alternative sanctioning regime for corporations engaging in good corporate conduct since most corporations, which self-report, avoid formal conviction especially for financial crimes and other crimes involving fraud.[1075]

1064 See *supra* at chapter 5, C. II. 2.
1065 The demise of Arthur Andersen is an example of such effects (cf. *Garrett*, 97 Va. L. Rev. 1775 (2011), p. 1794). See also *infra* at chapter 16, A. I. 2. a) (4).
1066 *Arlen*, 2011b, p. 34; cf. *Garrett*, 93 Va. L. Rev. 853 (2007), p. 855.
1067 *Arlen*, 2011b, p. 32 et seq.
1068 *Arlen*, 2011b, p. 34.
1069 See *supra* at chapter 5, B.
1070 Cf. *U.S. v. Ionia Management* S.A., 555 F.3d 303 (2d Cir. 2009).
1071 Cf. *Twardy/Wenner*, 2009; *Garrett*, 93 Va. L. Rev. 853 (2007), p. 855.
1072 *Arlen*, 2011a, p. 10 et seq. See also *infra* at chapter 16, B. I. 2. d).
1073 *Arlen*, 2011a, at fn. 29.
1074 *Arlen*, 2011b, p. 5.
1075 *Arlen*, 2011b, at fn 19.

The DOJ enforcement policy is reflected in various memoranda. In 1999 for the first time, then-Deputy Attorney General *Eric H. Holder* issued the memorandum on Federal Prosecution of Corporations, commonly known as the Holder Memo, setting out guidelines for prosecutors whether to bring charges against corporations.[1076] In 2003, the Holder Memo has been revised by then-Deputy Attorney General *Larry D. Thompson* issued the memorandum on Principles of Federal Prosecution of Business Organizations, commonly known as the Thompson Memo, which sets main focuses on cooperation and effective corporate governance issues including compliance programs.[1077] In 2006, then-Deputy Attorney General *Paul J. McNulty* issued the revised memorandum on Principles of Federal Prosecution of Business Organizations, commonly known as the McNulty Memo, initiating more stringent criteria for prosecutors to request privileged information and instructs prosecutors not to consider corporations' advancements of attorneys' fees to employees when making a charging decision.[1078] The McNulty Memo also set a focus on preexisting compliance programs. In 2008, then-Deputy Attorney General *Mark R. Filip* revised the McNulty Memo by further heighten the standard regarding the waiver the of attorney-client privilege forbidding prosecutors to ask for such a waiver, and by transferring the Principles of Federal Prosecution of Business Organizations into the USAM[1079], commonly known as the Filip Memo, which is binding on all federal prosecutors within the DOJ.[1080] In 2015, then-Deputy Attorney General *Sally Q. Yates* issued a memorandum on Individual Accountability for Corporate Wrongdoing, commonly known as the Yates memo, refocusing the DOJ prosecution policy to the accountability of individuals as corporate wrongdoers and requiring corporations to provide to the DOJ "all relevant facts about individual misconduct" in order to be eligible for any credit for cooperation.[1081]

In case misconduct occurred within a corporation, prosecutors may credit corporations for engaging in the named actions by offering non- or deferred prosecution agreements instead of indicting the corporation. Through such agreements, the DOJ ensures the enforcement of the law while eliminating the adverse effects of indictment (USAM 9-28.1100). The

1076 DOJ, Holder Memo.
1077 DOJ, Thompson Memo.
1078 DOJ, McNulty Memo; DOJ, Press Release 2006.
1079 See DOJ, USAM, Filip Memo.
1080 DOJ, Press Release 2008.
1081 DOJ, Yates Memo.

DOJ enforces the law by imposing penalties including remediation and forfeiture as well as further requirements on corporations through non- and deferred prosecution agreements.[1082] Obtaining non- or deferred prosecution agreements depends on the discretion of the prosecutor who needs to produce in a pragmatic and reasoned way a fair outcome, taking into consideration, among other things, the DOJ's need to promote and ensure respect for the law (USAM 9-28.1100). Moreover, prosecutors require corporations through such agreements to implement compliance programs fulfilling a DOJ-concept for these programs, to alter the structure of the board of directors, and to accept and pay for an outside monitor[1083] which altogether has been termed as "structural reforms"[1084] The DOJ sets out guidelines how monitors will be selected and used in non- and deferred prosecution agreements to ensure consistency of the selection.[1085]

The wide discretion of prosecutors[1086] leads to strong incentives for corporations to cooperate.[1087] The incentives for cooperation raise concerns regarding self-incrimination of employees. The policy of the several enforcement agencies especially the DOJ to provide incentives for corporations to cooperate, including efforts to encourage employees to cooperate, potentially coerces employees to incriminate themselves by providing information which might be used against them at trial.[1088] In general, the policy is intended to use corporate efforts including internal investigations to obtain information to prosecute individual wrongdoer of the corporation. Hence, employees are increasingly indicted and convicted while only few corporations have been charged.[1089] The policy has been named "awkward partnering of governmental investigations with private corporate compliance efforts" leading to outsource corporate criminal investigations.[1090] While enforcement agencies depend on corporate policing efforts to effectively enforce the law[1091] and corporations have all rights to investi-

1082 *Arlen*, 2011b, p. 5 et seq.

1083 *Arlen*, in: Prosecutors in the Boardroom, p. 62. See *Garrett*, 93 Va. L. Rev. 853 (2007), p. 893 et seq.

1084 *Garrett*, 97 Va. L. Rev. 1775 (2011), p. 1797; *Garrett*, 93 Va. L. Rev. 853 (2007), p. 854 et seq.

1085 DOJ, Memo on Monitors.

1086 *Garrett*, 93 Va. L. Rev. 853 (2007), p. 913 et seq.

1087 *Garrett*, 97 Va. L. Rev. 1775 (2011), p. 1788.

1088 Cf. *Griffin*, 82 N.Y.U. L. Rev. 311 (2007), p. 311.

1089 *Griffin*, 82 N.Y.U. L. Rev. 311 (2007), p. 329 et seq.

1090 *Griffin*, 82 N.Y.U. L. Rev. 311 (2007), p. 311.

1091 See *infra* at chapter 16, B. I. 1.

gate their own business, employees have to be protected from incriminating themselves[1092]. Prosecutors and courts should not be allowed to circumvent the elementary privilege against self-incrimination through private investigations.[1093] In this regard, it has to be differentiated between investigations aiming on gathering information and documents absent the involvement of employees suspected of criminal conduct, and interrogating suspected employees as part of internal investigations initiated by the corporation. Corporate investigators have to be trained and required to advise suspected employees to their right to obtain own counsel. Such warnings have been named the *Upjohn* warnings[1094] which advise interrogated employees that corporate counsel represents the corporation and that information from conversations and interviews are only subject to the attorney-client privilege as far as the corporation does not choose to waive such privilege.[1095] In an internal investigation, the suspected employees face a dilemma of either remaining silent risking to be fired or fully cooperating risking indictment and conviction and most probably being fired after conviction.[1096] In this context, the changes within the Deputy Attorney General Memos regarding the attorney-client privilege are important. The guidance of the various memoranda regarding the waiver of the attorney-client privilege as part of the cooperation has been subject to several changes. In the Holder Memo and in the Thompson Memo, the waiver of the attorney-client privilege has been a vital part of the prosecutors' considerations.[1097] As mentioned above, the McNulty Memo restricted prosecutors to ask for such waiver and the Filip Memo forbade it altogether. With the Filip Memo, corporations are not under pressure to waive the attorney-

1092 Cf. *Griffin*, 82 N.Y.U. L. Rev. 311 (2007), p. 311.

1093 It has been argued that the criteria for the Fifth Amendment protections apply in the context of compliance investigations (*Griffin*, 82 N.Y.U. L. Rev. 311 (2007), p. 353). See for more details *Griffin*, 82 N.Y.U. L. Rev. 311 (2007), p. 358 et seq.

1094 The *Upjohn* warnings are named after the case *Upjohn v. United States*, 449 U.S. 383 (1981). While the case does not directly address the need to warn an employee, it addresses the criteria of internal corporate communication between employees and the GC being protected by the attorney-client privilege (*Id.*, p. 394 et seq.) and, thereby highlighted the limited reach of the attorney-client privilege for the employee, in case the corporation decides to waive its privilege, leading to the *Upjohn* warnings in order to set a clear framework for the internal investigation.

1095 *Griffin*, 82 N.Y.U. L. Rev. 311 (2007), p. 337.

1096 Cf. *Griffin*, 82 N.Y.U. L. Rev. 311 (2007), p. 356.

1097 Cf. DOJ, Holder Memo, at VI, B; DOJ, Thompson Memo, at VI, B.

client privilege which allows internal investigators to assure employees the privilege of their information easing the dilemma for suspected employees. Thus, employees do no longer face the cost of conviction based on self-incrimination leaving their choice of cooperation with internal investigators between non-cooperation with the threat of losing their job and cooperation also with the possibility of losing their job. In essence, without the threat of self-incrimination, the cost of telling the truth is "sharply" reduced leading to more truthful information.[1098] In this regard, however, the Yates memo with its emphasis on the accountability of individual corporate wrongdoers and the demand of the DOJ to be provided with all relevant facts about individual misconduct has the potential to undermine the willingness of corporate individuals to cooperate with internal investigators.

I. USAM Principles of Federal Prosecution of Business Organizations and the Incentive Structure to Comply with these Principles

In order to determine whether to indict a corporation, prosecutors have to consider general factors also applicable to individuals such as the sufficiency of the evidence and further factors set out in the USAM Principles of Federal Prosecution of Business Organizations accommodate for the "nature of the corporate 'person'" (USAM 9-28.300). The prosecutors have to consider ten corporation-specific factors according to USAM 9-28.300: (1) the nature and seriousness of the offense, (2) pervasiveness of wrongdoing within the corporation and complicity of management, (3) corporation's history of similar misconduct, (4) the corporation's willingness to cooperate in the investigation, (5) existence and effectiveness of an pre-existing compliance program, (6) timely and voluntary disclosure of misconduct, (7) remedial actions including any efforts to implement an effective corporate compliance program or to improve an existing one, to replace responsible management, to discipline or terminate wrongdoers, to pay restitution, and to cooperate with government agencies, (8) collateral consequences including harm caused, (9) adequacy of civil or regulatory enforcement actions, and (10) adequacy of prosecuting individuals. In essence, these factors resemble the factors set out in the USSG[1099] and by the

1098 *Griffin*, 82 N.Y.U. L. Rev. 311 (2007), p. 377.
1099 See *supra* at chapter 5, C. II.

SEC[1100] especially with regard to self-policing, self-reporting, remediation, and cooperation.

As depicted above, corporations have incentives to affect the factors prosecutors have to consider in order to increase the possibility to obtain leniency. Not all the factors, however, can be equally affected by corporations. With regard to the seriousness of the offense, an effective compliance program including monitoring will deter corporate crime. While management may set a focus of such program on serious offenses, such offenses will, nevertheless, occur showing the limited opportunities of management to affect the seriousness of the offense. Nevertheless, due to the focus of the DOJ and also the SEC on fraud and corruption[1101], corporations have to set a focus within their compliance programs on such crimes. Similarly, the pervasiveness of misconduct including the complicity of management may be affected to some extent through an effective compliance program in particular through the culture of compliance and the tone at the top as these elements of a compliance program may reduce or prevent misconduct throughout the corporation and within management. The corporation's history of similar misconduct can also be affected through a compliance program as its deterrence effect will reduce the likelihood of an extensive history of misconduct and management may set a focus of such program on preventing previous misconduct. With regard to disclosure and cooperation, corporations have to predetermine means to ensure timely disclosure of misconduct and voluntary and comprehensive cooperation with enforcement agencies. Cooperation with the prosecutors is an essential factor to avoid indictment. A reporting system as part of the compliance system is important to ensure that information about misconduct will reach appropriate divisions within the corporation to ensure timely disclosure of such misconduct to the appropriate enforcement agency. While cooperation only becomes relevant after prosecutors commenced their investigations, it is essential for corporations to prepare cooperation in advance by assigning authority for coordinating the cooperation to the GC or CCO and by establishing policies for how to cooperate and how to address employee cooperation. The policy for how to cooperate has to include procedures regarding the attorney-client privilege and the work product protection especially in regard to internal investigations. The DOJ values such important privileges and does not seek corporations to waive them but is interested in such information if the corporation voluntarily chooses to

1100 See *infra* at chapter 5, E.
1101 See *supra* at chapter 5, A. II.

convey privileged information to the prosecutors (USAM 9-28.710). Receiving credits for cooperation is not contingent upon any waiver of privileges (USAM 9-28.750). Rather, timely disclosure of the relevant facts of the misconduct is important (USAM 9-28.720).[1102] In most cases, corporations will obtain such facts through internal investigations (USAM 9-28.720(a)). While cooperation is an important mitigating factor for whether to indict a corporation, it is not by itself decisive so that a non-cooperative corporation may not be indicted and a comprehensively cooperating corporation may be indicted (USAM 9-28.720 and 9-28.740). An obvious sign of non-cooperation is engaging in obstructing the investigation which corporations have to address in its policies especially regarding employee cooperation. Advancing or reimbursing attorneys' fees or providing counsel to employees, officers, or directors under investigation or indictment does not jeopardize receiving credit for cooperation as long as such payments do not conflict with the criminal obstruction of justice statutes e.g. sec. 1503 of title 18 USC (USAM 9-28.730).

As mentioned above, an important factor for receiving credit is that corporations established an effective compliance program. Prosecutors may consider a corporation's timely and voluntary disclosure in evaluating the adequacy of the compliance program and management's commitment to such program (USAM 9-28.900). While a corporation may still be indicted despite an established compliance program[1103], the DOJ recognizes that no compliance program will prevent all misconduct (USAM 9-28.800). The decisive factors for the prosecutors to evaluate the program are whether it is "adequately designed for maximum effectiveness in preventing and detecting wrongdoing by employees and whether corporate management is enforcing the program or is tacitly encouraging or pressuring employees to engage in misconduct to achieve business objectives" (USAM 9-28.800). For evaluating the appropriateness of the compliance program, prosecutors have to consider similar factors as for considering to indict corporations and those factors set out in sec. 8B2.1 USSG.[1104] While the effectiveness of the compliance program is important within the DOJ enforcement policy,

---

1102 Such facts include how and when did the alleged misconduct occur, who promoted or approved it, and who was responsible for committing it. Further cooperation includes "providing non-privileged documents and other evidence, making witnesses available for interviews, and assisting in the interpretation of complex business records" (USAM 9-28.720, at fn. 1).

1103 Cf. *Arlen*, 2011b, p. 7.

1104 USAM 9-28.800 at fn. 1. See *supra* at chapter 5, C. II. 1. See also DOJ, Evaluation of Corporate Compliance Programs.

the DOJ does not require any specific elements for the compliance program. Moreover, prosecutors may consider whether the corporation has established corporate governance mechanisms such as independent and comprehensive reviews of corporate actions conducted by the directors, independent and accurately operating internal audit, and an information and reporting system which ensures timely and accurate information of directors to allow for informed decisions as required by *In re Caremark International Inc. Derivative Litigation* (USAM 9-28.800).[1105] With regard to restitution and remediation, corporations have to engage in such practices especially by improving the compliance program or disciplining wrongdoers for enhancing the likelihood to receive credit for such actions (USAM 9-28.1000). Prosecutors will also consider the collateral consequences of a corporate criminal conviction or indictment for deciding the appropriate actions in light of corporate misconduct. In this regard, widespread misconduct and complicity of high-level management are factors leading more likely to indictment (USAM 9-28.1100) which corporations may affect through effective compliance programs. Finally, prosecutors also have to consider whether appropriate civil or regulatory alternatives exist. Corporations may seek civil or regulatory enforcement actions for misconduct in order to avoid criminal indictment if such actions seem preferable. Whether such approach will be successful, however, is difficult to predict. Even though the factors prosecutors have to consider whether to indict a corporation are binding, all factors are only indicative and corporations cannot rely on the factors to avoid indictment. Hence, corporations having an effective compliance program or fully cooperated may still be indicted.[1106] Conversely, corporations may still receive full leniency even though they had no effective compliance program in place.[1107]

It follows that corporations have rather weak incentives to engage in effective *ex ante* policing measures such as the compliance program since the DOJ enforcement policy to grant non- and deferred prosecution agreements does not provide for reliable means to offset the detriments associated with the litigation dilemma.[1108] Moreover, the DOJ enforcement policy lacks to require benchmarks and external audits necessary to evaluate the effectiveness of the compliance program. Similar to courts in the USSG-context, prosecutors are likely to lack the expertise to assess the effective-

1105 698 A.2d 959 (Del. Ch. 1996). See *infra* at chapter 5, F. I.
1106 *Arlen*, 2011b, p. 7; *id.*, 2011a, p. 53.
1107 *Arlen*, 2011b, p. 33.
1108 See *supra* at chapter 5, B. II.

ness of compliance programs.[1109] Hence, corporations will "mimic" the DOJ requirements for a compliance program to receive leniency. Due to the focus of the DOJ on fraud and anti-corruption, corporations will engage in compliance programs with a focus on fraud and anti-corruption measures due to the increased enforcement but they do not have sufficient incentives to engage in truly effective anti-corruption compliance programs. Only implementation of a monitor required by an agreement with the DOJ ensures that the corporation engages in a more effective compliance program. Due to the DOJ enforcement policy of non- and deferred prosecution agreements, corporations have strong incentives to engage in *ex post* policing measures.

II. Conclusion

The DOJ provides with its policy, reflected in the USAM Principles of Federal Prosecution of Business Organizations, incentives for corporations to engage in self-policing, self-reporting, remediation, and cooperation which are similar to the USSG. Through non- and deferred prosecution agreements, the DOJ enforces the law without indicting corporations avoiding severe collateral penalties which is an important advantage compared to the USSG. While the DOJ enforcement policy is binding for prosecutors, the single factors to consider are only indicative rendering the decisions of prosecutors whether to indict unpredictable. The DOJ has used its wide discretion to require structural reforms within corporations. Corporations have strong incentives to adhere to the DOJ enforcement policy by engaging in *ex post* policing measures. The incentives to engage in effective compliance programs which fulfill the requirements of the USSG compliance and ethics program and focus on corruption and fraud, are weaker due to unpredictable decisions to receive leniency for engaging in *ex ante* policing measures. Nevertheless, corporations have incentives to implement means for cooperation, a reporting system, and corporate governance mechanisms.

1109 See also *Engelhart*, Sanktionierung, p. 236.

E. SEC Enforcement Policy: Seaboard Report

The SEC enforcement and sentencing policy will provide insight for corporations for how to receive leniency in case of misconduct and when to expect harsh punishments. In 2001, the SEC published in its investigation report Release No. 44969, commonly known as the Seaboard Report, criteria it will employ to determine whether to bring actions against listed corporations for violations of securities law or how to credit corporations for good corporate behavior.[1110] Similarly, the SEC provides for determinants it will consider exercising its corporate penalty authority.[1111] Both documents provide incentives for corporations to engage in favorable behavior with regard to the provided criteria. In essence, both documents align their criteria with the structure and requirements of the USSG[1112]. The SEC aims to encourage self-policing efforts and tries to foster self-reporting, remediation, and cooperation.[1113] Moreover, through corporate penalties, the SEC tries to achieve effective deterrence to encourage the implementation of compliance programs.[1114] Through self-policing and especially through self-reporting and cooperation, the SEC will receive needed information to enforce securities law. In general, SEC enforcement faces enormous difficulties to learn from potential securities law violations and to receive information from suspected corporations since corporations have greater incentives to conceal and hide information in light of potential sanctions.[1115] With regard to securities law violations of provisions which are audited by the external auditors, the SEC can also rely on the external auditors to provide information which may lead to SEC enforcement actions. In order to increase the effectiveness of SEC enforcement, the SEC provides incentives for corporations to engage in self-policing, self-reporting, and cooperation. In contrast to the USSG, the SEC has less need to provide for incentives for corporations to implement effective internal controls including compliance programs as these systems are mandatory with regard to disclosure controls and procedures and internal control over financial reporting as required by SOX. Hence, the SEC states that providing more transparency on how it determines sanctions as the reason to publish

1110 SEC Release No. 44969.
1111 SEC Statement Concerning Financial Penalties.
1112 See *supra* at chapter 5, C. II.
1113 SEC Release No. 44969.
1114 SEC Statement Concerning Financial Penalties.
1115 See *supra* at chapter 5, B. II.

its statement on corporate penalties.[1116] With the provided guidance on sanctioning, corporations will better understand how they will profit from self-policing leading to more accurate compliance with the mandates for internal controls and compliance programs. In addition, the SEC provides guidance on how to receive credit for self-reporting and cooperation.

In the Seaboard Report, the SEC identifies factors it will consider to credit corporations for good corporate behavior, i.e. to provide incentives for corporations to proactively respond to the discovery of any misconduct[1117]. Such credit may reach from the "extraordinary" step to take no enforcement actions at all, to bringing reduced charges, or seeking lighter sanctions.[1118] The four key factors the SEC will consider are: self-policing, self-reporting, remediation, and cooperation.[1119] The SEC lists criteria and questions it will consider to determine whether and how to credit corporations. In order to receive such credit, corporations have to align their compliance efforts with the following criteria. With regard to self-policing, the SEC will consider the duration, extent and willfulness of the misconduct, the damage caused to investors, the effectiveness of the tone at the top, whether senior personnel was involved, and the effectiveness of the compliance program especially with regard to detecting and responding to violations.[1120] It follows from these criteria that corporations have to have an effective compliance program including an appropriate tone at the top which ensure prevention and timely detection of violations in order to minimize misconduct in general and especially from senior management, and to minimize the harm caused. With regard to self-reporting, the SEC will consider the timeliness and completeness of the corporation's disclosure of the misconduct including the efforts taken to fully investigate potential misconduct and completely providing the results and documents to the SEC.[1121] The SEC prefers the internal investigation to be conducted by outside counsel unfamiliar with the corporation and supervised by the outside directors.[1122] With regard to remediation, the SEC credits efforts of the corporation to strengthen controls and procedures to prevent the reoccurrence of similar misconduct and compensation efforts for the victims.[1123]

1116 SEC Statement Concerning Financial Penalties.
1117 Cf. *Frey*, 2002.
1118 SEC Release No. 44969.
1119 SEC Release No. 44969.
1120 SEC Release No. 44969; cf. *Frey*, 2002.
1121 SEC Release No. 44969.
1122 SEC Release No. 44969.
1123 SEC Release No. 44969.

With regard to cooperation, the SEC expects the corporation to cooperate in a complete and timely manner, and to ask and encourage employees to cooperate with the SEC.[1124] In addition, the SEC statement on how the SEC will exercise its corporate penalty authority provides insight for corporations on the SEC determinants. In essence, the SEC will consider similar factors as indicated by the Seaboard Report. Factors leading to a high corporate penalty are: need of corporate penalty to compensate victims other than shareholders including large extent of harm done to innocent parties; need of deterring similar conduct; widespread complicity in the violation throughout the corporation; intentional, fraudulent behavior; violation difficult to detect leading to the need of a high level of deterrence through a corporate penalty; no remedial steps taken; no reporting of violations; and no cooperation.[1125] In order to influence the determinants, corporations have to take the same measures as noted with regard to the Seaboard Report. An effective compliance program will deter criminal behavior and provides for timely detection of the remaining violations, mostly committed by single individuals, preventing a large extent of harm caused. Remedial steps as well as self-reporting and cooperation are essential for receiving leniency.

Imposing a high sanction on corporations for violations which are difficult to detect, however, does not provide much benefit since higher deterrence only provides for more incentives for the corporation to try to detect such violations. Since such violations are still difficult to detect, more effort on detection will not provide much benefit. Corporations will then try to put more effort into the prevention of such violations which will provide some benefits as some potential violators will be deterred from committing such violations but since they are still difficult to detect, deterring potential violators has its limits. Thus, the SEC should consider whether corporations maintained an effective compliance program with regard to violations which are difficult to detect, and, if so, should accept the limits of these programs without imposing a higher sanction with limited use on corporations. With the taken approach to provide for guidance on its enforcement considerations, the SEC ensures that each corporation may be able to determine how to comply with the SEC criteria and, therefore, avoids a one-size-fits-all approach.

1124 SEC Release No. 44969.
1125 SEC Statement Concerning Financial Penalties.

Similar to the USSG[1126], the information on misconduct produced by internal controls and compliance programs has to be immediately reported to the SEC for receiving leniency.[1127] In light of the litigation dilemma, the SEC has to provide for sanction mitigation which equals the effect of an effective compliance program on the probability that any crime committed will be detected and sanctioned in order to induce corporations to optimally engage in *ex ante* policing measures. In contrast to the USSG, securities law requires the implementation of effective internal controls combined with a sanction for failing to do so which tremendously reduces the amount of needed sanction mitigation to induce corporations to engage in effective internal controls compared to the USSG. Nevertheless, the SEC has to account for the increased probability that the SEC will investigate, based on the reported misconduct, that the corporation failed to implement effective internal controls leading to an increase expected liability for failing to comply with the internal control related mandates.

SEC does not provide for a more detailed guidance on how it will calculate sentences in contrast to the USSG. But previous SEC enforcement actions provide insight how the SEC will credit cooperation and punishes non-cooperation. The enforcement actions after the Seaboard Report demonstrate that the SEC "will severely penalize a [corporation] that does not cooperate"[1128] and will take "no action, or settle on non-fraud charges, based at least in part on the [corporations'] cooperation"[1129]. A comprehensive study analyzing the conditions under which the SEC exercises leniency revealed that cooperation increases the likelihood for corporations of being sanctioned but cooperation and prompt disclosure lower the monetary penalty.[1130] This finding is in line with the multi-tiered duty-based liability regime[1131] requiring to unbundle the granting of leniency for each policing measures so that leniency will be provided for each policing measure separately leading to a reduced sanction. Therefore, corporations have incentives to engage in cooperation despite failing to receive leniency for other policing measures. In general, the insight into the SEC enforcement actions shows that corporations have incentives to comply with

1126 See sec. 8C2.5 (f)(2) USSG and *supra* at chapter 5, C. I.
1127 SEC Release No. 44969.
1128 *McDermott/Smith*, 2007, p. 2. See e.g. SEC Release No. 2002-52; SEC Release No. 2004-104.
1129 *McDermott/Smith*, 2007, p. 4. See e.g. SEC Release No. 52370; SEC Release No. 2006-2.
1130 *Files*, 2011.
1131 See *infra* at chapter 16, B. I. 2. d).

the provided guidance since the SEC will grant leniency if the corporation's compliance performance meets the SEC's thresholds while the SEC has to ensure sufficient sanction mitigation for corporations in order to increase the effectiveness of its enforcement. Thus, corporations have incentives to engage in effective self-policing, self-reporting, remediation, and cooperation in light of securities law violations.

F. General Corporate Law of Delaware

In the U.S., state corporate law regulates the internal corporate governance structure of corporations.[1132] The General Corporate Law of Delaware (DGCL) is widely regarded as the most important corporate law in the U.S.[1133] The majority of all U.S. corporations is incorporated in Delaware.[1134] While the DGCL does not apply to German corporations listed on the NYSE, its dominance within the U.S. shapes U.S. best practice and provides insight into the cultural background of corporate governance in the U.S. which is relevant for the impact analysis.

Prior to the corporate scandals of the 2000s, Delaware did not impose strict rules on directors or officers regarding the governance of corporations[1135] and only few rules for the board of directors and the audit committee existed[1136]. Even, in light of the corporate scandals, Delaware kept mainly silent in addressing the issues revealed by the scandals.[1137] Nevertheless, Delaware courts aggravated their corporate governance standards after the scandals. *In re Walt Disney Co.*[1138] which involves executive compensation and the duty of care of directors, the Delaware Court of Chancery denied a motion to dismiss. The defendants moved for this motion on the basis that the plaintiff shareholders did neither demand the board to enforce a corporate right nor that such a demand had been excused based on futility.[1139] Despite some undisputed involvement of the

---

1132 Cf. *Grossman*, 12 Fordham J. Corp. & Fin. L. 393 (2007), p. 396.

1133 Cf. *Thompson*, 40 Hous. L. Rev. 99 (2003), p. 108; *Bebchuk/Cohen*, 46 J. L. & Econ. 383 (2003), p. 391.

1134 Cf. *Grossman*, 12 Fordham J. Corp. & Fin. L. 393 (2007), p. 396 et seq.; *Langevoort*, 42 Wake Forest L. Rev. 627 (2007), p. 631.

1135 *Sale*, 89 Cornell L. Rev. 456 (2004), p. 458.

1136 *Moeller*, SOX Internal Controls, p. 29.

1137 Cf. *Sale*, 89 Cornell L. Rev. 456 (2004), p. 458.

1138 825 A.2d 275 (Del. Ch. 2003).

1139 See on futility *Aronson v. Lewis*, 473 A.2d 805, p. 812 (Del. 1984).

board in the compensation package, the court held that the directors failed to exercise "*any* business judgment or [make] *any* good faith attempt to fulfill [their] fiduciary duties".[1140] It can be argued that, absent the scandals, the motion to dismiss had been granted. Thus, *Disney* illustrates a shift in Delaware's attitude towards directors.[1141] The second case in which a Delaware court ruled on a corporate governance issue is *In re Oracle Corp.*[1142] which involves the independence of special litigation committees. In order to address a shareholder derivatives suit, that four directors were engaged in insider trading, the corporation formed a special litigation committee which decided to dismiss the action. The court denied a motion to dismiss due to the lack of independence of the special litigation committee deciding upon the derivative suit.[1143]

Delaware statutory law mandates that the board of directors is the ultimate governing body of the corporation which "shall be managed by or under the direction of a board of directors" (sec. 141(a) DGCL). Thus, the directors have the duty to control the corporation.[1144] This duty encompasses internal controls and compliance with law.[1145] The Delaware corporate statute itself, however, does not provide for specific insight into the duties of directors and management regarding internal control or compliance. It mainly addresses the general corporate governance structure but leaves the incorporators or those who are able to amend the certificate of incorporation or the by-laws with significant power to structure the corporate governance. Only "markets or private ordering"[1146] may set a constraint to this power.[1147] This leaves the board of directors with broad discretion to manage and control the corporation.

1140 *In re Walt Disney*, 825 A.2d 275 (Del. Ch. 2003), p. 287 (emphasis in original).

1141 *Johnson/Sides*, 30 Wm. Mitchell L. Rev. 1149 (2004), p. 1203.

1142 824 A.2d 917 (Del. Ch. 2003).

1143 *Id.* at p. 948.

1144 *Sale*, 89 Cornell L. Rev. 456 (2004), p. 460 et seq.; *Veasey*, 28 Iowa J. Corp. L. 441 (2003), p. 444.

1145 See *In re Caremark International Inc. Derivative Litigation*, 698 A.2d 959 (Del. Ch. 1996); *Stone v. Ritter*, 911 A.2d 362 (Del. 2006).

1146 *Thompson*, 40 Hous. L. Rev. 99 (2003), p. 109.

1147 Especially in widely held public corporations, the power to set the governance structure is highly likely to stay with the management due to a lack of unified interests among shareholders. Thus, the governed can choose their rules of governance which contains a significant conflict of interest. Henceforth, the current law is a recipe for moral hazard derived from the separation of ownership and control (in general: *Berle/Means*, Corporation).

In fulfilling their task, directors owe duties to the corporation and its shareholders, i.e. the fiduciary duty of loyalty and the duty of care. The duty of loyalty requires directors to act in a good faith effort to advance the interests of the corporation including the "corporate opportunity doctrine"[1148] and "conflicting interest transactions"[1149]. In the case *Stone v. Ritter*, it became clear that good faith is not a separate fiduciary duty but a component of the duty of loyalty.[1150] With regard to the duty of care, directors have to act with the care of a prudent person in a like position would do. Mainly, courts test if the duty of care has been breached by applying the business judgment rule. The standard of care under the business judgment rule for director liability is "gross negligence".[1151] Due to the business judgment rule, it is presumed that directors acted on an informed basis, in good faith and in the best interest of the corporation when making business decisions.[1152] Therefore, directors have to inform themselves "prior to making a business decision, of all material information reasonably available to them".[1153] In order to rebut this presumption, plaintiffs have to show that the directors were interested in the transaction or disloyal to the corporation.[1154] In some decisions, the courts also use the criterion of independence in order to determine if the directors are protected by the business judgment rule.[1155] If a majority of directors is regarded as disinterested or independent in a transaction, the business judgment rule generally prevails.[1156] Since the statutory law of Delaware does not address internal control and compliance with law, the Delaware courts scrutinize the conduct of directors in light of the named duties.

I. Case Law Addressing Internal Control and Compliance with Law

Delaware case law addresses the issues of internal controls and compliance. The first case in which a Delaware court addressed the issues, especially the

1148 See *O'Kelley/Thompson*, Corporations, p. 247 et seq.
1149 See *O'Kelley/Thompson*, Corporations, p. 270 et seq.
1150 911 A.2d 362, p. 370 (Del. 2006).
1151 *Smith v. van Gorkom*, 488 A.2d 858, p. 873; *Aronson v. Lewis*, 473 A.2d 805, p. 812.
1152 *Aronson v. Lewis*, 473 A.2d 805, p. 812.
1153 *Smith v. van Gorkom*, 488 A.2d 858, p. 870.
1154 *Id.* at p. 812.
1155 See e.g. *id.* at p. 816.
1156 *Abikoff*, Corporate Governance, § 3.02.

directors' duty to oversee legal compliance, is the seminal case *In re Caremark International Inc. Derivative Litigation*.[1157] The court finds that directors have an "obligation to be reasonably informed" and the duty "to exercise reasonable oversight"[1158]. Therefore, information and reporting systems have to exist in the corporation which are reasonably designed to provide management and the board of directors with timely, accurate information to reach informed judgments about "the corporation's compliance with law and its business performance".[1159] Following this case, directors breach their duty of care if they do not have a compliance structure in place which assures proper monitoring and oversight of the corporation.[1160] The *Caremark* case strengthened corporate governance and in particular internal control requirements since the directors cannot exclusively rely on reports that reach them. The board has to set up a structure which actually ensures that the directors receive information regardless of any reports from the officers. Therefore, the *Caremark* ruling is different from the earlier Delaware Supreme Court case *Graham v. Allis-Chalmers Mfg. Co.*[1161] which held that directors are immune from liability under the duty to supervise, unless they are notified, if they rely on the officers' assurance that no problem exist. As the increase of duty for directors due to *Caremark* implies, the liability of directors should also increase. In *Caremark*, however, it is held that directors are only liable for failing "to attempt in good faith to assure that a corporate information and reporting system, which the board concludes is adequate, exists, [...] render[ing] a director liable for losses caused by non-compliance with applicable legal standards"[1162], i.e. if the directors acted in bad faith. In this regard, bad faith requires inaction amounting to a sustained or systematic failure of the board of directors in exercising reasonable oversight[1163] shielding directors largely from liability[1164].

In a subsequent case, the Delaware Supreme Court ruled in *Brehm v. Eisner*[1165] that "corporate governance practices for boards of directors that go beyond the minimal legal requirements of the corporation law are highly

---

1157 698 A.2d 959 (Del. Ch. 1996).
1158 *Id.* at p. 970.
1159 *Id.* at p. 970.
1160 *Arlen*, 2008, p. 3.
1161 188 A.2d 125, p. 130 (Del. 1963).
1162 698 A.2d 959 (Del. Ch. 1996), p. 970.
1163 698 A.2d 959 (Del. Ch. 1996), p. 971.
1164 *Arlen*, 2008, p. 4; cf. 698 A.2d 959 (Del. Ch. 1996), p. 971.
1165 746 A.2d 244 (Del. 2000).

desirable. But they are not required by the corporation law and do not define standards of liability"[1166]. This ruling clearly illustrates Delaware's position on corporate governance up until the scandals of the 2000s. Moreover, corporations are able to opt into an exculpation of liability for the directors by a vote of the shareholders pursuant to sec. 102(b)(7) DGCL which reduces the liability. Even though most directors might be exculpated in light of sec. 102(b)(7) DGCL, they still have to act in good faith and within their duty of loyalty in order to be exculpated. Also, a knowing violation of law is not covered by this exculpation either.[1167] Thus, directors could be exculpated from liability with regard to *Caremark* duties since *Caremark* located such duties within the duty of care. In the *Guttman v. Huang*[1168] case, however, the Chancery Court of Delaware relocated the so-called *Caremark* claims from the duty of care to the duty of loyalty which has been affirmed by *Stone v. Ritter*[1169].[1170] Thus, the *Caremark* claims can no longer be exculpated by sec. 102(b)(7) DGCL.

In the case of *Stone v. Ritter*[1171], the Delaware Supreme Court affirmed the ruling of *Caremark*. The Court held that "where directors fail to act in the face of a known duty to act, [...], they breach their duty of loyalty [...]"[1172]. Thus, plaintiffs have to show that the directors had knowledge of breaching their duty of loyalty which includes to act in good faith.[1173] Thereby, the Supreme Court established the duty to monitor as being part of the duty of loyalty in contrast to *Caremark*. The duty of loyalty requires directors to implement information and reporting systems and actually have to use such systems.[1174] But the efforts are not very high which the board of directors has to take. The Court held that the conditions for director oversight liability are either "(a) the directors utterly failed to implement any reporting or information system or controls; *or* (b) having implemented such a system or controls, consciously failed to monitor or oversee its operations thus disabling themselves from being informed of risks or problems requiring their attention".[1175] In affirming *Caremark*, the

1166 *Id.* at p. 256.
1167 *Chandler/Strine*, 152 U. Pa. L. Rev. 953 (2003), at fn. 90.
1168 823 A.2d 492, p. 506 (Del. Ch. 2003).
1169 911 A.2d 362, p. 365.
1170 Cf. *Bainbridge*, 34 J. Corp. L. 967 (2009), p. 975 et seq.
1171 911 A.2d 362, p. 369 (Del. 2006).
1172 *Id.* at p. 370.
1173 *Id.*
1174 *Id.*
1175 911 A.2d 362, p. 370 (emphasis in original).

Supreme Court shows that Chancellor Allen's decision to enhance the duties of directors regarding corporate governance and internal controls is in line with Delaware law. Nevertheless, the threshold for plaintiffs to actually pass the pleading stage is very high.[1176] They have to show that a pre-suit demand had been futile by showing that the directors would not have been independent to decide upon legal proceedings of the corporation.[1177] In order to show this, plaintiffs have to allege facts that the directors knowingly breached their duty of loyalty.[1178] It is not sufficient, however, to show that the internal controls of the corporation are inadequate.[1179] The high standard mostly eliminates the threat of liability and, therefore, any incentive to fulfill the required duty to monitor.[1180] The case *American International Group v. Greenberg* shows, however, that pleading a breach of the duty of loyalty based on the failure to monitor is feasible.[1181]

The liability risk for directors, especially for outside directors[1182], is further reduced, if not eliminated, through D&O insurance. Due to sec. 145(g) DGCL, corporations are empowered to purchase D&O insurance. There are no statutory limits on the coverage of such insurance.[1183] In most cases, the insurance contract will exclude coverage for deliberate fraud or personal profit[1184] but the exclusions are narrower than the duty of loyalty exculpation of sec. 102(b)(7) DGCL[1185] and insurance corporations seem to be eager to substantially participate in settlements despite the contractually exculpation of fraud[1186]. Also, costs of litigation are likely to be borne by the corporation.[1187] Since direct monetary costs of liability seem to be negligible for directors, the only remaining significant cost for failing to

---

1176 Cf. *Aronson v. Lewis*, 473 A.2d 805, p. 812 (Del. 1984).
1177 *Id.*
1178 *Id.*
1179 911 A.2d 362, p. 365.
1180 *Arlen*, 2008, p. 4 et seq.; *Pan*, 38 Fla. St. U. L. Rev. 209 (2011), p. 210.
1181 *American International Group v. Greenberg*, 965 A.2d 763, p. 799.
1182 Cf. *Black/Cheffins/Klausner*, 58 Stan. L. Rev. 1055 (2006).
1183 *Pan*, 2011, p. 245.
1184 *Pan*, 2011, p. 245; *Black/Cheffins/Klausner*, 58 Stan. L. Rev. 1055 (2006), p. 1086; cf. *O'Kelley/Thompson*, Corporations, p. 400; *Langevoort*, 42 Wake Forest L. Rev. 627 (2007), p. 651.
1185 *Black/Cheffins/Klausner*, 58 Stan. L. Rev. 1055 (2006), p. 1086.
1186 *Langevoort*, 42 Wake Forest L. Rev. 627 (2007), p. 651.
1187 *Pan*, 38 Fla. St. U. L. Rev. 209 (2011), p. 246.

comply with the duty to monitor is loss of reputation[1188] which has not been sufficient to induce appropriate compliance of directors with their duty to monitor[1189]. A further important aspect leads to insufficient director oversight. Delaware case law does not provide for details on the mandates for reporting and information systems.[1190] Therefore, *Caremark* and *Ritter* do not induce directors to adequately monitor legal compliance due to the lack of requiring specific mandates for how to monitor and due to insufficient incentives for complying with the duty to monitor resulting from the bad faith liability standard.[1191]

Despite the lack of requiring specific mandates, directors have to implement a compliance system constituting of information and reporting systems in order to fulfill the duty to monitor which they conclude – protected under the business judgment rule – to be adequate and which enables the directors to receive inside and outside information in order to respond to red flags.[1192] Thereby, the compliance system does not have to "prevent all losses" for being adequate.[1193] Receiving information includes that directors have to request and receive appropriate information from management in a timely manner and prior to board meetings.[1194] In that way, the good-faith obligation requires more than the implementing and monitoring a compliance system. Instead, directors have to be vigilant with regard to their corporation and others in the industry and have to interrogate further as indicated especially in face of red flags.[1195]

A further important case of Delaware regarding internal controls, compliance with law, and risk assessment, is *In re Citigroup Inc. Shareholder Derivative Litigation*[1196]. In this case Chancellor Chandler's view of Delaware's law demonstrates that the courts are not willing to further enhance the duties of directors particularly with regard to internal control issues. The plaintiff in *Citigroup* tried to extend the so-called *Caremark*

1188 *Pan*, 38 Fla. St. U. L. Rev. 209 (2011), p. 246 et seq.; cf. *Black/Cheffins/Klausner*, 58 Stan. L. Rev. 1055 (2006), p. 1099. See also *Langevoort*, 42 Wake Forest L. Rev. 627 (2007), passim; *Fich/Shivdasani*, 2006, passim; *Alexander*, 42 J.L. & Econ. 489 (1999).

1189 Cf. *Arlen*, 2008, p. 22.

1190 *Caremark*, 698 A.2d 959 (Del. Ch. 1996), p. 970; cf. *Bainbridge*, 34 J. Corp. L. 967 (2009), p. 986; *Arlen*, 2008, p. 3.

1191 *Arlen*, 2008, p. 22.

1192 Cf. *Sale*, 32 Del. J. Corp. L. 719 (2007), p. 733.

1193 698 A.2d 959 (Del. Ch. 1996), at fn. 27.

1194 Cf. *Sale*, 32 Del. J. Corp. L. 719 (2007), p. 743 et seq.

1195 *Sale*, 32 Del. J. Corp. L. 719 (2007), p. 734.

1196 964 A.2d 106 (Del. Ch. 2009).

claims to the board's failure to properly monitor the corporation's business risk.[1197] The court denied the extension of the *Caremark* claims by noting that "[t]here are significant differences between failing to oversee employee fraudulent or criminal conduct and failing to recognize the extent of a [corporation]'s business risk."[1198] The court argues that the assessment of business risk is part of business judgment and states that "[o]versight duties under Delaware law are not designed [...] to properly evaluate business risk".[1199] Despite the ruling in *Citigroup*, it has been argued that *Caremark* claims for failing to adopt and use risk management systems are, nevertheless, feasible since risk management "does not differ in kind" but "does differ in degree" from compliance with law cases.[1200] But, *Caremark* claims on the ground of a failing risk management system would be "the most difficult variant of *Caremark* claims".[1201] This view is not without merit but remains mostly theoretical since *Citigroup* has been followed by *In re Goldman Sachs Group, Shareholder Litigation*[1202] underlining the reluctance of Delaware's courts to find monitoring business risks to be part of the duty to monitor. The Court did not reach this issue, however, since plaintiffs failed to establish *Caremark* claims altogether, leaving at least the theoretical possibility for *Caremark* claims on the ground of failing to monitor business risks. While this theoretical possibility exists, *Goldman* shows that it is currently highly unlikely that such claims will succeed. *Caremark* and affirmative *Stone v. Ritter* definitely changed the perception of directors towards internal controls and compliance with law. The two cases provide a starting point to develop standards of internal control systems of significant magnitude. *Citibank* and *Goldman*, on the contrary, show the generally presumed reluctance of Delaware courts to aggravate the standards of corporate governance and in particular the standards for internal controls and risk assessment. Since risk assessment is one vital part of COSO I, the reluctance of Delaware's courts to require directors to monitor and assess the corporation's business risk shows that the internal control requirements of Delaware corporate law are not sufficient, at least with regard to large, listed corporations, to address the issues related to internal controls appropriately.

1197 *Id.* at p. 123.
1198 964 A.2d 106, p. 130.
1199 *Id.* at p. 131.
1200 *Bainbridge*, 34 J. Corp. L. 967 (2009), pp. 979 and 990.
1201 *Bainbridge*, 34 J. Corp. L. 967 (2009), p. 990 (emphasis in original).
1202 2011 Del. Ch. LEXIS 151, p. 71 et seq.

II. Conclusion

The current law of Delaware imposes a duty on directors to monitor as part of the duty of loyalty by using information and reporting systems. The likelihood of liability for failing to comply with the duty to monitor, however, is very low since all decisions related to the duty to monitor are protected by the business judgment rule, and D&O insurance eliminates most of the remaining monetary risks. Only the cost of reputational losses mainly remains as an incentive for directors to adequately monitor which has not proven to be sufficient to induce appropriate monitoring by directors. The recent case history suggests that the current status of Delaware law will only change in long time rather than in short time, if at all.

Chapter 6: Key Aspects of and Incentives to Engage in Internal Control Systems

The forgoing analysis considered important aspects of the respective U.S. regulatory regime regarding internal control systems and incentives for corporations to engage in internal control. Before addressing the overall incentives for corporations to engage in internal control systems, key aspects of effective internal control systems will be depicted.

A. Key Aspects of Internal Control

The conducted analysis shows an important aspect for corporations listed on the NYSE. Most of the U.S. regulation either builds on COSO I, has been influenced by COSO I, or at least resembles COSO I, so that none of the required elements is contradictory. It follows that the design of internal control systems should be built on COSO I considering the specific regulatory mandates and best practice as portrayed in Chapters 4 and 5. Besides the elements of internal control, the effectiveness and efficiency of internal control and the functions and responsibilities within internal control are important aspects.

I. Effectiveness and Efficiency of Internal Control

The effectiveness of internal control is essential. Effective internal control is important to adhere to the SOX requirements and to receive leniency for violations of laws. In general, the effectiveness of internal control encompasses design and operation and depends largely on the skills and effort of the people within the corporation. Effective internal controls need personnel qualified for executing controls and sensitive for irregularities, good reporting lines, active officers designing internal control and addressing these irregularities, capable mid level management for monitoring and executing received directives, and an active and investigative board of directors. The design effectiveness and the continuing effectiveness of internal control depend on the effort of officers to design effective internal control and to adjust the design to changes, and on the oversight of the board of directors. The operation effectiveness of internal control depends to a large degree on the personnel executing the controls and mid management involved in the execution and day-to-day monitoring. Appropriate execution is essential as well as reporting of any red flag which enables the officers to address the raised issues. A system has to ensure that red flags are not neglected or disregarded and has to be able to capture, process, and evaluate red flags. Also, management has to ensure that all controls are operated by personnel equipped with the necessary authority and competence.

The determination whether internal control is effective depends on the judgment of the board of directors and management that they have reasonable assurance that the corporation's operations objectives are achieved, the financial statements are prepared reliably, and the laws and regulations are complied with. COSO I does not provide for thresholds preventing management to conclude internal control to be effective.[1203] With regard to SOX's internal control over financial reporting, management is prevented from concluding internal control over financial reporting to be effective if management's assessment of the effectiveness identified one or more material weaknesses. In light of the definition of material weakness, management has to determine whether there is a reasonable possibility that the deficient controls will fail to prevent or detect a misstatement of a financial statement. A system is effective if risks are addressed by at least one adequate control operating effectively.

With regard to efficient internal control, the documentation process and monitoring are important. Documentation is most efficiently carried out during the implementation process and only those controls have to be documented which management considered adequate and sufficient to address risks. Most importantly, focusing on monitoring provides an efficient approach to evaluate the effectiveness of internal control for reporting purposes. Monitoring reduces the costs of gaining continued assurance that internal control operates effectively.

II. Functions and Responsibilities within Internal Control Systems

An important element of internal control is to clearly assign responsibilities. With regard to the board of directors, the audit committee, the officers, the CCO, the GC and internal audit, best practice evolved regarding internal control specific functions and related scope of responsibility. For

1203 *Gupta/Leech*, 3 Int. J. Disclosure and Governance 27 (2006), p. 33.

effective compliance related internal control, building a strong partnership between internal audit, and the compliance and legal divisions is essential[1204] which requires clear assignments of responsibilities for the different divisions. In this regard, the audit committee together with a strong internal audit is best equipped to identify and act in instances when management overrides internal controls or seeks to misrepresent financial results.

1. Board of Directors and the Audit Committee

The board of directors has the duty to control the corporation which includes internal control and compliance with law. Thereby, monitoring is important including to launch investigations, if indicated.[1205] One part of the oversight activities of the board of directors is to determine whether the internal control system including compliance implemented by management is effective by understanding the risks of the corporation and how the officers manage and mitigate those risks together with the assessment of the officers' determination of the effectiveness of the internal control system. The overall responsibility for compliance related internal controls has to be assigned to at least one independent director or to the audit committee in which one member should have a leading position regarding compliance. The directors have to promote a culture of compliance that encourages ethical conduct and a commitment to compliance with law, and have to use their influence on management in order to establish the adequate amount of integrity and ethical values within the internal control system. Since management might be able to override controls, and ignore or stifle communications, the board of directors has to have unrestricted upwards communication channels to all personnel of the corporation including the internal auditors, and further communication channels to the external auditors and legal counsel.[1206] In general, the board of directors needs to have the expertise, resources, and willingness to provide for the necessary governance, guidance, and oversight which has to be ensured by training of the board of directors. Qualified directors are also important for adequately fulfilling their task within the internal control system.[1207]

1204 *Biegelman*, in: FCPA Guidebook, p. 257.

1205 See regarding ineffective director oversight: *Prentice*, 91 Cornell L. Rev. 775 (2006), p. 828.

1206 COSO I, mar. 491 et seq.

1207 Cf. *Oxley*, 2011, at 01:03:15.

With regard to the audit committee, it has the main purpose to assist the board of directors' oversight of the financial reporting process and the compliance with law and regulation. The audit committee has the important responsibility to oversee management's duty to implement effective and efficient internal controls. An effective audit committee has to have the authority to question management regarding financial reporting responsibilities and practices, and has to ensure that corrective actions are taken as appropriate. The audit committee needs to be comprised of solely independent members of the board of directors.

With regard to assigning specific tasks of the board of directors to specialized committees, corporations are encouraged to implement a compliance committee composed entirely of independent directors or assigning the responsible for compliance to another committee e.g. the audit committee. The compliance committee should assess the key legal requirements impacting the corporation and the current level of compliance, the processes to achieve compliance and the risks of non-compliance, the evolving legal compliance and best practice standards trends that might impact the corporation, and the steps taken to monitor.[1208] The compliance committee should also perform routine reviews of disciplinary cases involving the compliance related internal control in order to avoid the development of double standards and to assess the effectiveness of the disciplinary measures. Corporations are also encouraged to implement a compensation committee or assigning the responsible for compensation to another committee e.g. the audit committee which should consider incentives related to internal controls as a part of the incentive based compensation.

2. CEO and CFO – Signing Officers

The CEO and the CFO are responsible for designing, establishing and maintaining internal control, and for evaluating its effectiveness. They have to establish and live rules and guidelines of the control environment to set a good tone at the top. With regard to the CEO, she has general oversight of the monitoring process of internal control and must promptly notify the NYSE in case an executive officer becomes aware of any non-compliance of Rule 303A NYSE-LCM. With regard to the CFO, she has to head the evaluation team of internal control over financial reporting and has to

1208 Cf. *Moeller*, SOX Internal Controls, p. 367.

receive all internal control related matters. She should have a critical role within the internal control system. She should be a key person for establishing the corporation's objectives, deciding on strategies and managing changes affecting the corporation, and analyzing risks as well as monitoring and follow up activities. She needs broad responsibilities exceeding standard areas of financial reporting and treasury including the responsibility to establish good communication between regional financial officers.

3. Chief Compliance Officer

Each corporation should have an officer responsible for compliance issues. The following tasks provide an overview on the scope of responsibilities a CCO may be assigned. A CCO should assume the responsibility of the compliance related internal control including the day-to-day operations and the compliance program. In order to fulfill her duties, the CCO should be given adequate resources, appropriate authority and direct access to the board of directors or the audit committee, and should use the internal audit in particular to assess compliance risks and the effectiveness of the compliance system. The CCO has to have direct reporting obligations to management and the board of directors or the audit committee. At least annually, the CCO has to report to the board of directors or the audit committee with regard to the implementation and effectiveness of compliance related internal control. As best practice, it has been suggested that the CCO should be responsible to monitor and report on the compliance efforts of the corporation on regular basis and by means of ad hoc report on specific issues such as misconduct of senior managers[1209] and to guide the board of directors and senior management on compliance issues.[1210] The CCO may be responsible to develop, maintain, and revise policies and procedures related to the compliance related internal control.[1211] With regard to multi-national corporations, regional CCOs have to be installed in order to address the need of country-specific knowledge since laws and regulation may be different in different countries.[1212]

1209 *Driscoll/Hoffman/Murphy*, 99 Business and Society Rev. 35 (1998), p. 43.

1210 *Moeller*, SOX Internal Controls, p. 362; cf. *Talukdar*, 6 U.C. Davis Bus. L. J. 45 (2005), p. 67 et seq.

1211 *Moeller*, SOX Internal Controls, p. 362.

1212 *Biegelman*, in: FCPA Guidebook, p. 260.

4. General Counsel

The GC also plays a vital role within internal control and compliance. Compliance related internal control and investigations are part of the GC's role. Also, the GC has to report to the audit committee on the financial reporting obligations. Depending on the preference of each corporation, the GC may become more involved into day-to-day operation of internal control by having the CCO report to the GC. Differently, having the CCO report to the CFO leaves the GC to concentrate more on investigations and providing legal input for the compliance related internal control. In most corporations, the CCO reports to the GC.[1213] In any case, the GC has to be involved in enforcement proceedings and decisions about self-reporting and cooperation with enforcement agencies. As a specific duty, the GC has to receive and act on the reports of evidence of a material violation of securities laws or breach of fiduciary duty or similar violation by the corporation by e.g. informing the board directors, if indicated.

5. Internal Audit

Every listed corporation has to have an independent and accurately operating internal audit function. The function encompasses helping the corporation to achieve compliance.[1214] Internal audit traditionally serves two functions within the corporation as an independent reviewer of internal controls and as an independent consultant to the corporation.[1215] Also, internal auditors play an important role in evaluating the effectiveness and monitoring of internal control due to their organizational position and authority in the corporation.[1216] In order to fulfill its task, internal audit should have unrestricted access to a senior officer not directly responsible for preparing the financial statements with sufficient authority to ensure appropriate audit coverage and to follow up on findings and recommendations.[1217] Internal audit should also have a direct reporting line to the audit

1213 *Rostain*, 21 Georgetown Journal of Legal Ethics 456 (2008), p. 481.
1214 *Moeller*, SOX Internal Controls, p. 316.
1215 *Moeller*, SOX Internal Controls, p. 316.
1216 COSO I, mar. 514 et seq.
1217 COSO I, mar. 517.

committee. The internal auditors should be objective by not being placed in a position of subordinating their audit judgment to that of others.[1218]

In light of SOX, internal audit received a more prominent role within the evaluation process of internal control over financial reporting performing work the external auditors rely on implying the importance of internal audit for the external auditors.[1219] In order to effectuate the compliance program especially with regard to the anti-bribery components, internal audit has to have the authority to inspect all the books and records within the corporation and has to report its findings to the responsible officers such as the GC, CCO, or CFO and the audit committee. In addition, internal audit has to be responsible for red flag reviews.

B. Incentives for Corporations to Engage in Internal Control Systems

The incentives for corporations to engage in elements of internal control systems especially with regard to financial reporting and compliance with law are manifold. Incentives to engage in comprehensive internal control as embodied in COSO I are given by enhanced operational efficiency including a more capable workforce. Since COSO I controls may be used for all of its three categories, corporations benefit from implementing SOX-required financial reporting controls and USSG, DOJ and SEC-induced compliance controls by obtaining an internal control structure which also improves operational controls. NYSE best practice and NYSE enforcement also provides for an incentive for the board of directors and management to implement an effective internal control system including the devotion of adequate resources, periodic reviews, and an appropriate risk management. Also, comprehensive internal control enables corporations to comply with all analyzed regulation at the same time. All other incentives are fragmentary and only address specific elements of internal control.

With regard to financial reporting, the aim of each corporation is to maintain effective internal control regarding financial reporting addressing financial and non-financial information in order to comply with the SOX mandates. The incentives scheme for management to implement SOX mandated internal control consisting of the personal liability of the CEO and CFO together with the increased enforcement actions of the SEC provide strong incentives for management to comply with the SOX mandates.

1218 COSO I, mar. 519.

1219 *Smith/Drake/Shaub*, 2009.

While non-optimal incentives to implement effective internal controls may be attributed to the agency problem, the attestation of the external auditors (sec. 404(b) SOX) and the tendency of management to overspend on internal control as well as the benefits of lower costs of capital provide generally for sufficient incentives for management to engage in effective internal control as required by SOX. Nevertheless, the implementation of internal controls is also subject to the principal-agent problem so that all internal control related processes have to be overseen by the board of directors. Moreover, SOX-related internal controls are generally beneficial for corporations providing further incentives to implement effective internal control. Similar to the SOX mandates, corporations have incentives to comply with the NYSE mandates and best practice for corporate governance structures due to the sanctions for failing to comply with NYSE listing standards and federal securities law and regulations.

With regard to compliance, corporations aim to engage in prevention measures, *ex ante* policing measure monitoring including compliance programs and *ex post* policing measures to ensure compliance with laws and regulations. In contrast to SOX-related internal control over financial reporting and disclosure controls and procedures, general compliance programs are not specifically mandated by law. Thus, every regulator with sanctioning authority needs to induce policing measures within his jurisdiction so that various leniency provisions exist leading to scattered requirements for compliance with law. The main incentives are penalties associated with breaching laws and regulations and the sanction mitigation offered by the USSG, the DOJ enforcement policy, the SEC enforcement policy, and the NYSE enforcement policy. With regard to prevention measures, corporate criminal liability provides optimal incentive to control their agents through these measures, but only provides non-optimal incentives for corporations to engage in *ex ante* policing measures including compliance programs. Also, the incentives from the USSG do not induce corporations to engage in truly effective compliance programs. The lack to provide for sufficient benefits to offset the detriments of the litigation dilemma leads corporations to implement ineffective "paper-tiger" compliance programs. Due to the DOJ enforcement policy to grant non- and deferred prosecution agreements, corporations have more incentives to implement more sophisticated compliance programs in order to ensure that the prosecutors will consider the implemented program as part of their decision to enter in such agreement. The incentives to receive the benefits of an effective compliance program based on the DOJ enforcement policy are stronger compared to the incentives provided by the USSG, which only apply after an indictment, since corporations mostly fear the negative effects of being indicted. Nevertheless, the DOJ enforcement policy fails to provide for reliable means to offset the detriments associated with the litigation dilemma. Nonetheless, due to the focus of the DOJ and also the SEC on fraud and corruption, corporations have to set a focus within their compliance programs on such crimes. Moreover, the USSG, the DOJ enforcement policy, the NYSE enforcement policy, and SEC enforcement policy provide some incentives to provide for measures enabling the corporation to engage in the required *ex post* policing measures self-reporting, cooperation, and acceptance of responsibility. Besides non-optimal incentives for corporations to engage in compliance programs, they have incentives to implement more effective anti-corruption measures into the general compliance program due to the FCPA but they do not have sufficient incentives to engage in a truly effective anti-corruption compliance program.

Following from the SEC related guidance, corporations have incentives to engage in more effective compliance programs than induced by the USSG and DOJ enforcement policy. The SEC expects corporations to include in management's evaluation process of internal control over financial reporting not only financial reporting elements but all elements the underlying control framework describes as necessary for an internal control system to be effective.[1220] Since COSO I is the predominant framework used by corporations, corporations have to include in their sec. 404(a) SOX evaluation also elements of internal control related to compliance. Due to the expectation of the SEC to include compliance elements in the evaluation process, corporations have incentives to engage in compliance elements which are effective in light of the COSO I. Hence, corporations subject to the sec. 404(a) SOX evaluation requirement have incentives to engage in more effective compliance programs than currently induced under the USSG. Since most of the requirements of an effective compliance and ethics program of sec. 8B2.1 USSG correspond with the requirements of COSO I, corporations have incentives to engage in more effective compliance programs vis-à-vis the incentives without SOX. In addition, the assessment of management's evaluation of the effectiveness of internal control over financial reporting by the external auditor pursuant to sec. 404(b) SOX also includes all elements of the underlying control framework necessary for the effectiveness further increasing the level of incentives to implement more effective compliance measures. While the audits increase the incentives to implement more effective compliance programs, the costs as-

1220 SEC Release No. 8810, at II, A. See also *supra* at chapter 4, A. II. 2. b) (1).

sociated with the litigation dilemma remain constant preventing corporations to implement truly effective compliance programs.

Due to corporate criminal liability, corporations have non-optimal incentives to engage in the required *ex post* policing measures. The USSG are also insufficient to provide for incentives for corporations to implement optimal policing measures since they do not provide for sufficient sanction mitigation to offset the undermining effects of the litigation dilemma. Similarly, the USSG incentives for reporting are weak since corporations have to be prepared to plead guilty. Nevertheless, the USSG provide incentives for cooperation and accepting responsibility absent reporting, or for accepting responsibility when even not cooperating. The DOJ enforcement policy is similar to the USSG with the important difference that the USSG only apply after indicting a corporation while the DOJ enforcement policy intervenes prior to indictment. As the USSG aim to provide incentives for corporation to engage in *ex post* policing measures, the severe adverse effects of indicting a corporation contradict these incentives. Since corporations do not have a guarantee of never being indicted, the USSG still provide incentives to implement effective compliance programs and to engage in *ex post* policing measures. Differently, the magnitude of sanction mitigation available for federal prosecutors based on the DOJ enforcement policy is significantly greater than the amount available under the USSG. Due to the DOJ enforcement policy of non- and deferred prosecution agreements, corporations have strong incentives to engage in *ex post* policing measures.

In essence, the overall incentives to comply with the mandates for engaging in effective financial reporting controls are sufficient albeit being high enough to induce officers to overspend on financial reporting controls. The incentives to engage in compliance related prevention and policing measures are based on the incentive frameworks of the various regulators. Each incentive framework itself does not provide for sufficient and predictable sanction mitigation to induce corporations to engage in effective policing measures. The USSG provide insufficient sanction mitigation to offset the impact of the litigation dilemma leading to insufficient incentives to engage in effective policing measures. The DOJ enforcement policy of non- and deferred prosecution agreements unsuccessfully tries to compensate the shortcomings of the USSG. Moreover, the DOJ enforcement policy is unpredictable for corporations. But since corporations fear the consequences of indictment, corporations have, nonetheless, strong incentives to comply with the DOJ requirements of *ex post* policing in order to receiving leniency. The NYSE enforcement policy and the SEC enforcement policy still have to prove that they will provide for sufficient sanction mitigation to offset the litigation dilemma. While each incentive framework has potential or actual shortcomings, corporations have strong joint incentives to engage in prevention and *ex post* policing measures but non-optimal incentives to engage in *ex ante* policing measures such as compliance measures.

Chapter 7: Conclusion

German corporations listed on the NYSE have to follow a massive amount of U.S. regulation with regard to internal control and compliance. In the U.S., regulators aim to ensure the accuracy of financial reporting and the deterrence of corporate crime by using internal controls including compliance measures. Various regulators focus on the internal control categories financial reporting and compliance with law. In light of the corporate scandals of the 2000s, Congress built on the existing concept of the FCPA to prevent and detect false financial reporting through internal controls and enacted SOX requiring adequate and effective internal controls. Similarly, the corporate scandals led to a review of the USSG regarding compliance with law. The main issue remains of how to optimally induce corporations to engage in effective prevention and policing measures. All U.S. regulations for internal control combined address the requirements, evaluation, incentives, effectiveness, and efficiency of internal control. Since every regulator regulates within his authority, U.S. internal control mandates and requirements, however, resemble a patchwork rug. Nevertheless, most of the U.S. regulation either builds on COSO I, has been influenced by COSO I, or at least resembles COSO I, so that none of the required elements is contradictory. It follows that the design of internal control systems should be built on COSO I.

With regard to financial reporting, SOX and related SEC regulation mandate corporations to implement effective internal controls comprised of disclosure controls and procedures and internal control over financial reporting with a specific emphasis on fraud controls, and to evaluate the effectiveness of these internal controls. Moreover, SOX requires the external auditors to attest to management's evaluation of internal control over financial reporting. Hence, PCAOB AS 5 provides further insight for the design of internal control over financial reporting and the evaluation of its effectiveness. For the design of internal control, the SEC does not provide comprehensive guidance and requires using a suitable framework for which COSO I evolved as best practice. In addition, the NYSE listing standards address financial reporting but focus on corporate governance elements affecting internal control. The professional standards for internal and external auditors also affect internal control. With regard to compliance, the FCPA, USSG, DOJ enforcement policy, SEC enforcement policy, and NYSE enforcement policy provide incentives for corporations to engage in prevention and policing measures. Corporate criminal liability provides the underlying incentive regime. Moreover, the DGCL represents best practice for German corporations listed on the NYSE. In addition to internal control related compliance measures, regulators require *ex post* policing measures. Since financial reporting related regulation does only require *ex ante* policing, the remaining *ex post* policing measures self-reporting, remediation and cooperation are only induced through sanction mitigation by e.g. the Seaboard report.

In order to fulfill all internal control requirements provided by all regulators, corporations have to implement an internal control system reflecting the mandates and considering best practice for the design of internal control including functions and responsibilities. Implementing and operating effective internal control is essential to fulfill SOX-related mandates regarding the internal control category financial reporting and to receive leniency in light of corporate sanctions. Effectiveness of internal control is the core issue for regulators. In this regard, all analyzed regulations recognize the inherent limitations of internal control and only require reasonable assurance to achieve internal control objectives. Management is required by SOX to evaluate the effectiveness of disclosure controls and procedures and internal control over financial reporting considering the concept of material weakness for the latter. In order to efficiently evaluate the effectiveness of internal control, management has to put strong emphasis on monitoring to maintain effective internal control and to receive assurance regarding the effectiveness out of the system itself. Hence, effective monitoring will lead to effective and efficient internal control. In general, internal control is an ongoing process which includes the execution, monitoring, and re-adjustment of internal control. The audit committee together with a strong internal audit has to be equipped to identify and act in instances when management overrides internal controls or seeks to misrepresent financial results as well as engages in other misconduct such as fraud. Moreover, ethical behavior within the executive level has to be fostered through compensation and other means in order to prevent misconduct first hand. In light of the financial crisis of 2008, corporate-wide risk management has become a focus of management induced by the SEC and NYSE.

The main driving factors to implement internal controls are SOX together with the NYSE listing requirements and increased FCPA enforcement. The increased scrutiny of the SEC and NYSE enforcement divisions leads to higher incentives to implement effective internal controls. While corporations generally have sufficient incentives to engage in effective internal control regarding financial reporting and in prevention measures, they lack incentives to engage in truly effective *ex ante* policing measures including compliance measures, but they have incentives to focus on fraud and corruption. With regard to *ex post* policing, corporations have generally strong incentives to engaging in these measures especially cooperation.

Part Two German Requirements for Internal Control Systems and Compliance

In Germany, the issue of internal control systems and risk management systems came on the agenda prior to SOX. In 1998, KonTraG has been enacted as a result of corporate scandals.[1221] Different to the FCPA, KonTraG[1222] addresses in sec. 91(2) AktG general measures to timely detect developments endangering the survival of the corporation. The scope of such early warning system has been the main focus of academic debate. In 2009, the BilMoG[1223] mainly addressed financial reporting issues including references to internal control and risk management reviving the debate of the scope of the early warning system. The debate on the scope of the early warning system also includes the important issue of corporate compliance. In light of the major corporate scandals in the second half of the 2000s, the question whether corporations have the duty to implement compliance measures moved into the academic focus. In the recent years, further corporate scandals[1224] unveiled the necessity to address corporate misconduct and to increase compliance efforts.

Even though the issues of internal control and risk management systems including compliance are part of German law and in particular of the academic debate, the mandates and requirements for internal control and risk management systems including compliance are not as advanced as in the U.S. Comprehensive internal controls are not required. Nevertheless, mandates for accurate financial reporting and compliance with law exist. While U.S. law provides a rather detailed set of rules in which SOX addresses financial reporting and the USSG and the DOJ enforcement policy mainly induce compliance with law through incentives, German law follows a more principle-based approach leading to less detailed statutory mandates.

1221 *Seibert*, FS Bezzenberger, 427, 428: naming the scandals of Balsam, Schneider, and Metallgesellschaft.

1222 *Gesetz zur Kontrolle und Transparenz im Unternehmensbereich* dated April 27, 1998, BGBl. I, p. 786.

1223 Begr RegE BilMoG, BT-Drucks. 16/10067, p. 1.

1224 See *supra* at chapter 1.

In light of the financial crisis of 2008, the question has been raised if the German legal requirements for internal control are still sufficient.[1225]

The German part is structured by addressing the law applicable for large, listed corporations (chapter 8), best practice (chapter 9), and the overall incentive structure (chapter 10). In the following, the regulatory framework for internal control regarding financial reporting and compliance with law will be analyzed including the mandates of EU law, corporate law, commercial law, law on administrative offences, criminal law, and best practice including specific law of regulated industries including BaFin guidance, the German Corporate Governance Code (GCGC), IDW auditing standards and concepts for profound risk management systems with regard to the legal mandates and requirements as well as best practice for internal control regarding financial reporting and compliance with law. In contrast to NYSE listing rules, the listing rules of e.g. the Frankfort Exchange do not require corporations to follow any specific corporate governance mandates. The exchange only requires German corporations to comply with the AktG and especially with sec. 161 AktG requiring a declaration regarding the GCGC. In order to facilitate the analysis, EU directives will be addressed although not directly applicable for corporations.

1225 Cf. *Spindler*, FS Hüffer, 985. See *supra* at chapter 4, G.

Chapter 8: Law Applicable to Large, Listed Corporations

A. *EU Law Addressing Internal Control, Risk Management and Compliance*

The European Commission considers establishing and maintaining an effective internal control system essential for corporate governance.[1226] In 2006, the EU issued amending Directive 2006/46/EC to the fourth and seventh Company Law Directives (accounting directives). The amending directive requires to describe the main features of internal control and risk management systems in relation to the financial reporting process (art. 46a Directive 2006/46/EC). In Germany, BilMoG implemented sec. 289(5) HGB (now sec. 289(4) HGB[1227]) to effectuate art. 46a Directive 2006/46/EC. Also in 2006, the EU issued amending Directive 2006/43/EC (*Abschlussprüferrichtlinie*) to the eighth Company Law Directive. Due to art. 41 Directive 2006/43/EC, each corporation should monitor the financial reporting process, the effectiveness of internal control, internal audit and risk management systems.[1228] With regard to the amending directive, internal control encompasses financial, operational and compliance risks.[1229] Hence, the concept of effective internal control of the directive is similar to COSO I.[1230] It is the goal of Directive 2006/43/EC to foster financial reporting.[1231] In contrast to compliance, financial reporting has not been a focus in Germany. Art. 41 Directive 2006/43/EC has been transposed into German law by BilMoG in sec. 107(3) and 171(1)(s. 2) AktG. In general, both directives do not require to implement profound internal control and risk management systems.[1232] Nevertheless, the directives led to an increase of

1226 Cf. Commission, Action Plan 2003, p. 12, at fn. 13.

1227 Renumbering according to CSR-Richtlinie-Umsetzungsgesetz, dated April 11, 2017, BGBl. I, p. 802.

1228 See on supervisory directors: Commission, 2005/162/EC, p. 51; Commission, Action Plan 2003, p. 15.

1229 Directive 2006/43/EC recital 24.

1230 Cf. Commission, 2007, p. 4, at fn. 2; Commission, Action Plan 2003, p. 12, at fn. 13; Commission, Green Paper, p. 10 regarding COSO I component 'control environment'; also *Dreher*, FS Hüffer 161, 169 et seq.; *van der Elst/van Daelen*, 2009, p. 28 et seq.

1231 Directive 2006/43/EC recital 24; cf. *Lanfermann/Röhricht*, BB 2009, 887.

1232 *Kort*, ZGR 2010, 440, 465; *Dreher*, FS Hüffer, 161, 166. Different: *Spindler*, in: Münch Komm AktG, sec. 91, mar. 46 arguing for an implicit duty to imple-

the requirements for the internal control and risk management systems beyond the early warning system of sec. 91(2) AktG.[1233]

In 2014, the EU adopted Directive 2014/95/EU[1234], commonly known as the Corporate Social Responsibility (CSR) Directive, to promote a change towards a sustainable global economy for which the EU views the disclosure of non-financial information by large, listed corporations as "vital".[1235] The CSR Directive Transposition Act transposed the Directive 2014/95/EU into German law.[1236]

Also in 2014, Directive 2014/56/EU amended Directive 2006/43/EC. Art. 1 no. 32 Directive 2014/56/EU replaced art. 41 Directive 2006/43/EC by art. 39 with a transposition deadline on June 17, 2016. With regard to internal control, art. 39(6)(b) requires the audit committee to "monitor the financial reporting process and [to] submit recommendations or proposals to ensure its integrity" and art. 39(6)(c) requires the audit committee to monitor the effectiveness of the internal quality control and risk management systems as well as internal audit regarding financial reporting. It seems that the term 'internal quality control' actually means 'internal control' as this term has been used in former art. 41 Directive 2006/43/EC.[1237] Thus, while the wording slightly changed and the audit committee has to submit recommendations or proposals to ensure the integrity of the financial reporting process, no further changes exist to the audit committee's function regarding internal control. The AReG transposed the Directive 2014/56/EU into German law.[1238]

---

ment profound internal control and risk management systems; cf. *Spindler*, FS Hüffer, 985, 991.

1233 *Spindler*, FS Hüffer, 985, 992.

1234 Directive 2014/95/EU amends Directive 2013/34/EU which amended Directive 2006/43/EC.

1235 Directive 2014/95/EU recital 3.

1236 CSR-Richtlinie-Umsetzungsgesetz, dated April 11, 2017, BGBl. I, p. 802. See *infra* at chapter 8, C. II.

1237 This conclusion follows from the German version of the directive which reads '*internes Kontrollsystem*'. Furthermore, the Commission's proposal for Directive 2014/56/EU (COM(2011) 778 final) includes the entire deletion of chapter X of Directive 2006/43/EC including art. 41. Only at the first reading of the European Parilament (P7_TC1-COD(2011)0389), chapter X has been reintroduced. Since the first reading also introduced a reference in recital 24 Directive 2014/56/EU to the Commission's recommendations on the role of the audit committee (Commission, 2005/162/EC) which addresses the 'effectiveness of internal control', it is conclusive that 'internal quality control' should actually read 'internal control'.

1238 Abschlussprüfungsreformgesetz (AReG), dated May 10, 2016, BGBl. I, p. 1142.

With effect of June 17, 2016, the statutory auditor will have to provide an additional report to the audit committee pursuant to art. 11(2)(j) Regulation (EU) No 537/2014 on any significant deficiencies of the internal financial control system and whether or not management has resolved such deficiencies as well as a report, pursuant to art. 11(2)(k), on any significant matters involving actual or suspected non-compliance with laws and regulations or articles of association which were identified in the course of the audit, in so far as they are considered to be relevant in order to enable the audit committee to fulfill its tasks. Art. 11(2)(j)(s. 1) is more or less similar to sec. 171(1)(s. 2) AktG despite the information regarding management's response to such deficiencies (art. 11(2)(j)(s. 2). In light of art. 11(2)(j)(s. 2), management already had incentives to address such deficiencies in order to avoid that the external auditor would report these deficiencies to the audit committee.[1239] In addition, the external auditor has to inform the audited corporation about any irregularities including fraud with regard to the financial statements in case she suspects that such irregularities may occur or have occurred and has to invite the corporation to investigate the matter and to take remediation measures, if indicated, according to art. 7(1) Regulation (EU) No 537/2014. In case the corporation does not investigate the matter, the external auditor has to report this to the respective authority (art. 7(2) Regulation (EU) No 537/2014). With regard to irregularities and fraud, the external auditor has to describe the assessed risks of material misstatements due to fraud (art. 10(2)(c)(i) Regulation (EU) No 537/2014) and has to explain to what extent the audit was considered capable of detecting irregularities, including fraud (art. 10(2)(d) Regulation (EU) No 537/2014) in the audit report. Fraud detection including the information of the corporation in case of signs of irregularities has already been part of the German external auditing.[1240]

B. Corporate Law

In Germany, corporate law is federal law. All German stock corporations are subject to the *Aktiengesetz* (AktG). With regard to corporate governance, corporate law addresses the structure of the corporation including the rights and duties of the organs. The management board of the corporation has the general duty to manage the corporation (sec. 76 AktG) and the

---

1239 See *infra* at chapter 8, B. III.
1240 Cf. *Berndt/Jeker*, BB 2007, 2615. See *infra* at chapter 9, C.

supervisory board has to supervise the management board (sec. 111 AktG). Corporate law addresses internal control with regard to financial reporting and compliance with law only peripheral. With regard to the duties of the management board, the corporation has to keep adequate books and records (sec. 91(1) AktG). The early warning system of sec. 91(2) AktG addresses elements of internal control. In general, internal control and compliance are aspects of the duty to manage the corporation (sec. 76 combined with sec. 93 AktG). With regard to the supervisory board, BilMoG implemented the duty to supervise and monitor the audit process, the effectiveness of the internal control system, the effectiveness of the risk management system, and the effectiveness of the internal audit system (sec. 107(3)(s. 2) AktG). With regard to the auditing process, the external auditor has to report significant deficiencies of the internal control system and the risk management system with regard to financial reporting to the supervisory board (sec. 171(1)(s. 2) AktG). As indicated above, no statutory mandate specifically addresses to implement internal control, compliance measures, or risk management besides the early warning system of sec. 91(2) AktG. Against this background, the main issue in corporate law is the scope of the early warning system, whether duties exist for corporations to implement an internal control system, a risk management system, or a compliance organization, and, if so, the scope of such duties. The analysis of corporate law will continue with the management board's duties regarding internal control and compliance and will be followed by the analysis of the respective supervisory board's duties. Then, the incentive structure of corporate law to implement internal control and compliance measures as an important element to achieve effective internal control and compliance will be analyzed.

I. Management Board's Duties Regarding Internal Control and Compliance

1. Books and Records – Section 91(1) AktG

The basis for internal control regarding financial reporting is that the management board has to keep adequate books and records pursuant to sec. 91(1) AktG. According to commercial law, the duty to keep books and records is also a duty of the corporation (sec. 6, 238 et seq., 264(2) HGB). The accounting provisions of sec. 150 et seq. AktG also require to keep books and records. The management board is collectively responsible keep books and records for accurate accounting in accordance with applicable accounting standards.

2. Early Warning System – Section 91(2) AktG

Corporate law requires the management board to implement an early warning system pursuant to sec. 91(2) AktG. In sec. 91(2) AktG, the general duty of the management board to manage the corporation (sec. 76 AktG) is specified.[1241] It is an essential element of corporate governance.[1242] Due to sec. 91(2) AktG, the management board has to implement adequate measures, especially a monitoring system for detecting developments endangering the survival of the corporation at an early stage. The risks concerning the survival of the corporation include risky dealings, inaccurate financial reporting, and substantial violations of accounting law.[1243] It is not the scope of sec. 91(2) AktG to prevent corporations to take risks.[1244] Taking risks is inherent in doing business[1245] and cannot be eliminated[1246].

a) Scope of Early Warning System and Relation to Internal Control of BilMoG

The main academic debate focuses on the scope of the early warning system mandated by sec. 91(2) AktG. While economists and accountants predominantly favor a wide scope requiring management to implement a profound risk management system[1247], legal scholars predominately favor a

1241 *Mertens/Cahn*, in: Köln Komm AktG, sec. 91, mar. 1; *Kort*, in: Großkomm AktG, sec. 91, mar. 1; cf. Begr RegE KonTraG, BT-Drucks. 13/9712, p. 15.

1242 *Kort*, in: Großkomm AktG, sec. 91, mar. 2.

1243 Begr RegE KonTraG, BT-Drucks. 13/9712, p. 15.

1244 *Seibert*, FS Bezzenberger, 427, 438.

1245 *Weber/Weißenberger/Liekweg*, DStR 1999, 1710; *Henselmann*, in: Risikomanagement, pp. 29 and 38.

1246 *Lück*, DB 1998, 8.

1247 *Mertens/Cahn*, in: Köln Komm AktG, sec. 91, mar. 20; *Schoberth/Servatius/Thees*, BB 2006, 2571, 2574; *Lück*, DB 1998, 8, 9 and 12 et seq.; *Kromschröder/Lück*, DB 1998, 1573; *Kless*, DStR 1998, 93, 95 et seq.; *Eggemann/Konradt*, BB 2000, 503, 504 et seq.; *Preußner/Becker*, NZG 2002, 846, 848. Differentiating: *Henselmann*, Risikomanagement, pp. 29 and 36 et seq.; cf. *Krieger/Sailer*, in: Schmidt/Lutter, sec. 91, at fn. 43 for further references.

stricter scope limited to an early warning system addressing risks concerning the survival of the corporation.[1248] According to the economic literature, a profound risk management is based on a wide risk concept which defines risk as speculative risk including risk of loss and chances.[1249] Also, a profound risk management would require the early warning system to provide for the complete identification, assessment, and communication of all risks within the business without any reference to their potential damage.[1250] Furthermore, a profound risk management would include counter measures.[1251] Nevertheless, the economic literature accepts a divergence between the legal requirements of sec. 91(2) AktG and the desirable economic requirements of a profound risk management system.[1252] Different from the issue of the legal scope of sec. 91(2) AktG, it is undisputed that, out of an economic viewpoint, a risk management system as well as an internal control system of a corporation may need to be more proficient than legally required by sec. 91(2) AktG.[1253]

The predominant legal view holds that sec. 91(2) AktG requires an early warning system which should only provide the management board with information concerning the risks of management's decisions in order to enable the management board to decide on an informed basis.[1254] It has been argued that the implementation of sec. 91(2) AktG by KonTraG did not enhance the existing duties of the management board regarding internal controls but clarified the existing duties pursuant to sec. 76 AktG com-

---

1248 *Mertens/Cahn*, in: Köln Komm AktG, sec. 91, mar. 19 et seq.; *Immenga*, 2009, p. 201.

1249 Cf. *Kless*, DStR 1998, 93; *Kromschröder/Lück*, DB 1998, 1573; *Weber/Weißenberger/Liekweg*, DStR 1999, 1710; *Tüllner*, PwC Guidance 2010, p. 9.

1250 *Mertens/Cahn*, in: Köln Komm AktG, sec. 91, mar. 20; *Lück*, DB 1998, 8, 11; *Lück*, DB 1998, 1925, 1927 et seq.

1251 *Lück*, DB 1998, 8, 13; *Lück*, DB 1998, 1925, 1927; *Weber/Weißenberger/Liekweg*, DStR 1999, 1710, 1715; *Henselmann*, in: Risikomanagement, p. 29, 39; *Kless*, DStR 1998, 93, 95 et seq.; *Eggemann/Konradt*, BB 2000, 503, 506; *Preußner/Becker*, NZG 2002, 846, 850. See on avoiding, reducing and managing risk: *Baums*, ZGR 2011, 218, 237 et seq.

1252 *Henselmann*, in: Risikomanagement, p. 29, 35 et seq.; *Weber/Weißenberger/Liekweg*, DStR 1999, 1710, 1716; cf. IDW PS 340, mar. 5; *Kuhl/Nickel*, DB 1999, 133, 134.

1253 Cf. *Kort*, in: Großkomm AktG, sec. 91, mar. 63.

1254 *Mertens/Cahn*, in: Köln Komm AktG, sec. 91, mar. 20; *Spindler*, in: Münch Komm AktG, sec. 91, mar. 27; *Seibert*, FS Bezzenberger, 427, 437; *Kort*, in: Großkomm AktG, sec. 91, mar. 51; *Hüffer*, AktG, sec. 91, mar. 9; *Kort*, FS Roth, 407, 412 et seq.; OLG Celle, AG 2008, 711.

bined with sec. 93 AktG.[1255] The wording only requires to implement adequate measures to detect developments endangering the survival of the corporation.[1256] Neither the wording nor the intention of sec. 91(2) AktG indicate that corporations need to implement a profound risk management system.[1257] Rather, sec. 91(2) AktG only mandates an early warning system.[1258] A further argument has been raised that the scope of the early warning system is a strict one by referring to the duty of the external auditor to audit the early warning system of sec. 91(2) AktG pursuant to sec. 317(4), 321(4) HGB.[1259] For listed corporations, the external auditor has to assess if the management board has fulfilled the duties of sec. 91(2) AktG. Risk management measures, however, are part of the business judgment of the management board. But the audit of the discretion of the management board is not part of the annual audit of sec. 316 et seq. HGB but, pursuant to sec. 111 AktG, the duty of the supervisory board.[1260] Hence, the duty of sec. 91(2) AktG cannot encompass a profound risk management system. Furthermore, the use of the term "risk management" in sec. 289(2)(no. 2)(a), 315(2)(no. 2)(a) HGB does not indicate that sec. 91(2) AktG requires to implement a risk management system pursuant to the wide economic view. That is, because the term is not used within sec. 91(2) AktG and the economic understanding of sec. 91(2) AktG does not predetermine the legal understanding of sec. 91(2) AktG.[1261] Moreover, the law concerning the management board prescribes the scope of the duty of the management board.[1262] It has also been pointed out that the constitutionally protected freedom to organize a business organization and the legislative history contradict an understanding of sec. 91(2) AktG to require establishing a profound risk management system.[1263] In general, the wording, legislative history and context of sec. 91(2) AktG support the finding that sec. 91(2) AktG does only require to implement an early warning system and not a

1255 Cf. Begr RegE KonTraG, BT-Drucks. 13/9712, p. 15; *Kuhl/Nickel*, DB 1999, 133; *Seibert*, FS Bezzenberger, 427, 437.
1256 Cf. *Kort*, in: Großkomm AktG, sec. 91, mar. 51, 63.
1257 *Spindler*, in: Münch Komm AktG, sec. 91, mar. 16; *Dreher*, FS Hüffer, 161, 162.
1258 *Seibert*, FS Bezzenberger, 427, 437.
1259 *Mertens/Cahn*, in: Köln Komm AktG, sec. 91, mar. 20. See on sec. 317(4) AktG *infra* at chapter 8, C. V.
1260 *Mertens/Cahn*, in: Köln Komm AktG, sec. 91, mar. 20.
1261 *Mertens/Cahn*, in: Köln Komm AktG, sec. 91, mar. 20.
1262 *Kort*, ZGR 2010, 440, 451 et seq.
1263 *Kort*, in: Großkomm AktG, sec. 91, mar. 62 et seq.

profound risk management system. Further controversies regarding the requirements of the early warning system will be addressed subsequently.

With the enactment of BilMoG, some authors revived the issue whether the scope of sec. 91(2) AktG includes more than only an early warning system arguing that BilMoG implicitly requires listed corporations to implement a profound risk management system.[1264] Prior to BilMoG, only no. 5.3.2 GCGC recommended for the audit committee to address risk management.[1265] In line with Directive 2006/43/EC, the internal risk management system of sec. 107(3)(s. 2) AktG encompasses a general risk management system.[1266] Based on the new responsibilities of the audit committee, the question arises whether such responsibilities change the scope of the early warning system of sec. 91(2) AktG so that the management board would be required to implement all the systems enumerated in sec. 107(3)(s. 2) AktG. While the supervisory board has to monitor all enumerated systems, neither the wording nor the legislative reasoning indicate any mandate for the management board to implement a profound risk management system due to 91(2) AktG.[1267] Rather, sec. 107(3)(s. 2) AktG addresses exclusively the supervisory board[1268] and the legislative reasoning expressively states that sec. 107(3)(s. 2) AktG does not mandate to implement a profound risk management system[1269]. Due to these reasons, the enactment of BilMoG did not change the scope of sec. 91(2) AktG.[1270] The legislator leaves the decision whether to implement any of the enumerated systems and, if implemented, the specific elements of such systems to the management board.[1271] Likewise, the supervisory board will require the management board to implement any of the systems enumerated in sec.

1264 *Spindler*, WM 2008, 905, 907; *Hommelhoff/Mattheus*, BB 2007, 2787, 2788.

1265 *Lanfermann/Röhricht*, BB 2009, 887, 889. See *infra* at chapter 9, B.

1266 Begr RegE BilMoG, BT-Drucks. 16/10067, p. 102; cf. *Habersack*, in: Münch Komm AktG, sec. 107, mar. 113; *Hoffman-Becking*, in: Münch Hdb GesR, vol. 4, sec. 32, mar. 26.

1267 *Dreher*, FS Hüffer, 161, 164 et seq.; *Ernst/Seidler*, ZGR 2008, 631, 664; cf. Begr RegE BilMoG, BT-Drucks. 16/10067, p. 76.

1268 Cf. *Kort*, 2010, 440, 449.

1269 Begr RegE BilMoG, BT-Drucks. 16/10067, p. 102; cf. *Kort*, ZGR 2010, 440, 452; *Fleischer*, in: Spindler/Stilz, AktG, sec. 91, mar. 35; *Dreher*, FS Hüffer, 161, 166; *Ernst/Seidler*, ZGR 2008, 631, 664.

1270 *Mertens/Cahn*, in: Köln Komm AktG, sec. 91, mar. 20; *Kort*, ZGR 2010, 440, 441, 452. Different: *Spindler*, in: Münch Komm AktG, sec. 91, mar. 46; *id.*, WM 2008, 905, 907; *Hommelhoff/Mattheus*, BB 2007, 2787, 2788. Unclear: *Weber-Rey*, AG 2008, 345, 350.

1271 Begr RegE BilMoG, BT-Drucks. 16/10067, p. 102 et seq.

107(3)(s. 2) AktG with adequate measures to eliminate any potential violations of the supervisory board's duties.[1272] The legislative reasoning states that necessary supplements, enhancements, or improvements of the enumerated systems have to be determined by the supervisory board.[1273] It has been stated that the legislator assumes that listed corporations will implement a compliance organization reflecting international best practice.[1274]

For the interpretation how sec. 91(2) relates to sec. 107(3)(s. 2) AktG, it is important to note that the internal control and risk management systems of sec. 107(3)(s. 2) AktG have a different basis than the early warning system of sec. 91(2) AktG. The early warning system of sec. 91(2) AktG does not have the scope of the internal control and risk management systems[1275] but is a part of such systems[1276]. While the early warning system may be part of the internal control and risk management systems, the latter does not build on the former. The early warning system of sec. 91(2) AktG originates from KonTraG aiming to address *inter alia* risk taking leading to bankruptcy or close-to-bankruptcy of corporations.[1277] Differently, the duty to supervise the internal control and risk management systems of sec. 107(3)(s. 2) AktG originate from BilMoG transposing Directive 2006/43/EC which draws from the EU Commission's recommendation on the role of non-executive directors[1278]. The directive has the one-tier board structure in mind[1279] and – more important – builds on COSO I and COSO II for internal control and risk management[1280]. While the early warning system may be seen as a safety net around the corporation trying to prevent developments endangering the survival of the corporation, internal control and risk management are management tools interwoven as a net with business processes throughout the corporation. Since the early

1272 Begr RegE BilMoG, BT-Drucks. 16/10067, p. 103.

1273 Begr RegE BilMoG, BT-Drucks. 16/10067, p. 102 et seq.; cf. *Kort*, ZGR 2010, 440, 469.

1274 *Schaefer/Baumann*, NJW 2011, 3601.

1275 Cf. *Spindler*, FS Hüffer, 985, 992; *Bussmann/Matschke*, wistra 2008, 88, 89.

1276 Begr RegE BilMoG, BT-Drucks. 16/10067, p. 102; cf. *Kort*, ZGR 2010, 440, 462: *Förschle/Almeling*, in: Beck'scher Bilanz-Komm, sec. 317, mar. 82.

1277 Cf. *Weber/Weißenberger/Liekweg*, DStR 1999, 1710; *Seibert*, FS Bezzenberger, 427, 428 naming the scandals of Balsam AG, Schneider, and Metallgesellschaft AG.

1278 Commission, 2005/162/EC.

1279 *Spindler*, FS Hüffer, 985, 991.

1280 Cf. Commission, 2007, p. 4, at fn. 2; Commission, Green Paper, p. 10 regarding COSO I component 'control environment'; also *Dreher*, FS Hüffer, 161, 169 et seq.

warning system also needs measures within business processes to gather and assess events[1281], it may be integrated into the internal control and risk management systems. In essence, sec. 91(2) AktG and sec. 107(3)(s. 2) AktG have a similar starting point and do not contradict, but they are different in origin and scope. Thus, BilMoG did not change the scope of the early warning system.

The issue whether the management board of a listed corporation has the duty to implement more proficient internal control and risk management systems than required by sec. 91(2) AktG is rather an issue of the management board's duty to manage the corporation pursuant to sec. 76 combined with sec. 93 AktG which is influenced by BilMoG.[1282] Similarly, within the debate whether corporations have to implement compliance measures, some authors argue that such duty is part of sec. 91(2) AktG. The issue of compliance will also be discussed further below within the management board's duty to manage the corporation.[1283]

b) Requirements of the Early Warning System

Besides the scope of the early warning system, the requirements to fulfill the mandates of sec. 91(2) AktG are at issue. Almost every aspect of sec. 91(2) AktG has been analyzed and criticized in detail. In general, the management board has to ensure that developments concerning the survival of the corporation will be identified at an early stage.[1284] It is the responsibility of the entire management board.[1285]

(1) Adequate Measures Including Internal Audit

Pursuant to sec. 91(2) AktG, the management board has to implement adequate measures which detect developments endangering the survival of the corporation. The term "monitoring system" as an enumerative example of the measures to be taken provides for a mandatory[1286] minimum stan-

---

1281 See *infra* at chapter 8, B. I. 2. b) (2).
1282 Differntly: *Spindler*, FS Hüffer, 985, 992. See *infra* at chapter 8, B. I. 3. a) (2).
1283 See *infra* at chapter 8, B. I. 3. b).
1284 Cf. *Mertens/Cahn*, in: Köln Komm AktG, sec. 91, mar. 22.
1285 *Spindler*, in: Münch Komm AktG, sec. 91, mar. 2.
1286 *Kort*, in: Großkomm AktG, sec. 91, mar. 49.

dard the management board has to comply with. Thus, systematic measures have to be taken.[1287] Sec. 91(2) AktG does not prescribe a specific economic model for the early warning system due to the managerial discretion of the management board and the freedom to organize a business organization pursuant to the right to property in art. 14 GG.[1288] The undetermined term "measures" indicates that the management board is not limited to any kind of measures. Hence, designing the early warning system including the risk management and internal audit is subject to a wide discretion of the management board.[1289] The board has to consider the size, branch, structure, and access to capital markets of the corporation[1290] as well as its specific characteristics so that each corporation will have its specific early warning system. In order to fulfill its discretionary duty, the management board has to assess the different risks of the business.[1291] Based on this information, it has to consider available measures prior to taking actual measures.[1292] The assessment of the business risks has to be periodically in order to adapt the system to changes.[1293] Management has to install measures which list and assess the relevant business risks including the status quo or baseline, and has to compare their development over

1287 *Mertens/Cahn*, in: Köln Komm AktG, sec. 91, mar. 26.

1288 *Spindler*, in: Fleischer, Hdb Vorstandsrecht, sec. 19, mar. 57.

1289 *Mertens/Cahn*, in: Köln Komm AktG, sec. 91, mar. 25; *Spindler*, in: Münch Komm AktG, sec. 91, mar. 17, 24; *Fleischer*, in: Spindler/Stilz, AktG, sec. 91, mar. 33; *Hüffer*, AktG, sec. 91, mar. 7; *Huth*, BB 2007, 2167; *Blasche*, CCZ 2009, 62; cf. *Spindler*, in: Münch Komm AktG, sec. 91, mar. 16 et seq.

1290 *Mertens/Cahn*, in: Köln Komm AktG, sec. 91, mar. 25; Begr RegE, BT-Drucks. 13/9712, p. 15; *Spindler*, in: Münch Komm AktG, sec. 91, mar. 24; *Fleischer*, in: Spindler/Stilz, AktG, sec. 91, mar. 32.

1291 *Spindler*, in: Münch Komm AktG, sec. 91, mar. 17; *Kort*, in: Großkomm, sec. 91, mar. 39; *Henselmann*, in: Risikomanagement, p. 29, 36; cf. LG Berlin AG 2002, 682, 683 et seq.

1292 *Spindler*, in: Münch Komm AktG, sec. 91, mar. 17; cf. *Huth*, BB 2007, 2167, 2168. See also *Huth*, Risikoüberwachung, 2007, p. 199 et seq. on the interesting concept of principles of proper risk monitoring. The concept, however, is limited to risks of non-compliance with law and regulation and does not encompass operational or financial risks endangering the survival of the corporation. Moreover, the concept includes to assess all risks not only risks endangering the survival of the corporation. While the proposed concept provides useful guidance on how to design an early warning system pursuant to sec. 91(2) AktG, it is on the one side too limited and on the other side too broad to be exclusively used to design such system.

1293 Cf. *Spindler*, in: Münch Komm AktG, sec. 91, mar. 17.

time with projected key figures such as revenue or earnings.[1294] These risks are e.g. market risks, financial risks, legal risks, management risks, production risks, logistical risks, or risks of research and development.[1295] Risks endangering the survival of the corporation do usually not evolve unexpectedly but develop over time. Therefore, also essential risks for the corporation have to be taken into account[1296] which may develop into risks endangering the survival of the corporation. The measures taken by the management board may be organizational, procedural, or personnel-wise.[1297] The measures have to ensure that risks endangering the survival of the corporation will be systematically revealed.[1298] Moreover, the measures have to address these risks in all business processes and units.[1299]

The circumstances for the measures to be adequate are disputed. The adequacy depends on the judgment of the management board.[1300] In light of the responsibility of the management board to manage the corporation with the care of a prudent businessman (sec. 76 combined with sec. 93 AktG), the measures are adequate if, based on experience, the management board expects that it will receive the necessary information in a timely manner.[1301] It has been indicated that measures are adequate if experience shows that the required information reaches the management board in time.[1302] Some commentators hold that a positive testing of these measures is sufficient to show their adequacy[1303], while others remark that a positive testing might be accidental[1304]. A test addressing the evaluation of controls will be discussed below.[1305]

The minimum requirements of sec. 91(2) AktG derive from the legislative reasoning of the legislator stating that the management board has

---

1294 *Mertens/Cahn*, in: Köln Komm Aktg, sec. 91, mar. 22; *Krieger/Sailer*, in: Schmidt/Lutter, sec. 91, mar. 8; *Kort*, in: Großkomm AktG, sec. 91, mar. 34; *Spindler*, in: Münch Komm, sec. 91, mar. 20.

1295 *Kort*, in: Großkomm AktG, sec. 91, mar. 21.

1296 *Vogler/Gundert*, DB 1998, 2377, 2378.

1297 *Mertens/Cahn*, in: Köln Komm AktG, sec. 91, mar. 25; *Hüffer, J.*, FS Imhoff, 1998, p. 91, 101.

1298 *Mertens/Cahn*, in: Köln Komm AktG, sec. 91, mar. 25; *Huth*, Risikoüberwachung, 2007, p. 91 et seq.; *Drygala/Drygala*, ZIP 2000, 297, 299.

1299 *Kort*, in: Großkomm, sec. 91, mar. 39.

1300 See *infra* at chapter 16, B. IV. 1.

1301 *Krieger/Sailer*, in: Schmidt/Lutter, sec. 91, mar. 12.

1302 *Hüffer*, AktG, sec. 91, mar. 7.

1303 *Hüffer*, AktG, sec. 91, mar. 7.

1304 *Mertens/Cahn*, in: Köln Komm AktG, sec. 91, mar. 25.

1305 See *infra* at chapter 16, B. IV. 2.

the duty to provide for appropriate risk management and internal audit as well as controlling.[1306] Any measure is sufficient which achieves the goal of sec. 91(2) AktG to detect developments endangering the survival of the corporation at an early stage[1307] as long as they fulfill the function of a risk management and an internal audit. Thus, with regard to sec. 91(2) AktG, the management board has to ensure that these two measures are designed that risks concerning the survival of the corporation will be detected and reported to the management board. The early warning system should be controlled by the internal audit and controlling.[1308]

The corporation has to implement an adequate internal audit as part of the early warning system.[1309] Internal audit has the duty to assess the adequacy, effectiveness, and efficiency of the early warning system[1310], even though, it may not be objective to evaluate the system if it designed and implemented the system[1311]. The specific design of the internal audit function depends on the specific needs of the corporation. The management board should consider the professional standards for internal audit. In 1998, the *Deutsche Institut für interne Revision* (DIIR) adopted the IIA standards for internal audit[1312] which are mandatory for the members of the DIIR constituting best practice. The IIA principles for internal auditors are integrity, objectivity, confidentiality, and competency.[1313] The IIA standards have already been depicted within the U.S. part.[1314] The adaptation of the IIA standards shows that internal audit is under pressure from international regulation.[1315] As further best practice for the internal audit of German corporations has been named that listed corporations need to implement an adequate internal audit for which clearly set management and monitoring duties have to be defined; that internal audit needs unrestricted access to information and unrestricted auditing privileges; that internal audit has to provide objective auditing to improve the effectiveness of business

---

1306 Begr RegE KonTraG, BT-Drucks. 13/9712, p. 15; cf. *Kort*, in: Großkomm AktG, sec. 91, mar. 62; *Spindler*, in: Fleischer, Hdb Vorstandsrecht, sec. 19, mar. 57; Reasoning of 1st draft of KonTraG printed in *Seibert*, FS Bezzenberger, 427, 430.

1307 *Spindler*, in: Münch Komm AktG, sec. 91, mar. 16.

1308 *Spindler*, in: Fleischer, Hdb Vorstandsrecht, sec. 19, mar. 16.

1309 Begr RegE KonTraG, BT-Drucks. 13/9712, p. 15.

1310 *Dreher*, FS Hüffer, 161, 175; *AEIÜU Schmalenbach-Ges.*, DB 2006, 225.

1311 *Withus/Hein*, CCZ 2011, 125, 128.

1312 *Amling/Bantleon*, DStR 2008, 1300.

1313 Cf. IIA Code of Ethics.

1314 See *supra* at chapter 4, E.

1315 Cf. *Marx/Korff/Kläne*, ZIR 2009, 47.

processes and the internal control and risk management systems; that internal audit should use a risk-based approach; that internal audit needs adequate resources and direct reporting duties to the management board in order to provide for independent and objective auditing; that the reporting duties should include significant risks and compliance issues; that internal audit should issue an internal audit report including the scope of the audits, purpose, evidence, result, evaluation, and recommendations at least annually; that the work of the internal audit has to be documented to allow for review by e.g. the external auditor; that the scope of the auditing duties of internal audit should be established in the internal audit manual; and that internal audit should work with the external auditor to achieve efficiency if the external auditor uses the audits of internal audit.[1316]

With regard to controlling, the corporation needs to implement administrative capacities with the responsibility to execute processes of the early warning system.[1317] Controlling should not be integrated into operational processes.[1318] It is the aim of controlling to establish and maintain capacities to react, adopt, and coordinate.[1319] With regard to risk management, controlling has to set risk limits, protection quotas, and risk reporting.[1320] In order to fulfill its duties, controlling needs to use an appropriate information system such as the management information system.[1321]

Besides internal audit and controlling, minimum requirements include to clearly assign competences and to implement precise reporting duties as well as communication[1322].[1323] Responding to risks is not part of the early warning system.[1324] Measures to respond to the identified risks may be required by sec. 76 combined with sec. 93 AktG.[1325] In general, the measures to be taken by the management board remain unclear.[1326]

1316 Cf. *AEIÜU Schmalenbach-Ges.*, DB 2006, 225 et seq.

1317 *Dreher*, FS Hüffer, 161, 167; cf. BaFin, MaRisk (VA), at 7.2.1.

1318 *Dreher*, FS Hüffer, 161, 167.

1319 *Lück*, DB 1998, 1925, 1929.

1320 *Lück*, DB 1998, 1925, 1929.

1321 *Lück*, DB 1998, 1925, 1929.

1322 LG München I, NZG 2008, 319.

1323 Cf. *Krieger/Sailer*, in: Schmidt/Lutter, sec. 91, mar. 13; *Kort*, in: Großkomm AktG, sec. 91, mar. 47, 51; *Hüffer*, AktG, sec. 91, mar. 8.

1324 *Kort*, ZGR 2010, 440, 443; *Krieger/Sailer*, in: Schmidt/Lutter, sec. 91, mar. 12; *Kort*, in: Großkomm AktG, sec. 91, mar. 62.

1325 *Kort*, ZGR 2010, 440, 443; *Krieger/Sailer*, in: Schmidt/Lutter, sec. 91, mar. 12.

1326 *Kort*, in: Großkomm AktG, sec. 91, mar. 26; cf. *Huth*, BB 2007, 2167.

(2) Developments Endangering the Survival of the Corporation

The measures taken by the management board have to detect developments endangering the survival of the corporation at an early stage. It has been argued that the early warning system has to address only unfavorable developments over time instead of every single risk of the business processes.[1327] Most scholars favor to restrict the scope of the early warning system to developments instead of abstract risks.[1328] The developments have to be specific which means that a negative development has already been initiated.[1329] Developments are processes and changes regarding risks.[1330] While it is undisputed that not every single business process has to be addressed by the early warning system[1331], developments include risks[1332] as developments are the materialization of risks. In order to detect developments endangering the survival of the corporation at an early stage, corporations have to monitor those risks potentially leading to such developments.[1333] Hence, all but highly unlikely events have to be gathered and assessed by the early warning system[1334] and their development has to be monitored over time.[1335] Also risk concentration has to be considered.[1336]

Furthermore, different opinions exist for the threshold of risks potentially endangering the survival of the corporation which have to be addressed. As thresholds of risks have been named risks potentially leading to

1327 *Mertens/Cahn*, in: Köln Komm AktG, sec. 91, mar. 21; *Spindler*, in: Fleischer, Hdb Vorstandsrecht, sec. 19, mar. 8; *Spindler*, in: Münch Komm AktG, sec. 91, mar. 22.

1328 *Seibert*, FS Bezzenberger, 427, 437; *Spindler*, in: Fleischer, Hdb Vorstandsrecht, sec. 19, mar. 8; cf. *Kort*, in: Großkomm AktG, sec. 91, mar. 30; *Hüffer*, AktG, sec. 91, mar. 8.

1329 *Seibert*, FS Bezzenberger, 427, 437; *Spindler*, in: Fleischer, Hdb Vorstandsrecht, sec. 19, mar. 8.

1330 *Kort*, in: Großkomm AktG, sec. 91, mar. 30; *Spindler*, in: Münch Komm AktG, sec. 91, mar. 20.

1331 *Spindler*, in: Hdb Vorstandsrecht, sec. 19, mar. 10; *Kort*, in: Großkomm, sec. 91, mar. 33.

1332 *Mertens/Cahn*, in: Köln Komm AktG, sec. 91, mar. 21.

1333 Cf. *Spindler*, in: Münch Komm AktG, sec. 91, mar. 20.

1334 *Seibert*, FS Bezzenberger, 427, 437; *Mertens/Cahn*, in: Köln Komm AktG, sec. 91, mar. 22; *Huth*, Risikoüberwachung, p. 74 et seq., p. 86 et seq.

1335 *Mertens/Cahn*, in: Köln Komm AktG, sec. 91, mar. 22; *Spindler*, in: Münch Komm AktG, sec. 91, mar. 20; *Huth*, Risikoüberwachung, p. 86; *Drygala/Drygala*, ZIP 2000, 297, 299.

1336 *Krieger/Sailer*, in: Schmidt/Lutter, sec. 91, mar. 9.

bankruptcy[1337], risks which are relevant within sec. 264(2) HGB[1338], and risks which endanger the stable profitability[1339]. But risks which are relevant within sec. 264(2) HGB are not risks concerning the survival of the corporation.[1340] Even though the lack of a stable profitability may lead indirectly to the endangerment of the corporation, risks concerning the stable profitability are beyond the wording of sec. 91(2) AktG.[1341] The legislative reasoning further suggests three main aspects constituting *inter alia* developments concerning the survival of the corporation: risky dealings, inaccurate financial reporting, and non-compliance with legal accounting statutes which have a substantial impact on the corporation's assets, financials, and revenue.[1342]

(3) Timely Warning

The identification of risks endangering the survival of the corporation has to be early enough to enable the management board to launch countermeasures which prevent these risks to unfold.[1343] Based on the provided information, the management board has to address the identified events. The countermeasures themselves are not part of the early warning system[1344] but the early warning system enables management to engage in prevention measures.

1337 *Seibert*, FS Bezzenberger, 427, 437; *Spindler*, in: Münch Komm, sec. 91, mar. 21; *Id.*, in: Fleischer, Hdb Vorstandsrecht, sec. 19, mar. 9; *Mertens/Cahn*, in: Köln Komm AktG, sec. 91, mar. 23; *Krieger/Sailer*, in: Schmidt/Lutter, sec. 91, mar. 9; *Kort*, in: Großkomm, sec. 91, mar. 36; cf. *Baums*, ZGR 2011, 218, 263 et seq.

1338 *Hüffer*, AktG, sec. 91, mar. 6.

1339 Cf. *Hüffer, J.*, FS Imhoff, p. 91, 100.

1340 *Spindler*, in: Fleischer, Hdb Vorstandsrecht, sec. 19, mar. 9.

1341 *Spindler*, in: Fleischer, Hdb Vorstandsrecht, sec. 19, mar. 9; *Kort*, in: Großkomm, sec. 91, mar. 37; *Spindler*, FS Hüffer, 985, 990.

1342 Begr RegE KonTraG, BT-Drucks. 13/9712, p. 15; cf. *Kort*, in: Großkomm AktG, sec. 91, mar. 30.

1343 *Mertens/Cahn*, in: Köln Komm AktG, sec. 91, mar. 24; Begr RegE KonTraG, BT-Drucks. 13/9712, p. 15; LG München I, NZG 2008, 319, 320.

1344 *Kort*, in: Großkomm AktG, sec. 91, mar. 44.

(4) Monitoring System

In sec. 91(2) AktG, a monitoring system is enumerated as an example of the adequate measures which the management board has to implement. Within the legal literature, the purpose of the monitoring system of sec. 91(2) AktG is debated.[1345] Some authors favor a very narrow and limited view regarding the mandates for a monitoring system. It has been argued that it would only require to monitor if the measures taken by management are adhered to.[1346] The monitoring system should control if an internal audit and controlling is appropriately implemented and that the information reaches the management board.[1347] The narrow interpretation of sec. 91(2) AktG is mainly based on the term monitoring system ("*Überwachungssystem*"). In an earlier version of the draft bill of KonTraG, the monitoring system actually had the function to only control if the measures taken by the management board are adhered to.[1348] Due to editorial reasons, the wording of the proposed legislation was shortened.[1349] Thus, the legislative history of the term monitoring system may indicate that it has currently the same meaning as in the draft bill. It is stressed that the editorial revision did not intend to materially change the provision.[1350] The mandates of the draft bill required two things: an early warning system and a system to control the adherence to this system. Otherwise, the wording of sec. 91(2) AktG indicates that the monitoring system is only a part of the early warning system and is not limited to monitor if the measures are taken.[1351] Likewise, it is argued that a monitoring system without any measures to monitor for developments endangering the survival of the corporation would not be functional.[1352] In order to decide on the mea-

1345 *Mertens/Cahn*, in: Köln Komm AktG, sec. 91, mar. 21.

1346 *Krieger/Sailer*, in: Schmidt/Lutter, sec. 91, mar. 13; *Kort*, in: Großkomm AktG, sec. 91, mar. 51; *Hüffer*, AktG, sec. 91, mar. 8; cf. LG Berlin AG 2002, 682, 683.

1347 *Kort*, in: Großkomm AktG, sec. 91, mar. 51; *Krieger/Sailer*, in: Schmidt/Lutter, sec. 91, mar. 13.

1348 Sec. 93(1)(s. 3) AktG-E of the draft bill of KonTraG, printed in ZIP 1996, 2129, 2130 et seq., reads as follows: "Thereto, the implementation of a monitoring system is required with the purpose to monitor the adherence of the measures taken pursuant to sentence 2." Sentence 2 of the draft bill required the management board in lengthy words to do basically the same as is required in the current sec. 91(2) AktG.

1349 Cf. *Hüffer*, AktG, sec. 91, mar. 8.

1350 *Hüffer*, AktG, sec. 91, mar. 8.

1351 *Mertens/Cahn*, in: Köln Komm AktG, sec. 91, mar. 26.

1352 *Kort*, in: Großkomm AktG, sec. 91, mar. 28.

sures for the early warning system, the management board has to know which risks endangering the survival of the corporation exist within the business.[1353] Hence, sec. 91(2) AktG requires an early warning system which detects risks endangering the survival of the corporation. A self-evident part of this system is to control if the measures taken are adhered to.[1354] Therefore, the monitoring function needs to encompass the detection of risks concerning the survival of the corporation.[1355] The intent of the legislator and the wording of sec. 91(2) AktG do not leave sufficient leeway for a different interpretation. An effective monitoring system has to have both aspects. It is not sufficient to have a risk detection system without any measures to control if the implemented system is adhered to, thus, to control its effectiveness. It is neither sufficient, however, to have a control system without any detection measures. In practice, all these differentiations will only lead to marginally different results.[1356]

(5) Documentation

The early warning system has to be documented.[1357] While the wording of sec. 91(2) AktG does not require any documentation of the early warning system[1358], appropriate documentation is essential as the documentation serves three functions: in case of doubt, the management board can prove the adherence to their duties; the documentation prevents loss of information, and the documentation has to serve the statutory accountant for her assessment duty of sec. 317(4) HGB[1359].[1360] As best practice, the documentation should illustrate the responsible person or unit for each business

1353 *Kort*, in: Großkomm AktG, sec. 91, mar. 28.
1354 *Mertens/Cahn*, in: Köln Komm AktG, sec. 91, mar. 26.
1355 *Kort*, in: Großkomm AktG, sec. 91, mar. 28.
1356 *Spindler*, in: Münch Komm AktG, sec. 91, mar. 26; *Kort*, in: Großkomm AktG, sec. 91, mar. 28; *Mertens/Cahn*, in: Köln Komm AktG, sec. 91, mar. 21.
1357 *Kort*, ZGR 2010, 440, 444; *id.*, in: Großkomm AktG, sec. 91, mar. 52; LG München I, NZG 2008, 319, 320; *Theusinger/Liese*, NZG 2008, 289, 290; *Mertens/Cahn*, in: Köln Komm AktG, sec. 91, mar. 25; VG Frankfurt a.M., AG 2005, 264, 266; *Kromschröder/Lück*, DB 1998, 1573, 1576; *Kuhl/Nickel*, DB 1999, 133; cf. *Krieger/Sailer*, in: Schmidt/Lutter, sec. 91, mar. 13; *Hüffer*, AktG, sec. 91, mar. 8.
1358 *Hillebrand*, Früherkennungs- und Überwachungssystem, p. 131.
1359 See also *Kuhl/Nickel*, DB 1999, 133, 135.
1360 Cf. *Kromschröder/Lück*, DB 1998, 1573, 1576; *Kless*, DStR 1998, 93, 94.

division.[1361] In general, the management board needs to document at least the code of conduct, the delegation of managerial authority, and all aspect of any existing risk management system.[1362]

c) Summary

It is widely accepted that the scope of the early warning system of sec. 91(2) AktG is limited to risks endangering the survival of the corporation. The risk management system of sec. 91(2) AktG does not encompass a comprehensive risk management as resembled by COSO II. The enactment of BilMoG did not affect the scope. The early warning system of sec. 91(2) AktG has to provide for an information and reporting system including monitoring ensuring the timely detection of developments endangering the survival of the corporation. The measures of risk management have to address risks potentially leading to such developments. The monitoring system has to include two elements: monitoring for such developments and monitoring whether the early warning system operates as designed. As part of the early warning system, internal audit and controlling functions have to be implemented. The early warning system has to be documented. In general, sec. 91(2) AktG does not mandate any details for the early warning system. The management board only has to adhere to broad concepts resulting in wide discretion and little guidance to design the early warning system.

3. Duty to Manage the Corporation – Section 76 combined with Section 93 AktG

The management board has the duty to manage the corporation pursuant to sec. 76(1) AktG. In executing such duty, the management board has to adhere to the standard of care of a prudent businessman pursuant to sec. 93(1)(s. 1) AktG. The provisions addressing the duty to manage the corporation are rather broad and unspecific. Therefore, general considerations provide the basis to specify the elements of the duty considering the care of a prudent businessman. The following analysis will determine the scope of the duty to manage the corporation with regard to implementing internal

1361 *Kuhl/Nickel*, DB 1999, 133, 135.
1362 *Theisinger/Liese*, NZG 2008, 289, 290.

control and risk management systems including a compliance organization. The separation of the two issues internal control together with risk management and the compliance organization follows the separation of these two issues within U.S. law and underscores the current academic focus on compliance in Germany.

a) Internal Control and Risk Management Systems

Within corporate law, the debate rests on the issues whether corporations have to implement internal control and risk management systems, the scope of this duty, and the effectiveness of these systems which will be addressed in the following subparts.

(1) Duty to Implement Internal Control and Risk Management Systems

Corporate law does not explicitly mandate to implement an internal control and risk management system. Rather, pursuant to sec. 76 combined with sec. 93 AktG, the management board has a duty to appropriately organize the corporation including monitoring duties[1363] and to adequately detect and assess risks within the corporation.[1364] In order to perform the managing duty, the management board has to provide for an organization which enables the board to always obtain the necessary overview over the economic and financial situation of the corporation.[1365] As part of the monitoring duty, the management board has to provide for means to prevent violation of duties of subordinates.[1366] Due to such duty of organizing the corporation, the management board may have a duty to implement internal control and risk management systems beyond the early warning sys-

---

1363 *Fleischer*, in: Fleischer, Hdb Vorstandsrecht, sec. 8, mar. 1; *Schneider*, NZG 2009, 1321, 1323; *Lück*, DB 1998, 8; cf. BGHZ 127, 336, 347.

1364 *Spindler*, in: Fleischer, Hdb Vorstandsrecht, sec. 19, mar. 6; *Lorenz*, in: Grundlagen des Risikomanagements, p. 11; cf. *Wiesner*, in: Münch Hdb GesR, vol. 4, sec. 25, mar. 8; *Spindler*, in: Münch Komm AktG, sec. 76, mar. 73 et seq.

1365 BGH, decision of February 20, 1995 - II ZR 9/94, at recital 7; cf. *Seibert*, FS Bezzenberger, 427, 430.

1366 *Fleischer*, in: Fleischer, Hdb Vorstandsrecht, sec. 8, mar. 36.

tem of sec. 91(2) AktG.[1367] This duty also includes internal control regarding compliance measures[1368] as will be shown below.

The duty to implement an early warning system similar to the requirements of sec. 91(2) AktG has already been inherent in the duty of the management board to manage the corporations with the care of a prudent businessman prior to KonTraG.[1369] Nevertheless, sec. 91(2) AktG purpose is beyond a mere repetition of the duty of sec. 76 combined with sec. 93 AktG as it specifies such duty[1370] and highlights the need of an early warning system. Even though sec. 91(2) AktG specifies the minimum duties of the management board pursuant to sec. 76 combined with sec. 93 AktG, it does not preclude sec. 93 AktG so that the mandates of sec. 76 combined with sec. 93 AktG may reach further than the mandates of sec. 91(2) AktG.[1371] Therefore, risks which do not fall into the categories of sec. 91(2) AktG have to be detected and dealt within the ordinary course of the business due to sec. 93 AktG.[1372] If the management board violates this duty, it might be liable pursuant to sec. 93 AktG.[1373]

(2) Scope of Internal Control System

The scope of the duty for the management board to implement an internal control and risk management system is not addressed by statute and only inherent in the general duty to manage the corporation pursuant to sec. 76 combined with sec. 93 AktG representing legislation in the style of principle instead of rule. It has been reasoned that this duty does not encompass that corporations have to implement a profound risk management system.[1374]

1367 *Spindler*, in: Fleischer, Hdb Vorstandsrecht, sec. 19, mar. 60; cf. *Kort*, ZGR 2010, 440, 454.

1368 See *infra* at chapter 8, B. I. 3. b).

1369 *Mertens/Cahn*, in: Köln Komm AktG, sec. 91, mar. 14.

1370 *Kort*, ZGR 2010, 440, 454.

1371 *Spindler*, in: Münch Komm AktG, sec. 91, mar. 3.

1372 *Spindler*, in: Münch Komm AktG, sec. 91, mar. 22.

1373 *Kort*, ZGR 2010, 440, 456; *Lorenz*, in: Grundlagen des Risikomanagements, p. 12; cf. *Bachmann*, VGR, 2008, 65, 73 et seq.

1374 *Kort*, ZGR 2010, 440, 454; *id.*, in: Großkomm AktG, sec. 91, mar. 64; *Meyer*, DB 2014, 1063, 1068. Different: *Hopt/Roth*, in: Großkomm AktG, sec. 111, mar. 223. Similar: *Spindler*, in: Münch Komm AktG, sec. 91, mar. 46 arguing for an implicit duty to implement profound internal control and risk management systems; cf. *Spindler*, FS Hüffer, 985, 991.

The enactment of BilMoG[1375] revived the issue whether corporations have to implement profound internal control and risk management systems. While it has been noted that BilMoG contains an implicit duty of the management board to implement a profound internal control system as well as a risk management system[1376], BilMoG neither changed the duties regarding internal control and risk management systems[1377] nor mandates to implement profound internal control and risk management systems[1378]. Likewise, neither BilMoG nor the EC directives expressive require to implement profound internal control and risk management systems.[1379] Rather, BilMoG is believed to foster the implementation of a comprehensive internal control and risk management system not limited to financial reporting.[1380] Since no legal mandate requires to implement a profound risk management system, BilMoG only influences the management board's duty to manage the corporation including the duty to monitor the corporation (sec. 76 combined with sec. 93 AktG)[1381] without setting a standard requiring a specific scope of internal control and risk management systems. BilMoG is only an indicator for the general necessity of effective internal control and risk management systems but does not mandate to implement such systems. Also the legislator stated that the decisions whether and how to implement internal control and risk management systems rests with the management board.[1382] The board has to consider the specific needs of the corporation including the business strategy, the scope of the business and effectiveness and efficiency issues.[1383]

The scope of the duty to implement internal control and risk management systems pursuant to sec. 76 combined with sec. 93 AktG depends on the specific circumstance of each corporation its size, branch, structure, and access to capital markets of the corporation. Depending on the scope and size of the business, implementing a proficient risk management sys-

1375 See on BilMoG also *infra* at chapter 8, B. II. 1. and chapter 8, C. I.

1376 *Weber-Rey*, AG 2008, 345, 350; cf. *Spindler*, in: Münch Komm AktG, sec. 91, mar. 46.

1377 *AKEU/AKEIÜ Schmalenbach-Ges.*, DB 2009, 1279.

1378 Begr RegE BilMoG, BT-Drucks. 16/10067, p. 102.

1379 Different: *Lutter*, FS Goette, 289, 296 et seq. noting that the EC directives require the implementation of a risk management system.

1380 *Windbichler*, FS Hopt, 1505, 1511; *Wolf*, DStR 2009, 920, 925.

1381 *Spindler*, FS Hüffer, 985, 991; cf. Begr RegE BilMoG, BT-Drucks. 16/10067, p. 102 et seq. See for incentives *infra* at chapter 8, B. III.

1382 Begr RegE BilMoG, BT-Drucks. 16/10067, p. 76 and p. 102.

1383 Begr RegE BilMoG, BT-Drucks. 16/10067, p. 76.

tem including internal controls may be a legal duty for the corporation.[1384] The standard to determine the scope of the internal control and risk management system is sec. 93 AktG, i.e. the management board to manage the corporations with the care of a prudent businessman (sec. 93 AktG). As part of the internal control system, the management board has to implement means to fulfill their reporting duty of sec. 90(1) AktG to the supervisory board. The reporting duty of sec. 90(1) AktG includes the measures of the sec. 91(2) AktG early warning system and any compliance measures.[1385] In general, corporations have the duty to document the important elements of the internal control and risk management systems.[1386] Moreover, the different needs of internal control regarding the ownership structure of the corporation reaching from block holdings to dispersed ownership have to be considered.[1387] In a dispersed ownership setting, internal control has to focus on management fraud such as earnings management. In a blockholding structure, internal control addressing these issues is not as important. Within a blockholding structure, internal control has to focus on minority protection.[1388]

For large, listed corporations, this standard requires to implement internal control and risk management systems in order to manage and control the corporation.[1389] Without such controls, the sheer size and complexity of the organization will lead to uninformed decisions and lack of knowledge of the operations and risks within the corporation. With the increasing level of delegating authority and responsibility, a corresponding level of control and monitoring has to accompany such increase. Even for large, listed corporations, the duty to manage the corporation does not generally include to implement a profound internal control and risk management systems. While the standard of such systems within large, listed corporations has to be higher than in an average corporation, sec. 76 combined with sec. 93 AktG does not require to follow specific frameworks or thresholds. Nevertheless, the level of proficiency for the internal control and risk management systems has to match the challenges of the size and complexity of the corporation. Therefore, regarding very large corporations or cor-

---

1384 *Kort*, ZGR 2010, 440, 456.

1385 *Hüffer*, AktG, sec. 90, mar. 2; *Mertens/Cahn*, in: Köln Komm AktG, sec. 91, mar. 34.

1386 *AKEIÜ Schmalenbach-Ges.*, DB 2011, 2101, 2103; *AKEU/AKEIÜ Schmalenbach-Ges.*, DB 2009, 1279, 1281.

1387 See *infra* at chapter 12, B. I. 1. c) (4).

1388 *Wackerbarth*, ZGR 2005, 686, 707.

1389 *Kort*, ZGR 2010, 440, 470; *Casper*, Libor Amicorum Winter, 77, 87.

porations with a high level of complexity, the minimum legal standard to manage the corporation converges towards best practice for internal control and risk management systems.

In order to specify the scope of the duty to manage the corporation regarding internal control and risk management, all implications of the statutory provisions addressing internal control and risk management issues as well as the GCGC, auditing standards, and best practice itself have to be considered. The standard to manage the corporation as a prudent businessman acting on an informed basis includes to consider all relevant aspects of internal control. In this regard, the statutory provisions provide the starting point for the management board followed by other regulatory frameworks and best practice. German law addresses internal control issues within several provisions of corporate law applicable for the supervisory board including sec. 107(3)(s. 2) AktG, sec. 171(1) AktG, and sec. 111 AktG[1390] as well as several provisions of commercial law including sec. 289(4) HGB and sec. 317 HGB[1391] applicable for the annual audit. Also, specific law of regulated industries including BaFin Guidelines[1392] and the law addressing corporate liability for crimes and offences[1393] address internal control aspects. Moreover, the GCGC[1394] and the auditing standards of the IDW[1395] address internal control issues as well as the general best practice for internal control[1396]. The two elements of internal control which received greater statutory attention – 'internal control regarding financial reporting'[1397] and 'compliance'[1398] – will be dealt with in more detail below. In addition, the statutory provisions provide incentives for the management board to consider their requirements for the internal control system which will also be dealt with further below.[1399]

In order to fulfill the duty to implement internal control and risk management systems, corporations should use a recognized control framework such as COSO I or COSO II which have been depicted above[1400]. The law

1390 See for a detailed analysis *infra* at chapter 8, B. II.
1391 See for a detailed analysis *infra* at chapter 8, C.
1392 See for a detailed analysis *infra* at chapter 8, D.
1393 See for a detailed analysis *infra* at chapter 8, E.
1394 See for a detailed analysis *infra* at chapter 9, B.
1395 See for a detailed analysis *infra* at chapter 9, C.
1396 See for a detailed analysis *infra* at chapter 9, D.
1397 See for a detailed analysis *infra* at chapter 8, C.
1398 See for a detailed analysis *infra* at chapter 8, B. I. 3. b).
1399 See *infra* at chapter 8, B. III.
1400 See *supra* at chapter 4, C.

does not require to use any specific framework and the management board has wide discretion on this issue. Nevertheless, the decision to use a specific framework has to be taken with the care of a prudent businessman. Choosing the COSO frameworks to implement profound internal control and risk management systems fulfills the requirements of the duty to manage the corporation since IDW PS 261 which includes elements of COSO I[1401] and IDW PS 980 which refers to COSO II[1402] as well as the referencing to the COSO frameworks by scholars[1403] and the worldwide acceptance of the COSO frameworks[1404] also as German best practice[1405].

(3) Effectiveness of the Internal Control and Risk Management Systems and the Evaluation of the Effectiveness

In order to fulfill the duty of the management board to design and implement an internal control and risk management systems exercising business judgment in light of sec. 76 combined with sec. 93 AktG[1406], it has been reasoned that these systems have to be effective.[1407] Also, BilMoG especially through sec. 107(3)(s. 2) AktG underscores and highlights the already existing minimum standard for large, listed corporations to implement effective internal control, risk management, and internal audit. Nevertheless, BilMoG does neither provide for thresholds constituting effective internal control and risk management systems nor requires corporations to define benchmarks representing effective systems nor the management board to evaluate the effectiveness.[1408]

Even though BilMoG does not require to define benchmarks, it is inevitable and part of best practice to define benchmarks in order to evaluate the effectiveness.[1409] Since the duty to monitor the corporation pursuant to

1401 See *infra* at at chapter 9, C.
1402 See *infra* at at chapter 9, C.
1403 *Sybon*, ZIR 2011, 93, 94; *Hillebrand*, Früherkennungs- und Überwachungssystem, p. 42 et seq. and p. 154 et seq.
1404 See *infra* at chapter 12, A. IV.
1405 See *infra* at chapter 9, D.
1406 *Lanfermann/Röhricht*, BB 2009, 887, 889; cf. Begr RegE BilMoG, BT-Drucks. 16/10067, p. 102.
1407 *Withus*, DB 2009, Beilage 5, 82, 84.
1408 *Wolf*, DStR 2009, 920, 925.
1409 *Withus*, DB 2009, Beilage 5, 82, 85. Similar: *Nonnenmacher/Pohle/v. Werder*, DB 2009, 1447, 1451; *Powilleit*, GWR 2010, 28. See *infra* at chapter 16, B. IV. 2.

sec. 76 combined with sec. 93 AktG for large, listed corporations converges towards best practice, the management board has the duty to define benchmarks. For defining such benchmarks and in particular to design internal control and risk management systems, best practice includes to use the well established frameworks COSO I and COSO II[1410] which have also been used by the EU commission[1411].[1412] Moreover, the concept of effective internal control in Directive 2006/43/EC[1413] and art. 266 Delegated Regulation (EU) 2015/35 is similar to COSO I. Since neither sec. 91(2) AktG nor BilMoG requires to implement profound internal control and risk management systems, the frameworks will provide guidance to design and operate such systems, but using COSO I or COSO II is not mandatory under German law.[1414] On the other hand, the minimum requirements for internal control systems of large, listed corporations converge towards best practice considering the COSO frameworks[1415], the COSO frameworks have to be considered for setting the performance level for the effectiveness of the compliance organization of large, listed corporations. The necessary elements to achieve effective internal controls and to evaluate their effectiveness will be discussed further below.[1416] With regard to the evaluation, the management board has incentives to evaluate the effectiveness.[1417]

b) Compliance Organization

An important issue within the duty to manage the corporation pursuant to sec. 76 combined with sec. 93 AktG is compliance. While corporate law does not specifically address the issue[1418], it is the general understanding that corporations have to adhere to the applicable laws and regulation

---

1410 Cf. *Withus*, DB 2009, Beilage 5, 82, 85; *AKEU/AKEIÜ Schmalenbach-Ges.*, DB 2009, 1279, 1282; *Hufnagel/Tönnissen*, ZIR 2010, 110, 117; *Tönnissen*, Revision der IT-Governance, p. 285 et seq.

1411 Cf. Commission, 2007, p. 4, at fn. 2.

1412 *Withus*, DB 2009, Beilage 5, 82, 85.

1413 Cf. Directive 2006/43/EC recital 24. See also *supra* at chapter 8, A.

1414 Cf. *Withus*, DB 2009, Beilage 5, 82, 85 et seq. For economic models in general: *Spindler*, WM 2008, 905, 909; *Spindler*, in: Münch Komm AktG, sec. 93, mar. 29; *Dreher/Hoffmann*, ZGR 2016, 445, 452 et seq.

1415 See *supra* at chapter 8, B. I. 3. a) (2).

1416 See *infra* at chapter 16, B. IV.

1417 See *infra* at chapter 8, B. III.

1418 *Fleischer*, in: Spindler/Stilz, AktG, sec. 91, mar. 47; *Winter*, FS Hüffer, 1103, 1104.

known as the principle of legality – *Legalitätsprinzip*.[1419] The principle of legality and the following duty to implement compliance measures has to include foreign law.[1420] Otherwise, the management board would be able to avoid liability due to sec. 93 AktG by incorporating in Germany and conducting business only in a foreign state without any ties to Germany which is feasible, at least in Europe, due to the doctrine of incorporation. The extent to which foreign law is part of the principle of legality has to be determined by using the general principles of German and international conflict of laws.[1421] For the purpose of the thesis, however, part II has to be limited to German law excluding any foreign law in order to enable the impact analysis of part III.[1422]

Compliance is a broad term which has been defined as encompassing all measures in order to ensure lawful behavior of the corporations, management, and employees regarding all statutory orders and prohibitions.[1423] As main aspects of compliance have been named prevention of harm and protection of reputation.[1424] Furthermore, compliance aims to ensure that the members of the boards and the employees comply with the law and to maintain the confidence of investors.[1425] So far, multiple understandings exist with regard to what is compliance reaching from being limited to the mere duty to comply with the law to compliance concepts including the internal control system and the risk management system as reflected in sec. 23, 29, 30 VAG[1426].[1427] The different understandings do not contradict. Compliance as such only states the need for corporations to ensure that the

---

1419 *Bachmann*, VGR, 2008, 65, 76; BGHZ 133, 370, 375; *Hüffer*, AktG, sec. 93, mar. 4; *Spindler*, in: Münch Komm AktG, sec. 93, mar. 63 et seq.; *Winter*, FS Hüffer, 1103, 1108; *Liese*, BB 2008, Beilage 5, 17, 18; *Reichert/Ott*, ZIP 2009, 2173; LG München I, decision of December 10, 2013 – 5 HK O 1387/10, juris at recital 89.

1420 *Bachmann*, VGR, 2008, 65, 97; cf. *Mertens/Cahn*, in: Köln Komm AktG, sec. 93, mar. 73; *Cichy/Cziupka*, BB 2014, 1482 et seq.; LG München I, decision of December 10, 2013 – 5 HK O 1387/10, juris at recital 89.

1421 *Bachmann*, VGR, 2008, 65, 97.

1422 See *supra* at chapter 1, D.

1423 *Schneider*, ZIP 2003, 645, 646; *Immenga*, 2009, p. 199.

1424 *Bürkle*, BB 2005, 565, 566; *Bürkle*, BB 2007, 1797, 1798; *Fleischer*, in: Spindler/Stilz, AktG, sec. 91, mar. 48; cf. *Schneider*, ZIP 2003, 645, 648; *Kremer/Klahold*, ZGR 2010, 113, 117 and 127; *Hauschka*, in: Haschka, Corporate Compliance, sec. 1, mar. 24.

1425 *Schneider*, ZIP 2003, 645, 648; cf. *Moosmayer*, Compliance, mar. 70.

1426 See *infra* at chapter 9, A. I.

1427 Cf. *Hauschka*, VGR, 2008, 51 et seq.; *Hüffer*, FS Roth, 299, 302; *Kramer/Klahold*, ZGR 2010, 113, 117; *Bergmoser/Theusinger/Gushurst*, BB 2008, Beilage 5, 1, 2.

people of the corporation especially management and employees adhere to the applicable laws and regulation. Depending on the organizational needs, the corporation has to use management tools such as internal control systems and risk management systems to ensure compliance throughout the complex structure of midsize and large corporations. Hence, compliance may reach from simple checks of the owner-manager in small corporations to a sophisticated compliance organization. In light of these management tools, economists ascribe four functions to compliance: limiting risk of sanctions, providing information, controlling the corporation and management, and marketing.[1428] In order to design compliance programs, the corporation may and should utilize the management tools internal control and risk management. The COSO frameworks – COSO I (internal control) and COSO II (enterprise risk management) – each include as one of their objectives 'compliance with laws and regulation' providing elements to design compliance programs.[1429] In light of the COSO frameworks, the internal control system may be integrated into risk management. At the end, the question what constitutes compliance is corporation-specific which includes legal mandates specifying the scope of compliance. Within regulated industries, sec. 33 WpHG, sec. 25a KWG and sec. 23, 29, 30 VAG are examples of such statutory mandates. In general, all approaches to compliance share the requirement that corporations have to comply with the law.

The differences between the approaches are foremost attributed to the scope of the compliance organization reflected in different levels of requirement reaching from no requirements to requiring proficient internal control and risk management systems. On the one hand, these differences reflect the different needs of corporations regarding the sophistication of the compliance programs and, on the other hand, to a certain degree the situation of an evolving field of law including the lack of a comprehensive concept leading to require internal control and risk management even though risk management may include internal control. In general, compliance encompasses the duty to comply with laws and regulation and the elements to achieve such compliance. The level of sophistication for the elements of the compliance organization depends on the specific circumstances of each corporation. A further aspect of compliance is how to achieve that corporations comply with the requirements for the compliance organization. In this regard, the issue of compliance within corporate

1428 *Bergmoser/Theusinger/Gushurst*, BB 2008, Beilage 5, 1, 2.
1429 See *supra* at chapter 4, C.

law encompasses three aspects: the duty to comply, the needed elements for the compliance organization, and the incentives to comply with the requirements for the compliance organization. The incentives to implement internal control and compliance measures are included in the analysis of the incentives from corporate law conducted below.[1430]

(1) Duty to Implement Compliance Measures

At first, the main debate centered on the issue whether or not corporations have a duty to implement compliance measures.[1431] It has been argued that the duty to implement a compliance organization might be based on corporate law for each individual case.[1432] In the recent years, the duty for the management board of listed corporations to implement compliance measures has been established which includes to implement measures ensuring the compliance with legal mandates and internal guidelines[1433].[1434] Now the main debate centers on the legal basis for such duty. Some scholars reason that the scope of the early warning system of sec. 91(2) AktG needs to

---

1430 See *infra* at chapter 8, B. III.

1431 See *Schneider*, ZIP 2003, 291; *Hauschka*, ZIP 2004, 877; cf. *Bachmann*, VGR, 2008, 65, 76; *Liese*, BB 2008, Beilage 5, 17.

1432 *Spindler*, in: Fleischer, Hdb Vorstandsrecht, sec. 19, mar. 60; cf. *Hauschka*, ZIP 2004, 877, 878.

1433 *Sieber*, FS Tiedemann, 449, 469 et seq.: arguing that internal guidelines define negligence standards for offences. Different *Hüffer*, FS Roth, 299, 302: excluding internal guidelines from legally mandated compliance demonstrating the difference between minimum legal requirements and economically preferable compliance. In order to ensure that employees follow specific instructions *inter alia* aiming to avoid misconduct, the corporation has high incentives to include internal guidelines into the compliance organization.

1434 *Fleischer*, in: Spindler/Stilz, AktG, sec. 91, mar. 47, 50; *Hüffer/Schneider*, ZIP 2010, 55; *Dreher*, FS Hüffer, 161, 168 et seq.; *Kort*, NZG 2008, 81, 84; *Fleischer*, in: Fleischer, Hdb Vorstandsrecht, sec. 8 mar. 40 et seq.; *Hüffer*, AktG, sec. 76, mar. 9a; *Mertens/Cahn*, in: Köln Komm AktG, sec. 91, mar. 34 et seq.; *Spindler*, in: Münch Komm AktG, sec. 91, mar. 35 et seq.; *Bürkle*, BB 2007, 1797, 1798; *v. Busekist/Hein*, CCZ 2012, 41; *Withus/Hein*, CCZ 2011, 125, 127; *Vetter*, FS v. Westphalen, 719, 721; LG München I, decision of December 10, 2013 – 5 HK O 1387/10, juris at recital 89. Different: *Böttcher*, NZG 2011, 1054; *Kremer/Klahold*, ZGR 2010, 113, 119; *Bachmann/Prüfer*, ZRP 2005, 109, 111; *AKEIÜ Schmalenbach-Ges.*, DB 2010, 1509, 1510 et seq.; *Engelhart*, Sanktionierung, p. 511; *Vetter*, FS v. Westphalen, 719, 727 et seq.

be enhanced to include compliance measures.[1435] Other scholars extract a general duty to implement a compliance organization from the legal mandates of various fields of specific law such as AktG, OWiG, and WpHG.[1436] More specifically, the duty to implement compliance measures has been derived from the mandates of sec. 30, 130 OWiG.[1437] Mainly, scholars favor to extend the existing duty to manage and monitor the corporation pursuant to sec. 76 combined with sec. 93 AktG to require compliance measures.[1438] Especially for listed corporations, the duty to monitor requires more than only single actions to monitor if employees comply with the law[1439] leading to a quasi duty to implement compliance measures based on sec. 93(1) AktG[1440].

With regard to the duty to monitor the corporation, *Hüffer* argues to add the aspect that the management board has the duty to implement a compliance organization in light of the external relationship with the state since sec. 76 combined with sec. 93 AktG would only address the internal duties of the management board.[1441] This argument rests on the assumption that implementing a compliance organization would be related to the state as the legislator[1442] representing the overarching demand of the state that its laws have to be followed. To the contrary, the duty to implement a compliance organization is the very own duty of the management board to manage the corporation which includes to ensure that the employees comply with the law. If the structure of the corporation is too complex to achieve compliance without specific compliance measures, then, more so-

1435 *Dreher*, ZGR 2010, 496, 519; *id.*, FS Hüffer, 161, 169; *Spindler*, WM 2008, 905, 907. Undecided: *Fleischer*, in: Fleischer, Hdb Vorstandsrecht, sec. 8, mar. 43 and fn. 188; *Fleischer*, CCZ 2008, 1, 2; *Fleischer*, AG 2003, 291, 299. With regard to anti-corruption measures arguably: *Berg*, AG 2007, 271, 274 et seq.

1436 *Dreher*, ZGR 2010, 496, 519; *Schneider*, ZIP 2003, 645, 649; *id.*, NZG 2009, 1321, 1332; *Schneider, S.*, 2006, 225 et seq.

1437 *Mertens/Cahn*, in: Köln Komm AktG, sec. 93, mar. 80; cf. *v. Busekist/Hein*, CCZ 2012, 41, 43.

1438 *Mertens/Cahn*, in: Köln Komm AktG, sec. 91, mar. 35; *Mertens/Cahn*, in: Köln Komm AktG, sec. 93, mar. 71, 80; *Fleischer*, in: Spindler/Stilz, AktG, sec. 91, mar. 47; *Immenga*, 2009, p. 202; *Bachmann*, VGR, 2008, 65, 73; *Winter*, FS Hüffer, 1103, 1104; *Hüffer*, FS Roth, 299, 304; *Kindler*, FS Roth, 2011, 367, 370; *Fleischer*, BB 2008, 1070, 1072; cf. *Gelhausen/Wermelt*, CCZ 2010, 208, 210; *v. Busekist/Hein*, CCZ 2012, 41, 43; *Reichert/Ott*, ZIP 2009, 2173; *Kort*, NZG 2008, 81, 84; *Bürkle*, BB 2005, 565, 567. Indicating: *Fleischer*, AG 2003, 291, 299.

1439 Cf. *Fleischer*, in: Fleischer, Hdb Vorstandsrecht, sec. 8, mar. 40.

1440 *Kremer/Klahold*, ZGR 2010, 113, 121.

1441 *Hüffer*, FS Roth, 299, 304.

1442 *Hüffer*, FS Roth, 299, 304.

phisticated management tools, such as internal control or compliance programs, have to be used to manage the corporation. This notion is in line with the finding that the compliance organization is generally in the interest of the corporation.[1443]

Locating the duty to implement compliance measures within sec. 76 combined with sec. 93 AktG reflects the structure of corporate law. The specific provision of sec. 91(2) AktG mandates only an early warning system which encompasses compliance only as far as non-compliance endangers the survival of the corporation. The duty to implement internal control and risk management systems beyond an early warning system is not part of sec. 91(2) AktG.[1444] Since the compliance organization may be part of internal control and risk management[1445] or is at least similar to internal control, the duty to implement compliance measures is likewise not part of sec. 91(2) AktG.[1446] Instead of extending a specific norm, the general norm, which includes the standard of liability, provides for the needed flexibility to require different levels of sophistication of compliance organizations depending on the needs of a corporation. The early warning system of sec. 91(2) AktG mandates the minimum standard for every corporation while more sophisticated compliance measures may be required due to the specific needs of a corporation derived from the standard of liability.

(2) Scope and Requirements of Compliance Organization

The scope of the required compliance organization is only about to take shape.[1447] The mandates and requirements for a compliance organization depend on the circumstances of each individual case.[1448] In general, the compliance organization has preventive and detective functions.[1449] It has

1443 Cf. *Kindler*, FS Roth, 2011, 367, 377.

1444 See *supra* at chapter 8, B. I. 2. a).

1445 Similar: *Dreher*, FS Hüffer, 161, 168 et seq. Different: *Weber-Rey*, AG 2008, 345, 348 arguing that compliance is not part of risk management. But compliance includes a risk of non-compliance which can be addressed by the risk management. (See on COSO II *supra* at chapter 4, C. III.).

1446 See *supra* at chapter 8, B. I. 2. a).

1447 Cf. *Fleischer*, in: Spindler/Stilz, AktG, sec. 91, mar. 47; *Hüffer/Schneider*, ZIP 2010, 55.

1448 *Mertens/Cahn*, in: Köln Komm AktG, sec. 93, mar. 80; *Bachmann*, VGR, 2008, 65, 68; cf. *Hauschka*, in: Hauschka, Corporate Compliance, sec. 1, mar. 23.

1449 *Schneider*, NZG 2009, 1321, 1325; *Hüffer/Schneider*, ZIP 2010, 55; cf. *Reichert/Ott*, ZIP 2009, 2173 et seq.

to prevent damages and has to include risk prevention.[1450] So far, the scope of the compliance organization depends on the risk profile of the specific corporation[1451] which includes the size, applicable provisions, and prior misconduct in the corporation.[1452] The duty to implement compliance measures does not require to implement a profound compliance organization[1453] but adequate measures[1454], since the duty is limited by necessity and appropriateness.[1455] It follows that the necessary scope of the compliance organization depends on a cost-benefit analysis weighing the costs of a particular level of compliance against the benefits of such level of compliance.[1456] For most corporations, the cost-benefits analysis will reveal that they do not have to implement a profound compliance organization.[1457] The compliance organization should focus on fields of law prone to misconduct such as capital markets law, antitrust law, anti-corruption law, and environmental law.[1458] Also, the corporation has to implement an organization to ensure to comply with tax law and social security law.[1459] The compliance organization has to ensure that every payment transaction can be tracked.[1460]

The management board has the responsibility for establishing adequate and effective compliance measures and has to monitor for the adequacy

1450 Cf. *Fleischer*, AG 2003, 291, 299.

1451 *Fleischer*, in: Spindler/Stilz, AktG, sec. 91, mar. 50; *Mertens/Cahn*, in: Köln Komm AktG, sec. 91, mar. 36; *Hüffer*, AktG, sec. 76, mar. 9a.

1452 *Fleischer*, in: Spindler/Stilz, AktG, sec. 91, mar. 50; *Kort*, NZG 2008, 81, 83; *Fleischer*, AG 2003, 291, 299 et seq.; LG München I, decision of December 10, 2013 – 5 HK O 1387/10, juris at recital 89 et seq.; cf. *AKEIÜ Schmalenbach-Ges.*, DB 2010, 1509, 1511 et seq.; *Bürkle*, in: Haschka, Corporate Compliance, sec. 8, mar. 8.

1453 *Vetter*, FS v. Westphalen, 719, 726: arguing for the need of a statutory mandate for such a duty.

1454 *Weber-Rey*, AG 2008, 345, 346; *Kort*, NZG 2008, 81, 83; cf. *Bürkle*, BB 2007, 1797, 1798.

1455 *Fleischer*, in: Spindler/Stilz, AktG, sec. 91, mar. 53; *Habersack*, in: Münch Komm, sec. 107, 113 et seq.; *Dreher*, FS Hüffer, 161, 174; *Bachmann*, VGR, 2008, 65, 78; *Fleischer*, AG 2003, 291, 300.

1456 *Bachmann*, VGR, 2008, 65, 79; cf. *Dreher/Hoffmann*, ZGR 2016, 445, 491 "efficiency audit".

1457 *Spindler*, in: Münch Komm AktG, sec. 91, mar. 38; *Kort*, Großkomm AktG, sec. 91, mar. 65; *Fleischer*, in: Spindler/Stilz, AktG, sec. 91, mar. 53.

1458 *Fleischer*, in: Spindler/Stilz, AktG, sec. 91, mar. 50; *id.*, CCZ 2008, 1, 2 et seq.

1459 *Bürkle*, BB 2005, 565, 567; *Liese*, BB 2008, Beilage 5, 17; BGHZ 133, 370, 374 et seq.

1460 LG München I, decision of December 10, 2013 – 5 HK O 1387/10, juris at recital 94.

and effectiveness of the implemented measures.[1461] While the entire management board is responsible for the compliance organization[1462], the responsibility for the compliance organization should be assigned to one member of the management board.[1463] With regard to the structure of the compliance organization, no centralized compliance measures regarding legal risks have to be taken[1464], so that labor and employment law issues may be dealt with by the human resources department. In many corporations however, the compliance function is part of the legal department.[1465] The scope of the compliance organization does not encompass a general duty to conduct standardized compliance trainings or to appoint a compliance officer.[1466] For large, listed corporations, the entity-wide coordination of the compliance measures may be necessary within due course of business[1467] including a clear assignment of responsibility regarding compliance within the management board with authority to take appropriate actions[1468]. Also for large corporations, appointing a CCO might be useful and may be legally mandatory if a certain risk profile exists.[1469] Otherwise, it has been argued that listed corporations have the duty to appoint a CCO.[1470] The CCO should have the responsibility to design, improve, doc-

1461 *Fleischer*, in: Spindler/Stilz, AktG, sec. 91, mar. 54 and 60; LG München I, decision of December 10, 2013 – 5 HK O 1387/10, juris at recital 97 et seq.; *Withus/Hein*, CCZ 2011, 125, 128; *Winter*, FS Hüffer, 1103, 1106; cf. *Liese*, BB 2008, Beilage 5, 17, 22.

1462 *Mertens/Cahn*, Köln Komm AktG, sec. 91, mar. 36; cf. *Spindler*, in: Münch Komm AktG, sec. 93, mar. 149.

1463 LG München I, decision of December 10, 2013 – 5 HK O 1387/10, juris at recital 98; *Hauschka*, ZIP 2004, 877, 881; *Hauschka*, NJW 2004, 257, 259; *Fleischer*, in: Spindler/Stilz, AktG, sec. 91, mar. 58; *Kort*, NZG 2008, 81, 83; *Fleischer*, CCZ 2008, 1, 3; *Kremer/Klahold*, ZGR 2010, 113, 125; cf. *Fleischer*, in: Fleischer, Hdb Vorstandsrecht, sec. 8, mar. 44.

1464 *Spindler*, in: Münch Komm AktG, sec. 91, mar. 38.

1465 *Dreher*, FS Hüffer, 161, 172; *Kremer/Klahold*, ZGR 2010, 113, 125 et seq.

1466 *Spindler*, in: Münch Komm AktG, sec. 91, mar. 38.

1467 *Mertens/Cahn*, Köln Komm AktG, sec. 91, mar. 36; *Hauschka*, ZIP 2004, 877, 878.

1468 LG München I, decision of December 10, 2013 – 5 HK O 1387/10, juris at recital 98 et seq.

1469 *Spindler*, in: Münch Komm AktG, sec. 91, mar. 38; *Kremer/Klahold*, ZGR 2010, 113, 120.

1470 *Dreher*, FS Hüffer, 161, 172; *Kort*, NZG 2008, 81, 83; *Weber-Rey*, AG 2008, 345, 346; *Fleischer*, in: Spindler/Stilz, AktG, sec. 91, mar. 58; cf. *id.*, in: Fleischer, Hdb Vorstandsrecht, sec. 8, mar. 44; *Schneider*, ZIP 2003, 645, 650. Against a general duty to appoint a CCO: *Kort*, FS Roth, 407, 410. See for an overview on the CCO: *Bürkle*, in: Haschka, Corporate Compliance, sec. 8, mar. 23 et seq.

ument, and report on the compliance organization.[1471] It has been argued that the CCO needs to have the right to report directly to the supervisory board, if indicated.[1472] In this regard, the issue of direct communication lines to the supervisory board will be dealt with further below.[1473] If a member of the management board is suspected of misconduct, the CCO has to inform another member of such board, or the supervisory board or the audit committee.[1474] Depending on the assumed responsibilities, the CCO may have the legal obligation to report known criminal behavior to the supervisory board.[1475] Otherwise, the CCO may be subject to prosecution.[1476]

Similar to the scope of the compliance organization, no general understanding exists on the requirements for the compliance organization.[1477] The management board has rather broad discretion protected by sec. 93(1) (s. 2) AktG on how to design the compliance organization.[1478] It has been argued that the discretion should not be limited through mandatory minimum requirements.[1479] Nevertheless, minimum requirements have been formulated for the compliance organization such as corporation-specific compliance standards including a code of conduct[1480], training programs[1481], monitoring, disciplining of misconduct[1482], hotlines, appropriate risk analysis, communication through a mission statement of the management, presentations, newsletters and information material, assigning re-

1471 *Fleischer*, in: Spindler/Stilz, AktG, sec. 91, mar. 58; *Bürkle*, BB 2007, 1797, 1799.

1472 *Lösler*, WM 2007, 676, 679; *Illing/Umnuß*, CCZ 2009, 1, 5.

1473 See *infra* at chapter 8, B. II. 1. c).

1474 *Rodewald/Unger*, BB 2007, 1629, 1632.

1475 BGH, decision of July 17, 2009 - 5 StR 394/08, CCZ 2009, 239; cf. *Pietzke*, CCZ 2010, 45, 51.

1476 See *infra* at chapter 8, E. I. 3.

1477 *Fleischer*, in: Spindler/Stilz, AktG, sec. 91, mar. 51.

1478 *Fleischer*, in: Spindler/Stilz, AktG, sec. 91, mar. 53; *Kort*, NZG 2008, 81, 83; *Fleischer*, AG 2003, 291, 299; *Kremer/Klahold*, ZGR 2010, 113, 121; *Reichert/Ott*, ZIP 2009, 2173, 2175; in: Haschka, Corporate Compliance, sec. 8, mar. 15.

1479 *Mertens/Cahn*, Köln Komm AktG, sec. 91, mar. 36 et seq.; cf. *Hauschka*, ZIP 2004, 877, 878; *Winter*, FS Hüffer, 1103, 1104 and 1105.

1480 Cf. *Fleischer*, in: Spindler/Stilz, AktG, sec. 91, mar. 55; *AKEIÜ Schmalenbach-Ges.*, DB 2010, 1509, 1512. Against the need and effect of code of conduct: *Kort*, FS Roth, 407, 411.

1481 Cf. *Pauthner/de Lamboy*, CCZ 2011, 106, 109; *id.*, CCZ 2011, 146 et seq.

1482 *Fleischer*, in: Spindler/Stilz, AktG, sec. 91, mar. 56; *Bussmann/Matschke*, CCZ 2009, 132, 136.

sponsibilities, skilled personnel, and documentation.[1483] These minimum requirements for compliance programs resemble U.S. compliance concepts.[1484] The compliance organization has to ensure that the management board is constantly and profoundly informed with regard to suspicious activities. It is also the duty of the management board to inform itself of such activities.[1485]

The code of conduct should enumerate all relevant legal mandates applicable to the corporation such as labor and employment law, environmental law, antitrust law, and capital markets law as well as corporation-specific guidelines.[1486] Ongoing monitoring activities of the compliance organization including to monitor its appropriateness and effectiveness have to be part of the compliance organization as well as compliance reporting.[1487] Monitoring also has to include taking corrective measures, if indicated.[1488] With regard to potential misconduct, measures have to be in place to address any misconduct in order to prevent further harm and to evaluate the harm caused.[1489] In general, the compliance organization has to be documented especially to enable audits and to provide evidence in case of lawsuits.[1490] The legal duty to document does not encompass to document every detail of the compliance organization.[1491] Especially with regard to

1483 *Schneider*, ZIP 2003, 645, 649 et seq.; *Bürkle*, BB 2005, 565; *Hauschka*, ZIP 2004, 877, 882; cf. *Mertens/Cahn*, Köln Komm AktG, sec. 91, mar. 37; *Lampert*, in: Hauschka, Corporate Compliance, sec. 9, mar. 13 et seq.; *Immenga*, 2009, p. 203; *Kremer/Klahold*, ZGR 2010, 113, 128 et seq.; *Hauschka*, VGR, 2008, 51, 57 et seq.; *Winter*, FS Hüffer, 1103, 1106 et seq.; *Kindler*, FS Roth, 2011, 367, 370; *Hauschka*, ZIP 2004, 877, 880; *AKEIÜ Schmalenbach-Ges.*, DB 2010, 1509, 1512 et seq. See for corruption-specific elements: BMI, Praktsiche Hilfestellungen für Antikorruptionsmaßnahmen, 2013; BMI, Empfehlungen zur Korruptionsprävention in der Bundesverwaltung, 2012; ICC, Code of Conduct.

1484 See *infra* at chapter 12, A. III.

1485 LG München I, decision of December 10, 2013 – 5 HK O 1387/10, juris at recital 101.

1486 *Schneider*, ZIP 2003, 645, 648; cf. *Hauschka*, ZIP 2004, 887, 880. Different: *Kort*, FS Roth, 407, 411.

1487 *Fleischer*, in: Spindler/Stilz, AktG, sec. 91, mar. 54; *Reichert/Ott*, ZIP 2009, 2173; *Moosmayer*, Compliance, p. 89; *AKEIÜ Schmalenbach-Ges.*, DB 2010, 1509, 1517; cf. *Liese/Schulz*, BB 2011, 1347 et seq.

1488 *Reichert/Ott*, ZIP 2009, 2173, 2177; *Moosmayer*, Compliance, p. 89.

1489 *Fleischer*, in: Spindler/Stilz, AktG, sec. 91, mar. 55; *Kremer/Klahold*, ZGR 2010, 113, 127.

1490 *Bachmann*, VGR, 2008, 65, 82; cf. BGH, decision of February 22, 2011 – II ZR 146/09, CCZ 2011, 233, 235 (annotated by *Schubert*).

1491 *Bachmann*, VGR, 2008, 65, 82.

large, listed corporations, a whistleblowing system has been named a core element of a compliance organization.[1492] Therefore, implementing an ombudsman for handling whistleblower complaints has been suggested.[1493] The corporation has to implement procedures to handle alleged misconduct. The CCO should investigate the circumstances and facts of the alleged misconduct, report to appropriate management level, decide on defensive measures including self-reporting to law enforcement authorities, instruct the public relation office, and evaluate the whole process after the case has been closed.[1494]

Implementing compliance programs has become best practice within large, listed corporations.[1495] The management board has the duty to adhere to the minimum requirements to design the compliance organization with regard to the specific needs of the corporation. For large, listed corporations, the minimum legal standard for the compliance organization converges towards best practice considering *inter alia* the COSO frameworks. In light of the newly established auditing standard on compliance management systems (IDW PS 980[1496]), the management board should consider the elements of the auditing standard to design the compliance organization which will receive an unqualified attestation in case of a voluntary audit of the compliance organization. In general, it is essential that corporations do not stop short in implementing compliance programs. Rather, compliance is an ongoing issue which requires monitoring and corrective measures.[1497]

(3) Effectiveness of the Compliance Organization

The effectiveness of the compliance organization is an important issue[1498] as only an effective compliance organization will provide for the necessary measures to optimally prevent and detect misconduct. In general, a com-

1492 *Fleischer*, ZGR 2011, 155, 175; *Berndt/Hoppler*, BB 2005, 2623; *Mengel/Hagemeister*, BB 2007, 1386. Different: *Kort*, FS Roth, 407, 412. See for more details on whistleblowing *infra* at chapter 8, D. I. 2. and D. II.

1493 *Kremer/Klahold*, ZGR 2010, 113, 134.

1494 *Rodewald/Unger*, BB 2007, 1629, 1634 et seq.

1495 *Kremer/Klahold*, ZGR 2010, 113, 121.

1496 See *infra* at chapter 9, C.

1497 *Rodewald/Unger*, BB 2006, 116, 117.

1498 See *infra* at chapter 16, B. IV. 1.

pliance organization needs to be effective and efficient.[1499] Besides the need to prevent and detect misconduct effectively, it has been stated that compliance departments have to justify the costs of the compliance organization by measuring its effectiveness.[1500] The main question is: what elements of a compliance organization are needed to consider the organization effective?[1501] The elements of a compliance program constituting the current best practice in Germany are: culture of compliance[1502] including tone at the top with a commitment of management to adhere to compliance[1503], compliance structure, and compliance program including the information of employees, identification of risks, and reporting.[1504] In order to inform employees, a code of conduct explaining the applicable laws and regulation may be used.[1505] Training employees is also an important part of the compliance program including reiterating onside sessions and e-learning.[1506] The compliance program should include general whistleblower hotlines.[1507] Monitoring activities such as audits should be part of a compliance system[1508] as well as to improve the system in case of identified deficiencies[1509]. An information system for communication is also essential for the compliance organization.[1510] German best practice reflects elements of COSO I and the USSG.[1511] The current best practice resembles more or less the named minimum requirements for a compliance organization.

1499 Cf. *Bergmoser/Theusinger/Gushurst*, BB 2008, Beilage 5, 1, 6 et seq.; *AKEIÜ Schmalenbach-Ges.*, DB 2010, 1509, 1514.

1500 *Benz/Klindt*, BB 2010, 2977.

1501 Cf. *Lösler*, WM 2007, 676.

1502 *Wendt*, in: Hauschka, Corporate Compliance, sec. 9; *Bussmann*, CCZ 2016, 50, 52 et seq.; *Pape*, CCZ 2009, 223; *Itzen*, BB 2008, Beilage 5, 12, 14.

1503 Cf. *Sieber*, FS Tiedemann, 449, 477; *Wendt*, in: Hauschka, Corporate Compliance, sec. 9, mar. 1.

1504 *Kremer/Klahold*, ZGR 2010, 113, 123; cf. *Sieber*, FS Tiedemann, 449, 458 and 477.

1505 *Kremer/Klahold*, ZGR 2010, 113, 128 et seq. Suspecting a preventive effect of codes of conduct: *Theile*, ZIS 2008, 417 et seq.

1506 *Kremer/Klahold*, ZGR 2010, 113, 130 et seq.

1507 *Kremer/Klahold*, ZGR 2010, 113, 131.

1508 *Kremer/Klahold*, ZGR 2010, 113, 132.

1509 *Kremer/Klahold*, ZGR 2010, 113, 136.

1510 *Buck-Heeb*, in: Haschka, Corporate Compliance, sec. 2, mar. 15 et seq.; *Rodewald/Unger*, BB 2007, 1629 et seq. and at fn. 16 citing Siemens AG; *Dreher/Hoffmann*, ZGR 2016, 445, 480 et seq.

1511 See *infra* at chapter 12, A. III.

The effectiveness of certain elements of best practice has been evaluated indicating that the compliance measures have the potential to be effective in preventing and detecting misconduct but only if the people of the corporation are truly committed to the corporate culture of compliance.[1512] The findings show that the elements of compliance programs currently reflecting best practice have the potential to provide for an effective compliance organization. It is important to note, however, that a compliance organization is only effective if the design and the operation are effective.[1513]

Without any reference to a legal statute, it has been stated that the compliance organization is effective if it is able to detect and especially prevent intentional behavior.[1514] Also, the district court of Munich held that the compliance organization has to prevent misconduct and it seems that the court expects a compliance organization to be effective if no further misconduct would be reported to the management board.[1515] This standard is too high. It requires an almost perfect system without any deficiencies which is able to detect or preferably prevent all intentional and unintentional behavior. The standard does not account for the difficulties to prevent and detect intentional behavior especially from the management board[1516] and the inherent limitations of internal control and compliance measures[1517]. It is important to note, that deliberate non-compliance of employees may not prejudice the conclusion that compliance measures are ineffective.[1518] The occurrence of occasional reports of alleged misconduct does not by itself justify the conclusion that the compliance organization is ineffective.[1519] Although, a constant flow of reports of alleged misconduct

---

1512 Cf. *Sieber/Engelhart*, Compliance Programs Survey, p. 207 et seq.; *Bussemann*, PwC Study 2010, p. 37 et seq.; *Bussmann/Salvenmoser*, CCZ 2008, 192, 194; *Pape*, CCZ 2009, 223; *Sieber*, FS Tiedemann, 449, 474; *Lösler*, WM 2007, 676, 677; and with regard to U.S. studies: *Pape*, Corporate Compliance, p. 219 et seq. (appendix). Different: *Schünemann*, FS Tiedemann, 429, 444 citing: *Laufer*, 1999. See *infra* at chapter 16, A. I. 2. a) (2).

1513 See for more details *infra* at chapter 16, B. IV.

1514 *AKEIÜ Schmalenbach-Ges.*, DB 2010, 1509, 1514.

1515 LG München I, decision of December 10, 2013 – 5 HK O 1387/10, juris at recital 103, 105 and 114.

1516 See *supra* at chapter 4, A. II. 1. c).

1517 See *supra* at chapter 4, C. I. 1. b). Also *Voet v. Vormizeele*, CCZ 2009, 41, 48.

1518 *Kremer/Klahold*, ZGR 2010, 113, 118; BGH, decision of March 11, 1986 – KRB 7/85, WuW/E BGH 2262 ("*Aktenvermerk*"); cf. *Fleischer*, in: Fleischer, Hdb Vorstandsrecht, sec. 8, mar. 45.

1519 Cf. *Bachmann*, ZIP 2014, 579, 580; *Grützner*, BB 2014, 850, 851.

may be a strong indication of an ineffective compliance organization.[1520] Moreover, under the constraint of efficiency, no compliance organization will be able to prevent all misconduct. In essence, the suggested standard lacks the consideration of the general capability of compliance organization and, more important, any reference to a legal statute requiring such high standard for effectiveness of compliance organizations. Even the high standard of the SEC with regard to the effectiveness of internal control over financial reporting only requires such controls to be without material weaknesses to be considered effective.[1521] In reference to sec. 171(1) AktG and IDW PS 261, the systems might be deemed effective if no significant deficiencies exist. The criterion for effectiveness including the four pillars of an effective internal control and compliance system will be depicted below.[1522]

(4) Evaluation of the Effectiveness of the Compliance Organization

As part of the duty to manage the corporation pursuant to sec. 76 combined with sec. 93 AktG, the management board has to ensure that the effectiveness of the compliance organization is monitored and has to take appropriate measures in case the ineffectiveness of the compliance organization becomes apparent.[1523] The management board has to evaluate the effectiveness of the compliance organization especially in case of numerous cases of suspected criminal activities within the corporation.[1524] Also, the management board has to use periodic reports including results of internal investigations for its evaluation of the effectiveness.[1525] In case of an appar-

1520 Cf. LG München I, decision of December 10, 2013 – 5 HK O 1387/10, juris at recital 99.

1521 See *supra* at chapter 4, A. II. 2. b) (3).

1522 See *infra* at chapter 16, B. IV. 1.

1523 *Fleischer*, in: Spindler/Stilz, AktG, sec. 91, mar. 60; LG München I, decision of December 10, 2013 – 5 HK O 1387/10, juris at recital 101; *Merkt*, DB 2014, 2331.

1524 LG München I, decision of December 10, 2013 – 5 HK O 1387/10, juris at recital 97; cf. *Fleischer*, in: Spindler/Stilz, AktG, sec. 91, mar. 60; *Dreher/Hoffmann*, ZGR 2016, 445, 491.

1525 Cf. LG München I, decision of December 10, 2013 – 5 HK O 1387/10, juris at recital 101.

ent ineffectiveness, management has to act without unreasonable delay to address the ineffectiveness of the compliance organization.[1526]

As measures to safeguard and evaluate the effectiveness of the compliance program have been named: documentation of training, self-assessments, knowledge tests for employees, surveys, evaluation of appropriateness of resources for compliance organization, and evaluation of whistleblower systems through testing.[1527] Furthermore, the CCO, internal audit and external experts need to conduct assessments of the compliance organization.[1528]

While the named measures and assessments are valuable elements for the evaluation of the effectiveness of the compliance organization, the corporation has to define benchmarks and key performance indicators which the compliance organization has to achieve considering the COSO frameworks in order to be able to evaluate the effectiveness of the compliance organization.[1529] In order to develop compliance benchmarks and key performance indicators, corporations have to define a compliance strategy and policy.[1530] Using the COSO frameworks is consistent with the performance level required by the general liability standard for managing the corporation (sec. 93(1) AktG). Since the law does not require a specific performance level for the compliance organization of corporations not subject to the specific regulatory law, the general liability standard for managing the corporation (sec. 93(1) AktG) has to be used to derive the specific performance level of the compliance organization which the compliance organization has to achieve in order to be considered effective, i.e. the standard of sec. 93(1) AktG equals the minimum requirements of the performance level. Thus, the general standards for the benchmarks and key performance indicators for each corporation depend on the liability standard of sec. 93(1) AktG to manage the business with due diligence of a prudent businessman. Since the minimum requirements for compliance organizations of large, listed corporations converge towards best practice considering the COSO frameworks[1531], the COSO frameworks have to be considered for

1526 LG München I, decision of December 10, 2013 – 5 HK O 1387/10, juris at recital 101.

1527 *Moosmayer*, Compliance, p. 89; cf. *Pape*, CCZ 2009, 223, 234.

1528 *Moosmayer*, Compliance, p. 90.

1529 See *infra* at chapter 16, B. IV. Also *Withus*, DB 2009, Beilage 5, 82, 85; cf. *Pauthner/de Lamboy*, CCZ 2011, 106, 107. Similar: *Nonnenmacher/Pohle/v. Werder*, DB 2009, 1447, 1451; *Powilleit*, GWR 2010, 28.

1530 *Pauthner/de Lamboy*, CCZ 2011, 106, 107. See *infra* at chapter 16, B. IV. 1.

1531 See *supra* at chapter 8, B. I. 3. a) (2).

setting the performance level for the effectiveness of the compliance organization of large, listed corporations.

Moreover, for defining benchmarks and key performance indicators, the corporation has to consider all legal mandates regarding the performance of the compliance organization in order to ensure that the compliance organization meets the requested performance. Thus, the benchmarks and key performance indicators have to reflect the mandates of sec. 91(2) AktG that the compliance organization ensures to detect developments endangering the survival of the corporation due to non-compliance.[1532] Likewise, the benchmarks and key performance indicators have to reflect the mandates of sec. 130 OWiG that the compliance organization includes monitoring measures which prevent or materially aggravate to commit infringements of duties within the scope of the corporation.[1533]

(5) Internal Investigations

In the wake of the debate on compliance, internal investigations are a new development in Germany.[1534] Internal investigations encompass mostly forensic investigations by law firms on behalf of the corporation to investigate alleged corporate misconduct.[1535] In case of investigations, the compliance program will provide useful information to avoid loss of reputation due to public relation issues.[1536] In the U.S., internal investigations are mainly used to provide information to enforcement agencies in order to receive leniency for cooperation.[1537] In addition and prior to self-reporting or cooperation, internal investigations provide detailed and objective information for the management board and the supervisory board whether, and if so, what kind of corporate misconduct occurred. Also, corporations use internal investigation to protect the corporation against any damages reaching from theft to disclosure of corporate secrets.[1538] Moreover, corporations should conduct internal investigations in order to verify whether

---

1532 See *supra* at chapter 8, B. I. 2. b).
1533 See *infra* at chapter 8, E. III. 2.
1534 Cf. *Wagner*, CCZ 2009, 8.
1535 Cf. *Wagner*, CCZ 2009, 8.
1536 Cf. *Kremer/Klahold*, ZGR 2010, 113, 138.
1537 See *supra* at chapter 5, C. II. 2. and D. I. and E. Also *Wagner*, CCZ 2009, 8, 9. For more details on the impact of the U.S. practice on German corporations see *infra* at chapter 12, B.
1538 *Dann/Gastell*, NJW 2008, 2945.

the compliance organization is still adequate and to eliminate the possibility of reoccurrences of misconduct by taking corrective actions, if indicated.[1539] The management board may be required to conduct internal investigations in light of sec. 76 combined with sec. 93 AktG in order to investigate alleged corporate crime.[1540] Similarly to the compliance organization, internal investigations have to adhere to the law mainly labor and employment law, data protection law and criminal law.[1541]

As part of the attempt to investigate corporate misconduct, amnesty programs may be used for lower level employees to foster cooperation with the internal investigators.[1542] Within law enforcement proceedings, sec. 46b StGB provides incentives for corporate wrongdoers to cooperate with law enforcement by providing leniency for contributing to solve a case. It has been stressed that sec. 46b StGB may lead to hastily self-reporting of potential suspects to law enforcement agencies which may be contrary to the corporation's attempt to avoid investigations by law enforcement.[1543] In order to avoid uncontrolled self-reporting, corporations need to investigate potential misconduct as part of the effective compliance organization.[1544]

With regard to internal investigation and cooperation with law enforcement agencies, corporations have to prepare its employees for internal and external investigations and cooperation.[1545] A contingency plan has to be implemented and needs to include elements such as information regarding the duties and rights of employees during investigation proceedings, instruction manual, crisis team, defensive strategy, selection of appropriate conference room, public relations, notification of management, notification of lawyers, eligibility check of prosecutorial investigators, check of search warrant, check of investigation report, no statements without legal advisor, communication, illegal behavior, report by corporation, notifica-

1539 *Schürrle/Olbers*, CCZ 2010, 102, 107.

1540 *Wagner*, CCZ 2009, 8, 13; *Fleischer*, AG 2003, 291, 294.

1541 Cf. *Dann/Gastell*, NJW 2008, 2945 et seq.; *Schneider*, NZG 2010, 1201 et seq.; *Göpfert/Merten/Siegrist*, NJW 2008, 1703, 1705 et seq.; *Klengel/Mückenberger*, CCZ 2009, 81, 82 et seq. See for details on labor law issues: *Vogt*, NJOZ 2009, 4206 et seq.; *Mengel*, Compliance und Arbeitsrecht, ch. 4, B. See for details on data protection issues: *Vogel/Glas*, DB 2009, 1747 et seq.

1542 Cf. *Mengel*, Compliance und Arbeitsrecht, ch. 5, VI; *Benz/Klindt*, BB 2010, 2977, 2979. See on elements of amnesty programs: *Annuß/Pelz*, BB 2010, Beilage 4, 14, 15 et seq.

1543 *Dann*, CCZ 2010, 30, 33.

1544 *Sahan/Berndt*, BB 2010, 647, 652.

1545 *Campos Nave/Bonenberger*, BB 2008, 734, 736; *Kremer*, FS Schneider, 701, 702.

tion of clients, feedback within crisis team, contacting the media, and evaluation and improvement of contingency plan after investigations.[1546] As far as the contingency plan includes rules regarding the organization of the workplace within the corporation (sec. 87(1)(no. 1) BetrVG), the works council has to participate in the implementation process.[1547]

c) Summary

The duty to manage the corporation pursuant to sec. 76 combined with sec. 93 AktG requires the management board to implement internal control and risk management systems beyond the early warning system of sec. 91(2) AktG depending on the circumstances of the specific corporation. Nevertheless, the duty to manage the corporation does not generally require to implement profound internal control and risk management systems. Also, with regard to large, listed corporations, the duty to manage the corporation does not generally require to implement profound internal control and risk management systems. Nevertheless, the minimum legal standard to manage the corporation for large, listed corporations converges towards best practice for internal control and risk management systems. The duty to manage the corporation includes in any case monitoring and compliance measures, effectiveness and efficiency considerations, measures to fulfill the reporting duty of sec. 90(1) AktG, and documenting the important elements of the existing internal control and risk management systems. In order to be able to evaluate the effectiveness of internal control and risk management systems, the management board has to define benchmarks by using COSO I or COSO II. These frameworks may also be used to design and operate such systems.

The duty to manage the corporation includes to take compliance measures. The duty does not encompass to implement profound compliance measures but adequate measures which are effective. The scope of the compliance organization depends on the specific needs of the corporation. The management board has wide discretion to decide on the appropriate compliance measures. In general, the responsibility for the compliance function should be assigned to a CCO and one member of the management board should assume the responsibility for compliance. Further minimum requirements for the compliance organization have been named including

1546 *Campos Nave/Bonenberger*, BB 2008, 734, 736 et seq.
1547 With regard to codes of conduct see also *infra* at chapter 8, D. I. 1.

a code of conduct, training programs, ongoing monitoring, disciplining of misconduct, hotlines, appropriate risk analysis, communication, assigning responsibilities, skilled personnel, and documentation. To prepare internal investigations, corporations need to establish a contingency plan as part of compliance organization. For large, listed corporations, a whistleblowing system is an essential additional measure of the compliance organization. Moreover, the minimum legal standard for the compliance organization of large, listed corporations converges towards best practice considering the *inter alia* the COSO frameworks and the auditing standard IDW PS 980. For designing and operating the compliance organization as well as for conducting internal investigations, the corporation has to adhere to the legal mandates especially of the labor and employment law and data protection law.

The effectiveness of the internal control and risk management system including compliance measures is important. In order to achieve an effective compliance organization, the people of the corporation have to be committed to compliance reflected in the corporate culture. Besides this element, the effectiveness of the compliance organization is corporation-specific. Each corporation has to set its specific compliance benchmarks and key performance indicators for the design and operation of the compliance organization. For defining these thresholds, the corporation has to adhere to the performance level required by the compliance-related mandates of sec. 91(2) AktG, the mandates of sec. 130 OWiG, and the corporation-specific performance level derived from the minimum legal requirements for the compliance organization pursuant to sec. 76 combined with sec. 93 AktG which converge for large, listed corporations towards best practice.

4. Conclusion

The management board's duties regarding internal control and compliance are based on two provisions encompassing the early warning system of sec. 91(2) AktG and the duty to manage the corporation pursuant to sec. 76 combined with sec. 93 AktG. Neither of these duties generally require the management board to implement profound internal control or risk management systems nor a profound compliance organization. Nevertheless, depending on the specific circumstances especially of large, listed corporations, the management board may have the duty pursuant to sec. 76 combined with sec. 93 AktG to implement effective internal control and risk management systems including a compliance organization reflecting best practice for such systems. With regard to the scope of the early warning system, internal control, and risk management, BilMoG highlights the importance of internal control, risk management, and compliance but does not change the scope of the management board's duties.

The duty to implement an early warning system with the function to timely detect risks endangering the survival of the corporation provides for the rudimentary control structure to address risks within the corporation including the risk of non-compliance as far as it concerns the survival of the corporation. As part of the early warning system, corporations have to implement *inter alia* a monitoring system, risk management, and internal audit. While the design and operation of the early warning system depends on the specific needs of each corporation, the general scope of sec. 91(2) AktG is limited to an early warning system.

The duty to manage the corporation provides the needed flexibility to require different level of sophistication for the internal control and risk management systems including compliance measures depending on the specific needs of each corporation including the ownership structure. The management board has wide discretion to design and operate the internal control and risk management systems but has to adhere to the legal mandates of specific law such as labor and employment law and data protection law. Within large, listed corporations, the early warning system will be absorbed into the internal control and risk management systems. As part of the internal control regarding financial reporting, corporations have to implement books and records keeping measures pursuant to sec. 91(1) AktG. The duty to manage the corporation includes ensuring that all people of the corporation comply with laws and regulation.

In essence, the duties for the management board regarding internal control, risk management, and compliance require corporations to implement elements of effective internal control and risk management systems including compliance measures. Large, listed corporations need to implement proficient measures considering the COSO frameworks as well as the mandates of the OWiG. The minimum requirements of internal control and risk management systems including compliance converge towards best practice for these corporations. For evaluating the effectiveness, corporations have to define benchmarks and key performance indicators for the implemented internal control and compliance measures.

II. Supervisory Board's Duties Regarding Internal Control and Compliance

In its capacity to supervise the management board pursuant to sec. 111 AktG, the general duty of the supervisory board includes to supervise the early warning system of sec. 91(2) AktG and any other measures taken by the management board regarding internal control, risk management, and compliance. In 2009, BilMoG introduced sec. 107(3) and 171(1) AktG mainly addressing financial reporting and oversight duties of the supervisory board regarding internal control and risk management. In the following, the supervisory board' duties regarding internal control and compliance will be analyzed.

1. Audit Committee – Section 107(3) AktG

In sec. 107(3)(s. 2) AktG, BilMoG introduced into the statute the option for the supervisory board to implement an audit committee which may have the responsibility to supervise and monitor the financial reporting process, the effectiveness of the internal control system, the effectiveness of the risk management system, and the effectiveness of the internal audit system as well as the effectiveness of the annual audit especially with regard to the independence of the external auditor.[1548] In light of former art. 41(2) Directive 2006/43/EC, the internal control and risk management systems encompass all aspects of risk management not only financial reporting.[1549] In accordance with the directive, internal control has to encompass financial, operational, and compliance risks.[1550] It is the duty of supervisory board to supervise the effectiveness of the systems enumerated in sec. 107(3)(s. 2) AktG[1551] and the compliance organization[1552]. Moreover, the supervisory board has to determine whether a risk management system has

1548 Cf. Begr RegE BilMoG, BT-Drucks. 16/10067, p. 102. See on the audit committee: *Windbichler*, Hdb Corporate Governance, 825, 831 et seq.

1549 Begr RegE BilMoG, BT-Drucks. 16/10067, p. 102.

1550 Directive 2006/43/EC recital 24; cf. *AKEU/AKEIÜ Schmalenbach-Ges.*, DB 2009, 1279, 1281; *Spindler*, FS Hüffer, 985, 992; *Spindler*, WM 2008, 905, 906 et seq. See for the general duty to monitor for compliance: *Schneider*, ZIP 2003, 645, 647.

1551 *Kort*, ZGR 2010, 440, 469.

1552 *Spindler*, in: Spindler/Stilz, AktG, sec. 107, mar. 131. Different: *Merkt*, DB 2014, 2271, 2272.

to be implemented in case no system exists within the corporation.[1553] In accordance with Directive 2014/56/EU, the audit committee may submit recommendations or proposals to ensure the integrity of the financial reporting process (sec. 107(3)(s. 3) AktG.

If the supervisory board does not implement an audit committee the entire board has to assume the indicated responsibilities.[1554] It is common amongst large, listed German corporations to implement an audit committee.[1555] In case the supervisory board implements an audit committee, sec. 107(4) AktG requires that the members fulfill the requirements of sec. 100(5) AktG. According to sec. 100(5) AktG, one member of the supervisory board has to have specific knowledge within the areas of accounting and annual auditing. The knowledge may be acquired by professional experience or other occupation.[1556] Moreover, the members of the audit as a whole need to be competent regarding the sector in which the corporation is operating (sec. 100(5) AktG).

a) Assessment of Effectiveness

With regard to the duty of the supervisory board to monitor the effectiveness of the systems enumerated in sec. 107(3)(s. 2) AktG, the main issue within sec. 107(3)(s. 2) AktG is the scope of the evaluation of the effectiveness and the requirements to consider such systems effective. In general, the determination whether the enumerated systems are effective depends on the judgment of the audit committee. In this regard, the audit committee has to evaluate whether the systems are adequate for the corporation and whether they have been operated as envisioned.[1557] For the assessment, the audit committee has to receive a report of the management board regarding the effectiveness which the audit committee has to evaluate.[1558] The audit committee does not have a general duty to conduct own investi-

---

1553 *Ernst/Seidler*, ZGR 2008, 631, 664.

1554 Begr RegE BilMoG, BT-Drucks. 16/10067, p. 102; *Kort*, ZGR 2010, 440, 449; *Ernst/Seidler*, BB 2007, 2557, 2564; *Ernst/Seidler*, ZGR 2008, 631, 662 et seq.; *Spindler*, FS Hüffer, 985, 986; *Preußner*, NZG 2008, 574.

1555 *Lanfermann/Röhricht*, BB 2009, 887; *Weber-Rey*, AG 2008, 345, 348.

1556 *Hüffer*, AktG, sec. 100, mar. 12.

1557 *Habersack*, in: Münch Komm, sec. 107, 113 et seq.

1558 *Nonnenmacher/Pohle/v. Werder*, DB 2009, 1447, 1451; *Kort*, ZGR 2010, 440, 462; *Withus*, DB 2009, Beilage 5, 82, 84 (suggesting a questionnaire on p. 89); cf. *Wohlmannstetter*, ZGR 2010, 472, 483.

gations or to commission further audits.[1559] In case further information is needed, the audit committee has to request such information.[1560] The audit committee should also use reports of internal audit.[1561] The audit committee may commission further audits to internal audit requested through the management board or to external experts[1562] pursuant to sec. 111(2) (s. 2) AktG.[1563] In case of doubt regarding the information provided by the management board, the audit committee has a duty to use its rights pursuant to sec. 90(3) and sec. 111(2)(s. 1) AktG which includes to commission own investigations.[1564]

The legislative documents state that the audit committee should inquire whether additions, enhancements, or improvements are necessary using *inter alia* the findings of the external auditor regarding the significant deficiencies of the internal control system and the risk management system but only with regard to financial reporting (sec. 171(1)(s. 2) AktG).[1565] In an attempt to specify the general evaluation duty, it has been indicated that the evaluation is beyond verifying that risk manuals and an early warning system exist within the corporation.[1566] The audit committee should at least evaluate the functionality of the implemented systems.[1567] Also, it has been noted that the assessment would be similar to a profound validity check.[1568] With regard to the evaluation of the early warning system by the external auditor (sec. 317(4) HGB), the scope of this evaluation is limited to verify the functionality and not the entrepreneurial appropriateness of the early warning system which is part of the supervisory board's duties of

1559 OLG München, NZG 2010, 784 et seq. Different: *Gros/Velte*, DStR 2012, 2243, 2245.

1560 *Nonnenmacher/Pohle/v. Werder*, DB 2009, 1447, 1451; cf. *Wohlmannstetter*, ZGR 2010, 472, 483; *Dreher/Hoffmann*, ZGR 2016, 445, 495 et seq.

1561 Cf. *AKEU/AKEIÜ Schmalenbach-Ges.*, DB 2009, 1279, 1282; *Nonnenmacher/Pohle/v. Werder*, DB 2009, 1447, 1451.

1562 See *infra* at chapter 9, C.

1563 Cf. *Nonnenmacher/Pohle/v. Werder*, DB 2009, 1447, 1451; *Wohlmannstetter*, ZGR 2010, 472, 483.

1564 *Habersack*, in: Münch Komm AktG, sec. 111, mar. 47 and 66 et seq.; *Spinder*, in: Spindler/Stilz, AktG, sec. 111, mar. 21; OLG München, NZG 2010, 784, 785. Different: *Arnold*, ZGR 2014, 76, 100 et seq. arguing that the supervisory board may only commission own investigations in case the management board obstructs the supervision of the supervisory board.

1565 Begr RegE BilMoG, BT-Drucks. 16/10067, p. 102 et seq.; cf. *Withus*, DB 2009, Beilage 5, 82, 87.

1566 *Preußner*, NZG 2008, 574, 575.

1567 *Lanfermann/Röhricht*, BB 2009, 887, 890.

1568 *Vetter*, ZGR 2010, 751, 767, 169; *Wohlmannstetter*, ZGR 2010, 472, 484.

sec. 111 AktG.[1569] From this finding, it has been concluded that the evaluation would include the entrepreneurial appropriateness of the internal control and risk management systems.[1570] With regard to internal control regarding financial reporting, it has been noted that the audit committee may not conclude its effectiveness solely based on the report of the external auditor pursuant to sec. 171(1)(s. 2) AktG that no significant deficiencies have been found.[1571]

While these general statements point to the right direction for the evaluation, the requirements to consider the enumerated systems effective are not straight forward. Corporate law does neither provide for a definition of effectiveness nor for any specific threshold or requirements[1572] which the internal control and risk management systems need to fulfill in order to be considered effective representing legislation in the style of principle instead of rule. Without any specific thresholds or requirements for the level of effectiveness, the performance level for the effectiveness of the internal control and risk management systems are the general requirements for these systems. The assessment of the effectiveness pursuant to sec. 107(3)(s. 2) AktG has only to ensure that the management board fulfills its duties regarding internal control and risk management systems derived from sec. 91(2) AktG and from the duty to manage the corporation (sec. 76 combined with sec. 93 AktG).[1573] Thus, the general duty to manage the corporation pursuant to sec. 76 combined with sec. 93 AktG provides for the minimum requirements which the internal control and risk management systems have to adhere to in order to be considered effective.[1574]

Furthermore, it has been noted that the monitoring of the effectiveness of the systems enumerated in sec. 107(3)(s. 2) AktG should not be limited to a materiality standard, such as significant deficiency, in line with the wording of sec. 107(3)(s. 2) AktG and the legislative documents requiring "profound" monitoring.[1575] Instead of a materiality standard, the general corporate law principle of proportionality (*Verhältnismäßigkeitsgrundsatz*)

1569 *Kort*, in: Großkomm AktG, sec. 91, mar. 24.
1570 *AKEIÜ Schmalenbach-Ges.*, DB 2011, 2101, 2102; cf. *Preußner*, NZG 2008, 574, 575.
1571 *Withus*, DB 2009, Beilage 5, 82, 88; *Dreher/Hoffmann*, ZGR 2016, 445, 461 and 489.
1572 Cf. *AKEIÜ Schmalenbach-Ges.*, DB 2011, 2101.
1573 Cf. *Kort*, ZGR 2010, 440, 469; *Dreher/Hoffmann*, ZGR 2016, 445, 456.
1574 See *supra* at chapter 8, B. I. 3. c).
1575 *Dreher/Hoffmann*, ZGR 2016, 445, 461 et seq.; cf. Begr RegE BilMoG, BT-Drucks. 16/10067, p. 102 "*umfassend*".

should be applied so that the assessment of the effectiveness does not lead to require 'perfect' systems.[1576] Therefore, the relevant criteria for the assessment of the effectiveness would be "suitable", "necessary", and "reasonable". With regard to the auditor-coined materiality standard of significant deficiency, it has been stressed that non-material deficiencies would not reach the audit committee leading to an undue filtering of information.[1577] Filtering as well as selecting and processing information is necessary, however, to allow the audit committee to focus on the important aspects. Also under the principle of proportionality, not all deficiencies of the systems enumerated in sec. 107(3)(s. 2) AktG are relevant for the assessment of the effectiveness. In case a combination of non-significant deficiencies or the cumulation of non-significant deficiencies constitute a significant deficiency[1578], this information has to reach the audit committee. Thus, a materiality standard, such as significant deficiencies, has to encompass the combination of non-significant deficiencies as well as the cumulation of such deficiencies.

Using the principle of proportionality to determine the scope of the duty to monitor the effectiveness according to sec. 107(3)(s. 2) AktG and to determine the criterion of effectiveness is important to highlight that the level of proficiency, required to determine that the systems are effective, is not to require perfect systems. The same result can be achieved, however, by using a materiality standard such as significant weakness[1579] which is e.g. used in sec. 171(1)(s. 2) AktG. Since the general duty to manage the corporation pursuant to sec. 76 combined with sec. 93 AktG provides for the minimum requirements in order to consider the systems effective, the corporate law principle of proportionality is also included in the minimum requirements.

The main aspect to determine whether the systems are effective is to determine whether they actually achieve their aims.[1580] While specific measures such as sample testing and audits[1581] will give an indication on the performance, the evaluation, based on the principle of proportionality, whether the results of these measures provide sufficient insight into the performance of the systems, warranting to determine the systems to be ef-

1576 *Dreher/Hoffmann*, ZGR 2016, 445, 462.

1577 *Dreher/Hoffmann*, ZGR 2016, 445, 462 et seq. stating that a large number of small deficiencies may lead to a significant deficiency due to cumulation.

1578 See also *supra* at chapter 4, A. II. 2. b) (3).

1579 See *supra* at chapter 4, C. I. 3.

1580 Cf. *Dreher/Hoffmann*, ZGR 2016, 445, 448 and 491.

1581 *Dreher/Hoffmann*, ZGR 2016, 445, 491.

fective, is rather subjective. Defining performance levels *ex ante* by defining benchmarks and key performance indicators, however, provides a setup to evaluate the effectiveness which is less prone to subjective judgment.[1582]

In order to enable the audit committee to evaluate the effectiveness of the internal control system, the risk management system and the internal audit system, the management board needs to define for each of the elements of these systems benchmarks and key performance indicators with regard to the operation of the systems.[1583] The benchmarks and key performance indicators objectify the judgment on the effectiveness. The supervisory board has to ensure that the management board fulfills its duty to define benchmarks and key performance indicators which are adequate for the specific corporation in light of the minimum legal requirements reflecting the expectations of the supervisory board. It is the duty of the supervisory board to supervise whether the management board is compliant with its legal duties.[1584] Moreover, while sec. 107(3)(s. 2) AktG does not directly mandate to define any benchmarks for the enumerated systems, the spirit of the law requires a comprehensive evaluation which is only feasible with predefined benchmarks and key performance indicators. In addition, the duty to supervise a large, listed corporation pursuant to sec. 111(1) combined with sec. 93 AktG also converges towards best practice similar to the duty to manage the corporations for large, listed corporations pursuant to sec. 76 combined with sec. 93 AktG. In light of the necessity for the evaluation, best practice requires to define benchmarks and key performance indicators.

For defining the benchmarks and as a general reference point for the audit committee to assess the effectiveness of the systems, it has been suggested to use the recognized frameworks COSO I and COSO II.[1585] These frameworks, however, are not explicitly mandated by law but may be used as guidance. Yet, they constitute best practice. Thus, the COSO frameworks should be considered for setting the performance level for the effectiveness of the enumerated systems of large, listed corporations. With regard to large, listed corporations, the duty to manage the corporation requires

---

1582 See *infra* at chapter 16, B. IV.

1583 Similar: *Nonnenmacher/Pohle/v. Werder*, DB 2009, 1447, 1451; *Powilleit*, GWR 2010, 28; *Benz/Klindt*, BB 2010, 2977, 2978.

1584 *Hüffer*, AktG, sec. 111, mar. 5.

1585 *AKEIÜ Schmalenbach-Ges.*, DB 2011, 2101, 2102; *Withus*, DB 2009, Beilage 5, 82, 86; *Hufnagel/Tönnissen*, ZIR 2010, 110, 117; *Nimwegen*, ZFRC 2010, 161; cf. *AKEU/AKEIÜ Schmalenbach-Ges.*, DB 2009, 1279, 1282. See *supra* at chapter 8, B. I. 2. a).

more specific measures for the internal control and risk management systems compared to the average corporation. Therefore, the supervisory board has to use such heightened minimum standard to evaluate the effectiveness of systems the enumerated in sec. 107(3)(s. 2) AktG.

b) Ability of the Audit Committee to Cope with the Assigned Task

The ability of the audit committee to cope with the assigned task in sec. 107(3)(s. 2) AktG has been questioned. It has been pointed out that the audit committee may be swamped by the duty to evaluate the effectiveness of the systems enumerated in sec. 107(3)(s. 2) AktG due to frequency of four meetings per year[1586] and the fact that the supervisory board will receive its information mainly from the biased management board and does not routinely have direct access to internal audit.[1587] With regard to the frequency of meetings, it has to be noted, however, that the frequency of meetings is sufficient especially with regard to internal control regarding financial reporting, since some controls are only used at the end of the fiscal year[1588] and the external auditor will report on any significant deficiencies of the internal control and the risk management systems with regard to financial reporting (sec. 171(1)(s. 2) AktG)[1589]. In light of the SEC rules on management's evaluation of the effectiveness of internal control over financial reporting, a profound evaluation once per year is sufficient reflecting costs and benefits of such evaluation.[1590] During the fiscal year, it is sufficient for the audit committee to assess at least twice per period of six months any changes to the systems enumerated in sec. 107(3)(s. 2) AktG or other material aspects regarding internal control or risk management.[1591] Moreover, audit committees of large, listed corporations tend to meet more often sometimes; even on a monthly basis.

1586 *Nonnenmacher/Pohle/v. Werder*, DB 2009, 1447, 1452 suggesting at least four meetings per year which reflects the legal duty of meetings for the supervisory board of listed corporations (sec. 110(3) AktG) applied to the audit committee (cf. *Habersack*, in: Münch Komm AktG, sec. 107, mar. 147).

1587 *Wohlmannstetter*, ZGR 2010, 472, 483 et seq.

1588 See *supra* at chapter 4, A. II. 3.

1589 See *infra* at chapter 9, B. II. 2.

1590 See *supra* at chapter 4, A. II. 2.

1591 See *supra* at chapter 4, A. II. 3.

With regard to the issue of biased information, direct communication lines[1592] to the audit committee for the CCO and internal audit to report alleged misconduct especially within the management board, such as circumvention of controls or deficiencies of the internal control and risk management systems, are important for receiving accurate information for the assessment and to foster monitoring of the management board.[1593] Moreover, the possibility of further audits will discipline the management board and will provide necessary information, if needed. In general, while the duty to monitor and assess the effectiveness of the systems enumerated in sec. 107(3)(s. 2) AktG is challenging, the audit committee is the only organ besides the entire supervisory board to exercise such duty. Through sec. 107(4) combined with sec. 100(5) AktG, the law aims to ensure sufficient expertise on the audit committee to fulfill the task.[1594] Nevertheless, without commissioning further audits by internal audit or external auditors, the audit committee will not be able to assess the information and reports regarding the effectiveness of the internal control and risk management systems provided by the management board. In light of sec. 404(b) SOX, internal or external audits of the internal control and risk management systems seem inevitable to enforce the mandates for the management board.

c) Direct Communication Lines to the Supervisory Board and Audit Committee

The issue of direct communication lines to the supervisory board has been raised as a measure for the audit committee to receive information and to evaluate the effectiveness of internal control and risk management systems. In general, the supervisory board needs information to carry out its supervisory duties[1595] and to reduce the issues associated with the information asymmetry[1596]. According to the corporate law principle reflected in sec. 90 AktG, the management board is the primary source of information for

1592 See on the issue of direct reporting lines *infra* at chapter 8, B. II. 1. c).
1593 Cf. *Withus*, DB 2009, Beilage 5, 82, 87.
1594 See *Langenbucher*, ZGR 2012, 314 on the issue of the composition of the supervisory board.
1595 Cf. *Dreher*, FS Ulmer, 87, 92.
1596 See *supra* at chapter 1, A.

the supervisory board[1597] either through reports of the management board pursuant to sec. 90(1) AktG or by fulfilling information requests of the supervisory board pursuant to sec. 90(3) AktG. This general setup of the information regime follows from the separation of power within the corporate governance between the management board with its duty to manage the corporation (sec. 76(1) AktG) and the supervisory board with its duty to supervise the management board (sec. 111(1) AktG) leading to a monopoly[1598] of the management board with regard to providing information. The main problem with this setup is that the management board, as the controlled, gathers, filters, selects and presents the information which the supervisory board, as the supervisor, uses to conduct its duty providing the management board with the opportunity to control information in light of the self-serving bias. It is of critical importance, however, that the supervisory board receives unbiased information.

With regard to receiving information, the supervisory board has to use *inter alia* its right to request information pursuant to sec. 90(3) AktG including group related issues (sec. 90(1)(s. 2) AktG) in order to conduct its monitoring duty.[1599] In this regard, the supervisory board may issue an information manual specifying the issues, scope, and frequency of information which the management board has to provide to the supervisory board according to such manual.[1600] The information provided by the external auditor pursuant to sec. 171(1) AktG will be addressed subsequently.

With regard to receiving unbiased information, the supervisory board may directly use the general information system of the corporation only in extreme cases, such as misconduct of members of the management board[1601], to receive information circumventing the management board due to the principle of separation of power.[1602] Therefore, the issue of direct communication lines to the supervisory board and especially to the au-

1597 *Dreher*, ZGR 2010, 496, 517; *Spindler*, in: Spindler/Stilz, AktG, sec. 111, mar. 36.

1598 *Habersack*, in: Münch Komm AktG, sec. 111, mar. 68.

1599 *Kort*, ZGR 2010, 440, 467.

1600 *Habersack*, in: Münch Komm AktG, sec. 111, mar. 44; cf. *Winter*, FS Hüffer, 1103, 1114.

1601 *Bürkle*, CCZ 2010, 4, 9 et seq.; *Dreher*, ZGR 2010, 496, 517; cf. *Lutter*, Information im Aufsichtsrat, mar. 319.

1602 *Spindler*, FS Hüffer, 985, 997 et seq.; *Bachmann*, VGR, 2008, 65, 93; *Fleischer*, in: Spindler/Stilz, AktG, sec. 90, mar. 43 et seq.; *Spindler*, WM 2008, 905, 913; *Winter*, FS Hüffer, 1103, 1116; *Spindler*, in: Spindler/Stilz, AktG, sec. 107, mar. 132; *Rodewald/Unger*, BB 2007, 1629, 1632 exhibit 4; *Hopt/Roth*, in: Großkomm AktG, sec. 111, mar. 511 et seq.; cf. *Dreher*, FS Goette, 43, 53. For a strict under-

dit committee is also important with regard to the design of internal control and risk management systems. In difference to the independent directors of U.S. corporations, the supervisory board does not have direct responsibility for and access to internal audit as a source for information.[1603] Nevertheless, the audit committee should use its right of sec. 90(3) AktG more actively and routinely to obtain more information on the issues which the committee has to supervise.[1604]

Contrasting the predominant view upholding the principle of separation of power with regard to information, it has been held that the supervisory board should have the right to question employees to receive independent information based on a modern understanding of corporate governance.[1605] In the more recent literature, authors assume without hesitation the need that the CCO reports monthly or at least annually directly to the supervisory board.[1606] It has been stressed that the right to question employees may be based on sec. 109(1)(s. 2) AktG[1607] which would not include the right, however, to request from the management board to establish an independent information channel bypassing the same.[1608] Otherwise, it has been held that the supervisory board may summon executive staff, such as the GC, CCO and head of internal audit, without the consent of the management board and regardless of any suspicion[1609], in order to fulfill its duty to monitor the management board[1610]. A specific issue within the debate of direct communication lines to the supervisory board con-

standing of the information regime: *Sünner*, CCZ 2008, 56, 59; cf. *v. Rosen*, AG 2008, 537. See for details on the history of the separation of power and information regime: *Roth*, AG 2004, 1 et seq.

1603 *Spindler* in: Spindler/Stilz, AktG, sec. 107, mar. 132; *Wohlmannstetter*, ZGR 2010, 472, 484; *Seibt*, Hdb Corporate Governance, 391, 399 et seq. Different favoring direct access to internal audit: *Velte*, NZG 2011, 1401, 1403.

1604 *Wohlmannstetter*, ZGR 2010, 472, 485.

1605 *Schneider, S. H.*, Informationspflichten, p. 107; *Leyens*, Aufsichtsrat, p. 191 et seq. and p. 348 et seq.

1606 *Lutter*, FS Hüffer, 617, 619 (monthly); *Nonnenmacher/Pohle/v. Werder*, DB 2007, 2412, 2415 (at least annually). Different: *Dreher*, FS Ulmer, 87, 93 no institutionalized contacts.

1607 *Dreher*, ZGR 2010, 496, 521 et seq.

1608 *Dreher*, FS Ulmer, 87, 98.

1609 *Habersack*, in. Münch Komm AktG, sec. 109, mar. 19; *id.*, in: Münch Komm AktG, sec. 111, mar. 68; cf. *Theisen*, Berichterstattung des Aufsichtsrats, pp. 10 and 24.

1610 *Habersack*, in: Münch Komm AktG, sec. 111, mar. 68; *Hopt/Roth*, in: Großkomm AktG, sec. 111, mar. 254, 519 et seq.; cf. *Marsch-Barner*, FS Schwark, 219, 226.

cerns information regarding criminal behavior of employees or the management board. In these cases, employees need to address the supervisory board circumventing the management board.[1611] For such communication, the internal control system needs to provide for standardized mechanisms.

Despite any specific right to establish communication lines and to question employees, the supervisory board and the management board may mutually agree on an information manual specifying reporting duties of executive staff such as the CCO, GC, and head of internal audit to the supervisory board or the audit committee.[1612] It is best practice that the CCO regularly reports to the audit committee and the head of accounting reports to the supervisory board regarding the annual report.[1613] In difference to an ad-hoc request, the predefined, recurring reporting duties to the supervisory board have less potential to endanger the trustful relationship between the supervisory board and the management board, which is mostly raised as an argument against direct contacts[1614], since the reporting is routinely and not triggered by any suspected misconduct. Moreover, against the background that transparency is regarded as an important element of good corporate governance, the argument of the potential damage of the trustful relationship is eroding.[1615]

In general, the strong opinion upholding the information regime in the two-tier structure including the monopoly of the management board to provide information to the supervisory board is eroding in light of good corporate governance and the need of the supervisory board for unbiased information. Direct communication lines and the right for the supervisory

1611 *Lutter*, Information im Aufsichtsrat, mar. 319; *Marsch-Barner*, FS Schwark, 219, 222; cf. *Hopt/Roth*, in: Großkomm AktG, sec. 111, mar. 508; *Dreher*, FS Goette, 43, 49 et seq.; *Leyens*, Aufsichtsrat, p. 199 et seq.

1612 Cf. *Dreher*, ZGR 2010, 496, 523; *Hüffer*, AktG, sec. 90, mar. 11; *Fleischer*, in: Spindler/Stilz, AktG, sec. 90, mar. 44; *Spindler*, in: Spindler/Stilz, AktG, sec. 107, mar. 131; *Roth*, AG 2004, 1, 9 et seq.; *Seibt*, Hdb Corporate Governance, 391, 407 et seq.; *Marsch-Barner*, FS Schwark, 219, 228 et seq.; *Hopt/Roth*, in: Großkomm AktG, sec. 111, mar. 182, 516 et seq.

1613 Cf. *Thomas*, ZGR 2010, 591, 595; *Dreher*, ZGR 2010, 496, 514; *AKEU/AKEIÜ Schmalenbach-Ges.*, DB 2009, 1279, 1282; *Lutter*, Information im Aufsichtsrat, mar. 320; *Schäfer*, ZGR 2004, 416, 428. See in general for direct contact: *Dreher*, FS Ulmer, 87, 88.

1614 Cf. *Dreher*, FS Ulmer, 87, 93; *Börsig/Löbbe*, FS Hoffmann-Becking, 125, 137 et seq.

1615 *Hopt/Roth*, in: Großkomm AktG, sec. 111, mar. 512 et seq.; *Roth*, AG 2004, 1, 7 et seq.; *Leyens*, Aufsichtsrat, p. 179 et seq.

board to directly question employees is essential to enable the supervisory board to receive information first hand in order to reduce the impact of the information asymmetry between the supervisory board and management board. Direct communication is especially important against the background that more than 20% of corporate crime is committed by top management.[1616] In order to account for the general two-tier structure, the direct communication lines and the right to question employees should be limited to executive staff such as the GC, CCO, and head of internal audit.

2. Audit of Annual Report – Section 171(1) AktG

The supervisory board has to audit the annual report (sec. 171(1)(s. 1) AktG) as well as the non-financial information statement (sec. 171(1)(s. 4) AktG). During the session of the supervisory board or the audit committee, the external auditor has to report on the results of its audit especially with regard to significant deficiencies of the internal control system and the risk management system but only with regard to financial reporting (sec. 171(1)(s. 2) AktG). The report provides information for the supervisory board to conduct its evaluation pursuant to sec. 107(3)(s. 2) AktG. Sec. 171(1)(s. 2) AktG only specifies the reporting duties of the external auditor[1617] and does not prescribe how the external auditor has to conduct its audit with regard to the internal control system and the risk management system. Therefore, the external auditor is not required to evaluate the internal control and risk management systems regarding financial reporting against any benchmarks but has to state whether these systems are generally adequate for the corporation.[1618] Thus, the supervisory board will only receive information regarding any red flags within the internal control and risk management systems regarding financial reporting. Since the external auditor will conduct its audit pursuant to the professional standards of external auditors, the external auditor will report on significant deficiencies revealed during this routine test in light of IDW PS 261.[1619] These are deficiencies of the internal control system which are relevant for the moni-

---

1616 *Bussmann/Matschke*, CCZ 2009, 132, 135; *Bussmann/Salvenmoser*, NStZ 2006, 203. 206.

1617 Begr RegE BilMoG, BT-Drucks. 16/10067, p. 104.

1618 *Spindler*, FS Hüffer, 985, 996.

1619 See *infra* at chapter 9, C.

toring function of the supervisory board.[1620] But, the external auditor only conducts sample testing and not a profound investigation. Moreover, the effectiveness of the internal control and risk management systems is not a primary focus of the external audit[1621] and the external audit has limits especially with regard to the assessment of internal controls being management tools[1622]. Therefore, the supervisory will need to conduct or commission further investigations to receive more detailed information on the reported deficiencies.

Similar to the debate regarding sec. 107(3) AktG, the reporting duty of the external auditor raises the issue if the management board has to implement a profound risk management system.[1623] The implementation of sec. 171(1)(s. 2) AktG only aims to specify the reporting duties of the external auditor.[1624] Hence, the reporting duty of the external auditor does not change any mandates for the management board to implement a risk management system.[1625] Nevertheless, the reporting duty of the external auditor will influence the internal control and risk management systems regarding financial reporting of the corporation. The supervisory board will use the provided information of the significant deficiencies of the internal control and risk management systems to execute its monitoring duty of these systems enumerated in sec. 107(3)(s. 2) AktG. Therefore, the identified significant deficiencies will influence the requests of the supervisory board to the management board regarding changes to the financial reporting related internal control and risk management elements. In this regard, the standards of the external auditor to evaluate the internal control and risk management systems regarding financial reporting provide insight into the requirements for the proficiency of these systems but also into the limits of the audit.[1626]

1620 Cf. IDW PS 261, mar. 89.
1621 See *infra* at chapter 9, C.
1622 See on the limits of external audits in corporate governance: *Windbichler*, FS Rokas, 1389, 1395 et seq.
1623 Cf. *Kort*, ZGR 2010, 440.
1624 Begr RegE BilMoG, BT-Drucks. 16/10067, p. 104.
1625 *Kort*, ZGR 2010, 460.
1626 See *infra* at chapter 9, C.

3. General Duties – Section 111 AktG

The supervisory board has to supervise the management of the corporation pursuant to sec. 111(1) AktG. As part of good corporate governance, the duties of the supervisory board encompass to advise the management board and to participate in the general decisions with regard to the business and the corporation which include internal control and risk management issues as well as compliance issues. The supervisory board is involved in defining the general scope of the internal control and risk management systems including compliance. With regard to the duty of the supervisory board to supervise, the scope of such duty is less than the duty of the management board to oversee and monitor the entire corporation.[1627] The supervisory board has to monitor only the managing activities of the management board.[1628] This includes whether the management board is compliant with its legal duties.[1629] The monitoring of the supervisory board is particularly important with regard to intentional misconduct of the management board such as fraud.[1630] One drawback for the supervisory board is that it mainly depends on information provided by the management board.[1631] In order to reduce the dependency on the management board, the supervisory board has to advise the management board on establishing direct communication lines of the executive staff such as GC, CCO and head of internal audit and has to question executive staff, if indicated.[1632] Besides these measures, the supervisory board has the right to access the books and records pursuant to sec. 111(2)(s. 1) AktG including reports of internal audit.[1633] Moreover, sec. 111(2)(s. 2) AktG includes the right to a third party expert opinion.[1634] The supervisory board may commission a special audit by an external auditor to audit the internal control and risk management systems.[1635] *Lutter* opines that the supervisory board of large,

---

1627 *Winter*, FS Hüffer, 1103, 1112.
1628 *Winter*, FS Hüffer, 1103, 1112.
1629 *Hüffer*, AktG, sec. 111, mar. 5.
1630 Cf. *Nimwegen*, ZFRC 2010, 161. See *supra* at chapter 4, A. II. 1. c).
1631 *Winter*, FS Hüffer, 1103, 1113.
1632 See *supra* at chapter 8, B. II. 1. c).
1633 *Lanfermann/Röhricht*, BB 2009, 887, 890; *Hüffer*, AktG, sec. 111, mar. 11; *Withus*, DB 2009, Beilage 5, 82, 87.
1634 Cf. *Withus*, DB 2009, Beilage 5, 82, 87.
1635 *Lanfermann/Röhricht*, BB 2009, 887, 890; *Habersack*, in: Münch Komm, sec. 111, mar. 74 and 78. See also *supra* at chapter 8, B. II. 1. a).

listed corporations has the duty to routinely commission such special audit.[1636]

In order to receive information on specific business dealings, the supervisory board has the opportunity to require prior approval (sec. 111(4)(s. 2) AktG). Requiring prior approval is generally subject to limits[1637] but does encompass aspects of managing the corporation including decisions on personnel[1638]. With regard to internal control, the supervisory board should require prior approval of decisions regarding the appointment of the GC, CCO, and the head of internal audit in order to prevent the dismissal of unpleasant advocates of compliance by the management board. The supervisory board may also consider prior approval for decisions regarding the design and operation of the internal control and risk management systems such as major overhauls and changes to these systems.

4. Summary

The supervisory board has the main duty to advise the management board and to participate in the important decisions with regard to internal control and risk management systems including compliance. The board should use its specific rights of sec. 111(2) and (4) AktG to execute its oversight. With the enactment of BilMoG, the duties of the supervisory have been specified in sec. 107(3)(s. 2) AktG to include supervising and monitoring the financial reporting process, the effectiveness of the internal control system, the effectiveness of the risk management system, and the effectiveness of the internal audit system. In order to assess the effectiveness, the supervisory board has to ensure that the management board fulfilled its duties derived from sec. 91(2) AktG and from the duty to manage the corporation (sec. 76 combined with sec. 93 AktG). For the evaluation, the supervisory board needs to require the management board beforehand to implement benchmarks and key performance indicators for the enumerated systems. The supervisory board should consider COSO I and COSO II as reference points for the evaluation.

As part of effective internal control and risk management systems, the supervisory board should have direct access to the information provided by the internal control and risk management systems which should include

1636 *Lutter*, FS Hüffer, 617, 623.

1637 Cf. *Hüffer*, AktG, sec. 111, mar. 18.

1638 *Habersack*, in: Münch Komm AktG, sec. 111, mar. 111.

direct communication lines to the audit committee but limited to executive staff such as the GC, CCO, and head of internal audit. Besides direct communication lines, the supervisory board will receive reports on significant deficiencies of the internal control and risk management systems regarding financial reporting from the external auditor due to sec. 171(1) (s. 2) AktG. In general, the supervisory board needs to receive unbiased information to supervise the management board through effective internal control and risk management systems as well as the external auditor, and by using its statutory rights. The effectiveness of the internal control and risk management systems is important to ensure the flow of information. In light of the complex issue of evaluating the effectiveness of the internal control and risk management systems, the audit committee needs to commission external audits of the systems in order to ensure the execution of its mandates by the management board.

III. Incentives from Corporate Law to Implement Internal Control and Compliance Measures

The incentive structure from corporate law for the management board and the supervisory board to implement internal control including compliance measures provides insight if and to which extent management will implement these measures. One of the apparent incentives for the management board to adhere to the mandates of corporate law is liability. Pursuant to sec. 93(2)(s. 1) AktG, the management board is collectively liable for violations of the duty to implement an adequate early warning system of sec. 91(2) AktG[1639] and internal control measures due to sec. 76 combined with sec. 93 AktG. Even though the management board may divide the responsibilities in departments, no member of the management board is able to avoid liability.[1640] The implementation and designing of the internal control system and the compliance organization, i.e. the decision if and how to implement these systems, are generally protected by the business judg-

1639 Cf. *Spindler*, in: Fleischer, Hdb Vorstandsrecht, sec. 19, mar. 5; *Mertens/Cahn*, in: Köln Komm AktG, sec. 91, mar. 15.

1640 *Spindler*, in: Münch Komm AktG, sec. 93, mar. 149; *Mertens/Cahn*, in: Köln Komm AktG, sec. 91, mar. 15; LG München I, decision of December 10, 2013 – 5 HK O 1387/10, juris at recital 98 et seq.

ment rule.[1641] But, the decision whether to implement internal control and compliance measures is only protected by sec. 93(1)(s. 2) AktG in case no duty to implement such systems exists.[1642] Since large, listed corporations have the duty to implement internal control and compliance measures, the business judgment rule does not apply with regard to the decision whether to implement such systems.[1643] The decision how to design internal control and the compliance organization, however, is protected by the business judgment rule besides the minimum requirements for these systems which are also mandated by law.[1644] Pursuant to sec. 93(2)(s. 2) AktG, each manager has the burden of proof to show that she did not act negligently. With regard to sec. 91(2) AktG, an unqualified attestation of the external auditor pursuant to sec. 317(4), 321(4) HGB[1645] is important. Otherwise, it will be very difficult to establish such proof.[1646]

The liability pursuant to sec. 93(1) AktG provides incentives for the management board to implement an early warning system, internal control, and a compliance organization fulfilling the minimum requirements applicable for the corporation. The implementation of compliance measures should reduce the risk of liability for the management and supervisory board.[1647] Due to the principle of legality, this duty would also include all foreign law applicable to the corporations.[1648] For the purpose of the thesis, however, U.S. law is excluded from part II of the thesis in order to enable the impact analysis of part III.[1649] The incentive level for the management board to fulfill such minimum requirements depends on the expected liability which mainly depends on the supervisory board to pursue claims against the management board for violating managerial duties. Vari-

---

1641 *Kort*, ZGR 2010, 440, 456; *Kremer/Klahold*, ZGR 2010, 113, 121; *Spindler*, FS Hüffer, 985, 993; *Bachmann*, VGR, 2008, 65, 85 et seq.; *Blasche* CCZ 2009, 62, 63.

1642 *Kort*, ZGR 2010, 440, 456.

1643 Cf. *Lorenz*, in: Grundlagen des Risikomanagements, p. 23.

1644 *Kort*, ZGR 2010, 440, 456.

1645 Regulation (EU) No 537/2014 does not address the audit of the early warning system pursuant to sec. 91(2) AktG but rather the internal financial control system in art. 11(2)(j) so that sec. 317(4) HGB still applies to the audit of large, listed corporations (cf. sec. 317(3a) HGB).

1646 *Mertens/Cahn*, in: Köln Komm AktG, sec. 91, mar. 39; *Spindler*, in: Fleischer, Hdb Vorstandsrecht, sec. 19, mar. 66; cf. LG Berlin AG 2002, 682, 683.

1647 *Hauschka*, NJW 2004, 257, 259; cf. *Fleischer*, in: Fleischer, Hdb Vorstandsrecht, sec. 8, mar. 44.

1648 See *supra* at chapter 8, B. I. 3. b).

1649 See *supra* at chapter 1, D.

ous aspects, however, provide incentives for the supervisory board not to pursue any recourse claims against the management board including the difficulties to establish damages[1650], costs of investigation and the question if these costs may be recovered[1651], difficulties in proving the failure to manage the corporation by implementing adequate internal control and compliance measures pursuant to sec. 76 combined with sec. 93 AktG[1652], personal ties to the management board[1653], further loss of reputation[1654] due to the continuation of the scandal, potential of deterring adequate candidates to join the corporation, and hiding own shortcomings of supervision. Also, the scope of the duty to implement internal control is not straight forward and may be difficult to determine preventing a clear decision whether the management board violated their duty to implement internal control leading the supervisory board to refrain from recourse claims unless in case of an ostensible violation of the duty. Therefore, the supervisory board will only intervene if the management board ostensibly violates its duties pursuant to sec. 93(1) AktG leading to an expected liability for the management board which is rather low except for ostensible violations of the sec. 93(1) AktG duties.

In light of the BGH case ARAG/Garmenbeck which established the duty of supervisory board to assess any recourse claims against members of the management board for damages in light of a breach of duty, the expected civil liability for violations of sec. 91(2) AktG and sec. 76 combined with sec. 93 AktG increased.[1655] Following from the case, the supervisory board has to follow several steps to decide on claiming recourse: evaluation of the facts, damages, objective violation of duty, fault, expected verdict, and prospect of collecting damages, as well as if such recourse claim is in favor of the corporation.[1656] At the end, it remains a business decision of the supervisory board whether to pursue any recourse claims.[1657] While the su-

---

1650 See *Kindler*, FS Roth, 367 not accounting for damages such as e.g. loss of reputation. Different: *Lorenz*, in: Grundlagen des Risikomanagements, p. 22; cf. *Meier-Greve*, BB 2009, 2555, 2558 et seq.

1651 *Meier-Greve*, BB 2009, 2555, 2558 et seq.

1652 Cf. *Fleischer*, NZG 2014, 321, 327 et seq.; *Meier-Greve*, BB 2009, 2555, 2360.

1653 Cross-relations among big German corporations are common. See *Wackerbarth*, ZGR 2005, 686, 706 et seq.

1654 Cf. *Werner*, CCZ 2011, 201, 202; *Bussmann*, PwC Study 2011; *Semler*, FS Goette, 499, 500. See also *infra* at chapter 8, E. III.

1655 *Hauschka*, ZIP 2004, 877, 848; BGHZ 135, 244.

1656 *Goette*, 2011.

1657 *Goette*, 2011.

pervisory board has the duty to assess any recourse claims, the fact that it remains a business decision whether to pursue such claims and the adverse incentives for the supervisory board to pursue such claims substantially limit the increase of expected liability of the management board.[1658] It follows that the management board has only incentives to implement internal control and compliance measures which appear to fulfill minimum requirements in order to avoid recourse claims. Hence, management has incentives to implement internal controls and compliance measures pursuant to sec. 93(1) AktG fulfilling minimum requirements *prima facie* to avoid ostensible violations of sec. 93(1) AktG leading to ineffective measures.

In addition, the management board has incentives to implement monitoring measures only *prima facie* since these measures increase the expected civil liability for management pursuant to sec. 93 AktG. Monitoring measures identify and disclose information of corporate misconduct that could be used in governmental proceedings or civil lawsuits.[1659] This fact is known as the litigation dilemma.[1660] With regard to civil lawsuits based on sec. 93 AktG, the corporation may use any information produced by the monitoring measures in recourse claims against members of the management board since this information is owned by the corporation. In this regard, differences in U.S. and German procedural law, especially with regard to the U.S. doctrine of discovery[1661], do not change the impact of the litigation dilemma on the expected liability of the management since the corporation does not need to obtain information through discovery. Due to the litigation dilemma, the management board has an incentive to refrain from implementing effective monitoring measures as part of internal control and the compliance organization. The incentives to refrain from implementing effective monitoring measures in light of the litigation dilemma are even higher due to one of the main issues within the incentive structure for the management board. The issue is that courts may use hindsight knowledge wrongly to judge on the decisions of the management board so that they are subject to the hindsight bias. Although the business judgment rule implemented in sec. 93(1)(s. 2) AktG aims *inter alia* to avoid

---

1658 Cf. *Meier-Greve*, BB 2009, 2555, 2560: "partial immunity" of the management board.

1659 See *supra* at chapter 5, B. See on civil liability for management: *Rieble*, CCZ 2010, 1, 2 et seq.; *Lackhoff/Schulz*, CCZ 2010, 81.

1660 See *supra* at chapter 5, B. II.

1661 See on the U.S. doctrine of discovery *supra* at chapter 5, B. II.

second guessing by the courts on business decisions with hindsight knowledge, it has been indicated that courts tend to use hindsight knowledge to judge whether corporate leaders fulfilled their duties.[1662] In light of the duties to implement an adequate early warning system and internal control as well as a compliance organization, the occurrence of misconduct may stipulate the finding in hindsight that if something went wrong the implemented controls must have been ineffective.[1663] The *Neubürger* case is a prominent example.[1664] Thus, the management board had not fulfilled its duties and would be subject to civil liability. In contrast to this finding in hindsight, the occurrence of misconduct itself does not indicate that the management board did not implement sufficient internal controls or compliance measures.[1665] Disregarding this fact, courts use hindsight knowledge to determine if management fulfilled its duties amplifying the potential for the management board to be punished increasing the incentive for the management board to refrain from implementing monitoring measures due to the increase of the expected liability through such measures. This scenario is especially burdensome in case management is liable pursuant to sec. 93(2) AktG for fines due to sec. 130, 30 OWiG[1666] since courts and law enforcement agencies generally do not grant leniency for the implemented monitoring measures[1667] in order to offset the detriments of the litigation dilemma. Without granting leniency, the fine is higher compared to the scenario with granting leniency increasing the expected liability especially when civil courts use hindsight knowledge to determine if management violated its duties. Thus, management has less incentives to implement monitoring measures since these measures produce information and the courts are reluctant to reward any efforts to foster compliance. Hence, absent any clear policy to honor the implementation and operation of effective internal controls and compliance measures together with pro-

---

1662 See on the issue of the hindsight bias: *Fleischer*, NZG 2008, 371, 372; *Rotsch*, ZIS 2010, 614, 616; *Fleischer*, FS Wiedemann, 827, 832; *Bachmann*, ZIP 2014, 579, 581.

1663 *Kremer/Klahold*, ZGR 2010, 113, 139 et seq.

1664 LG München I, decision of December 10, 2013 – 5 HK O 1387/10, juris at recital 105.

1665 *Fleischer*, in: Spindler/Stilz, AktG, sec. 91, mar. 64; *id.*, CCZ 2008, 1, 3; *id.*, AG 2003, 291, 300; cf. *Bachmann*, ZIP 2014, 579, 580; *Grützner*, BB 2014, 850, 851. See *supra* at chapter 4, C. I. 1. b).

1666 *v. Busekist/Hein*, CCZ 2012, 41; *Werner*, CCZ 2010, 143. See *supra* at chapter 4, C. I. 1. b).

1667 See *infra* at chapter 8, E. IV.

viding insufficient leniency for implemented monitoring measures leads corporations to implement ineffective "paper tiger" compliance measures.[1668]

The enactment of BilMoG, especially sec. 107(3)(s. 2) and sec. 171(1)(s. 2)[1669] AktG, affects the incentive structure of the management board even though these sections do not address management board's duties. Due to sec. 107(3)(s. 2) AktG, the supervisory board has to monitor *inter alia* the effectiveness of the internal control and risk management systems and in particular whether the management board has fulfilled its duties regarding internal control and risk management.[1670] Also, the audit committee may submit recommendations or proposals to ensure the integrity of the financial reporting process (sec. 107(3)(s. 3) AktG. But the duty of the supervisory board does not encompass to suggest any enhancements.[1671] Nevertheless, the supervisory board should consider to inquire whether additions, enhancements, or improvements are necessary in order to avoid liability.[1672] The suggested scrutiny of the supervisory board leads to an increased awareness of internal control and risk management issues.[1673] Due to BilMoG, the perceived and actual liability risk and the risk of loss of reputation of the members of the supervisory board increased.[1674] In general, the supervisory board has incentives to avoid personal liability pursuant to sec. 116 AktG combined with sec. 93 AktG especially in light of increasing potential of legal[1675] and prosecutorial proceedings[1676] against members of the supervisory board. In order to avoid liability pursuant to sec. 116 AktG combined with sec. 93 AktG, the supervisory board has incentives to require more proficient internal control, risk management, and internal audit than required by corporate law[1677] especially with regard to

1668 See *supra* at chapter 5, C. III.

1669 See for more detail on sec. 171(1)(s. 2) AktG *infra* at chapter 8, C. VIII.

1670 See *supra* at chapter 8, B. II. 1.

1671 *Kort*, ZGR 2010, 440, 469; cf. *AKEU/AKEIÜ Schmalenbach-Ges.*, DB 2009, 1279, 1280.

1672 Begr RegE BilMoG, BT-Drucks. 16/10067, p. 102 et seq.; cf. *Withus*, DB 2009, Beilage 5, 82, 87; *AKEIÜ Schmalenbach-Ges.*, DB 2011, 2101, 2103.

1673 Cf. *Kort*, ZGR 2010, 440, 466; *Withus*, DB 2009, Beilage 5, 82, 83; *AKEU/AKEIÜ Schmalenbach-Ges.*, DB 2009, 1279, 1280.

1674 Cf. *AKEU/AKEIÜ Schmalenbach-Ges.*, DB 2009, 1279, 1280; *Wohlmannstetter*, ZGR 2010, 472, 480; cf. *Vetter*, ZGR 2010, 751, 769.

1675 Cf. *Bachmann*, ZIP 2014, 579, 581.

1676 *Wagner/Spemann*, NZG 2015, 945.

1677 Begr RegE BilMoG, BT-Drucks. 16/10067, p. 103; cf. *Wohlmannstetter*, ZGR 2010, 472, 476 et seq.; *Preußner*, NZG 2008, 574, 575.

the effectiveness of these systems including to require the management board to define benchmarks and key performance indicators. In particular, the supervision of the effectiveness will lead the supervisory board to require that the management board enhances the effectiveness of the relevant systems beyond the rudimentary requirements of sec. 91(2) AktG and to fulfill the minimum standard for large, listed corporations pursuant to sec. 76 combined with sec. 93 AktG. That is because if the supervisory board seeks advice from experts with regard to the internal control and risk management related duties, such advice is likely to reflect a profound risk management system rather than an early warning system, since best practice requires to implement a profound risk management system.[1678] Effective internal control, risk management, and internal audit require more than an early warning system. But the detriments of the litigation dilemma also affect the expected liability of the supervisory board pursuant to sec. 116 combined with sec. 93 AktG leading to less than optimal incentives for the supervisory board to require truly effective systems. It follows that the supervisory board will require more proficient systems but not truly effective systems. In order to provide sufficient incentives for the management board to fulfill the requirements of the supervisory board, it is important that the management board expects the supervisory board to control its mandates with adequate audits. Since the supervisory board is mostly unable to conduct profound investigations, the supervisory board would need to commission further audits of the internal control and risk management systems including the compliance organization to internal audit or external auditors.

Due to the incentives from BilMoG for the supervisory board to require more proficient systems, the management board has incentives to ensure that internal control and risk management seem to fulfill the expectations of the supervisory board in order to avoid that any testing will find that it did not comply with the requirements. These incentives for the management board, however, fail to induce the management board to implement effective internal control and risk management systems. The foremost priority of the management board is to implement internal control and risk management systems which pass any routine test of the systems by the audit committee and – limited to financial reporting – by the external auditor (sec. 171(1) AktG and art. 11(2)(j) Regulation (EU) No 537/2014). From sec. 171(1)(s. 2) AktG and art. 11(2)(j) Regulation (EU) No 537/2014

1678 Cf. *Withus*, DB 2009, Beilage 5, 82, 86; *Hufnagel/Tönnissen*, ZIR 2010, 110, 117; *AKEU/AKEIÜ Schmalenbach-Ges.*, DB 2009, 1279, 1282.

follow incentives for the management board to implement internal control regarding financial reporting without significant deficiencies reflecting the requirements of IDW PS 261 which the external auditor would find during routine testing. The management board has only incentives to fulfill its statutory duties and the expectations of the supervisory board up to the point in which the assessment of the systems does not reveal the failing to comply with the expectations of the supervisory board or any significant deficiencies with regard to financial reporting. Similar incentives exist for the management board in order to avoid any loss of reputation or standing, vis-à-vis the supervisory board, for failing to comply with its duties. Absent comprehensive oversight, the management board has only incentives to implement "paper tiger" systems which satisfy the testing requirements but fall short of being truly effective.[1679] It remains questionable if the supervisory board is strong enough to ensure comprehensive oversight especially due to its limited capacities and its reliance on the management board for information.[1680]

Besides liability, members of the management board have further incentives to comply with the named duties to implement internal control since they face dismissal and the termination of the employment contract with immediate effect for the violation of duties.[1681] Also, their reappointment may be at risk. A more general incentive follows from the fact that effective internal control will adequately provide information[1682] needed to avoid liability since the business judgment rule requires that the management board acted on an informed basis.

The incentive structure has three additional aspects: the agency problem and, less important, compensation and D&O insurance. In the context of implementing internal control and compliance measures, the agency problem is one of the main reasons for the need of internal control and compliance measures.[1683] The management board has incentives to leave internal control and the compliance organization less than optimal to provide for sufficient leeway to conceal self-interested or even fraudulent behavior which is of particular interest for the management board since internal control and compliance measures provide the opportunity for the supervi-

1679 See *infra* at chapter 16, A. I. 2. a) (2).

1680 See *supra* at chapter 8, B. II. 1. b).

1681 *Mertens/Cahn*, in: Köln Komm AktG, sec. 91, mar. 27; *Spindler*, in: Münch Komm AktG, sec. 91, mar. 39; *Bürkle*, ZIP 2004, 877, 879; *Fleischer*, DB 2014, 345, 350.

1682 *Gelhausen/Wermelt*, CCZ 2010, 208, 210.

1683 See *supra* at chapter 4, A. III.

sory board to assess management's actions and performance. In order to address these incentives, designing and operating internal control and the compliance organization have to be executed under the guidance and oversight of the supervisory board.

The compensation policy also provides incentives for the management board. For listed corporations, sec. 87(1)(s. 2) AktG requires the supervisory board to structure the compensation of the members of the management board to foster sustainable growth of the corporation. In this regard, the supervisory board may consider incentives regarding internal control and compliance as part of the incentive-based compensation.[1684] For financial institutions subject to the KWG, the *Instituts-Vergütungsverordnung* (InstitutsVergV) requires in sec. 3(3) InstitutsVergV that the compensation of the management board should not be contrary to any monitoring functions such as compliance (sec. 3(3) combined with sec. 2(no. 9) InstitutsVergV). For corporations not subject to the KWG, the law does not require to consider internal control and compliance as part of the incentive-based compensation. Nevertheless, the supervisory board may consider the provisions of the InstitutsVergV and other incentives with regard to internal control and compliance to structure the compensation policy.

With regard to D&O insurance, most corporations purchase D&O insurance for the members of the management board which impacts the incentive structure. In general, D&O insurance provides for coverage in case members of the management board violate any of their duties to manage the corporation. In light of the financial crisis in 2008, the VorstAG[1685] implemented sec. 93(2)(s. 3) AktG requiring for D&O insurances purchased by the corporation to include a deductable of at least 10% of the damage limited to at least the amount of one and half times the fixed annual compensation of the member of the management board in order to prevent excessive risk taking.[1686] The implementation of sec. 93(2)(s. 3) AktG affects the incentive structure with regard to risk taking by providing more incentives for the management board to implement measures to control risk taking in order to avoid liability. Due to the rather limited scope of the required deductable and the opportunity for alternative insurance[1687], the additional incentive for the management board to implement risk controls is rather limited. Moreover, D&O insurance generally does not cover liability

1684 Cf. *Moosmayer*, Compliance, 81 et seq.
1685 Beschlussempfehlung des Rechtsausschusses BT-Drucks. 16/13433.
1686 Beschlussempfehlung des Rechtsausschusses BT-Drucks. 16/13433, p. 11.
1687 *Koch*, AG 2009, 637, 646.

due to criminal or administrative fines[1688] reducing its impact on the incentive structure.

For improving the systems prior to a test, the management board has incentives to assess the effectiveness of the internal control and risk management prior to reporting to the audit committee. Similarly, the management board incentives to evaluate the effectiveness to report to the supervisory board on the effectiveness.

In essence, the management board has only incentives to implement "paper tigers" systems, which fulfill minimum requirements to avoid ostensible violations of sec. 93 AktG and pass any routine testing, if the supervisory board fails to require the management board to implement truly effective systems reflecting the minimum legal requirements and the expectations of the supervisory board and, more importantly, if the supervisory board fails to ensures effective oversight by commissioning external audits. Due to adverse incentives for the supervisory board especially due to the litigation dilemma, the supervisory board will refrain from ensuring that the management board has incentives to implement truly effective systems.

IV. Conclusion

Corporate law only partially addresses internal control and risk management as well as compliance. It does not provide a comprehensive framework especially with regard to the specific needs of large, listed corporations. Nevertheless, the legal mandates and best practice in Germany for internal control systems are quite proficient even though no statutory mandate clearly expresses a duty of the corporation to implement comprehensive internal control in the sense of COSO I. The early warning system of sec. 91(2) AktG does not have the scope of internal control. The goal of the early warning system is to detect risks endangering the survival of the corporation focusing on risky dealings, inaccurate financial reporting, and non-compliance with legal accounting statutes including fraud. The system has to provide for controls evaluating whether detection measures have been implemented but does not need to provide for prevention measures or risk responds measures.

The duty of the management board to manage the corporation pursuant to sec. 76 combined with sec. 93 AktG requires corporations to implement

1688 Cf. *Seibt/Cziupka*, DB 2014, 1598.

an internal control system. The scope and requirements depend on the specific circumstances of each corporation. Since the legal mandates are corporation-specific, the law does not require specific thresholds or requirements. The duty to implement internal control does not include how to fulfill this duty. Each corporation has wide discretion how to design and operate internal control. The ownership structure of the corporation is one of the most important factors to consider for designing internal control. Even though not required by law, using one of the COSO frameworks will fulfill the requirements of the duty to manage the corporation. For large, listed corporations, the level of the duty to manage the corporation converges towards best practice. With regard to German best practice, corporations have to implement proficient internal control reflecting all three categories of COSO I or COSO II, i.e. operations, financial reporting, and compliance with laws. Corporations may use these frameworks to design, operate, and evaluate internal control. The assessment of the adequacy and effectiveness of internal control is also part of best practice. Furthermore, best practice includes to implement an audit committee and to appoint a CCO. It has been suggested that the supervisory board should commission voluntary audits of the effectiveness of the internal control system since the task to evaluate the effectiveness generally would exceed the capacity and competence of the audit committee.

The internal control and risk management systems including the compliance organization have to be effective. The effectiveness of the systems depends on the judgment of the management board supervised by the supervisory board. The boards are only allowed to determine the systems effective if they fulfill minimum legal requirements. In order to reach a reasonable conclusion, objective criteria have to be used. The management board needs to define benchmarks and key performance indicators for the internal control and risk management systems including the compliance organization, which the systems have to achieve, to justify the determination that the systems are effective. The benchmarks and key performance indicators have to be adequate for the specific corporation in light of the minimum legal requirements. Best practice requires the corporation to define benchmarks considering COSO I and COSO II. Since the law does not provide for a level of effectiveness of internal control, the standard for effectiveness is the general standard of liability in sec. 93(1) AktG.

With the enactment of BilMoG, several provisions address internal control issues. The AktG requires in sec. 107(3) AktG that the supervisory board monitors *inter alia* the audit process, the effectiveness of the internal control system, and the effectiveness of the internal audit system. But, the law does not mandate that corporations have to implement profound internal control. Rather, the suggested scrutiny of the supervisory board will lead to an increased awareness of internal control issues and the supervisory board is expected to require the management board to implement more proficient and effective internal control, if indicated. For large, listed corporations, all these systems have to be implemented leaving to the management board only the issue of the specific design. With regard to sec. 171(1) (s. 2) AktG, the external auditor has to report on significant deficiencies of internal control regarding financial reporting and has to state whether internal control regarding financial reporting are generally adequate.

The incentive structure from corporate law does not induce management to implement effective internal control and risk management systems including compliance measures. The management board has incentives to implement internal control and compliance measures fulfilling minimum requirements *prima facie* which will pass any routine testing. The incentives from sec. 93(1) AktG only lead the management board to implement systems fulfilling minimum requirements as long as ostensible violations of the duty to manage the corporation will be prevented. The expected civil liability for violating sec. 93(1) AktG is rather low beyond ostensible violations. The small increase of expected liability pursuant to the BGH case ARAG/Garmenbeck does not change this finding. Moreover, the detriments of the litigation dilemma affect the incentive structure. Due to BilMoG, the awareness regarding the effectiveness of internal control and risk management systems increased. Despite the unchanged legal mandates for internal control and risk management systems, the proficiency of the implemented internal control and risk management systems will rise due to incentives for the supervisory board to focus on internal control and risk management systems including compliance measures. While the supervisory board has incentives to require the management board to implement benchmarks and key performance indicators, it lacks incentives to require truly effective systems due to the detriments of the litigation dilemma. In addition, absent stringent oversight of the supervisory board, management has incentives to leave the internal control and compliance systems less than optimal. Thus, the management board has incentives to implement the minimum legal requirements for internal control and risk management systems including the compliance organization which seem only effective on paper.

C. Commercial Law – Accounting Provisions

In the accounting provisions, the commercial law (HGB) addresses bookkeeping, internal control and risk management as well as corporate governance issues. BilMoG implemented various changes to the accounting provisions of the commercial law, besides the changes to corporate law, which affect internal control and risk management as well as corporate governance including the mandates to describe the internal control and risk management systems regarding financial reporting in the management report (sec. 289(4) HGB) and to disclose a corporate governance statement (sec. 289f HGB former sec. 289a HGB)[1689]. In addition, the auditing mandates with regard to bookkeeping (sec. 317(1) HGB), the management report (sec. 317(2) HGB), and the early warning system of sec. 91(2) AktG (sec. 317(4) HGB) influence the management board in its decision how to design and operate internal control and risk management.

I. Management Report – Section 289(4) HGB

In the annual report, the management board has to include a management report (sec. 264(1) HGB) in which corporations have to describe the essential elements of the internal control system and the risk management system with regard to financial reporting (sec. 289(4) combined with sec. 264d HGB).[1690] For sec. 289(4) HGB purposes, the internal control system regarding financial reporting encompasses the principles, procedures and measures to ensure the effectiveness and efficiency of appropriate auditing and to ensure the compliance with the relevant legal mandates.[1691] With regard to the financial reporting, internal audit is regarded as a part of the internal control system.[1692]

Similar to sec. 107(3)(s. 2) and sec. 171(1)(s. 2) AktG, the question arises if sec. 289(4) HGB mandates the management board to implement a profound risk management system.[1693] The wording of sec. 289(4) HGB, however, neither constitutes a legal duty to implement nor specifies how to de-

---

1689 See for details: *Bachmann*, ZIP 2010, 1517.

1690 See for the essentials of the description in the management report: *Withus*, KoR 2009, 440.

1691 Begr RegE BilMoG, BT-Drucks. 16/10067, p. 77.

1692 Begr RegE BilMoG, BT-Drucks. 16/10067, p. 77.

1693 Cf. *Kort*, ZGR 2010, 440, 453.

sign an internal control system or a risk management system.[1694] In the extreme case that no such systems exist within a corporation, this fact has to be reported in the management report.[1695] Hence, no profound risk management system has to be implemented due to sec. 289(4) HGB.[1696] The management report only has to describe any existing internal control and risk management systems regarding financial reporting which may include elements of the early warning system of sec. 91(2) AktG, but the early warning system is otherwise detached from sec. 289(4) HGB. The management report has to describe all existing internal control and risk management elements and not only the elements mandated by law.

Also, the corporation needs to address in the management report how specific risk concerning financial instruments are handled (sec. 289(2) (no. 1) HGB). This element of the management report may be integrated into the general description of the internal control and risk management systems pursuant to sec. 289(4) HGB.[1697]

II. Non-Financial Statement – Sections 289b and 289c HGB

Large, listed corporations have to include in the management report a non-financial statement with regard to CSR-related matters according to sec. 289b and 289c HGB. The non-financial statement has to contain *inter*

1694 Begr RegE BilMoG, BT-Drucks. 16/10067, p. 76; *Kort*, ZGR 2010, 440, 453.

1695 Begr RegE BilMoG, BT-Drucks. 16/10067, p. 76; *Kort*, ZGR 2010, 440, 453.

1696 *Kort*, ZGR 2010, 440, 456. Different: *Hommelhoff/Mattheus* reason to interpret sec. 91(2) AktG in light of Directive 2006/46/EC to mandate the implementation of a profound risk management system in order to avoid any deception of investors since the corporation has to describe systems different from the legal mandate of an early warning system of sec. 91(2) AktG (*Hommelhoff/Mattheus*, BB 2007, 2787, 2788). Any potential for deception has been rebutted, however, on the grounds of a circular reasoning (*Dreher*, FS Hüffer, 161, 164 et seq.). Moreover, sec. 289(5) (now sec. 289(4)) HGB only requires to describe the actually implemented systems. Thus, the corporation may indicate that the implemented systems encompass the legal mandates of sec. 91(2) AktG but implemented, in addition to these mandates, elements of the enumerated systems. With this description, no investor will be misled. It has to be noted that the internal control and risk management systems have to be separately dealt with from the early warning system. Otherwise, the legislative reasoning would "allow" the corporation to breach its duty of sec. 91(2) AktG, since the corporation is allowed, and required, to indicate if no internal control and risk management systems exist (Begr RegE BilMoG, BT-Drucks. 16/10067, p. 76).

1697 *Kleindiek*, in: Münch Komm Bilanzrecht, sec. 289, mar. 81.

alia information on the business model of the corporation (sec. 289c(1) HGB), on environmental matters, employee matters, social matters, the respect of human rights, and the combat of corruption and bribery (sec. 289c(2) HGB). The non-financial statement also has to include information necessary for an understanding of the corporation's development, performance, position and impact of its activity relating to the matters listed in sec. 289c(2) HGB including a description of the policies, pursued by the corporation in relation to these matters, and the implemented due diligence processes (sec. 289c(3)(no. 1) HGB), the outcome of these policies (sec. 289c(3)(no. 2) HGB), and the principal risk, due to the business activities of the corporation and its products and services, related to these matters likely to cause adverse impacts in these areas and how the corporation manages these risks (sec. 289c(3)(no. 3) and (no. 4) HGB). With regard to the preparation of the non-financial statement, the corporation may use a national, European or international framework according to sec. 289d HGB. In such case, the non-financial statement has to include a statement which framework has been used by the corporation.

With regard to the scope of the thesis on internal control and corporate compliance, the CSR-related mandates of German law will only be taken into account as far as they concern this scope. With regard to internal control and corporate compliance, the disclosure mandate of sec. 289b and 289c HGB sets a focus on the matters listed in sec. 289c(2) HGB by requiring corporations to report on their efforts and actions in regard to these matters. Especially the obligation to provide information on the combat of corruption and bribery pursuant to sec. 289c(2)(no. 5) HGB, the reporting obligation concerns internal control and compliance aspects. Nevertheless, sec. 289c(2) HGB does neither constitute a legal duty to implement internal control or compliance measures nor specifies how to design these measures. Moreover, sec. 289c(3)(no. 1) HGB does neither mandate to perform a specific due diligence process[1698] nor how to design such process. Rather, the due diligence process overlaps with the risk management system and internal control system addressed in sec. 289 HGB especially with regard to the principal risks and how to manage these risks.[1699]

With regard to the framework addressed in sec. 289d HGB, no specific framework has been mandated.[1700] It has to be noted that the legislator

---

1698 Begr RegE CSR-Richtlinien-Umsetzungsgesetz, BT-Drucks. 18/9982, p. 49.
1699 Begr RegE CSR-Richtlinien-Umsetzungsgesetz, BT-Drucks. 18/9982, p. 49 et seq.
1700 Begr RegE CSR-Richtlinien-Umsetzungsgesetz, BT-Drucks. 18/9982, p. 52.

suggests rather CSR-specific frameworks in light of sec. 289d HGB[1701] which do not have a scope similar to an internal control framework such as COSO I or enterprise risk management framework such as COSO II. COSO I internal controls, however, will facilitate or may even be used to prepare the non-financial statement and/or to conduct the due diligence process. Such controls are generally capable to gather information, assess risks, and control these risks.[1702] Internal controls may be used to implement the policies to address the matters in light of sec. 289a(2) HGB or to monitor the compliance with these policies. Moreover, internal controls may be part of these policies especially with regard to the prevention and detection of non-compliance with e.g. environmental law, employee matters, anti-corruption law, and anti-bribery law.

III. Corporate Governance Statement – Section 289f HGB

Listed corporations have to include a corporate governance statement within their management report pursuant to sec. 289f HGB (former sec. 289a HGB). This statement has to include *inter alia* all relevant information regarding corporate governance exceeding statutory law (sec. 289f(2) (no. 2) HGB) which includes compliance measures and risk management.[1703] But in the corporate governance statement, corporations only have to name the implemented policies and do not need to describe them in detail.[1704] Moreover since the minimum legal standard for the compliance organization of large, listed corporations converges towards best practice, it is rather questionable which compliance measures fall under the scope of sec. 289f(2)(no. 2) HGB.[1705] It has to be noted, however, that corporations combine the corporate governance statement of sec. 289f HGB with the corporate governance report of the GCGC, as recommended in no. 3.10 GCGC,[1706] so that the content of this combined reporting will exceed the legal mandates of sec. 289f(2)(no. 2) HGB.

1701 Begr RegE CSR-Richtlinien-Umsetzungsgesetz, BT-Drucks. 18/9982, p. 52 naming the frameworks set out in Directive 2014/95/EU recital 9.

1702 See *supra* at chapter 4, C. I.

1703 *Lange*, in: Münch Komm HGB, sec. 289a (former version), mar. 10 and fn. 18; *Bachmann*, ZIP 2010, 1517, 1519.

1704 *Lange*, in: Münch Komm HGB, sec. 289a (former version), mar. 11.

1705 Cf. *Bachmann*, ZIP 2010, 1517, 1519.

1706 Cf. *Hüffer*, AktG, sec. 161, mar. 24a.

IV. Auditing of Bookkeeping – Section 317(1) HGB

The audit of the annual report includes the bookkeeping of the corporation (sec. 317(1)(s. 1) HGB). In order to assess the reliability of the financial data, the external auditor uses IDW PS 261 which addresses the effectiveness of the internal control system.[1707] With regard to sec. 317(1) HGB, the audit of the internal control system is limited to financial reporting in contrast to the early warning system of sec. 91(2) AktG.[1708] In order to evaluate the risk for errors within financial reporting, the external auditor relies on IDW PS 261. While the auditing standard does not mandate to evaluate the effectiveness of internal control system, the external auditor has to consider the effectiveness of internal control regarding financial reporting since the level of effectiveness affects the level of control risks.[1709] If the external auditor concludes that the internal control system is rather ineffective, she has to conduct more sample testing[1710] and has to report in the audit report (sec. 321(1) and (2) HGB) on significant deficiencies of the internal control system regarding financial reporting[1711] and also on significant deficiencies relating to non-financial reporting aspects of internal control which the external auditor detected during the audit[1712]. For the audit, the effectiveness of the internal control system is mainly relevant to consider the level of risk of errors within the financial statements and to plan the audit accordingly.[1713] A non-effective internal control system regarding financial reporting becomes relevant if the external auditor concludes that the deficiencies of the internal control system may lead to material misstatements of the financial statements.[1714] Then, she has to consider in light of sec. 322 HGB whether the deficiencies of the internal control system regarding financial reporting warrant to issue a qualified attestation or to refrain from issuing an attestation altogether or to include in the unqualified attestation an additional description of the deficiencies pursuant

1707 *Hopt/Merkt*, in: Baumbach/Hopt, HGB, sec. 317, mar. 2, 5, 10; *Schoberth/Servatius/Thees*, BB 2006, 2571, 2575. See *infra* at chapter 9, C.
1708 *Hopt/Merkt*, in: Baumbach/Hopt, HGB, sec. 317, mar. 10.
1709 Cf. IDW PS 261, mar. 6.
1710 IDW PS 261, mar. 7.
1711 Cf. IDW PS 450, mar. 47.
1712 Cf. IDW PS 261, mar. 93.
1713 Cf. IDW PS 261, mar. 35.
1714 IDW PS 261, mar. 91.

to sec. 322(3)(s. 2) HGB. Further details of the sec. 317(4) HGB audit will be discussed below within IDW PS 261.[1715]

Also, the audit of the external auditor has to encompass whether the corporation complied with the legal mandates and additional mandates of the articles of association or the by-laws (sec. 317(1)(s. 2) HGB) which would otherwise materially affect the financial situation of the corporation in light of sec. 264(2) HGB. This audit of compliance is limited to financial reporting considering the abilities of the external auditor.[1716]

V. Auditing of the Management Report – Section 317(2) HGB

The external auditor has to audit the management report pursuant to sec. 317(2) HGB. With the implementation of sec. 289(4) HGB, the management report contains the description of the implemented internal control and risk management systems with regard to financial reporting. The external auditor has to verify whether this statement accurately portrays the situation of the corporation. The audit of the management report with regard to the internal control and risk management systems is connected to the reporting duty of the external auditor pursuant to sec. 171(1) AktG. If the corporation portrays the internal control system further than required by sec. 289(4) HGB the external auditor has to assess if the statement is correct[1717], but the assessment does not include a complete evaluation of the effectiveness.[1718] The corporate governance statement of sec. 289f HGB is not part of the audit of the management report (sec. 317(2)(s. 3) HGB).

VI. Auditing of the Early Warning System – Section 317(4) HGB

Pursuant to sec. 317(4) HGB, the external auditor has to audit whether the management board has implemented an early warning system required by sec. 91(2) AktG comprised of adequate measures and an effective monitoring system.[1719] The external auditor has to audit the early warning sys-

1715 See *infra* at chapter 9, C.

1716 *Ebke*, in: Münch Komm HGB, sec. 317, mar. 66.

1717 *Kort*, ZGR 2010, 440, 466.

1718 *Melcher/Mattheus*, DB 2009, Beilage 5, 77, 79.

1719 Since 2002, sec. 317(4) AktG applies to all listed corporations after its extension by TransPuG (*Kort*, in: Großkomm AktG, sec. 91, mar. 23). See for the requirements of the early warning system *supra* at chapter 8, B. I. 2. b).

tem regarding adequate design and functionality.[1720] In the audit report, the external auditor has to include suggestions for improvements of the early warning system, if indicated (sec. 321(4) HGB). The management board may comment on these suggestions (sec. 321(5) HGB). The audit is limited to the early warning system of sec. 91(2) AktG and does not include the internal control and risk management systems[1721] or the compliance organization[1722]. Furthermore, the audit does not include the entrepreneurial appropriateness of the early warning system which is part of the supervisory board's duties of sec. 111 AktG.[1723] Based on sec. 317(4) HGB, no profound risk management system is required.[1724] Since most internal control systems of listed corporations exceed the legal requirements of sec. 91(2) AktG, it has to be assessed which parts of the system have to be audited pursuant to sec. 317(4) HGB.[1725] Further details of the sec. 317(4) HGB audit will be discussed below within IDW PS 340.[1726]

VII. Duty to Implement Internal Control Regarding Financial Reporting

The duty to implement internal control regarding financial reporting is not specifically addressed by commercial law. Nevertheless, it has been argued that corporations have the duty to implement internal control regarding financial reporting based on sec. 238(1)(s. 1), 243(1) HGB combined with German generally accepted accounting principles.[1727] While sec. 238(1)(s. 1), 243(1) HGB do not mandate to implement internal control regarding financial reporting, the management board is responsible for accurate accounting in accordance with the applicable accounting standards.[1728] This duty together with the reporting, auditing and disclosure

1720 *Kort*, in: Großkomm AktG, sec. 91, mar. 24; *Ebke*, in: Münch Komm HGB, sec. 317, mar. 82; cf. *Spindler*, in: Fleischer, Hdb Vorstandsrecht, sec. 19, mar. 59.
1721 *Ebke*, in: Münch Komm HGB, sec. 317, mar. 82.
1722 *Immenga*, 2009, p. 201; cf. *Kremer/Klahold*, ZGR 2010, 113, 120.
1723 *Kort*, in: Großkomm AktG, sec. 91, mar. 24.
1724 *Kort*, in: Großkomm AktG, sec. 91, mar. 25, 59.
1725 Cf. *Kuhl/Nickel*, DB 1999, 133, 134.
1726 See *infra* at chapter 9, C.
1727 *Melcher/Mattheus*, DB 2009, Beilage 5, 77, 79.
1728 *Mertens/Cahn*, in: Köln Komm AktG, sec. 91, mar. 5. See *supra* at chapter 8, B. I. 1.

obligations of sec. 289(4), 317(1), and 317(4) HGB lead to a *de facto* duty to implement internal control regarding financial reporting.[1729]

VIII. Scope of Internal Control Regarding Financial Reporting

In order to design internal control regarding financial reporting, the management board is *de facto* required to consider the auditing standard IDW PS 261 since the external auditor will audit internal control regarding financial reporting (sec. 317(1) HGB) in order to obtain confidence in the provided numbers of the corporation.[1730] In order to enable the auditor to verify the statements of the corporation, the implemented internal control and risk management systems have to be adequately documented[1731] since the auditor might request additional documents to verify the corporate statements. Moreover, the reporting obligations of the external auditor to the audit committee on significant deficiencies of internal control regarding financial reporting pursuant to sec. 171(1) AktG and art. 11(2)(j) Regulation (EU) No 537/2014 have to be considered. It has been suggested that internal control regarding financial reporting should be focused on essential risks such as risks endangering the survival of the corporation (sec. 91(2) AktG), legal and reputational risks including fraud, and risk concerning the internal controls of the financial reporting process.[1732] Also, taxes are an important element of financial reporting so that internal control has to focus on effective tax reporting.[1733] It has to be noted, however, that IDW PS 261 does not by itself consider effective internal control regarding financial reporting a primary goal.[1734]

1729 Cf. *Windbichler*, FS HU-Juristische Fakultät, 1079, 1091; *Melcher/Mattheus*, DB 2009, Beilage 5, 77, 79.

1730 Cf. *Schoberth/Servatius/Thees*, BB 2006, 2571; *Müller/Ergün*, ZRFC 2012, 102, 103: referring to *Stute*, IFRS, p. 191 et seq. See *infra* at chapter 9, C.

1731 *Melcher/Mattheus*, DB 2009, Beilage 5, 77, 80; *Wolf*, DStR 2009, 920, 924.

1732 *Wolf*, DStR 2009, 920, 925.

1733 *Büssow/Taetzner*, BB 2005, 2437, 2440.

1734 See *infra* at chapter 9, C.

IX. Incentives to Implement Internal Control Regarding Financial Reporting and Compliance Measures

For implementing internal control regarding financial reporting, the management board has specific incentives from commercial law apart from the general incentives to implement internal control. Failing to provide for accurate accounting will result in liability pursuant to sec. 331(no. 1) HGB. In order to ensure accurate accounting and to avoid liability, the management board has incentives to implement control measures ensuring accurate accounting.

Due to sec. 289(4) HGB combined with sec. 264d HGB, management has to consider its reporting obligation on the essential elements of the internal control system regarding financial reporting. Even though sec. 289(4) HGB does not mandate to implement an internal control system or a risk management system, the duty of the management board to describe the internal control system and the risk management system is an incentive for the management board to deal with these systems including the question of their effectiveness[1735] in order to meet the expectations of investors and the capital market. The disclosure required by sec. 289(4) HGB is especially important for investors. In order to satisfy the expectations of investors, the corporation has to implement proficient internal control and risk management systems including internal audit. While sec. 289(4) HGB does not mandate to evaluate the effectiveness of the systems and disclose any results[1736], the management board has incentives to deal with the effectiveness in light of sec. 107(3)(s. 2) AktG[1737] and to disclose its evaluation since only effective systems will be credited by investors. The capital market will favor those corporations who have a proficient internal control system[1738] because proficient internal controls will better protect the investment from fraud and other illegal acts.[1739] Hence, the disclosure require-

---

1735 *Kort*, ZGR 2010, 440, 457; *Windbichler*, FS Hopt, 1505, 1512; Begr RegE BilMoG, BT-Drucks. 16/10067, p. 76.

1736 Begr RegE BilMoG, BT-Drucks. 16/10067, p. 76; *Kort*, ZGR 2010, 440, 456; *Strieder*, BB 2009, 1002, 1004.

1737 *Spindler*, FS Hüffer, 985, 989. See *supra* at chapter 8, B. III.

1738 *Powilleit*, GWR 2010, 28; *Campos Nave/Bonenberger*, BB 2008, 734; *Bergmoser/Theusinger/Gushurst*, BB 2008, Beilage 5, 1; cf. *Melcher/Mattheus*, DB 2009, Beilage 5, 77, 79 et seq., *Schaefer/Baumann*, NJW 2011, 3601, 3605; *Weber/Lentfer/Köster*, ZCG 2007, 53; *Kremer/Klahold*, ZGR 2010, 113, 138.

1739 See also *infra* at chapter 13, A.

ments will lead to the implementation of internal control and risk management systems.[1740]

The duty of the external auditor to audit the management report (sec. 317(2) HGB) does not add a significant layer of auditing onto the more specific and extensive scope of the sec. 171(1) AktG and art. 11(2)(j) Regulation (EU) No 537/2014 related reporting duties of the external auditor. Hence, the audit of the management report provides no further incentives for the corporation.

Also, the regulatory framework for the external auditor provides incentives for the management board.[1741] The external auditor has to audit financial reporting (sec. 317(1) HGB). In order to evaluate the risk for errors within financial reporting, the external auditor relies on IDW PS 261 which includes to consider the effectiveness of the internal control system limited to financial reporting. A non-effective internal control system regarding financial reporting becomes relevant if the external auditor concludes that the deficiencies of the internal control system may lead to material misstatements of the financial statements.[1742] Then, she has to consider the effects on the attestation according to sec. 322 HGB.[1743] Since an unqualified attestation of the external auditor depends *inter alia* on the assessment of the effectiveness of the internal control system pursuant to IDW PS 261, the management board has an incentive to provide for internal control regarding financial reporting which pass the IDW PS 261 audit. In practice, however, refraining from issuing an unqualified attestation is almost never based on the ineffectiveness of the internal control system.[1744] Thus, the incentive level for management is not high.

Moreover, the external auditor has to report on significant deficiencies of the internal control system regarding financial reporting and also on any detected significant deficiencies relating to non-financial reporting aspects of internal control in the audit report (sec. 321(1) and (2) HGB). Also

---

1740 Cf. *Melcher/Mattheus*, DB 2009, Beilage 5, 77, 79; *Kort*, ZGR 2010, 440, 468.

1741 See also *infra* at chapter 9, C.

1742 IDW PS 261, mar. 91.

1743 Cf. IDW PS 261, mar. 91. See *supra* at chapter 8, C. IV.

1744 According to the summaries of qualified or supplemented attestations attached to the reports of the Chamber of Public Accountants regarding the supervision of annual auditors of the years 2005 to 2015, only one attestation has been qualified or denied based *inter alia* on the ineffectiveness of the internal control system. In one case, the unqualified attestation has been supplemented due to significant deficiencies of the internal control system (*WPK*, Summaries 2005-2015).

pursuant to sec. 171(1)(s. 2) AktG and art. 11(2)(j) Regulation (EU) No 537/2014, the external auditor has to report significant deficiencies of internal control regarding financial reporting to the audit committee and has to state whether these controls are generally adequate. But the external auditor does not have the duty to conduct an extensive evaluation of the effectiveness so that the testing is rather *en passant* than thorough. From sec. 171(1)(s. 2) AktG and art. 11(2)(j) Regulation (EU) No 537/2014 as well as the audit report follow incentives for the management board to implement internal control regarding financial reporting without significant deficiencies reflecting the requirements of IDW PS 261 which the external auditor would find during routine testing. With regard to non-financial reporting aspects of internal control, the incentive level for the management board is substantively lower due to the scope and limits[1745] of the audit. Following from the scope and limits, it is rather unlikely that the external auditor will be concerned with the non-financial reporting aspects of internal control as part of the regular audit. Absent ostensible significant deficiencies, it is rather unlikely that the external auditor will address these aspects in the audit report.[1746] Any report of significant deficiencies also induces the supervisory board as well as the management board to engage in corrective actions since inaction in light of a known significant deficiencies violates the duty pursuant to sec. 76 combined with sec. 93(1) AktG.[1747] Hence, both boards have incentives to implement internal control regarding financial reporting which meet the expectations of investors and the capital market in general and which do not have any significant deficiencies which the external auditor would find during routine testing.

Due to the scope of the external audit pursuant to sec. 317(1)(s. 2) HGB, management has incentives to comply with the legal mandates and additional mandates of the articles of association or the by-laws so that the financial situation of the corporation in light of sec. 264(2) HGB are not materially affected.

1745 See on the scope and limits of the audit *supra* at B. II. 2.

1746 According to the summaries of qualified or supplemented attestations attached to the reports of the Chamber of Public Accountants regarding the supervision of annual auditors of the years 2005 to 2015, only one attestation (unqualified) has been supplemented *inter alia* due to significant deficiencies of the internal control system mainly addressing financial reporting deficiencies (*WPK*, Summaries 2005-2015). It is questionable whether non-financial reporting aspects have been addressed at all by this supplement.

1747 See *supra* at chapter 8, B. I. 3. b).

Due to the audit of the early warning system (sec. 317(4) HGB), the board has further incentives to align the design of the early warning system with the auditing standards of the external auditor to receive an unqualified attestation and to avoid any suggestions for improvements pursuant to sec. 321(4) HGB.[1748]

With regard to compliance measures, management has to consider its reporting obligation pursuant to sec. 289c(2) HGB, in particular on bribery and corruption, in the same way as its reporting obligations pursuant to sec. 289(4) HGB. Furthermore, sec. 289f(2)(no. 2) HGB provides for incentives to implement compliance measures in order to fulfill the expectations of investors. The information regarding risk management and compliance is important for the capital markets since the risk management system and the compliance system have a "high significance" for actual or potential investors[1749]. While sec. 289c(2)(no. 5) HGB provides incentives for the management board to focus on anti-bribery and anti-corruption measures, the incentives from sec. 289f(2)(no. 2) HGB to implement compliance measures are rather low. Nevertheless, the corporate governance statement of sec. 289f HGB provides a platform for corporations, in particular if combined with the corporate governance report of the GCGC, to communicate to investors their compliance-related efforts which are aimed to fulfill the expectations of investors.

X. Conclusion

The accounting provisions of the commercial law influence the internal control and risk management systems of corporations. The duty for the management board to describe the essential elements of the internal control and the risk management systems provides incentives to implement proficient internal control and risk management systems fulfilling the expectations of investors with regard to these systems. Since the external auditor will assess the description in light of sec. 107(3) AktG, the management board has incentives to implement internal control regarding financial reporting which do not have any significant deficiencies which the external auditor would find during routine testing. For the designing of internal control regarding financial reporting, the management board has incentives to fulfill the requirements of IDW PS 261. With regard to the early

1748 *Berg*, AG 2007, 271, 275.
1749 *Weber/Velte*, DStR 2011, 1141, 1144 and 1146.

warning system of sec. 91(2) AktG, the management board has incentives to comply with the mandates of sec. 91(2) AktG and to fulfill the requirements of IDW PS 340. In essence, the auditing provisions together with the related auditing standards influence the management board to implement internal control and risk management systems fulfilling the expectations of the external auditor even though most provisions are only applicable for the external auditor.

D. *Specific Law Important for Internal Control and the Compliance Organization*

For designing and operating internal control including the compliance organization as well as for conducting compliance-related internal investigations, the corporation has to comply with the mandates and limits of specific law which limits the discretion of the management board. Labor and employment law and data protection law are the most critical in this regard. With regard to labor and employment law, codes of conduct and whistleblower protection will be addressed and within data protection law a focus will be set to anonymous reporting. For listed corporations, capital markets law is also important. Nevertheless, the specific law does not provide for mandates or requirements on how to structure internal control and the compliance organization. Since the thesis focuses on the elements of internal control and compliance and since the specific law rather defines the boundaries of these elements, the specific law will only be depicted as far as necessary to conduct the impact analysis of U.S. law on German corporations and as far as the specific law addresses general aspects of internal control and compliance elements. For each element, various possibilities to design such element exist which will not be analyzed in detail if they conflict with specific law. Within the thesis, the issue will only be raised so that corporations are aware of the general limits applicable for internal control and compliance elements. Despite labor and employment law and data protection law, compliance measures especially monitoring may be subject to the *Telekomunikationsgesetz* (TKG) so that corporations have to consider the limits provided by TKG for their monitoring and investigatory activities.[1750]

1750 *Schmidt*, BB 2009, 1295, 1296 et seq.; *Behling* BB 2010, 892.

I. Labor and Employment Law

1. Codes of Conduct

Corporations have to consider the requirements and limits provided by labor and employment law for designing and operating the compliance organization.[1751] For the implementation of specific compliance measures, the works council has to participate with regard to these measures as far as they represent rules regarding the organization of the workplace within the corporation (sec. 87(1)(no. 1) BetrVG) or address electronic monitoring (sec. 87(1)(no. 6) BetrVG).[1752] The implementation of a code of conduct requiring to report misconduct needs the participation of the works council.[1753] With regard to the duty to report misconduct established in a code of conduct, the labor courts ruled that such duty is invalid without the participation of the works council.[1754] In any case, the aspects of a code of conduct are case specific with regard to codetermination.[1755]

German corporations may have incentives to implement a code of conduct due to their listing on the NYSE or the listing of their parent corporation on the NYSE.[1756] It has to be noted that SOX does only require to implement a code of conduct for senior financial officers which does not have to include any whistleblower duty (sec. 406 SOX).[1757] So far, German labor courts dealt *inter alia* with the whistleblowing provisions in codes of conduct. The particular codes of conduct mandated to report misconduct.[1758] Such duty, however, is not required by SOX. Due to U.S. mandates, corporations only have to provide for means to allow for anonymous

---

1751 See *Mengel*, Compliance und Arbeitsrecht; *Mengel/Hagemeister*, BB 2006, 2466; *Mengel/Hagemeister*, BB 2007, 1386; *Wisskirchen/Jordan/Bissels*, DB 2005, 2190; *Müller-Bonanni/Sagan*, BB 2008, Beilage 5, 28, 29 et seq.

1752 *Kremer/Klahold*, ZGR 2010, 113, 137; *Bachmann*, VGR, 2008, 65, 90; *Mengel/Hagemeister*, BB 2006, 2466, 2467 et seq.; *Mengel/Hagemeister*, BB 2007, 1386, 1392.

1753 BAG NZA 2008, 1248, 1254; cf. *Kremer/Klahold*, ZGR 2010, 113, 137.

1754 LAG Hessen, CCZ 2008, 73; LAG Düsseldorf, ZIP 2006, 436; cf. *Bachmann*, VGR, 2008, 65, 90. See on codes of conduct: *Kock*, ZIP 2009, 1406.

1755 Cf. BAG NZA 2008, 1248, 1253.

1756 See *supra* at chapter 4, D. I. 2.

1757 See *supra* at chapter 4, A. IV. 3. Misleading: *Bachmann*, VGR, 2008, 65, 90 at fn. 133 indicating that a duty to blow the whistle is a SOX-related duty.

1758 LAG Düsseldorf v. 14.11.2005 - 10 TaBV 46/05, BB 2006, 335; cf. *Wisskirchen/Körber/Bissels*, BB 2006, 1567. See also *Schulz*, BB 2011, 629 on the issue if employees have the duty to blow the whistle based on the employment contract.

reporting. It rather reflects U.S. culture to require to report misconduct. With regard to a whistleblowing duty established in a code of conduct, it has to be noted that each employee has a general duty to prevent harm from its employer as far as possible and appropriate.[1759] The employer may specify such duty insofar as the employees have to use a whistleblower or compliance hotline for reporting any suspicious conduct.[1760] The reporting duty has to adhere to the principle of proportionality[1761] and has to comply with the data protection law[1762]. Moreover, employees must not be required to indict themselves.[1763] In addition, the code of conduct should consider cultural aspects especially in multinational corporations.[1764] In essence, labor law does not preclude codes of conduct but restricts their scope and may require the participation of the works council for certain provisions of the code.

2. Whistleblower Protection

Under German law, no explicit statutory provision protects whistleblower against retaliation.[1765] Whether a dismissal based on internal or external whistleblowing contradicts sec. 612a BGB rendering the dismissal void will be determined on a case by case basis[1766] leading to immanent legal uncertainty[1767]. With regard to external whistleblowing, the courts will determine whether the external reporting was merited and will weigh the interests of the employer against the interests of the employee and the public to inform external third parties, such as law enforcement, in order to determine whether the external whistleblowing has been legitimate rendering a

1759 *Preis*, in: Erfurter Komm ArbR, BGB, sec. 611, mar.744; LAG Hessen, CCZ 2008, 73, 75 (annotated by *Umnuß*).

1760 *Mengel/Hagemeister*, BB 2007, 1386, 1389; cf. *Klasen/Schaefer*, BB 2012, 641 et seq.

1761 *Bachmann*, VGR, 2008, 65, 91; cf. *Mengel/Hagemeister*, BB 2007, 1386, 1389.

1762 *Mengel/Hagemeister*, BB 2007, 1386, 1389.

1763 *Mengel/Hagemeister*, BB 2007, 1386, 1389.

1764 *Nezmeskal-Berggötz*, CCZ 2009, 209.

1765 *Forst*, NJW 2011, 3477; *Zimmer/Seebacher*, CCZ 2013, 31, 32; *Leuchten*, ZRP 2012, 142; cf. *Niemann*, in: Erfurter Komm ArbR, BGB, sec. 626, mar. 64b.

1766 *Joussen*, BeckOK Arbeitsrecht, sec. 612a BGB, mar. 15a. See for leading cases: *Forst*, NJW 2011, 3477.

1767 Cf. *Abraham*, ZRP 2012, 11.

dismissal void.[1768] Elements in the weighting process include the severity of the corporate misconduct and the possibility of appropriate internal resolution process.[1769] In this regard, courts have to take the European Convention on Human Rights and the rulings of the European Court of Human Rights into account.[1770] It follows that management has incentives to provide appropriate internal resolution processes in order to keep whistleblowing internally.

II. Data Protection Law – Especially Anonymous Whistleblowing

One of the critical aspects for the compliance organization with regard to specific law is whistleblowing. As part of the compliance organization, whistleblowing has been a catch phrase in the business world important especially for corporations subject to SOX.[1771] The main issues for whistleblowing systems derive from data protection law in particular anonymous reporting and, as discussed above[1772], labor law which corporations have to consider for implementing whistleblowing systems.[1773] The issue of anonymous reporting reflects historical resentments in Europe and Germany due to denunciation.[1774] Therefore, anonymous reporting has a negative reputation due to the inability of the accused person to protect himself against the accuser.[1775] It has to be differentiated between internal and external whistleblowing.[1776] The main focus of whistleblowing in the compliance context is internal whistleblowing.[1777] In general, no legal requirement ex-

1768 *Niemann*, in: Erfurter Komm ArbR, BGB, sec. 626, mar. 64 et seq.; *v. Busekist/Fahrig*, BB 2013, 119, 121; *Klasen/Schaefer*, BB 2012, 641, 643 et seq.

1769 *Niemann*, in: Erfurter Komm ArbR, BGB, sec. 626, mar. 64a; *v. Busekist/Fahrig*, BB 2013, 119, 121 et seq.

1770 BVerfG, *Beschluss*, 2 BvR 1481/04 of October 14, 2004; cf. ECtHR, *Heinisch v. Germany*, no. 2827/08, Judgment of July 21, 2011 (Fifth Section). See also on the debate regarding protection of whistleblower *infra* at chapter 20, A. II. 3.

1771 Cf. *Mahnhold*, NZA 2008, 737 and 739. See on whistleblowing *supra* at chapter 4, A. IV. 4.

1772 See *supra* at chapter 8, D. I. 2.

1773 Cf. *Mahnhold*, NZA 2008, 737; *Reufels/Deviard*, CCZ 2009, 201, 206.

1774 Cf. *Mahnhold*, NZA 2008, 737, 739; *Berndt/Hoppler*, BB 2005, 2623.

1775 Cf. *Reifels/Devirad*, CCZ 2009, 201, 204; *Rauhofer*, 2007, p. 6.

1776 *Kort*, MMR 2011, 294, 296.

1777 *Fleischer*, ZGR 2011, 155, 175.

ists on how to design whistleblowing systems. Likewise, no specific regulation on data protection exists with regard to whistleblowing.[1778]

For implementing whistleblowing systems, corporations have to adhere to the *Bundesdatenschutzgestz* (BDSG).[1779] For whistleblowing systems, sec. 32 BDSG may be applicable allowing the collection of personal data of an employee to investigate criminal acts only if actual indications have been documented that the employee committed a criminal act.[1780] Otherwise, sec. 28(1)(no. 2) BDSG may justify the collection of personal data.[1781] Similar to art. 7 of the Data Protection Directive (Directive 95/46/EC), both sections require a legitimate interest and to consider the personal interests of the accused person. It has been argued that a whistleblowing system allowing for anonymous reporting for all aspects may not be justified by sec. 28(1)(no. 2) BDSG without limitations such as suggested by the 'Art. 29 Working Party'.[1782] In general, any whistleblowing system has to account for the mandates of the BDSG. For whistleblowing systems operated by external providers, sec. 11 BDSG has to be considered if the corporation does not assign the complete whistleblowing function to the external provider.[1783] Each corporation has to ensure that the whistleblowing system adheres to the proportionality principle and protects the interests of the accused person. Such protection is also required due to the duty of the employer to protect its employees especially in light of the general right of personality (*allgemeines Persönlichkeitsrecht*) based on art. 2(1) combined with art. 1(1) GG.[1784] In order to protect such interests, procedural measures, such as a first glance plausibility check prior to proceed with any investigation in light of alleged misconduct especially in case of anonymous reporting, have to be used.[1785] By assigning case specific numbers, the anonymous whistleblower may stay in contact with the corporation.[1786] While upholding the important principles of data protection, corporations

1778 *Kort*, MMR 2011, 294, 297.

1779 See *Maschmann*, NZA-Beilage 2012, 50.

1780 Cf. *Reufels/Deviard*, CCZ 2009, 201, 206 et seq.; *Gola/Schomerus*, BDSG, sec. 32, mar. 16.

1781 *Wank*, in: Erfurter Komm ArbR, BDSG, sec. 28, mar. 9; *Reufels/Deviard*, CCZ 2009, 201, 206; *Wisskirchen/Körber/Bissels*, BB 2006, 1567, 1568.

1782 *Wisskirchen/Körber/Bissels*, BB 2006, 1567, 1570.

1783 *Reufels/Deviard*, CCZ 2009, 201, 206.

1784 *Joussen*, BeckOK Arbeitsrecht, sec. 611, mar. 240; cf. *Riesenhuber*, in: BeckOK Datenschutz, BDSG, sec. 32, mar. 125 on the general right of personality.

1785 See also *Salvenmoser/Hauschka*, NJW 2010, 331, 335; *Schürrle/Fleck*, CCZ 2011, 218, 221; *Düsseldorfer Kreis*, 2007, p. 4.

1786 Cf. *Nezmeskal-Berggötz*, CCZ 2009, 209, 214.

have to be able to use internal whistleblowing systems including measures for anonymous reporting[1787] as an important aspect of prevention and detection measures especially with regard to intentional behavior such as fraud[1788] and corruption[1789].[1790] The effect of whistleblowing systems is to increase the risk of detection which is important since the current risk of detection is "extremely low".[1791] For detecting misconduct, tips are most important, followed by internal audit which detects considerable less misconduct, and law enforcement agencies having only a minor role in detection.[1792] In this regard, the *Bundeskriminalamt* (BKA) names the implementation of compliance systems which facilitated whistleblowing eminent to fight corruption.[1793]

In order to ensure personal rights of the accused and in light of the sec. 28 BDSG as well as the general right of personality to justify the collection of data, corporation have to exercise caution and due diligence when deciding whether to pursue investigations only based on anonymous tips.[1794] Moreover, corporations may avoid the data protection issue by limiting the collected data through anonymous reporting to the unit or working group in which the suspected misconduct may have occurred. Thereby, internal investigations may be directed towards alleged misconduct within the corporation without using data of specific employees. While the use of these fragmentary tips may be limited, the corporation avoids the data protection law issue. Depending on the risk profile of the corporation with regard to intentional misconduct, such limited scope of anonymous reporting may be sufficient.

German data protection law is in line with on the Data Protection Directive. In order to collect data, art. 7 of the directive requires a legal mandate or legitimate interest. Due to art. 29 of the directive, the Art. 29 Working Party has been established providing for non-binding, independent counsel on data protection issues. With regard to the whistleblowing require-

---

1787 In favor of anonym reporting: *Bürkle*, DB 2004, 2158, 2161; *Schürrle/Fleck*, CCZ 2011, 218, 220; *Wybitul*, BB 2009, 111, 112.

1788 *Arlen*, 23 J. Legal Stud. 833 (1994), p. 835; cf. *Fleischer*, ZGR 2011, 155, 178; ACFE Report 2012, p. 14. See *supra* at chapter 4, A. IV. 4.

1789 Cf. *Reufels/Deviard*, CCZ 2009, 201, 203, 205.

1790 Cf. *Bussmann/Salvenmoser*, NStZ 2006, 203, 208; *Bussmann/Matschke*, CCZ 2009, 132, 135 et seq.

1791 *Bussmann/Matschke*, CCZ 2009, 132, 135.

1792 *Bussmann/Matschke*, CCZ 2009, 132, 135 et seq.

1793 BKA, Korruptionsbericht 2015, p. 13; BKA, Korruptionsbericht 2011, p. 20.

1794 *Casper*, Libor Amicorum Winter, 77, 94.

ments of SOX, the Art. 29 Working Party concluded that only EU law may provide for a legal mandate but SOX represents in general a legitimate interest.[1795] The justification of the collection of data also requires to consider the interests of accused person under the proportionality principle.[1796] With regard to anonymous reporting, German corporations would be allowed to provide for anonymous reporting but are not allowed to encourage anonymous reporting.[1797] Since sec. 301(4) SOX only requires for anonymous reporting with regard to financial reporting issues, the Art. 29 Working Party concludes that the whistleblowing system should only provide for anonymous reporting as far as required by U.S. law.[1798]

In recent years, various scandals regarding illegal monitoring methods violating *inter alia* data protection law show that corporations have to design and operate their compliance organization within the limits provided by law.[1799] Therefore, corporations have to be aware of the limits imposed by data protection law and should refrain from monitoring measures which the public may regard as spy systems endangering their reputation.[1800] In order to encourage internal whistleblowing, corporations have to ensure that legitimate and non-abusive whistleblowing is protected from retaliation.

III. Capital Markets Law – Reporting Obligations

Capital markets law is important for listed corporations especially the reporting obligations. Complying with these obligations requires a system to obtain the necessary information. While the information for reporting financial information is covered by internal control regarding financial reporting, the following section will focus on reporting non-financial infor-

1795 *Art. 29 Working Party*, 2006, p. 7 et seq.; cf. *Reufels/Deviard*, CCZ 2009, 201, 203.

1796 *Art. 29 Working Party*, 2006, p. 8 et seq.; cf. *Riesenhuber*, in: BeckOK Datenschutz, BDSG, sec. 32, mar. 125; *Reufels/Deviard*, CCZ 2009, 201, 203.

1797 *Art. 29 Working Party*, 2006, p. 11; cf. *Mahnhold*, NZA 2008, 737, 743; *Düsseldorfer Kreis*, 2007, p. 4 et seq.

1798 Cf. *Art. 29 Working Party*, 2006, p. 5.

1799 See *Overwetter*, NZA 2008, 609; *Salvenmoser/Hauschka*, NJW 2010, 331, 332; *Schmidt*, BB 2009, 1295, 1297 et seq.

1800 *Moosmayer*, Compliance, p. 99 citing the cases of Deutsche Bahn, Telekom, Deutsche Bank, Lidl or HSH Nordbank (*id.*, at fn 193); cf. *Wybitul*, BB 2009, 1582.

mation and the incentives to implement internal control regarding non-financial information.

1. Reporting of Non-Financial Information

Capital markets law provides for numerous reporting obligations of listed corporations. The information necessary for reporting has to be gathered from within and outside the corporation. Providing for an information system which gathers and assess such information has been named to be mostly an issue of business organization rather than law.[1801] In Germany, no statutory mandate exists that requires corporations to implement internal controls addressing non-financial information which has to be disclosed pursuant to capital markets law.[1802] While the non-financial statement in the management report with regard to CSR-related matters pursuant to sec. 289c HGB shares the terminology, the scope is different so that neither the due diligence processes addressed in sec. 289c(3)(no. 1) HGB nor the frameworks addressed in sec. 289d HGB will provide the information which has to be disclosed pursuant to capital markets law. Nevertheless, corporations have to ensure to comply with the reporting obligations in light of the general duty to comply with the law pursuant to sec. 76 combined with sec. 93 AktG. Following from such duty, the management board has to implement a compliance organization which also has to address non-financial information subject to reporting obligations[1803]. While it has been reasoned that no legal duty to implement internal control regarding non-financial information subject to reporting obligations follows as an appendix from the duty to report such information[1804], the management board particularly of large, listed corporations has the duty to implement internal control regarding non-financial information subject to reporting obligations pursuant to the general duty to manage the corporation of sec. 76 combined with sec. 93 AktG. Similar to the reasoning requiring large, listed corporations to implement internal control and risk

1801 Cf. *Schneider, S.H.*, in: Habersack/Mülbert/Schlitt, Hdb Kapitalmarktinformation, sec. 3, mar. 8.

1802 *Schneider, S.H.*, in: Habersack/Mülbert/Schlitt, Hdb Kapitalmarktinformation, sec. 3, mar. 46.

1803 *Schneider, S.H.*, in: Habersack/Mülbert/Schlitt, Hdb Kapitalmarktinformation, sec. 3, mar. 40 et seq.

1804 *Schneider, S.H.*, in: Habersack/Mülbert/Schlitt, Hdb Kapitalmarktinformation, sec. 3, mar. 52.

management systems[1805], this duty corresponds to the difficulties of managing the corporation resulting from the sheer scope and complexity to gather and assess such information especially within large, listed corporation[1806]. It follows that large, listed corporations have to implement a compliance program with a specific focus on non-financial information subject to reporting obligations. In light of sec. 107(3) AktG, the effectiveness of these controls should be evaluated.

With regard to the scope of the information system regarding non-financial information subject to reporting obligations, the specific requirements depend on the specific circumstances of the corporation.[1807] In this regard, the specific disclosure requirements will shape the focus of the information system to gather the information which needs to be disclosed.[1808] General aspects of the system include information guidelines, procedural guidelines, testing, monitoring, and reporting on the information system.[1809] Besides these general aspects, corporations should consider best practice including the COSO frameworks. Also, the requirements for the general compliance program have to be considered.[1810] In addition, corporations may consider the U.S. elements of disclosure controls and procedures of sec. 302 SOX.[1811] Since no further guidelines exist, management has wide discretion to design an information system regarding non-financial information subject to reporting obligations.

2. Incentives to Implement Internal Control Regarding Non-Financial Information

Implementing internal control regarding non-financial information subject to reporting obligations follows in general the same incentives structure as to implement the general compliance program. Complying with the reporting obligations of the capital markets law is not different from

---

1805 See *supra* at chapter 8, B. I. 3. a) (2).
1806 Cf. *Schneider, S.H.*, in: Habersack/Mülbert/Schlitt, Hdb Kapitalmarktinformation, sec. 3, mar. 41.
1807 *Schneider, S.H.*, in: Habersack/Mülbert/Schlitt, Hdb Kapitalmarktinformation, sec. 3, mar. 80.
1808 *Windbichler*, FS Hopt, 1505, 1511.
1809 *Schneider, S.H.*, in: Habersack/Mülbert/Schlitt, Hdb Kapitalmarktinformation, sec. 3, mar. 81 et seq.
1810 See *infra* at chapter 8, B. I. 3. b) (2).
1811 See *supra* at chapter 4, A. I.

complying with other legal mandates. In particular, corporations have incentives to implement effective controls in order to avoid liability pursuant to sec. 38 et seq. WpHG for failing to comply with reporting obligations.[1812] It has been stated that corporations should be exculpated from liability if appropriate internal controls had been implemented even though the corporation failed to provide such information in due time.[1813] This proposal corresponds with the U.S. concept of granting leniency for effective compliance programs.[1814]

One specific aspect of non-financial information subject to reporting increases the expected liability. Due to a higher likelihood attributed to the capital market that information will become public later on which the corporation would have had to report, corporations have more incentives to implement internal control regarding non-financial information subject to reporting obligations compared to the incentives to implement general compliance measures. Since the statutory requirements of the reporting obligations are not straight forward[1815], corporations need to focus on internal control regarding non-financial information subject to reporting obligations in order to receive sufficient information for the decision whether to report the received information.

E. *Corporate Liability for Crimes and Offences*

Imposing liability on corporations for criminal acts of their organs and employees is a repeated subject brought up especially after major corporate scandals. So far, the scope of corporate liability for criminal acts of corporate agents and employees in Germany is rather limited since criminal liability for corporations does not exist.[1816] The main provision to sanction corporations is sec. 30 OWiG which sanctions corporations for crimes and offences but only if committed by members of the management board and employees with specific management duties. Besides the OWiG, general criminal law affects the corporation and the compliance organization through individual criminal liability of members of the management

1812 *Schneider, S.H.*, in: Habersack/Mülbert/Schlitt, Hdb Kapitalmarktinformation, sec. 3, mar. 53 et seq.
1813 *Schneider, S.H.*, in: Habersack/Mülbert/Schlitt, Hdb Kapitalmarktinformation, sec. 3, mar. 61 et seq.
1814 See *supra* at chapter 5, C. II. 1.
1815 See *Herfs*, DB 2013, 1350 et seq.
1816 Cf. *Ransiek*, NZWiSt 2012, 45; *Schneider*, CCZ 2008, 18.

board and the supervisory board. Also, corporations may be subject to fines based on regulatory law for instance within antitrust law (sec. 81 GWB) which will be touched on in an *excursus*.

In 1998, the issue was brought up whether to implement corporate criminal liability in Germany[1817] leading to the appointment of the commission regarding the reform of the system for criminal sanctions which concluded in its final report in 2000 that the existing measures to sanction corporations through sec. 130, 30 OWiG were sufficient[1818] despite minor doubts that prosecuting individual crimes may be difficult within the context of corporate crime[1819]. The commission concluded that the available sanctions in Germany correspond with the recommendation of Committee of Ministers of the European Council on corporate liability.[1820] In 2012, the issue of corporate criminal liability has been set on the federal agenda again.[1821] In October 2012, the maximum fines of sec. 30(2) OWiG and of sec. 130(2) OWiG have been increased to ten million euro from one million euro in order to address concerns that a maximum fine of one million might have been inadequate.[1822]

I. Criminal Law – Incentives from Individual Criminal Liability

Criminal law is relevant for corporations as far as their organs and employees commit crimes for the benefit of the corporation. Since no corporate criminal liability exists, the incentive structure mainly consists of individual criminal liability. In general, criminal liability of members of the man-

---

1817 Cf. Antw Reg, BT-Drucks. 13/11425; *Ransiek*, ZGR 1999, 613.

1818 Similar: *Peglau*, ZRP 2001, 406; *Theile/Petermann*, JuS 2011, 496, 501; *v. Rosen*, in: Unternehmensstrafrecht, 263; *Weber-Rey*, in: Unternehmensstrafrecht, 321, 331.

1819 *Kommission zur Reform des strafrechtlichen Sanktionensytems*, Abschlussbericht, p. 191 et seq.

1820 *Kommission zur Reform des strafrechtlichen Sanktionensytems*, Abschlussbericht, p. 191; cf. *Council of Europe*, R (88) 18.

1821 See *Jahn*, F.A.Z. of August 13, 2012; *Reichling*, LTO of May 22, 2012 citing *Bundesministerium der Justiz*, Diskussionsentwurf zur Änderung des Ordnungswidrigkeitengesetzes (OWiG), April 27, 2012; *WDR*, WESTPOL of September 16, 2012; *Spiegel Online*, December 18, 2012; *Körner*, LTO of April 9, 2012; *Moosmayer/Gropp-Stadler*, NZWiSt 2012, 241.

1822 Beschlussempfehlung und Bericht, BT-Drucks. 17/11053, p. 9 et seq.

agement board is underestimated in Germany.[1823] The same holds for members of the supervisory board especially with regard to embezzlement pursuant to sec. 266 StGB.[1824] It follows that German corporations have mostly been ignorant to the threat of criminal liability and generally did not implement compliance programs until 2007[1825]. Only corporations which are listed on the NYSE and/or subject to the FCPA as well as corporations suffering from recent major compliance scandals started to engage in compliance measures. Mainly due to an increased awareness regarding the issue of compliance as well as market expectations, almost all large German corporations had implemented compliance programs in 2016.[1826] Similar to the expected civil liability, the expected criminal liability of members of the management board for corporate misconduct increased due to an increase of prosecuting corporate misconduct[1827] and together with increased fines for corporate misconduct lead to higher incentives for corporations to implement preventive measures[1828]. Nevertheless, the risk that misconduct will be detected has been named to be "extremely low".[1829]

1823 *Bussmann/Salvenmoser/Jeker*, CCZ 2016, 235, 237 noting that *Bussmann*, PwC Study 2016 revealed an overall perception of a rather low criminal liability risk with significant differences depending on the industry sector; *Bussmann/Salvenmoser*, CCZ 2008, 192, 193 et seq. noting that a PwC study in 2007 revealed an underestimation of the criminal liability risk. Similar: *Kremer/Klahold*, ZGR 2010, 113, 140. See for a list of German laws providing for criminal sanctions: *Schemmel/Minkoff*, CCZ 2012, 49, 50.

1824 *Wagner/Spemann*, NZG 2015, 945.

1825 *Bussmann/Salvenmoser*, CCZ 2008, 192, 193 referring to a PwC study in 2007 revealing that German corporations generally lacked prevention efforts especially through compliance programs.

1826 *Bussmann/Salvenmoser/Jeker*, CCZ 2016, 235 et seq. referring to *Bussmann*, PwC Study 2016.

1827 Cf. *Kremer/Klahold*, ZGR 2010, 113, 114 et seq.; *Hauschka*, VGR, 2008, 51, 56; *Pietzke*, CCZ 2010, 45, 49; *Hüffer*, FS Roth, 299, 301; *Wybitul*, BB 2009, 2590, 2591; *Lackhoff/Schulz*, CCZ 2010, 81, 83.

1828 Cf. *Hüffer*, FS Roth, 299, 301; *Kremer/Klahold*, ZGR 2010, 113, 117.

1829 *Bussmann/Matschke*, CCZ 2009, 132, 135; cf. *Hastenrath*, CCZ 2011, 32, 37: "overreaction" on BGH, decision of July 17, 2009 – 5 StR 394/08, NZG 2009, 1356; *Rünnau/Schneider*, ZIP 2010, 53, 61: "no change to already existing liability". Due to the complexity of corporate criminal cases, the prosecution uses favorable deals for managers to terminate investigations (cf. *Schumacher/Seiwert/Bergermann/Berke*, Wirtschaftswoche, p. 48, 50) reducing the expected liability for managers. Also, the increase of prosecution led to exceeding the capacities of the prosecutors endangering effective prosecution (cf. *Schumacher/Seiwert/Bergermann/Berke*, Wirtschaftswoche, p. 48) which will lead to counter effect the increase of prosecution with regard to the expected liability.

1. Embezzlement, Bankruptcy, and Violations of the Duty of Accurate Accounting

Criminal liability for embezzlement pursuant to sec. 266 StGB may result from the failure to implement a risk management system reflecting not even minimum requirements.[1830] Also, the creation or continuation of slush funds is a criminal offence under sec. 266 StGB.[1831] In addition, the members of the management board may be subject to criminal sanctions for violations of commercial law resulting in bankruptcy (sec. 283(1)(no. 5 to 7), 283a, 283b StGB) and for violating the duty of accurate accounting (sec. 400 AktG and sec. 331 HGB)[1832] demonstrating a variety of liability risks. The members of the management board and the supervisory board have limited incentives to address these issues within the compliance organization due to low expected criminal liability and the detriments of the litigation dilemma.

2. Corruption

Corruption is a pressing issue in Germany and worldwide.[1833] In 2011, the OECD acknowledged the increased enforcement regarding corruption but encourages further action to fight corruption.[1834] It is one of the main issues driving the debate on corporate compliance and corporate criminal liability. Currently, German criminal law addresses corruption with regard to state officials in sec. 331 to 336 StGB[1835] and with regard to commerce in sec. 299 StGB.

1830 *Preußner/Pananis*, BKR 2004, 347, 351 et seq.

1831 BGH, decision of August 29, 2008 - 2 StR 587/07 (Siemens-Decision), CCZ 2009, 38; cf. *Wybitul*, BB 2009, 111; *Schürrle/Olbers*, CCZ 2010, 102, 103. For more details on the criminal law aspects see *Satzger*, NStZ 2009, 297; *Marxen/Taschner*, EWiR 2009, 253.

1832 *Mertens/Cahn*, in: Köln Komm AktG, sec. 91, mar. 12; *Fleischer*, in: Spindler/Stilz, AktG, sec. 91, mar. 25 et seq.; cf. *Hefendehl*, FS Tiedemann, 1065, 1067. Different: *Spindler*, in: Münch Komm AktG, sec. 91, mar. 12.

1833 Cf. *Ernst & Young*, 12th Global Fraud Survey, p. 2; *KPMG*, 2011, p. 1; *Hauschka/Greeve*, BB 2007, 165; *Kremer/Klahold*, ZGR 2010, 113, 115.

1834 OECD, Report on Germany, p. 2 et seq.; cf. *Schumacher/Seiwert/Bergermann/Berke*, Wirtschaftswoche, p. 48, 50. See for details on the OECD recommendations for compliance measures *supra* at chapter 5, A. I.

1835 Note the extentions by *EU-Bestechungsgesetz* and *Gesetz zur Bekämpfung internationaler Bestechung*.

In general, it has been stressed that corporations have to address corruption by using the tools of the general compliance program including concepts of the COSO frameworks.[1836] Preventive compliance measure include internal control such as mandatory job rotation or separation of authority by the two-man rule, raising corruption awareness of employees through a code of ethics and training, and whistleblower protection.[1837] The increased focus on corruption led to issues such as the value of small business presents not falling under the criminal statutes addressing corruption.[1838] The code of ethics should address this topic.

a) Incentives due to Provisions Against Corruption

Corporations may be liable for corrupt behavior of their employees pursuant to sec. 130, 30 OWiG.[1839] Recently, corruption has been an important crime leading to corporate liability either pursuant to sec. 30 OWiG or sec. 130, 30 OWiG. Due to corruption, corporations face damages, loss of reputation and debarment from governmental contracts.[1840] The main incentive for corporations to engage in prevention measures to address corruption, however, is loss of reputation. Hence, corporations have in general an incentive to focus on corruption within their prevention measures. A more detailed analysis of the incentives deriving from loss of reputation will be discussed further below.[1841]

In light of the recently increased scrutiny and enhanced enforcement actions against corruption, corporations have set a high priority within their general compliance program to target corruption.[1842] Nevertheless, it has been noted that corporations underestimate the risk of liability due to cor-

---

1836 Cf. *Sahan/Berndt*, BB 2010, 647, 651; *Hauschka/Greeve*, BB 2007, 165, 167 et seq.; *KPMG*, 2011, p. 2; BDI, Drucks. 390; Transparency International, Checkliste. See for corruption-specific elements: BMI, Praktsiche Hilfestellungen für Antikorruptionsmaßnahmen, 2013; BMI, Empfehlungen zur Korruptionsprävention in der Bundesverwaltung, 2012; ICC, Code of Conduct.

1837 *Bachmann/Prüfer*, ZRP 2005, 109, 112.

1838 Cf. *Marschlich*, CCZ 2010, 110.

1839 Cf. *Bachmann/Prüfer*, ZRP 2005, 109, 110. See Staatsanwaltschaft München I, Bußgeldbescheid Siemens, p. 11 and *infra* at chapter 8, E. III. 2.

1840 *Kremer/Klahold*, ZGR 2010, 113, 139; *Bock*, ZIS 2009, 68, 69 et seq.

1841 See *infra* at chapter 8, E. III. 3.

1842 Cf. Transparency International, Corporate Reporting; *Sieber/Engelhart*, Compliance Programs Survey, p. 40 et seq.

ruption[1843] suggesting that they do not address the such risk appropriately. In any case, even a quantitative priority does not provide any information on the sophistication to target corruption especially in light of the litigation dilemma.

The main issue for addressing corruption, however, is that it is difficult to detect leading to a low probability of detection and sanctioning so that sanctions do hardly deter corruption.[1844] It has been stated that corporations do not have sufficient incentives to implement anti-corruption compliance measures.[1845] Thus, in order to induce corporations to engage in anti-corruption compliance measures, the incentive structure would need to be changed[1846] by implementing effective sanctions for corporations regarding corruption.[1847] In this regard, the detriments of the litigation dilemma have to be considered.

b) Increased Numbers of Cases of Corruption and Exemplary Cases

The findings are further supported by the increased numbers of registered cases of corruption in Germany. The number of registered cases of corruption fluctuated from 1994 to 2015 between 6,000 and 10,000 with tremendous spikes in case of the revealing of major corruption scandals leading to highs in 2005 of nearly 15,000 cases, in 2010 of more than 15,000 cases, in 2011 of staggering almost 47,000 cases, and in 2014 of about 20,000.[1848] The BKA attributes the increase of corruption cases especially in the years 2011 and 2014 to single enforcement measures rather than to an overall increase of the overall level of corruption but acknowledges difficulties regarding the assessment of the impact of these single enforcement actions with regard to the overall level of corruption which includes a "large" number of unknown cases.[1849] The revealing of major corruption scandals, shown by the tremendous increase of the number of cases in the respective

1843 *Bussmann/Salvenmoser/Jeker*, CCZ 2016, 235, 237 referring to *Bussmann*, PwC Study 2016.
1844 *Bachmann/Prüfer*, ZRP 2005, 109, 110.
1845 *Bachmann/Prüfer*, ZRP 2005, 109, 111.
1846 See *infra* at chapter 16, B.
1847 *Bachmann/Prüfer*, ZRP 2005, 109, 112.
1848 Cf. BKA, Korruptionsbericht 2015, p. 4; BKA, Korruptionsbericht 2011, p. 7; BKA, Korruptionsbericht 2006, p. 5; BKA, Korruptionsbericht 2002, p. 10.
1849 Cf. BKA, Korruptionsbericht 2015, p. 13; BKA, Korruptionsbericht 2011, p. 20; BKA, Korruptionsbericht 2010, p. 21.

year, indicates that while the awareness regarding corruption increased[1850] and whistleblowing measures facilitate reporting, it seems that corporations have not entirely banned the use of corruption as a 'regular element of doing business' in the sense of "structural corruption".[1851] It also suggests that the implemented compliance measures are only *prima facie* and not effective especially because a culture of compliance has not been implemented[1852] besides empurpled commitments of the management board. The corporations did not walk the talk. The finding that corporations only engage in ineffective compliance measures is further supported by the fact that the number of cases remained more or less constant despite spikes when major scandals were revealed. If proficient compliance measures had been implemented, the control paradox suggests that a constant increase of corruption cases would occur followed by a constant reduction of corruption cases. The phenomenon known as the control paradox describes the fact that enhanced measures and scrutiny will reveal more crime prior to reducing the overall crime rate[1853], as shown in the context of SOX[1854]. This is not the case in Germany suggesting that corporations did not engage in proficient compliance measures. In general, corruption is still a pressing issue. While the awareness regarding corruption increased, corporations do not seem to have not changed their attitude towards corruption and the compliance efforts are ineffective.

This finding is also supported by the example of the corruption scandal of ThyssenKrupp in 2012.[1855] Prior to the revealing of the scandal, the management board of ThyssenKrupp issued a compliance commitment in 2007 demonstrating its attitude not to accept any violations of antitrust law or corruption.[1856] In 2010, the compliance officers of ThyssenKrupp published a profound article on compliance programs demonstrating their knowledge on the issue.[1857] In 2011, KPMG issued an unqualified IDW PS 980 attestation for ThyssenKrupp stating that the compliance program of

---

1850 Cf. BKA, Korruptionsbericht 2015, p. 13; BKA, Korruptionsbericht 2006, p. 17 et seq.

1851 Cf. BKA, Korruptionsbericht 2015, p. 13.

1852 Cf. *Bussmann*, CCZ 2016, 50.

1853 Cf. *Bussmann/Matschke*, Crime, Law and Social Change 2008, 349, 356 et seq.

1854 See *infra* at chapter 13, B. III.

1855 See for an overview of the scandal *Ott*, Süddeutsche.de, 2012; *Wildhagen*, Wirtschaftswoche, p. 52.

1856 ThyssenKrupp, Compliance Program.

1857 See *Kremer/Klahold*, ZGR 2010, 113.

ThyssenKrupp was effective.[1858] In 2012, however, a major corruption scandal at ThyssenKrupp was revealed leading to the dismissal of the former CCO and the need to overhaul the entire internal control system including the culture of compliance at ThyssenKrupp, as stated by the new CCO.[1859] Thus, it seems that ThyssenKrupp implemented internal controls and compliance measures only fulfilling the standards of IDW PS 980 *prima facie* but failed to implement effective internal control including a culture of compliance as shown by the fact that an entire overhaul of the systems has been indicated. While even an effective compliance program will not prevent all crime, an entire overhaul precludes considering the system effective and indicates that the system has only been a "paper tiger".

c) Corruption Register

A corruption register will provide needed information to effectuate debarments from government contracts and will add a further layer on the incentive for corporations to avoid loss of reputation and business opportunities due to the stigma of being registered. The State of North Rhine-Westphalia implemented in 2004 the Law on Fighting Corruption (*Korrptionsbekämpfungsgesetz*) including a corruption register, the State of Berlin implemented in 2006 the Corruption Register Law (*Korruptionsregistergesetz*) and the State of Bremen implemented in 2011 the Corruption Register Law of Bremen (*Bremisches Korruptionsregistergesetz*) providing for an opportunity to obtain information on the reliability of businesses within public tender procedures in order to fight and prevent corruption.[1860] Despite these laws, it has been noted that such registers are rarely used in Germany.[1861] As early as 2002, the German Bundestag passed a law on establishing a register concerning unreliable businesses which has been halted

1858 *KPMG*, Report IDW PS 980 on ThyssenKrupp, p. 9. *Bussmann* notes that corporate wrongdoing within large international corporatations despite implemented compliance measures and IDW PS 980 attestations may be attributed to the difficulties in assessing the culture of compliance (CCZ 2016, 50).

1859 Cf. *Wildhagen*, Wirtschaftswoche, p. 52 and quoteing the new CCO Christoph Klahold.

1860 See Gesetzentwurf, BT-Drucks. 17/11415, p. 6.

1861 Cf. *Dörr*, in: Unternehmensstrafrecht, 24, 32.

by the German Bundesrat.[1862] Nevertheless, the issue of a national corruption registers has been put on the agenda again.[1863]

d) Summary

Corruption is a pressing issue but the current incentive regime of criminal law does not induce corporations to implement effective compliance measures to fight corruption as the increased numbers of registered cases and the example of ThyssenKrupp suggest. A corruption register provides a further layer to the incentive structure, but only if used, and it does not address the pressing issue within the incentive structure, i.e. the detriments of the litigation dilemma.

3. Criminal Liability of the CCO

In light of the so-called "top-down" jurisdiction of the BGH[1864], managers may be culpable for criminal acts of their subordinates due to command responsibility (*Organisationsherrschaft*) as an indirect offender (sec. 25(1) (alt. 2) StGB)[1865] and, more important for the honorable businessman, due to forbearance (sec. 13 StGB) based on liability of the principal (*Geschäftsherrenhaftung*) as a duty of guarantor (*Garantenpflicht*)[1866]. While the duty of guarantor does not lead to a general duty within criminal law to prevent crime, managers have to address dangers from unlawful conduct of subordinates if they have assumed responsibility for a specific operational field.[1867] The element of assuming responsibility to prevent crime is important for a duty of guarantor as has been shown by the BGH case regarding a CCO.[1868] The BGH decided that the CCO has a duty of guarantor and may commit a crime due to forbearance if she did not act to terminate

1862 Cf. Gesetzentwurf, BT-Drucks. 17/11415, p. 6.

1863 See Deutscher Bundestag, Hearing February 25, 2013; Gesetzentwurf, BT-Drucks. 17/11415.

1864 Cf. *Rotsch*, ZIS 2010, 614, 616; *Wittig*, 2011.

1865 BGH NJW 2004, 375, 378; BGH NZG 2004, 717, 722; cf. *Wittig*, 2011.

1866 *Stree/Bosch*, in: Schönke/Schröder, StGB, sec. 13, mar. 53; *Wittig*, 2011; *Rünnau/Schneider*, ZIP 2010, 53, 55 et seq.

1867 *Stree/Bosch*, in: Schönke/Schröder, StGB, sec. 13, mar. 53.

1868 *Stree/Bosch*, in: Schönke/Schröder, StGB, sec. 13, mar. 53; *Wybitul*, BB 2009, 2590, 2591; cf. BGH, decision of July 17, 2009 - 5 StR 394/08, CCZ 2009, 239.

known corporate misconduct.[1869] The CCO may be criminally liable for failing to prevent corporate crime despite her reasonable ability to do so.[1870] In this regard, it is important to note the inherent limitations of a compliance organization.[1871] The court held that the requested but forborne action of the CCO needs to have prevented the crime with near certainty.[1872] The court assumes such duty of guarantor only if a person has assumed the responsibility to prevent misconduct and particularly crimes.[1873] Such duty of guarantor may also be applicable for members of the management board if they do not act to terminate known corporate misconduct.[1874] The verdict has been described as case specific[1875] and may not necessarily be regarded as a general rule of law.[1876] In order to limit the danger for CCOs with regard to the duty of guarantor, the duties of the CCO should be established in detail and also documented.[1877] While the case provides incentives to engage in prevention measures, it does not induce to engage in *ex ante* policing measures such as monitoring. Management has rather low incentives to monitor for corruption to avoid knowledge of corporate misconduct which would trigger potential individual criminal liability.

Furthermore, the corporation may have a duty of guarantor to prevent harm from consumers which may lead to criminal sanctions of the management in case of management refraining to act while knowing that harm

---

1869 BGH, decision of July 17, 2009 – 5 StR 294/08 NGZ 2009, 1356; cf. *Raum*, CCZ 2012, 197. Critizising the decision: *Rübenstahl*, NZG 2009, 1341, 1342 et seq. See general on the duty of guarantor for the CCO: *Kraft/Winkler*, CCZ 2009, 29, 31 et seq.

1870 *Wybitul*, BB 2009, 2590. See on potential civil liability: *Favoccia/Richter*, AG 2010, 137, 144 et seq.

1871 See *supra* at chapter 4, C. I. 1. b). Also *Voet v. Vormizeele*, CCZ 2009, 41, 48.

1872 BGH, decision of July17, 2009 - 5 StR 394/08, CCZ 2009, 239, 240 (annotated by *Thomas*); cf. *Deutscher*, WM 2010, 1387, 1392 et seq.; *Campos Nave/Vogel*, BB 2009, 2546, 2550.

1873 BGH, decision of July17, 2009 – 5 StR 294/08, NZG 2009, 1356, 1358, at, recital 26 et seq.; cf. *Wybitul*, BB 2009, 2590, 2592; *Campos Nave/Vogel*, BB 2009, 2546, 2548.

1874 *Fleischer*, in: Spindler/Stilz, AktG, sec. 91, mar. 63; *Kremer/Klahold*, ZGR 2010, 113, 140; *Schneider*, NZG 2009, 1321, 1322.

1875 *Hüffer*, FS Roth, 299, 306; *Rieder*, FS Goette, 413, 421 and 423.

1876 See on the limits of criminal liability: *Bürkle*, CCZ 2010, 4.

1877 *Hüffer*, FS Roth, 299, 306; *AKEIÜ Schmalenbach-Ges.*, DB 2010, 1509, 1511; *Wybitul*, BB 2009, 2590, 2593. See for the aspects of the employment law: *Krieger/Günther*, NZA 2010, 367.

may occur.[1878] The "top-down" jurisdiction of the BGH induces the management board to implement compliance measures to avoid liability.[1879] Nevertheless, the impact of the BGH case on compliance departments is in general rather low.[1880]

4. Forfeiture (Section 73 StGB) and Confiscation (Section 74 StGB)

Illegally obtained gain may be forfeited (sec. 73 StGB) and illegally generated objects may be confiscated (sec. 74 StGB), if the corporation is the beneficiary of the illegal act (sec. 73(3) StGB)[1881] or specific corporate personnel acted to generate the illegal objects (sec. 75 StGB), seemingly providing incentives for corporations to refrain from engaging or tolerating corporate crime. Based on sec. 73(1) StGB, courts may order the forfeiture of gross profit deterring corporations from accepting criminal sanctions as a cost of business.[1882] Forfeiture and confiscation are no classic sanction since it is mostly only taken from corporations what they have not legally obtained.[1883] Nonetheless, sec. 73 StGB is hardly used in Germany.[1884] The prosecution needs to prove an illegal act of an individual person acting within the sphere of the beneficiary which is similar to sec. 30(1) OWiG.[1885] In difference to sec. 30 OWiG, the prosecution does not have to prove that the element of *mens rea*. But proving an illegal act to the benefit of the corporation is likewise difficult against the background that the prosecution needs to prove the illegal act of a specific individual person. Without information received from the corporation, such proof has proven to be extremely difficult.

The same holds for the opportunity of courts to confiscate criminally obtained objects pursuant to sec. 74 StGB. The term objects in sec. 74 StGB includes not only things but also rights such as bank deposits, mort-

---

1878 *Hauschka*, ZIP 2004, 877, 881; *Schneider*, NZG 2009, 1321, 1322; BGH NStR 1990, 587.

1879 *Rotsch*, ZIS 2010, 614, 616.

1880 Cf. *Hastenrath*, CCZ 2011, 32 et seq.

1881 *Eser*, in: Schönke/Schröder, StGB, sec. 73, mar. 35.

1882 *Roxin*, in: Unternehmensstrafrecht, 37, 38; BGHSt 47, 369, 373 et seq.

1883 See for the difference of foreiting gain gross or net: *Eser*, in: Schönke/Schröder, StGB, Vorbem. sec. 73, mar. 18 et seq.

1884 *Roxin*, in: Unternehmensstrafrecht, 37.

1885 *Eser*, in: Schönke/Schröder, StGB, sec. 73, mar. 37.

gages, and co-ownership shares.[1886] The connecting criminal act has to be illegal and committed culpably (*mens rea*).[1887] Criminally obtained assets of the corporation may be subject to confiscation pursuant to sec. 75 StGB if the act of the crime has been committed by management, employees with specific management duties, authorized officers or persons with supervisory responsibility within the corporation. In general, forfeiture and confiscation based on criminal law do not deter corporate crime and, since these provisions are hardly used in Germany, corporations can accept criminal sanctions as a cost of business since a monetary sanction may be paid by the illegally obtained profits.

5. Conclusion

The incentive structure of criminal law to induce corporations to engage in compliance measures is rudimentary at best. Despite the underestimation of criminal liability, the awareness regarding the issue of compliance as well as market expectations lead German corporations to implement compliance programs.[1888] Even though, corporations are mainly aware of the costs and detriments of corporate crime, they hardly invest in effective compliance programs which generally include prevention and *ex ante* policing measures. This is mainly attributed to insufficient liability to engage in prevention measures and to insufficient rewarding for engaging in policing measures. It has been noted that the level of liability is not sufficient to induce corporations to engage in prevention measures compared to stricter U.S. liability rules.[1889] This finding still holds against the recent development that corporations have set a high priority within their general compliance program to target corruption. Management tends to overspend on *prima facie* compliance measures in light of the low expected individual criminal liability since the members of the management board only share a fraction of the costs, if at all, and profit substantially from compliance measures. But management mainly faces criminal liability only for failing to act to terminate known corporate misconduct. Therefore, management has rather low incentives to monitor effectively for corporate wrongdoing

1886 *Eser*, in: Schönke/Schröder, StGB, sec. 74, mar. 6 et seq.
1887 *Eser*, in: Schönke/Schröder, StGB, sec. 74, mar. 3.
1888 *Bussmann/Salvenmoser/Jeker*, CCZ 2016, 235 et seq. referring to *Bussmann*, PwC Study 2016.
1889 *Bussmann/Salvenmoser*, CCZ 2008, 192, 193.

such as corruption in order to avoid knowledge of corporate misconduct. The only incentive for corporations to focus their prevention measures on corruption is loss of reputation. Criminal law does not, however, provide incentives to engage in policing measures.

II. *Excursus*: Antitrust Law

The formation of cartels is a second driving factor with regard to corporate compliance and corporate criminal liability besides corruption. Antitrust law is a specific field of law in which isolated legal regimes apply providing for a specific incentive structure. Due to the specifics of antitrust law and the subsequent limited insight for the general issues of internal control and corporate compliance, the thesis will only touch on antitrust law. Antitrust law does not require any particular elements for internal control or the compliance organization. Preventing and detecting antitrust law violations has to be part of the general compliance program.[1890] Due to corporate liability for violations of antitrust law (sec. 81 GWB and art. 23(2)(a) VO 1/2003) and incentives for corporations to report antitrust law violations by granting leniency for self-reporting and cooperation, management has incentives to set a focus on antitrust law within the compliance program. Recently increased enforcement action by the EU Commission[1891] increases the expected liability for antitrust violations increasing the incentives to implement compliance measures.

On the European level, the EU commission issued guidelines on the method of setting fines imposed for antitrust law violations.[1892] Corporations will receive a reduced fine for effective cooperation with the EU commission.[1893] Also, for self-reporting, corporations may qualify for a reduced fine or no fine at all under the leniency program.[1894] In Germany, a similar regime exists pursuant to the notice of the *Bundeskartellamt* based on sec. 81(7) GWB.[1895] But, both regimes only provide leniency for antitrust-specific regulatory offences not for criminal offences such as fraud (sec. 263

1890 Cf. *Fleischer*, BB 2008, 1070, 1071.
1891 Cf. *Voet v. Vormizeele*, CCZ 2009, 41.
1892 Commission, 2006/C 210/02.
1893 Commission, 2006/C 210/02, recital 29.
1894 Commission, 2006/C 210/02, recital 34; Commission, 2006/C 298/11.
1895 Cf. Bundeskartellamt, Bußgeldzumessung; Bundeskartellamt, Bonusregelung.

StGB), restricting competition through agreements in the context of public bids (sec. 298 StGB), or embezzlement (sec. 266 StGB).[1896]

III. Law on Administrative Offences (OWiG)

The OWiG is the only law in Germany providing for measures to hold corporations liable for criminal acts of their organs and employees. The scope is limited and under reiterating review whether the scope is still sufficient. The OWiG provides for an opportunity to hold corporations administratively liable for misconduct of their employees characterizing an exception from the principle that German law does not provide for corporate criminal liability.[1897] Based on sec. 30 OWiG, corporations may be liable for crimes and offences committed by management and employees with specific management duties. One of the most important offences in this context is sec. 130 OWiG which requires corporations to take necessary monitoring measures to prevent infringements of duties within the scope of the corporation. In recent years, corruption has been an important underlying crime for corporate administrative liability based on sec. 30 and sec. 130, 30 OWiG. For the following analysis, group law issues in the context of sec. 130 OWiG are excluded.[1898]

1. Scope of Corporate Administrative Liability – Section 30 OWiG

The scope of corporate administrative liability derives from sec. 30 OWiG. Pursuant to sec. 30(1) OWiG, corporations may be liable for crimes or offences either within the scope of the corporate duties or for the profit, at least intended, of the corporation committed by members of the management board or employees with specific management duties. Such crimes and offences include for example fraud, embezzlement, corruption, money laundering, and, most importantly, violations of the monitoring duty of

---

1896 *Cramer/Pananis*, in: Loewenheim/Meessen/Riesenkampff, Kartellrecht, GWB, sec. 81, mar. 76.

1897 *Bussmann/Matschke*, CCZ 2009, 132; cf. *Rogall*, in: Karlsruher Komm OWiG, sec. 130, mar. 6. See for details *Engelhart*, Sanktionierung, p. 320 et seq. and p. 346 et seq.

1898 See for details: *Koch*, AG 2009, 564.

sec. 130 combined with sec. 9(1) OWiG[1899].[1900] The act of management or an employee with specific management duties constituting the crime or offence has to be illegal and culpably (*mens rea*) committed.[1901] Potential sanctions for corporations are fines up to ten million euro (sec. 30(2) OWiG) and disgorgement of profits (sec. 30(3) combined with sec. 17(4) OWiG).[1902] Due to sec. 17(4) OWiG, the imposed fine should exceed the profits obtained by the offence or crime and may exceed the maximum fines provided by OWiG so that the minimum fine equals the profits obtained by the offence or crime and the maximum fine equals such profits plus the maximum fine provided by OWiG.[1903] In sec. 30(4) OWiG, the law provides for an opportunity to independently fine corporations even if no proceedings have been brought for the connecting crime or offence, such proceedings have been ceased, or the penalty for such crime or offence has been waived. This independent fine may not be imposed on corporations if the connecting crime or offence cannot be prosecuted based on legal grounds (sec. 30(4)(s. 3) OWiG).

In case of illegally obtained gain due to an offence, such gain may be forfeit pursuant to sec. 29a(1) OWiG, if no fine has been imposed for the offence (sec. 30(5) OWiG), even if the corporation is the beneficiary of the underlying offence (sec. 29a(2) OWiG). The forfeiture of illegally obtained gain may also be ordered independently pursuant to sec. 29a(4) OWiG in case proceedings are either ceased or not brought.

2. Monitoring Duty – Section 130 OWiG

The OWiG requires in sec. 130(1) that a corporation takes the necessary monitoring measures to prevent occupational non-compliance. Otherwise, the corporation commits an offence if infringements of duties within the scope of the corporation occur and the corporation failed to take necessary monitoring measures which would have prevented or materially aggravated to commit such infringements. The infringements consist of the illegal acts constituting a crime or offence which violate duties within the scope

1899 Cf. *Rogall*, in: Karlsruher Komm OWiG, sec. 30, mar. 21.
1900 *Rogall*, in: Karlsruher Komm OWiG, sec. 30, mar. 75 et seq.
1901 *Bohnert*, OWiG, sec. 30, mar. 7.
1902 *Hauschka*, ZIP 2004, 887, 879; *Powilleit*, GWR 2010, 28; cf. *Rogall*, in: Karlsruher Komm OWiG, sec. 30, mar. 115 et seq.
1903 Cf. *Mitsch*, in: Karlsruher Komm OWiG, sec. 17, mar. 140.

of the corporation, for example, violations of environmental protection law, fraud, corruption, and embezzlement.[1904] The offence pursuant to sec. 130 OWiG is the main connection offence with regard to sec. 30 OWiG[1905], also shown by the Siemens case[1906]. For law enforcement agencies, the requirements to prove an infringement of a corporate duty to establish a violation of sec. 130 OWiG which then leads to liability pursuant to sec. 30 OWiG are less than to prove a violation of a crime or offence committed by management or employees with specific management duties[1907] in order to directly establish corporate liability based on sec. 30 OWiG. In contrast to direct corporate liability for an individual crime or offence pursuant to sec. 30 OWiG, sec. 130 OWiG applies already in case infringements of corporate duties occurred within the corporation. Law enforcement does not have to prove that a specific individual person committed a crime or offence as long as it can be shown that the crime or offence has been committed by an employee.[1908] Thus, enforcement agencies do not have to prove all requirements of an individual crime or offence necessary to impose liability on a corporation pursuant to sec. 30 OWiG but only have to prove that infringements of corporate duties occurred and that the corporation failed to provide for necessary monitoring measures. Hence, in light of corporate misconduct, convicting corporations based on sec. 130, 30 OWiG for infringements of corporate duties are more likely to succeed since law enforcement agencies do not have to convict an individual manager or employee with specific management duties of a crime or offence.

With regard to monitoring duties of the management board due to corporate law, sec. 130 OWiG provides guidance for the scope of such duties.[1909] Nevertheless, the guidance is rather limited. The monitoring duties of sec. 130 OWiG, established by the courts, encompass to assign reasonable responsibility to employees, to provide adequate instructions, to conduct random tests, to document the taken measures, to emphasize that misconduct will not be tolerated, to investigate in case of red flags, to mon-

1904 *Rogall*, Karlsruher Komm OWiG, sec. 130, mar. 75 and 79.
1905 *Rogall*, Karlsruher Komm OWiG, sec. 30, mar. 20.
1906 Staatsanwaltschaft München I, Bußgeldbescheid Siemens, p. 2.
1907 Cf. *Engelhart*, Sanktionierung, p. 624 et seq. reflecting on the opportunity of individuals to disguise their criminal actions within the corporate structure.
1908 *Rogall*, Karlsruher Komm OWiG, sec. 130, mar. 94.
1909 *Fleischer*, in: Fleischer, Hdb Vorstandsrecht, sec. 8, mar. 4.

itor, and to punish misconduct.[1910] Also, the management board has to ensure that all employees receive information on the applicable laws and regulation.[1911] The monitoring duty of sec. 130 OWiG does not include to implement a comprehensive monitoring system since the employment relationship is generally believed to be characterized by trust.[1912] Similarly, the monitoring system has to respect the dignity of the employees so that monitoring measures should not be intrusive.[1913] In this regard, the compliance organization has to account for the individual responsibility of the employees with regard to monitoring.[1914] In general, the specific design of the monitoring measures depends on the scope, size and organization of the business.[1915] Besides the named requirements, the courts do not further specify the minimum requirements of sec. 130 OWiG with regard to compliance programs.[1916] As best practice, minimum requirements for sec. 130 OWiG have been developed reflecting IDW PS 980.[1917] It has been argued that an effective compliance management system should be sufficient to eliminate liability due to sec. 130 OWiG[1918] especially if the system has received an unqualified attestation pursuant to IDW PS 980[1919].[1920]

In essence, the minimum requirements for the monitoring duty of sec. 130 OWiG are not high.[1921] Thus, even if corporations fulfill the minimum requirements, the required level of monitoring is very low leading corporations to implement only a rudimentary compliance program mostly incapable to deter corporate crime effectively.

1910 *Mertens/Cahn*, in: Köln Komm AktG, sec. 93, mar. 77; *Schneider*, NZG 2009, 1321, 1325; *Fleischer*, AG 2003, 291; *Liese*, BB 2008, Beilage 5, 17, 19 et seq.; *Bussmann/Matschke*, CCZ 2009, 132, 133 et seq.; *Rogall*, in: Karlsruher Komm OWiG, sec. 130, 40 et seq.; cf. *Rettenmaier/Palm*, NJOZ 2010, 1414.

1911 *v. Busekist/Hein*, CCZ 2012, 41, 44; *Rogall*, in: Karlsruher Komm OWiG, sec. 130, 55.

1912 *Fleischer*, AG 2003, 291, 294; cf. *Immenga*, 2009, p. 200.

1913 *Fleischer*, AG 2003, 291, 294.

1914 *Bussmann/Matschke*, CCZ 2009, 132, 137.

1915 *Rogall*, in: Karlsruher Komm OWiG, sec. 130, 41.

1916 *Kort*, NZG 2008, 81, 82; *Pampel*, BB 2007, 1636.

1917 See *v. Busekist/Hein*, CCZ 2012, 41 and *v. Busekist/Schlitt*, CCZ 2012, 86 and *infra* at chapter 9, C.

1918 *Sieber*, FS Tiedemann, 449, 470 et seq.; cf. *Engelhart*, Sanktionierung, p. 403 et seq.

1919 *Gelhausen/Wermelt*, CCZ 2010, 208, 209.

1920 *Withus/Hein*, CCZ 2011, 125, 129.

1921 *Gelhausen/Wermelt*, CCZ 2010, 208, 209.

3. Incentives due to the Law on Administrative Offences

In light of corporate misconduct, the incentive regime of OWiG is mainly based on sec. 30, sec. 130 OWiG, disgorgement of profits, costs especially due to loss of reputation, and personal liability of management. Due to sec. 30 OWiG, corporations may be sanctioned for crimes and offences committed by management and employees with specific management duties. Corporate administrative liability for these individual crimes and offences leads seemingly to incentives for the corporation to engage in prevention and policing measures to avoid sanctions. The expected liability for corporations of sec. 30 OWiG, however, is low due to a low probability of being sanctioned and a relatively low maximum fine. The low probability of being sanctioned results from the main issue for enforcement agencies to prove a connecting crime or offence of management or employees with specific management duties. In particular, identifying the culpable individual is difficult especially in large corporations.[1922] Enforcement agencies are mostly dependent on information received from corporations regarding individual wrongdoing.[1923] Without such information, the probability is low that individual corporate crime will be prosecuted. It follows that law enforcement agencies are most of the time only able to prosecute ostensible corporate crime. The difficulties to prove individual crime or offences is shown by the fact that corporations are mostly sanctioned in light of corporate crime for their own offence of failing to provide accurate monitoring pursuant to sec. 130 OWiG combined with sec. 30 OWiG.[1924] Neither the recent increase of sections in 2012 nor the recent increase of enforcement actions[1925] do change this finding since these increases do not affect the information deficit of enforcement agencies so that the probability of being sanctioned is hardly affected and corporations are still not induced to engage in prevention and policing measures.

The limited scope of sec. 30 OWiG to crimes and offences committed by management and employees with specific management duties does not significantly lead to a decrease of incentives to implement prevention and policing measures because employees with no specific management duty

1922 *Meyer*, in: Criminal Responsibility, p. 130; cf. *Beale/Adam*, 8 Buffalo Crim. L. Rev. 89 (2005), p. 123 et seq.

1923 Cf. BKA, Korruptionsbericht 2011, p. 20. See *infra* at chapter 16, B. I. 1. and *Schumacher/Seiwert/Bergermann/Berke*, Wirtschaftswoche, p. 48.

1924 *Rogall*, Karlsruher Komm OWiG, sec. 30, mar. 20.

1925 Cf. *Hugger*, BB 2012, 2125.

mainly do not have any authority to commit relevant corporate crimes and offences by using the corporate structure to hide their behavior. Moreover, offences and crimes not committed by management or employees with specific management duties may result in corporate liability pursuant to sec. 130, 30 OWiG if the corporation had not fulfilled its monitoring duties pursuant to sec. 130 OWiG. In addition, it is believed that many employees are considered to have specific management duties with regard to sec. 30 OWiG minimizing the limitations of the provision.[1926]

Besides sec. 30 OWiG, sec. 130 OWiG provides for incentives regarding prevention and policing measures. Due to sec. 130, 30 OWiG, corporations may be liable for failing to engage in monitoring measures fulfilling the minimum requirements in case infringements of corporate duties occur. In contrast to other connecting crimes and offences to establish corporate liability pursuant sec. 30 OWiG, sec. 130 OWiG applies already in case infringements of corporate duties occurred within the corporation which enforcement agencies are more likely to prove compared to prove individual crimes or offences.[1927] Since violations of sec. 130 OWiG are easier to prove, the expected liability regarding sec. 130, 30 OWiG is higher compared to the expected liability of sec. 30 OWiG together with a connecting crime or offence other than sec. 130 OWiG.

The main issue with regard to sec. 130 OWiG is that even the higher expected sanction due to sec. 30 OWiG for violating sec. 130 OWiG is not significant for large corporations. The expected sanction for violations of sec. 130 OWiG induces corporations to fulfill the minimum requirements for monitoring measures only if marginal costs for such measures are less than the expected liability disregarding other incentives inducing corporations to implement monitoring measures. In most cases concerning large corporations, the expected sanction will not exceed marginal costs to implement the minimum monitoring measures. This finding is illustrated by the fact that the German prosecution issued a penalty notice in the Siemens case of 395 million euro consisting of 394,750,000 euro for disgorgement of (estimated) profits and a fine of only 250,000 euro.[1928] While disgorgement of profits is no sanction (in a technical sense)[1929] and only takes from the corporation what it did not legally obtain, the sanction of 250,000 euro shows

1926 Cf. *Rogall*, Karlsruher Komm OWiG, sec. 30, mar. 51 et seq.

1927 See *supra* at chapter 8, E. III. 2.

1928 Staatsanwaltschaft München I, Bußgeldbescheid Siemens, pp. 1, 12, and 13.

1929 Cf. *Eser*, in: Schönke/Schröder, StGB, Vorbem. sec. 73, mar. 18 et seq. on forfeiting gain net.

that corporations have hardly any incentives to invest in monitoring measures due to the OWiG since the expected sanction is lower than the costs to implement anti-corruption measures.

Even in light of the recent increase of enforcement actions as well as the increase of the maximum fines, the expected sanction remains low. While the recent increase of enforcement action led to reveal several major cases of corporate non-compliance, prosecutors are still dependent on information from within the corporation so that the recent increase of the expected sanction by the factor ten does not lead to an expected sanction sufficiently high to induce corporations to engage in prevention and policing measures. Moreover, prosecutors have wide discretion whether to initiate investigations, since they are not required to investigate alleged violations of OWiG due to sec. 47 OWiG (*Opportunitätsprinzip*), further reducing the probability of being sanctioned especially in light of insufficient capacities of law enforcement agencies. Due to these circumstances, the probability of being sanctioned is reduced resulting in a reduced expected liability for corporations. With regard to the maximum fines of the OWiG, it has to be noticed that the amounts are low compared to U.S. fines especially for large corporations. Thus, the low probability of being sanctioned multiplied by a low maximum fine results in an negligible expected sanction for large corporations. Hence, the expected sanction of sec. 130, 30 OWiG does not induce corporations to even engage in the minimum monitoring requirements of sec. 130 OWiG. In this regard, a survey found in 2013 that only 25% of German corporations had implemented compliance measures fulfilling the rather low standard of sec. 130 OWiG.[1930]

Besides insufficient incentives from the expected liability, the low minimum requirements of sec. 130 OWiG limit the scope of sec. 130 OWiG as a connecting offence for sec. 30 OWiG since corporations may easily exculpate from sanctions due to sec. 130, 30 OWiG by fulfilling the minimum requirements. For exculpation, corporations have to convince courts that they have fulfilled the monitoring requirements of sec. 130 OWiG. To establish this, corporations have to show that their implemented monitoring measures would have prevented or materially hindered the infringement of corporate duties. This level of effectiveness required by sec. 130 OWiG is rather high. Nevertheless, courts have difficulties to determine whether the implemented measures fulfilled this level of effectiveness[1931] in light of oc-

1930 *Bussmann*, PwC Study 2013, p. 5.

1931 See in general on the issue for courts to determine the effectiveness *infra* at chapter 16, A. I. 2. a) (2).

curred misconduct absent any requirements for external testing or setting benchmarks[1932]. It follows that corporations have incentives to engage in monitoring measures which fulfill the requirements *prima facie*, i.e. the measures are only "paper tigers"[1933], since effective measures would produce information increasing the expected liability. But, as will be shown below[1934], corporations will generally not receive leniency for having implemented effective monitoring measures to offset the increase of expected liability so that corporations will only engage in monitoring measures *prima facie* to exculpate from sec. 130 OWiG liability. Hence, if corporations decide to implement any monitoring measures at all despite insufficient incentives to do so, they have only incentives to implement monitoring measures which fulfill the requirements of sec. 130 OWiG *prima facie* up to a level which ensures that courts will accept these measures in light of sec. 130 OWiG to exculpate from liability.

Besides the incentives deriving from the expected sanction due to sec. 30 and sec. 130, 30 OWiG, corporations have incentives to engage in prevention and policing measures to avoid costs incurred for example due to internal and prosecutorial investigations, debarment from government contracts, and liability of management through recourse.[1935] The most important incentive for corporations to engage in prevention and policing measures, however, is to avoid any loss of reputation[1936] due to publicly known prosecutorial investigations and indictment.[1937] The factors affecting the reputation are numerous[1938] but their effect is hard to measure so that the magnitude of the costs due to the loss of reputation are almost unquantifiable[1939]. An important incentive in this regard are expectations of investors and contractors that corporations engage in effective compliance measures.[1940] In light of the expectations of investors and contractors, corporations have incentives to engage in prevention measures *prima facie* in order to satisfy the expectations *ex ante* and to argue *ex post* that compliance measures had been in place in order to reduce the impact of the corporate

---

1932 See *infra* at chapter 16, B. IV. 2.
1933 See with regard to "paper tigers" *supra* at chapter 5, C. III.
1934 See *infra* at chapter 8, E. IV.
1935 *Hauschka*, VGR, 2008, 51, 55 et seq.
1936 See *supra* at chapter 8, C. III.
1937 Cf. *Moosmayer*, Compliance, mar. 69.
1938 Cf. *Werner*, CCZ 2011, 201, 202; *Bussmann*, PwC Study 2011; *Semler*, FS Goette, 499, 500.
1939 *Bannenberg*, in: Hdb Wirt-SteuerStR, sec. 12, mar. 28.
1940 *Moosmayer*, Compliance, mar. 70.

wrongdoing on the reputation. Similar to prosecutors and courts, investors and contractors have also difficulties, however, to assess whether the corporation engaged in truly effective compliance measures or only in *prima facie* measures and whether to "grant leniency" by continuing the investment or contract despite the corporate wrongdoing. In difference to prosecutors and courts, investors and contractors are not bound by legal concepts such as "probable cause" or "beyond reasonable doubt" and may act on rumors and belief. Despite all uncertainty, corporations have to assess the expected costs of the loss of reputation. Due to the incentives deriving from potential loss of reputation, corporations have incentives to engage in prevention measures up to the point when marginal costs exceed marginal benefits. Since the possibility of being indicted is rather low, the incentives to engage in prevention measures are also low. Moreover, since the provisions on forfeiture and confiscation are hardly used, the gain from corporate wrongdoing may exceed the expected costs of the loss of reputation so that these costs may be tolerated or even accepted as a cost of business further reducing the incentives to engage in prevention measures.

Corporations have generally no incentive, however, to engage in policing measures including monitoring, internal investigations, and self-reporting. In contrast, corporations have incentives to refrain from producing information and to hold back such information in order to avoid prosecutorial investigations and indictment. Only if prosecutorial investigations are imminent or after prosecutors initiated investigations, corporations have incentives to self-report and cooperate with law enforcement agencies as well as initiate internal investigations with the aim to avoid or terminate prosecutorial investigations.[1941] The recent increase of enforcement induces corporations to further refrain from producing information and to hide information.

Regardless of the foregoing, corporations may want to show their commitment to compliance.[1942] Especially against the background that it has been highlighted that cooperation is part of good corporate citizenship.[1943] But corporations have only incentives to show their commitment to compliance by implementing compliance measures *prima facie* in order to obtain the benefits of showing this commitment since *prima facie* measures are sufficient to show good corporate citizenship. Corporations have no in-

---

1941 Cf. *Klengel/Mückenberger*, CCZ 2009, 81, 87.

1942 *Dann*, CCZ 2010, 30, 33; *Klengel/Mückenberger*, CCZ 2009, 81, 87.

1943 Cf. *Moosmayer*, Compliance, p. 106. See with regard to corporate social responsibility: Commission, Strategy for Corporate Social Responsibility.

centives, however, to implement effective monitoring measures to show their commitment to compliance since monitoring measures increase the expected liability, i.e. the litigation dilemma. Corporations may only produce information in order to cooperate with law enforcement agencies through internal investigations after prosecutorial investigations are imminent or initiated. Corporations will engage in non-effective compliance measures *prima facie* to satisfy public opinion, investors, and prosecutors in order to achieve the benefits and to avoid the detriments of the litigation dilemma.[1944]

Disregarding the previous findings with regard to sec. 30 and sec. 130, 30 OWiG, disgorgement of profits has been proclaimed to be particularly effective to deter corporate crime in combination with the recently increased enforcement actions.[1945] So far, disgorgement of profits has been the almost exclusively used sanction.[1946] Disgorgement of profits, however, mainly aims to prevent corporations to factor in sanctions as a cost of business. But imposing a sanction for corporate crime is necessary since corporations will not be deterred to engage in corporate crime only by the prospect of losing profits which would not have been made without the crime. With regard to disgorgement of profits, corporations only face the chance that enforcement agencies calculate the profits too low, then the crime would have paid off, and the risk that enforcement agencies calculate profits too high resulting in an unintended fine for the corporation. Moreover, disgorgement of profits is not a sanction, as the rationale of sec. 17(4) OWiG shows, but takes from the corporation what it has not been legally obtained. Hence, disgorgement of profits is an important supplement of fines but does not deter corporate crime. Thus, corporations need to face punishment within a correctly structured incentive regime as an element to deter corporate crime.[1947] Similar to disgorgement of profits based on sec. 30(4) combined with sec. 17(4) OWiG, forfeiture of profits may be ordered, pursuant to sec. 29a OWiG, if no sanction has been imposed on the corporation for the specific act (sec. 30(5) OWiG). The findings regarding disgorgement of profits based on sec. 30(4) combined with sec. 17(4) OWiG also hold for sec. 29a OWiG.

1944 See on the issue *supra* at chapter 8, B. III.

1945 Cf. *Hugger*, BB 2012, 2125.

1946 *Moosmayer/Gropp-Stadler*, NZWiSt 2012, 241, 242; cf. *Hauschka*, VGR, 2008, 51, 55.

1947 See *infra* at chapter 20, B. I. 1.

In addition to the depicted incentives, management faces personal liability for sec. 130 OWiG violations pursuant to sec. 130 combined with sec. 9(1) OWiG and sec. 93(2) AktG. Any fine the corporation may receive due to a violation of sec. 130 OWiG may be transferred to the management board pursuant to sec. 93(2) AktG for violating its duty of monitoring the corporation.[1948] Also, management may be liable for violating their monitoring duty pursuant to sec. 130 combined with sec. 9(1) OWiG in case of corporate misconduct.[1949] Due to such liability, management has incentives to implement monitoring systems fulfilling the requirements of sec. 130 OWiG. The incentives for management are similar to the incentive for corporations with regard to sec. 130 OWiG. In difference to the corporation, management does not bear the costs of the monitoring measures. Hence, management seems to have incentives to ensure that the corporation complies with the rudimentary duties of sec. 130 OWiG but not with any proficient prevention and policing measures. As part of the agency problem[1950], ineffective monitoring measures leave management sufficient leeway to conceal self-interested or even fraudulent behavior which is of particular interest for management since monitoring provides the opportunity for monitors to assess management's actions and performance.[1951] Moreover, self-reporting and cooperation would reveal potential self-interested and fraudulent behavior. Hence, also management has only incentives to fulfill the monitoring duties of sec. 130 OWiG *prima facie* in order to avoid personal liability.

4. Summary

The OWiG does not deter corporate crime. The current incentive regime of OWiG does hardly provide incentives for corporations to engage in prevention and policing measures. To the contrary, corporations have incentives to hold back information and to refrain from producing internal information due to the prospect of being subject to prosecutorial investigations and indictment. Corporations have only incentives to engage in prevention

---

1948 *v. Busekist/Hein*, CCZ 2012, 41; *Werner*, CCZ 2010, 143. See *supra* at chapter 8, B. III.

1949 *Fleischer*, in: Spindler/Stilz, AktG, sec. 91, mar. 63; *Rogall*, in: Karlsruher Komm OWiG, sec. 9, mar. 87; *Fleischer*, AG 2003, 291, 294; *Bussmann/Matschke*, CCZ 2009, 132.

1950 See *supra* at chapter 1, A.

1951 See *supra* at chapter 4, A. III.

measures to avoid loss of reputation and to cooperate with law enforcement agencies after investigations are imminent or initiated.

Corporate liability pursuant to sec. 30 OWiG fails to induce corporations to engage in effective prevention and policing measures mainly because the connecting crime or offence are difficult to prove for enforcement agencies and the amount of sanctions is low especially for large corporations. In sec. 130 OWiG, the law requires *de facto* to implement monitoring measures. The expected sanction for failing to engage in the minimum monitoring requirements of sec. 130 OWiG, however, does mostly not induce corporations to engage in such measures even though it might generally be easier for law enforcement agencies to prove violations of sec. 130 OWiG to establish sec. 30 OWiG liability since law enforcement agencies do not have to prove all elements of an individual crime or offence. Even if corporations fulfill the minimum requirements, the required level of monitoring is very low leading corporations to implement only a rudimentary compliance program incapable to deter corporate crime effectively. The corporation and management have generally three reasons to comply with the monitoring requirements of sec. 130 OWiG, but only *prima facie*. The low minimum requirements of sec. 130 OWiG lead corporations to easily exculpate from sanctions due to sec. 130, 30 OWiG. Also, corporations may want to show their commitment to compliance. Moreover, the personal liability of management.

Even in light of the increased enforcement action and the recent increase of the maximum fines, the expected sanction is not high enough for large corporations since the probability of being sanctioned is low, due to the difficulties of law enforcement to prove connecting crimes or offences, and the low level of the maximum fines. Moreover, disgorgement or forfeiture of profits as well as confiscation of assets do not deter corporate crime. These measures are not sanctions since corporations are only deprived of what has not been legally obtained. These measures, however, are necessary to prevent corporations to factor in corporate crime as a cost of business.

IV. Leniency within the Incentive Regime of Corporate Liability for Crimes and Offences for Compliance Programs, Self-Reporting, and Cooperation

One important aspect of the incentive regime is the issue of granting leniency for corporations in light of corporate crime and the litigation dilemma. The current situation in Germany with regard to corporations receiving leniency in light of corporate crime is blurry at best. Despite many opportunities within German law to grant leniency, the law does not provide certainty and clear guidelines for the requirements to receive leniency. The following analysis will focus on incentives for corporations to engage in prevention and policing measures such as compliance programs, self-reporting, and cooperation to deter corporate crime.[1952]

In contrast to the findings of the U.S. research with regard to the litigation dilemma[1953], it has been argued that corporations would have a genuine interest to investigate misconduct in order to prevent further misconduct.[1954] This finding may be right with regard to minor issues within the corporation. The same authors argue further that a corporation would have to assess the risk of sanctions prior to self-reporting and cooperation with law enforcement agencies.[1955] The two statements do not directly contradict but it seems that the authors do not calculate for the increase of the expected sanction due to any internal investigations. Internal investigations increase the risk of fines for a corporation based on sec. 30 OWiG as well as forfeiture of assets pursuant to sec. 29a OWiG and sec. 73 StGB, and the risk of further claims against the corporation since business partners may find evidence for potential claims of damages using their right to examine prosecutorial files pursuant to sec. 406e StPO[1956] if the documents of the internal investigations reach the prosecution.[1957] Also, management may be personally liable due to sec. 93 AktG and sec. 9 OWiG. The internally obtained information is generally not protected by the attorney-client privilege. Documents from counsel in the possession of the corporation are only partially privileged in case of investigations of law enforcement.[1958] Only documents necessary for defense are privileged pursuant to sec. 97 StPO.[1959]All other documents are subject to confiscation.[1960] Hence, cor-

1952 See on details regarding prevention and policing measures *supra* at chapter 5, B. I.

1953 See *supra* at chapter 5, B. II.

1954 *Kremer/Klahold*, ZGR 2010, 113, 126; cf. *Wessing*, in: Hauschka, Corporate Compliance, sec. 46, mar. 4.

1955 *Kremer/Klahold*, ZGR 2010, 113, 135; cf. also *Wessing*, in: Hauschka, Corporate Compliance, sec. 46, mar. 171; *Reichert/Ott*, ZIP 2009, 2173, 2177.

1956 Regarding documents related to the amnesty program of the antitrust law: cf. *Dück/Eufinger/Schultes*, EuZW 2012, 418 et seq.

1957 Cf. *Annuß/Pelz*, BB 2010, Beilage 4, 14, 19.

1958 *Schürrle/Olbers*, CCZ 2010, 102, 105.

1959 *Schürrle/Olbers*, CCZ 2010, 102, 105; *Nack*, in: Karlsruher Komm StPO, sec. 97, mar. 24; cf. *Annuß/Pelz*, BB 2010, Beilage 4, 14, 18.

1960 *Schürrle/Olbers*, CCZ 2010, 102, 105.

porations have few incentives to produce unprivileged information by internal investigations or other compliance measures. While cooperation may have a positive impact on the corporation[1961], the management board has to value the pros and cons of self-reporting and cooperation by considering *inter alia* the need of further investigations, impact on prevention, restoral of the working atmosphere, or impact of self-reporting on public relations.[1962] The most important aspect corporations will consider is whether the benefits of self-reporting, internal investigations, and cooperation with law enforcement agencies exceed the increase of the expected sanction due to these acts. In most cases without receiving leniency, this will only be the case if prosecutorial investigations are imminent or initiated.

In general, German and European law enforcement agencies do not grant leniency for effective compliance programs especially with regard to violations of antitrust law.[1963] Only in 2013, the *Bundeskartellamt* issued sentencing guidelines for proceedings regarding regulatory cartel offences which only allow to consider acceptance of responsibility to grant leniency.[1964] Rather, sanctions may be increased for corporate misconduct despite an implemented compliance program[1965] especially in case corporations implemented "window-dressing" compliance programs[1966]. The assump-

---

1961 *Reichert/Ott*, ZIP 2009, 2173, 2177.

1962 *Reichert/Ott*, ZIP 2009, 2173, 2180; cf. *Klengel/Mückenberger*, CCZ 2009, 81, 87.

1963 *Kremer*, FS Schneider, 701, 704; *Kremer/Klahold*, ZGR 2010, 113, 139; *Moosmayer/Gropp-Stadler*, NZWiSt 2012, 241, 242; *Dannecker/Biermann*, in: Immenga/Mestmäcker, EU-WettbewerbsR, VO (EG) 1/2003 Art. 23, mar. 201, 217; *Pampel*, BB 2007, 1636, 1639; *Bosch/Colbus/Harbusch*, WuW 2009, 740, 743; cf. *Itzen*, BB 2008, Beilage 5, 12, 16; *Pietzke*, CCZ 2010, 45, 50; *Krebs/Eufinger/Jung*, CCZ 2011, 213, et seq.; cf. Commission, 2004, p. 10: the Commission does not even consider cooperation between law enforcement agencies and corporations. Granting leniency for effective compliance programs has to be differeniated from the leniency programm of the Commission for reporting antitrust law violations pursuant to art. 23(2)(a) Regulation No 1/2003 combined with the Guidelines on the method of setting fines imposed pursuant to Article 23(2)(a) of Regulation No 1/2003 (Commission, 2006/C 210/02, recital 34) combined with the Commission Notice on Immunity from fines and reduction of fines in cartel cases (Commission, 2006/C 298/11, recital 8 et seq.).

1964 Bundeskartellamt, Bußgeldzumessung, mar. 18.

1965 *Dannecker/Biermann*, in: Immenga/Mestmäcker, EU-WettbewerbsR, VO (EG) 1/2003 Art. 23, mar. 201; *Voet v. Vormizeele*, CCZ 2009, 41, 43 et seq.; *Bosch/Colbus/Harbusch*, WuW 2009, 740, 744: indicating that it might have been an exceptional case.

1966 *Engelhart*, Sanktionierung, p. 441 et seq.

tion presumes that a compliance program is not effective in case misconduct occurred[1967] so that granting leniency would be not an option. The conclusion drawn from this assumption is that corporations would need to be punished more severely if corporate crime occurred all the more since a compliance program existed. Such kind of reasoning builds on a hindsight perspective by assuming that if corporate crime occurred, the compliance system would obviously not have been effective.[1968] The higher sanction would be justified since the corporation knew about the need to address potential corporate crime, as shown by the implemented compliance program, but did not invest enough to prevent the crime despite that knowledge. Such kind of reasoning assumes, however, that a compliance program has to prevent all corporate crime in order to be considered effective. In contrast, as it has been shown above[1969], no compliance program will be able to prevent and detect all corporate crime. A compliance program may still be considered effective even though it failed to prevent or detect all corporate crime.

Regardless of the finding that the reasoning to refrain from granting leniency or even to increase the sanction despite an implemented compliance program is not conclusive, law enforcement agencies are in general reluctant to grant leniency. Moreover, German and EU law enforcement policies do not consider the benefits of compliance programs as a prevention measure.[1970] Differently, sanctions may be increased on the European level for failing to cooperate or for obstructing investigations.[1971]

Under current law, the prosecution has the opportunity to grant leniency by opting for an order of summary punishment (*Strafbefehl*) pursuant to sec. 46(1) OWiG combined with sec. 444(2)(s. 2) combined with sec. 438(1)(s. 1), sec. 407(2)(no. 1) StPO. Furthermore, in order to reward corporations for self-reporting and cooperation, the prosecution may refrain from issuing a penalty notice in light of sec. 30(4) OWiG by refraining from indictment and may instead order forfeiture of profits pursuant to sec. 29a OWiG.[1972]

1967 *Kremer/Klahold*, ZGR 2010, 113, 139; cf. *Bosch/Colbus/Harbusch*, WuW 2009, 740, 754.
1968 Cf. *Rotsch*, ZIS 2010, 614, 616. See also *supra* at chapter 8, B. I. 3. b).
1969 See *supra* at chapter 4, C. I. 1. b).
1970 *Bosch/Colbus/Harbusch*, WuW 2009, 740, 745.
1971 *Kremer/Klahold*, ZGR 2010, 113, 140.
1972 *Moosmayer*, Compliance, p. 110.

In the Siemens case for example, the prosecution considered greatly the extraordinary cooperation of Siemens as a factor to grant leniency.[1973] In light of this occasion to grant leniency, law enforcement agencies and courts might grant leniency in light of corporate misconduct if the corporation implemented an effective compliance system. Thus, effective compliance systems have the potential to reduce liability or eliminate liability e.g. in the context of sec. 17(3) OWiG.[1974] In sec. 17(3) OWiG, the sentencing of offences provides for the opportunity to grant leniency by considering corporate conduct after the offence as a mitigating factor such as to voluntarily cease the malfeasance, to compensate for the harm done, or to confess the malfeasance.[1975] But reduced or no sanctions due to an effective compliance program are currently not certain.[1976] Due to the uncertainty to receive leniency, the current law does not provide for sufficient incentives to balance out the increase of expected liability resulting from compliance measures, self-reporting, and cooperation. Thus, corporations have incentives to refrain from engaging in such measures unless prosecutorial investigations are imminent or initiated.

V. Conclusion: Corporate Liability for Crimes and Offences

Under the corporate administrative liability regime for crimes and offences, corporations are in general liable for crimes and offences committed by management and employees with specific management duties pursuant to sec. 30 OWiG which is an offence but no crime. German law does not provide for corporate criminal liability although the topic has repeatedly been set on the agenda. So far, the federal legislator constantly concluded that the current corporate liability regime is adequate. In light of the recent corporate scandals, only minor adjustments to the maximum fines have been implemented into the OWiG. Nevertheless, criminal law provides for incentives to engage in prevention measures up to the point when marginal costs exceed marginal benefits in order to minimize the

1973 Cf. Staatsanwaltschaft München I, Bußgeldbescheid Siemens, p. 12 et seq.

1974 *Gelhausen/Wermelt*, CCZ 2010, 208; *Böttcher*, NZG 2011, 1054, 1057; *Rieder/Jerg*, CCZ 2010, 201, 202; *Withus/Hein*, CCZ 2011, 125, 127.

1975 Cf. *Mitch*, in: Karlsruher Komm OWiG, sec. 17, mar. 62 et seq.

1976 Cf. *Gelhausen/Wermelt*, CCZ 2010, 208, 209; *Böttcher*, NZG 2011, 1054, 1057; *Rieder/Jerg*, CCZ 2010, 201, 207; *Sieber*, FS Tiedemann, 449, 473. See also *Schemmel/Minkoff*, CCZ 2012, 49, 51 et seq.

costs of the loss of reputation from corporate criminal conduct but lacks to provide incentives for corporations to engage in policing measures.

One of the most important connection offences for corporate administrative liability pursuant to sec. 30 OWiG is the violation of the monitoring duties of the corporation pursuant to sec. 130 OWiG. Sec. 130 OWiG imposes a quasi-duty on corporations to implement the monitoring measures fulfilling the minimum standards. Compared to proficient or even effective compliance programs, the minimum standards of sec. 130 OWiG are low.

Regardless of corporate administrative liability and the quasi-duty to implement monitoring measures, the OWiG does not deter corporate crime. The incentive regime following from corporate liability does not induce corporations to engage in effective prevention and policing measures. The expected liability due to sec. 30 OWiG and especially sec. 130, 30 OWiG only induces corporations to engage in the required monitoring measures *prima facie* resulting in ineffective compliance programs. The lack of provisions, which render the granting of leniency certain for corporations, leads corporations to refrain from engaging in policing measures such as monitoring, self-reporting, and cooperation due to the increase of the expected liability resulting from such measures. Corporations have only incentives to engage in self-reporting and cooperation as well as internal investigations if prosecutorial investigations are imminent or initiated. Prior to any investigations, corporations have incentives to refrain from producing sensitive information through monitoring or internal investigations and will hold back information on alleged or actual corporate misconduct. Thus, law enforcement agencies will receive essential information to prosecute individual wrongdoer rather late, if at all.

The Siemens case illustrates the shortcomings of the incentive structure even better.[1977] The management board withheld pressing information on slush funds and corruption in general from the supervisory board.[1978] Siemens failed to increase compliance measures despite the known misconduct.[1979] Then, Siemens cooperated with law enforcement and initiated internal investigations only after prosecutorial investigations were initiated and the dimension of misconduct had been revealed. The main incentives for Siemens to implement the current comprehensive internal control and

---

1977 See for more details on the Siemens case *infra* at chapter 14.

1978 *U.S. v. Siemens*, Statement of Offense, mar. 56 and 60; cf. *Leyendecker/Ott*, Süddeutsche Zeitung, 2008.

1979 Staatsanwaltschaft München I, Bußgeldbescheid Siemens, p. 5 et seq.

compliance program result, however, from the incentives of U.S. law and its enforcement.[1980]

The recently increased enforcement actions revealed numerous scandals. Nevertheless, the prosecution only seems to have revealed obvious and unrestricted violations of law which the implemented *prima facie* compliance measures did not prevent or hardly detect. Law enforcement revealed such violations demonstrating the ineffectiveness of the current corporate liability regime to induce corporations to engage in effective prevention and policing measures. The increased enforcement actions and subsequent heightened awareness regarding corruption only led corporations to address corruption by implementing *prima facie* compliance systems mainly to avoid loss of reputation due to prosecutorial investigations and to demonstrate their efforts to be a good corporate citizen by showing their commitment to compliance. Despite the increased enforcement actions and heightened awareness regarding corruption, the situation of corruption in Germany has hardly changed. The prosecution still depends on information from within the corporation. On the surface, evident crime has been revealed through increased enforcement and will probably be prevented due to the increased awareness of corruption and since corporations will cease such obvious behavior. Also, *prima facie* compliance programs will be implemented since management has incentives to overspend on compliance measures to prevent individual criminal liability. Besides such cosmetic measures, the incentive structure remains ineffective to induce corporations to implement effective prevention and policing measures despite the increased enforcement actions.

1980 See *infra* at chapter 14.

Chapter 9: German Best Practice Addressing Internal Control and Compliance

Internal control and risk management systems including compliance measures are especially addressed in specific law of regulated industries which is not applicable to general corporations but constitutes best practice for general corporations. Specific law together with the BaFin guidance provide insight into the higher standards for regulated industries with regard to internal control and risk management systems. The GCGC, the IDW auditing standards and German best practice regarding profound internal control systems will also be considered.

A. Specific Law of Regulated Industries Including BaFin and EIOPA Guidance

Regulated industries are addressed by specific law mandating more specific requirements for internal control and risk management systems as well as compliance for the regulated corporations than required by corporate law. In addition to the legal mandates for financial corporations (sec. 25a KWG), investment firms (art. 21 et seq. Delegated Regulation (EU) 2017/565 and sec. 80 WpHG[1981] (former sec. 33 WpHG)) and insurance corporations (art. 258 et seq. Delegated Regulation (EU) 2015/35 and sec. 23 et seq. VAG), the regulatory agency, BaFin, published guidance on risk management and compliance. While specific law does not apply to general corporations, the issue has been raised if and to which extent the specific law impacts general corporate law.[1982] Specific law provides guidance on how to structure risk management and compliance and sets best practice.[1983] Hence, the specific law impacts risk management and the compliance organization of general corporations.[1984] The specific mandates of the

---

1981 Cf. RegE, Entwurf eines Zweiten Gesetzes zur Novellierung von Finanzmarktvorschriften auf Grund europäischer Rechtsakte (Zweites Finanzmarktnovellierungsgesetz – 2. FiMaNoG), BT-Drucks. 18/10936).

1982 Cf. *Dreher*, ZGR 2010, 496 et seq.; *Weber-Rey*, ZGR 2010, 591 et seq.

1983 *Fleischer*, in: Spindler/Stilz, AktG, sec. 91, mar. 52; *id.*, NZG 2014, 321, 325; *Lorenz*, in: Grundlagen des Risikomanagements, p. 18; *Weber-Rey*, AG 2008, 345, 358.

1984 *Kort*, NZG 2008, 81, 82; cf. *Wiederholt/Walter*, BB 2011, 968, 969.

regulatory law cannot be used, however, to prescribe the duty for general corporations to implement profound risk management since the European and German legislator refrained from mandating such specific mandates for general corporations.[1985] With regard to the impact of the specific law on the early warning system of sec. 91(2) AktG, it has been argued that the specific law should generally not be used as guidance for general corporations[1986], since banking specific rules are not useful for general corporations[1987], and the mandates of art. 21 et seq. Delegated Regulation (EU) 2017/565 and sec. 80(1) WpHG are too specific for general corporations to provide much guidance.[1988] Otherwise, it has been pointed out that the principles of sec. 25a KWG may be used to interpret the requirements for a risk management system of sec. 91(2) AktG.[1989] Thereby, the intention to provide for a higher standard within the KWG setting has to be considered. Thus, only general ideas and reduced standards of sec. 25a KWG may be used for sec. 91(2) AktG purposes.[1990] Similarly, only general ideas and reduced standards of art. 21 et seq. Delegated Regulation (EU) 2017/565 and sec. 80(1) WpHG should be used for sec. 91(2) AktG purposes.[1991] In light of the necessary reductions, the required organizational elements of art. 22 Delegated Regulation (EU) 2017/565 for general corporations should include appropriate design for the flow of information, selection and training of employees, appropriate financial reporting pursuant to sec. 238 et seq. HGB, and the protection of the corporation's assets by the two-man-principle or the limitation of authority.[1992] Specific law should only be used as guidance for general corporations acknowledging the specific circumstances of the regulated industries.[1993]

1985 *Dreher*, ZGR 2010, 496, 532.

1986 *Mertens/Cahn*, in: Köln Komm AktG, sec. 91, mar. 30; *Krieger/Sailer*, in: Schmidt/Lutter, sec. 91, mar. 15; *Weber-Rey*, ZGR 2010, 543, 571.

1987 Cf. *Wohlmannstetter*, ZGR 2010, 472, 479. Different: VG Frankfurt decision of 08.07.2004 – 1 E 7363/03, WM 2004, 2157, 2156.

1988 Cf. *Mertens/Cahn*, Köln Komm AktG, sec. 91, mar. 33 with regard to sec. 33 WpHG.

1989 *Spindler*, in: Fleischer, Hdb Vorstandsrecht, sec. 19, mar. 19.

1990 Cf. *Mertens/Cahn*, in: Köln Komm AktG, sec. 91, mar. 31.

1991 Cf. *Spindler*, in: Fleischer, Hdb Vorstandsrecht, sec. 19, mar. 41 with regard to sec. 33 WpHG.

1992 Cf. for required elements of art. 22 Delegated Regulation (EU) 2017/565 prescribing the elements of former sec. 33(1)(no. 1) WpHG: *Spindler*, in: Fleischer, Hdb Vorstandsrecht, sec. 19, mar. 47 with regard to sec. 33 WpHG.

1993 Cf. *Spindler*, FS Hüffer, 985, 998.

I. Requirements of Specific Law for Financial Institutions, Investment Firms, and Insurance Corporations

With regard to financial institutions, sec. 25a(1)(s. 1) KWG requires the prudent organization of the business which includes to ensure the compliance with applicable laws and regulation and in particular an adequate and effective risk management. Pursuant to sec. 25a(1)(s. 3) KWG, risk management has to include strategies and measures to assess and assure the sustainability regarding risk (no. 1); measures to assess and safeguard the risk bearing ability (no. 2); the implementation of internal control and internal audit (no. 3) including processes with clear assignment of responsibilities (no. 3(a)), processes to identify, assess, manage, monitor, and communicate risks (no. 3(b)), and a risk controlling function and a compliance function (no. 3(c)); adequate staffing and resources (no. 4); an adequate contingency plan including IT systems (no. 5); and adequate, transparent and sustainable compensation policies (no. 6). The scope of the risk management system depends on the aspects, scope, complexity, and risk magnitude (sec. 25a(1)(s. 4) KWG). The financial institute has to assess periodically the adequacy and effectiveness of risk management (sec. 25a(1)(s. 5) KWG). Moreover pursuant to sec. 25a(1)(s. 6)(no. 3) KWG, the prudent organization of the business requires to provide for a whistleblowing process which allows employees to report violations of various financial laws and regulations under safeguarding their identity.

Investment firms have to comply with the mandates for an adequate and effective risk management of sec. 25a(1) KWG pursuant to sec. 80(1) WpHG[1994]. In addition, investment firms are subject to the mandates of Delegated Regulation (EU) 2017/565, supplementing Directive 2014/65/EU (MiFID II), and have to establish and maintain a permanent and effective compliance function ensuring the compliance with the obligations under Directive 2014/65/EU (art. 22 Delegated Regulation (EU) 2017/565). The CCO has to report at least annual to the management board and the supervisory board on the implementation and effectiveness of the overall control environment for investment services and activities, on the risks that have been identified and on the complaints-handling reporting as well as remedies undertaken or to be undertaken (art. 22(2)(c) Delegated Regulation (EU) 2017/565) and on an ad hoc basis in case of a

1994 See also the requirements of the *Verordnung zur Konkretisierung der Verhaltensregeln und Organisationsanforderungen für Wertpapierdienstleistungsunternehmen* (WpDVerOV).

significant risk of failure to comply with the obligations under Directive 2014/65/EU (art. 22(3)(c) Delegated Regulation (EU) 2017/565). The adequacy and effectiveness of the compliance measures have to be monitored and regularly assessed and corrective measures have to be taken, if indicated (art. 22(2)(a) Delegated Regulation (EU) 2017/565). Moreover, investment firms need to implement and maintain adequate risk management (art. 23 Delegated Regulation (EU) 2017/565) and an internal audit function (art. 24 Delegated Regulation (EU) 2017/565). With regard to the audit committee of an investment firms, it has the duty to supervise financial reporting (sec. 114 et seq. WpHG). Also according to art. 16(1) Regulation (EU) 596/2014 combined with art. 3 Delegated Regulation (EU) 2016/957, investment firms are required to implement compliance measures regarding the prevention and detection of market abuse. Since these measures address the specific requirements of a trading venue, they hardly provide guidance to general corporations, if any at all.

Insurance corporations are subject to the mandates of Delegated Regulation (EU) 2015/35, supplementing Directive 2009/138/EC (Solvency II), and have to provide for an adequate and effective system of governance (art. 258 et seq. Delegated Regulation (EU) 2015/35) including the risk management system (art. 259 Delegated Regulation (EU) 2015/35) and the internal control system (art. 266 Delegated Regulation (EU) 2015/35) as well as the risk management function (art. 269 Delegated Regulation (EU) 2015/35), the compliance function (art. 270 Delegated Regulation (EU) 2015/35), and the internal audit function (art. 271 Delegated Regulation (EU) 2015/35). The specific requirements of Directive 2009/138/EC with regard to risk management, internal control including compliance measures have been transposed into German law in particular in sec. 23, 26, 29, 30 VAG. Compared to former sec. 64a VAG, a specific compliance function is a new requirement for insurance corporations. In general, sec. 23, 26, 29, 30 VAG mandate in more detail the requirements for risk management compared to sec. 25a KWG and sec. 80 WpHG.[1995] Pursuant to sec. 23 VAG, insurance companies have to provide for an appropriate system of governance. Pursuant to sec. 26 VAG, insurance corporations have to implement an effective risk management system which has to consider the informational needs of the management of the insurance corporation and which has to identify, assess, monitor, and control risks. Also, a risk controlling function needs to be implemented (sec. 26(8) VAG). Insurance corporations also have to implement an effective internal control system pur-

---

1995 Cf. *Weber-Rey*, AG 2008, 345, 358 with regard to former sec. 64a VAG.

suant to sec. 29 VAG. The internal control system has to provide the necessary information to be reported to any supervising agency as required by the VAG (sec. 29(3) VAG). Also, insurance corporations have to provide for an effective and independent internal audit pursuant to sec. 30 VAG which has to audit the whole business organization in particular the appropriateness and effectiveness of the internal control system.

With regard to former sec. 64a VAG, it has been argued that no real difference exists between the material risk of art. 259(1)(d) Delegated Regulation (EU) 2015/35 (former sec. 64a(1)(s. 4)(no. 3c) VAG) and the risk endangering the survival of the corporation of sec. 91(2) AktG.[1996] The concept of materiality in art. 259(1)(d) Delegated Regulation (EU) 2015/35, however, does only exclude non-material risks.[1997] Therefore, the scope of material risks encompasses all risks besides non-material, i.e. irrelevant risks, which includes significantly more than only risk endangering the survival for the corporation. As a result, the scope of the risk management system pursuant to art. 259(1)(d) Delegated Regulation (EU) 2015/35 has to be far greater than the scope of the early warning system of sec. 91(2) AktG.

II. BaFin Guidance on Risk Management and Compliance – MaRisk, MaGo and MaComp and EIOPA Guidelines on System of Governance

The Federal Financial Supervisory Authority (*BaFin*) issued circulars on minimum requirements for risk management including a compliance of corporations subject to sec. 25a KWG (MaRisk (BA)[1998]) and on minimum requirements for the compliance function of sec. 63 et seq. WpHG (MaComp[1999]) as well as minimum requirements for the governance system of insurance corporations (MaGo)[2000] providing guidance for the regulated industries. Neither MaRisk (BA) nor MaComp nor MaGo are applicable for general corporations. Nevertheless, they are believed to provide guidance for the design of internal control, risk management, and compliance

1996 *Dreher*, ZGR 2010, 496, 533.

1997 Cf. *Gehringer*, in: Bürkle, Compliance in Versicherungsunternehmen, sec. 6, mar. 14 with regard to former sec. 64a VAG.

1998 BaFin, MaRisk (BA).

1999 BaFin, MaComp.

2000 BaFin, MaGo. MaGo superceded MaRisk (VA) in light of the transposition of Directive 2009/138/EC (Solvency II) into German law.

systems of general corporations[2001] and the interpretation of the mandates of sec. 91(2) AktG[2002].

With regard to the potential and scope of providing guidance for the internal control and risk management systems of general corporations including the early warning system of sec. 91(2) AktG the guidance of the BaFin circulars, however, is rather limited. Due to such limited guidance, the content of such BaFin circulars will not be further depicted as the compliance measures of regulated industries have been done been analyzed in detail elsewhere[2003]. The main shortcoming of all three BaFin circulars is that they follow a functional approach by requiring corporations to implement functions such as risk management, internal control systems, compliance function, and internal audit. The minimum requirements of risk management including internal control as well as the compliance function of MaRisk (BA), MaGo and MaComp, however, do not have the scope of COSO I[2004] regarding internal control or COSO II[2005] regarding enterprise risk management. One main focus is to regulate how specific operational risks have to be handled within the banking and financial industries. Especially with regard to internal control and compliance systems, the BaFin circulars are rather functional and does not provide guidance on how to design compliance measures. Moreover, MaComp is limited to violations of the Securities Trading Act and, therefore, rather limited for providing guidance on general compliance measures. Thus, the BaFin circulars may pinpoint general corporations on the need for the functions risk management, internal control and compliance, but falls short of providing further guidance. Nevertheless, the required elements of the BaFin regarding risk management and compliance may be used as a starting point to design and implement risk management and internal control addressing all three components of COSO I and COSO II. Especially since all three BaFin circulars do not contradict COSO I or COSO II so that the COSO frameworks may be used for designing the required functions.

In general, the potential of the three BaFin circulars for guiding general corporations on the issues of risk management, internal control, internal audit, or compliance is limited to indicating the needed functions as such

2001 Cf. *Lösler*, WM 2010, 1917, 1923.
2002 *Spindler*, in: Fleischer, Hdb Vorstandsrecht, sec. 19, mar. 3.
2003 See for more details the dissertations by *Harm*, Compliance Wertpapierdienstleister on compliance of investment service providers and by *Wundenberg*, Compliance Bankengruppen on compliance within banking groups.
2004 See for details on COSO I *supra* at chapter 4, C. I.
2005 See for details on COSO II *supra* at chapter 4, C. III.

including some minor aspects such as independence or sufficient resources.

Similar to the BaFin circulars, the guidelines on the system of governance issued by the European Insurance and Occupational Pensions Authority (EIOPA)[2006] have a strong focus on operational risk management and risk inherent in insurance corporations but does not provide great insight more specific requirements of the internal control and compliance system.

III. Conclusion

The specific law of regulated industries in sec. 25a KWG, art. 21 et seq. Delegated Regulation (EU) 2017/565 and sec. 80 WpHG, and art. 258 et seq. Delegated Regulation (EU) 2015/35 and sec. 23 et seq. VAG including the BaFin guidance of MaRisk (BA), MaGO, and MaComp as well as the guidance of EIOPA provide guidance for general corporations on risk management, internal control, and compliance. The specific law addresses basic elements of risk management, internal control, and compliance. An important aspect of the specific law is the requirement to periodically assess the adequacy and effectiveness of risk management and compliance which is important to ensure that the implemented systems fulfill their function. The basic elements are rudimentary compared to the scope of the COSO frameworks. Hence, the specific law does not provide much guidance on how to design internal control, risk management, and the compliance organization.

Furthermore, neither the specific law nor the BaFin circulars require any level of effectiveness which the implemented systems have to achieve in order to be considered effective. In essence, the specific law and the BaFin circulars emphasize the need of specific functions without prescribing how to design these functions. In order to design risk management, internal control and compliance, corporations may use COSO I or COSO II.

B. German Corporate Governance Code

The German Corporate Governance Code (GCGC) addresses issues regarding corporate governance, internal control, risk management, and compli-

2006 EIOPA, Guidelines.

ance. Being soft law, the code is not binding for corporations but reflects best practice[2007] which corporations generally have incentives to follow in order to satisfy the expectations of the capital market. Due to sec. 161 AktG, the corporation has to declare to which extent it follows the code and has to explain why it does not follow any recommendations of the code, if any. Sec. 289f HGB ensures that the information regarding the comply-or-explain-approach of sec. 161 AktG will be provided to investors at a prominent place within the annual report. In the management report of the annual report, the corporation has to include a corporate governance statement (sec. 289f HGB) addressing *inter alia* the declaration of sec. 161 AktG regarding the corporate governance code (sec. 289f(2)(no. 1) HGB).

In no. 3 GCGC, the code addresses the cooperation between management board and supervisory board. One important aspect within internal control and risk management is that the supervisory board receives appropriate information to supervise the management board. This may be ensured by adequate and effective internal control and risk management systems which reduce the magnitude of the information asymmetry.[2008] In this regard, no. 3.4(2) GCGC highlights the opportunity for the supervisory board to specify the information and reporting duties of the management board with regard to internal control and risk management.

In no. 4.1 GCGC, the code deals with the tasks and responsibilities of the management board. In no. 4.1.3 GCGC, the code addresses compliance stating that the management board ensures the compliance with all provisions of law and internal policies. The main aspect of no. 4.1.3 GCGC is not to highlight the duty of the corporation to comply with the law. Rather, it raises the awareness of management regarding the implementation of compliance measures.[2009] The code regards compliance as a legal duty of the management board.[2010] Moreover, the code recommends that the management board ensures to implement appropriate measures, i.e. a compliance management system, which considers the risk profile of the business. Also, the code recommends to disclose the main features of such system. Furthermore, employees and third parties should have the possibility to report indications of corporate wrongdoing in protected manner. Due to no. 4.1.4 GCGC, the management board ensures to provide for an

---

2007 *Lorenz*, in: Grundlagen des Risikomanagements, p. 14.
2008 See *infra* at chapter 20, B. I. 2. c. (1).
2009 Cf. *Hüffer*, FS Roth, 299, 302; *Kremer/Klahold*, ZGR 2010, 113, 117.
2010 *Kort*, NZG 2008, 81, 83.

appropriate risk management system. This requirement, however, does not predetermine the interpretation of sec. 91(2) AktG since no. 4.1.4 GCGC does only state the current statutory mandates and does not have statutory authority.[2011] While it has been stated that the code goes beyond the scope of the statutory law by requiring risk controlling[2012], no. 4.1.4 GCGC does not suggest to implement a profound risk management system.

In no. 5 GCGC, the code addresses the supervisory board. No. 5.2(3) GCGC specifies for the flow of information between the chairman of the supervisory board and the management board that the chairman of the supervisory board should consult with the management board with regard to the risk situation, risk management, and compliance. The code recommends in no. 5.3.2 GCGC to implement an audit committee with the responsibility to monitor the accounting, the accounting process, the effectiveness of the internal control system and the internal audit system, and the audit of the annual financial statements including the annual report.

In general, the GCGC highlights the general importance of internal control, risk management, and compliance. It encourages implementing an audit committee. Also, the compliance management system and protected whistleblowing are highlighted. Nevertheless, besides highlighting the necessity of appropriate information in the corporate governance context, the code does not add much to the incentive structure for listed corporations. This holds also in light of the recommendation to disclose the main features of the compliance management system. While the usefulness of the ever increasing amount of disclosed information is questionable[2013], disclosing the elements of a "paper tiger" compliance program will fulfill the recommendation. Moreover, disclosing the main features of the compliance management system addresses more the issue of whether or not the corporation implemented such system than the issue of how the corporation designed and operate its compliance management system. The disclosure of the main features will not allow to assess whether or not the implemented system is appropriate in light of the specific circumstances of the corporation.

2011 *Mertens/Cahn*, in: Köln Komm AktG, sec. 91, mar. 20, 38; *Kort*, ZGR 2010, 440, 454; *id.*, in: Großkomm AktG, sec. 91, mar. 71; *Dreher*, FS Hüffer, 161, 163; cf. *Ringleb*, in: Ringleb, DCGK, mar. 617.

2012 *Spindler*, in: Fleischer, Hdb Vorstandsrecht, sec. 19, mar. 2; cf. *Preußner*, NZG 2004, 303, 307.

2013 *Windbichler*, FS Hopt, 1505, 1507 et seq.

C. Auditing Standards – IDW PS

The *Institut der Wirtschaftsprüfer* (IDW) sets professional auditing standards for the external auditor. The IDW auditing standards have no legal authority.[2014] Nevertheless, they are influential for the management board[2015] as management has incentives to fulfill the IDW auditing standards, mandatory for the external auditors, to receive an unqualified attestation in the sense of sec. 322(2)(no. 1) HGB more easily and to avoid any supplements to the attestation in light of sec. 322(3)(s. 2) HGB.[2016] In addition, management has incentives to seek advice from auditors[2017] for how to design and operate internal control systems in order to avoid any deficiencies which the external auditor would find during routine testing. Such consulting activities of auditors pose an issue with regard to independency which is beyond the scope of the thesis.[2018] Also, the International Standards on Auditing (ISA) will be excluded from the thesis as they will only become mandatory for external auditors pursuant to sec. 317(5) HGB once the EU Commission has adopted the standards on an individual basis, which is not yet the case, and since the IDW auditing standards and the ISA are to a great extent similar[2019]. The IDW addresses in its standards: the early warning system (IDW PS 340), internal control system (IDW PS 261), the compliance management system (IDW PS 980), and internal audit (IDW PS 321).

For the auditing of the early warning system of sec. 91(2) AktG required by sec. 317(4) HGB, the external auditor has to apply IDW PS 340. Pursuant to IDW PS 340[2020], the early warning system does only encompass a partial aspect of risk management. It does not encompass to manage risks or the measures taken by the management board to address any reported risks. The external auditor has to audit the early warning system with regard to the elements: addressing the risks of all business units; identification and analysis of predefined and undefined risks which requires appropriate risk awareness of the employees; communication of unmanaged risks including thresholds for reporting risks and flexibility of risk reporting; assignment of duties and responsibility; monitoring system to detect

2014 *Kort*, ZGR 2010, 440, 450 et seq.; *Spindler*, FS Hüffer, 985, 990.
2015 Cf. *Windbichler*, FS HU-Juristische Fakultät, 1079, 1091.
2016 Cf. *Lorenz*, 2007, p. 9; *Binder*, ZGR 2010, 489, 493. See *supra* at chapter 4, B.
2017 Cf. *Windbichler*, FS Rokas, 1389, 1398.
2018 See for regulation e.g. art. 5 Regulation (EU) No 537/2014 and sec. 201 SOX.
2019 *Hopt/Merkt*, in: Baumbach/Hopt, HGB, sec. 317, mar. 13.
2020 IDW PS 340, mar. 4 et seq.

and communicate risks endangering the survival of the corporation; internal audit; and documentation of the taken measures including a risk manual.[2021] The standards for the early warning system provided by IDW PS 340 have to be adapted to the specific requirements of each corporation.[2022] IDW PS 340 states only general requirements. Hence, IDW PS 340 is not the standard for sec. 91(2) AktG[2023] but provides guidance for corporations on the design of an early warning system.[2024] IDW PS 340 provides basic elements for the early warning system reflecting, but falling short of, the requirements of the COSO frameworks. It has been argued that the efficiency of the risk management system cannot be assessed by the accountants and that no objective assessment of risk management or controlling would be possible.[2025]

In addition to IDW PS 340, the external auditor has to assess the risk of misstatements in financial reporting during the annual audit pursuant to IDW PS 261.[2026] An essential part of determining the risk of misstatements is the internal control system of the corporation. The risk of misstatements correlates with the effectiveness of the internal control system.[2027] The external auditor has to assess the functionality including appropriateness of the system using a risk-based approach.[2028] In order to enable the external auditor to understand the internal control system of the audited corporation, IDW PS 261 provides a general example for an internal control system.[2029] Such example system is closely derived from COSO I[2030] including all three categories: effectiveness and efficiency of operations, reliability of financial reporting and compliance with applicable laws and regulations. Hence, the internal control system also needs to address important operational risks.[2031] IDW PS 261 limits the scope of the assessment of the internal control system with regard to operations to the protection of assets in-

2021 IDW PS 340, mar. 11 et seq.
2022 *Spindler*, in: Fleischer, Hdb Vorstandsrecht, sec. 19, mar. 58.
2023 *Spindler*, in: Münch Komm AktG, sec. 91, mar. 27.
2024 *Spindler*, in: Fleischer, Hdb Vorstandsrecht, sec. 19, mar. 16; *Blasche*, CCZ 2009, 62, 67; *Berg*, AG 2007, 271, 275.
2025 *Spindler*, in: Fleischer, Hdb Vorstandsrecht, sec. 19, mar. 58.
2026 IDW PS 261, mar. 1.
2027 IDW PS 261, mar. 9.
2028 IDW PS 261, mar. 10 and 18.
2029 IDW PS 261, mar. 19 et seq.
2030 Cf. *Bungartz*, IKS, p. 38; *Withus*, DB 2009, Beilage 5, 82, 85; *Schoberth/Servatius/Thees*, BB 2006, 2571.
2031 *Schoberth/Servatius/Thees*, BB 2006, 2571, 2572.

cluding fraud detection.[2032] With regard to compliance, the scope of the internal control system is limited to laws and regulation addressing the annual report e.g. tax law, labor and employment law, social security law, and competition law.[2033] The assessment does not include to verify that the corporation complies with the law.[2034] The aim of the evaluation of the effectiveness of the internal control system regarding financial reporting is predominantly to provide the external auditor with the needed level of sample testing.[2035] As a minor aspect, the external auditor has to report on significant deficiencies impacting the effectiveness of internal control regarding financial reporting[2036] and also on any significant deficiencies relating to non-financial reporting aspects of internal control which the external auditor detected during the audit[2037]. Thereby, a significant deficiency is a deficiency of the internal control system which the external auditor considers as being relevant for the supervisory board.[2038] In this regard, IDW PS 261 acknowledges the inherent limitations of internal control including relative cost-benefit considerations of management.[2039] In case the external auditor concluded that the deficiencies of the internal control system may lead to material misstatements of the financial statements, she has to consider the effects on the attestation according to sec. 322 HGB.[2040] Both determinations of the external auditor have a rather broad scope and provide ample leeway for the external auditor to rule in favor of management.[2041] Due to this leeway, effective internal control regarding financial reporting is not a primary goal of IDW PS 261. In general, IDW PS 261 provides incentives for corporations to implement an effective internal control system using COSO I with the main focus on financial reporting[2042] also with regard to the categories operations and compliance within the limits of IDW PS 261. With regard to fraud detection, the external auditor has to focus the audit on serious misconduct such as financial statement fraud and management override of the internal control system in light of IDW PS

2032 IDW PS 261, mar. 21; cf. IDW PS 210.
2033 IDW PS 261, mar. 23; cf. IDW PS 201, mar. 9.
2034 IDW PS 201, mar. 9, 11.
2035 IDW PS 261, mar. 7.
2036 IDW PS 450, mar. 47.
2037 IDW PS 261, mar. 93.
2038 Cf. IDW PS 261, mar. 89.
2039 IDW PS 261, mar. 25.
2040 Cf. IDW PS 261, mar. 91. See *supra* at chapter 8, C. IV.
2041 See *infra* at chapter 12, B. I. 1. c) (3).
2042 Cf. IDW PS 261, mar. 24.

210.[2043] The result of the fraud detection audit influences the IDW PS 261 evaluation of the internal control system. With regard to the IT components in the internal control system, the external auditor has to apply IDW PS 330 for the audit.[2044]

In 2011, IDW PS 980 has been issued for voluntary audits of compliance management systems. The auditing standard is not applicable for systems which are addressed in specific auditing standards such as IDW PS 340.[2045] Three different scopes for an audit of the design of the implemented compliance management system are feasible either with regard to the evaluation of the effectiveness, the functionality, or the appropriateness.[2046] IDW PS 980 is based on international frameworks including COSO II and the USSG.[2047] In general, the compliance management system is comprised of seven elements[2048] including the culture of compliance, the compliance structure, compliance objectives, compliance risks, compliance program, compliance communication, and compliance monitoring and enhancement. The compliance management system needs to be documented.[2049] The elements of the compliance management system resemble the COSO II components.[2050] Hence, the elements of IDW PS 980 only resemble general requirements for an effective compliance management system which have to be adapted to the specific corporation.[2051] The adaptation is subject to the discretion of the management board.[2052] In light of IDW PS 980, authors aim to establish legal minimum requirements for a compliance management system.[2053] Within IDW PS 980, significant deficiencies of the compliance management system exist preventing the external auditor to issue an unqualified attestation if the corporation did not use adequate guidelines to design the system, deficiencies exist within the design so that not all risks of misconduct are addressed, the system lacks regular adjustments, insufficient resources are attributed to the system, the system is inadequately communicated and monitored, and the system is inade-

---

2043 *Berndt/Jeker*, BB 2007, 2615; cf. IDW PS 210, 5 et seq.
2044 IDW PS 330, mar. 9.
2045 IDW PS 980, mar. 2
2046 Cf. IDW PS 980, mar. 14.
2047 Cf. IDW PS 980, exhibit 1.
2048 IDW PS 980, mar. A10 et seq.
2049 IDW PS 980, mar. 61 et seq.
2050 See *supra* at chapter 4, C. III. 1.
2051 *Withus/Hein*, CCZ 2011, 125, 126.
2052 *Withus/Hein*, CCZ 2011, 125, 126.
2053 See. *v. Busekist/Hein*, CCZ 2012, 41 and *v. Busekist/Schlitt*, CCZ 2012, 86.

quately implemented or enforced.[2054] While IDW PS 980 provides guidance for corporations regarding the elements of a compliance management system[2055], it has been noted that it requires far too much for an ordinary corporation and only sets a best practice for corporations.[2056] IDW PS 980 may only set the best practice standard for large, listed corporations but would not provide for a legal standard.[2057]

In general, IDW PS 980 provides good guidance for corporations on general aspects of compliance management systems. It falls short, however, to provide guidance to implement truly effective systems. The IDW PS 980 attestation does not require corporations to set benchmarks and key performance indicators. Hence, the evaluation of the effectiveness of the compliance system based on IDW PS 980 will provide only insight whether the system fulfills general aspects of an effectively designed and operated compliance systems but lacks to require to define benchmarks and key performance indicators necessary to evaluate the effectiveness of the corporate-specific compliance system leading to truly effective systems.[2058]

With regard to the voluntary attestation of IDW PS 980, it has been pointed out that an attestation of such system will not affect substantive law.[2059] The advantage of an unqualified attestation is rather procedural.[2060] The audit may provide the necessary basis for the management board to establish that it acted on an informed basis in light of the business judgment rule of sec. 93(1)(s. 2) AktG.[2061] Furthermore, the attestation may provide proof that the management board fulfilled its duty to monitor the corporation by implementing and operating an effective compliance management system especially if the potential violation of such duty may have occurred years ago.[2062] Otherwise, such far reaching effect of a IDW PS 980 attestation has been called into question.[2063]

2054 *Wolf*, DStR 2011, 997, 1000; cf. IDW PS 980, mar. A28.

2055 *Wolf*, DStR 2011, 977, 1002; *Schemmel/Minkoff*, CCZ 2012, 49; *Böttcher*, NZG 2011, 1054, 1056.

2056 Cf. *Klindt/Pelz/Theusinger*, NJW 2010, 2385, 2387; *Böttcher*, NZG 2011, 1054.

2057 Cf. *Fleischer*, NZG 2014, 321, 325; *Merkt*, ZIP 2014, 1705, 1713.

2058 See *infra* at chapter 16, B. IV.

2059 *v. Busekist/Hein*, CCZ 2012, 41, 42; *Böttcher*, NZG 2011, 1054, 1057.

2060 *Withus/Hein*, CCZ 125, 128 et seq.; cf. *v. Busekist/Hein*, CCZ 2012, 41, 42.

2061 *Withus/Hein*, CCZ 2011, 125, 127 et seq. See more general: *Merkt*, DB 2014, 2271; *id.*, DB 2014, 2331.

2062 *Withus/Hein*, CCZ 2011, 125, 128 et seq.

2063 *Merkt*, DB 2014, 2331, 2335 et seq.

With regard to internal audit, IDW PS 321 requires the external auditor to assess internal audit regarding the skills of the internal auditors, monitoring activities, documentation, gathered evidence, the assessment of the evidence, the conclusion of such assessment, the responds to unusual issues, and the monitoring of the adherence to suggestions of internal audit.[2064] Due to this audit, corporations have incentives to focus on internal audit.

In essence, the IDW auditing standards provide incentives for the management board to implement internal control, risk management, compliance measures, and internal audit using the auditing standards as guidance. All depicted IDW auditing standards reflect, to a different degree, elements of COSO I and COSO II. Hence, in light of the IDW PS standards, corporations may use the COSO frameworks to design internal control, risk management, and compliance system as well as elements of the internal audit function. But the guidance following from the auditing standards is rather general and lacks to induce corporations to define benchmarks and key performance indicators necessary to achieve truly effective internal control and risk management systems including compliance.

D. *Profound Internal Control and Risk Management Systems Including COSO I and COSO II*

In Germany, corporations implement profound internal control and risk management as best practice.[2065] The German best practice is influenced by legal authors and mainly by consulting firms and auditors and exceeds the recommendations of the GCGC and the measures induced by the auditing standards. Within corporate law and specific regulatory law, risk management and internal control are addressed as either two separate systems (sec. 107(3), 171(1) AktG and sec. 26, 29 VAG) or as one system in which internal control is a part of risk management (sec. 25a(1) KWG). The latter setup resembles the risk management framework of COSO II.[2066] Similar to the debate regarding the legally required elements of internal control and risk management, different concepts for profound risk management systems exist which require different elements.

2064 Cf. *Amling/Bantleon*, DStR 2008, 1300, 1305 et seq.
2065 *Lorenz*, in: Grundlagen des Risikomanagements, p. 11.
2066 See *supra* at chapter 4, C. III. 2.

Scholars have named minimum requirements for a risk management system such as risk identification, risk analysis, risk assessment and risk communication including managing and controlling risk.[2067] These requirements resemble IDW PS 340. Similarly, a risk management system would include an early warning system, a risk monitoring system, crisis management, and crisis follow-up treatment.[2068] It has also been pointed out that the internal control system should be comprised of the early warning system together with the reporting of risk, compliance, and internal audit.[2069] The internal control and risk management systems should address essential processes within a business such as procurement, production, sales, fixed assets, staff, accounting, finance, taxes, and IT-systems.[2070] Similarly, a profound risk management system would require to assess all risks, risk analysis, communication and documentation of risks, and measures to manage risks such as risk avoidance, risk reduction, risk mitigation, and risk compensation.[2071] In addition, a profound risk management system should include an information system for standardized reporting and ad-hoc reporting.[2072] Further elements of a profound risk management system have been depicted above by portraying the wide interpretation of sec. 91(2) AktG of economists.[2073]

In essence, a profound risk management system is a management tool to address risks within corporations encompassing loss and chances.[2074] In order to achieve effective and efficient risk management, corporations need to integrate existing elements of risk management such as the compliance system or internal control over financial reporting into one comprehensive risk management system.[2075] It is essential that the risk management system adapts to changes in the corporation and the market environment.[2076] Further important elements of risk management are to align risk manage-

---

2067 *Kort*, Großkomm AktG, sec. 91, mar. 56; *Spindler*, in: Fleischer, Hdb Vorstandsrecht, sec. 19, mar. 16 et seq.

2068 *Preußner/Becker*, NZG 2002, 846, 848.

2069 *Dreher*, FS Hüffer, 161, 167 et seq.

2070 Cf. *Bungartz*, IKS, p. 412.

2071 *Preußner/Becker*, NZG 2002, 846, 848 et seq.

2072 *Weber/Weißenberger/Liekweg*, DStR 1999, 1710, 1714.

2073 See *supra* at chapter 8, B. I. 2. a).

2074 *Tüllner*, PwC Guidance 2010, p. 9

2075 *Tüllner*, PwC Guidance 2010, p. 11.

2076 *Tüllner*, PwC Guidance 2010, p. 9 and p. 13: in this regard, PwC terms risk management as "Dynamic Risk Management". The PwC guidance resembles to a large extent COSO II.

ment with the corporate strategy[2077], the tone at the top[2078], the exchange of information[2079], and technology to prioritize risks[2080]. The management board should continuously evaluate the effectiveness of the internal control and risk management systems to fulfill its duty of care.[2081]

All named settings for profound internal control and risk management systems provide a reasonable starting point to design internal control and risk management systems and mainly include all necessary elements resembling to different degrees the COSO frameworks. Nevertheless, the COSO frameworks – COSO I and COSO II – provide an even more comprehensive approach to internal control and risk management and constitute best practice in Germany. The consulting firms and the auditors strongly suggest to use COSO I and COSO II for internal control and risk management.[2082] Especially COSO II provides for "maximum flexibility" to design internal control and risk management systems.[2083] Currently, COSO I serves as the standard for internal control systems with acceptance worldwide.[2084] It has been pointed out that corporations should define parameter and tolerance ranges for their risk management system.[2085] Benchmarks and key performance indicators are necessary to evaluate the effectiveness of the internal control and risk management systems.[2086] A detailed analysis of the requirements of COSO I including an overview of COSO II has been conducted above.[2087]

2077 *Tüllner*, PwC Guidance 2010, p. 12.
2078 *Tüllner*, PwC Guidance 2010, p. 17.
2079 *Tüllner*, PwC Guidance 2010, p. 28.
2080 *Tüllner*, PwC Guidance 2010, p. 30.
2081 See *Wolf*, DStR 2009, 920, 924.
2082 *AKEIÜ Schmalenbach-Ges.*, DB 2011, 2101; 2102; *Withus*, DB 2009, Beilage 5, 82; *AKEU/AKEIÜ Schmalenbach-Ges.*, DB 2009, 1279; *Hufnagel/Tönnissen*, ZIR 2010, 110; cf. *Bungartz/Strobl*, ZIR 2012, 138; *Withus*, ZIR 2010, 99 et seq.; *Sybon*, ZIR 2011, 93, 95 et seq.; *Nimwegen/Koelen*, DB 2010, 2011. Regarding COSO I: *Lanfermann/Röhricht*, BB 2009, 887, 889.
2083 *Withus*, ZIR 2010, 99, 101. See for details on COSO II *Brünger*, COSO ERM.
2084 *Withus*, DB 2009, Beilage 5, 82, 85; *Hofmann*, Hdb Anti-Fraud-Management, p. 377 et seq.
2085 *Powilleit*, GWR 2010, 28.
2086 See *infra* at chapter 16, B. IV. 2.
2087 See *supra* at chapter 4, C. I.

Chapter 10: Incentives to Engage in Internal Control and Compliance Measures

In the following section, all incentives for corporations to implement internal control will be depicted with regard to financial reporting and compliance mirroring the COSO I categories. The analysis includes the costs and benefits of internal control systems.

A. *Internal Control Regarding Financial Reporting*

Corporations have incentives to implement internal control regarding financial reporting from corporate law and commercial law. Due to corporate law, corporations have incentives to implement internal control regarding financial reporting pursuant to sec. 93(1) AktG only fulfilling minimum requirements *prima facie* which satisfy the non-optimal expectations of the supervisory board and the testing requirements in light of sec. 171 AktG and art. 11(2)(j) Regulation (EU) No 537/2014 but fail to be truly effective.[2088] Also, the management board has incentives from commercial law to implement internal control regarding financial reporting which do not have any significant deficiencies which the external auditor would find during routine testing. In light of art. 7 Regulation (EU) No 537/2014, the management board has incentives to focus on financial reporting fraud considering the extent to which the statutory audit is capable to detect fraud and to investigate and remedy, if indicated, any reported irregularities in order to avoid that the external auditor reports any reluctance to do so to the authorities. With regard to best practice, corporations have incentives to implement internal control regarding financial reporting reflecting best practice as signal to capital markets in order to reduce the cost of capital.

2088 See *supra* at chapter 8, B. III.

B. Compliance

With regard to compliance measures, the expected liability of the management board for corporate crime is in general not sufficient to induce the management board to implement proficient compliance measures. Only in light of the recent corporate compliance scandals, the general need for compliance measures became apparent to corporations. While the recent increase in enforcement actions led to a focus on compliance, insufficient liability and in particular the policy of courts and agencies to refrain from granting leniency for compliance measures as well as the potential for being punished for taking any of these measures provide incentives to refrain from implementing optimal compliance measures. The incentives from corporate law do not induce management to implement effective internal control and risk management systems including compliance measures. The management board has only incentives to implement compliance measures fulfilling minimum requirements *prima facie*.

The incentive structure from corporate liability for crimes and offences includes incentives from criminal law and the OWiG. Criminal law provides for incentives to focus on prevention measures but lacks to provide incentives for corporations to engage in policing measures. From OWiG, corporations have hardly incentives to engage in prevention measures and to implement monitoring measures which only fulfill the requirements of sec. 130 OWiG *prima facie* up to a level which ensures that courts will accept these measures in light of sec. 130 OWiG to exculpate from liability.

Due to the incentives deriving from potential loss of reputation, corporations have incentives to engage in prevention measures up to the point when marginal costs exceed marginal benefits. Corporations have generally no incentive, however, to engage in policing measures including monitoring, internal investigations, and self-reporting. In contrast, corporations have incentives to refrain from producing information and to hold back such information in order to avoid prosecutorial investigations and indictment. Only if prosecutorial investigations are imminent or after prosecutors initiated investigations, corporations have incentives to self-report and cooperate with law enforcement agencies as well as initiate internal investigations.

With regard to internal control regarding non-financial information subject to reporting obligations, corporations have incentives to focus their compliance measures on such non-financial information in order to receive sufficient information for the decision whether to report the received information. The specific circumstance of the capital markets increase the incentives to implement these controls compared to the incentives to implement general compliance measures. With regard to compliance measures, sec. 289f HGB provides a platform for corporations, in particular if combined with the corporate governance report of the GCGC, to communicate to investors their compliance-related efforts which are aimed to fulfill the expectations of investors.

The main incentives to implement non-effective compliance measures follow from sec. 93(1) AktG. In addition, large, listed corporations have incentives to focus on compliance with law with regard to e.g. anti-corruption and anti-bribery measures including related due diligence processes in light of sec. 289b und 298c HGB. In light of best practice, corporations have incentives to implement compliance measures reflecting best practice as signal to the capital markets and to communicate these measures to the market.

C. Costs and Benefits of Internal Control Systems Including Compliance Measures

Internal control systems including compliance measures are a cost factor. While the actual costs are corporation-specific, costs for implementing and maintaining these controls occur. Nevertheless, internal control also provide for benefits. In Germany, internal control including compliance measures are mostly regarded as a cost factor neglecting the benefits of an effective internal control system.[2089] In this regard, the experience of SOX shows that implementation costs may be high but operating costs are relatively low.[2090] Since almost all large corporation already implemented compliance measures to some degree, these costs are sunk costs and need to be excluded from a forward looking cost-benefit analysis.

The compliance measures will provide benefits[2091], especially if embedded in enterprise risk management like COSO II, which have to be balanced against the costs.[2092] The benefits include prevention of crime and the opportunity to learn from prior misconduct to prevent reoccur-

2089 *Görtz/Roßkopf*, ZRFC 2010, 150.
2090 See *infra* at chapter 13, B. I.
2091 *Bussmann*, PwC Study 2011; cf. *Bungartz/Strobl*, ZIR 2012, 138 et seq. See on benefits also *infra* at chapter 13, B. III.
2092 *Görtz/Roßkopf*, ZRFC 2010, 150, 154; cf. *Sahan/Berndt*, BB 2010, 647, 651; *Hindelmeier/Maier*, ZIR 2009, 119 et seq.

rence.[2093] Any reduction of the costs of corporate misconduct is a benefit provided by the compliance measures. Corporations face costs due to corporate misconduct encompassing costs directly caused by the misconduct such as compensation of damages, costs to deal with the corporate crime[2094], and costs linked to the crime such as loss of reputation. Costs to deal with the corporate crime, such as working time dedicated to manage the incident and working time used for a lawsuit, have been named to be the most important cost factors followed by costs linked to the crime such as loss of reputation, impairments of business relationships, or higher scrutiny of enforcement agencies.[2095] In light of alleged corruption, costs occur due to the disruption of the business through comprehensive investigation and confiscation of documents by prosecutors, testimony of employees, and investigations against management for violating the monitoring duties of sec. 130, 30, 9 OWiG.[2096] In case of conviction, the corporation faces fines, disgorgement of profits, and debarment from governmental contracts.[2097] These costs will be mitigated by implementing internal controls including compliance measures.

Effective internal control and compliance measures may also provide benefits through lower cost of capital if the implemented systems fulfill the requirements expected by investors.[2098] Moreover, compliance measures will reduce the risk of personal liability of members of the management board[2099] which is likely to lead the management board to overspend on compliance since the members of the management board only share a fraction of the costs, if at all, and profit substantially from compliance measures. The management board is likely to overspend on compliance only to avoid liability which does not mean that they will implement an optimal compliance organization. Also, it has been noted that corporations generally do not miss on business opportunities due to implemented anti-corruption programs[2100] contradicting the general assumption that such programs cost business opportunities.

2093 *Bussmann/Matschke*, CCZ 2009, 132, 138.

2094 Cf. *Meier-Greve*, BB 2009, 2555, 2558.

2095 *Bussmann/Salvenmoser*, CCZ 2008, 192, 193. See also *Görtz/Roßkopf*, ZRFC 2010, 150, 154 et seq.

2096 *Bürkle*, ZIP 2004, 877, 879.

2097 *Bürkle*, ZIP 2004, 877, 879.

2098 See also *Bussmann*, FS Achenbach, 57, 60 et seq. on market pressure to implement compliance. See *infra* at chapter 13, B. III. and *supra* at chapter 8, C. I.

2099 *Schürrle/Olbers*, CCZ 2010, 102, 107.

2100 *Bussmann/Salvenmoser*, CCZ 2008, 192, 194; *Lambsdorff*, 2007, p. 174 et seq.

In essence, costs and benefits of internal control including compliance measures are specific for each corporation. One should not underestimate the benefits of internal control providing incentives to implement these measures. Since marginal expected costs of wrongdoing are generally low, however, marginal benefits are also low.

D. Conclusion

In general, corporations have only incentives to engage in prevention measures to avoid loss of reputation up to the point when marginal costs exceed marginal benefits. Since the possibility of being indicted is rather low, the incentives to engage in prevention measures are also low. Besides prevention measures, management has only incentives to implement internal control and risk management systems including compliance measures fulfilling minimum requirements *prima facie* leading to non-effective "paper-tiger" programs except for the early warning system and internal control regarding financial reporting. These two aspects of internal control do not optimally prevent and detect corporate crime.

The lack of providing leniency for implemented policing measures leads management to implement non-effective "paper-tigers" since the costs associated with the litigation dilemma outweigh the benefits generally connected to internal control. The argument of high costs against the implementation of internal control usually falls short in light of the benefits of such measures providing incentives to implement these measures but only up to the point when marginal benefits equal martial costs. The benefits do not provide for sufficient incentives, however, to induce the management board to implement optimal internal control and compliance measures. This holds especially against the background of the incentives for the management board to leave internal control and the compliance organization less than optimal. The compensation policy may be used to counteract some of the incentives to refrain from implementing internal control and compliance measures.

Chapter 11: Conclusion

German law and best practice address internal control and compliance rather rudimentary. Only the specific law of regulatory industries requires to implement internal control and risk management systems including compliance measures but these provisions are not applicable for general corporations and constitute only best practice.

In the recent years, the corporate scandals lead to crystallize the duty to implement compliance measures. Before these developments, only an early warning system and internal control regarding financial reporting were generally regarded as mandatory. Corporate law still lacks to require a specific level of effectiveness for these controls. While BilMoG requires the audit committee to monitor the effectiveness, the lack of a specific level of effectiveness leads corporations to implement ineffective internal controls and compliance measures unless the supervisory board requires to implement optimal benchmarks and key performance indicators and conducts further audits of internal control. Absent those additional requests, the incentives structure of corporate law provides hardly incentives for the management board to implement effective internal control and compliance measures besides internal control regarding financial reporting and the early warning system. Despite the duty to implement effective internal control and compliance measures, the insufficient incentive structure for the members of the supervisory board and the management board induces to implement at best minimum requirements instead of optimal measures. Hence, large, listed corporations will implement internal control and risk management systems including compliance measures *prima facie* but lack the incentive to optimally comply with these mandates leading to non-effective systems except for the early warning system and internal control regarding financial reporting. Moreover, a focus will be set to the reporting obligations of the capital market regarding non-financial information. Besides corporate law, commercial law induces corporations to implement internal control regarding financial reporting which are conform with the general expectations of the external auditor. The effectiveness of internal control regarding financial reporting, however, is not a major concern of the external auditor.

The incentive structure from corporate liability for crimes and offences is dominated by the OWiG since no corporate criminal liability exists in

Germany. The incentives are rather limited for corporations to implement effective policing measures including a compliance program and the incentives to engage in prevention measures are only a little higher.

The insight form German best practice consisting of specific law on regulated industries, the GCGC, and auditing standards is rather limited. The auditing standards and best practice reflect elements of COSO I and COSO II which may be used by corporations to design internal control and risk management systems. But, only best practice regarding profound internal control measures with requirements to define benchmarks and key performance indicators provides insight how to design and operate effective internal controls. But the incentives to implement profound systems, however, are limited to signaling to the public and the capital market that the corporation engages in a truly effective internal control system.

Part Three Impact of Being Listed on the NYSE

Chapter 12: Impact Analysis of U.S. Law on German Corporations

The impact of being listed on the NYSE will be analyzed three in steps. First, the law and economics impact analysis of the impact of U.S. law on German corporations listed on the NYSE will be conducted followed by a cost-benefit analysis of being cross-listed in chapter 13. At last, the Siemens case will be portrayed concisely as a prominent example of the impact (chapter 14).

The impact on German corporations listed on the NYSE may be twofold. First, U.S. concepts regarding internal control and compliance may have become legal transplants within German or European law affecting German corporations. The impact on EU law is important since German corporations are either directly subject to EU law or indirectly in case EU law has been transposed into German law. In order to provide for a comprehensive analysis, the impact of U.S. legal transplants on the international level will also be considered. Second, German corporations listed on the NYSE are subject to U.S. law leading to a direct impact. In order to consider all aspects, best practice will be included in the impact analysis.

In step one of the impact analysis, European and German law as well as German and international best practice will be analyzed for already existing U.S. elements of internal control and compliance which, if any, will be carved out of the receiving legal framework. The impact of these U.S. legal transplants will be analyzed by defining the remaining legal framework as the stable basis in which the U.S. legal transplants will be inserted as variables. For the second step, the German legal framework regarding internal control and compliance for German corporations will be defined as the stable basis in which all U.S. mandates and requirements regarding internal control and compliance, which German corporations listed on the NYSE have incentives to comply with, will be inserted as variables.

A. *U.S. Law and U.S. Best Practice Impacting German Corporations through Legal Transplants in EU Law, German Law, German Best Practice, and International Best Practice*

The impact analysis of the first step starts with the impact of U.S. law as well as U.S. best practice on EU and German law.[2101] It will be followed by the impact analysis of U.S. law and best practice on German best practice since significant impact has occurred on this level. Finally, the impact analysis will address the U.S. impact on the international level.

I. Impact of U.S. Law and Best Practice within EU Law

For the analysis, it has to be differentiated between transplants of U.S. concepts of internal control and compliance and the statutory mandates of SOX which is often not clearly separated within the scholarly debate leading to irritations regarding the scope and influence of SOX. The Directives 2006/43/EC and 2006/46/EC addressed internal control and compliance issues after the enactment of SOX and in close cooperation of EU and U.S. authorities[2102]. In 2014, Directive 2006/43/EC has been amended by Directive 2014/56/EU replacing art. 41 Directive 2006/43/EC by art. 39 Directive 2014/56/EU slightly changing the wording and introducing the duty of the audit committee to submit recommendations or proposals to ensure the integrity of the financial reporting process.[2103] Since art. 39 Directive 2014/56/EU is essentially similar to former art. 41 Directive 2006/43/EC, the findings regarding art. 41 Directive 2006/43/EC are still valid. With regard to the amending Directive 2006/43/EC and amending Directive 2006/46/EC, several authors have reasoned they have been influenced by SOX[2104], especially former art. 41 Directive 2006/43/EC by sec. 404 SOX[2105]. Also, an Americanization of EU law has been noted.[2106]

2101 See for an initial overview of the U.S. impact on EU and German law *Bussmann/Matschke*, wistra 2008, 88.

2102 Commission, Action Plan 2003, p. 5.

2103 See also *supra* at chapter 8, A.

2104 *v. Rosen*, AG 2008, 537; *Willems*, ZRFC 2007, 79, 86; cf. Commission, Action Plan 2003, p. 5; *v. Hulle/Maul*, ZGR 2004, 484, 502 et seq. (the authors drafted the directives); *Hütten/Stromann*, BB 2003, 2223; *Förster*, ZIP 2006, 162, 163. See on the EU action plan: *v. Hulle/Maul*, ZGR 2004, 484, 486.

2105 *Sünner*, CCZ 2008, 56, 57; *Schoberth/Servatius/Thees*, BB 2006, 2571, 2573.

2106 *Martín*, FS Tiedemann, 485, 500.

While the aim of both the directives and SOX has been to improve financial reporting after numerous scandals in the U.S. and Europe[2107], the influence of SOX on EU Law, however, is only marginal[2108] and limited to the fact that SOX highlighted the importance of effective internal control for accurate financial reporting. The directives seize on the issue of financial reporting and highlight the importance of an audit committee and effective internal control to address financial, operational, and compliance risks.[2109] But the directives do not include SOX provisions. Due to former art. 41 Directive 2006/43/EC, each corporation should have an audit committee which shall *inter alia* monitor the financial reporting process, the effectiveness of the corporation's internal control, internal audit and risk management systems. Likewise, SOX highlights in sec. 301 and sec. 404 the importance of the audit committee and effective internal control for the financial reporting process. SOX does not specifically mandate, however, that the audit committee has to monitor the financial reporting process and the effectiveness of internal control, internal audit and risk management systems. Rather, these duties are not particularly addressed by SOX but have already been duties of the U.S. audit committee prior to SOX. SOX's main aim has been to improve the financial reporting process and to emphasize the responsibility of the CEO and CFO for financial reporting. The EU legislator, however, has not adopted the most important aspects of SOX: requiring to implement effective internal control over financial reporting including a level of effectiveness and effective internal control regarding non-financial information subject to the reporting obligations of securities law, by mandating management's evaluation regarding these internal control aspects as well as to require the external auditors to attest to the evaluation of management.

Moreover, Directive 2006/43/EC requires in former art. 41(1) that at least one member within the supervisory board or the audit committee, if such committee exists, has to be a financial expert. The requirement resembles sec. 407 SOX which imposes a comply-or-explain duty on corporations regarding the fact that at least one member of the audit committee is a financial expert[2110]. The general idea of requiring expertise on financial reporting within the audit committee is identical with SOX. In detail, the two

2107 *Lanfermann/Röhricht*, BB 2009, 887.
2108 Cf. *Glaum/Thomaschewski/Weber*, Studien des Deutschen Aktieninstituts 2006, p. 111.
2109 Directive 2006/43/EC recital 24.
2110 See *supra* at chapter 4, A. IV. 1.

mandates differ. While former art. 41(1) Directive 2006/43/EC mandates that an expert serves on the audit committee, sec. 407 SOX only mandates a comply-or-explain-approach. While the EU legislator has not specifically referred to sec. 407 SOX, the influence of sec. 407 SOX on former art. 41(1) Directive 2006/43/EC is obvious.

Moreover, Directive 2006/46/EC requires in art. 46a that corporations report on the main features of the internal control and risk management systems in relation to the financial reporting process. In sec. 404, SOX also requires to report on internal control over financial reporting. In difference to the directive, U.S. corporations need to report on management's assessment of the effectiveness of internal control over financial reporting. The only similarity between the directive and SOX is that both require corporations to report on internal control over financial reporting. The directive requires to provide descriptive information of the elements of the implemented internal control as well as risk management system while SOX requires to provide evaluative information. The influence of SOX regarding art. 46(a) Directive 2006/46/EC is limited to highlighting the general importance of internal control regarding financial reporting for investors.

The directives are influenced by SOX regarding its focus on financial reporting, the reporting obligation on internal control regarding financial reporting, and the requirement of a financial expert serving on the audit committee. But the directives do not mandate the requirements nearly as far reaching as sec. 302 and 404 SOX. In essence, SOX requires to implement effective internal control over financial reporting as well as effective internal control regarding non-financial information by using COSO I, and to perform recurring evaluations of the effectiveness. In addition, the external auditors have to attest to the evaluation. This attestation together with increased liability provides for sufficient incentives for management to adhere to the mandates of SOX. Thereby, the main aspect of SOX is to implement sufficient enforcement for internal control concepts which already existed in the U.S. prior to SOX. The scope and magnitude of sec. 302 and 404 SOX mandates exceed the EU mandates by far as it has been demonstrated by the extent of the conducted analysis[2111] and by the fact that even the SEC tremendously underestimated the impact of the SEC rules effectuating SOX's mandates.

For the directives, the EU legislator mainly refrained from transplanting provisions of SOX into EU law. Rather, it seizes on the corporate governance concept 'audit committee' and the internal control concept of the

---

2111 See *supra* at chapter 4, A.

COSO frameworks but lacks to implement substantial enforcement elements similar to the SOX provisions. By requiring in former art. 41 Directive 2006/43/EC the audit committee or the supervisory board to supervise and monitor *inter alia* the financial reporting process, the effectiveness of the internal control system, and the effectiveness of the risk management system, the EU legislator stipulates corporations to implement an audit committee and clearly builds the internal control concept of the COSO frameworks[2112]. The impact becomes evident due to the wording especially in the English version of Directive 2006/43/EC.[2113] The impact of COSO I on EU law has also been concluded based on the finding that EU law regards compliance as part of internal control.[2114]

A further example of the U.S. law influencing European law is sec. 922 Dodd-Frank Act requiring the SEC to launch a program to reward whistleblowers.[2115] In art. 32(4) Regulation (EU) No 596/2014, the EU Commission provides the opportunity for member states to provide financial incentives for whistleblowers.

In essence, SOX builds on the concept 'audit committee' within a one-tier board system[2116] as well as the COSO frameworks and highlights the issue of internal control but does not influence the directives besides the requirement of having a financial expert on the audit committee and the importance on providing information on internal control regarding financial reporting to investors. Rather, member states incorporated the underlying concepts of SOX, i.e. the audit committee and the internal control concept of the COSO frameworks constituting U.S. best practice, into their national law by transposing the directives. In difference to the U.S., the directives also include risk management. While the issue of compliance is an integral part of the COSO frameworks, there is no evidence that any further U.S. concept of compliance such as the USSG has influenced EU legislation. Within EU law, transplants of U.S. concepts regarding internal control and compliance are limited in nature and scope. Since the directives have to be transposed, German corporations are not directly impacted by the directives. The indirect impact of U.S. law and best practice on German

2112 See *supra* at chapter 8, A.
2113 See for the wording of Directive 2014/56/EU *supra* at chapter 8, A.
2114 Cf. *Dreher*, FS Hüffer, 161, 169 et seq.
2115 See *supra* at chapter 4, A. IV. 4.
2116 Cf. *Windbichler*, ZGR 1985, 50.

corporations through European legislation with regard to internal control and corporate compliance is rather small.[2117]

II. Impact of U.S. Law and Best Practice within German Law

U.S. law may impact German corporations through German law in two different ways: directly, or indirectly through EU directives. In 2002, the German Governmental Commission on Corporate Governance issued a ten point plan to improve corporate integrity and investor protection as a reaction *inter alia* to SOX.[2118] But the ten point plan does not include any measures to improve internal control or compliance. While the German legislator was aware of SOX, U.S. legislation did not directly influence German law.

With regard to an indirect influence of U.S. law on German law through EU directives, the above findings illustrate that the U.S. corporate governance concept 'audit committee' and the U.S. concept of internal control reflecting the COSO frameworks influenced the directives 2006/43/EC and 2006/46/EC. SOX itself only influenced the requirement to report on internal control regarding financial reporting and the requirement of a financial expert on the audit committee. Besides these two aspects, SOX only highlighted the general importance of the audit committee, internal control and reporting for accurate financial reporting. Through the directives, these U.S. concepts regarding corporate governance including internal control became part of German law. In order to transpose the directives into German law, BilMoG has been enacted in 2009. BilMoG sections containing elements of U.S. concepts are sec. 107(3) AktG, sec. 100(5) AktG, and sec. 289(4) HGB. BilMoG transposes the minimum mandates of the directives and does not add any further mandates regarding the audit committee, internal control, or compliance so that the impact of U.S. law and best practice on EU law also applies to the U.S. impact on German law. BilMoG uses the provided opportunity in former art. 41(5) Directive 2006/43/EC to refrain from mandating corporations to implement an audit committee.

In contrast to EU law, German corporations are directly affected by the U.S. concepts inherent in BilMoG. Especially sec. 107(3)(s. 2) AktG affects corporations by increasing the awareness of internal control issues within

2117 Similar: *Hellwig*, ECFR 2007, 417, 419 reasons that the U.S. approach had no influence on European law.

2118 Cf. *Seibert*, BB 2003, 693.

the corporation including incentives for the supervisory board to require the management board to implement more proficient internal control.[2119] Due to sec. 107(3)(s. 2) AktG, German corporations will most likely implement an audit committee, in case it had not been implemented before.[2120] With regard to the impact of the audit committee, this issue is mainly beyond the scope of the thesis as far as it is not related to internal control and compliance. From an internal control and compliance perspective, it is important that the supervisory board receives information and deals with internal control and compliance issues. For internal control and compliance, the structure of the supervisory board is only important with regard to the expertise of its members receiving and dealing with internal control and compliance issues and the appropriateness to deal with the provided information. Due to these considerations, most corporations will establish specialized committees within the supervisory board even though it is not mandated by BilMoG.

More important for internal control and compliance, the suggested scrutiny of the supervisory board will lead to an increased awareness of internal control issues within the corporation. The effect of increased awareness of internal control and risk management is only based on the increased awareness of the supervisory board, its advisors, and external auditors, as well as the impact of the evolving best practice in German corporations listed on the NYSE which reflects U.S. best practice[2121]. COSO I elements of internal control will become more prominent in Germany since the internal control concept of the underlying Directive 2006/43/EC resembles the COSO frameworks.

The COSO I framework is already part of German financial controls as illustrated by IDW PS 261 but mostly limited to financial reporting.[2122] The broader scope of the internal control system of sec. 107(3) AktG, in relation to the early warning system of sec. 91(2) AktG, includes besides financial reporting the COSO I categories operations and compliance. Especially with regard to compliance, implementing comprehensive and effective compliance measures impacts German corporations. Sec. 107(3) AktG magnifies the scope of the internal control system and affects the incentive structure of the management board to implement internal control includ-

2119 See *supra* at chapter 8, B. III.

2120 Also the GCGC recommends in no. 5.3.2 to implement an audit committee.

2121 See *infra* at chapter 12, A. III.

2122 See *supra* at chapter 9, C.

ing compliance measures.[2123] Especially the implementation of compliance measures leads to costs associated with the litigation dilemma. But sec. 107(3) AktG does not stand alone. In light of the requirement to implement compliance measures pursuant to sec. 76 combined with sec. 93 AktG, the U.S. concepts impact German corporations through sec. 107(3) AktG more on the issue how to design compliance measures rather than on the issue whether or not to implement these measures.

With regard to the requirement of sec. 100(5) AktG together with sec. 107(4) AktG, it imposes the duty on listed corporations that at least one member serving on the audit committee or on the supervisory board has to be an expert on accounting or auditing. The provision will increase the expertise on the audit committee resulting in better oversight of the management board with regard to internal control issues. Due to the required scope of expertise, the increase in oversight quality will most likely be limited to financial reporting.

Pursuant to sec. 289(4) HGB, listed corporations have to describe the essential elements of the internal control system and the risk management system with regard to financial reporting. Due to such duty, the management board has incentives to deal with these systems including their effectiveness subsequently leading to the implementation of these systems.[2124]

Also with regard to the protection of whistleblowers against retaliation, U.S. law has an impact on the German legislator. Even though not signed into law, German lawmakers and scholars referred heavily to the U.S. rules regarding the protection of whistleblowers against retaliation.[2125] Likewise, the State of North Rhine-Westphalia refers to U.S. law in its bill to implement corporate criminal liability in Germany. [2126]

III. Impact of U.S. Law and Best Practice on German Best Practice

Despite legislation, the concepts of internal control and especially compliance spread from the U.S. to Germany mostly not by codified law but by

---

2123 See *supra* at chapter 8, B. III.

2124 See *supra* at chapter 8, C. I.

2125 Cf. Gesetzentwurf der Fraktion Bündnis 90/Die Grünen, BT-Drucks. 18/3039, p. 12; Gesetzentwurf der Fraktion Bündnis 90/Die Grünen, BT-Drucks. 17/9782, p. 7; Gesetzentwurf der Fraktion der SPD, BT-Drucks. 17/8567, p. 6; *Abraham*, ZRP 2012, 11, 12; *Király*, ZRP 2011, 146. See *infra* at chapter 20, A. II. 3.

2126 *NRW-Justiz*, Gesetzentwurf Unternehmensstrafrecht, p. 22 and p. 53.

German scholars who referred to U.S. law and best practice in order to advance German best practice.[2127] In order to search for insight and guidance for the evolving debate on internal control and compliance in Germany, the distinct U.S. law and best practice have been seized on. It can be observed that economic scholars are more straight forward to use U.S. concepts within German corporations than legal scholars. Some[2128] only highlight the development of compliance in the U.S. as an example to foster and advance the debate in Germany while others[2129] use U.S. concepts of internal control and compliance to interpret German law and to provide guidance for German corporations for how to address these issues.

In this context, it has been noted that especially compliance would have been influenced by SOX.[2130] In most cases, SOX has been addressed to highlight the U.S. requirements for internal control and compliance. SOX itself, however, neither addresses compliance nor all aspects of internal control. Rather, it requires in sec. 302 and 404 SOX that management states its responsibility for internal control over financial reporting and internal control to ensure financial reporting as well as the duty of management to assess the effectiveness these aspects of internal control. Through the promulgated SEC rules enabling SOX, COSO I became the predominant framework providing measures to establish internal control. Similarly, with regard to compliance, the USSG and related DOJ-policies are the dominant factors in the U.S. while SOX only plays a small role. Most compliance measures reflect the mandates and requirements of the USSG and COSO I and not SOX. While the issue of internal control received highest attention with the enactment of SOX, this attention also stained on the issue of compliance. But SOX hardly addresses compliance. Only

---

2127 See for references: *Schneider*, ZIP 2003, 645, 648; *Fleischer*, AG 2003, 291, 297 et seq.; *Kort*, NZG 2008, 81; *Immenga*, FS Schwark, 199, 205 et seq.; *Withus*, DB 2009, Beilage 5, 82, 85 et seq.; *Berndt/Hoppler*, BB 2005, 2623; *AKEU/AKEIÜ Schmalenbach-Ges.*, DB 2009, 1279, at fn. 13 and 14; *Schoberth/Servatius/Thees*, BB 2006, 2571; *Liese/Schulz*, BB 2011, 1347, 1348 et seq.; *Roth*, AG 2004, 1; *Engelhart*, Sanktionierung, p. 711.

2128 *Schneider*, ZIP 2003, 645, 648; *Fleischer*, AG 2003, 291, 297 et seq.; *Immenga*, FS Schwark, 199, 205 et seq.; *Roth*, AG 2004, 1.

2129 *Lampert*, in: Hauschka, sec 9, mar. 13 et seq. listing compliance measures inherent in COSO I and U.S. best practice; *Withus*, DB 2009, Beilage 5, 82, 85 et seq.; *AKEU/AKEIÜ Schmalenbach-Ges.*, DB 2009, 1279, at fn. 13, 14; *Berndt/Hoppler*, BB 2005, 2623; *Schoberth/Servatius/Thees*, BB 2006, 2571; *Liese/Schulz*, BB 2011, 1347, 1348 et seq.; *Hopson/Koehler*, 2008, p. 213; *Bachmann/Prüfer*, ZRP 2005, 109, 113. In general: *Engelhart*, Sanktionierung.

2130 *Mengel*, Compliance und Arbeitsrecht, at Introduction, B.

COSO I as the underlying framework for the elements for effective internal control to fulfill the requirements of SOX and related SEC rules addresses compliance. In the U.S., the elements for compliance programs are based on the USSG and COSO I.[2131] Hence, SOX itself only plays a limited role with regard to the mandates of internal control and compliance systems. It is more precise to refer to the COSO I framework regarding internal control and to the USSG with regard to compliance programs when suggesting to use U.S. concepts for internal control and compliance systems within German corporations.

Due to the references by German scholars to U.S. law and best practice, the U.S. concepts and related best practice in particular COSO I regarding internal control and the USSG regarding compliance have partially become part of the German best practice regarding internal control and compliance. One example of this impact is the reference by German scholars regarding the debate on direct communication lines to the supervisory board.[2132] Hence, German corporations are indirectly impacted by U.S. concepts of internal control reflected in SOX and other U.S. regulation through German best practice.[2133] In this regard, specific SOX mandates have little impact on German corporations.

Besides the impact through reference, German best practice is impacted due to German corporations listed on the NYSE required to follow U.S. securities law. Especially with regard to compliance, the compliance program of Siemens has been used to provide guidance for German corporations on how to design compliance programs.[2134] Such guidance and the examples of the compliance programs of German corporations listed on the NYSE provide guidance to German corporations for designing their compliance

---

2131 See *supra* at chapter 6, A.

2132 See *infra* at chapter 12, B. I. 2. a).

2133 *Ringleb*, in: Ringleb, DCGK, mar. 647; cf. *Lorenz*, in: Grundlagen des Risikomanagements, p. 19; *Sybon*, ZIR 2011, 93, 98; *Bussmann/Matschke*, Crime, Law and Social Change 2008, 349, 354; cf. *Stadtmann/Wißmann*, ZRFG 2006, 16. See *Lampert*, in: Hauschka, Compliance, sec. 9, mar. 13 et seq. listing compliance measures inherent in COSO I and U.S. best practice; *Withus*, DB 2009, Beilage 5, 82, 85 et seq.; *AKEU/AKEIÜ Schmalenbach-Ges.*, DB 2009, 1279, at fn. 13, 14; *Berndt/Hoppler*, BB 2005, 2623; *Schoberth/Servatius/Thees*, BB 2006, 2571; *Liese/Schulz*, BB 2011, 1347, 1348 et seq.; *Engelhart*, Sanktionierung, p. 711.

2134 Cf. *Moosmayer*, Compliance: the guidance is based on the compliance organization of Siemens AG including an annex of the details of Siemens AG's compliance organization. To great extent, the guide portrays U.S. concepts and elements of compliance (cf. *Ringleb*, in: Ringleb, DCGK, mar. 647; *Schäfer*, ZGR 2004, 416 et seq.). See also *supra* at chapter 8, B. I. 3. b) (2).

program even though they are not subject to U.S. law resulting in the adaptation of U.S. concepts by German corporations. Moreover, the U.S. compliance concepts have become the global standard leading German corporations to implement U.S.-style compliance programs.[2135]

It has been argued that German corporations in the mid 2000s followed U.S. best practice with regard to compliance.[2136] At the end of the 2000s, they would follow the German standard at the capital market with a recent focus on risks regarding corruption and antitrust law violations.[2137] As the depicted impact of U.S. law and best practice on German best practice shows, U.S. concepts have largely become the German standard so that the German standard reflects to a certain degree U.S. best practice. Hence, the notion that German corporations follow now the German standard should not be misunderstood in the way that U.S. concepts are no longer part of this new German standard. As it has been shown, the situation is the other way round: U.S. standards have largely become the German standard. The impact of U.S. best practice is not limited to internal control and compliance. U.S. law such as SOX and FCPA also influences German internal audit[2138] demonstrated by the fact that the DIIR adopted the IIA standards.[2139]

In essence, the impact of U.S. law and best practice on German best practice occurs in three ways resulting in a comprehensive adaption of U.S. concepts within German best practice. First, German scholars refer to U.S. law as an example and for guidance. Second, German corporations listed on the NYSE provide with their U.S.-style compliance programs for guidance used by German corporations to design their compliance program. Third, the U.S. standard has become the worldwide standard which German corporations may not easily escape from. The best practice contains mostly elements of COSO I and the USSG and hardly any elements of SOX.

The reference of German scholars to U.S. concepts for internal control and compliance systems increases the required level of sophistication for these systems in Germany. But since the U.S. concepts are mainly based on or reflect COSO I[2140], they do not implement new regulation into German

2135 *Ringleb*, in: Ringleb, DCGK, mar. 622.
2136 Cf. *Klindt*, NJW 2006, 3399; *Benz/Klindt*, BB 2010, 2977.
2137 *Benz/Klindt*, BB 2010, 2977.
2138 *Buderath/Amling*, BB 2005, Beilage 3, 8, 9.
2139 *Amling/Bantleon*, DStR 2008, 1300. See also *supra* at chapter 8, B. I. 2. b) (1).
2140 See *supra* at chapter 6, A.

best practice. In Germany, internal control regarding financial reporting also draws on COSO I demonstrated by IDW PS 261. With regard to compliance, only rudimentary requirements existed, pursuant to sec. 130, 30 OWiG, prior to the debate concerning compliance programs and the following reference to U.S. concepts of compliance by German scholars. The formulated requirements for the compliance organization in Germany[2141] reflect to a large degree the U.S. requirements for these organizations[2142]. In general, the U.S. concepts do not contradict German law. Nevertheless, specific legal mandates such as following from data protection law[2143] have to be observed while implementing the compliance organization.

The increased level of sophistication for internal control and compliance systems affects the duty to manage the corporation pursuant to sec. 93(1) AktG. The enhanced systems provide benefits by increasing the reliability of financial reporting and the general compliance with law. At the same time, the implementation of more sophisticated internal control and compliance systems results in costs. Besides the costs for implementing and operating these systems, the increased level of sophistication leads to an increase of the expected liability due to the litigation dilemma especially with regard to compliance measures. Only an optimal incentive structure may offset these costs.[2144] Under the current liability regime in Germany, however, the costs of the litigation dilemma remain.[2145] Corporations neither receive sufficient leniency, if any, for implemented compliance measures nor does sec. 93(1) AktG provide for a sufficient increase of expected liability especially for failing to implement an appropriate compliance system. Thus, while the sophistication for internal control and compliance systems increased, corporations will not have sufficient incentives to implement these systems.

IV. Impact of U.S. Law and Best Practice on International Best Practice Particularly Japan

The impact of U.S. law is not limited to German corporations. The U.S. concepts of internal control and compliance have become the global stan-

2141 See *supra* at chapter 8, B. I. 3. b) (2).
2142 See e.g. *supra* at chapter 5, C. II. 1.
2143 See *supra* at chapter 8, D. II.
2144 See *infra* at chapter 16, B. I.
2145 See *supra* at chapter 10, D.

dard[2146] leading to a worldwide acceptance of SOX[2147], COSO I[2148], and U.S. compliance standards[2149].[2150] Hence, SOX and other U.S. legislation in the field of internal control and compliance constitute international best practice.[2151] Multinational corporations implement compliance programs fulfilling the highest standard of compliance programs even in countries with far less legal mandates for compliance programs due to simplification of the overall program and reputational considerations.[2152] A uniform compliance programs following a uniform standard reduces fixed costs of the compliance program for each country a corporation operates in leading to overall efficiency.[2153] The U.S. standards emerge as such a uniform standard. Nevertheless, corporations have to consider national specifics for designing and operating internal control and compliance.

The U.S. law did not only influence international best practice. It also stipulated codification. In Japan for example, SOX led to the implementation of the Financial Instruments and Exchange Act known as J-SOX which became effective on April 1, 2008. Following SOX, J-SOX requires listed corporations to report on the evaluation of internal control over financial reporting including material weaknesses.[2154]

V. Conclusion

German corporations are impacteded by U.S. concepts of internal control and compliance through Directives 2006/43/EC and 2006/46/EC and relat-

---

2146 *Ringleb*, in: Ringleb, DCGK, mar. 623.

2147 *Bussmann/Matschke*, Crime, Law and Social Change 2008, 349, 354. See for the worldwide influence of SOX: *Hopt*, ZHR 175 (2011), 444, 463.

2148 *Amling/Bantleon*, WPg 2014, 343, 345; *Dierks/Sandmann/Herre*, CCZ 2013, 164, 165; *Sybon*, ZIR 2011, 93, 94; *Hillebrand*, Früherkennungs- und Überwachungssystem, p. 42 et seq. and p. 154 et seq.

2149 *Bussmann/Matschke*, Crime, Law and Social Change 2008, 349 et seq.

2150 See in general for setting worldwide corporate governance standards through non-state actors: *Fleischer*, ZGR 2012, 160, 191 et seq.

2151 *Mengel*, Compliance und Arbeitsrecht, at Introduction, B; *Mengel/Hagemeister*, BB 2006, 2466, 2467. Anticipating: *Karmel*, 33 Stetson L. Rev. 849 (2004), p. 886; *Stoltenberg/Lacey/George/Cuthbert*, 53 Am. J. Comp. L. 457 (2005), p. 490; *Bussmann/Matschke*, wistra 2008, 88, 95.

2152 *Hohmann-Dennhardt*, in: Unternehmensstrafrecht, 7, 10; *Rosinus*, ZRFG 2008, 260, 282 et seq.; cf. *Ringleb*, in: Ringleb, DCGK, mar. 623.

2153 See also *infra* at chapter 13, D.

2154 *Shishido*, 2008, p. 9.

ed German law as well as German and international best practice. The U.S. impact is generally not through statutes but through reference by German scholars so that the notion of an Americanization of European law is not warranted. The impact of U.S. law and best practice on the European level is rather small. The directives include the U.S. understanding of internal control reflected in the COSO frameworks, and the corporate governance concept 'audit committee'. The impact of SOX is limited to the concept of a financial expert on the audit committee as well as the general ideas that the external auditors have to report on the corporation's internal control and that the corporation has to disclose information regarding internal control to investors. Besides the requirements of a financial expert on the audit committee and to report on internal control, all other U.S. elements within the directives are not specific attributes of SOX. Rather, they constitute general U.S. concepts of internal control and corporate governance which SOX builds on.

The German law transposing the directives, BilMoG, introduces the U.S. concepts included in the directives into German law without adding any further requirements. Different from the directives, the U.S. concepts impact German corporations through BilMoG. Most corporations will implement an audit committee, even though not mandated by BilMoG. BilMoG increases the awareness of German corporations regarding effective internal control reflecting the elements of the COSO frameworks with a special emphasis on effective financial reporting and provides for incentives to implement more proficient, yet not effective, internal control. Moreover, corporations have to have a financial expert on the audit committee and the external auditor has to report on internal control regarding financial reporting.

German best practice for internal control and especially for compliance is influenced by U.S. law and best practice through reference by German scholars. In addition, German corporations listed on the NYSE implemented compliance programs reflecting U.S. standards further shaping German best practice. The reference led to an increased level of sophistication for internal control and compliance systems affecting management and supervisory boards. While the sophistication for internal control and compliance systems increased, corporations will not have sufficient incentives to implement these systems.

On the international level, U.S. law and best practice are widely accepted. Hence, German corporations operating worldwide have incentives to comply with the U.S. standards even though they might exceed national requirements in order to reduce friction and costs.

B. Impact of U.S. Law and Best Practice on German Corporations Listed on the NYSE

In the second step of the impact analysis, the impact of U.S. law and best practice regarding internal control and compliance programs applicable for German corporations listed on the NYSE will be analyzed. Then, the impact of the additional elements and requirements of U.S. internal control and compliance programs will be analyzed as well as their impact on the incentive structure and occurring friction. Since internal control, especially regarding financial reporting, and compliance matters are addressed by two overlapping but separate regulatory frameworks in the U.S., the following analysis acknowledges this separation in order to facilitate the analysis. The impact analysis of U.S. law and best practice on German corporation listed on the NYSE will be conducted, first, by analyzing the impact of internal control provisions and, second, by analyzing the impact of compliance provisions. The impact on the incentive structure will be dealt with the end of each subpart. It follows an analysis of the U.S. impact on the corporate governance structure of German corporations as well as the finding that U.S. law had no impact on risk management.

As a rather obvious impact, SOX and the FCPA enforcement of the DOJ together with the accompanying rules and best practice increased the awareness of German corporations with regard to internal control and compliance. Moreover, German corporations have to follow massive amount of U.S. regulation including *inter alia* SOX, SEC rules, PCAOB, FCPA, USSG, DOJ, NYSE etc. demonstrated by the size of the U.S. part of the thesis.

I. Internal Control

With regard to internal control, both jurisdictions address the issue of implementing and operating effective internal control, especially internal control regarding financial reporting, differently. In Germany, no specific statutory mandates exist for establishing and maintaining effective internal control. Whereas in the U.S., sec. 302 and 404 SOX contain such mandates. Nevertheless, German law and best practice require large, listed corporations to establish internal control. The German legal mandates and best practice for internal control systems especially with regard to financial reporting are quite proficient even though no statutory mandate clearly expresses a duty to implement comprehensive internal control in the sense of

COSO I, representing legislation in the style of principle. The regulatory framework under German law addressing internal control includes the duty to manage the corporation pursuant to sec. 76 combined with sec. 93 AktG, the early warning system of sec. 91(2) AktG, the duty of the supervisory board to monitor the internal control system and related issues (sec. 107(3) AktG), the reporting obligation of the management board on the essential elements of the corporation's internal control regarding financial reporting pursuant to sec. 289(4) HGB, the duty of the external auditor to report on significant deficiencies of the internal control system (sec. 171(1) AktG and art. 11(2)(j) Regulation (EU) No 537/2014), the certification requirements of sec. 264(2) and sec. 245 HGB, and the audit of the financial statements pursuant to 317(1)HGB and related IDW PS 261, as well as the requirement that a financial expert serves on the audit committee (sec. 100(5) AktG). This regulatory framework constitutes the starting point of the impact analysis.

The U.S. regulatory framework constituting the variables with regard to internal control includes the statutory mandates of sec. 302 and 404 as well as sec. 301, 307, 406, 407, 806, 1107 SOX and sec. 922 Dodd-Frank Act, related SEC rules and regulation as well as SEC guidelines regarding internal control. The most important aspect is that management has to file the internal control report required by sec. 404 SOX each fiscal year and it has to report on any material changes in the foreign private issuer's internal control over financial reporting also every fiscal year. German corporations listed on the NYSE face an almost impervious maze of mandates and expectations especially due to the escalating rulemaking of the SEC. In addition, best practice composed of the PCAOB AS no. 5 and voluntary NYSE listing standards completes the regulatory framework regarding internal control. In addition, while this best practice is not mandatory, German corporations listed on the NYSE have incentives to adhere to these rules. The COSO frameworks especially COSO I are also part of best practice. Most corporations use COSO I to fulfill the requirements of sec. 404 and sec. 302 SOX. Therefore, corporations set the main focus within the COSO I framework on internal control regarding financial reporting. The two other categories, operational and compliance with laws and regulation, become relevant due to the SEC's expectation to consider all material aspects of the control framework, even beyond financial reporting areas, within management's evaluation of the effectiveness of internal control over financial reporting.[2155] Besides internal control regarding financial report-

---

2155 See *supra* at chapter 4, A. II. 2. b) (1).

ing, U.S. law and best practice also addresses compliance issues related to the COSO I category 'compliance with laws and regulation' which will be dealt with in the subsection on compliance further below.

1. Impact of U.S. Requirements for Internal Control on German Corporations

Several of the mandates and requirements of the U.S. regulatory framework exceed the German level of requirements for internal control impacting German corporations listed on the NYSE. The main impact relates to the internal control provisions of SOX, sec. 302 and 404, and related SEC rules and guidelines as well as PCAOB AS no. 5. Due to the wide flexibility of the German corporate law, German corporations are able to comply with most of the U.S. legal mandates especially SOX and requirements following from best practice.[2156] Nevertheless, some U.S. mandates contradict German law leading to friction which will be discussed further below.[2157]

a) The Impact of U.S. Internal Control on the Early Warning System – Section 91(2) AktG

Even though the early warning system of sec. 91(2) AktG does not have the scope of internal control in the sense of sec. 404 and 302 SOX as well as COSO I, the impact of U.S. internal control on the early warning system will briefly be touched on due to a focus of the German academic debate on sec. 91(2) AktG. In line with the prevailing opinion, sec. 91(2) AktG does not require to implement comprehensive internal control. If German law had only required to implement an early warning system, the impact of U.S. law and best practice regarding internal control would have been devastating. As it has been portrayed above[2158], the early warning system is rather a safety net around the corporation trying to prevent developments endangering the survival of the corporation, while internal control together with risk management are management tools interwoven as a net with the business processes throughout the corporation. Therefore, requiring to

---

2156 *Kersting*, ZIP 2003, 233, 242. See for more details: *Nicklisch*, Auswirkungen SOX.

2157 See *infra* at chapter 12, B. I. 2.

2158 See *supra* at chapter 8, B. I. 2. a).

implement effective management tools including to evaluate their effectiveness would have had no equivalent structure in German corporations.

b) The Impact of Disclosure Controls and Procedures – Section 302 SOX

German corporations listed on the NYSE have to comply with the certification requirement of sec. 302 SOX and related SEC rules.[2159] Since the analysis is limited to internal control issues, the certification requirements of sec. 302(a)(1-3) SOX and corresponding sec. 264(2) HGB are not part of the analysis. Due to sec. 302 SOX, the CEO and CFO will focus on the duties and obligations regarding internal control. This focus will further strengthen the position of the CEO and CFO within the management board. Pursuant to sec. 302(a)(4) SOX and related SEC rules, the CEO and CFO have to certify their responsibility to establish and maintain internal controls – defined by the SEC as disclosure controls and procedures – they have to ensure that non-financial information subject to the reporting obligations of securities law reaches the two officers, they have to evaluate the effectiveness of disclosure controls and procedures once per year and they have to present the conclusion of the effectiveness in the annual report. Due to sec. 302(a)(4) SOX, management has to implement disclosure control and procedures fulfilling the requirements depicted above.[2160] In essence, management has to implement a reporting system ensuring that non-financial information required to be disclosed by federal securities law reaches the CEO and CFO. The SEC does not require any particular procedure but recommends to implement a committee with responsibility for considering the materiality of information and determining disclosures obligations on a timely basis which could include the principal accounting officer, the general counsel, and the principal risk management officer. In general, the corporation should develop a review and evaluation process consistent with its business and internal management and oversight practices.[2161] Annually, management including the CEO and CFO has to evaluate the effectiveness of disclosure controls and procedures. The SEC expects the disclosure controls and procedures to provide at least reasonable assurance regarding their objectives for management's determination that disclosure controls and procedures are effective. In Item 307 Regu-

2159 See *supra* at chapter 4, A. I.
2160 See *supra* at chapter 4, A. I. 2.
2161 SEC Release No. 8124, at II, B, 3.

lation S-K, the SEC requires the corporation to disclose the conclusions of the CEO and CFO regarding the effectiveness of the corporation's disclosure controls and procedures.

In Germany, no equivalent statutory mandate exists for implementing and evaluating control procedures similar to 'disclosure controls and procedures.' Nevertheless, German corporations need to ensure complying with the reporting obligations of capital markets law by implementing controls which gather and process relevant information as part of the internal control system required by the duty to manage the corporation pursuant to sec. 76 combined with sec. 93 AktG.[2162] These controls may be part of the general compliance program addressing to comply with the German reporting duties. In light of sec. 107(3) AktG, the effectiveness of such controls should be evaluated. The incentives to evaluate these controls are by far not as straight forward as under sec. 302(a)(4)(C) SOX. Moreover, German law does not require to report on the evaluation.

The impact of sec. 302(a)(4) SOX on German corporations listed on the NYSE is to implement effective disclosure controls and procedures, to evaluate the effectiveness, and to report on the evaluation. Sec. 302(a)(4) SOX pinpoints the specific need to provide for controls ensuring that non-financial information will be gathered and reported which is also part of German law. It leads German corporations to implement more formalized and documented controls in order to enable the CEO and CFO to evaluate the effectiveness. The specific mandate to evaluate the effectiveness of disclosure controls and procedures together with the reporting obligation ensure that the CEO and CFO will actually implement disclosure controls and procedures and conduct the evaluation. Being subject to U.S. reporting obligations, German corporations have to implement controls specifically designed to gather and process information which has to be reported due to U.S. securities law. Fulfilling local reporting obligations comes with the listing on a foreign exchange. The U.S. controls will also gather information subject to the German reporting obligations. While the assessment whether to report such information depends on the German obligations, implementing U.S. disclosure controls and procedures provides the basis for German disclosure controls and procedures and increases their effectiveness. Nevertheless, the specifics of the respective German reporting obligations have to be observed. In general, being subject to sec. 302(a)(4) SOX will increase the awareness of the need for disclosure controls and procedures also for German reporting obligations. With regard to sec.

2162 See *supra* at chapter 8, D. III.

302(a)(5-6) SOX, the SEC considered these provisions to address financial information and assigned these mandates to internal control over financial reporting of sec. 404 SOX so that the impact of these provisions will be dealt with in the subsequent impact analysis of sec. 404 SOX.

In essence, the impact of sec. 302 SOX on German corporations listed on the NYSE includes the following. The certification requirement of sec. 302 SOX pinpoints the responsibility of the CEO and CFO for the accuracy of the annual report and for the implementation of effective disclosure controls and procedures which ensures that the responsibility may not be denied by these officers. Due to their specific responsibility, the CEO and CFO will focus on internal control. The CEO and CFO will ensure the implementation and evaluation of formalized and documented disclosure controls and procedures which will gather and process non-financial information which has to be reported pursuant to U.S. securities law. These elements of internal control may also be used to comply with German reporting obligations. In general, sec. 302 SOX raises the awareness of the need to implement disclosure controls and procedures also regarding German reporting obligations.

c) The Impact of Internal Control over Financial Reporting – Section 404 SOX

The most important provision of SOX regarding internal control over financial reporting is sec. 404 SOX which has three main mandates: implementing effective internal control over financial reporting (sec. 404(a)(1) SOX), evaluation of the effectiveness of internal control over financial reporting by management (sec. 404(a)(2) SOX), and the attestation of the external auditor on management's evaluation (sec. 404(b) SOX). In the following, the impact of each mandate on German corporations listed on the NYSE will be analyzed separately.

(1) Requiring Effective Internal Control over Financial Reporting – Section 404(a)(1) SOX

Due to sec. 404(a)(1) SOX and related SEC rules, German corporations listed on the NYSE need to implement adequate and effective internal control over financial reporting.[2163] The U.S. law provides for a strict mandate to implement such controls including a clear standard for effectiveness. These controls have to be adequately designed to address financial reporting risks by preventing or detecting material misstatements of financial statements. Also, management has to ensure and assess whether the controls actually operate effectively as planned. The definition of internal control over financial reporting in Exchange Act Rule 13a-15(f) reflects the definition of internal control by COSO I. According to the definition, corporations have to implement internal control over financial reporting which provides reasonable assurance regarding the reliability of financial reporting. Internal control over financial reporting provides reasonable assurance if there is only a remote likelihood that material misstatements will not be prevented or not be detected on a timely basis. Internal control over financial reporting is not effective in case of material weaknesses. A material weakness is a deficiency, or a combination of deficiencies, in internal control over financial reporting such that there is a reasonable possibility that a material misstatement of the annual report will not be prevented or detected on a timely basis. Due to inherent limitations of internal control over financial reporting, no absolute assurance is required by the SEC. These limitations do not affect the effectiveness. Nevertheless, in difference to COSO I[2164], relative costs and benefits are not accepted as an inherent limitation of internal control over financial reporting by the SEC[2165] or PCAOB[2166]. Thus, internal control over financial reporting does not have to provide for absolute assurance regarding the reliability of financial statements.

In order to avoid material weaknesses, all financial reporting risks potentially leading to a material misstatement in the financial statements have to be addressed by at least one adequate control which operates effectively. The core issue of management's efforts to achieve adequate and effective internal control over financial reporting is to accurately determine all financial reporting risks potentially leading to a material misstatement in the financial statements. Identifying financial reporting risk is of crucial importance for the effectiveness of internal control over financial reporting.[2167] In order to accurately address such financial reporting risks, man-

2163 See *supra* at chapter 4, A. II.
2164 See *supra* at chapter 4, C. I. 1. b).
2165 See *supra* at chapter 4, A. II. 1. a).
2166 See *supra* at chapter 4, B. I.
2167 See *supra* at chapter 4, A. II. 2. b) (3).

agement has to implement internal control over financial reporting using the comprehensive approach to internal control of the COSO I framework. Thereby, good documentation of internal control over financial reporting is a prerequisite for management's evaluation pursuant to sec. 404(a)(2) SOX.[2168]

Within internal control over financial reporting, the SEC expects corporations to maintain controls related to the prevention, identification, and detection of fraud.[2169] While internal control over financial reporting has considerable limits to prevent and detect fraud, corporations should implement a specific fraud risk management program as part of the overall compliance program.[2170] Moreover, the SEC considers direct reporting lines for the GC and head of internal audit to the audit committee essential for effective internal controls.[2171] Best practice also includes PCAOB AS no. 5.[2172] In light of this standard, the corporation's internal control system should include controls addressing fraud and management override; it should focus on entity-level controls; significant accounts have to have controls in place which address the risks of material misstatements; management needs to set control objectives; it should deal with risk factors which might result in a material weakness; and it should address indicators of material weaknesses. Moreover, the audit committee should have the oversight of the financial reporting process.

In difference to U.S. law, German law does not provide for an equivalent statutory provision requiring corporations to establish and maintain internal control regarding financial reporting. Nevertheless, the management board has the duty to manage the corporation pursuant to sec. 76 combined with sec. 93 AktG. This duty encompasses the responsibility for accurate financial reporting including to implement internal control regarding financial reporting. With regard to large, listed corporations, the duty to implement internal control regarding financial reporting converges towards best practice which includes to address fraud.[2173] Since the legal mandates are corporation-specific, the law does not require specific thresholds or requirements. Each corporation has wide discretion how to design and operate internal control. Even though not required by law, using one

2168 See *supra* at chapter 4, A. II. 1. d).
2169 SEC Release No. 8238, at II, B, d.
2170 See *supra* at chapter 4, A. II. 1. c).
2171 See *supra* at chapter 4, A. II. 1. a).
2172 See *supra* at chapter 4, B.
2173 See *supra* at chapter 8, C. VII.

of the COSO frameworks will fulfill the requirements of the duty to manage the corporation. In addition, sec. 107(3)(s. 2) AktG assigns the oversight of the financial reporting process to the audit committee. With regard to German best practice, corporations should implement proficient internal control reflecting all three categories of COSO I or COSO II on aspects of financial reporting. Moreover, best practice includes to implement an audit committee and to appoint a CCO. Even though the duty of large, listed corporations to implement internal control converges towards best practice, not every large, listed corporation is required to implement internal control addressing all aspects of internal control regarding financial reporting with the same level of proficiency. Depending on the specific characteristics of each corporation, the internal control system needs to focus on aspects prone to misstating financial statements. The ownership structure of the corporation is one of the most important factors to consider for designing internal control regarding financial reporting. A corporation with dispersed ownership is more prone to earnings management requiring strong financial controls while a corporation with concentrated ownership is more prone to the exploitation of minority shareholder requiring internal control to focus on minority protection.

In addition, management has to consider its reporting obligation on the essential elements of the corporation's internal control system regarding financial reporting pursuant to sec. 289(4) HGB combined with sec. 264d HGB. Even though sec. 289(4) HGB does not mandate to implement internal control system regarding financial reporting, the duty of the management board to describe the internal control system regarding financial reporting is an incentive for the management board to deal with the system including the question of its effectiveness in order to meet the expectations of investors and the capital market in general.

Also, the regulatory framework for the external auditor provides incentives for the management board. The external auditor has to audit financial reporting (sec. 317(1) HGB). In order to evaluate the risk for errors within financial reporting, the external auditor relies on IDW PS 261 which reflects COSO I. The auditing standard does not mandate to evaluate the effectiveness of internal control system. But the external auditor has to consider the effectiveness of the internal control system regarding financial reporting since the level of effectiveness of this system affects the level of control risks.[2174] If the external auditor concludes that the internal control

2174 Cf. IDW PS 261, mar. 6.

system is rather ineffective, she has to conduct more sample testing[2175] and has to report in the audit report (sec. 321(1) and (2) HGB) on significant deficiencies of the internal control system regarding financial reporting or to include in the unqualified attestation an additional description of the deficiencies pursuant to sec. 322(3)(s. 2) HGB. For the audit, the effectiveness of the internal control system is mainly relevant to consider the level of risk of errors within the financial statements and to plan the audit accordingly.[2176] IDW PS 261 acknowledges that internal control regarding financial reporting has inherent limitations which do not affect the appropriateness of the internal control system including that management refrains from certain measures due to relative costs and benefits.[2177] A non-effective internal control system regarding financial reporting becomes relevant if the external auditor concludes that the weaknesses of the internal control system may lead to material misstatements of the financial statements.[2178] Then, she has to consider in light of sec. 322 HGB whether the deficiencies of the internal control system regarding financial reporting warrant to issue a qualified attestation or to refrain from issuing an attestation. Hence, the management board has to ensure that the internal control system prevents material misstatements of the financial statements. In practice, however, refraining from issuing an unqualified attestation is hardly based on the ineffectiveness of the internal control system. Thus, the incentive level for management is not high.

Moreover, pursuant to sec. 171(1)(s. 2) AktG and art. 11(2)(j) Regulation (EU) No 537/2014, the external auditor has to report significant deficiencies of internal control regarding financial reporting to the audit committee and has to state whether internal control regarding financial reporting is generally adequate. But the external auditor does not have the duty to conduct an extensive evaluation of the effectiveness so that the testing is rather *en passant* than thorough. From sec. 171(1)(s. 2) AktG and art. 11(2)(j) Regulation (EU) No 537/2014 follow incentives for the management board to implement internal control regarding financial reporting without significant deficiencies reflecting the requirements of IDW PS 261 which the external auditor would find during routine testing. Due to IDW PS 261, significant deficiencies are deficiencies of the internal control system which are relevant for the monitoring function of the supervisory

2175 IDW PS 261, mar. 7.
2176 Cf. IDW PS 261, mar. 35.
2177 IDW PS 261, mar. 25.
2178 IDW PS 261, mar. 91.

board.[2179] It follows that the management board has incentives to use COSO I to implement internal control regarding financial reporting without any significant deficiencies which the external auditor would find during routine testing ensuring that no material misstatements of the financial statements occur reflecting the requirements of IDW PS 261. The report of significant deficiencies also induces the supervisory board as well as the management board to engage in corrective actions since inaction in light of a known significant deficiency violates the duty pursuant to sec. 76 combined with sec. 93(1) AktG.[2180] In light of art. 7 Regulation (EU) No 537/2014, the management board has incentives to focus on financial reporting fraud. Hence, both boards have incentives to implement internal control regarding financial reporting which meet the expectations of investors and the capital market in general and which do not have any significant deficiencies which the external auditor would find during routine testing.

With regard to the effectiveness of internal control regarding financial reporting, no express statutory mandate requires to implement effective internal control or provides for a threshold concerning the level of effectiveness. Absent a more specific standard, the general standard of liability requiring the members of the management and supervisory boards to act with the care of a prudent businessman represents the required level of effectiveness. It has been reasoned that internal control have to be effective and best practice includes to define benchmarks in order to enable the evaluation of the effectiveness. Nevertheless, effective internal control regarding financial reporting is not by itself a primary goal. In this regard, the auditing standard IDW PS 261 provides for the opportunity within the audit to compensate for a less effective internal control system by increasing the amount of sample testing. Only totally ineffective internal control regarding financial reporting will lead to severe consequences. The inexact requirements to refrain from issuing an unqualified attestation provide ample leeway for management to convince the external auditor that the deficiencies of the internal control system are not as severe.[2181] Similarly, the duty of the external auditor to report significant deficiencies depends on the dutifully exercised discretion of the external auditor whether a deficiency of the internal control system is relevant for the supervisory organ providing for ample room to discuss whether or not a deficiency is signifi-

2179 Cf. IDW PS 261, mar. 89.
2180 See *supra* at chapter 8, B. I. 3. b).
2181 Cf. *Wohlmannstetter*, ZGR 2010, 472, 486.

cant. In addition, the adequacy of the internal control system is not in jeopardy if the management board concludes that a control provides for relative more costs than benefits providing also for ample room to refrain from implementing controls. Following from the auditing standard, the management board has only incentives to implement an internal control system slightly fulfilling the expectations of the auditors. Only sec. 289(4) HGB provides for incentives to fulfill investor expectations. Furthermore, all information regarding the effectiveness of internal control regarding financial reporting remains within the corporation unless the management board chooses to disclose any information within the management report of sec. 289(4) HGB. Hence, the internal control system will reflect COSO I elements expected by investors and will be as effective as necessary to convince the external auditor that the deficiencies do not lead to material misstatements of financial statements and are not relevant for the supervisory board.

The most important impact of the U.S. mandate to implement effective internal control over financial reporting is to introduce the concept of effectiveness including the U.S. definition of material weakness into German corporations. The German concept of reporting significant deficiencies within internal control regarding financial reporting does not have a clear standard for determining whether a deficiency, or deficiencies, in internal control regarding financial reporting constitute a significant deficiency. Moreover, the existence of one or more significant deficiencies does not have a direct consequence such as being prevented from considering internal control regarding financial reporting effective. The German approach towards internal control regarding financial reporting neglects the aspect of effectiveness which is not a primary goal leading to minimum effective internal control. In contrast, the U.S. approach aims for maximum effective internal control regarding financial reporting considering minimum inherent constraints of these controls. In this regard, the SEC and the PCAOB do not expressly include relative costs and benefits within the inherent limitations of internal control over financial reporting in contrast to COSO I and IDW PS 261[2182] demonstrating the fact that effectiveness is less important in Germany compared to efficiency. The resulting increase of effectiveness of internal control over financial reporting potentially leads to more earnings restatement due to the control paradox but this does not have to be misunderstood as a sign of ineffective rulemaking.[2183]

2182 IDW PS 261, mar. 25.
2183 See *infra* at chapter 13, B. III.

In general, the U.S. approach follows a clear concept while the German approach does not have a clear statutory mandate and is blurry at best. The clear U.S. standards substantially increase the required level for effective internal control regarding financial reporting within German corporations listed on the NYSE. Only with regard to the oversight of the financial reporting process, both jurisdictions similarly require that the audit committee conducts the oversight.

Further differences between both approaches impact German corporations listed on the NYSE. The duty to document internal control in Germany is not as high as under sec. 404 SOX.[2184] The documentation in Germany has the purpose to allow the external auditor to assess the effectiveness of the internal control system in order to set the required level of testing and to conclude whether significant deficiencies of the internal control system regarding financial reporting exists which would need to be reported. Thus, management has incentives to document internal control regarding financial reporting to ensure that the external auditor does not conclude, as a result of her routine testing, that significant deficiencies of internal control regarding financial reporting exist. Since the external auditor is neither required to evaluate the effectiveness of internal control regarding financial reporting nor to attest to its effectiveness, the level of documentation does not need to serve this purpose as compared to the U.S.

Moreover, documentation of the early warning system is required as well as the important elements of internal control to allow the supervisory board to exercise its duties in light of sec. 107(3) AktG. Since management does not have the duty to evaluate the effectiveness of internal control over financial reporting, no documentation is required in this regard. Hence, German corporations listed on the NYSE have to adhere to the higher U.S. standard for documenting internal control over financial reporting.

The best practice of internal control of both jurisdictions requires corporations to address fraudulent behavior even though no statutory mandate exists. In difference to German best practice, the expectations of the SEC are more pointed to implement controls addressing fraud. Since technical financial controls are rather ineffective to prevent and detect intentional behavior especially of high-level management, internal control regarding financial reporting needs to focus on compliance elements of COSO I.[2185]

2184 Cf. *AKEU/AKEIÜ Schmalenbach-Ges.*, DB 2009, 1279, 1281; *Börsig/Löbbe*, FS Hoffmann-Becking, 125, 138 et seq.

2185 See *supra* at chapter 4, A. II. 1. c).

A specific fraud risk management program is advisable as part of the general compliance program. Hence, German corporations listed on the NYSE need to establish or increase their focus on fraud.

Also, in contrast to the German requirements, U.S. best practice requires corporations to implement direct reporting lines for the GC, CCO, and head of internal audit. These direct reporting lines are not part of German law. With regard to the traditional understanding, these reporting lines contradict German corporation law.[2186] The friction occurring between the contradicting provisions will be discussed below[2187] including the implications of sec. 301 SOX.

In order to establish internal control over financial reporting in the U.S., COSO I is the primarily used control framework. German internal control regarding financial reporting also builds on COSO I as reflected in IDW PS 261. Both, U.S. and German jurisdictions build on COSO I so that German corporations may easily follow U.S. mandates regarding internal control over financial reporting. Following from the overlap regarding COSO I for both jurisdictions, the respective concepts of reasonable assurance and material weaknesses are comparable. In order to comply with sec. 404 SOX, German corporations almost exclusively rely on COSO I.[2188] Prior to SOX, COSO I has hardly been known in Germany.[2189] Now, COSO I has become more prominent in Germany especially through reference by German scholars in light of SOX.[2190] Thus, the listings of German corporations on the NYSE increased the awareness of COSO I in Germany. But since elements of COSO I have already been part of German best practice regarding internal control regarding financial reporting, COSO I itself hardly impacts the German regulatory framework.

In essence, German corporations listed on the NYSE have to implement more proficient internal control over financial reporting fulfilling U.S. requirements resulting in a considerable impact regarding the proficiency of internal control regarding financial reporting including specific controls addressing fraud and direct reporting lines of the GC, CCO, and head of internal audit to the audit committee. German corporations have to adhere to the standard of effectiveness requiring that each financial reporting risk

2186 See *supra* at chapter 4, B. II. 1. c).

2187 See *infra* at chapter 12, B. I. 2.

2188 *Happ/Pott*, KoR 2007, 666, 671; cf. *Westhausen*, ZIR 2005, 98, 101; *Schäfer*, ZGR 2004, 416, 424.

2189 Cf. *Westhausen*, ZIR 2005, 98, 100.

2190 See *supra* at chapter 12, A. III.

has to be addressed by at least one adequate control operating effectively. In addition, more documentation of the controls is required to enable management's evaluation and its assessment by external auditors. Also, the awareness of COSO I increased within German corporations but it has already been part of the German regulatory framework.

(2) Management's Assessment of the Effectiveness – Section 404(a)(2) SOX

Pursuant to sec. 404(a)(2) SOX management has to evaluate the effectiveness of internal control over financial reporting by determining whether the design or operations have any material weaknesses using a recognized control framework. In the U.S., the pre-dominant framework used for the evaluation is COSO I. The evaluation is mandatory for all corporations including foreign private issuers. The results of the evaluation have to be reported as part of management's report on internal control over financial reporting pursuant to Item 308(a)(3) Regulation S-K. For the evaluation, the SEC expects that corporations consider all material aspects of the control framework including all categories even though SOX and related SEC rules are limited to financial reporting. In light of COSO I, the evaluation has to consider also the categories operational and compliance with laws and regulation. Following from the 2007 reforms[2191], corporations may conduct a top-down, risk-based evaluation.[2192] Also, management is only required to evaluate changes in risks and internal controls in an updated evaluation rather than recreating the entire process every fiscal year.

Corporations need to maintain evidential matter including documentation of the conducted evaluation providing reasonable support for the assessment.[2193] As a part of the evaluation process, the corporation has to document methods and procedures utilized to gather and evaluate the evidence and the design of the controls which adequately address the financial reporting risks including the entity-level controls and other elements necessary for effective internal control over financial reporting.[2194] Only those controls have to be documented which management considered adequate and sufficient to address financial reporting risks. Therefore, not all controls regarding financial reporting have to be documented.

2191 See *supra* at chapter 4, A. II. 2. a).
2192 See *supra* at chapter 4, A. II. 2.
2193 See *supra* at chapter 4, A. II. 2. b) (2).
2194 See *supra* at chapter 4, A. II. 2. b) (1).

Management has to evaluate whether internal control over financial reporting will achieve its objective. The SEC suggests to set control objectives in order to evaluate whether the controls actually meet these benchmarks. Management's evaluation of the adequacy of the controls is very import for the overall conclusion of effective internal control over financial reporting.[2195] Management has to evaluate and test the operational effectiveness only of the controls identified as adequate to address financial reporting risks.[2196] Besides direct tests, ongoing monitoring of predefined key performance indicators is an important element to evaluate the operational effectiveness of internal control over financial reporting. Due to Item 308 Regulation S-K, management is not permitted to conclude internal control over financial reporting to be effective if one or more material weaknesses exist. Following from sec. 302(a)(6) SOX, management also has to evaluate any changes to internal control over financial reporting.

Under German law, no provision explicitly requires management to evaluate the effectiveness of internal control regarding financial reporting. In sec. 107(3) AktG, the audit committee has the duty to supervise the effectiveness of the internal control system but sec. 107(3) AktG does not provide for any guidance on the level of effectiveness or on requirements regarding internal control. In light of sec. 107(3) and sec. 171(1) AktG and art. 11(2)(j) Regulation (EU) No 537/2014 as well as sec. 289(4) HGB, the management board has incentives to deal with the effectiveness of internal control regarding financial reporting in order to ensure that no significant deficiencies exist within the system. In order to evaluate the effectiveness of internal control, German best practice requires German corporation to define benchmarks considering COSO I and COSO II. The evaluation, however, is not as far reaching as the evaluation of required by sec. 404(a)(2) SOX.

In addition, German law does not require a specific level of proficiency and effectiveness for the implemented internal control system or a threshold to conclude internal control to be effective. Nevertheless, IDW PS 261 provides for an interpretation of the term "significant deficiencies" representing a deficiency of the internal control system which the external auditor considers as relevant for the supervisory board.[2197] Also, using one of the COSO frameworks to evaluate the effectiveness of internal control over financial reporting has been suggested. Absent a more specific standard,

---

2195 See *supra* at chapter 4, A. II. 2. b) (3).
2196 See *supra* at chapter 4, A. II. 2. b) (2).
2197 Cf. IDW PS 261, mar. 89.

the general standard of liability requiring the members of the management and supervisory boards to act with the care of a prudent businessman represents the required level of effectiveness. Hence, any internal control system may be considered effective which fulfills the minimum requirements for such system pursuant to sec. 76 combined with sec. 93 AktG.

The impact of sec. 404(a)(2) SOX on German corporations listed on the NYSE is high. Management is mandated to conduct and document an evaluation of the effectiveness of internal control over financial reporting considering an epic amount of guidance from the SEC.[2198] The incentives for management from German law to conduct an evaluation of the effectiveness do neither have the scope nor detailed guidelines to be followed. At least the wide scope of the internal control system addressed in sec. 107(3) AktG including all three COSO components for internal control correlates with the SEC expectations for the evaluation. The evaluation requirement leads the management board of German corporations listed on the NYSE to conduct the evaluation of internal control over financial reporting and to direct considerably more resources towards the evaluation process. In addition, the reporting requirement provides incentives to implement effective internal control over financial reporting.

(3) External Auditor's Attestation on Management's Assessment – Section 404(b) SOX

Due to sec. 404(b) SOX, the SEC promulgated rules for the external auditor's attestation on management's assessment of the effectiveness of internal control over financial reporting.[2199] The external auditor has to state the opinion whether, in all material respect, the corporation maintained effective internal control over financial reporting. Moreover, the external auditor also has to attest to the assessment of management complying with PCAOB AS 5.[2200] The corporation has to include the attestation report of the external auditor on the assessment of management's evaluation of the effectiveness of internal control over financial reporting within the annual report (Item 308(b) Regulation S-K).

In Germany, the evaluation of the effectiveness of internal control regarding financial reporting by the external auditor is rather limited. The

2198 See *supra* at chapter 4, A. II. 2. b).
2199 See *supra* at chapter 4, A. II. 5.
2200 See *supra* at chapter 4, B.

external auditor only has to evaluate the effectiveness in order to determine the scope of testing required for the audit (IDW PS 261) and to report significant deficiencies to the audit committee (sec. 171(1) AktG and art. 11(2)(j) Regulation (EU) No 537/2014). The auditing standard IDW PS 261, which also addresses significant deficiencies, builds on COSO I but does not include any benchmarks or key performance indicators to evaluate the effectiveness. In addition, the auditing standard provides for ample leeway to evaluate the effectiveness. In light of sec. 107(3)(s. 2) AktG, it has been stressed that the supervisory board does not have the means to directly access information from within the corporation leading to the suggestion to commission an enhanced audit including the systems enumerated in sec. 107(3)(s. 2) AktG.[2201] Such audit would also use the applicable auditing standards including IDW PS 261 and IDW PS 980 and would only intensify the audit with regard to the general elements of a compliance program. Since the level of proficiency for internal control regarding financial reporting of IDW PS 261 is not comparable with the sec. 404(a) SOX mandates, the suggested evaluation by commissioning an enhanced audit does not have a similar scope than sec. 404(b) SOX. Moreover, the corporation does not have to report on the commissioned audit.

The requirement to assess management's evaluation of the effectiveness of internal control over financial reporting by the external auditor pursuant to sec. 404(b) SOX provides for a high impact on German corporations listed on the NYSE. They have to provide for accurate documentation in order to allow the external auditor to conduct its assessment. Moreover, the attestation requirement together with detailed parameters for the evaluation including the duty to report the attestation leads management to actually implement effective internal control over financial reporting as required by sec. 404 SOX.

(4) Different Shareholder Structures in the U.S. and Germany

The impact level of sec. 404 SOX on German corporations listed on the NYSE depends on the shareholder structure of each specific corporation. In general, shareholder structures in the U.S. and Germany are different. In the U.S., dispersed ownership prevails while institutional blockholdings

2201 *Wohlmannstetter*, ZGR 2010, 472, 484; cf. *Nonnenmacher/Pohle/v. Werder*, DB 2009, 1447, 1451.

are more common in Germany.[2202] In addition, banks are also strong shareholders in German corporations exercising influence on management[2203] but usually did not hold more than 25%[2204]. The strong position of banks in Germany is a result of the German financial system which has been predominantly bank-based with regard to corporate finance and only within the last decade the German capital market developed taking its share in corporate finance.[2205] The difference in shareholder structure generates different corporate governance issues.[2206] In a dispersed ownership setting, shareholder control on management is especially limited due to the informational asymmetry[2207] and the free rider problem[2208] leading management to expropriate shareholders through earnings management induced by incentive-based compensation.[2209] In order to address the issues revealed by the 2000s scandals in the U.S., SOX has been enacted to repress earnings management through effective internal control over financial reporting and by restructuring the auditing "circuitry" within the corporation.[2210]

In an institutional blockholding shareholder structure also termed concentrated ownership structure, however, the controlling shareholder has a firmer grip on management and does not rely on "indirect mechanisms of control" to the same extent as in the dispersed ownership setting.[2211] Also, the controlling shareholder has "less interest in the day-to-day stock price" of the corporation and makes less use of incentive-based compensation.[2212] Nevertheless, concentrated ownership leads to a different type of expropri-

---

2202 *Wackerbarth*, ZGR 2005, 686, 692 et seq.; *Coffee*, 2005, p. 2; *Stoltenberg/Lacey/George/Cuthbert*, 53 Am. J. Comp. L. 457 (2005), p. 486 et seq.; cf. *Franks/Mayer*, 14 Rev. Financ. Stud. 943 (2001), p. 947; *Möllers*, ECFR 2007, 173, 174 et seq.

2203 *Stamm*, 32 Ga. J. Int'l & Comp. L. 813 (2004), p. 829 et seq.

2204 *Franks/Mayer*, 14 Rev. Financ. Stud. 943 (2001), p. 947.

2205 *Detzer/Dodig/Evans/Hein/Herr*, 2013, p. 20; *Rudolf*, in: Unternehmensfinanzierung, sec. 1, mar. 7 et seq. and mar. 71 et seq.; *Merkt*, AG 2003, 126, 127 et seq.; *Assmann*, FS Kümpel, 1, 3; *Schmidt/Tyrell*, 2003, p. 32; arguing for a shift from bank-based corporate finance to capital market-based corporate finance: *Fleischer*, ZIP 2006, 451, 453.

2206 *Davies/Hopt*, 2013, p. 42; *Hopt*, ZHR 175 (2011), 444, 449; *Stoltenberg/Lacey/George/Cuthbert*, 53 Am. J. Comp. L. 457 (2005), p. 486; *Coffee*, 2005, p. 15.

2207 *Davies/Hopt*, 2013, p. 42 noting the basic principal-agent conflict in a dispersed ownership setting.

2208 See *supra* at chapter 1, A.

2209 Cf. *Coffee*, 2005, p. 3 et seq.

2210 *Coffee*, 2005, p. 11 and p. 17.

2211 *Coffee*, 2005, p. 11.

2212 *Coffee*, 2005, p. 11.

ation: "the extraction of private benefits of control" to the detriment of minority shareholders.[2213] The controlling shareholder may dilute ownership followed by a tender offer or squeeze-out merger below fair market value or may engage in related party transactions to the detriment of the corporation.[2214] Such kind of fraud is less likely to be resolved by enhancing internal control.[2215] Rather, different regulation is required to address self-dealing.[2216] For the U.S. it has been noted that increasing auditor and audit committee independence is also less likely to restrain controlling shareholders since even independent auditors and independent directors "may serve at the pleasure of a controlling shareholder".[2217] Hence, enhancing the auditing process and internal control is less effective to tackle fraud occurring within concentrated ownership settings.[2218] Nevertheless, effective internal control is important within corporations with concentrated ownership since accurate financial statements are important to effectuate several measures protecting minority shareholders such as reporting on related party transactions pursuant to sec. 285(no. 21) HGB considering no. 7.1.4 GCGC, sec. 314(1)(no. 13) HGB, or sec. 315a(1) HGB combined with IAS 24 (related party disclosures)[2219], as well as to support evaluations of an adequate compensation e.g. in a squeeze-out according to sec. 327a AktG. Also, the general compliance program needs to focus on fraudulent behavior to the detriment of the minority shareholders. In essence, the focus of U.S. internal control provisions on financial reporting issues of corporations with dispersed ownership impacts German corporations listed on the NYSE, as far as their ownership structure is mainly characterized by blockholdings, by requiring these corporations to implement internal control over financial reporting with an unnecessary strong focus on financial fraud such as earnings management leading to inefficiencies within internal control over financial reporting.[2220] Otherwise, the SEC rules on the effectiveness of internal control over financial reporting do not mandate a specific set of controls providing flexibility for corporations for how to design and operate their internal control over financial reporting. German

---

2213 *Coffee*, 2005, p. 12. Similar: *Davies/Hopt*, 2013, p. 42.
2214 *Coffee*, 2005, p. 13 et seq.
2215 *Coffee*, 2005, p. 15 et seq.
2216 *Davies/Hopt*, 2013, p. 42 et seq. noting the example of German group law to address self-dealing.
2217 *Coffee*, 2005, p. 15 et seq.
2218 Cf. *Coffee*, 2005, p. 18.
2219 Cf. *Poelzig*, in: Münch Komm HGB, sec. 314, mar. 85.
2220 Similar: *Wackerbarth*, ZGR 2005, 686, 709.

corporations have the opportunity to design internal control over financial reporting with the needs of a corporation with concentrated ownership as long as every financial reporting risk is addressed by one adequate control assuring the effectiveness of internal control over financial reporting as defined by Exchange Act Rule 12b-2. The COSO I framework provides for the needed flexibility to design internal control over financial reporting suitable for concentrated ownership structures. Therefore, German corporations with concentrated ownership are generally able to use COSO I to design and operate internal control over financial reporting fulfilling the effectiveness criterion of the SEC without the inefficiencies of U.S.-style internal control over financial reporting designed for dispersed ownership structures. It follows that German corporations with concentrated ownership structure are able to reduce the inefficiencies associated with U.S.-style internal control over financial reporting. As long as the shareholder structure of the German corporation is dispersed, no additional impact occurs besides the already depicted impact of sec. 404 SOX.

d) The Impact of Section 301 SOX – Direct Communication Lines and Anonymous Reporting

With regard to the impact of the audit committee, the scope of the thesis is limited to aspects concerning internal control and compliance. Due to sec. 301 SOX, the audit committee has to be comprised of solely independent directors. The issue has been raised that employee representatives as members of the supervisory board would not fulfill the independence requirements of sec. 301 SOX to serve on the audit committee.[2221] The SEC, however, realized the issue and promulgated exceptions for foreign corporations regarding the independence requirement of employee representatives serving on the audit committee.[2222] Also, sec. 301 SOX transposed by Exchange Act Rule 10A-3 requires corporations to implement direct procedures for anonymous reporting of financial reporting issues. In light of the disclosure requirement of Item 407(f) Regulation S-K and Rule 303A.03 NYSE-LCM, the communication procedure of Rule 10A-3 Exchange Act should be extended from the audit committee to all non-management and independent directors and should be opened for shareholders. In difference to the independence requirement, sec. 301 SOX and related best prac-

2221 *Kersting*, ZIP 2003, 233, 238 et seq.
2222 See *supra* at chapter 4, A. IV. 1.

tice are not covered by the subordination rule of the Instruction no. 2 to Exchange Act Rule 10A-3. As it has been indicated above, direct communication lines from within the corporation contradict the general information regime in German corporate law causing friction between German and U.S. law.[2223] Within a two-tier board system, extending the communication lines from the audit committee to the whole supervisory board does not affect the friction since the whole board has collective responsibility for monitoring the management board. Likewise, shareholder communication to the supervisory board does not contradict German corporate law. It is part of good corporate governance that the owners of the corporation communicate with their representatives.[2224] Similar to direct communication lines, anonymous reporting causes difficulties under German law. The occurring friction due to direct reporting lines and anonymous reporting will be discussed below[2225].

In addition, in-house lawyers may be required, depending on the circumstances, to report evidence of material violations of U.S. securities law or breach of fiduciary duty or similar violations by the corporation or its agents to the audit committee in light of sec. 307 SOX leading to a similar impact as the procedures required by sec. 301 SOX. But German corporations may limit the impact of sec. 307 SOX with regard to non-U.S. in-house lawyers by requiring its in-house lawyers to always appear before the SEC "in consultation with" a U.S. lawyer in order to opt out of this reporting obligation.[2226] In addition, German corporations have incentives to limit the access of their U.S. in-house lawyers to information which these in-house lawyers would need to report pursuant to sec. 307 SOX. As far as the reporting concerns criminal behavior is concerned, the reporting obligation pursuant to sec. 307 SOX does not lead to further friction, since employees may directly report information regarding criminal behavior to the supervisory board according to German corporate law.[2227]

2223 See *supra* at chapter 12, B. I. 1. c) (1).
2224 Cf. *Hopt/Roth*, in: Großkomm AktG, sec. 111, mar. 538.
2225 See *infra* at chapter 12, B. I. 2. b).
2226 See *supra* at chapter 4, A. IV. 2.
2227 See *supra* at chapter 8, B. II. 1. c).

e) The Impact of Whistleblower Protection – Sections 806, 1107 SOX and Section 922 Dodd-Frank Act

With regard to whistleblower protection, corporations need to ensure whistleblower protection pursuant to sec. 806, 1107 SOX and sec. 922 Dodd-Frank Act. Under German law, no explicit statutory provision exists protecting whistleblowers against retaliation.[2228] Hence, U.S. law impacts German corporations listed on the NYSE by requiring whistleblower protection. From a U.S. standpoint, whistleblower protection is not limited to U.S. whistleblowers since sec. 922(a)(6) Dodd-Frank Act defines a whistleblower to be "any individual". Ensuring whistleblower protection limits the ability of the corporation to retaliate against any whistleblower due to any lawful act. Besides this limitation, no further impact or friction occurs for German corporations especially against the background that the main argument of German lawmakers against implementing whistleblower protection in Germany are concerns regarding the necessity of such protection.[2229]

Whistleblower protection and rewards for whistleblower aim to increase the incentives for individuals to blow the whistle. It follows that corporations listed on the NYSE have to consider the increased likelihood for whistleblowing.

f) The Impact of Further SOX Mandates and Best Practice

Other provisions of SOX and U.S. best practice address internal control issues. Corporations need to implement a code of ethics for senior financial personnel pursuant to sec. 406 SOX. Following from Rule 303A.10 NYSE-LCM, best practice requires German corporations listed on the NYSE to adopt a code of business conduct and ethics.[2230] Under German law, no statutory provision expressly requires to implement such code but implementing a code of conduct constitutes a minimum requirement for the compliance organization of German corporations.[2231] The elements of the code of ethics pursuant to sec. 406 SOX and the code of business conduct and ethics do not contradict German law and mostly state self-evident mat-

2228 See *supra* at chapter 8, D.
2229 See *infra* at chapter 20, A. II. 3.
2230 See *supra* at chapter 4, D. I. 1.
2231 See *supra* at chapter 8, B. I. 3. b) (2).

ters of ethical and lawful behavior. Hence, German corporations listed on the NYSE have to implement these codes, complying with German law, potentially improving the corporate culture, but no further impact will occur.

With regard to sec. 407(a) SOX, corporations are required to disclose whether the audit committee is comprised of at least one member who is a financial expert, as defined by the SEC[2232], or to explain why not. In Germany due to sec. 100(5) AktG, a financial expert in accounting or annual audit has to serve on the audit committee or the supervisory board, in case no audit committee exists, of a German corporation. How the person acquired her specific knowledge is irrelevant. While sec. 407 SOX constitutes a comply-or-explain approach, corporations have incentives to have a financial expert on the audit committee fulfilling the requirements set out by the SEC. The SEC requirements are more detailed and exceed the sec. 100(5) AktG spectrum by requiring specifically an understanding of internal controls and procedures for financial reporting as well as an understanding of audit committee functions.[2233] Vice versa, a financial expert fulfilling the SEC requirements will fulfill the German requirements if she has knowledge of IFRS besides the SEC required knowledge of U.S. GAAP. Hence, German corporations listed on the NYSE have to observe the higher and more detailed U.S. standard regarding the financial expert who must serve on the audit committee.

Besides statutory mandates, German corporations listed on the NYSE need to have an audit committee pursuant to Rule 303A.06 NYSE-LCM. While sec. 107(3) AktG does not mandate to implement an audit committee, the impact of Rule 303A.06 NYSE-LCM is marginal, since almost all large, listed German corporations have implemented an audit committee. In addition, U.S. best practice following from the NYSE-LCM includes that the purpose of the audit committee is to assist the board of director's oversight of integrity of the corporation's financial statements, the corporation's compliance with legal and regulatory requirements, and the performance of the corporation's internal audit function pursuant to Rule 303A.07(b)(i)(A) NYSE-LCM. Likewise, sec. 107(3)(s. 2) AktG has a similar scope of duties for the audit committee so that the requirements of Rule 303A.07(b)(i)(A) NYSE-LCM do not impact German corporations listed on the NYSE. Also, pursuant to Rule 303A.11 NYSE-LCM, listed foreign corporations must disclose any significant differences between the actual

2232 See SEC Release No. 8177, at II, 4, c and *supra* at chapter 4, A. IV. 1.
2233 See *supra* at chapter 4, A. IV. 1.

followed corporate governance practice and those followed by U.S. domestic corporations under NYSE listing standards. Besides the need to disclose existing difference, the Rule 303A.11 NYSE-LCM only induces corporations to follow U.S. best practice up to the point when marginal benefits of reducing the difference to U.S. domestic corporations for attracting U.S. investors equal marginal costs associated with U.S. best practice. At last, the mandate to notify the NYSE in case an executive officer becomes aware of any non-compliance with any applicable provision pursuant to Rule 303A NYSE-LCM requires German corporations listed on the NYSE to implement measures to ensure adequate reporting.

g) The Impact Regarding Internal Audit

In the U.S., corporations have to implement an independent and accurately operating internal audit function observing IIA standards.[2234] Internal audit has to provide for an ongoing assessment of the corporation's risk management process and internal control including separate evaluations and walkthroughs. With regard to internal control, internal audit has to evaluate the adequacy, effectiveness, and efficiency of internal control including the promotion of continuous improvements. Internal audit has to be a link between external auditors and management and has to provide accurate information to the audit committee.

In Germany, internal audit is required as part of the early warning system pursuant to sec. 91(2) AktG.[2235] Similar to the U.S., the IIA standards have been adopted by the DIIR and are also applicable in Germany. Therefore, the applicable professional standards are generally similar. The role of internal audit is more distinctive in the U.S. than in Germany especially regarding the duties concerning the audit committee. In Germany, the responsibility for internal audit rests with the management board and may not be transferred to the supervisory board.[2236] Likewise, internal audit may not focus its work on the monitoring duties of the supervisory board.[2237] Hence, the authority to issue instructions has to remain with the management board.[2238] The supervisory board may only require the man-

2234 See *supra* at chapter 4, E.
2235 See *supra* at chapter 8, B. I. 2. b) (1).
2236 *Lanfermann/Röhricht*, BB 2009, 887, 890.
2237 *Lanfermann/Röhricht*, BB 2009, 887, 890.
2238 *Lanfermann/Röhricht*, BB 2009, 887, 890.

agement board to implement an adequate internal audit and to provide information on the work of internal audit.[2239] Therefore, German corporations listed on the NYSE have to implement a more distinctive internal audit function fulfilling U.S. requirements. The friction regarding the direct reporting lines of internal audit to the audit committee will be discussed subsequently.

2. Friction Occurring Between German Law and U.S. Law

German corporations listed on the NYSE are not only impacted for being subject to U.S. law and best practice. Most of the U.S. provisions addressing internal control enhance the level of proficiency compared to the German standard and require measures not known to German law but do not interfere with the German regulatory framework. Two mandates of sec. 10A(m)(4)(A) Exchange Act – implemented by sec. 301 SOX and, pursuant to Exchange Act Rule 10A-3, part of the NYSE listing standards[2240] – associated with internal control as well as U.S. best practice, however, cause friction with German law. First, direct communication lines to the audit committee, and, second, the requirement to provide for means for anonymous reporting. These two mandates do not fit into German law. In the following, the extent to which these mandates cause friction will be analyzed.

a) Direct Communication Lines to the Audit Committee and Supervisory Board

Under German corporate law, the management board has the monopoly with regard to providing information within the corporation. It is one of the core obligations of the management board to report to the supervisory board. Due to such monopoly, the supervisory board may directly use the general information system of the corporation only in extreme cases, such as misconduct of members of the management board, to receive information circumventing the management board.[2241] In difference to the independent directors of U.S. corporations, the supervisory board does not

---

2239 Cf. *Lanfermann/Röhricht*, BB 2009, 887, 890.
2240 See *supra* at chapter 4, D. I. 1.
2241 See *supra* at chapter 8, B. II. 1. c).

have direct responsibility for and access to internal audit as a source of information. Therefore, direct communication lines for general information circumventing the management board is generally prohibited under German law. Only direct communication lines to the supervisory board concerning information regarding criminal behavior of employees or even the management board are acceptable which includes reporting due to sec. 307 SOX. In the more recent German literature, the general need of senior officers to report to the audit committee, mirroring the U.S. approach, has been claimed to represent good corporate governance[2242] demonstrating a further aspect of U.S. corporate governance impacting German corporate governance through reference by German scholars. Despite any specific right to establish communication lines and to question employees, the supervisory board and the management board may mutually agree on reporting duties of executive staff such as the CCO, GC, and head of internal audit to the supervisory board or the audit committee.[2243] These kind of reporting obligations have become best practice within German corporations.

For the analysis, it has to be pointed out that sec. 301 SOX and related regulation does not require direct communication lines to the audit committee concerning general information on the corporation. Sec. 301 SOX only requires communication lines for complaints limited to questionable matters concerning auditing and financial aspects of the corporation. Such kind of complaints affects potential non-compliance with accounting and auditing matters. Under German law, such concerns have to be raised primarily with supervisors, internal audit, or other appropriate offices below the supervisory board level. Nevertheless, even under the prerogative of information for the management board, the supervisory board does not have to be isolated from the corporation. The current process of developing German law regarding corporate governance towards more direct information, on general topics, for the supervisory board from within the corporation, with or without a closely involved management board, clearly shows that direct communication lines to the audit committee regarding questionable accounting and auditing matters does only lead to little or no fric-

2242 E.g. *Schneider, S. H.*, Informationspflichten, p. 107 (citing *Schwarz/Holland*, Enron, Worldcom… und die Corporate-Governance-Diskussion, ZIP 2002, 1661); *Leyens*, Aufsichtsrat, p. 191 et seq. and p. 348 et seq.; *Lutter*, FS Hüffer, 617, 619; *Nonnenmacher/Pohle/v. Werder*, DB 2007, 2412, 2415; cf. *Theisen*, Berichterstattung des Aufsichtsrats, pp. 10 and 24. Also *Dreher*, FS Ulmer, 87, 93.

2243 See *supra* at chapter 8, B. II. 1. c).

tion within German law. Despite this analysis, it has been suggested to comply with Exchange Act Rule 10A-3(b)(3) by using a staged approach limiting the accessibility of the audit committee.[2244] Such restrictions, however, contradict the mandates of Exchange Act Rule 10A-3(b)(3). Hence, German corporations listed on the NYSE have to implement direct communication lines.

In difference to the U.S. statutory mandates, U.S. best practice includes direct reporting lines for the GC, CCO, and head of internal audit to the audit committee comprised totally of non-executive or independent directors. While the U.S. and the German audit committee are functionally much alike[2245], direct reporting obligations cause no friction in a one-tier board setting but contradict the current setting of the German two-tier board system.[2246] As an impact of direct communication lines, loss of trust between supervisory board and management board has been named.[2247] The magnitude of the impact on corporation depends on the development in German law regarding direct communication lines. So far, direct reporting has only been established for the external auditor pursuant to sec. 107(3)(s. 2) and sec. 171(1) AktG and art. 11(2)(j) Regulation (EU) No 537/2014. Although based on European legislation, it provides a starting point for an understanding of corporate governance which strengthens the direct flow of information on important matters to the supervisory board as a fundamental part to monitor the management board. In light of the new best practice in Germany of mutually agreed communication and the recent literature on the issue, the impact of direct communication lines is not likely to be so strong any more. It seems that management boards have accepted such kind of communication. Standardized communication obligations with the knowledge of the management board may hardly affect the level of trust between the supervisory board and the management board since supervision and monitoring genuinely include to use means to receive unbiased information.[2248]

2244 *Gruson/Kubicek*, AG 2003, 337, 349.

2245 Cf. *Börsig/Löbbe*, FS Hoffmann-Becking, 125, 131 et seq.; *Cromme*, FS Hoffmann-Becking, 283; *Bezzenberger/Keul*, FS Schwark, 121, 124.

2246 See also *supra* at chapter 8, B. II. 1. c).

2247 *AKEU/AKEIÜ Schmalenbach-Ges.*, DB 2009, 1279, 1282; *v. Rosen*, AG 2008, 537, 538; *Marsch-Barner*, FS Schwark, 219, 226; *Mertens/Cahn*, Köln Komm AktG, sec. 90, mar. 52; cf. *Spindler*, in: Spindler/Stilz, AktG, sec. 109, mar. 22.

2248 Cf. *Hopt/Roth*, in: Großkomm AktG, sec. 111, mar. 512 et seq.

b) Anonymous Whistleblowing

Due to sec. 301 SOX and related rules including NYSE-LCM 303A.06, corporations have to provide for measures to allow anonymous whistleblowing. It has been concluded that U.S.-style anonymous whistleblowing does not fit into German law especially data protection law.[2249] Besides SOX, sec. 8B2.1 (b)(5)(C) USSG encourages, but does not require, anonymous reporting.[2250] The SEC expects all employees of corporations listed on the NYSE to have access to the whistleblowing system.[2251] In the U.S., whistleblowing, especially anonymous whistleblowing, is an important aspect of corporate governance. In Europe and Germany, however, it is associated with denunciation.[2252]

For implementing whistleblowing systems, corporations have to adhere to the BDSG.[2253] With regard to the whistleblowing requirements of SOX, the Art. 29 Working Party concluded that only EU law may provide for a legal mandate to collect data through anonymous reporting but SOX represents in general a legitimate interest to justify the collection.[2254] The justification of the collection of data also requires to consider the interests of accused person under the proportionality principle.[2255] With regard to anonymous reporting, German corporations would be allowed to provide for anonymous reporting but are not allowed to encourage anonymous reporting.[2256] Since sec. 301(4) SOX only requires for anonymous reporting with regard to financial reporting issues, the Art. 29 Working Party concludes that the whistleblowing system should only provide for anonymous reporting as far as required by U.S. law.[2257] The main issue of anonymous reporting remains unsolved despite an intervention of the Art. 29 Working Group by the SEC.[2258] Nevertheless, German law allows corporations in narrow limits to collect data resulting from anonymous tips.[2259] Corpora-

---

2249 *Mahnhold*, NZA 2008, 737, 740. See *supra* at chapter 8, D. II.

2250 See *supra* at chapter 5, C. II. 1.

2251 *Mahnhold*, NZA 2008, 737, 742.

2252 *Reufels/Deviard*, CCZ 2009, 201, 204; cf. *Seffer/Mayer-Wegelin*, ITRB 2009, 41.

2253 See *supra* at chapter 8, D. II.

2254 *Art. 29 Working Party*, 2006, p. 7 et seq.; cf. *Reufels/Deviard*, CCZ 2009, 201, 203.

2255 *Art. 29 Working Party*, 2006, p. 8 et seq.; cf. *Reufels/Deviard*, CCZ 2009, 201, 203.

2256 *Art. 29 Working Party*, 2006, p. 11; cf. *Mahnhold*, NZA 2008, 737, 743; *Düsseldorfer Kreis*, 2007, p. 4 et seq.

2257 Cf. *Art. 29 Working Party*, 2006, p. 5.

2258 Cf. *von Zimmermann*, WM 2007, 1060, 1062.

2259 See *supra* at chapter 8, D. II.

tions have to be aware of the limitations especially resulting from the personal rights of the accused.[2260] German corporations listed on the NYSE may implement communication lines required by sec. 301 SOX including anonymous reporting and are allowed to exercise broader discretion on collecting anonymously provided data against the background of SOX.[2261]

The provided solution under German law for corporations listed on the NYSE essentially yields to U.S. law eliminating the friction. The impact on German corporations listed on the NYSE remains, however, with regard to provide for anonymous reporting and the difficulties to determine how and when to collect data on anonymously provided tips. In addition, the issue of anticipating anonymous whistleblowing with denunciation due to the historical differences between the U.S. and Europe/Germany remains resulting in unease or stronger reactions of employees.

3. Impact on the Incentive Structure Regarding Internal Control

The impact on the incentive structure of German corporations listed on the NYSE with regard to internal control following from sec. 302 and 404 SOX is strong. The U.S. law provides for strong incentives to implement effective disclosure controls and procedures and to evaluate their effectiveness due to the reporting obligation of Item 307 Regulation S-K, liability pursuant to sec. 906 SOX and sec. 18(a) Exchange Act, and SEC enforcement.[2262] In Germany, the incentive structure to implement disclosure controls and procedures is similar to the incentive structure regarding the general compliance program since disclosure controls and procedures are measures to comply with the reporting obligations. Thus, corporations have only incentives to implement a non-effective "paper-tiger" compliance program.[2263] Due to the likelihood that information which the corporation has been required to report under capital markets law becomes public triggering investigations of the BaFin, corporations have higher incentives to implement controls addressing non-financial information required to be disclosed than to implement general compliance measures.

The U.S. incentive level to implement effective disclosure controls and procedures exceeds the German incentive level by far particularly due to

2260 *Casper*, Libor Amicorum Winter, 77, 94.
2261 Cf. *Casper*, Libor Amicorum Winter, 77, 93 et seq.
2262 See *supra* at chapter 4, A. III.
2263 See *supra* at chapter 10, D.

the specific statutory mandate to implement effective controls and SEC enforcement. In particular, liability for violating the duty to monitor pursuant to sec. 76 combined with sec. 93 AktG is less pinpointed than liability for violating sec. 302(a)(4) SOX. If German corporations follow U.S. incentives and implement enhanced disclosure controls and procedures, these controls produce more information within the corporation increasing the level of expected liability for the management board in light of the litigation dilemma. Following from this finding, one would expect that the combined incentive level settles between the U.S. and German level. To the contrary, the U.S. incentives to comply with the U.S. mandates induce full compliance regardless of the German incentives leading the U.S. incentives to dominate the combined incentive level. Hence, being listed on the NYSE shifts the incentive structure to implement internal controls addressing non-financial information subject to reporting obligations but only with regard to controls necessary for sec. 302 SOX-related disclosure controls and procedures.

With regard to internal control over financial reporting, U.S. law provides for even stronger incentives to implement effective internal control over financial reporting due to the required evaluation of management and the external auditor, reporting obligations of Item 308 Regulation S-K, liability pursuant to sec. 906 SOX and sec. 18(a) Exchange Act, and SEC enforcement.[2264] The German incentive structure does not provide for sufficient incentives for corporations to implement effective internal control and risk management systems.[2265] Corporations are only induced to implement internal controls fulfilling minimum legal requirements *prima facie* resulting in non-effective "paper-tiger" programs. With regard to internal control regarding financial reporting, the required attestation of the external auditor leads corporations to implement these controls slightly fulfilling the required auditing standards. As it has been shown above[2266], these standards only provide for an approach toward minimum effective internal control. Moreover regarding the liability pursuant to sec. 906 SOX, it has been noted that sec. 331(no. 3a) HGB provides for strong punishment in Germany.[2267] But sec. 331 HGB would not provide for a similarly severe punishment as sec. 906 SOX.[2268] Hence, the incentive structure for the

2264 See *supra* at chapter 4, A. III.
2265 See *supra* at chapter 10, D.
2266 See *supra* at chapter 12, B. I. 1. c) (3).
2267 *Möllers*, ECFR 2007, 173, 187 et seq.
2268 *Fleischer*, ZIP 2007, 97, 102.

management board of German corporations listed on the NYSE to provide accurate financial statements changes due to higher sanctions and probably additionally increased enforcement. From a German perspective considering that corporations with concentrated ownership are more common leading in general to less financial reporting fraud[2269], the high U.S. sanctions lead to over-deterrence and inefficiencies within German corporations with concentrated ownership.

Due to the listing on the NYSE, German corporations are subject to both incentive structures. Following from the strong U.S. incentives to implement effective internal control over financial reporting adhering to the U.S. standards, one might expect that the impact of the U.S. incentives will lead to an increase of the overall incentive level for these corporations resulting in a level higher than the German level but also lower than the U.S. level. Subsequently, German corporations listed on the NYSE would have suboptimal incentives to follow U.S. mandates leading to implement less than effective internal control over financial reporting. Likewise, these corporations would have suboptimal incentives to follow German mandates leading to implement more than required internal control regarding financial reporting. The result of an overall incentive level between the U.S. level and the German level builds on the assumption that both incentive regimes have the strength to influence one another. This is not the case. The U.S. incentive structure to implement effective internal control over financial reporting fulfilling the U.S. mandates does not provide any leeway not to comply with the mandates. Especially the strict level of effectiveness coupled with the dual audit and the reporting of the results of the audits ensure that corporations comply with the mandates. Therefore, the German incentive structure has no effect on the overall incentive structure of the corporation. Following from strong enforcement of the SEC[2270], German corporations listed on the NYSE adhere to the U.S. mandates.[2271] The U.S. incentive structure for internal control over financial reporting totally replaces the German incentive structure leading to complete U.S.-style internal control over financial reporting within German corporations listed on the NYSE negating German incentives.

Following from the U.S. incentives, German corporations will implement effective internal control over financial reporting. Likewise to U.S. corporations, German corporations are likely to overspend on SOX-related

2269 See *supra* at chapter 12, B. I. 1. c) (4).
2270 Cf. *Möllers*, ECFR 2007, 173, 182.
2271 Cf. *Sieber*, FS Tiedemann, 449, 478. See also *infra* at chapter 14.

internal control. From a German standpoint considering the German incentive structure to implement internal control regarding financial reporting slightly fulfilling the minimum requirements following from the auditing standards, corporations listed on the NYSE will enormously overspend on internal control over financial reporting which relativizes due to the U.S. listing. In addition, depending on the ownership structure of the corporation[2272], the U.S. incentive structure will induce German corporations listed on the NYSE to implement internal control over financial reporting with a sub-optimal focus on financial fraud such as earnings management in case of a concentrated ownership structure.

The U.S. mandates for internal control also impact the CEO and CFO. Following from sec. 302(a)(1) and 302(a)(4) SOX, both officers have direct responsibility for the effectiveness of disclosure controls and procedures and internal control over financial reporting. Due to the specific responsibility of the CEO and CFO, both officers will increase their focus on internal control compared to the German incentive structure based on the collective liability of the management board. Also, the management board has stronger incentives to deal with the effectiveness of internal control over financial reporting pursuant to sec. 404(a)(1) SOX compared to German incentive level particularly since BilMoG assigns the responsibility for the effectiveness of the internal control system to the audit committee and does not directly[2273] impact the responsibility of management. As a further aspect, it has been observed that SOX pushes management to exercise risk-averse business judgment.[2274] At least, management has less leeway to hide unfavorable business outcome.

With regard to the further mandates of SOX, German corporations listed on the NYSE implemented whistleblowing systems providing for anonymous reporting and unrestricted of topics.[2275] This fact indicates that German corporations have more incentives to adhere not even to SOX but to the U.S. best practice to allow for unrestricted anonymous reporting than to avoid data protection law issues in Germany.

The listing standards of the NYSE also impact the incentive structure of German corporations listed on the NYSE. Due to the listing, the German corporation faces several incentives to follow NYSE corporate governance

---

2272 See *supra* at chapter 12, B. I. 1. c) (4).

2273 Cf. *Wolf*, DStR 2009, 920, 924.

2274 *Shishido*, 2008, p. 12.

2275 *Reufels/Deviard*, CCZ 2009, 201, 208 et seq.; *Wisskirchen/Körber/Bissels*, BB 2006, 1567.

standards and NYSE best practice regarding internal control. The specific mandates of Rule 303A NYSE-LCM for German corporations are inevitable in order to be listed on the NYSE. German corporations have an incentive to follow the U.S. best practice in order to attract U.S. and foreign investors. Therefore, German corporations have to minimize the difference of their internal control system with regard to system of U.S. corporations. German corporations have to win the confidence of investors by adhering to the U.S. corporate governance standards which are believed to protect investors. Moreover, German corporations have to adhere to U.S. best practice in order to be able to advertize their compliance with these advanced standards. Since the mandates and best practice of NYSE-LCM hardly provides for an additional impact on German corporations listed on the NYSE compared to the impact of SOX[2276], German corporations have strong incentives to follow NYSE best practice.

4. Conclusion

Being listed on the NYSE impacts German corporations with regard to internal control in various ways. Due to sec. 404 SOX, German corporations have to implement more proficient internal control over financial reporting fulfilling U.S. requirements exceeding by far the early warning system of sec. 91(2) AktG and also exceeding substantially the requirements of internal control regarding financial reporting in light of IDW PS 261 especially with regard to effectiveness. Since both, U.S. and German, mandates for internal control regarding financial reporting are based on COSO I, the general structures of internal control regarding financial reporting are alike reducing the impact. Nevertheless, the U.S. approach towards internal control regarding financial reporting aims for maximum effective internal control while the German approach neglects the aspect of effectiveness leading to minimum effective internal control. The U.S. approach follows a clear concept substantially increasing the required level for effective internal control regarding financial reporting within German corporations listed on the NYSE. Corporations need to implement a fraud risk management system as part of general compliance program. Due to U.S. law, corporations need more documentation of internal control over financial reporting. German corporations are strongly impacted by the mandate to evaluate the effectiveness of internal control over financial reporting and

2276 See *supra* at chapter 12, B. I. 1. f).

the external auditor's attestation of the evaluation as well as the reporting obligation on the results. The enhanced level of effectiveness together with the twofold evaluation of internal control over financial reporting and the reporting obligation lead to truly effective internal control over financial reporting. Depending on the shareholder structure, the U.S. approach to internal control over financial reporting focusing of financial fraud such as earnings management lead to inefficiencies within the internal control system of German corporations with concentrated ownership. The inefficiencies may be reduced by designing and implementing internal control over financial reporting suitable for corporations with concentrated ownership. Due to the enhanced effectiveness and the control paradox, earnings restatements are likely to increase in the beginning.

With regard to sec. 302 SOX, the certification requirement will lead the CEO and CFO to focus on the accuracy of financial reporting and on the implementation of effective disclosure controls and procedures. With regard to the unproblematic, further requirements of SOX, the duty to implement a code of ethics may improve the corporate culture and observing the SEC requirements for the financial expert serving on the audit committee increases the qualification of this expert. Moreover, internal audit has a more distinctive role in the U.S. leading to a more distinctive role of internal audit in German corporations listed on the NYSE.

The problematic requirements of SOX and best practice concern direct reporting obligations to the audit committee including anonymous reporting causing friction with German law due to the two-tier board structure and data protection law. With regard to the direct reporting obligations, sec. 301 SOX communication lines of complaints regarding financial reporting issues is in line with German law allowing for direct access of the supervisory board in case of alleged criminal behavior. Hence, the main impact derives from U.S. best practice rather than from SOX. In light of the newly developed German best practice, considering the U.S. approach of direct reporting leads to reduce any further friction due to direct reporting obligations of senior officers on general information from within the corporation. Depending on the development of corporate governance in Germany, the remaining friction of direct reporting lines will further diminish or even vanish. With regard to anonymous reporting, German law yields to SOX allowing to consider SOX as part of the weighting to justify the collection of anonymously reported data. Nevertheless, German corporations are impact by the difficulties to determine how and when to collect data on anonymously provided tips. Also, German corporations have to cope with potential resentment of the work force regarding anonymous reporting resulting different the historical backgrounds in the U.S. and Germany.

Being listed on the NYSE also affects the incentive structure regarding internal control. The U.S. impact on the incentive structure is strong. The U.S. incentives mainly substitute the German incentives. Following from sec. 302 SOX, German corporations listed on the NYSE have incentives to implement disclosure controls and procedures but only with regard to the controls necessary to comply with sec. 302 SOX. This includes a focus of the CEO and CFO on the effectiveness of disclosure controls and procedures. In light of sec. 404 SOX, the U.S. incentive structure for internal control over financial reporting totally replaces the German incentive structure leading to complete U.S.-style internal control over financial reporting within German corporations listed on the NYSE negating German incentives. The management board has stronger incentives to deal with the effectiveness of internal control over financial reporting. In case of a concentrated ownership structure, the U.S. incentive structure will induce German corporations to implement internal control over financial reporting with a sub-optimal focus on financial fraud. With regard to U.S. best practice especially NYSE related best practice, German corporations have strong incentives to follow such practice.

II. Compliance

In difference to the legal mandates concerning internal control, statutory mandates hardly exist for compliance programs in both jurisdictions. In the U.S., specific mandates for compliance programs are only induced not mandated by the USSG and DOJ enforcement policy. Further elements and incentives derive from *Caremark*, FCPA, and SEC policy. The underlying framework of U.S. compliance is corporate criminal liability. Providing incentives for corporations to implement compliance programs is an important aspect of U.S. compliance. In Germany, the issue of compliance is only evolving and mainly addressed as an element of the duty to manage the corporation pursuant to sec. 76 combined with sec. 93 AktG and the law on administrative offences. Neither the concept of corporate criminal liability nor a comprehensive statutory framework addressing compliance exist within German law. So far, U.S. compliance serves as a role model in Germany.

1. Impact of U.S. Requirements for Compliance on German Corporations

In Germany, the management board has to implement a compliance organization as part of their duty to manage the corporation pursuant to sec. 76 combined with sec. 93 AktG.[2277] In light of sec. 91(2) AktG, compliance with law has to be addressed within the early warning system but only as far as compliance issues constitute a risk endangering the survival of the corporation. The management board has broad discretion for how to design the compliance program considering necessity and appropriateness of such program. Therefore, the board has to implement and operate adequate and effective compliance measures but not necessarily a profound compliance program. As minimum requirements for the compliance program have been named: code of conduct, training programs, monitoring, disciplining of misconduct, hotlines, and documentation. The monitoring duties of sec. 130 OWiG, established by the courts, are also relevant and encompass to assign reasonable responsibility to employees, to provide adequate instructions, to conduct random tests, to document the taken measures, to emphasize that misconduct will not be tolerated, to investigate in case of red flags, to monitor, and to punish misconduct. Furthermore, the compliance program has to address corruption with high priority and also antitrust law violations. For large, listed corporations, the minimum legal standards for the compliance organization converges towards the best practice considering *inter alia* the COSO frameworks and IDW PS 980 which includes to appoint a CCO, to implement whistleblowing measures, and to assess the adequacy and effectiveness of the compliance organization. In this regard, the culture of compliance is one of the most important factors to render compliance measures effective.

In the U.S., following from the FCPA[2278], corporations have incentives to implement an anti-bribery compliance system to ensure compliance with sec. 30A Exchange Act by using COSO I and elements derived from the DOJ enforcement policy including to appoint a CCO with direct reporting lines, independent audits by outside counsel and auditors of the anti-bribery compliance program to ensure its effectiveness; reporting system without fear of retaliation, an anti-bribery committee to supervise any retention process in a foreign jurisdiction; FCPA audits within the corporation with specific attention to FCPA related red flags; and ongoing identification of red flags. In order to assess corruption risks, management has to

2277 See *supra* at chapter 8, B. I. 3. b).
2278 See *supra* at chapter 5, A. I.

evaluate the detection and prevention controls regarding corruption. In addition, corporations have incentives to comply with the requirement of an effective compliance and ethics program following from the USSG[2279] and the DOJ enforcement policy[2280] which includes whistleblowing not exceeding SOX requirements for anonymous reporting.

Similarly, the SEC Seaboard Report[2281] induces essentially to implement a compliance program essentially fulfilling USSG requirements. Furthermore, U.S. best practice consists of Delaware law[2282] which established in *Caremark* the duty of directors to control the corporation including an effective internal control structure and compliance measures which include information and reporting systems. Also, Rule 303A.07(b)(i)(A) NYSE-LCM induces to include compliance as part of audit committee's duties.

The impact on German corporations listed on the NYSE with regard to compliance requirements started with the Siemens scandal. Prior, compliance was not on the agenda of German corporations despite numerous listings on the NYSE. Also, the extraterritorial application of the FCPA had been neglected. In the aftermath of the Siemens scandal, U.S. compliance has become a prominent role model in Germany. As a consequence of the listing of German corporations on the NYSE and the extraterritorial application of the FCPA, the current German best practice is mainly based on U.S. compliance concepts and reflects elements of COSO I and COSO II as well as the USSG.[2283] In particular, IDW PS 980 is *inter alia* based on COSO II and the USSG. It has also been suggested to use the USSG as reference points to design German compliance programs.[2284] Thus, the impact on German corporations has been high in the beginning but diminishes by the ratio of U.S. compliance concepts becoming part of German best practice. At present, the impact has become relatively low since the legal requirements for compliance in the U.S. and Germany have become similar in a process of convergence.

With regard to codes of conduct, the participation of the work councils may be required in Germany.[2285] While labor law may limit the scope of the codes of conduct, the plain mandates of SOX and the NYSE-LCM do not contradict German labor law. No U.S. legal mandate requires provi-

---

2279 See *supra* at chapter 5, C.
2280 See *supra* at chapter 5, D.
2281 See *supra* at chapter 5, E.
2282 See *supra* at chapter 5, F.
2283 See *supra* at chapter 12, A. III.
2284 *Engelhart*, Sanktionierung, p. 711; *Bachmann/Prüfer*, ZRP 2005, 109, 113.
2285 See *supra* at chapter 8, D. I.

sions for a code of conduct violating German labor law. Also in the aftermath of the Siemens scandal, internal investigations have evolved in Germany as an element to investigate suspicious behavior. While they are needed within the U.S. for providing information to law enforcement in order to receive leniency for cooperation, they may be required in light of sec. 76 combined with sec. 93 AktG in Germany to investigate alleged corporate crime.[2286]

2. Impact on the Incentive Structure Regarding Compliance

The impact of the U.S. incentive structure regarding compliance on the German incentive structure is strong. The U.S. incentive structure[2287] is characterized by inducing prevention and policing measures including compliance measures, self-reporting, cooperation, and remediation. The main underlying aspect of the U.S. incentive structure is corporate criminal liability linked with granting leniency. With regard to compliance measures, corporations have incentives to implement compliance programs which fairly fulfill the USSG requirements but lack sufficient incentives to implement truly effective compliance programs even though aspects of the compliance program should be part of the sec. 404(a) SOX evaluation. Also in light of *Caremark* reflecting best practice for German corporations listed on the NYSE, the incentive level does not lead corporations to implement "truly" effective compliance programs. While *Caremark* highlighted the need to do something and eliminated the option of directors to ignore compliance measures altogether, startling corporate America, the following case law clearly shows that the standard directors have to meet to avoid liability is still low.[2288] Differently, corporations have strong incentives to self-report, cooperate, and accept responsibility in order to obtain non- and deferred prosecution agreements especially with regard to FCPA violations as well as to obtain leniency. The compliance program will provide information necessary for self-reporting. Costs associate with the litigation dilemma remain since receiving leniency based on the DOJ enforcement policy is difficult to predict and not certain. Moreover, the *respondeat superior* principle applies to many federal criminal statues[2289] leading to a

2286 *Wagner*, CCZ 2009, 8, 10 and 13; *Fleischer*, AG 2003, 291, 294.
2287 See *supra* at chapter 6, B.
2288 See *supra* at chapter 5, F. I.
2289 *Garrett*, 97 Va. L. Rev. 1775 (2011), p. 1789.

broad scope of potential criminal charges and identifying the culpable agent is not strictly necessary.

In Germany, the management board of large, listed corporations has generally not sufficient incentives from civil and administrative liability to implement proficient compliance measures.[2290] While the incentive level increased as a result of the recent corporate scandals, the lack of providing leniency for implemented policing measures leads management to implement non-effective "paper-tiger" compliance organizations fulfilling minimum requirements *prima facie*. Likewise, the management board has hardly any incentives following from sec. 130 OWiG and sec. 30 OWiG to engage in effective policing measures.[2291] Incentives mainly exist from avoiding loss of reputation due to criminal acts of employees and through law enforcement investigations. In difference to U.S. corporate criminal liability[2292], the expected liability is even lower with regard to sec. 30 OWiG since enforcement agencies have to prove a connecting crime of a specific individual corporate agent.[2293] With regard to sec. 130 OWiG, identifying the culpable agent is also not strictly necessary.

With regard to *ex ante* policing measures including compliance measures, German corporations listed on the NYSE have incentives following from the U.S. incentive structure to engage in non-effective, window-dressing compliance programs in order to obtain leniency. Large, listed German corporations have similar incentives from German law to fulfilling minimum requirements *prima facie*. This finding also holds in light of *Caremark* since the German standard of care in corporate law is comparable to the standard established in *Caremark*.

The main difference between the incentives structures is that the DOJ enforcement policy and the USSG provide for leniency for implemented *ex ante* policing measures and the scope of potential criminal liability is broader due to *respondeat superior* principle. The situation in Germany is just the opposite. Instead of granting leniency for implemented *ex ante* policing measures, courts tend to use hindsight knowledge to judge whether an implemented monitoring system has been effective leading corporations to refrain from implementing monitoring systems. In addition, U.S. law enforcement seems in general more active than German law enforcement increasing the expected liability for German corporations list-

2290 See *supra* at chapter 10, B.
2291 See *supra* at chapter 8, E. III. 3.
2292 See *supra* at chapter 5, B.
2293 See *supra* at chapter 8, E. III.

ed on the NYSE. Hence, the incentives for German corporations to engage in non-effective, window-dressing *ex ante* policing measures including compliance programs increase compared to the German incentive structure.

With regard to *ex post* policing measures including self-reporting and cooperation, German corporations have hardly any incentives to engage in these measures following from German law due to the lack of provisions to grant leniency even though German corporations may be punished, despite the lack of corporate criminal liability, based on German administrative law[2294]. In contrast, German corporations have incentives to refrain from producing information and to hold back such information in order to avoid prosecutorial investigations and indictment. Only if prosecutorial investigations are imminent or after prosecutors initiated investigations, corporations have incentives to self-report and cooperate with law enforcement agencies as well as initiate internal investigations with the aim to avoid or terminate prosecutorial investigations. While it has been noted that sanctions in Germany and U.S. would be more or less the same[2295], U.S. criminal law is more penalizing than that of other countries providing substantial fines for corporations.[2296] These factors render cooperation with U.S. prosecutors inevitable.[2297] The Siemens case shows the strong incentives for foreign corporation to comply with U.S. regulation potentially prioritizing this regulation over domestic regulation.[2298] Hence, German corporations have incentives to implement compliance programs fulfilling the requirements *prima facie*. But the U.S. incentives for self-reporting, cooperation, and remediation have a strong impact on German corporations listed on the NYSE regardless of the lack of German law to provide for leniency.

III. Impact of U.S. Law and Best Practice on Corporate Governance

Due to SOX, the enlargement of internal audit departments[2299] and the installing CCOs[2300] are the most visible effects within the structural gover-

---

2294 *Beale/Adam*, 8 Buffalo Crim. L. Rev. 89 (2005), p. 123.
2295 *v. Rosen*, in: Unternehmensstrafrecht, 263, 264.
2296 *Garrett*, 97 Va. L. Rev. 1775 (2011), pp. 1778 and 1790.
2297 *Garrett*, 97 Va. L. Rev. 1775 (2011), p. 1778.
2298 *Garrett*, 97 Va. L. Rev. 1775 (2011), p. 1793.
2299 Cf. *Clark*, 22 Ga. St. U. L. Rev. 251 (2005), p. 264.
2300 *Carney*, 55 Emory L. J. 141 (2006), p. 146.

nance of corporations due to higher responsibilities within the overall auditing process, internal controls, and compliance. Their importance as gatekeepers and as a link between external auditors and management has increased fundamentally. Moreover, the requirements of implementing, evaluating, and auditing internal controls have the potential to break up the internal governance structure of corporations[2301] leading to greater transparency of the control efforts since more departments and employees are involved in the process[2302]. Due to the increase of transparency, risk taking will be closer moved into the spotlight requiring the internal governance structure to account for enterprise risk[2303] moving internal controls over financial reporting closer to risk management including compliance with law and operational controls.[2304]

Also with regard to the DOJ enforcement policy, corporations have to restructure their corporate governance. As part of the cooperating process, U.S. prosecution requires foreign corporations to restructure their corporate governance structure.[2305] Siemens is one prominent example of such practice. In its statement of offence, Siemens pledged to implement a new compliance program to detect and prevent FCPA violations, and hired a corporate monitor.[2306]

In light of NYSE-best practice, German corporations listed on the NYSE voluntarily follow(-ed) NYSE listing standards as far as permitted by German law except for the various committees only mandated for U.S. corporations.[2307]

IV. No Impact from U.S. Law and Best Practice on Risk Management

Despite the portrayed impact of U.S. requirements regarding internal control and compliance, U.S. law and best practice do not affect risk management. In contrast to the U.S., risk management is part of German corporate and regulatory law. In light of BilMoG sec. 107(3) AktG, the risk management system is also part of the duty to manage the corporation pur-

---

2301 *Langevoort*, 105 Mich. L. Rev. 1817 (2007), p. 1830.

2302 *Langevoort*, 31 J. Corp. L. 949 (2006), p. 969.

2303 See in general for enterprise risk management *supra* at chapter 4, C. III.

2304 *Langevoort*, 105 Mich. L. Rev. 1817 (2007), p. 1830 et seq.

2305 *Garrett*, 97 Va. L. Rev. 1775 (2011), p. 1783. See also *Kaal/Lacine*, 2014.

2306 Cf. *Garrett*, 97 Va. L. Rev. 1775 (2011), p. 1787; *U.S. v. Siemens*, Statement of Offense, attachment 1, mar. 1 et seq.

2307 See *supra* at chapter 4, D. I. 1.

suant to sec. 76 combined with sec. 93 AktG. Therefore, the terminology in Germany is closer to COSO II "risk management systems" than in U.S. COSO I "internal control". In the U.S., COSO II is not used for internal control and compliance.[2308] The finding holds especially in light of *Citigroup* holding that business risk is not part of *Caremark*.[2309]

V. Conclusion

Besides the obvious impact of adhering to the local law in case of being listed on the NYSE, the most important impact originates from sec. 404 SOX by requiring to implement effective internal control over financial reporting fulfilling the maximum approach of U.S. law. The evaluation and reporting mandates of sec. 302 and 404 SOX are also unknown to German corporations which ensure truly effective internal control. In addition, in case of concentrated ownership, the U.S. mandates will lead to inefficiencies of internal control over financial reporting. The occurring friction between U.S. and German law is rather limited and originates from side aspects of internal control. With regard to compliance, the impact had been high in the beginning of the Siemens scandal but diminishes since U.S. compliance concepts become part of German best practice. German corporations have incentives to implement compliance programs fulfilling the U.S. requirements *prima facie*. But the U.S. incentives for self-reporting, cooperation, and remediation have a strong impact on German corporations listed on the NYSE regardless of the lack of German law to provide for leniency. While there has been no impact on risk management systems, the U.S. impact on the governance structure of corporations is high.

2308 See *supra* at chapter 4, C. III.

2309 See *supra* at chapter 5, F.

Chapter 13: Costs and Benefits Analysis of Being Listed on the NYSE

The decision for German corporations to list on the NYSE depends on a cost-benefit analysis. Since the thesis concerns large, listed corporations, it is assumed that German corporations are also listed in Germany. Being listed on two or more exchanges is usually termed cross-listed. In the following, the costs and benefits of a cross-listing on the NYSE will be considered to determine the cross-listing premium which includes the aspect of agency costs. Special emphasis will be set on the regulatory framework including the costs and benefits related to SOX and the FCPA. At last, general benefits of U.S. internal control will be addressed. The analysis focuses mainly on aspects of the regulatory framework and neglects corporation-specific aspects whether to cross-list such as the relevance of a NYSE listing shown e.g. by traded shares volume[2310] or the need to diversify the access to capital. Since each corporation has its specific setup and resulting costs and benefits, the following chapter has the main purpose of being indicative and to provide corporations with substantive information for performing their specific cost-benefit analysis.

A. Costs and Benefits for Being Listed on the NYSE – Cross-Listing Premium

With regard to the NYSE market place, corporations face listing costs: a onetime initial listing fee of $125,000 to $250,000 and a continued listing fee of $42,000 to $500,000 both fees depending on the total shares outstanding.[2311] While the listing costs have to be considered, they will not be decisive for corporations in most cases since German corporations believe that indirect costs such as the additional SEC reporting obligations are more significant than listing costs.[2312]

2310 Cf. *Glaum/Thomaschewski/Weber*, Studien des Deutschen Aktieninstituts 2006, p. 103.

2311 Cf. NYSE Fees.

2312 *Glaum/Thomaschewski/Weber*, Studien des Deutschen Aktieninstituts 2006, p. 102.

The combined benefits associated with the cross-listing on the NYSE are generally referred to as the cross-listing premium. The benefits of being listed on the NYSE include prestige, increased liquidity, decreased exposure to domestic market risks, increased visibility through more analyst attention, reduced cost of capital[2313], obtaining acquisition currency, and stricter disclosure requirements compared to home country requirements together with strict enforcement of the SEC[2314] leading to a higher stock price[2315] resulting in an increase of value of the corporation through cross-listing[2316]. The decision whether to cross-list involves aspects such as "bonding, signaling, self-selection, and reduced informational asymmetry" as well as the level of enforcement in the foreign market further reducing the informational asymmetry leading to lower costs of equity.[2317] In particular, legal bonding provides a benefit for foreign private issuers.[2318] Legal bonding is a term of institutional law and economics referring to "the costs or liabilities that an agent or entrepreneur will incur to assure investors that it will perform as promised, thereby enabling it to market its securities at a higher price".[2319] Thus, corporations have to make investors confident that management will not scam them in order to raise money by implementing an appropriate governance structure.[2320] The better the structure the more investors are willing to pay, or put differently, corporations must compensate investors *ex ante* for inefficient governance rules.[2321] Studies have shown that institutional investors are willing to pay a premium for good corporate governance.[2322] Corporations may demand up to 18% more for their shares being a well-governed corporation.[2323] Therefore, an effective internal control structure will help corporations to

2313 Cf. *Glaum/Thomaschewski/Weber*, Studien des Deutschen Aktieninstituts 2006, p. 90.
2314 Cf. *Glaum/Thomaschewski/Weber*, Studien des Deutschen Aktieninstituts 2006, p. 88 et seq.
2315 Cf. *Prentice*, 29 Cardozo L. Rev. 703 (2007), p. 754; *Stefou*, Corporate Ownership & Control 2008, p. 153.
2316 *Coffee*, 102 Colum. L. Rev. 1757 (2002), p. 1779.
2317 *Coffee*, 2007; cf. *Prentice*, 91 Cornell L. Rev. 775 (2006), p. 832 et seq.
2318 *Berger/Li/Wong*, 2011, p. 28. Similar: *Li*, 2011, p. 5.
2319 *Coffee*, 102 Colum. L. Rev. 1757 (2002), p. 1767 at fn. 26 and p. 1780 et seq.
2320 *Easterbrook*, 95 Va. L. Rev. 685 (2009), p. 687 et seq.
2321 Cf. *Easterbrook* 2009, p. 687 et seq. and p. 689; *Dodwell*, CPA Journal 2008; *Prentice/Spence*, 95 Geo. L. J. 1843 (2007), p. 1902.
2322 *Prentice/Spence*, 95 Geo. L. J. 1843 (2007), p. 1863 et seq.; cf. *Coombes/Watson*, 2000; *Bushman/Smith*, 32 J. Acct. and Econ. 237 (2001), p. 241.
2323 *Coombes/Watson*, 2000.

assert investors that they will not be scammed leading to higher payments from investors or to a reduced risk premium resulting in lower cost of capital.[2324] Due to an U.S. listing, corporations are able to increase their share price and investor confidence[2325] and to lower the cost of additional equity.[2326] Since, the U.S. mandates for corporate governance and disclosure are viewed as the highest available standard, foreign markets reward corporations meeting these standards.[2327]

In light of the benefits of a high corporate governance standard, it has been argued that the increased sophistication of the European capital market renders the listing of European corporations on the NYSE obsolete to receive capital.[2328] The German and the European capital market gained attractiveness through liberalization as well as information and transaction costs have been reduced through the digital era.[2329] In this regard, it has been found that cross-listing has become less attractive for corporations subject to high disclosure standards and sophisticated capital markets in their home countries.[2330] Otherwise, it has been found that the cross-listing premium is positive for German corporations when listed on levels higher than over-the-counter.[2331] Also, the German capital market has been named to be underdeveloped and not liquid enough to finance all business adventures.[2332] An indicator for such underdevelopment has been the listing of large German corporations on the NYSE.[2333] The delistings of German corporations in the second half of the 2000s indicate that other alternatives especially at the London exchange evolved. The massive delistings of 15 German corporations in July 2005[2334] shows that the cross-listing pre-

---

2324 Cf. *Bedard/Graham/Hoitash/Hoitash*, CPA Journal 2007; *Prentice/Spence*, 95 Geo. L. J. 1843 (2007), pp. 1900 and 1902; *Coates*, 21 J. Econ. Perspectives 91 (2007), p. 92; *Ashaubgh-Skaife/Collins/Kinney*, 2008, p. 5 et seq.; *Ogneva/Subramanyam/Raghunandan*, 2006; *Hammersley/Myers/Shakespeare*, 2007; *Berger/Li/Wong*, 2011, p. 28; *Dhaliwal/Hogan/Wilkins*, 86 Acct. Rev. 1131 (2011).

2325 *Brown*, 90 Marq. L. Rev. 309 (2006), p. 327.

2326 *Coffee*, 102 Colum. L. Rev. 1757 (2002), p. 1763.

2327 *Brown*, 90 Marq. L. Rev. 309 (2006), p. 327.

2328 *Stoltenberg/Lacey/George/Cuthbert*, 53 Am. J. Comp. L. 457 (2005), p. 471.

2329 *Glaum/Thomaschewski/Weber*, Studien des Deutschen Aktieninstituts 2006, p. 103.

2330 *Marosi/Massoud*, 2006; cf. *Coffee*, 102 Colum. L. Rev. 1757 (2002), p. 1830.

2331 Cf. *Glaum/Thomaschewski/Weber*, Studien des Deutschen Aktieninstituts 2006, p. 89.

2332 *Wackerbarth*, ZGR 2005, 686, 689.

2333 Cf. *Wackerbarth*, ZGR 2005, 686, 701.

2334 Cf. *Glaum/Thomaschewski/Weber*, Studien des Deutschen Aktieninstituts 2006, p. 85.

mium for German corporations has been negative at least for the period from 2001 to 2005.[2335]

Due to the burdens of SOX, many foreign corporations would have liked to delist or actually delisted[2336] but other reasons such as improved capital markets in home countries are also factors for choosing to delist in the U.S.[2337] While it has been noted that there was a significant drop in listings of foreign corporations on U.S. exchanges between 2000 and 2005[2338], the SEC found in a comprehensive study on the sec. 404 SOX requirements that 26% of foreign corporations "very seriously" considered delisting from U.S. exchanges and 25% "somewhat" considered delisting.[2339] But the remaining corporations did not consider delisting. It has also been noted that "voluntary delistings by foreign corporations are not as frequent as SOX critics predicted".[2340] The drop in foreign listings may also be attributed to the fact that many foreign corporations were able to access the U.S. capital market through private transactions.[2341]

Otherwise, it has been found that the premium for trading on an U.S. exchange remained constant but the premium for being subject to U.S. regulation declined.[2342] Due to SOX, the overall cross-listing premium declined.[2343] After the enactment of SOX, the cross-listing premium is generally only available for large corporations since smaller corporations are not able to handle the high costs related to the listing requirements including SOX.[2344] While alternative capital markets render the listing on the NYSE less attractive, it follows from this finding that the main decisive factors whether to list on the NYSE is the costs and benefits associated with SOX and other regulation such as the FCPA and USSG depicted subsequently.

The benefits of a high corporate governance standard also include reduced agency costs. Through effective internal controls, supervisors are

---

2335 *Bianconi/Chen/Yoshino*, 2010, p. 16.

2336 *Prentice*, 29 Cardozo L. Rev. 703 (2007), p. 746; *Moeller*, SOX Internal Controls, p. 23; cf. *Romano*, 26 Yale J. on Reg. 229 (2009), p. 254; *Hostak/Lys/Yang/Karaoglu*, 2011, p. 2. German corporations delisted after SOX such as: Daimler AG, Telekom AG, Allianz SE and Siemens AG.

2337 *Prentice*, 29 Cardozo L. Rev. 703 (2007), p. 746 et seq., *Committee Capital Markets Reg.*, 2006, p. 4.

2338 *Newman/Oliverio*, 2006.

2339 SEC Study Sec. 404, p. 67.

2340 *Branson*, 58 S. C. L. Rev. 65 (2006), p. 75.

2341 *Newman/Oliverio*, 2006.

2342 *Litvak*, 105 Mich. L. Rev. 1857 (2007), p. 1861.

2343 *Litvak*, European Financial Management 2008, 875 et seq.

2344 Cf. *Srinivansan/Piotroski*, 2011, p. 5.

better able to oversee management reducing agency costs.[2345] While it has been suggested that agency costs in civil law countries are less within listed corporations compared to U.S. corporations since civil law countries generally have more concentrated ownership compared to common law systems' dispersed ownership[2346], the general issue of agency costs still exists[2347]. With regard to reduced agency costs, corporations with dispersed ownership have an incentive to list on an exchange with high disclosure standards as the share price is important for these corporations.[2348] As it has been shown, investors are willing to pay a premium for good governance. For corporations with concentrated ownership, however, a high share price is often less important than the benefits of the controlling shareholders.[2349] The presence of a controlling shareholder leads to the issue of the expropriation of the control premium to the detriment of minority shareholders.[2350] This will be more difficult with effective internal controls.[2351] But agency costs also exist within concentrated ownership due to the separation of ownership and control. While controlling shareholders will invest more in monitoring reducing agency costs, the general issue of information asymmetry between the management board, on the one side, and the supervisory board as the agent for the shareholders together with the controlling shareholder, on the other side, still exists leading to the need of internal control to address the information asymmetry. Thus, a controlling shareholder has an interest to actively monitor the corporation but also to extract the control premium. In general, corporations with controlling shareholders do not seek exchanges with high disclosure standards and minority shareholder protection.[2352]

Due to reduced agency problem, corporations with concentrated ownership profit less from an increased governance standard. For the cost-benefit analysis of being listed on the NYSE, it follows that the magnitude of

---

2345 Cf. *Langevoort*, 31 J. Corp. L. 949 (2006), p. 964; *Ribstein*, 2006, p. 369 (questioning if the benefits exceed the costs for more monitoring); *Hostak/Lys/Yang/Karaoglu*, 2011, p. 2; *Quall*, CPA Journal 2004.

2346 *Coffee*, 102 Colum. L. Rev. 1757 (2002), p. 1827 at fn. 286; cf. *Wackerbarth*, ZGR 2005, 686, 708.

2347 Cf. *Wackerbarth*, ZGR 2005, 686, 710 et seq.

2348 *Coffee*, 102 Colum. L. Rev. 1757 (2002), p. 1764.

2349 *Coffee*, 2005, p. 11; *Coffee*, 102 Colum. L. Rev. 1757 (2002), p. 1764.

2350 Cf. *Coffee*, 2005, p. 11 et seq.

2351 See *supra* at chapter 12, B. I. 1. c) (4).

2352 *Coffee*, 102 Colum. L. Rev. 1757 (2002), p. 1765; cf. *Prentice*, 29 Cardozo L. Rev. 703 (2007), p. 754 et seq.; *Hostak/Lys/Yang/Karaoglu*, 2011, p. 2.

benefits of an enhanced internal control structure depends on the shareholder structure of each corporation. The benefits of being listed on the NYSE due to reduced agency costs of corporations with concentrated ownership is less compared to the agency costs of corporations with dispersed ownership.

As further arguments in favor of cross-listing have been named by German corporations: "limitations of non-German institutional investors to their national capital market; implementation of stock option plans for non-German employees; facilitation of acquisitions by using own shares; operational advantages within procurement and sales markets through media coverage; specific knowledge of investors and analysts with regard to new technologies; and positive signal for capital markets to follow stricter capital market rules".[2353] German corporations attribute significance to the following aims for being listed on U.S. exchanges: increase of investor basis, increase of reputation regarding U.S. business partners, increase of brand and product awareness, easing the recruiting employees in the U.S., easing of implementation of stock option plans for non-German employees, creating shares to be used within acquisitions.[2354] German corporations believe to have achieved only the aims: increase of investor basis, increase of reputation regarding U.S. business partners, increase of brand and product awareness, easing the recruiting employees in the U.S., and easing of implementation of stock option plans for non-German employees.[2355]

B. *Costs and Benefits of SOX*

The following illustration of the costs and benefits of SOX internal controls will provide greater clarity on their costs, cost factors, and benefits. Also, SOX-related costs and benefits for German corporations will be depicted.

2353 *Glaum/Thomaschewski/Weber*, Studien des Deutschen Aktieninstituts 2006, p. 80 et seq.

2354 *Glaum/Thomaschewski/Weber*, Studien des Deutschen Aktieninstituts 2006, p. 92.

2355 *Glaum/Thomaschewski/Weber*, Studien des Deutschen Aktieninstituts 2006, p. 94.

I. Costs

The costs of SOX have been subject to various studies. Nevertheless, despite plentiful effort, many of the costs attributed to SOX will be impossible to measure accurately.[2356] In addition, the empirical studies of SOX's effects are "preliminary" since legislation needs time to be absorbed from corporations.[2357] The studies also faced difficulties to attribute findings to SOX since market conditions surrounding SOX were "very noisy".[2358] These may be reasons for the different results of the studies. Various studies analyzed the implementation costs in 2004 which has been the first year corporations were subject to sec. 404 SOX. Foreign corporations became subject to sec. 404 SOX as of July 2006.[2359] One study found implementation costs for sec. 404 SOX to be $5.9 million per sample corporation plus $1.9 million for the external auditors leading to sec. 404 SOX costs of $7.8 million per corporation.[2360] Another study found the average implementation to cost $5.1 million.[2361] A further study found sec. 404 SOX costs in 2004 to average $4.26 million per corporation.[2362] The FEI survey found the implementation costs to averaged $4.36 million comprised of total costs for compliance $1.34 million, external costs $1.72 million, and auditor fees $1.30 million.[2363] For implementation costs, a further survey did not provide average costs but provided cost ranges for different sizes of corporations. Of the corporations with revenues greater than $20 billion, 85% invested more than $10 million dollars including more than 30% of these corporations which invested at least $25 million.[2364] While implementation costs of sec. 404 SOX are significant, it has been noted that critics "tend to exaggerate" sec. 404 SOX costs and ignore the benefits of effective

2356 *Prentice/Spence*, 95 Geo. L. J. 1843 (2007), p. 1845.
2357 *Langevoort*, 105 Mich. L. Rev. 1817 (2007), p. 1819.
2358 *Langevoort*, 105 Mich. L. Rev. 1817 (2007), p. 1819; *Coates*, 21 J. Econ. Perspectives 91 (2007), p. 106. The noisiness of the market may explain the finding that stock price negatively reacted to SOX (cf. *Zhang*, 2007).
2359 SEC Release No. 8545.
2360 *Charles River Associates*, 2005, p. 2.
2361 See *Murdock*, 39 Loy. U. Chi. L. J. 525 (2008), p. 548.
2362 *Committee Capital Markets Reg.*, 2006, p. 5.
2363 FEI, 2005.
2364 *Ernst & Young*, 2005, p. 20. The survey provides more data in the categories of corporations with less than $1 billion, $1 to $5 billion, and $5 to $20 billion in revenue which shows a wider span of sec. 404 SOX implementation costs.

internal controls.[2365] In 2005, the FEI survey found the sec. 404 SOX costs declined to average $3.8 million comprised of total costs for compliance $1.18 million, external costs $1.3 million, and auditor fees $1.32 million mainly attributed to initial investment costs in 2004.[2366] A further study found average total compliance costs for the period from 2003 to 2005 of $2.2 million.[2367] For 2005, a survey found sec. 404 SOX costs only for external resources to average $1.8 million per $1 billion in sales for small corporations with sales of $2 billion or less and $10 million per $1 billion in sales for large corporations with average sales between $7 billion and $10 billion.[2368] Also for 2005, a survey found total costs for large corporations of $4.8 million comprised of internal costs of $2.2 million, external costs of $1 million, and auditor fees of $1.6 million.[2369] The 2006 FEI survey found the sec. 404 SOX costs further declined to average $2.9 million comprised of total costs for compliance of $0.8 million, external costs $0.9 million, and auditor fees $1.2 million.[2370] The 2006 FEI survey also revealed that centralized operations are more cost effective since sec. 404 SOX costs for corporations with centralized operations were $1.7 million compared to $4.0 million for corporations with decentralized operations.[2371] The 2007 FEI survey names total average costs of $1.7 million with an average of $1.3 million for corporations with a centralized organization and 1.9 million for corporations with decentralized corporations.[2372] The SEC noted that surveys found the early compliance costs for relatively large corporations to range from $860,000 to $5.4 million per corporation.[2373] Also, it has been observed that SOX leads to an increase of audit fees and internal audit cost of about $1 million per $1 billion in revenue with a ratio of audit costs declining as corporation size rises.[2374] In 2009, the SEC published a comprehensive study of its office of economic analysis on the sec. 404 SOX requirements including the effects of the 2007 reforms and efficiency in regard to total and component compliance costs, changes in costs over time,

---

2365 *Prentice*, 29 Cardozo L. Rev. 703 (2007), p. 703; cf. *Langevoort*, 105 Mich. L. Rev. 1817 (2007), p. 1819.

2366 FEI, 2006.

2367 *Krishnan/Rama/Zhang*, 2007.

2368 *arc morgan*, 2005, p. 6.

2369 *Charles River Associates*, 2006, p. 3.

2370 FEI, 2007 (partial amounts rounded).

2371 FEI, 2007.

2372 FEI, 2008.

2373 SEC Release No. 8809, at VI, A.

2374 *Coates*, 21 J. Econ. Perspectives 91 (2007), p. 107.

and factors explaining higher or lower costs for different corporations.[2375] The general findings are that compliance costs are higher for larger corporations, decrease with more compliance experience, and decreased after the 2007 reforms especially for larger corporations.[2376] For 2008, the SEC study found total average costs of $2.4 million comprised of compliance costs of $1.4 million, external costs of $0.3 million, and auditor fees of $0.7 million.[2377] Large corporations incurred total costs of $4 million comprised of compliance costs of $2.4 million, external costs of $0.5 million, and auditor fees of $1.1 million.[2378] A study in 2009 of the net realized costs of SOX including direct and indirect costs investigated SOX's impact on corporations' cash-flow profitability finding costs for smaller corporations of $6 million and $39 million for larger corporations.[2379] In general, smaller corporations, low-growth opportunity corporations, and corporations with more complex operations face higher costs.[2380] While implementation costs declined after 2004, the study finds continuous costs implying that other than direct implementation costs of SOX are more significant.[2381] In 2011, a study found that 12% of the corporations had a total annual budget for compliance activities of $10 million or more and 14% of $3 million to $9.9 million while the remaining 74% had less than $3 million.[2382] The numbers show, however, that the average costs for sec. 404 SOX declined after the initial implementation costs which have been named to be sunk costs since 2007.[2383] The costs decreased substantially after initial implementation, which is more expensive than annual maintenance.[2384] A study found a 44% drop for larger corporations and a 30% drop for smaller firms.[2385] In 2010, a survey found that SOX compliance costs across corporations dropped by 50% compared to the implementation costs.[2386] Costs are assumed to continue to decline due to the SEC 2007 reforms aimed to

---

2375 SEC Study Sec. 404, p. 1.

2376 SEC Study Sec. 404, p. 2.

2377 SEC Study Sec. 404, p. 43.

2378 SEC Study Sec. 404, p. 47.

2379 *Ahmed/McAnally/Rasmussen*, 2009, p. 2 et seq. and p. 25. The authors acknowledge the failure to capture the full cost-benefit trade off of SOX (p. 34).

2380 *Ahmed/McAnally/Rasmussen*, 2009, p. 4.

2381 *Ahmed/McAnally/Rasmussen*, 2009, p. 4 et seq.

2382 Cf. *PwC/Compliance Week*, 2011, p. 11.

2383 Prof. *Eric Talley* in a meeting at Berkeley Law in 2011.

2384 See *Brown*, 90 Marq. L. Rev. 309 (2006), p. 321 et seq.

2385 *Prentice*, 29 Cardozo L. Rev. 703 (2007), p. 728.

2386 *protiviti*, 2010, p. 2.

reduce costs by clarifying what the SEC expects under sec. 404 SOX[2387] and the coordinated issuing of AS 5 by the PCAOB.

With regard to audit costs, they increased due to SOX.[2388] Audit fees increased in case corporations reported internal control weaknesses[2389] but also decreased for corporations with strong internal controls providing corporations with the opportunity to reduce audit fees by improving internal controls.[2390] The audit fee increase is to some point attributed to the broad understanding of internal controls rules by auditors – assisted by the SEC and the PCAOB – leading to higher responsibility and workload of auditors.[2391] Due to the reduced effort of management to evaluate internal control over financial reporting as a result of the 2007 reforms, audit fees may increase since external auditors may no longer base their assessment to the same extent on management's evaluation so that auditors might engage in additional tests.[2392]

In order to reduce costs, management should work with the external auditor to define the scope of management's assessment of sec. 404 SOX internal controls.[2393] For example, choosing the right amount of locations for the multi-location testing approach is important factor of minimizing costs.[2394] Improving training, streamlining SOX-related processes, and automating controls are further means to reduce SOX costs.[2395]

II. Factors of Costs

The primary factors of costs have been identified to be the scope of the internal control audit and the amount of the performed testing by management.[2396] Thus, the number of controls identified for testing mainly correlates with the costs for the sec. 404 SOX assessment.[2397] Easily identifiable

2387 *Prentice*, 29 Cardozo L. Rev. 703 (2007), p. 728 et seq.
2388 *Iliev*, 2009, p. 5; *Clark*, 22 Ga. St. U. L. Rev. 251 (2005), p. 266.
2389 *Shakespeare*, 3 J. Bus. & Tech. 333 (2008), p. 336.
2390 Cf. *Bedard/Graham/Hoitash/Hoitash*, CPA Journal 2007; also *Hoitash/Hoitash/Bedard*, 2007.
2391 *Langevoort*, 31 J. Corp. L. 949 (2006), p. 967.
2392 SEC Release No. 8809, at VI, B.
2393 *O'Brien*, CPA Journal 2006b.
2394 *O'Brien*, CPA Journal 2006a.
2395 *O'Brien*, CPA Journal 2006a.
2396 *O'Brien*, CPA Journal 2006a.
2397 *O'Brien*, CPA Journal 2006a.

costs of internal controls are audit fees, working hours of line, compliance and internal audit personnel[2398], and costs attributed to intrusive control actions causing opportunity costs and distractions, as well as costs attributed to accurate documentation.[2399] In addition to specific costs, the possibility of more abstract costs such as reduced employee motivation and opportunity costs have been raised by authors. Opportunity costs related to the review of the internal controls by the CEO and CFO decreasing their working time for running the business has been named as one of the more significant costs of sec. 404 SOX.[2400] These costs are difficult to determine accurately.[2401] Employee monitoring through internal controls has the potential of diminishing the benefits of internal controls by reducing the motivation of employees.[2402] If employees are monitored too closely and intrusively as well as unevenly and unfairly, the powerful motivating factor of autonomy decreases leading to rising opportunity costs of internal controls.[2403] A further factor of opportunity costs is related to requiring the board of directors and the audit committee in particular to supervise internal controls adding a further layer of responsibility to the traditional role of supervising the business strategy of management.[2404] Such further layer of responsibility will reduce the available time of directors to deal with other issues of the corporation.[2405] The requirements documentation, monitoring, verifying, and reporting have been named as being burdensome for the assessment process of internal control over reporting.[2406] With regard to documentation, it is especially burdensome when a corporation newly becomes subject to SOX depending on the accuracy of existing documentation. As further factors of costs have been named: "[s]maller profit margins and retarded economic growth from management compliance costs, higher audit fees, and the opportunity costs of forging more productive activities", "[c]ertain redundancy between the work of management and the [external] auditor", and "SOX work conducted after the ini-

2398 Cf. *Carney*, 55 Emory L. J. 141 (2006), p. 151.
2399 *Langevoort*, 31 J. Corp. L. 949 (2006), p. 959.
2400 *Coates*, 21 J. Econ. Perspectives 91 (2007), p. 107 et seq.; *Brown*, 90 Marq. L. Rev. 309 (2006), at fn. 65; *financial executives research foundation*, 2005, p. 6.
2401 *Coates*, 21 J. Econ. Perspectives 91 (2007), p. 108; *Brown*, 90 Marq. L. Rev. 309 (2006), at fn. 65.
2402 *Langevoort*, 31 J. Corp. L. 949 (2006), p. 959.
2403 Cf. *Langevoort*, 31 J. Corp. L. 949 (2006), p. 971.
2404 Cf. *Langevoort*, 105 Mich. L. Rev. 1817 (2007), p. 1831.
2405 Cf. *Langevoort*, 105 Mich. L. Rev. 1817 (2007), p. 1831.
2406 *O'Brien*, CPA Journal 2006a.

tial implementation tends to yield diminishing returns in succeeding years after control weaknesses are corrected".[2407] Diminishing returns for correcting control weaknesses, however, are attributed to a reduced marginal benefit of further correcting control weaknesses in an internal control system approaching the status of having no weakness. In general, requiring more disclosure leads to more information which increases the costs to process such information.[2408]

Some of the high costs can be attributed to rent-seeking by external auditors[2409], lawyers, and other consultants.[2410] It has been noted that involved parties of the sec. 404 SOX process have an interest to exaggerate such costs.[2411] With regard to the auditor attestation of sec. 404(b) SOX, the auditors have a greater incentive than management to increase the identification of material weaknesses since they are less likely to bear fixing costs, rather, they may benefit from additional spending to fix control weaknesses.[2412] Similarly, as shown above,[2413] management has incentives to identify and remediate material weaknesses in order to avoid liability for failing to disclose material weaknesses or consequences of disclosing material weaknesses. A further cost of SOX has been named that management will reduce their risk appetite due to SOX and will lose competitiveness especially with regard to corporations not subject to SOX.[2414] The personal liability for officers has been named to undermine the risk-bearing advantages of modern capital markets since individuals have to bear the liability risk instead of the shareholders which are better able to bear the risk due to the opportunity of owning a diversified portfolio.[2415] Also, the enhanced officer liability increased D&O insurance premiums by 100%.[2416]

With regard to sec. 302 SOX, costs have been named to be minimal for U.S. corporations since they had already been required to include Ex-

---

2407 *Dodwell*, CPA Journal 2008.

2408 *Manne*, 58 Ala. L. Rev. 473 (2007), p. 473 et seq.; *Paredes*, 81 Wash. U. L. Q. 417 (2003), p. 417 et seq.

2409 *Romano*, 26 Yale J. on Reg. 229 (2009), p. 298; *Grundfest/Bochner*, 105 Mich. L. Rev. 1643 (2007), p. 1647 et seq.

2410 *Prentice*, 29 Cardozo L. Rev. 703 (2007), p. 729; *Langevoort*, 105 Mich. L. Rev. 1817 (2007), p. 1838.

2411 *Prentice*, 29 Cardozo L. Rev. 703 (2007), p. 726.

2412 *Coates*, 21 J. Econ. Perspectives 91 (2007), p. 103 et seq.

2413 See *supra* at chapter 4, A. III.

2414 Cf. *Langevoort*, 105 Mich. L. Rev. 1817 (2007), p. 1852 et seq.

2415 *Ribstein*, 2006, p. 372; *Bargeron/Lehn/Zutter*, 2008.

2416 *Linck/Netter/Yang*, 2008; cf. *Carney*, 55 Emory L. J. 141 (2006), p. 147; *Cohen/Dey/Lys*, 2007.

change Act Rule 13a-14 certifications in their quarterly and annual reports.[2417] Nevertheless, German corporations have to consider these costs within a cost-benefits analysis of being listed on the NYSE. These costs include factors such as implementing disclosure controls and procedures to gather information needed to be reported under U.S. securities laws and management's evaluation of the effectiveness of these controls. Since COSO I may also be used for disclosure controls and procedures, synergy effects exists with regard to existing internal control structures. Also, the ability to report under IFRS reduces costs.

III. Benefits

The benefits of SOX depend largely on its acceptance by corporate leaders and employees.[2418] It "has the potential to have substantial beneficial influence in creating a culture of compliance" so that the involved parties of a corporation are truly committed to ethical behavior and accurate financial reporting.[2419] Due to the improved corporate culture, employees may increasingly consider violations of accounting rules or the code of ethics illegitimate and will report such behavior up within the corporate compliance system.[2420] Implementing internal controls as mandated by sec. 302 and 404 SOX provides benefits for corporations and a great opportunity to enhance the efficiency and value of corporations.[2421] Some of SOX's main benefits are corporate transparency and accountability in general and specifically improvements to the quality of financial reporting.[2422] Benefits include that employees will be encouraged by evaluations to improve their efficiency and, thereby, become a more capable workforce.[2423] The overall efficiency of corporations can be enhanced by documenting proce-

2417 Cf. SEC Release No. 8238, at V, B.

2418 *Prentice*, 29 Cardozo L. Rev. 703 (2007), pp. 705 and 762; *Langevoort*, 105 Mich. L. Rev. 1817 (2007), p. 1844.

2419 *Prentice*, 29 Cardozo L. Rev. 703 (2007), p. 705.

2420 Cf. *Langevoort*, 105 Mich. L. Rev. 1817 (2007), p. 1844.

2421 *Quall*, CPA Journal 2004; *Campos*, 55 Case W. Res. J. Rev. 527 (2005), p. 531; *Coates*, 21 J. Econ. Perspectives 91 (2007), p. 92; cf. *Bedard/Graham/Hoitash/Hoitash*, CPA Journal 2007.

2422 *Committee Capital Markets Reg.*, 2006, p. xiii; *Coates*, 21 J. Econ. Perspectives 91 (2007), p. 92.

2423 *Quall*, CPA Journal 2004.

dures.[2424] Documentation allows for reviews eliminating pointless or redundant processes.[2425] Within the evaluation process of internal controls, efficiency considerations are an important factor which has been elaborated above.[2426] Moreover, documentation provides value for training new employees and as a disaster recovery backup.[2427] Also, enhanced job-description documentation will benefit the corporation during employee absences and periods of high turnover.[2428] Clear responsibility for business processes is an important element of internal controls and facilitates training, oversight, and performance evaluations.[2429] Due to the documentation efforts, employees will get a better understanding of operations including the opportunity for their enhancement.[2430] In addition, corporations use SOX as an opportunity to bring operations under better control while driving compliance costs down.[2431] Moreover, large corporations view compliance mandates as a tool to advertise their compliance efforts as a competitive advantage.[2432] The SEC study of 2009 found benefits of sec. 404 SOX such as improved quality of internal controls, improved confidence by the audit committee in the corporation's internal control over financial reporting, improved quality of the corporation's financial reporting, and improved ability of the corporation to prevent and detect fraud.[2433] As the typical organization loses 5% of its annual revenues to occupational fraud and abuse,[2434] the benefit of internal controls regarding fraud are sizeable. In general, corporations anticipate value by sec. 404 SOX through enhanced accountability and ownership of controls, enhanced financial processes, systems enhancements, and leverage of sec. 404 SOX as a platform to address risks beyond financial reporting.[2435] Also, SOX internal controls prevent and detect financial misstatements and to a lesser extent fraud. It

2424 Cf. *Dodwell*, CPA Journal 2008; *Coates*, 21 J. Econ. Perspectives 91 (2007), p. 92.
2425 *Quall*, CPA Journal 2004.
2426 See *supra* at chapter 4, A. II. 2. a) and *infra* at chapter 17.
2427 *Dodwell*, CPA Journal 2008.
2428 *Wagner/Dittmar*, 2006, p. 4.
2429 *Wagner/Dittmar*, 2006, p. 4.
2430 *Wagner/Dittmar*, 2006, p. 4.
2431 Cf. *Wagner/Dittmar*, 2006.
2432 Former-Congressman *Michael G. Oxley* mentioned at the reception after his speech at Berkeley Law (see *Oxley*, 2011) that General Electric uses its "standard setting" compliance efforts as an advertising tool viewing the costs as negligible for the benefits.
2433 SEC Study Sec. 404, p. 56.
2434 ACFE Report 2010, p. 8.
2435 *Ernst & Young*, Survey 2005, p. 60.

has been suggested that sec. 302 and 404 SOX controls actually deter fraud.[2436] This finding seems to be supported by a large drop in securities fraud litigation after the implementation phase remaining on a low level from 2007 to 2009.[2437] But since securities fraud litigation alleging internal control weaknesses increased in 2010 to the 2006-level and remained on this level since then[2438], the ability of sec. 302 and 404 SOX controls to deter fraud is questionable. With regard to sec. 302 SOX, studies found this section to be beneficial by providing useful information to investors[2439], restoring investors' confidence in the market, and rewarding corporations with better internal controls.[2440] Also, investors use the information of internal control weaknesses from sec. 302 SOX reports to evaluate risks.[2441] Likewise, sec. 404 SOX reports provide important information for capital markets.[2442] In general, research indicates that sec. 302 and 404 SOX improve financial reporting.[2443]

A further benefit of SOX internal controls is to prevent negative effects of non-effective internal controls. Due to reporting of material weaknesses, the corporation's capitalization and reputation may be affected[2444] as one cost of insufficient internal controls is represented in the finding that the initial disclosure of material weaknesses in internal controls leads to a negative stock market reaction.[2445] Since corporations with material weaknesses of their internal controls are more likely to restate their financial report-

---

2436 *Prentice*, 29 Cardozo L. Rev. 703 (2007), p. 723 et seq. Even though fraud detection might be modest (cf. *Clark*, 22 Ga. St. U. L. Rev. 251 (2005), p. 294).

2437 Cf. *Cornerstone Research*, 2009, p. 27.

2438 Cf. *Cornerstone Research*, 2016, p. 9; *Cornerstone Research*, 2012, p. 6.

2439 *De Franco/Guan/Lu*, 2005, p. 25.

2440 *Prentice/Spence*, 95 Geo. L. J. 1843 (2007), p. 1900 et seq.; *Lord & Benoit*, 2006, p. 4.

2441 *Prentice*, 29 Cardozo L. Rev. 703 (2007), p. 717; cf. *Ashbaugh-Skaife/Collins/Kinney*, 2008, p. 2.

2442 *Prentice*, 29 Cardozo L. Rev. 703 (2007), p. 719; *Langevoort*, 105 Mich. L. Rev. 1817 (2007), p. 1827; cf. *Lord & Benoit*, 2006, p. 4.

2443 See *Prentice*, 29 Cardozo L. Rev. 703 (2007), p. 715 et seq.; *Coates*, 21 J. Econ. Perspectives 91 (2007), p. 92.

2444 *Barker/Hedin*, in: The Metropolitan Corporate Counsel. See on reputation: *Desai/Hogan/Wilkins*, 81 Acct. Rev. 83 (2006).

2445 *Zhang/Pany*, CPA Journal 2008; *Shakespeare*, 3 J. Bus. & Tech. 333 (2008), p. 335; *Prentice/Spence*, 95 Geo. L. J. 1843 (2007), p. 1902; *Desai/Hogan/Wilkins*, 81 Acct. Rev. 83 (2006), p. 84 (finding that the market imposes a substantial penalty on those companies that engage in earnings manipulation and have to restate financials); *Kinney/McDaniel*, 11 J. Acct. and Econ. 71 (1989), p. 71 (finding that company profitability is negatively associated with restatements);

ing[2446], and since the failure to comply with SOX affects stock price, borrowing rates, and bond ratings, as well as debt contracting[2447], corporations have an incentive to maintain higher quality internal controls and corporate governance leading to an increase of investor assurance.[2448] Due to these findings, SOX lead numerous corporations to disclose their internal control deficiencies[2449] and especially their discovered material weaknesses.

The disclosure of such deficiencies contributed to a dramatic rise in the number of financial restatements until 2005.[2450] The interpretation of the increasing number of financial restatements is controversial. Some commentators view this development as a sign that internal control systems do not work since the number shows that wrong information leading to restatements is increasing rather than diminishing.[2451] Other reasons, however, may explain the increase of financial restatements. It has been observed that several factors may have prompted more corporations to restate previously reported financial results.[2452] This includes financial reporting requirements of SOX, especially sec. 302 and 404 SOX, increased scrutiny from the then-newly formed PCAOB through its inspections of registered public accounting firms, and increased staffing and review by the SEC.[2453] In addition, empirical evidence suggests that corporations with poor internal controls tend to restate earnings more often[2454] indicating that higher

---

cf. *Bedard/Graham/Hoitash/Hoitash*, CPA Journal 2007; *Prentice*, 29 Cardozo L. Rev. 703 (2007), p. 716.

2446 Cf. *Bedard/Graham/Hoitash/Hoitash*, CPA Journal 2007; *Shakespeare*, 3 J. Bus. & Tech. 333 (2008), pp. 335 and 348.

2447 *Costello/Wittenberg-Moerman*, 2010.

2448 *Dodwell*, CPA Journal 2008.

2449 Cf. *Zhang/Pany*, CPA Journal 2008.

2450 Cf. *Dodwell*, CPA Journal 2008; cf. GAO, 2006, p. 12.

2451 E.g. *Beecher-Monas*, 55 Admin. L. Rev. 357 (2003).

2452 *Prentice*, 29 Cardozo L. Rev. 703 (2007), 733; *Brown*, 90 Marq. L. Rev. 309 (2006), p. 328; *Krishnan/Visvanathan*, 2005 (finding that an active and financially experience audit committee performing its duties is more likely to find and report internal control weaknesses); *Bédard*, 2006 (finding that the formal internal control assessment process of sec 404 SOX improved internal controls and/or increased audit effort of auditors); *Hoitash/Hoitash/Bedard*, 2008 (finding that an experienced audit committee reduces the likelihood of disclosing material weaknesses).

2453 GAO, 2006, p. 12.

2454 *Prentice/Spence*, 95 Geo. L. J. 1843, (2007), p. 1902; *Kinney/McDaniel*, 11 J. Acct. and Econ. 71 (1989), p. 72 (finding that a restatement may indicate problems with the internal control system).

scrutiny reveals already existing deficiencies in internal controls. This phenomenon is known as the control paradox.[2455] Thus, the increasing number of financial restatements shows that the internal control systems actually work indicated by the detection of deficiencies and the increased attention of officers towards financial reporting.[2456] In 2006, the number of restatements by large corporations fell by 20%.[2457] This number indicates with regard to large corporations the internal control systems start to work properly.[2458] In general, the reporting of internal control deficiencies decreased in the subsequent years after SOX.[2459] As financial restatements after the implementation phase of SOX decreased, SOX clearly contributed to increase the effectiveness of financial reporting. The increase of disclosure of material weaknesses is in line with the goals of SOX since disclosure creates strong incentives for corporate leaders to fix the weaknesses.[2460] The subsequent corrections and disclosures inspire greater investor confidence leading to more efficient capital allocation leading to reduced costs of capital.[2461] Thus, the market values disclosure of material weaknesses.[2462] Moreover, earnings management was reduced after the enactment of SOX[2463] which led to an increase of investor confidence[2464]. It follows that investor and the market are beneficiaries of effective internal controls.[2465] The following groups also benefit from accurate financial reporting fostered by effective internal controls the board of directors, management, employees, lenders, customers, and regulators.[2466]

2455 Cf. *Bussmann/Matschke*, Crime, Law and Social Change 2008, 349, 356.

2456 *Prentice*, 29 Cardozo L. Rev. 703 (2007), 730; *Wade*, 39 Loy. U. Chi. L. J. 595 (2008), p. 603 et seq.

2457 *Grothe*, 2007b, p. 2; *Reilly*, 2007, C7; cf. *Prentice*, 29 Cardozo L. Rev. 703 (2007), p. 730; *Jonas/Rosenberg/Gale/Hedges*, 2007, p. 2.

2458 *Prentice*, 29 Cardozo L. Rev. 703 (2007), p. 730; *Aguilar*, 2007; cf. *Langevoort*, 105 Mich. L. Rev. 1817 (2007), p. 1824.

2459 Cf. *Zhang/Pany*, CPA Journal 2008; *Bedard/Graham/Hoitash/Hoitash*, CPA Journal 2007.

2460 *Coates*, 21 J. Econ. Perspectives 91 (2007), p. 103.

2461 Cf. *Dodwell*, CPA Journal 2008; *Coates*, 21 J. Econ. Perspectives 91 (2007), p. 92; *Lord & Benoit*, 2006, p. 4; *Campos*, 55 Case W. Res. J. Rev. 527 (2005), p. 531.

2462 *Hammersley/Myers/Shakespeare*, 2007.

2463 *Coates*, 21 J. Econ. Perspectives 91 (2007), p. 106; *Cohen/Dey/Lys*, 2005; *Cohen/Dey/Lys*, 2007.

2464 *Coates*, 21 J. Econ. Perspectives 91 (2007), p. 107; *Jain/Kim/Rezaee*, 2006.

2465 Cf. *Langevoort*, 31 J. Corp. L. 949 (2006), p. 964; *Committee Capital Markets Reg.*, 2006, p. xiii.

2466 Cf. *Langevoort*, 31 J. Corp. L. 949 (2006), p. 964 et seq.

Quantifying the benefits of the internal control mandates of SOX has always been difficult.[2467] Estimating the benefits of SOX internal controls is more challenging than capturing the costs especially since benefits may only come to light years after the implementation of SOX controls.[2468] Nevertheless, the SEC received numerous supporting comments regarding the benefits of the internal control amendments of SOX.[2469] Investing in internal controls will be beneficial for corporations as they improve the corporation's business by highlighting weaknesses but only if the investment is directed toward the material aspects of the business.[2470] With the 2007 reforms allowing a top-down, risk-based approach, the benefits of effective internal control clearly outweigh the cost at least for large corporations. In 2012, a survey found that almost 50% of U.S. corporations, especially large corporations, believe that the benefits outweigh the costs.[2471] Similarly, corporations should not focus on only complying with SOX mandates since they will miss on the benefits of a corporation-wide comprehensive approach for internal controls as represented by COSO I.[2472] Also, since the mandates of the FCPA and sec. 404 SOX are overlapping, some sec. 404 SOX costs will be mitigated due to the existing obligation to maintain an adequate system of internal accounting controls.[2473]

In essence, corporations are better off with good internal controls.[2474] The benefits of "improved market efficiency, better asset allocation, and fraud avoidance"[2475] as well as "greater investor confidence, greater market liquidity, more accurate corporate reporting, fewer restatements, lower capital costs, and improved fraud detection and prevention" exceed the costs of implementing sec. 404 SOX.[2476]

2467 *Prentice*, 29 Cardozo L. Rev. 703 (2007), p. 723; *Carney*, 55 Emory L. J. 141 (2006), p. 142; cf. SEC Release No. 8238, at V, A.

2468 Cf. *Bedard/Graham/Hoitash/Hoitash*, CPA Journal 2007; *Langevoort*, 31 J. Corp. L. 949 (2006), p. 960; *Prentice/Spence*, 95 Geo. L. J. 1843 (2007), p. 1845; *Coates*, 21 J. Econ. Perspectives 91 (2007), p. 92; *Nelson*, 31 Academy of Management Rev. 30 (2006), p. 33.

2469 SEC Release No. 8238, at V, A.

2470 *Langevoort*, 105 Mich. L. Rev. 1817 (2007), p. 1839.

2471 *protiviti*, 2012, p. 3.

2472 Cf. *Quall*, CPA Journal 2004.

2473 SEC Release No. 8238, at V, B.

2474 *Prentice*, 29 Cardozo L. Rev. 703 (2007), p. 711; *Campos*, 55 Case W. Res. J. Rev. 527 (2005), p. 531.

2475 *Prentice*, 29 Cardozo L. Rev. 703 (2007), p. 725.

2476 *Prentice*, 29 Cardozo L. Rev. 703 (2007), p. 732; cf. *Campos*, 55 Case W. Res. J. Rev. 527 (2005), p. 531.

IV. SOX-Related Costs and Benefits for German Corporations

With regard to foreign private issuers, SOX relates to the general benefits of being listed on the NYSE since SOX accounts to a large degree for the high disclosure standards and enforcement. All of the SOX-required internal control and compliance measures have been considered by German corporations listed on the NYSE to have increased investor confidence including the implementation of an audit committee, reports of management on the adequacy of financial reporting, and the implementation and documentation of an internal control system including a code of ethics and whistleblower protection.[2477] Some German corporations even voluntarily follow sec. 404 SOX as best practice[2478] in order to signal their compliance with U.S. standards[2479].

Similar to U.S. corporations, German corporations incur costs to establish and evaluate SOX-related internal control.[2480] For some European corporations, the costs of being listed on the NYSE especially due to SOX may exceed the benefits of such listing.[2481] The costs to implement and operate internal control over financial reporting pursuant to sec. 404 SOX have been high.[2482] German corporations estimated their expenses to be listed on the NYSE in 2004 to reach from 30 million to 80 million Euros.[2483] Total costs for German corporations listed on the NYSE to become compliant with sec. 404 SOX have been estimated in 2004-2005 to average about seven million euro per corporation.[2484] In 2004-2005, German corporations listed on the NYSE believed that the costs of SOX outweigh the benefits.[2485] Most German studies regarding costs due to SOX, however, describe the situation prior to the 2007 reforms of SOX-related rules of the SEC and the PCAOB, while U.S. studies also cover the period after the

2477 *Glaum/Thomaschewski/Weber*, Studien des Deutschen Aktieninstituts 2006, p. 33.

2478 *Happ/Pott*, KoR 2007, 666, 669; cf. *Schäfer*, ZGR 2004, 416, 419.

2479 Cf. *Fleischer*, ECFR 2005, 378, 387.

2480 Cf. *Stoltenberg/Lacey/George/Cuthbert*, 53 Am. J. Comp. L. 457 (2005), p. 461 et seq.; *Glaum/Thomaschewski/Weber*, Studien des Deutschen Aktieninstituts 2006, p. 32.

2481 Cf. *Stoltenberg/Lacey/George/Cuthbert*, 53 Am. J. Comp. L. 457 (2005), p. 470.

2482 *Ringleb*, in: Ringleb, DCGK, mar. 649.

2483 *Stoltenberg/Lacey/George/Cuthbert*, 53 Am. J. Comp. L. 457 (2005), p. 470 et seq.

2484 *Glaum/Thomaschewski/Weber*, Studien des Deutschen Aktieninstituts 2006, p. 76.

2485 *Glaum/Thomaschewski/Weber*, Studien des Deutschen Aktieninstituts 2006, p. 41.

2007 reforms. Similar to U.S. corporations, German corporations over fulfilled the documentation duties of SOX providing leeway to reduce costs after the implementation of more principle-based rules in the 2007 reforms. The costs of SOX prior to the 2007 reforms also exceeded the benefits of SOX for U.S. corporations. With the 2007 reforms, the benefits of SOX generally outweigh the costs of SOX so that also German corporations may obtain a positive cross-listing premium. Nevertheless, it has been found that the costs of SOX generally exceed the benefits provided by SOX for foreign private issuers especially for foreign corporations from well-governed countries with high-disclosure capital markets.[2486] Also, it has been found that being subject to SOX does hardly provide any synergy effects within German corporations concerning the existing risk management system and internal control over financial reporting.[2487] This finding is not surprising since the requirements of sec. 91(2) AktG and sec. 317(4), 321(4) HGB are not equivalent to sec. 404 SOX requirements.[2488] As it has been shown above[2489], the SOX requirements exceed the German mandates of internal control regarding financial reporting[2490] and SOX does not mandate to implement risk management[2491]. But U.S. and German internal control regarding financial reporting are COSO I based, fulfilling U.S. requirements also leads to fulfilling German requirements.

For German corporations, the general factors determining whether SOX-related costs exceed the benefits are the shareholder structure and the friction incurred by complying with U.S. law, regulation, and best practice. With regard to friction, the conducted analysis demonstrates that being subject to two different legal regimes concerning corporate governance and internal control in particular does only result in minor friction[2492] leading to minor opportunity costs in this regard. With regard to the shareholder structure, the impact analysis revealed that the sec. 404 SOX internal control over financial reporting lead to inefficiencies for German cor-

2486 *Litvak*, 2007, p. 4; *Litvak*, 105 Mich. L. Rev. 1857 (2007), p. 1860; *Litvak*, European Financial Management 2008, 875; *Berger/Li/Wong*, 2011, p. 28; cf. *Li*, 2011, p. 5.

2487 *Happ/Pott*, KoR 2007, 666, 671; *Stadtmann/Wißmann*, ZRFG 2006, 16, 18.

2488 *Stadtmann/Wißmann*, ZRFG 2006, 16, 18; cf. *Gruson/Kubicek*, AG 2003, 393, 399. Different: *Kort*, in: Großkomm AktG, sec. 91, mar. 107.

2489 See *supra* at chapter 12, B. I. 1. c).

2490 Also *Gruson/Kubicek*, AG 2003, 393, 395.

2491 See *supra* at chapter 12, B. IV.

2492 See *supra* at chapter 12, B. I. 2.

poration with concentrated ownership.[2493] German corporations with a blockholding structure face higher costs due to this increased inefficiency compared to corporations with dispersed ownership. The findings indicate that for German corporations with dispersed ownership similar to the general ownership structure in the U.S., the benefits of SOX generally exceed the costs as it is the case for U.S. corporations. For German corporations with concentrated ownership, the impact analysis showed[2494] that U.S.-style internal control over financial reporting with a focus on financial fraud such as earnings management is less efficient for corporations with concentrated ownership indicating that the costs of SOX are more likely to exceed the benefits reducing or even eliminating the cross-listing premium. Otherwise, the SEC rules on the effectiveness of internal control over financial reporting do not mandate a specific set of controls providing flexibility for corporations for how to design and operate their internal control over financial reporting. German corporations have the opportunity to design internal control over financial reporting with the needs of a corporation with concentrated ownership. The COSO I framework provides for the needed flexibility to design internal control over financial reporting suitable for concentrated ownership structures. Thus, German corporations with concentrated ownership are generally able to use COSO I to design and operate internal control over financial reporting fulfilling the effectiveness criterion of the SEC without the inefficiencies of U.S.-style internal control over financial reporting designed for dispersed ownership structures. It follows that German corporations with concentrated ownership structure are able to reduce inefficiencies rendering it more likely that the SOX-related benefits exceed the costs.

C. FCPA and USSG-Related Costs and Benefits

Estimating the costs and benefits of a compliance program fulfilling the FCPA-related requirements of the USSG and the connected DOJ enforcement policy is even more difficult than estimating the costs and benefits of SOX. In difference to SOX, foreign corporations may be subject to the FCPA regardless of their listing on an U.S. exchange.[2495] Since most multinational corporations will mostly be subject to the FCPA even without be-

2493 See *supra* at chapter 12, B. I. 1. c) (4).
2494 See *supra* at chapter 12, B. I. 1. c) (4).
2495 See *supra* at chapter 5, A.

ing listed on an U.S. exchange, these corporations incur the costs to comply with FCPA and especially USSG and DOJ-related requirements for a compliance program regardless of being listed on the NYSE. Hence, most multi-national corporations have to exclude FCPA related costs from the cost-benefit analysis whether to list on the NYSE. Also, the costs of complying with USSG requirements is further reduced since German best practice of compliance programs includes more and more aspects of the USSG.[2496] Due to the impact of U.S. requirements on German best practice regarding compliance programs, corporations incur the costs to implement compliance programs fulfilling U.S. requirements in any case.

The benefits of a compliance program[2497] fulfilling the requirements of the USSG and DOJ-policy include avoiding harsh penalties, signaling to comply with U.S. standards, and COSO I-related benefits such as providing information within the corporation to assess the expected criminal and civil liability, to conduct more precise and target-aimed internal investigations, as well as reducing or eliminating corporate crime and subsequent fines including the risk of fraud and corruption. U.S. corporations aim to balance out the pros and cons of engaging in policing measures to fulfill USSG and DOJ requirements especially against the background of the litigation dilemma describing indirect costs due to the increase of the expected liability through a compliance program.[2498] Corporations have some influence on the FCPA and USSG-related costs particularly by implementing "paper-tiger" compliance programs.[2499] In general, the benefits of a compliance program are likely to outweigh the direct and indirect costs.[2500]

D. *General Benefits of U.S. Internal Control*

Corporations listed on the NYSE have to implement internal controls regarding financial reporting and are induced to implement internal controls regarding compliance with law. These requirements correspond with two of the three categories of COSO I. Since both USSG and SOX build on COSO I, corporations may reduce their overall costs for internal control over financial reporting and the compliance program by using elements of

2496 See *supra* at chapter 12, A. III.
2497 See *infra* at chapter 16, B. I. 2. c).
2498 See *infra* at chapter 16, A. I. 2. a) (3).
2499 See *supra* at chapter 5, C. III.
2500 See *infra* at chapter 16, B. I. 2. c).

their COSO I internal control structure for USSG and SOX purposes. By using COSO I internal control, corporation will comply with all relevant U.S. requirements regarding internal control and compliance.[2501] The trend of SOX and other U.S. standards including the COSO frameworks to become the international standard for internal control and compliance measures will further reduce the costs of internal control and, thus, being listed on the NYSE. Especially multi-national corporations will be able to operate worldwide using one internal control and compliance system instead of several national ones reducing the overall costs for internal control and compliance. Moreover, since corporations have incentives to implement two of the three COSO I categories, corporations may also implement the third COSO I category 'effective and efficient operations'.[2502] Thus, complying with SOX and USSG requirements provides the basis to enhance managerial control of the corporation at minimum costs.

E. Conclusion

The analysis for the costs and benefits of German corporations for being listed on the NYSE only addresses general aspects while a corporation-specific cost-benefit analysis has to consider the case-specific circumstances. The advantage of being listed on the NYSE as expressed in the cross-listing premium generally depends on the sophistication of the home country capital markets. A decisive factor for the cross-listing premium is the cost-benefit analysis of being subject to the U.S. regulatory framework. In this regard, SOX has been burdensome rendering similarly sophisticated alternative capital markets potentially attractive. Following the 2007 reforms, SOX has become beneficial for U.S. corporations. The same holds for large German corporations with dispersed ownership. For German corporations with concentrated ownership, the benefits of SOX are less obvious. But, the SEC rules provide for sufficient flexibility to implement internal control designed for the needs of corporations with concentrated ownership, i.e. a reduced focus on financial fraud and an increased focus on minority protection. With regard to the induced requirements of the USSG, the adoption of the requirements for German compliance programs and the extraterritorial application of the FCPA eliminate additional costs for being listed on the NYSE. In addition, implementing internal control using

2501 See *supra* at chapter 6, A.
2502 See *supra* at chapter 6, B.

COSO I enables corporations to comply with all relevant U.S. requirements regarding financial reporting and compliance with law and further provides the opportunity to reduce overall costs for internal control and particularly compliance programs for corporations subject to various national regulations since the U.S. mandates represent the worldwide standard.

Based on the U.S. mandates and induced requirements for internal control addressing financial reporting and compliance, corporations face little additional costs to implement comprehensive internal control in light of COSO I including managerial controls increasing the control of the corporations. Such kind of internal controls are beneficial as they will reduce agency costs and enhance minority protection if designed considering the specific shareholder structure. Especially large, listed corporations in Germany need internal control particularly with regard to financial reporting and compliance to control the corporation and to provide for timely and accurate information throughout the corporation.

Being listed on the NYSE is generally beneficial for German corporations with dispersed ownership. For corporations with concentrated ownership, the result of the cost-benefit analysis mainly depends on the ability to design internal control complying with U.S. standards while considering the implications of the concentrated shareholder structure. It follows that the cost-benefits analysis of each corporation whether to list on the NYSE has to take the existing and targeted shareholder structure into account. A corporation having or aiming for dispersed ownership will obtain more benefits when listed on the NYSE.

Chapter 14: Example of Impact – The Siemens Case

Starting in 2001, Siemens has been listed on the NYSE and was required to comply with the provisions of the FCPA.[2503] The Siemens case concerns violations of the internal control and book keeping provisions of the FCPA.[2504] The history of violations, as portrayed by the statement of offense of the U.S. District Court of Columbia[2505], includes that Siemens engaged in systematic efforts to falsify its corporate books and records and knowingly failed to implement and circumvent existing internal controls.[2506] In a period of approx. six years, Siemens made payments totaling $1.36 billion through various mechanisms of which $554 million were paid for unknown purposes including approx. $341 million in direct payments to business consultants.[2507] At least some of those payments were intended to be passed on to foreign government officials.[2508] The remaining sum was intended as direct corrupt payments to foreign officials through the payment mechanisms including cash desks and slush funds.[2509] Siemens maintained three cash desks within their offices where employees withdrew large sums of cash for corrupt payments.[2510] The same managers who submitted the requests for the cash were able to authorize the cash pickups. Until 2004, a Siemens company in South America created "slush funds" controlled by non-Siemens "trustees" and Siemens managers at offshore banks.[2511] Siemens used the slush funds to generate cash for corrupt payments.

Siemens was aware of the non-compliance and violations of laws since 2000[2512] and hired an external law firm in 2003 to investigate the ongoing practice at Siemens.[2513] The law firm reported several compliance is-

2503 *U.S. v. Siemens,* Statement of Offense, mar. 2.
2504 Cf. *Grau/Meshulam/Blechschmidt,* BB 2010, 652, at fn. 7.
2505 *U.S. v. Siemens,* Statement of Offense.
2506 *U.S. v. Siemens,* Statement of Offense, mar. 86.
2507 *U.S. v. Siemens,* Statement of Offense, mar. 87.
2508 Cf. *U.S. v. Siemens,* Statement of Offense, mar. 87.
2509 Cf. *U.S. v. Siemens,* Statement of Offense, mar. 87.
2510 *U.S. v. Siemens,* Statement of Offense, mar. 87 b.
2511 *U.S. v. Siemens,* Statement of Offense, mar. 87 f.
2512 Cf. *U.S. v. Siemens,* Statement of Offense, mar. 41.
2513 *U.S. v. Siemens,* Statement of Offense, mar. 55.

sues.[2514] These reports were ignored and buried by management which created a further compliance issue apart from bribery.[2515] Moreover, internal whistleblower reports were ignored which shows another compliance problem.[2516] In audit committee meetings, it has been falsely assured that "'no indication existed of any cash deposit accounts outside of Siemens which may be attributable to the company and in the case that any such indication existed, the company would look into this.'"[2517] In general, Siemens knew about their structural and specific compliance issues and were pressed several times by the external investigators[2518] to "fix" the compliance system and violations of law. As a result of the corruption scandal, Siemens paid $1.7 billion in fines, penalties, and disgorgement of profits to U.S. and German authorities[2519] as well as $1.3 billion in attorney and consultant fees[2520].

Besides the monetary impact on Siemens, the impact regarding the compliance organization and its corporate governance is even more significant. In its statement of offence, Siemens pledged to implement a new compliance program to detect and prevent FCPA violations, and hired a corporate monitor.[2521] The compliance program resembles to 100% the requirements of a FCPA compliance program. It has been noted that Siemens tried as hard as feasible under German law to fulfill all U.S. mandates.[2522] It follows that Siemens implemented an internal control structure which likely causes friction as shown above.[2523] Moreover, for legal and financial reporting, a global functional reporting structure was implemented.[2524] Now, all finance officers report to the CFO and all legal counsel report to the GC.[2525] In order to accommodate the magnitude of compliance functions, the compliance organization of Siemens swelled to about 600 employees.

2514 *U.S. v. Siemens,* Statement of Offense, mar. 65, 69, and 74.
2515 *U.S. v. Siemens,* Statement of Offense, mar. 56 and 60.
2516 Cf. *U.S. v. Siemens,* Statement of Offense, mar. 59.
2517 *U.S. v. Siemens,* Statement of Offense, mar. 72.
2518 Cf. *U.S. v. Siemens,* Statement of Offense, e.g. mar. 54.
2519 *Bieglman*, 2010, p. 2.
2520 Cf. *Laux*, Die Zeit, 2014.
2521 Cf. *Garrett*, 97 Va. L. Rev. 1775 (2011), p. 1787; *U.S. v. Siemens,* Statement of Offense, attachment 1, mar. 1 et seq.
2522 Cf. *Schäfer*, ZGR 2004, 416, 419.
2523 See *supra* at chapter 12, B. I. 2.
2524 *Siemens*, Statement 2008, p. 21.
2525 *Siemens*, Statement 2008, p. 21.

Chapter 15: Conclusion

The impact analysis of part III reveals that many aspects on different levels have to be considered for the impact of being listed on the NYSE with regard to internal control and compliance. The impact of U.S. law and best practice on German law is rather small by introducing U.S. concepts of internal control into German law. The main impact from U.S. law and best practice is on German best practice through references by German scholars. Also, the applicability of SOX for German corporations listed on the NYSE and the extraterritorial application of the FCPA paved the way for internal control and compliance measures of COSO I and the USSG into German corporations and German best practice.

With regard to the impact for corporations, the sheer magnitude of U.S. regulation which has to be followed is astonishing. Also, U.S. incentives negate German incentives in several aspects. Nevertheless, the amount of friction between both jurisdictions is rather low. The Siemens case illustrates the impact.

The cost-benefits analysis revealed that cross-listing on the NYSE is most probably only beneficial for large corporations with dispersed ownership seeking to profit from enhanced governance. Also, corporations subject to the FCPA and USSG regardless of a U.S. listing and multi-national corporations trying to establish worldwide compliance measures may profit from synergy effects.

Part Four Effective and Efficient Internal Control and Compliance Systems and the Evaluation of the Effectiveness

The main goal of internal control and compliance systems is to prevent and detect corporate crime as an element to deter corporate crime. The main issue is how to efficiently achieve effective internal control and compliance systems as part of effective deterrence of corporate crime. In order to determine how to achieve effective internal control and compliance systems to optimally deter corporate crime, the critique and shortcomings of the current approaches in the U.S. and Germany will be analyzed followed by the elements and requirements of an optimal approach to deter corporate crime. With regard to an optimal approach, a crucial element is the criterion of effectiveness and its evaluation. Also, the issue whether criminal or civil liability is required for an optimal approach and the options to structure a regulatory regime will be addressed. Before concluding, the analysis will focus on efficiency with regard to deterring corporate crime and achieving effective internal control and compliance systems.

Chapter 16: How to Achieve Effective Internal Control and Compliance Systems to Optimally Deter Corporate Crime?

A. *Critique and Shortcomings of the Current Approaches in the U.S. and Germany*

I. United States

In the U.S., two different approaches exist. With the enactment of SOX, a statutory approach has been chosen to require corporations to implement effective internal control over financial reporting and effective disclosure controls and procedures. Differently, the common law regime of corporate criminal liability together with the USSG and the DOJ enforcement policy induces corporations to implement effective compliance programs through granting leniency. Both approaches have been criticized.

1. Statutory Approach: Critique on SOX

Due to its far reaching legislation, it is no surprise that SOX has been criticized from early on for various reasons[2526] including costs and efficiency considerations which will be addressed subsequently. More general, SOX has been criticized by noting that "[...] frauds are not caught by auditors and internal controls", that SOX did not lead to a market rise "as it would have done if the statute solved a problem that injured investors"[2527], and that criminal law would take care of criminal managers "without any need for special rules of corporate law"[2528]. With regard to the market argument, the main goals of SOX were to restore investor confidence in the market and to reorganize external auditing.[2529] It is widely believed that SOX has

2526 E.g. *Ribstein*, 28 Iowa J. Corp. L. 1 (2002).
2527 *Easterbrook*, 95 Va. L. Rev. 685 (2009), p. 696. In contrast, a study found a negative stock price reaction (*Zhang*, 2007).
2528 *Easterbrook*, 95 Va. L. Rev. 685 (2009), p. 698.
2529 See *supra* at chapter 4, A.

been successful in achieving these goals.[2530] With regard to the argument that fraud would not be caught by internal controls, it has to be noted that effective internal controls will render fraudulent activity more difficult. While the inherent limitations of internal controls will not prevent or detect all fraudulent activity, using the general compliance program to address fraud[2531] improves the ability of corporations to prevent and detect fraud[2532].

a) Cost-Benefit Efficiency Especially Section 404 SOX

The most vigorously raised critique on SOX has been costs especially with regard to sec. 404 SOX.[2533] The costs and benefits of SOX have been analyzed above.[2534] While costs attributed to SOX have been higher than estimated, it is important to consider the average costs over a longer period of years instead of highlighting the undisputed high implementation costs leading to skewed results. The cost-benefit analysis of SOX and legislation in general faces major obstacles. These obstacles are e.g. how to interpret the obtained data, how to compare various studies with different methods used, and the problem of correlation and causation.[2535] Therefore, empirical evidence for evaluating major legislation should only be used as guidance.[2536] In this regard, it is not the purpose of the thesis to determine whether SOX has been beneficial.

After the 2007 reforms of the SEC, it is generally believed that the benefits of SOX outweigh the costs especially after the initial costs have been sunk.[2537] The finding remains controversial due to the difficulties to measure the benefits accurately. The 2007 reforms enhanced efficiency since management is only required to evaluate changes in risks and internal con-

2530 E.g. *Shakespeare*, 3 J. Bus. & Tech. 333 (2008), p. 355; *Brown*, 90 Marq. L. Rev. 309 (2006), p. 326; *Prentice/Spence*, 95 Geo. L. J. 1843 (2007), p. 1887; *Coates*, 21 J. Econ. Perspectives 91 (2007), p. 107.

2531 See *supra* at chapter 4, A. II. 1. c).

2532 See *supra* at chapter 13, B. III.

2533 Cf. *O'Brien*, CPA Journal 2006a; *Dodwell*, CPA Journal 2008; *Carney*, 55 Emory L. J. 141 (2006), p. 142; *Prentice/Spence*, 95 Geo. L. J. 1843 (2007), p. 1898; *Prentice*, 29 Cardozo L. Rev. 703 (2007), p. 703.

2534 See *supra* at chapter 13, B.

2535 *Cox*, 40 U.S.F. L. Rev. 823 (2006), p. 838 et seq.

2536 *Cox*, 40 U.S.F. L. Rev. 823 (2006), p. 833 et seq.

2537 See *supra* at chapter 13, B.

trols in an updated evaluation rather than recreating the entire process.[2538] In addition, management has to direct its efforts towards entity-level controls and automated controls rather than focusing on the details of informational infrastructure.[2539] Also, the SEC fostered a top-down, risk-based approach for the evaluation process. It is the belief of the SEC that the chosen approach will provide sufficient flexibility for corporations[2540], and will result in both effective and efficient evaluations of the effectiveness of internal control over financial reporting.[2541] Management can focus its evaluation and documentation for the overall assessment of internal controls on the business processes it determines to adequately address the risks of a material misstatement of the financial statements.[2542]

The notion that SOX is beneficial suggests that it is *Kaldor-Hicks* efficient. In this regard, the macroeconomic outcome of the cost-benefit analysis may be different from the outcome of a corporation-specific cost-benefit analysis. But according to *Kaldor-Hicks*, SOX is efficient when the macroeconomic outcome is beneficial even though the outcome for a specific corporation may not. If corporation-specific costs outweigh the benefits, corporations delist from the NYSE to avoid SOX.[2543]

b) Efficiency: One-Size-Fits-All? (Federal) Statutory Law vs. (State) Common Law

One of the main points of the critique on SOX is that federal law regulates indirectly the corporate governance structure of corporations[2544] which is a hotly debated issue in the U.S.[2545] For the first time, SOX overcame the clear distinction between federal securities law and state corporate law.[2546] Securities law has always been a highly regulated, statutory field of law

2538 See *supra* at chapter 4, A. II. 2. a).

2539 Cf. *Langevoort*, 31 J. Corp. L. 949 (2006), p. 972.

2540 SEC Release No. 8810, at I.

2541 SEC Release No. 8809, at II, A, 3; SEC Release No. 8810, at I.

2542 SEC Release No. 8810, at I.

2543 *Engel/Hayes/Wang*, 2004.

2544 Cf. *Romano*, 114 Yale L. J. 1521 (2005), p. 1540.

2545 Cf. *Johnson/Sides*, 30 Wm. Mitchell L. Rev. 1149 (2004), p. 1150; *Thompson*, 38 Wake Forest L. Rev. 961 (2003), p. 962; *Easterbrook*, 95 Va. L. Rev. 685 (2009), p. 699 et seq. See further *Thompson/Sale*, 56 Vand. L. Rev. 859 (2003); *Bainbridge*, 2003; *Brown*, 38 U. Rich. L. Rev. 317 (2004).

2546 *Johnson/Sides*, 30 Wm. Mitchell L. Rev. 1149 (2004), p. 1150. See also *Fisch*, 28 Harvard J. Law & Public Policy 39 (2004).

with its main purpose to foster disclosure and to provide necessary and accurate information to investors. Whereas corporate law, on the contrary, derives mainly from equity and is created by state courts dealing with the internal structure of corporations.[2547] Nevertheless, the finding that the General Corporate Law of Delaware is insufficient with regard to internal control and corporate compliance[2548] challenges the general argument of several commentators that state corporate law – as common law – would be more efficient[2549] than statutory law, and that case law is more flexible than statutory law since courts would be able to address each individual fact pattern and need not rely on an, allegedly, one-size-fits-all approach.[2550]

With regard to corporate governance, the notion in favor of common law is that the courts would only intervene if the directors violate their fiduciary duties of care and loyalty. A series of factual case by case decisions would leave more discretion for directors to determine the best corporate structure for each individual corporation. [2551] Each case would lead to a comprehensive development of case law which would then provide a more predictable standard for internal controls than statutory rules would be able to provide.[2552] In general, abstract fiduciary duties of care and loyalty would be more flexible to deal with different situations.[2553] Moreover, common law would provide a basis for competition for corporate charters characterized by a trial and error principle, allowing a bottom up approach rather than using a statutory top-down approach such as SOX.[2554] Thus,

2547 *Johnson/Sides*, 30 Wm. Mitchell L. Rev. 1149 (2004), p. 1151.

2548 See *supra* at chapter 5, F.

2549 See in favor of efficiency: e.g. *Posner*, Economic Analysis of Law, p. 604; *Rubin*, 6 J. Legal Stud. 51 (1977); *Bays*, 1996; *Rubin*, 13 Supreme Court Econ. Rev. 19 (2005). Also *Pan*, 2011, p. 247 et seq.; cf. *Steele/Verret*, 2 Va. L. & Bus. Rev. 189 (2007), p. 193 et seq.; *Veasey/Di Guglielmo*, 153 U. Pa. L. Rev. 1399 (2005), p. 1403 et seq. See for details on the fall of efficiency in the common law: *Zywicki*, 2003. The controversial issue whether common law is generally more efficient than statutory law is beyond the scope of the thesis.

2550 *Steele*, 52 N.Y.L. Sch. L. Rev. 503 (2007-2008), p. 504.

2551 *Johnson/Sides*, 30 Wm. Mitchell L. Rev. 1149 (2004), p. 1195. See *Scalia*, 56 U. Chi. L. Rev 1175 (1989), p. 1179 on 'rules constrain judges better than standards'.

2552 *Steele*, 52 N.Y.L. Sch. L. Rev. 503 (2007-2008), p. 504.

2553 *Steele*, 52 N.Y.L. Sch. L. Rev. 503 (2007-2008), p. 504.

2554 See e.g. *Romano*, 114 Yale L. J. 1521 (2005), p. 1529 and 1597 et seq.

state law is believed to be the only law to govern the internal structures of corporations.[2555]

With regard to the argument that case law is more flexible than statutory law, SOX has shown to foster flexibility by predetermining several different layers of lawmaking. With SOX, Congress provided a basis for internal controls but gave the SEC broad authority in sec. 3 SOX to "promulgate such rules and regulations, as may be necessary or appropriate in the public interest or for the protection of investors, and in furtherance of [SOX]". Therefore, the standard for internal controls is composed of various layers of legislation, regulation, and quasi-authoritative standard setting.[2556] The authority granted to the SEC provides that the SEC can react in a timely manner to promulgate changes to the standard, if indicated. The current system is probably more flexible than a common law rule. While one of the major criticisms of sec. 404 SOX is that it requires a one-size-fits-all approach towards internal controls, it has to be noted that the SEC believes that the top-down, risk-based approach together with the broad guidelines of the interpretive guidelines will prevent a one-size-fits-all approach.[2557] Also, the broad definition of 'internal control' within COSO I prevents a one-size-fits-all proposition.[2558]

2. Granting Leniency in the Context of Corporate Criminal Liability

In the context of corporate criminal liability, corporations are induced to implement effective compliance programs through leniency provisions within the USSG and DOJ enforcement policy. The USSG as well as the DOJ enforcement policy have been criticized.

a) Critique on the USSG-Approach

With regard to their purpose of deterring criminal conduct, the USSG have been criticized for their incentive structure aiming to induce corporations to prevent and detect corporate crime effectively. The critique on the USSG

2555 *Steele*, 52 N.Y.L. Sch. L. Rev. 503 (2007-2008), p. 507.

2556 *Stevelman*, 52, N.Y.L. Sch. L. Rev. 475 (2007-2008), p. 493.

2557 SEC Release No. 8810, at III, B; also *Coates*, 21 J. Econ. Perspectives 91 (2007), p. 103.

2558 See *supra* at chapter 4, C. I.

is not consistent and aims at different aspects of the USSG. The main critique mirrors the debate of the optimal regime for corporate criminal liability.[2559] Besides this main critique, facile praising and provoking notions complete the critique on the USSG. While some authors claim the approach to be successful[2560], others conclude that the sentencing guidelines for corporations are a "failure"[2561] or outdated[2562]. Moreover, the reliance of USSG-approach on compliance programs has been criticized based on the arguments that compliance programs have not been proven to be effective and that courts would lack the expertise to evaluate their effectiveness resulting in the implementation of mere "cosmetic" compliance programs.[2563] While some of the critique is merited, the following evaluation directs the focus on the key issues.

(1) Success of the USSG

The USSG have been characterized as "a milestone in federal criminal law and in organizational behavior" and "a real success story for the [USSC] in its work to deter crime and encourage compliance with the law".[2564] Moreover, it has been noted that the USSG "influenced many corporations to adopt compliance programs".[2565] Also, a study found that corporations have expended "vigorous efforts" in recent years to enhance "ethical performance and reduce organizational misconduct" since the enactment of the USSG-carrot-and-stick-approach.[2566] These findings, however, are mainly based on the fact that corporation have implemented compliance and ethics programs. Thus, the USSG have successfully raised the awareness of corporations for the need of effective compliance programs[2567], despite

2559 See *infra* at chapter 16, B.

2560 *Steer*, 2001, p. 21; *Murphy*, 87 Iowa L. Rev. 697 (2002), p. 719; USSC, Ad Hoc Report, p. 28.

2561 Cf. *Arlen*, 2011b.

2562 Cf. *Henning*, 116 Yale L. J. Pocket Part 312 (2007).

2563 Cf. *Krawiec*, 81 Wash. U. L. Quarterly 487 (2003); *Pape*, Corporate Compliance, p. 156.

2564 *Murphy*, 87 Iowa L. Rev. 697 (2002), p. 719. See also *Lytton/Swenson*, 2002, pp. 44 and 48.

2565 *Murphy*, 87 Iowa L. Rev. 697 (2002), p. 710.

2566 Ethics Resource Center, 2011, p. 29.

2567 *Webb/Molo*, 71 Wash. U. L. Q. 375 (1993), p. 375; *Steer*, 2001, p. 10; *Stansbury/Barry*, 2007, p. 2; *Driscoll/Hoffman/Murphy*, 99 Business and Society Rev. 35 (1998), p. 40; USSC, Ad Hoc Report, p. 35.

fears of corporate leaders, especially in the beginning, that courts would not determine compliance programs to be effective, and, therefore, would deny the mitigating factor of such program. These fears were attributed to the hindsight argument that a truly effective program would have prevented the criminal act to occur in the first place.[2568] Even today corporations cannot be sure if and how judges will apply the USSG, because the USSG are only advisory for the judge and provide considerable discretion with regard to the actually imposed fine.[2569]

(2) Ineffectiveness of the USSG

The USSG-approach has been criticized for being ineffective.[2570] For the main part, the criticism is based on the arguments that USSG-compliance programs would not have been proven to be effective[2571] and that courts would lack the expertise to determine the effectiveness of compliance programs.[2572] Thus, the main goal of the USSG to prevent and detect misconduct would not be achieved by the required compliance program. Based on these assumptions, the USSG only provide for incentives for corporations to implement "cosmetic" compliance programs – whose purpose is solely to comply with the USSG *prima facie* to receive leniency – intended to "mimic" the USSG requirements resulting in "social waste".[2573] Thus, corporations will only invest in compliance programs "that have sufficient content to persuade courts […] of their effectiveness, but they will not invest additional resources to make the programs fully effective in mitigating misconduct".[2574] The finding that corporations only invest in "paper tiger"

2568 *Webb/Molo*, 71 Wash. U. L. Q. 375 (1993), p. 396; cf. *Guthrie/Rachlinski/Wistrich*, 86 Cornell L. Rev. 777 (2001), p. 799.

2569 *Arlen*, 2011b, at fn. 16.

2570 Cf. *Krawiec*, 81 Wash. U. L. Quarterly 487 (2003), p. 487 et seq.

2571 *Krawiec*, 32 Fla. St. U. L. Rev. 571 (2005), p. 592 et seq.; *id.*, 81 Wash. U. L. Quarterly 487 (2003), p. 512 et seq.; *Kendall/DeMarr/Jones-Rikkers*, 37 Journal of Bus. Ethics 367 (2002), p. 380.

2572 *Krawiec*, 32 Fla. St. U. L. Rev. 571 (2005), p. 580; *id.*, 81 Wash. U. L. Quarterly 487 (2003), p. 536; *Fischel/Sykes*, 25 J. Legal Stud. 319 (1996), p. 329; *Khanna*, 2002, p. 16. See also *Langevoort*, 2002 Colum. Bus. L. Rev. 71, p. 118.

2573 *Krawiec*, 81 Wash. U. L. Quarterly 487 (2003), p. 491 et seq.; cf. *Pape*, Corporate Compliance, p. 216.

2574 *Aviram*, 32 Fla. St. U. L. Rev. 763 (2005), p. 768 commenting on *Krawiec*, 32 Fla. St. U. L. Rev. 571 (2005).

compliance programs has distinct standing.[2575] Corporations do not devote sufficient resources to implement best practice standards but implement only minimum requirements of compliance programs.[2576] A prominent example of a "paper tiger" compliance program is the Enron case since Enron's massive fraud was feasible despite Enron's code of conduct and compliance program.[2577]

The critique, stressing the lack of expertise of courts to determine compliance programs to be effective and the unproven effectiveness of such programs resulting in "paper tiger" compliance programs, aims at a central component of the USSG and targets the underlying corporate criminal liability regime of the USSG which is duty-based liability.[2578] The argument that compliance programs have not been proven to be effective mainly rests on the finding that the USSG-approach is ineffective in providing incentives to induce optimal compliance programs due to the ineffectiveness of the underlying corporate criminal liability regime of duty-based liability to induce effective policing.[2579]

The two arguments will be addressed separately. First, with regard to the ineffectiveness of the duty-based liability regime to induce effective policing, law and economics research suggests that a duty-based liability regime is able to induce optimal policing since government and courts are able to set an optimal standard of care.[2580] Therefore, the argument of unproven effectiveness of policing measures has still some standing since the effectiveness has not been proven yet, but substantially loses its standing due to the rebuttal of the underlying foundation of the argument a duty-based liability regime would be ineffective to induce effective policing measures. Moreover, research summarizing studies regarding the effectiveness of codes of conduct – an important element of policing measures – indicates that important elements of policing measures are in fact effective.[2581] In the same way, studies have shown that compliance programs reduce mis-

2575 See also *supra* at chapter 5, C. III.
2576 Ethics Resource Center, 2011, p. 70.
2577 Cf. USSC, Ad Hoc Report, p. 37.
2578 See also *supra* at chapter 5, C. III.
2579 Cf. *Krawiec*, 32 Fla. St. U. L. Rev. 571 (2005), pp. 580, 582 and 597. See also *supra* at chapter 5, C. III.
2580 See *infra* at chapter 16, B.
2581 Cf. *Pape*, Corporate Compliance, p. 219 et seq. (appendix): Out of 81 examined studies, 33.3% found a strongly positive and 13.6% slightly positive impact while 2.5% had a negative impact. Moreover, 30% of the studies found no meaningful and 13.6% inconsistent results.

conduct and increase employee reporting.[2582] Admittedly, the overall effectiveness of policing measures is still unproven and the empirical testing of the effectiveness of compliance programs remains difficult starting with the common problem of how to measure effectiveness.[2583] Nonetheless, there is no indication so far that compliance programs are *per se* non-effective. Moreover, noting *arguendo* that corporations only engage in "cosmetic" compliance programs, the finding that such compliance programs have not been proven to be effective is obvious. If corporations had never implemented effective compliance programs, no study would have been able to find such programs to be effective. It follows from that corporations have to be provided with sufficient incentives to implement effective compliance programs. Then, corporations will engage in effective compliance programs rendering the problems of "cosmetic" compliance programs and unproven effectiveness obsolete.

Second, with regard to the argument that courts would lack the expertise to assess the effectiveness of compliance programs, it has been noted that courts may have the ability to identify sham programs[2584] but mainly lack the resources to do so[2585]. While courts lack the expertise with regard to many issues they are confronted with, they usually have the opportunity to obtain the expertise of expert witnesses.[2586] Likewise, in light of the DOJ enforcement policy, entrusting prosecutors with the task of assessing the effectiveness of compliance programs has not been viewed as a better alternative.[2587] The need for courts to evaluate the effectiveness of compliance programs can only be avoided by a strict liability regime.[2588] As it has been shown, however, strict liability does not provide sufficient incentives for corporations to implement policing measures.[2589] In order to deal with the supposed issue of inadequate expertise of courts, courts have to be equipped with sufficient resources to fulfill their task. When courts are enabled to fulfill their task, corporations would get no benefit from engaging in "cosmetic" policing measures and would stop to do so. While it remains

2582 Ethics Resource Center, 2011, p. 81; cf. ERC, NBES 2009, p. 9.
2583 *Steer*, 2001, p. 9; *Pape*, Corporate Compliance, p. 156 et seq.; cf. USSC, Ad Hoc Report, p. 35; *PwC/Compliance Week*, 2011, p. 8. See for the evaluation of the effectiveness *infra* at chapter 16, B. IV. 2.
2584 *Aviram*, 32 Fla. St. U. L. Rev. 763 (2005), p. 769.
2585 *Krawiec*, 32 Fla. St. U. L. Rev. 571 (2005), p. 581.
2586 Cf. USSG, Commentary to sec. 8D1.4 no. 1.
2587 See *infra* at chapter 16, A. I. 2. b).
2588 Cf. *Krawiec*, 32 Fla. St. U. L. Rev. 571 (2005), p. 575 et seq.
2589 See *supra* at chapter 5, B. II.

a difficult task for courts to assess the effectiveness of compliance programs, it has to be noted that COSO I provides for a framework to assess the effectiveness of such programs.[2590] Moreover, a test for the effectiveness and its prerequisites will be suggested further below[2591] enabling courts and agencies to assess the effectiveness of compliance programs in order to grant leniency.

With regard to the raised critique that the USSG-approach is ineffective, it has to be conceded that assessing the effectiveness of compliance programs is a difficult task for courts, but courts are capable to fulfill this task if equipped with sufficient resources and by using the suggested test. With regard to the criticism of unproven effectiveness of compliance programs, research indicates that important elements of policing measures are effective such as codes of conduct. Moreover, the argument of unproven effectiveness, resting on the rebutted finding that duty-based liability is ineffective in inducing corporations to engage in effective policing, does not have sufficient substance to favor a strict liability regime. Since the arguments for criticizing the USSG-approach to be ineffective have at least strongly been weakened if not rebutted, the reasons for the correct finding that corporations tend to engage in "cosmetic" or minimum requirement compliance programs are neither the general ineffectiveness of compliance programs nor the lack of expertise of courts as the following subpart will show: a law and economics analysis of the USSG suggests a different cause.

(3) Failure of the USSG

One of the main purposes of the USSG is to induce corporations to engage in policing measures[2592] by providing for lower sanctions if corporations adopted effective policing measures. Accordingly, the USSG resemble the duty-based liability regime of corporate criminal liability which is the best choice for a corporate criminal liability regime.[2593] A recent law and economics analysis of the Sentencing Guidelines for Corporations of the USSG, however, concludes the USSG to be a "failure" to serve the objec-

---

2590 See *supra* at chapter 4, C. I.

2591 See *infra* at chapter 16, B. IV. 2.

2592 Cf. USSG, Introductory Commentary to chapter 8.

2593 Cf. *Arlen/Kraakman*, 72 N.Y.U.L. Rev. 687 (1997), p. 745. See *infra* at chapter 16, B. 2. c) and d).

tives of the duty-based liability regime.[2594] With regard to the requirements of an optimal duty-based liability regime, the USSG generally provide for the requested "large default sanction".[2595] Also, the mitigating provisions of the USSG inducing *ex ante* monitoring, and *ex post* cooperation and reporting are in general consistent with the first requirement of duty-based liability.[2596] Due to policing measures, the expected liability increases since such measures increase the likelihood of being sanctioned.[2597] Therefore, corporations face a higher expected sanction when engaging in corporate policing measures than when refraining from such measures.[2598] Reflected in the higher expected sanction is the higher probability for the corporation to be sanctioned.[2599] Unlike provided by the USSG, the "mitigation amount should be larger […] the greater the impact of optimal policing measures on the probability of detection" in order to induce optimal policing.[2600] The USSG, however, do not provide for sufficient mitigation to induce optimal policing.[2601] Thus, it has been suggested that the USSC abandons the USSG-approach of standardized sanctions and attempts to account for "the impact of policing measures on the probability of detection"[2602] leading to a flexible approach towards sanctioning.

The USSG also adhere to the second requirement of the duty-based liability regime that the mitigated sanction has to be still high enough to induce corporations to engage in optimal prevention measures[2603], because corporations receiving full sanction mitigation remain subject to a mitigated sanction under the USSG[2604]. The mitigated sanction of the USSG, however, does not necessarily equal the social cost of the crime divided by the probability of detection when the corporation engages optimally in policing as mandated by the second requirement.[2605] Thus, the USSG have

2594 Cf. *Arlen*, 2011b.

2595 *Arlen/Kraakman*, 72 N.Y.U.L. Rev. 687 (1997), p. 745.

2596 See *infra* at chapter 16, B. I. 2. d).

2597 *Arlen*, 2011b, p. 14; *id.*, 2011a, p. 38.

2598 *Arlen*, 2011b, p. 30 et seq.; cf. *Arlen/Kraakman*, 72 N.Y.U.L. Rev. 687 (1997), p. 707; *Arlen*, 23 J. Legal Stud. 833 (1994), p. 836.

2599 See *supra* at chapter 5, B. II.

2600 *Arlen/Kraakman*, 72 N.Y.U.L. Rev. 687 (1997), p. 746.

2601 *Arlen/Kraakman*, 72 N.Y.U.L. Rev. 687 (1997), p. 746; *Arlen*, 2011b, pp. 21-32. See *supra* at chapter 5, C. III.

2602 *Arlen/Kraakman*, 72 N.Y.U.L. Rev. 687 (1997), p. 747.

2603 See *infra* at chapter 16, B. I. 2. d).

2604 *Arlen/Kraakman*, 72 N.Y.U.L. Rev. 687 (1997), p. 745.

2605 *Arlen/Kraakman*, 72 N.Y.U.L. Rev. 687 (1997), p. 749. See *supra* at chapter 5, C. III.

to ensure sufficient sanction mitigation to offset the increase in the probability of being sanctioned provided by policing measures.[2606]

Furthermore, the USSG most intensely undermine the incentives to implement effective policing measures "when effective sanction mitigation is most needed".[2607] That is when managers of large firms are involved in wrongdoings.[2608] The USSG provide for even less optimal incentives to implement optimal policing measures in case of large corporations.[2609] As it will be shown, however, government relies on the help of corporations especially when high-level management is involved in criminal conduct and whenever corporations are large and complex.[2610] Therefore, the USSG should provide large corporations with higher incentives to implement policing measures especially with regard to criminal conduct of high-level management.[2611] Thus, despite the reasoning of the USSC regarding the higher culpability of large corporations, counterintuitive measures should be taken to provide sufficient incentives for large corporations to implement effective policing measures.

The law and economics analysis of corporate criminal liability demonstrates the need of a duty-based liability regime to induce corporations to optimally engage in prevention and policing measures. These measures are important to prevent and detect general and securities fraud especially with regard to high-level management. As the analysis shows, the USSG are in general structured to "help to deter crime if the provisions provided sufficient fine mitigation to induce [corporations] to police optimally".[2612] The current USSG, however, do not provide for sufficient incentives to induce corporations to implement effective policing measures.

(4) Relevance of the USSG

Besides the named critique on the USSG, their overall importance has been called into question. The main argument is that the prosecutorial

---

2606 *Arlen*, 2011b, pp. 15 and 17. See *id.*, 2011b, p. 20 et seq.; *Arlen/Kraakman*, 72 N.Y.U.L. Rev. 687 (1997), p. 751 et seq.

2607 *Arlen*, 2011b, p. 5.

2608 *Arlen*, 2011b, p. 5, p. 22 et seq., and p. 25 et seq.; cf. *Kraakman*, in: Encyclopedia of Law and Economics, p. 137.

2609 See *supra* at chapter 5, C. III.

2610 Cf. *Arlen*, 2011b, p. 11 and *infra* at chapter 16, B. I. 1.

2611 Cf. *Arlen*, 2011b, p. 20.

2612 *Arlen*, 2011b, p. 20.

policy of the DOJ to come to deferred and non-prosecution agreements can better "achieve the goal of reforming corporate cultures" than the USSG.[2613] The main difference between the DOJ-policy and the USSG is that the DOJ-policy interferes prior to an indictment in contrast to the USSG which are only involved in the end of a trial to determine the fine. The mere threat of an indictment, however, provides sufficient incentives for corporations to follow the dictates of the federal prosecutors since indicting a corporation may have severe adverse effects on a business.[2614] A classical example of the effects of an indictment is the Arthur Andersen case in the aftermath of the Enron scandal.[2615] In contrast to an indictment, the fines which may be imposed under the USSG are not as threatening to corporations.[2616] Moreover, corporations may agree to pay an agreed-upon amount as part of a DOJ-agreement[2617] rendering fine mitigation through the USSG less attractive. Therefore, corporations try hard to avoid an indictment by adhering to the DOJ-policy in order to obtain a deferred or non-prosecution agreement which allegedly renders the USSG "largely irrelevant".[2618]

The provoking notion of the irrelevance of the USSG draws the attention towards the severe consequences of indicting a corporation. These consequences lead to the DOJ-policy of non- and deferred prosecution agreements providing incentives for corporations to implement compliance programs. Regardless of the alleged irrelevance of the USSG, their benefit has been to provide for a structure to evaluate the "corporation's

---

2613 *Henning*, 116 Yale L. J. Pocket Part 312 (2007), p. 312. See *supra* at chapter 5, D.

2614 *Beale*, 46 Am. Crim. L. Rev. 1481 (2009), p. 1500; cf. *Henning*, 116 Yale L. J. Pocket Part 312 (2007), p. 312 et seq.; *Garrett*, 97 Va. L. Rev. 1775 (2011), p. 1794.

2615 Cf. *Henning*, 116 Yale L. J. Pocket Part 312 (2007), p. 313; *Garrett*, 97 Va. L. Rev. 1775 (2011), p. 1794. Arthur Andersen was the auditing firm of Enron which was indicted for obstruction of justice. In 2005, the U.S. Supreme Court (*Arthur Andersen LLP v. United States*, 544 U.S. 696 (2005)) overturned Arthur Andersen's conviction for obstruction of justice. Thus, Arthur Andersen has not been found guilty of a crime. Nevertheless, the corporation had already ceased its operations and did not resume its business after the acquittal. Arguably, even without an indictment, the firm's reputation had already been irrecoverable damaged due to its involvement in the Enron scandal.

2616 Cf. *Henning*, 116 Yale L. J. Pocket Part 312 (2007), p. 313. The Siemens case is also a good example that corporations will accept even high monetary fines (see *supra* at chapter 14).

2617 *Kaal/Lacine*, 2014, p. 3; *Henning*, 116 Yale L. J. Pocket Part 312 (2007), p. 314 et seq.

2618 *Henning*, 116 Yale L. J. Pocket Part 312 (2007), pp. 312 and 314.

culture and the authenticity of its response to wrongdoing by its employees".[2619] Moreover, the USSG served as the model for the DOJ-policy[2620] which still refers to the USSG.[2621] Thus, under the current regime, the DOJ-policy needs the USSG as its underlying reference. Despite the DOJ's policy of non-prosecution[2622], the USSG are still important for those corporations engaging in effective compliance programs which are anyhow convicted by prosecutors[2623] or which are not confident to benefit from the DOJ-policy[2624]. Due to general prevention of crime or other policy reasons, corporations may still be indicted even though they have an effective compliance program in place. Especially FCPA violations appear to be prosecuted despite full cooperation.[2625] Since corporations do not have a guarantee of never being indicted, the USSG still provide incentives to implement effective compliance programs. That the current incentives are not sufficient does not lead to the irrelevance of the USSG. Rather, their potential in inducing corporations to implement effective compliance programs has not been entirely used. Moreover, it has been concluded that the DOJ-policy is not sufficient to outweigh the detriments of USSG-shortcomings.[2626] If the DOJ-policy were to render the USSG irrelevant it would outweigh the detriments of the USSG-shortcomings. Thus, the DOJ-policy itself does not provide sufficient incentives to induce corporations to optimally engage in compliance programs.[2627] It can be conceded that the impact of the USSG has diminished due to the DOJ-policy. Nevertheless, the USSG provide the basis for the DOJ-policy and are still relevant for corporations.

(5) Conclusion

The USSG are in general suitable to induce corporations to engage in optimal prevention and policing measures including the implementation of ef-

---

2619 *Henning*, 116 Yale L. J. Pocket Part 312 (2007), p. 312.

2620 *Henning*, 116 Yale L. J. Pocket Part 312 (2007), p. 314; *Murphy*, 87 Iowa L. Rev. 697 (2002), p. 712; cf. *Steer*, 2001, p. 15.

2621 Cf. DOJ, Principles of Federal Prosecution of Business Organizations.

2622 See *supra* at chapter 5, D.

2623 *Arlen*, 2011b, p. 7.

2624 *Arlen*, 2011b, p. 18.

2625 *Arlen*, 2011b, at fn. 22.

2626 *Arlen*, 2011b, p. 35.

2627 See *supra* at chapter 5, D. I.

fective compliance programs. Thereby, the USSG have the potential to foster their goal of preventing and detecting corporate crime. Nevertheless, their success until now is indistinct as the inconsistent critique shows. In contrast to the long-lasting failure of the FCPA[2628] to induce corporations to engage in policing measures between its implementation and its recent revival[2629], the USSG were successful in raising the awareness of the need for effective compliance programs. Their success so far is limited, however, to raising the awareness of corporations regarding compliance programs.

The existence of ineffective "cosmetic" compliance programs and the DOJ-policy are the result of important shortcomings of the USSG. The reasons for the shortcomings have been revealed by the law and economics research finding the current USSG to provide for insufficient incentives for corporations to implement optimal prevention and policing measures. The existence of "cosmetic" compliance programs has been used to argue against the duty-based liability regime, on which the USSG are based, in favor of strict liability. The argument of unproven effectiveness, however, rests on the rebutted finding that duty-based liability is ineffective in inducing corporations to engage in effective policing. Therefore, it does not have sufficient substance to favor a strict liability regime. On the contrary, as the analyzed research shows, the duty-based liability approach of the USSG is generally suitable to induce optimal prevention and policing. Therefore, the observation that corporations tend to engage in "cosmetic" compliance programs finds support in the analyzed research but the conclusion to dismiss the USSG-approach in favor of an adjusted strict liability regime has been rebutted. On the contrary, corporations have to be provided with optimal incentives to engage in effective policing measures. Thereby, the USSG play an important role.

The depicted shortcomings of the USSG have to be viewed against the background that the concept of inducing corporations to deliberately engage in policing measures is fairly new. Prior to USSG, no standardized approach of sanction mitigation existed to induce corporations to engage in policing measures. In the U.S., the predominant corporate liability regime has been vicarious strict liability to deter corporate crime without the concept of inducing corporations to engage in policing measures through sanction mitigation. In addition, it seems that the USSC introduced the provisions of sanction mitigation into the USSG in 1991 based on the

2628 See *Seligman*, 80 Notre Dame L. Rev. 1159 (2005), p. 1182; *Newman/Oliverio*, 2006.

2629 See *supra* at chapter 5, A. II.

"philosophical" idea that corporations are less culpable and, therefore, the appropriate sanction should be reduced in case corporations engaged "prior to the offense [in] prevent[ing] and detect[ing] criminal conduct".[2630] Thus, the steps taken by a corporation prior to its agents' wrongdoing to prevent and detect criminal conduct were primarily designed to determine the culpability of a corporation and not to induce effective policing measures. As a supplement effect, the determination of the culpability also induces corporations to engage in steps to prevent and detect criminal conduct. While the purpose of the current USSG is also to induce corporations to prevent and detect corporate crime, the USSG-requirements were not designed, however, to offset the undermining effects of the litigation dilemma in order to optimally induce corporations to engage in policing measures. Providing for reduced sanctions was a side effect and not the primary goal of the USSG leading to the current ineffectiveness in providing for optimal sanction mitigation in light of inducing corporations to engage in optimal policing measures. The notion of the Ad Hoc Advisory Group of 2003, indicating that resolving the litigation dilemma would be beyond the scope of the USSC[2631], clearly shows that the USSG are currently not designed with the goal of providing sufficient sanction mitigation to offset the litigation dilemma.

Moreover, as the lack of enforcement of the FCPA up until recently shows, enforcement is an important factor to effectively deter corporate crime. Since law enforcement agencies rely on policing measures of corporations to prevent and detect corporate crime, ceasing the USSG-approach in favor of strict liability is not promising despite the ineffectiveness of the current USSG. Hence, rendering the USSG effective is an important and ongoing task. As the recent research[2632] shows, the magnitude of the issue of ineffective USSG has not been fully apprehended.

2630 USSC, Suppl. Report, p. 4 et seq.
2631 Cf. USSC, Ad Hoc Report, p. 120.
2632 See *Arlen*, 2011a and *id.*, 2011b.

b) Critique on the DOJ Enforcement Policy

The DOJ enforcement policy has been criticized for the wide discretion of prosecutors[2633] which is hardly subject to any judicial review.[2634] Also, the practice of the DOJ has been criticized as prosecutors substitute with their own judgment the judgment of the board of directors and civil regulators for how to optimally structure internal corporate governance.[2635] Through such substitution, prosecutors stepped out of their traditional role to obtain convictions.[2636] It has been argued to leave the issue of imposed structural reforms including outside monitors to civil regulators since civil regulators are more likely to have the necessary expertise than prosecutors.[2637] With regard to DOJ practice to require the implementation of an external monitor as part of non- and deferred prosecution agreements, the usefulness of monitors for achieving the goal of ensuring that the corporation meets the terms of the settlement agreement has been analyzed.[2638] It has been found that monitors generally serve an important function to ensure that corporations implement effective internal controls and compliance programs but monitors have to be qualified for the job to be successful.[2639] It has been suggested as an important element of monitorships that fiduciary duties should apply to monitors to the extent of the powers ranging from being very influential to being significant advisors in order to reflect the extent of vulnerability of shareholders to the powers of monitors.[2640] In light of the argument to leave structural reforms to civil regulators, it has been noted that properly structured corporate criminal liability would render imposed structural reforms obsolete.[2641]

Currently, the DOJ enforcement policy is used to offset the shortcomings of the USSG. It will not be needed, however, if incentives for corporations are structured optimally.

2633 *Garrett*, 93 Va. L. Rev. 853 (2007), p. 913 et seq.

2634 *Garrett*, 93 Va. L. Rev. 853 (2007), p. 919 et seq.; *id.*, 97 Va. L. Rev. 1775 (2011), p. 1788.

2635 See *Arlen*, in: Prosecutors in the Boardroom, p. 63 et seq.; *Garrett*, 93 Va. L. Rev. 853 (2007), p. 859 et seq. and on the effect of deferred and non-prosecution agreements: *Kaal/Lacine*, 2014.

2636 Cf. *Garrett*, 93 Va. L. Rev. 853 (2007), p. 936.

2637 *Arlen*, in: Prosecutors in the Boardroom, p. 63.

2638 See *Ford/Hess*, 34 J. Corp. L. 679 (2009), p. 679 et seq.

2639 *Ford/Hess*, 34 J. Corp. L. 679 (2009), p. 737.

2640 *Khanna/Dickinson*, 105 Mich. L. Rev. 1713 (2007), p. 1742 et seq.

2641 *Arlen*, in: Prosecutors in the Boardroom, p. 78. See *infra* at chapter 16, B.

II. Shortcomings of German Law to Achieve Effective Internal Control and Compliance

The German legal system does not provide an optimal setup to induce German corporations to implement effective internal control including an effective compliance program.[2642] This is foremost due to an insufficient incentive structure for corporations to implement truly effective internal control including compliance measures. With regard to internal control regarding financial reporting, inducing such kind of internal control is not a primary goal in Germany. With regard to corporate compliance, no concept exists to provide leniency for corporations to offset the litigation dilemma. Moreover, no standard is mandated to evaluate the effectiveness of internal control. Also, no official guidelines for internal control or compliance programs exist in Germany.

With regard to corporate law, issues are neglected within sec. 76 combined with sec. 93 and sec. 91(2) AktG such as the agency problem including non-optimal incentives for managers to implement effective internal control. Also, the supervisory board has to enhance its oversight duty by providing guidance to scrutinize the decisions of the management board regarding internal control and the early warning system. With such enhanced scrutiny, the agency problem will be reduced fostering good corporate governance.

Also from the incentive regime of corporate liability for crimes and offences, corporations do not have sufficient incentives to implement effective compliance measures due to the low expected sanction of OWiG and the deterring effect attributed to the litigation dilemma. Corporations have only incentives to implement prevention measures up to the point when marginal costs exceed marginal benefits. Since the possibility of being indicted is rather low, the incentives to engage in prevention measures are also low.

B. *Optimal Approach to Deter Corporate Crime*

The aim of optimally deterring corporate crime is ambitious but necessary in light of the magnitude of corporate wrongdoing as shown by the numerous corporate scandals. Law and economics research, in particular by

2642 See *supra* at chapter 10, D.

Jennifer Arlen[2643], has been conducted analyzing the different approaches of corporate criminal liability to deter corporate crime. In the following, the essential elements of this research will be portrayed. Then the questions will be addressed whether corporate civil liability would provide similar results compared to corporate criminal liability and which regulatory regime is advisable. An important element of internal control is the criterion of effectiveness which will be addressed before turning to a similar important element to achieve effective internal control: the evaluation of the effectiveness. A two steps test will be suggested for the evaluation.

I. Corporate Criminal Liability

In the U.S., corporate criminal liability has the main purpose to deter corporate crime in order to maximize social welfare.[2644] In order to achieve effective prevention and deterrence of corporate crime, government has to ensure that crime does not pay by making sure that expected penalties exceed the benefits from committing crime. In this context, cost-effective detection of wrongdoing and identification of wrongdoers is essential.[2645] In order to effectively prevent and deter corporate crime, the structure of corporate criminal liability is of utmost importance. While legislators and judges sometime seem to act on the simple equation that higher penalties would lead to less corporate crime[2646], law and economics research shows that this simple equation does not hold.[2647] The knowledge of how corporate criminal liability has to be structured to provide for optimal incentives to prevent and deter corporate crime is important for government and courts to understand how their sentencing rules and decisions will affect corporate behavior in order to avoid suboptimal incentives regarding the deterrence of corporate crime.

2643 See *Arlen*, 2011b; *id.*, 2011a; *Arlen/Kraakman*, 72 N.Y.U.L. Rev. 687 (1997); *Arlen*, 23 J. Legal Stud. 833 (1994).

2644 *Arlen*, 2011b, p. 8.

2645 *Arlen*, 2011b, p. 1.

2646 *Arlen*, 1994, p. 833.

2647 Cf. *Arlen*, 2011a, p. 42; *Arlen/Kraakman*, 72 N.Y.U.L. Rev. 687 (1997), p. 707 et seq.; *Arlen*, 23 J. Legal Stud. 833 (1994), p. 847 et seq. See *Laufer*, 52 Vand. L. Rev. 1343 (1999).

1. Need for Individual and Corporate Criminal Liability

Under the classic economic model – representing a "perfect world" –, government would be able to deter corporate crime optimally by using a strict liability regime imposing liability either on individual wrongdoers or on corporations.[2648] The assumptions of a perfect-world-model are that states and corporations can impose optimal sanctions on wrongdoers at zero marginal cost, corporations and employees contract without costs, labor markets ensure that corporations bear their employees' expected costs of working for the corporation including liability, and all parties are perfectly informed about the expected costs and benefits of each other's actions.[2649] Thus, there would be no need for prevention or policing measures by corporations to deter corporate crime.[2650] In contrast to a perfect world, however, government cannot optimally deter corporate crime in a "real world" through individual liability.[2651] Due to significant costs of investigations for government and since *ex post* sanctions do not deter all crime, government "may find that it can deter crime at lower cost by inducing [corporations] to intervene *ex ante* to prevent wrongs".[2652] Since government is unable to optimally deter corporate crime, optimal deterrence can only be achieved through "corporate expenditures on prevention and policing".[2653] Therefore, government needs to induce corporations to engage in prevention and policing measures.[2654] In this regard, it is noteworthy that corporate liability deters crime differently than individual liability.[2655]

While individual liability has direct influence on individuals, corporate liability falls on the owners of the corporation and not directly on the wrongdoer. Especially in situations of separation of ownership and control, as in most large corporations, corporate liability does not address

2648 *Arlen*, 2011a, p. 14 et seq.

2649 Cf. *Arlen*, 2011a, p. 23.

2650 *Arlen*, 2011a, p. 24.

2651 *Arlen*, 2011a, p. 24; cf. *Arlen/Kraakman*, 72 N.Y.U.L. Rev. 687 (1997), p. 691 et seq. In a real world, deterrence is costly and government will have expenditures on enforcement (*Arlen*, 2011a, p. 24; cf. *Driscoll/Hoffman/Murphy*, 99 Business and Society Rev. 35 (1998), p. 49).

2652 *Arlen*, 2011a, p. 24; cf. *Arlen/Kraakman*, 72 N.Y.U.L. Rev. 687 (1997), p. 701 et seq.

2653 *Arlen*, 2011a, p. 24; *Arlen/Kraakman*, 72 N.Y.U.L. Rev. 687 (1997), p. 700.

2654 *Arlen*, 2011a, p. 25; cf. *id.*, 2011b, p. 12; *Arlen/Kraakman*, 72 N.Y.U.L. Rev. 687 (1997), p. 700.

2655 *Arlen*, 2011b, p. 8; *id.*, 2011a, p. 30.

those responsible for the crime which results in agency costs.[2656] In addition to corporate liability, government imposes individual criminal liability to deter intentional wrongdoing.[2657] Individual criminal liability is needed to deter crime sufficiently since individuals may not have sufficient funds to pay sanctions.[2658] Furthermore, individual liability is essential to supplement corporate liability by ensuring that individual wrongdoers are sanctioned in order to remedy agency costs.[2659] Thus, optimal deterrence of corporate crime requires government to impose both individual and corporate criminal liability.[2660]

Moreover, optimal deterrence requires effective enforcement. In order to ensure that wrongdoers are sanctioned, government depends on the efforts of corporations to deter, detect, or report wrongdoers[2661], especially for crimes such as securities fraud[2662]. Since corporations are in a remarkable position to deter crimes committed by employees through corporate policing[2663], corporate liability is important despite the perceived misallocation of corporate liability.[2664] With regard to securities fraud, corporations are almost always liable for fraud on the market[2665] of its agents.[2666] The justification of this liability is mostly based on the economic arguments made in the court's context that (1) corporate liability better serves the goals of optimal deterrence than agent liability, (2) corporate liability optimally spreads the risk of liability between the corporation and its agents, (3) and corporate liability optimally allocates the losses of a crime to the corporation rather than to the victims.[2667] These arguments have been criticized by noting that it is not the goal in torts to prevent all harms but to induce the

2656 *Arlen*, 2011a, p. 35; cf. *id.*, 2011b, p. 9. See *Oded*, Corporate Compliance, p. 160 et seq. and also *supra* at chapter 1, A.

2657 *Arlen*, 2011b, p. 9 et seq.

2658 *Kraakman*, in: Encyclopedia of Law and Economics, p. 135; cf. *Arlen/Kraakman*, 72 N.Y.U.L. Rev. 687 (1997), p. 695; *Fischel/Sykes*, 25 J. Legal Stud. 319 (1996), p. 322; *Langevoort*, 42 Wake Forest L. Rev. 627 (2007), p. 639.

2659 *Arlen*, 2011a, p. 35.

2660 *Arlen*, 2011a, p. 36.

2661 *Arlen*, 2011b, p. 10 et seq.

2662 *Arlen*, 23 J. Legal Stud. 833 (1994), p. 835.

2663 *Arlen*, 2011b, p. 9; *id.*, 2011a, p. 26; cf. *Arlen/Kraakman*, 72 N.Y.U.L. Rev. 687 (1997), p. 692.

2664 Cf. *Arlen*, 2011b, p. 9.

2665 *Basic, Inc. v. Levinson*, 485 U.S. 224 (1988); *Halliburton Co. v. Erica P. John Fund, Inc.*, 573 U.S. (2014).

2666 *Arlen/Carney*, in: Governance by Legal and Economic Measures, p. 147 et seq.

2667 *Arlen/Carney*, in: Governance by Legal and Economic Measures, p. 148; cf. *Langevoort*, 42 Wake Forest L. Rev. 627 (2007), p. 635.

actor to take the optimal level of care. In contrast hereto, fraud on the market is optimally deterred when agents refrain from fraud altogether.[2668]

Since corporations are the lowest cost provider for many prevention and policing measures, they can provide cost-effective deterrence.[2669] In this regard, reporting of wrongdoing ensures its detection and sanctioning, and, thereby, reduces the costs of detection for government.[2670] With regard to monitoring, corporations already collect a reasonable amount of information needed to detect criminal conduct in the ordinary course of business.[2671] Thus, corporations are more cost-effective to monitor crimes than government. Likewise, corporations can investigate criminal conduct at lower costs and more effectively than government since corporations know their operations, including potential areas prone to criminal conduct, and have immediate access to internal documents and employees.[2672] This is of particularly import with regard to large corporations with complex internal structures.[2673] Corporations are believed to be the lowest cost provider regarding the detection of crime, such as fraud, "when the crime does not produce an obvious harm and the boundary between the legitimate and criminal conduct depends on the employee's intent"[2674] rendering these crimes difficult to detect for government.[2675] Thus, corporations can deter crime through prevention and policing measures at lower costs rendering government's enforcement efforts more effective.

2. Corporate Criminal Liability Regimes

Through corporate criminal liability, corporations are induced to engage in prevention and policing measures to deter misconduct of corporate agents. In general, scholars discuss three corporate criminal liability regimes – strict vicarious liability, negligence, and composite liability – to

2668 *Arlen/Carney*, in: Governance by Legal and Economic Measures, p. 148 et seq.
2669 *Arlen*, 2011b, p. 11; *Arlen/Kraakman*, 72 N.Y.U.L. Rev. 687 (1997), p. 700; *Arlen*, 2011a, p. 2.
2670 *Arlen/Kraakman*, 72 N.Y.U.L. Rev. 687 (1997), p. 707.
2671 *Arlen*, 2011b, p. 11; *id.*, 2011a, p. 28; cf. *Baer*, 50 Boston College L. Rev. 949 (2009), p. 959.
2672 *Arlen*, 2011b, p. 11 et seq.
2673 *Arlen*, 2011b, p. 12.
2674 *Arlen*, 2011b, at fn. 37; cf. *Arlen/Kraakman*, 72 N.Y.U.L. Rev. 687 (1997), p. 706.
2675 *Arlen*, 2011a, p. 24.

address misconduct of corporate agents.[2676] Adjustments to strict vicarious liability based on privilege rules have also been suggested.[2677] In essence, the discussion revolves around the issue which regime provides for optimal incentives for corporations to engage in prevention and policing measures.

a) Vicarious Strict Liability

Under the principle of *respondeat superior*, corporations are subject to vicarious strict liability for criminal acts of their agents.[2678] Vicarious liability is the most common regime of corporate liability and deters crime optimally if agents act in the best interests of their principals because they either share the principals' interests or they act as requested.[2679] But if the alignment of interests of the corporation and its agents is not given, vicarious liability "may no longer be the preferred corporate incentive regime".[2680] Due to vicarious liability, corporations, as the principal of their agents, face the full expected costs of damages, regardless of any effort by the corporation to avoid the harm.[2681] Thus, corporations have an incentive to control their agents through optimal prevention and policing measures.[2682] The main advantage of vicarious liability is, therefore, to induce prevention measures by simply setting the corporation's expected sanction to the social cost of the crime.[2683] In addition, courts are not required to assess the effectiveness of the prevention and policing measures of corporations.[2684] As it has been shown above[2685], vicarious liability does not, however, in-

2676 See *Arlen/Kraakman*, 72 N.Y.U.L. Rev. 687 (1997), p. 695 et seq.; *Krawiec*, 32 Fla. St. U. L. Rev. 571 (2005), p. 575 et seq.; *Fischel/Sykes*, 25 J. Legal Stud. 319 (1996), p. 322 et seq.
2677 See *Arlen/Kraakman*, 72 N.Y.U.L. Rev. 687 (1997), p. 719 et seq.; *Krawiec*, 32 Fla. St. U. L. Rev. 571 (2005), p. 577 et seq.
2678 See *supra* at chapter 5, B. II.
2679 *Arlen/Kraakman*, 72 N.Y.U.L. Rev. 687 (1997), p. 690.
2680 *Arlen/Kraakman*, 72 N.Y.U.L. Rev. 687 (1997), p. 690.
2681 Cf. *Arlen/Kraakman*, 72 N.Y.U.L. Rev. 687 (1997), p. 718 et seq.; *Krawiec*, 32 Fla. St. U. L. Rev. 571 (2005), p. 575.
2682 *Kraakman*, in: Encyclopedia of Law and Economics, p. 135 et seq.; *Krawiec*, 32 Fla. St. U. L. Rev. 571 (2005), p. 576 (defined as: internal compliance structures).
2683 *Arlen*, 2011a, p. 30; *id.*, 2011b, p. 13; *Arlen/Kraakman*, 72 N.Y.U.L. Rev. 687 (1997), p. 703.
2684 Cf. *Arlen/Kraakman*, 72 N.Y.U.L. Rev. 687 (1997), p. 705.
2685 See *supra* at chapter 5, B. II.

duce corporations to optimally invest in *ex ante* and *ex post* policing mainly due to the detriments of the litigation dilemma.[2686] Even an increase of sanctions would be counterproductive within a vicarious liability regime as it would result in even less incentives to engage in policing measures.[2687]

In order to partially mitigate the risks imposed by the litigation dilemma, corporations have to adhere strictly to the requirements of the attorney-client privilege and the work product privilege or similar privileges provided by law excluding the use of protected information in administrative or court proceedings.[2688] With regard to the German attorney-client privilege, it has to be noted that the scope of the U.S. attorney-client privilege would exceed the scope of the German attorney-client privilege.[2689] Despite these privileges, the litigation dilemma still remains an important factor corporations have to consider. That is because of the limitations of the privileges and the remaining risk of their non-acceptance by the courts.[2690] Due to the litigation dilemma, policing measures are not as effective as possible.[2691]

In order to mitigate the detriments of the litigation dilemma, government needs to provide full recognition of policing measures and corporations have to be immune from exploitation in litigation.[2692] Corporate liability has to be structured by government "to ensure that [corporations] always face lower expected costs" when they optimally invest in policing measures than when they fail to do so.[2693] Thus, the expected criminal sanction with effective policing measures in place has to be lower than the expected criminal sanction without effective policing measures, even though corporate policing measures will increase the probability that the

2686 *Arlen*, 2011a, p. 37 et seq.; *id.*, 2011b, p. 13; *Arlen/Kraakman*, 72 N.Y.U.L. Rev. 687 (1997), p. 707; *Arlen*, 23 J. Legal Stud. 833 (1994), p. 847; cf. *Oded*, Corporate Compliance, p. 176 et seq.

2687 *Arlen/Kraakman*, 72 N.Y.U.L. Rev. 687 (1997), p. 708; *Arlen*, 23 J. Legal Stud. 833 (1994), p. 843.

2688 Cf. USSC, Ad Hoc Report, p. 108 et seq. and p. 121; *Goldsmith/King*, 50 Vand. L. Rev. 1 (1997), p. 379.

2689 *Schneider, H.*, ZIS 2016, 626, 633.

2690 See *infra* at chapter 16, B. I. 2. c).

2691 USSC, Ad Hoc Report, p. 116 et seq.: affected elements of compliance programs are training, monitoring, and auditing.

2692 Cf. *Driscoll/Hoffman/Murphy*, 99 Business and Society Rev. 35 (1998), p. 50. In the same direction, for the need to mitigate the detriments of the litigation dilemma: see USSC, Ad Hoc Report, p. 120.

2693 *Arlen*, 2011b, p. 14; *id.*, 2011a, p. 47; *Arlen/Kraakman*, 72 N.Y.U.L. Rev. 687 (1997), p. 728; *Arlen*, 23 J. Legal Stud. 833 (1994), p. 849 et seq.

corporation will be sanctioned.[2694] As will be depicted below, this can be achieved by a duty-based corporate liability regime which provides for smaller sanctions if the corporation engages in optimal policing measures.[2695] In theory, even strict liability is able to induce optimal policing measures and, thereby, mitigating the detriments of the litigation dilemma if the sanction is set correctly.[2696] But courts would face high information costs to determine optimal sanctions in order to try to induce corporations to optimal engage in policing under a vicarious liability regime.[2697] The optimal sanction regarding policing measures, however, would provide for non-optimal incentives regarding prevention measures. In essence, strict vicarious liability is able to optimally induce prevention measures but is unable to induce optimal policing measures at the same time.[2698]

b) Negligence-Based Liability

Under a negligence-based liability regime, a corporation will be held liable if a corporate agent commits a crime and the corporation does not meet the standard of due care.[2699] Usually, the standard includes to take sufficient measures by the corporation to avoid crime.[2700]

(1) Optimally Inducing Policing Measures

With regard to policing measures, a negligence-based liability regime induces corporations to optimally engage in *ex ante* and *ex post* policing measures.[2701] Optimal policing measures can be induced under a negligence-based regime, because policing measures do not increase the expected lia-

---

2694 *Arlen*, 2011b, p. 14: the expected criminal sanction is the criminal sanction multiplied by the probability that the government detects the violation and sanctions the corporation.

2695 *Arlen*, 2011b, p. 14. See *infra* at chapter 16, B. I. 2. d).

2696 *Arlen/Kraakman*, 72 N.Y.U.L. Rev. 687 (1997), p. 709 et seq.

2697 *Arlen/Kraakman*, 72 N.Y.U.L. Rev. 687 (1997), p. 711 and p. 725 et seq.; *Arlen*, 23 J. Legal Stud. 833 (1994), p. 847.

2698 *Arlen/Kraakman*, 72 N.Y.U.L. Rev. 687 (1997), p. 709 et seq.

2699 Cf. *Krawiec*, 32 Fla. St. U. L. Rev. 571 (2005), p. 579; *Arlen/Kraakman*, 72 N.Y.U.L. Rev. 687 (1997), p. 691; *Fischel/Sykes*, 25 J. Legal Stud. 319 (1996), p. 327 et seq.; *Arlen*, 23 J. Legal Stud. 833 (1994), p. 862.

2700 Cf. *Krawiec*, 32 Fla. St. U. L. Rev. 571 (2005), p. 579.

2701 *Arlen/Kraakman*, 72 N.Y.U.L. Rev. 687 (1997), p. 694.

bility of corporations in contrast to a strict liability regime[2702] since corporations are only liable if they breach their duty of policing. Moreover, a negligence-based regime ensures incentives for corporations to police so that employees expect the corporation to execute its policing measures.[2703] The more employees expect the corporation to execute its policing measures the more effective are such measures.[2704] Hence, a negligence-based liability regime renders policing measures more effective compared to a strict liability regime.[2705]

The negligence-based liability regime has been criticized for being ineffective for providing incentives to induce optimal policing measures.[2706] It has been stressed that setting a standard of due care is difficult and prone to judicial error.[2707] Therefore, it would be unlikely that government and courts set an optimal standard of care.[2708] In addition, courts would lack the expertise to determine if the policing measures of a corporation have fulfilled the standard of care requiring effectiveness.[2709] Due to the inability of courts to determine the effectiveness of policing measures, corporations would only engage in "cosmetic" policing measures with the effect of mitigated or no sanctioning of corporations although they were not engaging in effective policing.[2710] Furthermore, it has been stressed that inducing policing measures is ineffective since they have not been proven to be effective.[2711] These arguments, however, have been rebutted as shown above.[2712]

The ability of negligence-based liability to induce optimal policing measures largely depends on the sophistication of government and courts to

2702 *Arlen/Kraakman*, 72 N.Y.U.L. Rev. 687 (1997), p. 710; cf. *Arlen*, 2011a, p. 43 et seq.; *id.*, 2011b, p. 13 et seq.

2703 *Arlen/Kraakman*, 72 N.Y.U.L. Rev. 687 (1997), p. 713 et seq.

2704 *Arlen/Kraakman*, 72 N.Y.U.L. Rev. 687 (1997), p. 699.

2705 *Arlen/Kraakman*, 72 N.Y.U.L. Rev. 687 (1997), p. 712 et seq.

2706 *Krawiec*, 32 Fla. St. U. L. Rev. 571 (2005), p. 580.

2707 *Krawiec*, 32 Fla. St. U. L. Rev. 571 (2005), p. 580; *Fischel/Sykes*, 25 J. Legal Stud. 319 (1996), p. 329; *Khanna*, 2002, p. 16.

2708 *Krawiec*, 32 Fla. St. U. L. Rev. 571 (2005), p. 580.

2709 *Krawiec*, 32 Fla. St. U. L. Rev. 571 (2005), p. 580; *id.*, 81 Wash. U. L. Quarterly 487 (2003), p. 536; *Fischel/Sykes*, 25 J. Legal Stud. 319 (1996), p. 329; *Khanna*, 2002, p. 16.

2710 *Krawiec*, 32 Fla. St. U. L. Rev. 571 (2005), p. 580; *id.*, 81 Wash. U. L. Quarterly 487 (2003), p. 491 et seq.

2711 *Krawiec*, 32 Fla. St. U. L. Rev. 571 (2005), pp. 580 and 591; cf. *id.*, 81 Wash. U. L. Quarterly 487 (2003), p. 512 et seq.

2712 See *supra* at chapter 16, A. I. 2. a) (2).

define an optimal standard of care.[2713] This task, however, is not impossible for government and courts. On the contrary, law and economics research shows how a negligence-based liability regime has to be structured in order to optimally induce policing measures.[2714] COSO I provides *inter alia* for insight into the best practice of policing measures. Thus, the conducted research and COSO I provide the basis for government and courts to define an optimal standard of care. Despite the difficulties, negligence-based liability is superior to strict liability to induce policing measures.[2715] Even if the standard of care were set to a non-optimal level, corporations would still be induced to engage in at least "some policing [measures], in contrast to strict liability which may fail to induce any at all".[2716] Since only negligence-based liability is able to induce optimal policing measures, this liability regime is superior to a strict liability regime.

As it has been concluded above[2717], a negligence-based liability regime is able to induce optimal policing measures since government and courts are able to set an optimal standard of care and effective policing measures are feasible. With regard to the issue of evaluating the effectiveness of policing measures, the suggested two steps test for courts to assess the effectiveness of policing measures demonstrates that such assessment is feasible.[2718] It remains, nevertheless, a difficult task.

A further argument against a negligence-based liability regime is that monitoring is done by agents and is, thus, prone to error and wrongdoing. Therefore, the monitors would also have to be monitored leading to social costs even if monitoring would be effective.[2719] It has also been stressed, however, that the costs to society, due to suboptimal policing under a strict liability regime leading to more crime, will exceed the additional administrative costs of a negligence-based liability regime[2720] which would render negligence-based liability superior to strict liability. The argument of costs is always controversial. It is further depicted below.[2721]

2713 *Arlen/Kraakman*, 72 N.Y.U.L. Rev. 687 (1997), p. 711.

2714 *Arlen*, 2011b, p. 14 et seq.; *id.*, 2011a, p. 43 et seq.; *Arlen/Kraakman*, 72 N.Y.U.L. Rev. 687 (1997), p. 718 et seq.

2715 *Arlen/Kraakman*, 72 N.Y.U.L. Rev. 687 (1997), p. 711.

2716 *Arlen/Kraakman*, 72 N.Y.U.L. Rev. 687 (1997), p. 711.

2717 See *supra* at chapter 16, A. I. 2. a) (3).

2718 See *infra* at chapter 16, B. IV. 2.

2719 *Fischel/Sykes*, 25 J. Legal Stud. 319 (1996), p. 329.

2720 *Arlen/Kraakman*, 72 N.Y.U.L. Rev. 687 (1997), p. 711.

2721 See *infra* at chapter 16, B. I. 2. c).

(2) Optimally Inducing Prevention Measures

With regard to prevention measures, it is even more important for a negligence-based regime to determine the scope and form of prevention measures to ensure optimal deterrence of crime.[2722] In this regard, a negligence-based regime also faces difficulties in assessing the standard of care which makes it prone to judicial error.[2723] Due to such error, courts may impose too high penalties on corporations despite corporations implemented optimal prevention measures.[2724] This will lead to excessive expenditures on prevention measures[2725] and social waste by corporations due to their efforts to even fulfill a non-optimal standard of due care. Moreover, negligence-based regimes can achieve optimal deterrence only through higher administrative costs.[2726] Due to these increased costs, strict liability has been favored.[2727] In contrast, it has also been noted that "strict vicarious [...] liability either entails enormous administrative costs or is potentially inefficient or both".[2728] Nonetheless, it has been concluded that strict liability is superior to negligence-based liability for inducing prevention measures.[2729] Although negligence-based regimes are in theory able to induce an optimal level of prevention, the difficulties of determining accurately, whether the standard of care has been met, render this regime unpractical.[2730] This finding holds especially against the background that strict liability can better induce prevention measures than negligence-based liability. With regard to inducing policing measures, however, is has been shown that negligence-based liability is considerably superior to strict liability rendering negligence-based liability the best choice regime to induce policing measures.

2722 *Arlen/Kraakman*, 72 N.Y.U.L. Rev. 687 (1997), p. 705.

2723 Cf. *Arlen/Kraakman*, 72 N.Y.U.L. Rev. 687 (1997), p. 705; *Krawiec*, 32 Fla. St. U. L. Rev. 571 (2005), p. 580.

2724 Cf. *Fischel/Sykes*, 25 J. Legal Stud. 319 (1996), p. 328 et seq. *Fischel/Sykes* seem to not distinguish between policing and prevention measures and, thus, discuss "monitoring" as part of deterrence measures.

2725 Cf. *Fischel/Sykes*, 25 J. Legal Stud. 319 (1996), p. 329.

2726 *Arlen/Kraakman*, 72 N.Y.U.L. Rev. 687 (1997), p. 694.

2727 Cf. *Fischel/Sykes*, 25 J. Legal Stud. 319 (1996), p. 329 et seq.

2728 *Arlen*, 23 J. Legal Stud. 833 (1994), p. 849; cf. *Arlen/Kraakman*, 72 N.Y.U.L. Rev. 687 (1997), p. 711.

2729 *Arlen/Kraakman*, 72 N.Y.U.L. Rev. 687 (1997), p. 705.

2730 *Krawiec*, 32 Fla. St. U. L. Rev. 571 (2005), p. 580; cf. *Arlen/Kraakman*, 72 N.Y.U.L. Rev. 687 (1997), p. 705. See also *Fischel/Sykes*, 25 J. Legal Stud. 319 (1996), p. 330.

c) Mixed Regimes: Adjusted Strict Liability and Composite Liability

Since neither strict vicarious liability nor negligence-based liability regimes provide sufficient incentives for corporations to optimally engage in prevention and policing measures at the same time, "mixed" liability regimes have been explored in order to address the shortcomings.[2731] Two general forms of mixed liability have been examined: "adjusted strict liability" and "composite liability". By adjusting strict liability, it has been suggested to induce corporations to optimally engage in policing and cooperation "through some combination of evidentiary privilege rules and mitigated sanction for cooperation with government investigations" in order to address the shortcoming of strict liability to induce corporations to engage in optimal policing measures.[2732] This form of adjustment would leave the sanctions for corporations unchanged but it would lead to a constant probability of detection despite *ex ante* policing measures taken by corporations. Due to privilege rules, information produced by *ex ante* policing measures would be barred from use apart from prosecuting individual wrongdoing. Thereby, corporations would be induced to engage in such policing measures despite their usual downside of producing information which potentially leads to some detriment for the corporation.[2733] By providing sanction mitigation for *ex post* cooperation, corporations would be induced to cooperate with government. While adjusted strict liability will mitigate some of the shortcoming of strict liability, it still has downsides.[2734] In particular, privilege rules may work in theory, but they are difficult to implement into the existing U.S. law system which includes concepts such as discovery. Furthermore, corporations have to trust that neither government nor courts will use the produced information to their detriment in order to induce optimal policing. It is a doomed endeavor, however, to try to get corporations to fully trust in such privileges.[2735] Trusting privilege rules will be further undermined by the issue that the exact scope and applicability of such privileges will always remain uncertain to some degree. In addition, potential insolvency of corporations has been

2731 See *Arlen/Kraakman*, 72 N.Y.U.L. Rev. 687 (1997), p. 718 et seq.
2732 *Krawiec*, 32 Fla. St. U. L. Rev. 571 (2005), p. 577 et seq.
2733 *Arlen/Kraakman*, 72 N.Y.U.L. Rev. 687 (1997), p. 719 et seq.
2734 Cf. *Arlen/Kraakman*, 72 N.Y.U.L. Rev. 687 (1997), p. 718; *Krawiec*, 32 Fla. St. U. L. Rev. 571 (2005), p. 578.
2735 Cf. *Arlen/Kraakman*, 72 N.Y.U.L. Rev. 687 (1997), p. 719 et seq.

named a "central problem" for the privilege-approach.[2736] In case the probability of detection is low absent voluntary corporate policing, the fine necessary to induce optimal corporate policing would need to be "extraordinarily large" so that imposing such fine would almost always lead to the insolvency of the corporation. Such fines would not optimally induce corporate policing since corporations could avoid to actually pay such fine by filing for insolvency. A further form of adjusted strict liability reduces the sanctions for corporations continuously to counterbalance the increasing probability of detection through policing measures. While, compared to the privilege-approach, such adjusted strict liability regime can better provide for incentives to implement *ex ante* policing measures, it fails to provide optimal incentives to engage in *ex post* policing measures.[2737] Moreover, continuously reducing sanctions may work in theory, but in practice, it will be difficult to establish standards on the level of reduction. Other forms of adjusted strict liability are imaginable but unrewarding with regard to the objectives of corporate criminal liability.[2738] A critical downside of all forms of adjusted strict liability is that they do not provide for optimal incentives for policing.[2739] Moreover, depending on the form of adjusted strict liability, significant information costs occur; whereas the adjustment through privilege rules imposes the lowest information costs of all forms of adjusted strict liability.[2740] A further drawback of adjusted strict liability is that no standard of policing can be prescribed by government or courts. Corporations will have no official guidance on legal standards regarding policing measures which are only induced through indirect incentives. In essence, meddling with the strict liability regime, to render it somehow workable, does not provide for an optimal solution.

In contrast to adjusted strict liability, composite liability – a negligence-based liability regime with a layer of strict liability – renders corporations liable for their agents' crime and their own failure to fulfill their policing duties. Through the layer of strict liability, composite liability imposes optimal prevention, and, through negligence-based liability, optimal policing measures on corporations but only if courts are able to deal with the issue

2736 *Arlen*, 23 J. Legal Stud. 833 (1994), p. 866; *Arlen/Kraakman*, 72 N.Y.U.L. Rev. 687 (1997), p. 720.
2737 *Arlen/Kraakman*, 72 N.Y.U.L. Rev. 687 (1997), p. 726.
2738 See *Arlen/Kraakman*, 72 N.Y.U.L. Rev. 687 (1997), p. 723 et seq.
2739 *Arlen/Kraakman*, 72 N.Y.U.L. Rev. 687 (1997), p. 718.
2740 *Arlen/Kraakman*, 72 N.Y.U.L. Rev. 687 (1997), p. 719 et seq. and p. 723.

of determining the standards of care.[2741] Especially monitoring, as an *ex ante* policing measure, is an important feature for vicarious liability since vicarious liability is assumed to become more efficient the more principals are able to monitor and control their agents' risk-taking.[2742] Thus, combining strict liability with optimal incentives to monitor has the potential to lead to efficient deterrence. In addition, due to the negligence-based layer of composite liability, employees expect the corporation to execute its policing measures rendering them more effective.[2743] Despite these advantages, the composite liability regime faces the same detriments as the negligence-based regime. This includes anticipated high administration costs, difficulties to determine the standard of care, lack of expertise of courts to assess the effectiveness of policing measures, and the problems of "cosmetic" policing measures and unproven effectiveness of such measures. All these arguments have been dealt with above resulting in the strongly weakening or rebuttal of these arguments. In particular, it has been shown, that government and courts are able to set a standard of care for policing measures despite conceded difficulties to do so.[2744] In fact, it is an advantage of the composite liability regime that government and courts are able to prescribe the standard of due care rendering the composite liability regime more predictable for corporations and more straight forward.

Regardless of the foregoing, none of the two mixed liability regimes provide for a "perfect" solution to structure corporate liability.[2745] Adjusted strict liability, on the one hand, has the advantage of requiring less administrative information but lacks optimal incentives for policing. Composite liability, on the other hand, imposes optimal prevention and policing measures but only if government and courts are able to deal with the issue of determining the standards of care.[2746] It is more effective than adjusted strict liability since employees expect the corporation to execute its policing measures. While there are rare circumstances in which adjusted strict liability may be the primary corporate liability regime, composite liability better serves in general the need of optimally inducing prevention and

2741 *Arlen/Kraakman*, 72 N.Y.U.L. Rev. 687 (1997), p. 718; cf. *Arlen*, 2011a, p. 43; cf. *id.*, 23 J. Legal Stud. 833 (1994), p. 849 et seq.
2742 *Kraakman*, in: Encyclopedia of Law and Economics, p. 135.
2743 *Arlen/Kraakman*, 72 N.Y.U.L. Rev. 687 (1997), p. 730.
2744 See *supra* at chapter 16, A. I. 2. a) (2).
2745 *Arlen/Kraakman*, 72 N.Y.U.L. Rev. 687 (1997), p. 718; *Krawiec*, 32 Fla. St. U. L. Rev. 571 (2005), p. 578.
2746 *Arlen/Kraakman*, 72 N.Y.U.L. Rev. 687 (1997), p. 718.

policing measures.[2747] Hence, connecting two known liability regimes serves the objectives of corporate criminal liability better than meddling with one unsuitable regime to make it somehow workable.

In addition to the named arguments, costs are always raised as an argument. The choice between the adjusted strict liability regime and the composite liability regime has been commonly heated up to compare the costs of each regime, i.e. to the question if information costs are higher or lower than administrative costs.[2748] It has been stressed that adjusted strict liability may result in fewer costs than negligence-based liability.[2749] As noted before, it has also been stressed that the costs to society due to suboptimal policing under a strict liability regime leading to more crime will exceed the additional administrative costs of a negligence-based liability regime.[2750] Moreover, courts do not have to determine the optimal level of policing but only whether, for the case at hand, additional monitoring was cost-justified since policing is optimal under a negligence-based corporate liability regime when marginal costs of additional policing exceeds its marginal social benefit.[2751] This determination is less costly since less information is needed to calculate the optimal level of policing. Only in difficult cases, courts do actually have to determine "the cost and benefit of a marginal change in policing measures".[2752] Thus, the administrative costs are assumed to be not as high as it may have appeared first hand.[2753] But, since no research exists whether information costs are higher or lower than administration costs considering that administration costs might be lower than initially expected, the question whether adjusted strict liability or composite liability represent with regard to costs the superior corporate liability regime actually rests to a significant degree on the prerogative of interpretation. Either one assumes information costs or administration costs to be less. With regard to costs, however, "composite liability is the only

2747 Cf. *Arlen/Kraakman*, 72 N.Y.U.L. Rev. 687 (1997), p. 735.

2748 *Arlen/Kraakman*, 72 N.Y.U.L. Rev. 687 (1997), p. 730. For more details see *Arlen/ Kraakman*, 72 N.Y.U.L. Rev. 687 (1997), p. 730 et seq. and *Arlen*, 23 J. Legal Stud. 833 (1994), p. 847 et seq. and p. 866.

2749 *Arlen/Kraakman*, 72 N.Y.U.L. Rev. 687 (1997), p. 723.

2750 *Arlen/Kraakman*, 72 N.Y.U.L. Rev. 687 (1997), p. 711.

2751 *Arlen/Kraakman*, 72 N.Y.U.L. Rev. 687 (1997), p. 731 et seq.

2752 *Arlen/Kraakman*, 72 N.Y.U.L. Rev. 687 (1997), p. 733.

2753 Cf. *Arlen/Kraakman*, 72 N.Y.U.L. Rev. 687 (1997), p. 734. Otherwise, it has been noted that administrative costs of the public enforcement system are enormous (*Oded*, Corporate Compliance, p. 36) but self-reporting of corporations also reduces administrative costs (*id.*, p. 185).

[structure] of [corporate] liability" ensuring optimal prevention and policing but only for the price of "larger administrative costs".[2754] Thus, regarding arguments urging high costs, it has to be noted that preventing crime is not costless. With regard to *Kaldor-Hicks* efficiency, a liability regime is efficient if the advantages due to reduced corporate crime are higher than the costs.

In contrast to adjusted strict liability, composite liability provides for an opportunity to verify if corporations actually engage in effective policing. In many other areas of law, law does not trust individuals or corporations to engage in optimal behavior only by providing incentives without setting the required standard. Rather, law prescribes in many situations at least a framework for what is required and what is prohibited. While in theory, such as within law and economics models, sophisticated incentive regimes will lead to optimal results, these theoretical findings have to be reviewed for practicability and revised to better suit the needs of the real world. In this regard, the composite liability regime provides for an opportunity to assess whether corporations implement effective policing measures and if the standards of care are sufficient. Overall, a composite liability regime is superior to an adjusted strict liability regime due to optimal incentives for prevention measures, optimal incentives for *ex ante* and *ex post* policing, the opportunity to prescribe the standard of due care, and the possibility of judicial review of the prescribed standards; despite manageable difficulties in setting such standard and presumably higher costs of administration. Considering all arguments, a composite liability regime is the best choice for the structure of corporate criminal liability.

d) Structure of Composite Regime: Duty-Based Liability

A composite liability regime consists of two layers: negligence and strict liability. In the recent literature, composite liability is referred to as duty-based liability.[2755] In a duty-based liability regime, the corporation will be strictly liable for its agents' misconduct due to the strict liability layer of duty-based liability. Through the negligence-layer of duty-based liability, the corporation will be liable for its own failure to adhere to the set standard of care for policing measures.[2756] The duty-based liability regime may

2754 *Arlen/Kraakman*, 72 N.Y.U.L. Rev. 687 (1997), p. 730.
2755 See *Arlen*, 2011a.
2756 Cf. *Arlen/Kraakman*, 72 N.Y.U.L. Rev. 687 (1997), p. 726.

be two-tiered or multi-tiered. A two-tier duty-based liability system has to fulfill two requirements in order to be effective.[2757] As to the first requirement, sanction provisions have to ensure that corporations optimally engage in *ex ante* and *ex post* policing measures. As a first step, government needs to impose a duty-based sanction to induce optimal *ex ante* policing including monitoring as part of a compliance program.[2758] This sanction has to ensure that the expected costs of crime are lower for the corporation if it engages in *ex ante* policing measures than if it does not, but still has to be high enough to induce corporations to fulfill their policing duties first hand.[2759] Thereby, government has to consider that *ex ante* policing measures imposes direct costs on the corporation and increases the expected liability of the corporation.[2760] As a second step, for inducing optimal *ex post* policing, government must impose a higher sanction on corporations if they did not engage in *ex post* policing than if they did. The sanction for failing to engage in optimal *ex post* policing must be sufficiently high that the expected liability for any crime a corporation detects is higher if it does not report and cooperate than the reduced sanction if it does report and cooperate, since reporting will most certainly lead to the sanctioning of a crime the government might not detect otherwise.[2761] As to the second requirement, the mitigated sanction for corporations compliant with their policing duties has to be large enough to ensure that corporations implement optimal prevention measures.[2762] This mitigated sanction "should equal the social cost of [crime] divided by its probability of detection".[2763] The two requirements can be achieved through granting sanction mitigation if the corporation has met the standard of care for policing, i.e. duty-based liability.[2764]

In the context of structuring corporate sanctions, government has to impose duty-based liability on corporations besides the fact that corporations

2757 Cf. *Arlen/Kraakman*, 72 N.Y.U.L. Rev. 687 (1997), p. 727.

2758 *Arlen*, 2011a, p. 47; *id.*, 2011b, p. 14; *Arlen/Kraakman*, 72 N.Y.U.L. Rev. 687 (1997), p. 728; *Arlen*, 23 J. Legal Stud. 833 (1994), p. 849 et seq.

2759 *Arlen*, 2011a, p. 47; cf. *Arlen/Kraakman*, 72 N.Y.U.L. Rev. 687 (1997), p. 728.

2760 Cf. *Arlen*, 2011a, p. 47. See *supra* at chapter 5, B. II.

2761 *Arlen*, 2011a, p. 44; *Arlen/Kraakman*, 72 N.Y.U.L. Rev. 687 (1997), p. 728 et seq.

2762 *Arlen*, 2011a, p. 44; *Arlen/Kraakman*, 72 N.Y.U.L. Rev. 687 (1997), p. 727; cf. *Fischel/Sykes*, 25 J. Legal Stud. 319 (1996), p. 329.

2763 *Arlen/Kraakman*, 72 N.Y.U.L. Rev. 687 (1997), p. 727; cf. *Fischel/Sykes*, 25 J. Legal Stud. 319 (1996), p. 324; *Arlen*, 23 J. Legal Stud. 833 (1994), p. 847 et seq.

2764 Cf. *Arlen/Kraakman*, 72 N.Y.U.L. Rev. 687 (1997), p. 727.

are subject to market-based or reputational sanctions.[2765] Since market-based or reputational sanctions "operate as a form of strict corporate liability for certain types of crime", corporations face the same incentives to engage in non-optimal corporate policing.[2766] Therefore, optimal policing can only be accomplished through duty-based liability which has to take the market sanctions into account for determining the optimal sanction.[2767] In addition, in order to induce optimal deterrence, government has to ensure that "the total sanction (civil, criminal, and market-based) must equal the social cost of wrongdoing multiplied by one over the probability of detection".[2768] Otherwise, due to the litigation dilemma, which results from the increase of expected liability of corporations through policing measures [2769], corporations do not have optimal incentives to invest in policing measures if the expected sanction does not encompass all civil, criminal, and market-based sanctions. As a downside, the two-tier regime fails if corporations "perceive a significant risk" that sanction mitigation will not be grated either through "judicial error or an agency problem".[2770] Since it is difficult to determine the standard of care, there is some risk for judicial error or agents' wrongdoing.[2771] Therefore, in case of judicial error or agents' wrongdoing resulting in a breach of duty, or if agents deliberately fail to execute the policing duties, or if corporations otherwise breach one of their policing duties, corporations will receive no mitigation under the two-tiered regime for any other fulfilled duty probably leading to abandoning all other policing duties.

In contrast to a two-tiered duty-based liability regime, a "multi-tiered" duty-based regime is able to cope with the difficulties of determining the standard of care and the difficulties of implementing and controlling policing measures leading courts to possibly deny credit for policing.[2772] Such regime is also able to address non-compliant behavior of agents with

2765 *Arlen*, 2011a, p. 51.
2766 *Arlen*, 2011a, p. 51.
2767 *Arlen*, 2011a, p. 52; cf. *Arlen/Kraakman*, 72 N.Y.U.L. Rev. 687 (1997), p. 698.
2768 *Arlen/Kraakman*, 72 N.Y.U.L. Rev. 687 (1997), p. 750. See for further details: *Arlen*, 2011a, p. 5 et seq.
2769 See *supra* at chapter 5, B. II.
2770 *Arlen/Kraakman*, 72 N.Y.U.L. Rev. 687 (1997), p. 735; USSC, Ad Hoc Report, p. 106. At least shortly after the enactment of the USSG, fears of corporate leaders are documented that mitigation will not be granted (*Webb/Molo*, 71 Wash. U. L. Q. 375 (1993), p. 396).
2771 *Arlen/Kraakman*, 72 N.Y.U.L. Rev. 687 (1997), p. 735.
2772 *Arlen/Kraakman*, 72 N.Y.U.L. Rev. 687 (1997), p. 741.

regard to policing duties. A multi-tier regime achieves these advantages by unbundling the individual policing duties which, then, induce corporations to engage separately in each of the *ex ante* and *ex post* policing measures, i.e. corporations would benefit from acting optimally with regard to each policing measure independently[2773] preventing corporations from abandoning their policing duties. Therefore, "a multi-tiered regime is less vulnerable to errors in control and assessment of policing duties".[2774] In a multi-tiered regime, the structure of sanctions has to reflect the unbundling of policing duties.[2775] Therefore, sanctions should be imposed on corporations if they fail to monitor optimally. An additional sanction should be imposed but only if corporations fail to report detected wrongdoing. A further sanction should be imposed but only if corporations fail to fully cooperate with government. If corporations engage in optimal *ex ante* and *ex post* policing, they should avoid all these sanctions.[2776] The same two requirements of the two-tier regime hold for the multi-tiered regime with the difference that the mitigating provisions will be separately applied by the courts. If these sanctions are structured correctly, corporations will engage optimally in policing measures despite the increasing probability of being sanctioned.[2777]

A multi-tiered duty-based liability regime provides incentives for corporations to engage in optimal policing but only if corporations choose a policing regime that maximizes profits.[2778] In case management's incentives are connected to the corporation's well being, they should have optimal incentives to engage in optimal policing for the corporation as long as they "derive any benefit from higher corporate profits and do not expect to obtain a private benefit from crime".[2779] In case corporate governance is characterized by a separation of ownership and control, however, a profit maximizing policing regime may not have been chosen by manage-

2773 *Arlen*, 2011a, p. 43; cf. *Arlen/Kraakman*, 72 N.Y.U.L. Rev. 687 (1997), p. 735 et seq.

2774 *Arlen/Kraakman*, 72 N.Y.U.L. Rev. 687 (1997), p. 741.

2775 *Arlen*, 2011a, p. 43.

2776 *Arlen*, 2011a, p. 43.

2777 *Arlen*, 2011a, p. 43.

2778 *Arlen*, 2011a, p. 48.

2779 *Arlen*, 2011a, p. 49. Evidence suggests that corporations committing audit fraud and other financial disclosure violations the to have inside and outside directors who own proportionally less of the corporation's stock than boards of non-offending corporations (*id.*, 2011a, at fn. 101).

ment.[2780] In this situation, agency costs arise since the sanctions for corporate crime falls on shareholders and not on management. Then, managerial agency costs can undermine management's incentives to police optimally if managers either incur private costs e.g. spending additional effort on record-keeping due to corporate monitoring, obtain private benefits from any crime such as promotion or bonus, or hide poor corporate performance through committing securities fraud in order to safeguard their jobs.[2781] Especially securities fraud often occurs when executives have strong incentives to conceal their mismanagement in order to save their jobs, reputation, and investments in the corporation.[2782] In order to mitigate these incentives, corporations have to structure their promotion and compensation policies on long-run returns.[2783] Through these prevention measures, corporations are able to mitigate some of the undermining incentives for management to optimally engage in policing. With regard to outside directors and other gatekeepers not subject to the incentives to conceal mismanagement, the different incentive structure has to be considered to ensure vigorous monitoring and other controls.[2784] For outside directors, personal liability through claw backs plus the effect on their reputation may provide sufficient incentives.[2785]

Although agency costs complicate governmental efforts to induce optimal policing, the agency cost problem should be lower under the duty-based regime than under strict corporate liability since the duty-based regime provides shareholders and directors with information whether management engages optimally in policing, and, thus, helps shareholders and directors to hold managers accountable who fail to do so.[2786] In case agency costs are significant and undermine the governmental incentives to implement optimal policing, government should couple duty-based corporate sanctions with corporation-specific structural reform mandates requiring the corporation to detect wrongdoing and to adopt specific policing

---

2780 *Arlen*, 2011a, p. 49; cf. *Arlen/Kraakman*, 72 N.Y.U.L. Rev. 687 (1997), pp. 699 and 741.

2781 *Arlen*, 2011a, p. 49; cf. *Arlen/Kraakman*, 72 N.Y.U.L. Rev. 687 (1997), p. 704.

2782 *Arlen/Carney*, in: Governance by Legal and Economic Measures, p. 151; *Langevoort*, 42 Wake Forest L. Rev. 627 (2007), p. 635.

2783 See *supra* at chapter 5, B. I.

2784 *Langevoort*, 42 Wake Forest L. Rev. 627 (2007), p. 636.

2785 *Id.*

2786 Cf. *Arlen*, 2011a, p. 50; cf. *id.*, 2011b, at fn. 51.

measures under the supervision of government.[2787] Also, effective internal control will provide unbiased information to enhance supervision of agents. In general, while the two-tier system of duty-based liability is simpler than the multi-tiered system, the latter serves better the objective of corporate criminal liability to optimally induce corporations to engage in policing measures, especially with regard to large corporations mostly characterized by a corporate governance structure of separation of ownership and control.

3. Conclusion

In the U.S., corporate criminal liability has the main purpose to deter corporate crime and is needed besides individual liability to deter intentional wrongdoing of corporate agents. Since government cannot optimally deter corporate crime, government has to induce corporations to engage in prevention and policing measures for optimal deterrence. Corporations can deter crime *ex ante* by implementing prevention measures which may reduce benefits for wrongdoers, increase the direct cost of wrongdoing, or make wrongdoing more difficult to carry out. In addition to prevention measures, corporations can increase the effectiveness of government's efforts to deter corporate crime by intervening *ex ante* and *ex post* through policing measures such as *ex ante* monitoring as part of an ongoing compliance program, *ex post* investigation, cooperation, reporting, and auditing. For most prevention and policing measures, corporations are the lowest cost provider and, thus, provide for cost-effective deterrence. In order to optimally induce corporations to engage in prevention and policing measures, three corporate liability regimes – strict vicarious liability, negligence, and composite liability – are discussed. In addition, adjustments to strict liability have been suggested. As the most common regime, strict liability provides for optimal incentives for corporations to engage in prevention measures but lacks optimal incentives for policing measures since policing measures increase the expected liability of corporations due to the litigation dilemma. In contrast to strict liability, negligence-based liability provides for optimal incentives for policing measures. With regard to prevention measures, the negligence-based liability regime is theoretically able

2787 *Arlen*, 2011a, p. 51. In the U.S., the concept of corporate monitor exists and for Germany an external *Kurator* has been suggested *de lege ferenda* drawing on the U.S. concept (see *infra* at chapter 20, A. II. 2).

to induce an optimal level of prevention but is unpractical due to the difficulties of determining accurately the standard of care. In general, neither strict vicarious liability nor negligence-based liability regimes provide sufficient incentives for corporations to optimally engage in prevention and policing measures at the same time. Therefore, mixed liability regimes have been explored in order to address the shortcomings of these liability regimes.

Two general forms of mixed liability have been examined: adjusted strict liability and composite liability. Adjusted strict liability is based on privilege rules and mitigated sanctions for cooperation to provide for optimal incentives for policing. Due to application deficiencies of privilege rules, however, even adjusted strict liability does not provide for optimal incentives for policing. In contrast to adjusted strict liability, composite liability – a negligence-based liability regime with a layer of strict liability – imposes optimal prevention and policing measures. While there is currently no research whether adjusted strict liability imposes higher information costs than composite liability imposing administration costs, administration costs have to be accepted as necessary means to achieve optimal deterrence of corporate crime. Moreover, composite liability provides an opportunity for government and courts to prescribe standards of care and to verify whether corporations actually engage in effective policing through judicial review. Due to these advantages, composite liability is the best choice for the structure of corporate criminal liability.

Composite liability, recently referred to as duty-based liability, consists of two layers: negligence and strict liability. In order to be effective, duty-based liability has to fulfill two requirements. In order to provide for optimal incentives for corporations to engage in *ex ante* and *ex post* policing measures, a duty-based sanction has to impose an expected cost of crime which is lower for corporations if they engage in *ex ante* policing measures but which is still high enough to induce corporations to fulfill their policing duties first hand. In addition, the duty-based sanction for corporations for failing to engage in optimal *ex post* policing must be higher than for carrying out such policing. The sanction for engaging in *ex post* policing measures has to be lower than the expected liability when refraining from such measures. Furthermore, the mitigated sanction for corporations compliant with their policing duties has to be high enough to ensure that corporations implement optimal prevention measures by setting the sanction equal to the social costs of crime divided by its probability of detection. To ensure optimal deterrence in light of the litigation dilemma, this expected sanction has to encompass all civil, criminal, and market-based sanctions.

In order to address difficulties of the duty-based liability regime that corporations might not receive sanction mitigation for failing to fulfill one or more of their duties probably leading to the abandonment of all their other policing duties, the duty-based liability regime has to be multi-tiered. In a multi-tiered regime, all individual policing duties are unbundled, thereby, inducing corporations to engage separately in each of the *ex ante* and *ex post* policing measures. Thus, corporations will benefit from acting optimally with regard to each policing measure independently preventing corporations from abandoning their policing duties. A multi-tiered duty-based liability regime also addresses agency costs by providing shareholders with information, whether management engages optimally in policing, helping shareholders to sanction managers who fail to do so. Through promotion and compensation policies, corporations are also able to mitigate some of the undermining incentives for management to optimally engage in policing. Overall, a multi-tiered duty-based liability regime is the best choice to serve the objective of corporate criminal liability to optimally deter corporate crime.

II. Corporate Liability: Civil Liability vs. Criminal Liability

The law and economics research on an optimal approach to achieve effective internal control and corporate compliance is based on corporate criminal liability due to the existing regime of corporate criminal liability in the U.S. which is, however, not undisputed[2788] in the U.S. Against the background that corporate criminal liability may not be regarded as the preferable or optimal regime, the issue will be addressed whether the same results may be achieved with civil liability.

For inducing corporations to engage in prevention and policing measures, the level of incentives has to be appropriate. Generally, investing in these measures is desirable "up to the point at which [their] marginal cost would exceed the marginal social gain in the form of reduced social harm from criminal activity".[2789] To achieve this, the corporation should internalize the social cost of the harm caused by the corporate crime adjusted for the chance of non-detection.[2790] To achieve this, it is inevitable that corpo-

2788 See for an overview: *Beale*, 2013; *Beale*, ZStW 2014, 27.
2789 *Fischel/Sykes*, 25 J. Legal Stud. 319 (1996), p. 324.
2790 *Fischel/Sykes*, 25 J. Legal Stud. 319 (1996), p. 324.

rations are liable under a principle of *respondeat superior* either through civil or criminal liability.

In order to set the optimal level of incentives, one important factor is to mitigate the effects of the litigation dilemma.[2791] Moreover, the social cost of the crime should include costs of enforcement in addition to any direct costs to victims.[2792] By imposing civil corporate liability for corporate crime, corporations will bear the social cost of the harm caused by this crime. Imposing criminal corporate liability is not advantageous.[2793] Rather, corporate criminal liability may lead to overdeterrence leading to an inefficient high level of investment in deterrence measures.[2794] Collateral penalties such as reputational and market penalties[2795] may increase this effect.[2796] Since corporations may not be incarcerated[2797], the criminal penalty for corporations is necessarily a monetary fine which may also be achieved by civil liability.[2798] Even a mandate to liquidate a corporation as a kind of last resort in light of corporate wrongdoing results mostly in a loss of the investment opportunity for the owners besides the consequences for other stakeholders. Moreover, the often claimed reputational loss and social stigma due to a criminal fine vis-à-vis a civil fine has been questioned on the ground that the public hardly differentiates between a criminal or a regulatory fine.[2799] Otherwise, a criminal fine seems to provide slightly more incentives for corporate leaders than a civil fine.[2800] It has also been stated that the costs of a civil lawsuit of a governmental agencies are likely to be less than the administration costs of criminal proceed-

2791 Cf. *Fischel/Sykes*, 25 J. Legal Stud. 319 (1996), p. 326. See on the litigation dilemma *supra* at chapter 5, B. II.

2792 *Fischel/Sykes*, 25 J. Legal Stud. 319 (1996), p. 325; *Arlen*, 2011a, p. 56.

2793 *Fischel/Sykes*, 25 J. Legal Stud. 319 (1996), p. 321 et seq.; *Kraakman*, Anatomy of Corporate Law, p. 679; *Khanna*, 109 Harvard L. Rev. 1477 (1996), p. 1510.

2794 *Fischel/Sykes*, 25 J. Legal Stud. 319 (1996), p. 324.

2795 See *supra* at chapter 5, C. III.

2796 *Arlen*, 2011b, p. 34; cf. *Garrett*, 93 Va. L. Rev. 853 (2007), p. 855.

2797 See on the issue: *Fischel/Sykes*, 25 J. Legal Stud. 319 (1996), p. 322 et seq.

2798 *Fischel/Sykes*, 25 J. Legal Stud. 319 (1996), p. 331.

2799 Cf. *Peglau*, ZRP 2001, 406, 407; *Ransiek*, NZWiSt 2012, 45, 46 et seq.; *id.*, Unternehmensstrafrecht, 285, 288 et seq. See on the role of moral sanctions in Europe: *Beale/Adam*, 8 Buffalo Crim. L. Rev. 89 (2005), p. 154 et seq.

2800 Cf. *Sieber/Engelhart*, Compliance Programs Survey, p. 142: the empirical survey shows that the motivation of sanctions to create a compliance program is on average 8.1/10 and median 9/10 for criminal fines and 7.4/10 and 8.0/10 for civil fines respectively.

ings.[2801] In essence, there is hardly a good argument in favor of corporate criminal liability vis-à-vis corporate civil liability.[2802] At last, the corporation has to pay the social cost of the harm caused for the misconduct of its agents and its own failure to provide for effective preventive and policing measures.

The issue of criminal or civil liability also includes the issue of who conducts the litigation against the corporation in order to ensure an optimal level of expected liability. It has to be considered that the legal nature of corporate liability implies the legal nature of the litigation. While civil liability generally implies that individual plaintiffs sue the corporation, criminal liability is enforced by the law enforcement agencies. But the government could also act as a plaintiff in civil proceedings in cases when individual plaintiffs do not exist or have little incentive to sue the corporation such as (1) the government or nature are the victims of corporate wrongdoing, (2) failure of the corporation to comply with regulatory or reporting requirements when no harm occurred but compliance of the corporation *ex ante* is desirable, or (3) a diffuse group of victims with modest harm caused to each of them and, thus, little incentive for each to sue the corporation.[2803] A third option is administrative law enforced by state agencies. In this regard, it has been noted that European states traditionally rely on administrative regulation to ensure adequate enforcement of corporate wrongdoing.[2804]

The issue of who ensures enforcement of the liability is only a major issue with regard to civil liability as criminal liability is enforced by law enforcement agencies. This is the case within the U.S. criminal liability regime which resembles a duty-based liability regime in light of the USSG. By enforcing criminal law, law enforcement agencies ensure that corporations have incentives to comply with the USSG or the respective enforcement policy of the agency. The SOX-approach is different as it mandates to implement effective internal control over financial reporting and disclosure controls and procedures. The mandate is backed by personal liability of the responsible officers enforced by civil litigation of either the SEC

2801 *Khanna*, 109 Harvard L. Rev. 1477 (1996), p. 1512 et seq.; cf. *Kraakman*, Anatomy of Corporate Law, p. 679.

2802 *Kraakman*, Anatomy of Corporate Law, p. 679; *Khanna*, 109 Harvard L. Rev. 1477 (1996), p. 1510; *Fischel/Sykes*, 25 J. Legal Stud. 319 (1996), p. 322 et seq. *Arlen/Kraakman*, 72 N.Y.U.L. Rev. 687 (1997), p. 727; *Arlen*, 2011b, p. 13. Different: cf. *Beale*, 2013, p. 14; *Beale*, ZStW 2014, 27, 38 et seq.

2803 *Fischel/Sykes*, 25 J. Legal Stud. 319 (1996), p. 330 et seq.

2804 *Beale/Adam*, 8 Buffalo Crim. L. Rev. 89 (2005), p. 143 et seq.

(sec. 21 et seq. Exchange Act) or any other person (sec. 18 Exchange Act). In addition, external auditors attest to whether the corporation has fulfilled the mandates. Both U.S. approaches differ in the structure of how to induce corporations to engage in effective internal control and corporate compliance. The USSG and enforcement policies provide a carrot while SOX works with the stick. But in both cases, state agencies ensure enforcement.

It follows that from a corporate liability perspective, it does not matter whether the liability is civil or criminal. But, effective enforcement of the liability has to be ensured. In this regard considering the free rider problem[2805] and general shortcomings of private civil litigation, it is not sufficient to rely on shareholders or other private litigation. Rather, a state agency, as it is the case with the SEC, has to ensure enforcement. In this regard, it is generally irrelevant whether these proceedings are civil, criminal, or administrative as long as they are effective.

III. Regulatory Regime: Statutory Approach vs. USSG-Approach vs. Case Law

Various structures and regulatory approaches have been used in the U.S. to induce corporations to engage in effective internal controls. Most of these approaches have not been chosen from scratch and are path dependent considering the factual limitations of lawmaking. In the following, the different approaches will be portrayed in order to only touch on the issue of which approach might be more better suited than others to achieve effective internal control including compliance will provide further insight into the optimal regulatory structure. A profound analysis of the pros and cons of the different approaches especially of the dichotomy of statutory law vs. case law[2806], however, is beyond the scope of the thesis.

1. Statutory Approach

A statutory approach builds on parliamentary statutes rather than on agency guidelines. Corporations can be induced to implement optimal prevention and policing measures through statutory provisions, if the sanction for

2805 See *supra* at chapter 1, A.
2806 Cf. *Rubin*, 11 J. Legal Stud. 205 (1982). See also *supra* at chapter 16, A. I. 1. b).

failing to comply with such provision is structured correctly.[2807] Hence, inducing corporations to engage in optimal prevention and policing measures is not limited to the USSG-approach. In difference to the USSG, a statutory approach induces corporations to engage in the specific policing measures commonly through statutory sanctions and not through sanction mitigation, i.e. through the stick and not the carrot. But leniency provisions may also be statutory. While the USSG-approach is in general suitable to fulfill the requirements of the duty-based liability regime in order to induce optimal prevention and policing measures, a statutory approach may provide advantages by achieving optimal incentives at the same time. In this regard, it has been stressed that a legal obligation to implement compliance measures seems more effective than sanctioning the corporation for the lack of compliance in case of criminal acts by agents or providing leniency for the corporation in case the corporations had implemented compliance measures[2808] even though law and economics research does not support this notion.

In the following, the advantages and the different structures of a statutory approach to induce corporations to engage in effective internal control including compliance will be depicted including a carrot approach mainly mirroring the USSG, a combined carrot and stick approach mirroring SOX, and a stick approach probably the most controversial.

a) Advantages of a Statutory Approach

The advantages of a comprehensive statutory approach for inducing prevention and policing measures are manifold. A statutory approach has the advantage to prescribe specific requirements in greater detail providing at best a comprehensive framework for corporations for how to design and implement internal controls and compliance measures. Such comprehensive framework will become effective on the date as stated in the statute in contrast to a case by case approach of the common law which usually takes years and years to develop such a framework. A statutory standard also reduces a major concern of courts of second guessing business decisions when deciding on the violation of fiduciary duties.[2809] Since the legislator

---

2807 Cf. *Arlen*, 2011a, p. 43 et seq.; *id.*, 23 J. Legal Stud. 833 (1994), p. 862. See also *infra* at chapter 16, B. I. 2. d).

2808 *Sieber/Engelhart*, Compliance Programs Survey, p. 212 et seq.

2809 Cf. e.g. *Caremark*, 698 A.2d 959 (Del. Ch. 1996), p. 967 et seq.

has already set the standard for internal controls, courts do not have to evaluate business decisions with regard to such standards. Rather, they only have to verify if corporations have met those standards. This argument might be attacked on the notion that the legislature is no better in anticipating business decisions beforehand than courts are able to second guess business decisions afterwards. It is the role of the parliamentary legislature, however, to set standards and to foster social welfare by providing rules believed to foster this goal. Also, in contrast to the current USSG-approach, a statutory provision is binding for corporations and courts instead of just being advisable to comply with rendering the statutory approach more predictable compared to the USSG-approach. In the same way, a comprehensive statutory approach is more predictable for corporations compared to the common law approach since the case law of Delaware hardly provides for any guidelines for how to comply with the duty to monitor. Courts would still have a supplementary role in specifying the statutory requirements and sanctions but this is the common role of courts. Furthermore, since engaging in effective policing measures is required by law, government or the external auditors are able to control whether corporations comply with the law regardless of any investigations of potential agents' misconduct and prior to any indicted wrongdoing. Besides these advantages of the statutory approach, it faces, nonetheless, the difficulties of the duty-based liability regime to induce effective policing measures.

b) Structures of the Statutory Approaches

Inducing corporations to engage in effective internal control including compliance can be achieved through different statutory regulation. A prerequisite is that corporations are liable under a principle of *respondeat superior* either through civil or criminal liability.

(1) Carrot Approach – Granting Leniency

A statutory approach using a carrot, i.e. granting leniency, would prescribe the USSG-approach by law providing the opportunity to enact a cohesive legal framework to optimally induce effective internal control and corporate compliance considering the suggestions for reforming the USSG[2810].

2810 See *infra* at chapter 19.

(2) Combined Stick and Carrot Approach – SOX-Approach

A combined stick and carrot approach would mirror the SOX-approach. SOX only mandates to implement specific compliance components such as internal control over financial reporting and disclosure controls and procedures. Since SOX induces only *ex ante* monitoring with regard to financial reporting and reporting obligations, the SEC needs to induce *ex post* policing by granting leniency as set out in the Seaboard Report[2811] despite all SOX-related compliance mandates. Hence, a combined stick and carrot approach combines a mandate to implement comprehensive *ex ante* monitoring elements such as a compliance program, enforced by liability, and leniency provisions.

(3) Stick Approach: Composite Liability

In a stick approach, statutes mandate corporations to engage in specific *ex ante* and *ex post* policing measures enforced by sanctions for not engaging in these measures. The duties to engage in effective policing measures together with the imposed sanction for failing to engage in effective policing measures reverse the incentive structure of the of a carrot approach into the opposite. In order to be effective, the sanction for failing to engage in policing measures has to fulfill the first requirement of the duty-based corporate liability regime. In reference to the "multi-tiered" composite regime, each policing duty has to be provided with an independent sanction in order to induce corporations to engage in each single *ex post* policing measures even though they might have failed to engage in *ex ante* or one or more *ex post* policing measures. Therefore, corporations will have a duty to implement compliance measures, to investigate, to self-report, and to cooperate.

The imposed sanctions for failing to comply with these duties increase the overall expected liability. If the increase of the overall expected liability through sanctions for failing to engage in policing measures is structured correctly, i.e. if the increase of expected liability through such sanctions is equal or higher than the increase of the overall expected liability through policing measures, corporations have an incentive to engage in these policing measures absent any sanction mitigation. Then, corporations have sufficient incentives to engage in *ex ante* policing albeit the detriments of the

2811 See *supra* at chapter 5, E.

litigation dilemma. In order to induce effective prevention measures, the second requirement of the duty-based liability regime has to be fulfilled.[2812] Within the stick approach, effective prevention measures will be induced through strict liability for corporate agent's misconduct since the statutory provision of engaging in effective policing measures will not affect other sanctions in difference to the carrot approach.

(4) Additional Mandatory Attestation of the External Auditor

In order to ensure that corporations comply with a statutory mandate to implement effective *ex ante* policing measures, the legislator could require, at least for corporations reaching predefined thresholds such as large, listed corporations, that the external auditor has to attest to the effectiveness of such measures similar to the sec. 404(b) SOX-approach.[2813] Moreover, corporations could be required to assess the effectiveness of the compliance program and to disclose information similar to management's report on internal control over financial reporting similar to Item 308 Regulation S-K. In essence, the setup with regard to sec. 404 SOX could be used to ensure that corporations comply with the mandates.

2. USSG-Approach: Administrative Guidelines

Despite the advantages of a statutory approach, the USSG-approach is feasible to address the issue of inducing corporations to engage in effective policing measures. Despite the advantages of the statutory approach, the USSG-approach is probably more suitable for the U.S. In order to ensure that corporate misconduct is deterred nationwide, every corporation has to be subject to the incentives regime. In general, one would assume that corporate law would be most effective in prescribing policing measures. In U.S., however, corporate law would not be effective to do so. Since every U.S. State has its own corporate law, no comprehensive statutory approach would be feasible. In light of the corporate governance issues revealed by the scandals of the 2000s, most states and in particular the State of

2812 Cf. *supra* at chapter 16, B. I. 2. d).
2813 See also *infra* at chapter 19, B. I. 2.

Delaware remained reluctant to address these issues[2814] leading to the enactment of SOX. As the example of SOX shows, it is unlikely that all states would pursue legislation requiring corporations to engage in effective policing measures. This example also shows that the federal legislator regulated within the territory of the state legislators in order to address the revealed issues of the scandals. Such "crossing the line" between the federal level and the state level is a hotly debated issue in the U.S.[2815] rendering the chance of a federal initiative to mandate policing measures highly unlikely. Moreover, the example of SOX also shows that the federal legislator would be likely to choose securities law again as the platform to prescribe policing measures with the issue of limited application only for corporations subject to securities law. It follows that using sentencing guidelines in the U.S. to achieve effective corporate compliance is mainly attributed to the constraints of legislative power. The example of the USSG shows that the appropriate structure of a regulatory regime depends on the regulatory circumstances.

3. Case Law

With regard to case law, the example of Delaware case law shows that such kind of process is likely doomed to failure in the context of inducing corporations to engage in effective internal control to police corporate crime. Especially since courts face difficulties to determine the standard of care for policing measures accurately.[2816] With regard to corporate governance and internal controls and compliance with law in particular, the corporate scandals of the 2000s revealed the limitations of Delaware law.[2817] The portrayed Delaware case law shows the problems of the common law approach. It may take years and years to develop sufficient case law to comprehensively address new legal issues.[2818] In *Caremark*, then-Chancellor Allen used an *obiter dictum* to issue his "far-reaching opinion"[2819]. But he was, nonetheless, reluctant to provide details for how to comply with the duty to monitor and refrained from imposing meaningful consequences

2814 *Thompson*, 38 Wake Forest L. Rev. 961 (2003), p. 964 et seq.; cf. *Hern*, 41 Willamette L. Rev. 207 (2005). See *supra* at chapter 5, F. I.
2815 See *supra* at chapter 16, A. I. 1. b).
2816 See *supra* at chapter 16, A. I. 2. a) (2).
2817 Cf. *Arlen*, 2008, p. 5.
2818 See *supra* at chapter 5, F.
2819 Cf. *Arlen*, 2008, p. 3.

on directors for failing to comply with such duty. The subsequent cases took further years to approve and to elaborate the duty to monitor for directors. Nevertheless, even after the scandals, *Ritter* did not increase the duty to monitor and merely increased the consequences for directors. At last, *Citigroup* and *Goldman* show that courts are reluctant to comprehensively tackle the risk component of internal controls and compliance with law issues.

This finding holds more so in Germany. In Germany, judges are no genuine lawmaker. Rather, they have to interpret the law within the boundaries provided by the letter of the law. But judges in Germany interpret the law and undefined legal terms, such as effective internal controls in sec. 107(3)(s. 2) AktG, provide ample room to be filled by courts and create uncertainty, at least as long as various cases by the high court would provide more guidance to corporations. Also, the *Neubürger* case[2820] shows that judges are not in the position to provide a comprehensive framework to grant leniency to offset the detriments of the litigation dilemma needed when requiring corporations to engage in compliance measures. It is neither sufficient to leave the whole issue to the courts nor to enact broad rules leaving the interpretation to the courts. The issue of providing optimal incentives for corporations to engage in effective compliance measures is too complex to leave it to the courts. More precise guidance on how to design and operate effective internal control is needed to achieve the desired results.

In essence, developing law case by case is merited but reaches its limits when a new comprehensive framework of law is needed to address new issues such as internal controls, compliance with law, and related risk assessment. In this regard, a statutory approach is more promising than case law. Using *Caremark* and *Ritter* as a starting point to develop a comprehensive statutory framework for internal controls, compliance with law, and related risk assessment is more promising than waiting for another judge like then-Chancellor Allen to issue a far-reaching opinion such as *Caremark*. In light of *Citigroup* and *Goldman*, the waiting period is very likely to be long.

IV. Criterion of Effectiveness and its Evaluation

The criterion of effectiveness regarding the internal control and compliance system is crucial as only an effective system ensures deterrence of cor-

2820 *LG München I*, NZG 2014, 345.

porate crime. The criterion of effectiveness and the evaluation of the effectiveness are intertwined since the evaluation of the effectiveness depends on the predefined benchmarks and key performance indicators for the internal control and compliance system. In the following, the four pillars of an effective internal control and compliance system and a two steps test for the evaluation will be depicted.

1. Criterion of Effectiveness

The criterion of effectiveness constitutes one of the central elements of corporate policing and compliance in general as the focus on this criterion of the critique on the USSG points out. The USSC was also aware of the issue that corporation would implement merely "cosmetic" compliance programs[2821] and addressed it by requiring the compliance and ethics program to be effective.[2822] Besides the issue of evaluating the effectiveness of compliance programs for which the necessary steps will be outlined subsequently[2823], the underlying tremendous issue for corporations, courts, and government remains, however, of what actually are the general ingredients constituting an effective compliance program. This issue is not limited to the USSG but encompasses also SOX, COSO I, and internal controls in general.

An internal control and compliance system is effective if its design and operation are adequate for the specific corporation.[2824] This is the case, first, if the operation of the internal control and compliance system meet predefined benchmarks and key performance indicators and, second, if the design of the system is adequate. This is the case if the elements of the internal control and compliance system, the benchmarks, and the key performance indicators meet general standards including benchmarks and indicators of internal control and compliance system representing best practice, as well as applicable regulatory materiality standards, such as material weaknesses, or an applicable standard of care. For establishing its specific

2821 Even though the USSG have not been designed to provide primarily for sanction mitigation, the criterion of effectiveness is still needed to determine if corporations are less culpable. In both cases, corporations may try to obtain the advantage of reduced sanctions by engaging in "cosmetic" compliance programs.

2822 *Swenson/Clark*, 1 Corporate Conduct Quarterly 1 (1991).

2823 See *infra* at chapter 16, B. IV. 2.

2824 See *supra* at chapter 4, A. II. 2. b).

effectiveness, the corporation has to define its internal control and compliance vision and has to establish internal control and compliance objectives.[2825] Then, each corporation is able to define benchmarks and key performance indicators benchmarks necessary to conclude whether the internal control and compliance system operates effectively.[2826] In this regard, corporations have to consider the COSO frameworks.[2827] Since each corporation chooses its specific elements of the compliance program and defines the performance requirements of such elements, it follows that the whole process of establishing a compliance program including its effectiveness is corporation-specific and, thus, within the control of the corporation. From this finding, it follows an important observation regarding the effectiveness that each corporation "owns" the whole process of establishing an effective compliance program, i.e. by designing and implementing the specific standards and procedures of the internal control and compliance system, by setting the compliance vision and compliance objectives (compliance benchmarks), and by defining the key performance indicators to evaluate the effectiveness of the compliance program. Thus, each corporation itself defines what constitutes effectiveness for its internal control and compliance system. While corporations define what constitutes the specific effectiveness of their internal control and compliance system, they have to adhere to applicable regulatory standards or an applicable standard of care as well as general benchmarks and indicators of internal control and compliance system including best practice.

In general, an effective internal control and compliance system consists of four pillars: the elements of the compliance program, the compliance vision and objectives, key performance indicators, and the accurate operation of the compliance program. It follows that the effectiveness of a compliance program encompasses the elements of the compliance program, the performance requirements of such elements, and accurate execution. The key performance indicators constitute the performance requirements. Moreover, the effectiveness of internal control depends enormously on the staff responsible for its implementation.[2828]

2825 Cf. *PwC/Compliance Week*, 2011, p. 8; *Pauthner/de Lamboy*, CCZ 2011, 106, 107.

2826 Cf. *PwC/Compliance Week*, 2011, p. 8.

2827 See also *Withus*, DB 2009, Beilage 5, 82, 85; cf. *Pauthner/de Lamboy*, CCZ 2011, 106, 107. Similar: *Nonnenmacher/Pohle/v. Werder*, DB 2009, 1447, 1451; *Powilleit*, GWR 2010, 28. Skeptical with regard to COSO II: *Dreher/Hoffmann*, ZGR 2016, 445, 493.

2828 *Driscoll/Hoffman/Murphy*, 99 Business and Society Rev. 35 (1998), p. 48.

2. Evaluation of the Effectiveness: Using a Two Steps Test

The issue of how to evaluate the effectiveness using a verifiable test rather than purely judgment is important in order to objectify the evaluation. It has been called for a scientific method to evaluate the effectiveness of individual compliance programs.[2829] Also, it has been stressed that evaluating the effectiveness of compliance measures "requires consistency between organizational assessments of effectiveness and those of regulators, prosecutors, and courts".[2830] More importantly, the effectiveness of an internal control and compliance system can only be assessed by defining benchmarks and key performance indicators in order to set a performance level for the effectiveness.[2831] Since each corporation has its specific setup and, thus, specific internal control and compliance needs, it follows that also the effectiveness of its compliance program is unique. A test to evaluate the effectiveness has to account for this fact that each corporation "owns" the whole process of establishing an effective internal control and compliance system.

For evaluating the effectiveness, a two steps test is needed. First, courts or agencies have to determine if the corporation has met its predefined benchmarks for effectiveness by using the key performance indicators defined by the corporation. Second, the elements of the internal control and compliance system, the defined benchmarks and key performance indicators have to be assessed in order to determine whether they reflect general standards, benchmarks and indicators of internal control and compliance system including best practice and applicable regulatory standards or an applicable standard of care. Thus, if it is determined that the corporation failed to satisfy its own internal control benchmarks, or if the internal control benchmarks or the key performance indicators do not satisfy general standards for internal control, the corporation's internal control is not effective. Since each corporation defines what constitutes the effectiveness of its compliance program, the second prong of the test is of critical importance.

For the second step, courts and agencies may draw on the concept of material weakness especially for a standard of care as well as on the principle of proportionality. In light of the definition of material weakness, courts

---

2829 *Pape*, Corporate Compliance, p. 207.
2830 *Laufer*, 52 Vand. L. Rev. 1343 (1999), p. 1419.
2831 Cf. *PwC/Compliance Week*, 2011, p. 8; *Langevoort*, 31 J. Corp. L. 949 (2006), p. 955.

would have to determine whether there is a reasonable possibility that a deficient compliance program will fail to prevent or detect a material misconduct.[2832] Likewise, courts should orient their evaluation on the top-down, risk-based approach of the SEC for evaluating the effectiveness of internal control over financial reporting[2833] to enhance efficiency of the evaluation. If the court or agency determines that the corporation failed to satisfy its own compliance benchmarks, or if the compliance benchmarks or the key performance indicators do not satisfy a regulatory standard e.g. the USSG-standards for compliance programs, the corporation will not receive leniency for its compliance program. If the corporation failed to define its compliance benchmarks at all, it will likewise receive no leniency.

The two steps test reveals that courts and governmental agencies depend on general standards, benchmarks and indicators of internal control and compliance systems including best practice and applicable regulatory standards or an applicable standard of care to evaluate whether the specific corporation has implemented an effective compliance program. Therefore, the legislator, courts, and agencies must establish such general standards, benchmarks and indicators *ex ante* to evaluate if the design of the internal control and compliance system and its effectiveness defined by the corporation is reasonably believed to actually constitute an adequate system for the specific corporation. So far, the COSO I requirements provide a starting point for benchmarks. Further general benchmarks and key performance indicators have to be developed which is beyond the scope of this thesis.

So far, the following has been used by corporations to measure the effectiveness of compliance programs as compiled by the survey of *PwC* and *Compliance Week*: hotline activity, employee training data, audits of the compliance program, employee disclosure, material weaknesses and significant deficiencies, employee questionnaires, cost of compliance program activities, and cost of non-compliance.[2834] These statistics alone, however, only measure the activity and not the effectiveness of the compliance program.[2835] In addition, as revealed by the survey, corporations have used the following methods to measure the effectiveness of the compliance program: track incidents; track cases received, processed, and resolved; track training metrics; conduct employee interviews; conduct internal audits of

2832 See *supra* at chapter 4, A. II. 2. b) (3).
2833 See *supra* at chapter 4, A. II. 2.
2834 *PwC/Compliance Week*, 2011, p. 9.
2835 Cf. *PwC/Compliance Week*, 2011, p. 8.

the compliance program; risk assessment results; regulatory examinations; external assessments of compliance program effectiveness; and employee surveys.[2836] These findings show that measuring the activity regarding the compliance program alone does not provide much insight into the effectiveness of such program. Moreover, the methods used to evaluate the effectiveness of the compliance program also need key performance indicators to compare the results of the methods with the indicators. If the results meet or exceed the indicators, the compliance program is by definition effective.

In essence, the two steps test overcomes the difficulties[2837] to evaluate the effectiveness of individual internal control and compliance systems and concerns that "without metrics for assessing compliance effectiveness, regulators and prosecutors often rely on little more than corporate representations"[2838]. It remains, nevertheless, a difficult task.

2836 *PwC/Compliance Week*, 2011, p. 9.

2837 *Langevoort*, 2002 Colum. Bus. L. Rev. 71, p. 114; cf. *Pape*, Corporate Compliance, p. 208.

2838 *Laufer*, 43 Journal of Business Ethics 253 (2003), p. 254. See *supra* at chapter 5, C. III.

Chapter 17: Efficient Deterrence and Efficient Internal Control and Compliance Systems

Besides the issue of effective deterrence of corporate crime, efficiency considerations are also important. While effective internal control and compliance systems are one important aspect of effective deterrence, another main issue is how to efficiently deter corporate crime through effective internal control and compliance systems. For the thesis, efficiency is defined by the *Kaldor-Hicks* criterion.[2839] Therefore, a change of rules is more efficient and thus should be made if the increase in utility of the gainers is greater than the loss in utility of the losers in regard to the change.

With regard to the deterrence of corporate wrongdoing through internal control and compliance systems, society as a whole will gain from less corporate crime. In general, compliance with the law is beneficial since individual and general rights such as rights protecting the market or the environment are respected.[2840] But requiring corporations to invest into internal control and compliance measures as well as to evaluate the effectiveness, leads obviously to a loss for corporations since effective internal controls are not without costs.[2841] Moreover, individual corporations may be better off not complying with the law. On the other hand, other corporations may be better off in case competitors comply with the law. In addition, the cost-benefit analysis[2842] suggests that effective internal controls are in general beneficial for corporations. While it is difficult to determine, whether it is overall beneficial for corporations to invest in effective internal controls vis-à-vis the costs, the gain of society due to corporations being in compliance with the law will be high enough to compensate the loss of corporations in light of effective internal controls. This notion is based on the finding that corporations are able to deter corporate wrongdoing at lower costs than government[2843]. Hence, rules requiring corporations to invest in effective internal control and compliance systems are generally ef-

2839 See *supra* at chapter 2, A.

2840 See e.g. with regard to the effect of bribery on economic development *supra* at chapter 5, A.

2841 Cf. *Langevoort*, 31 J. Corp. L. 949 (2006), p. 959 et seq.

2842 See *supra* at chapter 13.

2843 See *supra* at chapter 16, II. B. 1.

ficient. In this regard, it has been noted that a regulatory regime is more efficient the better it induces corporations to engage in effective measures to deter corporate crime.[2844] Therefore, the composite liability regime is more efficient to achieve the goal of deterring corporate wrongdoing in contrast to the current regulatory regimes in the U.S. and Germany since it is the best choice to induce corporations to engage in effective prevention and policing measures.[2845]

The alternatives to the composite liability regime do not lead to more efficiency. One alternative would be to increase governmental investigations. But governmental investigations have several downsides. They are costly to society and they are detrimental to corporations especially with regard to loss of reputation[2846]. Moreover, governmental investigators are less familiar with the corporation which increases the costs of investigations. Another alternative would be to increase corporate fines. This does not lead to more efficiency, however, since higher fines do not induce corporations to engage in effective prevention and policing measures[2847] and since a liability regime is more efficient the better it induces effective measures. A further alternative would be to reduce the required level of effectiveness of such measures. Instead of requiring measures which comply with a materiality standard, such as material weaknesses or an applicable standard of care, a liability regime could only require corporations to implement cost-efficient measures considering costs and benefits. But such kind of lower level of effectiveness is likely to increase the costs of corporate wrongdoing on society since cost-efficient measures are less able to deter corporate wrongdoing compared to effective measures. In this regard based on the finding that a liability regime is more efficient the better it induces effective measures, requiring less than effective measures decreases efficiency.

Efficiency is undermined, however, if unnecessary burdens are placed on corporations. As the example the former PCAOB AS 2 regarding the evaluation of the effectiveness of internal control over financial reporting pursuant to sec. 404 SOX shows, ticking boxes places high burdens on corporations without a corresponding gain with regard to the effectiveness of internal control over financial reporting.[2848] Also, the use of a top-down, risk-based approach for the evaluation fosters efficiency. With regard to

2844 Cf. *Oded*, 2011.
2845 See *supra* at chapter 16, B. I. 2. d).
2846 See *supra* at chapter 8, E. III. 3.
2847 See *supra* at chapter 16, B. I.
2848 See *supra* at chapter 4, A. II. 2. a).

costs, the SOX example shows that initial investment cost might be high but the running costs are significantly lower so that the overall costs decrease over time.[2849]

In order to reduce the burdens on corporations, the specifics of each corporation will need to be taken into account in order to avoid inefficiencies due to one-size-fits-all mandates. In this regard, it is important to note that each corporation "owns" the effectiveness of its internal control and compliance system which reduces inefficiency due to one-size-fits-all mandates. Thereby, an important factor to consider is the ownership structure of corporations as a relevant factor for the design of internal control and compliance measures.[2850] In light of the burdens on corporations, the suggested four pillars of an effective internal control and compliance system provide flexibility needed to avoid "one-size-fits-all" and the suggested two steps test to evaluate the effectiveness considers that each internal control system will be different. The most important factor in light of efficiency is the fact, however, that the criterion of effectiveness does not require to implement "perfect" internal control and compliance systems. Rather, by setting a materiality standard which requires less than "perfect" systems, which are, nonetheless, considered effective[2851], efficiency is fostered to a great extent.

In essence, efficient deterrence and efficient internal control and compliance systems will be achieved by a set of rules which ensures effective internal control and compliance systems at least costs. The composite liability regime combined with the criterion of effectiveness and the suggested two steps test have the potential to induce corporations to engage in effective internal control and compliance systems at least costs.

2849 See *supra* at chapter 13, B. I.
2850 See *supra* at chapter 12, B. I. 1. c) (4).
2851 See *supra* at chapter 4, C. I. 1. b).

Chapter 18: Conclusion

The issue of how to achieve effective internal control and compliance systems to optimally deter corporate crime is difficult and controversial. By using the critique and shortcomings of the current approaches to induce corporations to engage in effective internal control and compliance systems, law and economics research suggests an approach for an optimal incentive regime. A duty-based liability regime will be the best choice regardless if it uses criminal corporate liability or civil corporate liability as long as enforcement by a state agency is ensured. The criterion of an effective internal control and compliance system consisting of four pillars and the suggested two steps test for the evaluation of the effectiveness provide useful insight regarding effective internal control and compliance systems. In light of the *Kaldor-Hicks* criterion, the portrayed regulatory regime to induce effective internal control and compliance systems is in general efficient.

Part Five Suggestions for Reforming the USSG and German Law

In this part, suggestions for reforming the USSG and German law will be addressed in order to achieve effective deterrence of corporate crime through effective internal control and compliance systems seizing on the findings of previous parts of the thesis. With regard to German law, also the main issues identified by the current academic debate regarding internal control, compliance, and corporate governance will be portrayed.

Chapter 19: Reforming the USSG

In light of the conducted research, the USSC may address the following suggestions in order to render the USSG more effective to induce corporations to engage in optimal prevention and policing measures. First, the USSG have to provide for optimal incentives to implement effective compliance programs by fulfilling the requirements of the duty-based corporate criminal liability regime. The USSG have to account for the impact of policing measures on the probability of detection. They have to encompass all sanctions not only the criminal sanction. Moreover, they have to provide sufficient incentives especially for large corporations to engage in optimal policing measures. Second, as a prerequisite to obtain leniency, the USSG have to require that corporations establish compliance benchmarks and key performance indicators in order to enable corporations and courts to evaluate the effectiveness of the compliance program using the suggested two steps test. Third, the USSG should provide for general benchmarks for compliance and key performance indicators to provide guidance for corporations to set such benchmarks and indicators and to provide guidance for corporations, government, and courts to evaluate the effectiveness of compliance programs. In this regard, courts will also develop such benchmarks and indicators as part of the process of setting a standard of care within a duty-based liability regime. In general, in order to fulfill the two requirements revealed by the law and economics research to provide for optimal incentives to induce prevention and policing measures, the USSG need to prescribe a flexible framework for sanctioning and sanction mitigation so that judges are able to decide for each case at hand on the optimal sanction. In order to fulfill their task appropriately, courts have to be aware of their function within the USSG.

With regard to the four pillars constituting an effective compliance program[2852], the requirements of the USSG for an effective compliance and ethics program of sec. 8B2.1 USSG fairly provide for a framework for the first and second pillar of an effective compliance program by addressing e.g. the standards and procedures (sec. 8B2.1 (2)(A) USSG), the responsibility and authority for the compliance program (sec. 8B2.1 (2)(B) and (C) USSG), the communication to and training of the employees (sec. 8B2.1

2852 See *supra* at chapter 16, B. IV. 1.

(4)(A) USSG), monitoring and auditing (sec. 8B2.1 (5)(A) USSG), and the promotion of the compliance program (sec. 8B2.1 (6) USSG). With regard to the evaluation of the compliance program, the USSG only require the corporation to evaluate periodically the effectiveness of the compliance and ethics program (sec. 8B2.1 (b)(5)(B) USSG) and do not provide any further guidance on how to evaluate the effectiveness. It follows, that the USSG set the basis for the effectiveness of compliance programs through the seven elements. The current USSG, however, do neither require corporations to define key performance indicators nor do they provide for any guidance on the third pillar, i.e. on general benchmarks of the performance of the elements of the compliance program.

Chapter 20: Reforming German Law

A. *Current Debate: Identified Issues of Internal Control and Compliance and Suggestions for Improvement*

The current debate of legal scholars in Germany centers mainly on compliance issues. Internal control especially regarding financial reporting is not a general issue and the debate of BilMoG with the minor topic of the influence of SOX on German corporations has faded away. The focus regarding internal control currently rests on European reforms of the annual audit[2853] which do not address the mandates for internal control over financial reporting and do not affect the incentive structure of corporations. Within corporate governance, the role of the supervisory board is at issue including the issue of providing adequate information to this board. With regard to compliance, the main focus of the debate rests on compliance programs, liability of the members of the supervisory and management boards, granting leniency, and implementing corporate criminal liability as well as the protection of whistleblowers.

I. Corporate Governance: Need of Information

Within the field of corporate governance, the issue of control in one- and two-tier board systems is dominant especially in light of a dispersed ownership structure.[2854] As a control mechanism, information is an important element in corporate law.[2855] One of the key conflicts of corporate governance within the two-tier board system is the flow of information between the management board and the supervisory board.[2856] In this regard, the antagonism between "too close to management" ensuring the flow of in-

2853 See Directive 2014/56/EU, Regulation (EU) No 537/2014, and *Abschlussprüfungsreformgesetz* (AReG).

2854 Cf. *Windbichler*, FS HU-Juristische Fakultät, 1079, 1086.

2855 *Windbichler*, FS HU-Juristische Fakultät, 1079, 1089; *Grundmann*, European Company Law, 2007, mar. 85 et seq.

2856 *Marsch-Barner*, FS Schwark, 219; *Seibt*, Hdb Corporate Governance, 391 et seq.; *Lutter*, Information im Aufsichtsrat, mar. 320; *Hopt/Roth*, in: Großkomm AktG, sec. 111, mar. 505.

formation, due to personal relations, and "independence" including the detriment of limited flow of information has been identified.[2857] So far, the access of the supervisory board to the internal control system has not been part of best practice in Germany.[2858] Receiving accurate information, however, is crucial for the supervisory board.[2859] It has been stated that effective internal controls are needed to achieve accurate flow of information to the supervisory board.[2860] Also the economic literature addresses the issue of providing information to the supervisory board.[2861] It has been noted, however, that information is no panacea especially in light of mandatory disclosure obligations.[2862] In this regard, costs, benefits and side effects will need to be considered as well as the impact of standardized disclosure forms.

A further issue within corporate governance is minority protection.[2863] In this regard, the protection of minority shareholders through legal action in light of sec. 147 AktG has hardly any effect due to high barriers preventing such claims.[2864] Therefore, the supervisory board would need to focus on minority protection especially within a concentrated shareholder setting[2865].[2866] Otherwise, it has been stressed that even independent directors would be unsuitable for protecting minority shareholders due to disinter-

2857 *Wackerbarth*, ZGR 2005, 686, 712. See for the constitution of the supervisory board: *Langenbucher*, ZGR 2012, 314 et seq.

2858 Cf. *Hopt/Roth*, in: Großkomm AktG, sec. 111, mar. 214; *Wohlmannstetter*, ZGR 2010, 472, 484. See *supra* at chapter 8, B. II. 1. c) and chapter 12, B. I. 2. a).

2859 *Davies/Hopt*, 2013, p. 27 et seq.; *Hopt*, FS Hoffmann-Becking, 563, 583; *Seibt*, Hdb Corporate Governance, 391 et seq.; BT-Drucks. 14/7515 mar. 19-32; *Marsch-Barner*, FS Schwark, 219; *Hopt/Roth*, in: Großkomm AktG, sec. 111, mar. 502; cf. *Semler*, FS Goette, 499, 501; *Roth*, ZGR 2012, 343, 372 et seq.; *Leyens*, Aufsichtsrat, pp. 114 and 198; cf. *Theisen*, ZGR 2013, 1 et seq.; *Schünemann*, FS Tiedemann, 429, 446. See in general on information: *Schneider, S.H.*, 2006; *Leyens*, Aufsichtsrat; *Jungmann*, ECFR 2006, 426, 453.

2860 *Hopt*, ECFR 2013, 167, 186.

2861 Cf. *Theisen*, ZGR 2013, 1 et seq. See in general: *Beckmann*, Informationsversorgung Aufsichtsrat; *Theisen*, Berichterstattung des Aufsichtsrats; *Grothe, P.*, Unternehmensüberwachung, p. 254 et seq.

2862 *Windbichler*, FS Hopt, 1505, 1507 et seq. and 1519.

2863 See in general: *Hommelhoff*, EBOR 2001, 61 et seq.

2864 *Hopt*, ECFR 2013, 167, 190.

2865 See *supra* at chapter 12, B. I. 1. c) (4).

2866 *Wackerbarth*, ZGR 2005, 686, 707; cf. *Cromme*, FS Hoffmann-Becking, 283, 289.

estedness.[2867] But since directors are subject to the duty of loyalty[2868], outside directors increase the protection of minority shareholders against self-dealings in the relationship between the corporation and its controlling shareholder[2869] if provided with sufficient information to decide on conflicted issues.[2870] This is in line with the notion that the duty of loyalty is best preserved by full disclosure of the relevant facts.[2871] With regard to conflicts of interests within groups of corporations, minority protection is addressed within group law.[2872] In order to protect minority shareholders against "tunneling" and to prevent conflicts of interest, organizational measures should be used within the corporation including a compliance organization[2873] and through disclosure and controls.[2874]

In essence, the debate regarding corporate governance with the raised issues has one underlying topic: the need of accurate information for the supervisor. Only the EU Commission follows a different path to address ongoing corporate governance issues. The EU Commission aims to strengthen the duties of shareholders within corporate governance.[2875] A legal obligation for boards to certify the effectiveness of internal control, however, has been named to be unnecessary at the EU level.[2876] This position is reflected in the directives addressing statutory audits and BilMoG implementing the directives.

2867 *Wackerbarth*, ZGR 2005, 686, 719.

2868 *Hopt*, ECFR 2013, 167, 175; *Möllers*, Hdb Corporate Governance, 423 et seq.; *Hopt*, in: Corporate Governance and Directors' Liabilities, p. 306 et seq.; cf. BGH NJW 1980, 1929.

2869 Cf. *Hopt*, ECFR 2013, 167, 177.

2870 *Hopt*, FS Hoffmann-Becking, 563, 583; *Hopt*, in: Corporate Governance and Directors' Liabilities, p. 320.

2871 *Hopt*, ECFR 2013, 167, 186.

2872 *Hopt*, ECFR 2013, 167, 177; *Hopt*, in: Corporate Governance and Directors' Liabilities, p. 311; *Hommelhoff*, EBOR 2001, 61 et seq.

2873 *Hopt*, ECFR 2013, 167, 188.

2874 *Conac*, ECFR 2013, 194, 224. See *Drygala*, AG 2013, 198, 207 et seq.

2875 Commission, Action Plan 2012, at 3; Commission, Green Paper, at 2.1; cf. *Seibert*, FS Hoffmann-Becking, 1101 et seq. Against: *Wilsing*, ZGR 2012, 291, 301.

2876 *European Corporate Governance Forum*, Risk Management and Internal Control, 2006, at recital 6.

II. Compliance

Within the debate regarding compliance, the need of compliance measures has been stressed to address the increased potential to harm society through the ability to hide personal behavior within the organizational structure of the corporation.[2877] In this regard, the issue has been raised which incentive structure is needed to achieve compliance.[2878] With regard to corporate liability for crimes and offences due to sec. 30, 130 OWiG, it has been proposed to adjust the amount of the penalty following sec. 81(4) (s. 2)(half sentence 2) GWB which allows for a penalty up to 10% of the revenue.[2879] Also, it has been suggested to implement a leniency provision within sec. 30 OWiG.[2880] Otherwise, it has been held that fines would not have a preventive effect and hardly any deterring effect.[2881] Moreover, it has been stated that German prosecution would not have sufficient resources to fight corporate crime.[2882]

Currently, the general duty to implement a compliance organization does not encompass any specifics on how to design a compliance organization. But members of the management board usually prefer more guidance even on the design of a compliance organization.[2883] Therefore, it has been postulated to provide more precise guidance on monitoring duties in order to enhance the predictability of law.[2884] Likewise, the legislator should provide for minimum standards of an effective compliance system in order to enhance the predictability of law.[2885] Moreover, legal mandates would better create trust of investors than voluntary rules.[2886] Otherwise, a strong

---

2877 Cf. *Semler*, FS Goette, 499, 500; *Sieber/Engelhart*, Compliance Programs Survey, p. 205; *Bussmann*, 2003 MschrKrim, 89, 91. Different: *Habersack*, FS Schneider, 429, 433 et seq.

2878 See *Benz/Klindt*, BB 2010, 2977.

2879 Transparency International Deutschland, 2012.

2880 *Nell*, ZRP 2008, 149, 151.

2881 *Schünemann*, FS Tiedemann, 429, 445 et seq.

2882 *Hoven/Wimmer/Schwarz/Schumann*, NZWiSt 2014, 201, 209; Antrag der Fraktion Bündnis 90/Die Grünen, BT-Drucks. 18/10038, p. 1; *Schumacher/Seiwert/Bergermann/Berke*, Wirtschaftswoche, p. 48 et seq. See also *Meyer*, in: Criminal Responsibility, p. 130.

2883 Cf. *Bachmann*, VGR, 2008, 65, 80; *Sieber/Engelhart*, Compliance Programs Survey, p. 210.

2884 *Bussmann/Matschke*, CCZ 2009, 132, 133; cf. *Hauschka/Greeve*, BB 2007, 165; *Hindelmeier/Maier*, ZIR 2009, 119.

2885 *Moosmayer/Gropp-Stadler*, NZWiSt 2012, 241, 242.

2886 *Köhler/Marten/Schlereth*, DB 2009, 1477, 1486.

opinion has been formed against the implementation of statutory duty to implement compliance measures due to fear of overregulation leading to one-size-fits-all regulation.[2887] Also, mandating to implement compliance measures has been named disproportional since most corporations would be law-abiding.[2888] Moreover, it has been stressed that a profound risk management system would lead to more bureaucracy without the assurance that the risk management system will be more effective.[2889] In this regard, SOX has been named as a bad example for such overregulation.[2890] At least, the law should not provide for specifications of how to design compliance measures.[2891] Thus, no legal minimum requirements should cripple corporations.[2892] Moreover, it has been argued that a statutory mandate of U.S.-style compliance requirements would be unconstitutional in Germany without a proper test to evaluate the effectiveness of compliance measures, due to a violation of the principle of certainty.[2893]

Furthermore, in light of internal investigations, self-reporting, and cooperation, it has been noted that the management board would not be a deputy of the prosecution and should not become one.[2894] Nevertheless, it has been stressed that prosecutors press corporations to launch internal investigations.[2895]

1. Debate on Granting Leniency

The debate whether to grant leniency in the context of corporate crime is fairly new in Germany and has mainly been started based on the experience of German corporations in the U.S. regarding investigations, sanctions, compliance, and leniency provisions. It has been reasoned that providing leniency for implemented compliance measures would not be necessary since the management board would have sufficient incentives to im-

2887 *Bachmann*, VGR, 2008, 65, 99; *Hauschka*, VGR, 2008, 51, 63; *Bachmann/Prüfer*, ZRP 2005, 109, 112; *Spindler*, Unternehmensorganisationspflichten, p. 548 et seq. and p. 598; cf. *Hüffer*, FS Roth, 299, 307; *Huth*, BB 2007, 2167.

2888 *Engelhart*, Sanktionierung, p. 645 and p. 653.

2889 Cf. *Spindler*, in: Fleischer, Hdb Vorstandsrecht, sec. 19, mar. 56.

2890 *Bachmann/Prüfer*, ZRP 2005, 109, 112.

2891 *Bachmann*, VGR, 2008, 65, 101.

2892 *Bock*, ZIS 2009, 68, 80.

2893 *Pape*, Corporate Compliance, p. 205 et seq.

2894 *Bachmann*, VGR, 2008, 65, 78; cf. *Lösler*, WM 2007, 676, 682.

2895 *Benz/Klindt*, BB 2010, 2977, 2979; *Schneider*, NZG 2010, 1201, 1202.

plement compliance measures regardless of providing leniency[2896] and that corporations would have an incentive to implement compliance measures to prevent any misconduct and to self-report and cooperate to avoid a penalty notice.[2897] Otherwise, granting leniency or increasing the expected liability for corporations has been named to induce corporations to implement effective compliance programs.[2898] Also, it has been suggested to implement leniency provisions similar to the USSG as well as to assign the investigation of corruption to an independent and specialized agency which is not the prosecutor's office in order to achieve effective prosecution.[2899] In order to provide incentives for corporations to implement compliance measures by granting leniency, it has been suggested to use the *Richtlinien für das Strafverfahren und das Bußgeldverfahren* (RiStBV) similarly to the USSG.[2900] In the same way, several authors advocate to consider compliance programs to grant leniency.[2901] Granting leniency for compliance programs would not contradict any other element of a leniency program.[2902] Rather, granting leniency for confessions is common within criminal law. In the OWiG-context, it has been suggested to consider compliance measures for determining the fine by granting leniency for effective compliance systems considering the policy rationale embodied in sec. 17(3) OWiG and sec. 153 StPO.[2903] Compliance organizations may be considered to determine the fine[2904] within the dutifully exercised discretion of the enforcement agency (sec. 47 OWiG)[2905]. In case of self-reporting and cooperation, it has been argued that law enforcement agencies should refrain from any sanctions.[2906]

With regard to precluding liability for effective compliance measures, the Committee of Ministers of the Council of Europe recommended as

---

2896 *Pampel*, BB 2007, 1636, 1639. Undecided: *Bachmann*, VGR, 2008, 65, 87.
2897 *Moosmayer*, Compliance, pp. 15 and 110.
2898 Cf. *Sieber*, FS Tiedemann, 449, 478; *Heine*, in: Schönke/Schröder, StGB, Vorbem. zu sec. 25, mar. 129.
2899 *Bachmann/Prüfer*, ZRP 2005, 109, 113.
2900 Cf. *Sieber*, FS Tiedemann, 449, 482.
2901 *Bosch/Colbus/Harbusch*, WuW 2009, 740, 746; *Lampert*, BB 2002, 2237, 2243.
2902 *Bosch/Colbus/Harbusch*, WuW 2009, 740, 746.
2903 *Sieber*, FS Tiedemann, 449, 471 et seq.; *Moosmayer/Gropp-Stadler*, NZWiSt 2012, 241, 242 et seq. Within the antitrust context: *Krebs/Eufinger/Jung*, CCZ 2011, 213, 214 et seq.; *Voet v. Vormizeele*, CCZ 2009, 41, 48; *Bosch/Colbus/Harbusch*, WuW 2009, 740, 746 et seq.; cf. *Bachmann*, VGR, 2008, 65, 84 et seq.
2904 *Gürtler* in: Göhler, OWiG, sec. 30, mar. 36; *Bock*, Criminal Compliance, p. 355.
2905 *Sieber*, FS Tiedemann, 449, 472 et seq.
2906 *Moosmayer/Gropp-Stadler*, NZWiSt 2012, 241, 243; *Dann*, CCZ 2010, 30, 34.

early as 1988 that corporations should not be criminal liable if the "management is not implicated in the offence and has taken all the necessary steps to prevent its commission".[2907] The recommendation emphasizes the general opinion on granting leniency. Thus, if corporations implemented effective compliance organizations, liability based on the duty to implement compliance measures should be precluded.[2908] In order to avoid liability, the compliance system would need to be effective in design and operation.[2909] For the evaluation, whether such system is effective, it has been suggested to use the scope of testing of the U.S. monitor including self-assessment, document review, interviews, and testing to analyze German compliance management systems.[2910] Furthermore, the adoption of IDW PS 980 started a debate whether an effective compliance management system with an unqualified attestation in light of IDW PS 980 will reduce or eliminate the liability of management for failing to comply with their monitoring duties of sec. 130 OWiG and sec. 76 combined with sec. 93 AktG.[2911] The ThyssenKrupp corruption scandal casts doubt on the significance of an IDW PS 980 attestation.[2912]

2. Implementing Corporate Criminal Liability in Germany?

The current debate on compliance centers on whether to implement corporate criminal liability in Germany seizing on the same debate in 1998 which the "Commission regarding the reform of the system for criminal sanctions" refused in 2000 arguing that the measures to sanction corporations through sec. 130, 30 OWiG were sufficient.[2913] In 2011, the Department of Justice of the State of North Rhine-Westphalia started the project: "Disgorgement of Profits and Sanctioning" which includes the aspect of

---

2907 *Council of Europe*, R (88) 18, p. 2.

2908 *Bachmann*, VGR, 2008, 65, 84; *Bosch/Colbus/Harbusch*, WuW 2009, 740, 742 and 748.

2909 *v. Busekist/Hein*, CCZ 2012, 41, 42; *Withus/Hein*, CCZ 2011, 125, 128 et seq.

2910 *Rieder/Jerg*, CCZ 2010, 201, 203.

2911 See *supra* at chapter 9, C.

2912 See *supra* at chapter 4, D. I. 2. b).

2913 *Kommission zur Reform des strafrechtlichen Sanktionensytems*, Abschlussbericht, p. 191 et seq. Similar: *Peglau*, ZRP 2001, 406; *Theile/Petermann*, JuS 2011, 496, 501; *v. Rosen*, in: Unternehmensstrafrecht, 263; *Weber-Rey*, in: Unternehmensstrafrecht, 321, 331. See also *supra* at chapter 8, D.

corporate criminal liability.[2914] In 2012, the issue of corporate criminal liability has been set on the federal agenda again.[2915] But the legislator only increased the maximum fines of sec. 30(2) OWiG and of sec. 130(2) OWiG in October 2012 in order to address concerns that the former maximum fine might have been inadequate.[2916] In 2013, North Rhine-Westphalia published a draft bill[2917] addressing corporate criminal liability which will be addressed in more detail below[2918].

As an argument in favor of corporate criminal liability, a deterring effect is claimed in case corporations are subject to a fine based on criminal law rather than regulatory law due to the stigma of a criminal sanction.[2919] Differently, it has been stated that there is hardly any difference between a criminal fine and a regulatory fine especially in the public opinion decisive for the deterring effect.[2920] Moreover, civil judgments may serve the same purpose to stigmatize the corporation.[2921]Also, it has been argued that corporations should not bear any additional reputational loss for failing to engage in prevention and policing measures to avoid overdeter-rence.[2922] In general, the issue of guilt as an element of justifying punishment within criminal law is a complex and controversial issue in the context of corporate crime which is beyond the scope of the thesis.[2923] In addition, it has

2914 See *NRW-Justiz*, Vermögensabschöpfung; *Kutschaty*, Das Unternehmen als Straftäter.

2915 See *Jahn*, F.A.Z. of August 13, 2012; *Reichling*, LTO of May 22, 2012 citing *Bundesministerium der Justiz*, Diskussionsentwurf zur Änderung des Ordnungswidrigkeitengesetzes (OWiG), April 27, 2012; *WDR*, WESTPOL of September 16, 2012; *Spiegel Online*, December 18, 2012; *Körner*, LTO of April 9, 2012; *Moosmayer/Gropp-Stadler*, NZWiSt 2012, 241; also Antrag der Fraktion der SPD, BT-Drucks. 17/13087.

2916 Beschlussempfehlung und Bericht, BT-Drucks. 17/11053, p. 9 et seq.

2917 *NRW-Justiz*, Gesetzentwurf Unternehmensstrafrecht.

2918 See *infra* at chapter 20, B. I. 2. d) (2).

2919 *Alwart*, HFR 2000, p. 8.

2920 Cf. *Peglau*, ZRP 2001, 406, 407; *Ransiek*, NZWiSt 2012, 45, 46 et seq.; *id.*, Unternehmensstrafrecht, 285, 288 et seq.

2921 *Fischel/Sykes*, 25 J. Legal Stud. 319 (1996), p. 332.

2922 *Fischel/Sykes*, 25 J. Legal Stud. 319 (1996), p. 332.

2923 See on the issue: *Sieber*, FS Tiedemann, 449, 463 et seq.; *Schünemann*, FS Tiedemann, 429 et seq.; *Sachs*, in: Unternehmensstrafrecht, 195; *Wohlers*, in: Unternehmensstrafrecht, 231; *Engelhart*, Sanktionierung, p. 599 et seq. See for an overview on the debate regarding corporate criminal liability: *Engelhart*, Sanktionierung, p. 346 et seq.

been argued that criminal law would be inadequate[2924] and should, therefore, not be used to influence human behavior by providing incentives.[2925]

In order to address corporate crime without implementing corporate criminal liability, it has been suggested to use regulatory law differentiating between minor and major offences and implementing different sets of procedural law for these two sets of offences acknowledging the need for a more sophisticated procedural law for major offences.[2926] A further approach draws on the U.S. concept of corporate monitor to increase the flow of information by implementing an external *Kurator* as a prevention measure.[2927] Moreover, it has been argued that corporations should not face a criminal fine but should only be liable for failing to implement compliance measures.[2928]

A further proposal includes that a corporation would be liable for corporate crime if its internal structure is inadequate to address the risks of its operation.[2929]

3. Whistleblower Protection

Fostering whistleblower protection has been raised in the political debate following the judgment of the European Court of Human Rights awarding damages to an individual applicant based on the violation of art. 10 of the Convention for the Protection of Human Rights and Fundamental Freedoms (right of freedom of expression) by Germany for a dismissal without notice on the grounds that the applicant had lodged a criminal complaint against her employer and the refusal of the domestic courts in the ensuing proceedings to order her reinstatement.[2930] Several draft bills[2931] have been introduced to promote the protection of whistleblower

---

2924 Cf. *Schünemann*, FS Tiedemann, 429, 445; *Ransiek*, NZWiSt 2012, 45, 51.

2925 *Hefendehl*, FS Tiedemann, 1065, 1083 et seq.

2926 *Achenbach*, in: Unternehmensstrafrecht, 271, 275 et seq.

2927 *Schünemann*, FS Tiedemann, 429, 446 et seq.; cf. *Ransiek*, NZWiSt 2012, 45, 47; *Kirch-Heim*, Sanktionen gegen Unternehmen, p. 213 et seq.

2928 *Ransiek*, NZWiSt 2012, 45, 51.

2929 Cf. *Beale/Adams*, 2004, p. 125.

2930 ECtHR, *Heinisch v. Germany*, no. 2827/08, Judgment of July 21, 2011 (Fifth Section).

2931 Cf. Gesetzentwurf der Fraktion Bündnis 90/Die Grünen, BT-Drucks. 18/3039; Gesetzentwurf der Fraktion Bündnis 90/Die Grünen, BT-Drucks. 17/9782; Gesetzentwurf der Fraktion der SPD, BT-Drucks. 17/8567.

against retaliation but the legislative process is still pending due to concerns regarding the necessity of such protection.[2932] Despite these concerns, resolution 1729 (2010) of the Parliamentary Assembly of the Council of Europe stressed the importance of whistleblowing and whistleblower protection. As the main argument for the need of whistleblower protection through statutes, the current lack of legal certainty has been named regarding the weighting process by courts, whether to protect the whistleblower, by balancing the interest of freedom to conduct a business of the employer and the interest of freedom of speech of the employee.[2933] Furthermore, the EU encourages Member States to ensure whistleblower protection.[2934]

B. *Suggestions for Reforming German Law*

The focus of this thesis is on the issue of how to prevent and detect corporate crime effectively by providing guidance and requirements.[2935] In the following, suggestions to reform German law will be addressed which are necessary to achieve effective internal control and compliance systems.

I. Achieving an Effective Internal Control and Compliance System

Within an optimal incentive regime to deter corporate crime, an internal control and compliance system is an important element as it includes prevention and *ex ante* policing measures. In this regard, it is more efficient to induce corporations to implement effective internal control and compliance measures in order to optimally deter corporate crime.[2936] The current legal regime, however, does not provide sufficient incentives for corporations to implement effective compliance measures.[2937] This finding is supported against the background that expectations of investors and the expectations of contractors within the supply chain are a strong factor for Ger-

2932 Cf. Minutes of the German Bundestag, 18/64, p. 6021(A), p. 6022(A), p. 6028(C), p. 6032(C); *Rosbach*, DLF; *Krempl*, heise-online. See also *v. Busekist/ Fahrig*, BB 2013, 119, 123 et seq.

2933 See *supra* at chapter 8, D. I. 2.

2934 Directive 2014/56/EU recital 17.

2935 This approach has been categorized as being U.S.-American (*Engelhart*, Sanktionierung, p. 650).

2936 See *supra* at chapter 16, B.

2937 See *supra* at chapter 16, A. II.

man corporations to implement compliance measures as well as the impact of U.S. regulation and U.S. law enforcement[2938] but not liability concerns deriving from German law or German law enforcement. Prior to the expectations of the market and the U.S. influence, German corporations had less control measures in place than U.S. corporations which has been mainly attributed to stricter U.S. regulation such as the FCPA and SOX as well as the USSG.[2939] Moreover, a survey in 2013 found that only 25% of German corporations had implemented compliance measures fulfilling the rather low standard of sec. 130 OWiG.[2940] In 2016, a survey found that most German corporations implemented compliance measures but (1) face struggles regarding the implementation of a culture of compliance or (2) do not attribute a high priority to the culture of compliance as well as (3) refrain from external evaluations of the compliance measures.[2941] Since the culture of compliance and evaluations are important factors for the effectiveness of compliance measures, the effectiveness of the implemented compliance measures is questionable.

Even though German corporations tend to focus their compliance efforts on corruption, fraud, asset protection, data protection, and antitrust violations[2942], it has been noted that it would be necessary to improve the legal requirements for corporations in order to improve corporate compliance in Germany.[2943] In this regard, it is important to note that transplanting rules similar to the USSG into German law will not provide for an effective and efficient solution as the findings with regard to the shortcomings of the USSG[2944] and the suggestions to their reform[2945] clearly demonstrate. The liability regime needs to be more differentiated to optimally induce corporations to engage in an effective internal control and compliance system as a measure of prevention and *ex ante* policing.[2946]

2938 *Bussmann/Salvenmoser/Jeker*, CCZ 2016, 235 et seq. referring to *Bussmann*, PwC Study 2016 and *id.*, PwC Study 2013.

2939 *Bussmann*, 2007 MschrKrim 260, 264 and 273 referring to a PwC survey in 2007.

2940 *Bussmann*, PwC Study 2013, p. 5.

2941 *Bussmann*, PwC Study 2016, p. 64.

2942 Cf. *Sieber/Engelhart*, Compliance Programs Survey, p. 40 et seq.

2943 Cf. *Bussmann*, 2007 MschrKrim 260, 275. Similar: *Schünemann*, FS Tiedemann, 429, 446; *Martín*, FS Tiedemann, 485, 500.

2944 See *supra* at chapter 16, A. I. 2. a).

2945 See *supra* at chapter 19.

2946 See *supra* at chapter 16, B. I. 2. d).

1. Regulatory Elements to Efficiently Achieve Effective Internal Control and Compliance

The regulatory elements are the essence of the law and economics research to achieve effective internal control and compliance conducted in the previous parts of the thesis. Within the model used for the analysis, they ensure the goal to induce corporations to engage in effective internal control and compliance systems as an element to deter corporate crime. The proposed elements are intended to provide the academic basis for needed legislation.

In order to prevent and detect corporate crime effectively, the law needs to induce corporations to engage in prevention as well as *ex ante* and *ex post* policing measures. Regardless of increased enforcement actions, law enforcement agencies depend on information from within the corporation. For optimal deterrence of corporate misconduct, a multi-tiered duty-based liability regime will provide incentives for corporations to engage in optimal prevention and policing measures. A multi-tiered duty-based liability regime requires strict civil or criminal corporate liability for the acts of its agents and an independent sanction for each policing duty. A duty-based liability regime with statutory requirements to implement effective policing measures, i.e. a stick approach, renders sanction mitigation obsolete and induces optimal policing if structured correctly.

Otherwise, regulators could also provide sufficient sanction mitigation through granting leniency, i.e. a carrot approach, in order to offset the effects of the litigation dilemma.[2947] A combined stick and carrot approach is also feasible.[2948] In order to induce optimal policing measures (monitoring, self-reporting, and cooperation), all involved agencies have to set the right amount of sanction mitigation considering the total sanction (civil, criminal, and market-based) which must equal the social cost of wrongdoing multiplied by one over the probability of detection.

Regardless of the regulatory regime, an effective internal control and compliance system consists of four pillars: the elements of the system, the compliance vision and objectives, key performance indicators, and the accurate operation of the system. Also, corporations need to be induced to define benchmarks and key performance indicators. Moreover, regulators need to provide regulatory standards or a standard of care as well as general benchmarks and indicators of internal control and compliance system.

2947 See *supra* at chapter 16, B. III. 1. b) (1).
2948 See *supra* at chapter 16, B. III. 1. b) (2).

For the evaluation of the effectiveness, the suggested two steps test should be used. In order to ensure sufficient incentives, a state agency has to ensure enforcement and needs to be equipped with sufficient resources. As it has been shown above, the suggested elements are efficient to induce an effective internal control and compliance system especially by using a top-down, risk- based approach for the evaluation.[2949] Furthermore, optimal deterrence of corporate crime requires government to impose both individual and corporate liability.[2950]

2. Issues to Consider

The depicted elements to achieve an effective internal control and compliance system derive from the conducted analysis which used an economic model including the assumptions of new institutional economics. In the following, issues will be addressed which are either attributed to the current academic debate, intended to stipulate further research, or beyond the scope of the thesis.

a) General Aspects Regarding Effectiveness

One important aspect to ensure the acceptance of the proposed elements within the German legal system would be to acknowledge that no "perfect" internal control and compliance system can be achieved efficiently.[2951] Especially in light of a "rogue employee", an internal control and compliance system can be effective even though corporate misconduct occurred. Accepting this fact is important so that courts and agencies are confident in rewarding a corporation for an effective internal control and compliance system despite the occurred misconduct. The suggested two steps test[2952] to evaluate the effectiveness may also foster this confidence. In this regard, the test and the acceptance that an internal control and compliance system may be effective but, at the same time, not perfect will reduce the issue of hindsight bias with regard to the common argument that if

2949 See *supra* at chapter 17.

2950 Cf. *Arlen*, 23 J. Legal Stud. 833 (1994), p. 858 et seq. Different: *Ransiek*, Unternehmensstrafrecht, 285, 308. See *supra* at chapter 16, B. I. 1.

2951 See *supra* at chapter 4, C. I. 1. b).

2952 See *supra* at chapter 16, B. IV. 2.

corporate misconduct occurred the compliance system would obviously not have been effective. Also, the suggested test may serve as the stipulated test to evaluate the effectiveness of compliance measures removing doubts regarding the constitutionality of statutory U.S.-style compliance requirements.

Moreover, it has to be noted that optimal incentives for corporations to engage in an effective internal control and compliance system potentially increase the number of reported misconduct which should not be misinterpreted as sign for ineffectiveness of the implemented systems. Rather, implementing effective compliance measures may increase the number of reported misconduct. This phenomenon is known as the control paradox describing the fact that enhanced measures and scrutiny will temporarily reveal more misconduct prior to reducing the overall rate of misconduct.[2953]

b) Regulatory Standards and Benchmarks for Internal Control and Compliance Systems

Prescribing general standards and benchmarks is a prerequisite to achieve effective internal control and compliance systems. In light of sec. 171(1) (s. 2) AktG or the SEC guidelines, a general standard could be set to require no significant deficiencies for the design and the operation in order to consider an internal control and compliance system effective. In this regard, the term 'significant deficiency' has to encompass the combination of non-significant deficiencies as well as the cumulation of such deficiencies. For setting general benchmarks, the COSO frameworks or IDW PS 980 may be used. The BaFin circulars (MaRisk (BA), MaGo and MaComp), however, are mainly functional requiring specific functions such as risk controlling, compliance-function, and internal audit but provides hardly any guidance on the content of the internal control and compliance system and, therefore, seems rather incomplete to be used for setting general benchmarks.

2953 Cf. *Bussmann/Matschke*, Crime, Law and Social Change 2008, 349, 356 et seq.

c) Internal Control – Corporate Governance

Within corporate governance, the role of the supervisory board has to be strengthened to control the management board. So far, the focus has been on structural improvements within corporate governance by providing the audit committee with specific obligations and rights. Now, the supervisory board including the audit committee has to get the instruments to fulfill its tasks. Comprehensive internal control is the instrument providing the supervisory board with information to supervise the management board.

(1) Direct Access for the Supervisory Board to the Information System and Direct Communication Lines

One of the main issues for supervising management is the antagonism between "too close to management" and "independence" including the detriment of limited flow of information[2954]. One of the main detriments within the corporate governance of German corporations is that the management board is the primary source of information for the supervisory board. Reducing the monopoly of the management board to provide information through effective internal control is an important element to reduce the dependency of the supervisory board on information from the management board. Similar to the rewiring of the "circuitry"[2955] in the U.S. through SOX, German corporate law needs to be rewired with regard to the flow of information within the corporation to the audit committee in a way which is appropriate for a two-tier board system. Thus, day-to-day management rests with the management board which includes to receive all information necessary. But, the AktG needs to further loosen the principle of the information regime that the management board is the primary source of information for the supervisory board including the control of the information which the supervisor receives falling short of easing the detriments of asymmetric information. Rather, the GC, CCO, and head of internal audit need to report periodically to the audit committee. The current principle of separating management and control has not always been that strict within the AktG.[2956]

2954 *Wackerbarth*, ZGR 2005, 686, 712.

2955 Cf. *Coffee*, 2005, pp. 11 and 17.

2956 *Hopt/Roth*, in: Großkomm AktG, sec. 111, mar. 563 et seq.; *Bezzenberger/Keul*, FS Schwark, 121, 125 et seq.

Also, communication lines to the audit committee regarding criminal behavior need to be implemented. In this regard, communication lines may also be termed reporting lines. Reporting in this context, however, should be understood as communication rather than in the sense of a 'chain of command'. These measures do not erode the relationship between the management board and the supervisory board since they are known for both sides. These kinds of communication lines do not contradict a two-tier board structure. It does only shift the balance of power between both boards. The need for more and unbiased information for the supervisory board is greatly accepted. Information is generally important for the supervisory board to carry out its monitoring duties and especially in light of minority protection. Effective internal control will provide for such information. It has to reach the supervisory board! Therefore, the law needs to require corporations to establish effective "wires", i.e. internal controls including information and reporting systems. The supervisory board or a designated committee such as the audit committee should have direct access to the information which the internal control system provides for the purpose of conducting its supervising duties according to sec. 111 AktG. While the general division of power between the management board and the supervisory board shall remain, the internal control system should provide direct two-way information lines for the supervisory board without the involvement of the management board so that the supervisory board has direct access to the internal control system and direct communication lines exist to the supervisory board. The direct flow of information within the internal control system should not „end" at the management board level from where the information is passed on to the ultimate supervisor. Through the design and operation of the internal control and risk management systems, the supervisory board has to ensure that it has the opportunity to receive unbiased information.

(2) Structure of Ownership

Different shareholder structures have to be taken into account since the shareholder structure influences the design and operation of the internal control system. Within a dispersed ownership setting, the internal control system has to focus on the potential for management to expropriate shareholders, while the potential of expropriating minority shareholders has to be a focus in a blockholding structure.[2957] Even though effective internal controls will also enhance minority protection, they are less effective for this purpose compared to addressing potential expropriation of shareholders by management. Thus, requiring effective internal control should be a primary goal at least for large, listed corporations with dispersed ownership.

(3) External Attestation of Effectiveness and Exempting Small Corporations

One issue to consider is whether to require external auditors to attest to the effectiveness of the internal control and compliance system. Several aspects are relevant in this regard. First, the attestation of external auditors would reduce the need for state resources to enforce the mandates of the regulatory regime to achieve effective internal control and compliance systems. Second, since the effectiveness of the internal control and risk management systems is not a primary focus of the external audit[2958] so that the testing of the effectiveness is rather *en passant* than thorough, requiring the external auditors to attest to the effectiveness would increase the level of testing. Third, in order to achieve an effective internal control and compliance system, it is import that the supervisory board requires the management board to define benchmarks and key performance indicators reflecting the legal requirements and the expectations of the supervisory board. But even this requirement is only effective if the supervisory board and the audit committee have adequate measures to verify whether the design and operation of the implemented system is effective. In order to ensure the effectiveness of the implemented system, the audit committee needs to commission further audits of the internal control and compliance system to external auditors. Otherwise, absent sufficient enforcement, requiring the management board to define benchmarks and key performance indicators does not change the incentive structure of the management board to refrain from implementing truly effective systems. Hence, unless an optimal level of state enforcement is ensured, external audits are highly recommended to achieve effective systems. Fourth, the limits of the external audit will need to be considered especially since the auditing of internal controls as management tools is more difficult than the assessment of num-

2957 See *supra* at chapter 12, B. I. 1. c) (4).
2958 See *supra* at chapter 9, C.

bers.[2959] In this regard, benchmarks and key performance indicators will facilitate the audits.

A further issue is whether to exempt small corporations from the requirement of evaluating the effectiveness. A main argument for requiring small corporations to evaluate the effectiveness is that these corporations are considered most prone to fraud and misconduct.[2960] The U.S. debate on this issue shows some of the issues to consider in particular as this debate on the burdens of SOX for small corporations dwarfs the general debate on costs of SOX.[2961] Since the mandates of sec. 404 SOX do not differentiate between the size of corporations, it has been argued that especially the upfront investments into internal control systems place a heavy burden on small corporations.[2962] As a result, small corporations were forced out of the market by SOX.[2963] The SEC tried to accommodate the needs of smaller corporations by postponing the application of sec. 404 SOX for smaller corporations.[2964] Exempting smaller corporations from the internal control requirements of sec. 404 SOX, however, has been rejected by the SEC since smaller corporations have the greatest problems maintaining effective internal controls.[2965] In the Dodd-Frank Act of 2010, the burdens of sec. 404 SOX for small corporations have been eased. Sec. 989G Dodd-Frank Act, adding sec. 404(c) into SOX, provides that non-accelerated filers are permanently exempt from the requirements of sec. 404(b) SOX to provide an auditor attestation report on the effectiveness of their internal control over financial reporting.[2966] Thus, the exemption of the Dodd-Frank Act only addresses small corporations with less than $75 million in worldwide market value.[2967]

2959 *Windbichler*, FS Rokas, 1389, 1396.

2960 Cf. *Steinbuch*, Wirtschaftswoche, p. 74.

2961 See as a result of the debate e.g.: SEC Study Sec. 404(b), COSO Guidance for Smaller Public Companies, and the report of the American Electronics Association (AeA, 2005).

2962 *Ribstein*, 3 NZ L. Rev. 365 (2005), p. 372.

2963 *Carney*, 55 Emory L. J. 141 (2006), p. 143; cf. *Hansen/Pownall/Wang*, 2008.

2964 *Prentice*, 29 Cardozo L. Rev. 703 (2007), p. 729.

2965 *Prentice*, 29 Cardozo L. Rev. 703 (2007), p. 730; cf. *Brown*, 90 Marq. L. Rev. 309 (2006), p. 322 et seq.

2966 See SEC Release No. 9142.

2967 The SEC defines an accelerated filer to meet an aggregate worldwide market value of $75 million but less than $700 million and a large accelerated filer to meet an aggregate worldwide market value of $700 million or more besides further conditions (cf. Rule 12b-2 (1) and (2) Exchange Act).

d) Compliance

With regard to issues generally coming under the heading of compliance, the finding of requiring corporations to engage in policing measures in order to optimally deter corporate crime provokes protest with regard to general principles such as the privilege against self-incrimination. Otherwise, providing incentives to confess by reducing the sentence is common in German criminal trials. As an efficiency argument, law and economics research suggests that law enforcement agencies depend on the efforts of the corporation to deter, detect, and report wrongdoers in order to ensure that wrongdoers are sanctioned.[2968] Since especially *ex post* policing measures such as internal investigations, self-reporting, and cooperation are not a central part of the thesis, the issue will only be raised to stipulate further research.

Within the corporate liability context, granting leniency is an important issue. As it has been shown above[2969], engaging in policing measures increases the expected liability for corporations, i.e. the litigation dilemma.[2970] Hence, in order to induce corporations to engage in the desirable compliance measures such as monitoring, self-reporting, and cooperation with law enforcement, the law needs to provide for incentives to offset the incentives for corporations to refrain from policing measures due to the increase of the expected liability. These counter-balancing incentives may be achieved by providing leniency. Receiving leniency has to be certain for corporations in order to achieve adequate incentives.[2971]

In order to offset the detriments of the litigation dilemma, the impact of the scope of the attorney-client privilege on the magnitude of the litigation dilemma has to be considered due to their direct relation[2972]. With regard to scope of the attorney-client privilege regarding the ombudsman and internal investigations by law firms in the context of prosecutorial confiscations, it has been noted that German district courts, being the final in-

---

2968 *Arlen*, 23 J. Legal Stud. 833 (1994), p. 835; cf. *Fleischer*, ZGR 2011, 155, 178. See *supra* at chapter 16, B. I. 1. Similar: *Bussmann*, FS Achenbach, 57, 66 et seq.; *Martín*, FS Tiedemann, 485, 501: arguing that corporations should partially bear the social costs of law enforcement by inventing in prevention measures. Different: *Lösler*, WM 2007, 676, 682.

2969 See *supra* at chapter 10, B.

2970 See *supra* at chapter 5, B. II.

2971 See *supra* at chapter 6, B.

2972 See *supra* at chapter 16, B. I. 2. a).

stance, have come to diametrically opposing rulings.[2973] Certainty and predictability of the scope of the attorney-client privilege is important, however, to achieve effective internal control and compliance systems.

(1) Criminal or Civil Corporate Liability?

The issue whether civil corporate liability leads to the same or at least similar results compared to corporate criminal liability has already been addressed above.[2974] From a law and economics perspective, the legal nature of the liability is not relevant under the condition that sufficient enforcement is ensured through a governmental agency. Besides the prosecution, the BaFin may be a suitable governmental agency due to the already existing expertise with regard to internal control and risk management systems of financial corporations, investment firms, and insurance corporations. In favor of criminal corporate liability, it has been stressed that the stigma of a criminal sanction would be necessary. On first glance, the situation in the U.S., that the mere threat of a DOJ indictment provides sufficient incentives for corporations to follow the dictates of the federal prosecutors[2975], seems to support this argument. It can be observed, however, that SEC investigation cause comparable concerns. Moreover, it has been observed that sanctions, such as debarment from government contracting, do not necessarily require a criminal sentence.[2976] They could also be imposed by e.g. administrative courts.

With regard to potentially doubtful enforcement of civil corporate liability, corporate criminal liability might be more effective under the principle of legality – *Legalitätsprinzip* of sec. 152 combined with sec. 160 StPO. Especially with regard to recourses and the ample leeway due to sec. 47 OWiG (*Opportunitätsprinzip*), the principle of legality may better serve the needs of providing optimal incentives if providing leniency is ensured. In this regard, it has been noted that German prosecutors generally have simi-

---

2973 See *Kottek*, CB 2016, 349 naming LG Hamburg, decision of October 15, 2010 - 608 Qs 18/10, NJW 2011, 942 (HSH Nordbank) and LG Braunschweig, decision of July 21, 2015 – 6 Qs 116/15, NStZ 2016, 308. Regarding ombudsman see: *Szesny*, CCZ 2017, 25.

2974 See *supra* at chapter 16, B. II.

2975 See *supra* at chapter 5, C. III.

2976 Cf. *Beale*, 46 Am. Crim. L. Rev. 1481 (2009), p. 1502.

larly broad discretion whether to indict corporations compared to U.S. prosecutors.[2977]

(2) Shortcomings of the Proposals to Implement Corporate Criminal Liability

Recently, one academic proposal and one proposal of the State of North Rhine-Westphalia for a draft bill to implement corporate criminal liability in Germany rendered the debate on implementing corporate criminal liability more specific. Without analyzing the proposals in detail, some problematic provisions will be highlighted.

The German approach to corporate crime is mainly focused on how to punish corporate crime.[2978] Thus, it has been argued that corporate responsibility should be part of criminal law (StGB) or the law on administrative offences (OWiG).[2979] The sanctioning of corporate crime should aim to prevent further criminal acts.[2980] In order to sanction corporations, a corporate sanction law (*Gesetz zur strafrechtlichen und ordnungswidrigkeitenrechtlichen Sanktionierung von Unternehmen - Unternehmenssanktionsgesetz*) has been proposed.[2981] In sec. 10 and sec. 30, corporate criminal liability depends on proving a criminal act of a specific corporate agent, i.e. a connecting crime. Without information from within the corporation, such proof is mostly very difficult as it is the case with regard to sec. 30 OWiG.[2982] Hence, the proposed draft bill does not address one of the main weaknesses of the current law of regulatory offences in Germany. With regard to implementing a compliance program, sec. 5 essentially lists the requirements of the USSG compliance program which exceed the requirements for monitoring of sec. 130 OWiG. As it has been shown, the USSG-approach is not without criticism and need of reform.[2983] In sec. 5, a compliance program is defined without any reference to its effectiveness. Only in sec. 14, the level of effectiveness is indirectly addressed within the mitigating circumstances which require a mostly sufficient ("*weitgehend zureichendes*") compliance program. The draft bill does neither require corpo-

2977 *Engelhart*, Sanktionierung, p. 231 et seq. especially at fn. 61.
2978 See *Engelhart*, Sanktionierung, p. 601 et seq.
2979 *Engelhart*, Sanktionierung, p. 689.
2980 *Engelhart*, Sanktionierung, p. 695.
2981 *Engelhart*, Sanktionierung, p. 720 et seq.
2982 See *supra* at chapter 8, D. III. 3.
2983 See *supra* at chapter 16, A. I. 2. a) and chapter 19.

rations to implement an effective compliance program nor to define benchmarks necessary to assess the effectiveness of the compliance program.[2984] Furthermore, the draft bill undermines the incentive structure for corporations to report criminal behavior and to cooperate with law enforcement, two crucial *ex post* policing measures to deter corporate crime[2985], since sec. 17 provides courts with the opportunity to require corporations to publish the verdict. The danger of a public trial and, more so, the danger of being required to public the verdict is one of main weaknesses of the USSG.[2986] Also, sec. 27 subsection 2 provides the organs of the corporation with a right to silence in order not to incriminate the corporation exceeding the right to silence of sec. 55 StPO in case of potential self-incrimination. It is disputed, however, if the right to silence is applicable to corporations and also its scope.[2987] This issue, however, is beyond the scope of this thesis.[2988]

While using USSG requirements does increase the minimum standard for compliance programs and provides guidance to such programs, it does not provide for sufficient incentives to implement effective programs and does not lead to "truly" effective compliance programs. Without sufficient incentives to implement effective compliance programs and without any threshold or requirements, corporations will not engage in effective compliance programs.

The draft bill[2989] proposed by North Rhine-Westphalia addresses the issue of proving individual crime in sec. 2(1) by sanctioning corporations for crimes of their agents even though multiple agents may have committed the crime alternatively[2990] and in sec. 2(2) by sanctioning corporations for failing to provide monitoring measures in case of a crime committed by their agents even though multiple agents may have committed the crime alternatively[2991]. Nevertheless, the draft bill does neither require to implement a compliance program nor does it address a level of effectiveness of any compliance measures. Only in sec. 5, the level of effectiveness is indirectly addressed within the mitigating circumstances which require adequate ("*ausreichend*") monitoring measures. Also, the draft bill does not

2984 See *supra* at chapter 16, B. IV.
2985 See *supra* at chapter 5, B. I.
2986 See *supra* at chapter 5, D. and chapter 16, A. I. 2. b).
2987 *NRW-Justiz*, Gesetzentwurf Unternehmensstrafrecht, p. 73.
2988 See on the issue within the U.S. *supra* at chapter 5, D.
2989 *NRW-Justiz*, Gesetzentwurf Unternehmensstrafrecht.
2990 *NRW-Justiz*, Gesetzentwurf Unternehmensstrafrecht, p. 43.
2991 *NRW-Justiz*, Gesetzentwurf Unternehmensstrafrecht, p. 46.

require corporations to define benchmarks necessary to assess the effectiveness of the compliance program. Furthermore, the draft bill undermines the incentive structure for corporations to report criminal behavior and to cooperate with law enforcement, since sec. 9 provides courts with the opportunity to require corporations to publish the verdict with the depicted consequences[2992] and sec. 18(1) provides a right to silence for corporate organs in the trial against the corporation.

(3) Need of Whistleblower Protection

Two aspects call to implement statutory protection of justified internal and, in extreme cases, external whistleblowing. First, protection against retaliation facilities the effectiveness of internal control and compliance measures since tips of insiders[2993] are important to reveal corporate misconduct increasing the expected liability. Second, statutory protection would be at least a symbolic act to overcome the historic anticipation towards whistleblowers as denunciators and would foster the view that justified whistleblowing is socially welcome[2994]. Moreover, employees need a clear statement that justified, but only justified, whistleblowing is protected.[2995] Unclear case law, which started to provide profound protection just recently[2996], does not fulfill this purpose.

II. Applying the Two Steps Test for Evaluations within Corporate Law

Besides the proposal to use the two steps test as part of the proposed elements to achieve an effective internal control and compliance system, the two steps test[2997] may also be used in current corporate law for the evaluation of the effectiveness of the internal control and risk management systems required by sec. 76 combined with sec. 93 AktG, the evaluation of the enumerated systems in sec. 107(3)(s. 2) AktG by the supervisory board as

---

2992 See *supra* at chapter 5, D. and chapter 16, A. I. 2. b).

2993 See *supra* at chapter 8, D. II. and chapter 4, A. IV. 4.

2994 See also *Abraham*, ZRP 2012, 11, 13.

2995 Cf. *Leuchten*, ZRP 2012, 142, 145.

2996 Cf. BVerfG, *Beschluss*, BvR 2049/00 of July 2, 2001, NZA 2001, 888; ECtHR, *Heinisch v. Germany*, no. 2827/08, Judgment of July 21, 2011 (Fifth Section).

2997 See *supra* at chapter 16, B. IV. 1.

well as the evaluation of the adequacy of the early warning system of sec. 91(2) AktG which is similar to the testing of the effectiveness.

For the second step of the evaluation, the minimum legal standards fulfilling the mandates of sec. 76 combined with sec. 93, sec. 107(3)(s. 2), and sec. 91(2) AktG respectively, constitute the general standards, benchmarks, and indicators considering the specific needs of the each corporation in light of the principle of proportionality. If the respective system or the benchmarks and key performance indicators defined by the specific corporation do not satisfy the minimum legal requirements, the respective system is not effective.

Chapter 21: Conclusion

The suggestions for reforming the USSG and German law seize on the findings of the thesis using the conducted research to propose more effective and efficient rules. As the German debate especially on corporate compliance is fairly new, the suggestions for reforms are more profound. Due to the scope of the thesis, not all issue revealed by the academic debate are addressed. Also, issues to consider which are outside of the economic model used for the thesis have only been touched on. Nevertheless, the suggestions provide a thorough academic basis for legislation and the highlighted issues may stipulate further research.

Conclusion

The magnitude of the conducted analysis, shown by the various aspects involved, is surprising considering the starting point of the thesis consisting of two simple questions, one provision, and the general concept of corporate compliance. The magnitude is primarily owed to the fact that various U.S. regulators address aspects of the U.S. concept of internal control. The extent of regulation demonstrates the usefulness of conducting a law and economics impact analysis with regard to legal transplants prior to their transplantation. More so, the impact analysis provides considerable insight when not only single provisions are intended to be transplanted into the receiving jurisdiction but when legal entities become subject to foreign law either through voluntary submission or extraterritorial application leading to *de facto* legal transplants. For conducting the impact analysis, the current status quo of U.S. and German regulation had to be complied providing insight into the requirements of how to design and operate internal control and compliance systems in the U.S. and Germany.

The main impact of U.S. law and best practice regarding internal control and corporate compliance on German *Aktiengesellschaften* listed on the NYSE results from this magnitude of regulation and its sophistication leading to a considerably high impact. A strong regime of SOX including SEC enforcement regarding internal control over financial reporting (sec. 404 SOX) and disclosure controls and procedures (sec. 302 SOX) induces corporate leaders to comply with the U.S. mandates leading to more effective internal control regarding financial and non-financial information. With regard to compliance, the impact of U.S. incentives for German corporations listed on the NYSE is also rather high especially with regard to the FCPA and its enforcement considering the low level of German law requirements and incentives regarding corporate compliance. But the impact regarding compliance diminishes since U.S. compliance concepts became part of German best practice. In this regard, a rather strong impact of U.S. law and best practice on German corporations exists on the German best practice level as numerous German scholars refer to U.S. regulation to enhance German corporate compliance. Nevertheless, the U.S. incentives for self-reporting, cooperation, and remediation have a strong impact on German corporations listed on the NYSE regardless of the lack of German law to provide for leniency. While there has been no impact on risk management systems, the U.S. impact on the governance structure is high.

Besides this huge impact, the friction occurring between U.S. and German law due to the fact that German corporations listed on the NYSE serve two masters is rather low. The issue of direct reporting lines to the audit committee is about to diminish as more and more German scholars postulate to loosen the principle of German corporate law regarding the prerogative of information for the management board. Also, the issue of anonymous whistleblowing seems manageable.

With regard to costs and benefits of being listed on the NYSE, the answer is corporation-specific. The findings suggest that large corporations with dispersed ownership and the need to access the U.S. capital markets will profit from being listed on the NYSE. Moreover, corporation with the ambition to signal their compliance with the sophisticated U.S. internal control mandates may consider a listing at a U.S. exchange. In general, effective internal control provides benefits for corporations especially after the implementation costs are sunk.

With regard to effective internal control and compliance systems, the analysis revealed shortcomings of the U.S. regime and, more so, of the German regime to induce corporations to engage in effective internal control and compliance systems. An effective internal control and compliance system is important as it provides unbiased information for the supervisory board reducing agency costs and is an essential part to deter corporate crime. With regard to internal control regarding financial reporting, it is surprising that the German regime does not consider effective controls as a primary goal. In order to address the revealed shortcomings, suggestions for reform draw on the law and economics research of a best choice corporate liability regime to optimally deter corporate crime, a multi-tiered duty-based liability regime, adding the findings that an effective internal control and compliance system consist of four pillars – the elements of the compliance program, the compliance vision and objectives, key performance indicators, and the accurate operation of the compliance program – and its effectiveness should be tested using the suggested two steps test. From a law and economics standpoint, no preference exists between criminal or civil liability for corporate liability as long as enforcement is ensured through a state agency.

Bibliography

A. Literature

I. Monographs

Abikoff, Kevin, Corporate Governance: Avoiding and Responding to Misconduct, New York loose-leaf 2008; cited: *Abikoff*, Corporate Governance, §

Beckmann, Stefanie, Die Informationsversorgung von Mitgliedern des Aufsichtsrats deutscher börsennotierter Aktiengesellschaften: theoretische Grundlagen und empirische Erkenntnisse, Wiesbaden 2009; cited: *Beckmann*, Informationsversorgung Aufsichtsrat

Berle, Adolph A./Means, Gradinier C., The Modern Corporation and Private Property, New York 1932; cited: *Berle/Means*, Corporation

Biegelman, Martin T./Bartow, Joel T., Executive roadmap to fraud prevention and internal control: creating a culture of compliance, Hoboken 2006; *Biegelman/ Bartow*, Culture of Compliance, p.

Bock, Dennis, Criminal Compliance, Baden-Baden 2011; cited: *Bock*, Criminal Compliance, p.

Brünger, Christian, Erfolgreiches Risikomanagement mit COSO ERM, Empfehlungen für die Gestaltung und Umsetzung in der Praxis, Berlin 2010; cited: *Brünger*, COSO ERM

Bungartz, Oliver, Handbuch Interne Kontrollsysteme (IKS): Steuerung und Überwachung von Unternehmen, Berlin 2010; cited: *Bungartz*, IKS, p.

Engelhart, Marc, Sanktionierung von Unternehmen und Compliance - Eine rechtsvergleichende Analyse des Straf- und Ordnungswidrigkeitenrechts in Deutschland und den USA, 2nd edition, Berlin 2012; cited: *Engelhart*, Sanktionierung, p.

Felderer, Bernhard/Homburg, Stefan, Makroökonomik und neue Makroökonomik, 9th edition, Berlin 2005; cited: *Felderer/Homburg*, Makroökonomik

Furubotn, Eirik G./Richter, Rudolf, Institutions and Economic Theory: The Contribution of the New Institutional Economics, Ann Arbor 1998; cited: *Furubotn/ Richter*, New Institutional Economics, p.

Green, Scott, Manger's Guide to the Sarbanes-Oxley Act - Improving Internal Controls to Prevent Fraud, Hoboken 2004; cited: *Green*, SOX Guide, p.

Grothe, Philip, Unternehmensüberwachung durch den Aufsichtsrat: ein Beitrag zur Corporate-Governance-Diskussion in Deutschland, Frankfurt a.M. 2006; cited: *Grothe, P.*, Unternehmensüberwachung, p.

Grundmann, Stefan, European Company Law: Organizations, Finance and Capital Markets, Antwerpen 2007; cited: *Grundmann*, European Company Law, 2007, mar.

Harm, Julian A., Compliance in Wertpapierdienstleistungsunternehmen und Emittenten von Finanzinstrumenten, Frankfurt a. M. 2008; cited: *Harm*, Compliance Wertpapierdienstleister, p.

Hillebrand, Werner, Das Früherkennungs- und Überwachungssystem bei Kapitalgesellschaften - Erfordernis und Mindestanforderungen aus juristischer und betriebswirtschaftlicher Sicht, Düsseldorf 2005; cited: *Hillebrand*, Früherkennungs- und Überwachungssystem, p.

Hofmann, Stefan, Handbuch Anti-Fraud-Management, Bilanzbetrug erkennen - vorbeugen - bekämpfen, Berlin 2008; cited: *Hofmann*, Hdb Anti-Fraud-Management, p.

Huth, Mark-Alexander, Die Vorstandspflicht zur Risikoüberwachung, Baden-Baden 2007; cited: *Huth*, Risikoüberwachung, p.

Kirch-Heim, Claudio, Sanktionen gegen Unternehmen, Rechtsinstrumente zur Bekämpfung unternehmensbezogener Straftaten, Berlin 2007; cited: *Kirch-Heim*, Sanktionen gegen Unternehmen, p.

Kraakman, Reinier/Armour, John/Paul, Davies/Enriques, Luca/Hansmann, Henry/ Hertig, Gerard/Hopt, Klaus/Kanda, Hideki/Rock, Edward, The Anatomy of Corporate Law - A Comparative and Functional Approach, 2nd edition, New York 2009; cited: *Kraakman*, Anatomy of Corporate Law, p.

Kreps, D.M., A Course in Microeconomic Theory, Princeton 1990; cited: *Kreps*, Microeconomic

Lambsdorff, Johann Graf, The Institutional Economics of Corruption and Reform, Theory, Evidence and Policy, Cambridge 2007; cited: *Lambsdorff*, 2007, p.

Leyens, Patrick C., Information des Aufsichtsrats, Tübingen 2006; cited: *Leyens*, Aufsichtsrat, p.

Lieth, Oliver, Die ökonomische Analyse des Rechts im Spiegelbild klassischer Argumentationsrestriktionen des Rechts und seiner Methodenlehre, Baden-Baden 2006; cited: *Lieth*, Ökonomische Analyse des Rechts

Lutter, Markus, Information und Vertraulichkeit im Aufsichtsrat, 3rd edition, München 2006; cited: *Lutter*, Information im Aufsichtsrat, mar.

Mengel, Anja, Compliance und Arbeitsrecht - Implementierung, Durchsetzung, Organisation, München 2009; cited: *Mengel*, Compliance und Arbeitsrecht

Mercuro, Nicholas/Medema, Steven G., Economics and the Law, Princeton 1997; cited: *Mercuro/Medema*, Economics and the Law

Moeller, Robert R., Sarbanes-Oxley Internal Controls: Effective Auditing with AS 5, CobiT, and ITIL, New Jersey 2008; *Moeller*, SOX Internal Controls, p.

Moosmayer, Klaus, Compliance, 2nd edition, München 2012; cited: *Moosmayer*, Compliance

Nicklisch, Anette C., Die Auswirkungen des Sarbanes-Oxley Act auf die deutsche Corporate Governance – Ein Beitrag zur Amerikanisierung des deutschen Aktienwesens, Berlin 2007; cited: *Nicklisch*, Auswirkungen SOX, p.

Oded, Sharon, Corporate Compliance: New Approaches to Regulatory Enforcement, Elgar 2013; cited: *Oded*, Corporate Compliance, p.

O'Kelley, Charles R./Thompson, Robert B., Corporations and Other Business Associations - Cases and Materials, 5th edition, New York 2006; cited: *O'Kelley/ Thompson*, Corporations, p.

Pape, Jonas, Corporate Compliance - Rechtspflichten zur Verhaltenssteuerung von Unternehmensangehörigen in Deutschland und den USA, Berlin 2011; cited: *Pape*, Corporate Compliance, p.

Posner, Richard A., Economic Analysis of Law, 7th edition, New York 2007; cited: *Posner*, Economic Analysis of Law

Ramos, Michael J., How to comply with Sarbanes-Oxley Section 404: assessing the effectiveness of internal control, 3rd edition, Hoboken 2008; cited: *Ramos*, SOX 404, p.

Root, Steven J., Beyond COSO - Internal Control to Enhance Corporate Governance, New York 1998; cited: *Root*, Beyond COSO

Schneider, Sven H., Informationspflichten und Informationssystemeinrichtungspflichten im Aktienkonzern, Berlin 2006; cited: *Schneider, S. H.*, Informationspflichten, p.

Sieber, Ulrich/Engelhart, Marc, Compliance Programs for the Prevention of Economic Crimes: An Empirical Survey of German Companies, Berlin 2014; cited: *Sieber/Engelhart*, Compliance Programs Survey, p.

Spindler, Gerald, Unternehmensorganisationspflichten - Zivilrechtliche und öffentlich-rechtliche Regelungskonzepte, Köln 2001; cited: *Spindler*, Unternehmensorganisationspflichten, p.

Stute, Andreas, IFRS: Lagebericht und Konzernlagebericht, Grundlagen und Darstellung, Berlin 2010; cited: *Stute*, IFRS, p.

Theisen, Manuel R., Information und Berichterstattung des Aufsichtsrats, 4th edition, Stuttgart 2007; cited: *Theisen*, Berichterstattung des Aufsichtsrats

Tönnissen, Stefan, Revision der IT-Governance mit CoBiT - Leitfaden für die Prüfpraxis, Berlin 2011; cited: *Tönnissen*, Revision der IT-Governance, p.

Watson, Allan, Legal Transplants, An Approach in Comparative Law, 2nd edition, Athens 1993; cited: *Watson*, Legal Transplants, p.

Wundenberg, Malte, Compliance und die prinzipiengeleitete Aufsicht über Bankengruppen, Tübingen 2012; cited: *Wundenberg*, Compliance Bankengruppen, p.

Zweigert, Konrad/Kötz, Hein, Einführung in die Rechtsvergleichung, auf dem Gebiet des Privatrechts, 3rd edition, Tübingen 1996; cited: *Zweigert/Kötz*, Rechtsvergleichung, p.

II. Commentaries and Handbooks

Baumbach, Adolf/Hopt, Klaus J. [eds.], Kommentar zum Handelsgesetzbuch, 35th edition, München 2012; cited: *Author*, in: Baumbach/Hopt, HGB, sec., mar.

Beck'scher Bilanz-Kommentar, *Ellrott, Helmut/Förschle, Gerharrt/Grottel, Bernd/ Kozikowski, Michael/Schmidt, Stefan/Winkeljohann, Norbert* [eds.], 8th edition, München 2012; cited: *Author*, in: Beck'scher Bilanz-Komm, sec., mar.

Beck'scher Online Kommentar Arbeitsrecht, *Rolfs, Christian/Giesen, Richard/Kreikebohm, Ralf/Udsching, Peter* [eds.], München; cited: *Author*, BeckOK Arbeitsrecht, sec., mar.

Beck'scher Online-Kommentar Datenschutzrecht, *Wolff, Heinrich Amadeus/Brink, Stefan* [eds.], 19th edition, München 2017; cited: *Author*, BeckOK Datenschutz, law, sec., mar.

Bohnert, Joachim, OWiG Kommentar zum Ordnungswidrigkeitengesetz, 3rd edition, München 2010; cited: *Bohnert*, OWiG, sec., mar.

Bürkle, Jürgen [ed.], Compliance in Versicherungsunternehmen – Rechtliche Anforderungen und praktische Umsetzung, München 2009; cited: *Author*, in: Bürkle, Compliance in Versicherungsunternehmen, sec., mar.

Erfurter Kommentar zum Arbeitsrecht, *Müller-Glöge, Rudi/Preis, Ulrich/Schmidt, Ingrid* [eds.], 12th edition, München 2012; cited: *Author*, in: Erfurter Komm ArbR, law, sec., mar.

Foreign Corrupt Practices Act Compliance Guidebook - Protecting Your Organization from Bribery and Corruption, *Biegelman, Martin T./Biegelman, Daniel R.* [eds.], New Jersey 2010; cited: *Author*, in: FCPA Guidebook, p.

Göhler, Erich [ed.], Gesetz über Ordnungswidrigkeiten, 16th edition, München 2012; cited: *Author*, in: Göhler, OWiG, sec., mar.

Gola, Peter/Klug, Christoph/Körffer, Barbara/Schomerus, Rudolf, Bundesdatenschutzgesetz, 11th edition, München 2012; cited: *Gola/Schomerus*, BDSG, sec., mar.

Großkommentar Aktiengesetz, *Hopt, Klaus J./Wiedemann, Herbert* [eds.], 4th edition, Berlin 2006; cited: *Author*, in: Großkomm AktG, sec., mar.

Habersack, Mathias/Mülbert, Peter O./Schlitt, Michael [eds.], Handbuch der Kapitalmarktinformation, München 2008; cited: *Author*, in: Habersack/Mülbert/Schlitt, Hdb Kapitalmarktinformation, sec., mar.

Habersack, Mathias/Mülbert, Peter O./Schlitt, Michael [eds.], Unternehmensfinanzierung am Kapitalmarkt, 3rd edition, Köln 2013; cited: *Author*, in: Unternehmensfinanzierung, sec., mar.

Handbuch des Vorstandsrecht, *Fleischer, Holger* [ed.], München 2006; cited: *Author*, in: Fleischer, Hdb Vorstandsrecht, sec., mar.

Handbuch des Wirtschafts- und Steuerstrafrechts, *Wabnitz, Heinz-Bernd/Janovsky, Thomas* [eds.], 4th edition, München 2014; cited: *Author*, in: Hdb Wirt-Steuer-StR, sec., mar.

Hauschka, Christoph E. [ed.], Corporate Compliance, Handbuch der Haftungsvermeidung im Unternehmen, 2nd edition, München 2010; cited: *Author*, in: Hauschka, Corporate Compliance, sec., mar.

Hüffer, Uwe, Aktiengesetz, 10th edition, München 2012; cited: *Hüffer*, AktG, sec., mar.

Immenga, Ulrich/Mestmäcker, Ernst-Joachim, Wettbewerbsrecht, volume 1, 5th edition, München 2012; cited: *Author*, in: Immenga/Mestmäcker, EU-WettbewerbsR, art., mar.

Karlsruher Kommentar zum Gesetz über Ordnungswidrigkeiten, *Senge, Lothar* [ed.], 3rd edition, München 2006; cited: *Author*, in: Karlsruher Komm OWiG, sec., mar.

Karlsruher Kommentar zur Strafprozessordnung mit GVG, EGGVG und EMRK, *Hannich, Rolf* [ed.], 6th edition, München 2008; cited: *Author*, in: Karlsruher Komm StPO, sec., mar.

Kölner Kommentar zum Aktienrecht, *Zöllner, Wolfgang/Noack, Ulrich* [eds.], volume 2 sec. 76 - 94 AktG, 3rd edition, München 2010; cited: *Author*, in: Köln Komm AktG, sec., mar.

Loewenheim, Ulrich/Meessen, Karl/Riesenkampff, Alexander, Kartellrecht, 2nd edition, München 2009; cited: *Author*, in: Loewenheim/Meessen/Riesenkampff, Kartellrecht, sec., mar.

Menzies, Christoph [ed.], Sarbanes-Oxley und Corporate Compliance: Nachhaltigkeit, Optimierung, Integration, Stuttgart 2006; *Author*, in: Menzies, Sarbanes-Oxley, p.

Münchener Handbuch des Gesellschaftsrechts, *Gummert, Hans/Weipert, Lutz* [eds.], 3rd edition, 2007; cited: *Author*, in: Münch Hdb GesR, vol., sec., mar.

Münchener Kommentar zum Aktiengesetz, *Goette, Wulf/Habersack, Mathias* [eds.], 3rd edition, München 2008; cited: *Author*, in: Münch Komm AktG, sec., mar.

Münchener Kommentar zum Bilanzrecht, *Hennrichs, Joachim/Kleindiek, Detlef/ Watrin, Christoph* [eds.], München 2013; cited: *Author*, in: Münch Komm Bilanzrecht, sec., mar.

Münchener Kommentar zum Bürgerlichen Gesetzbuch, *Säcker, Franz Jürgen/Rixecker, Roland/Oetker, Hartmut/Limperg, Bettina* [eds.], Internationales Privatrecht II vol. 11, Internationales Finanzmarktrecht, Grundlagen, 6th edition, München 2015; cited: *Author*, in: Münch Komm BGB, Int. Capital Markets Law, Basics, mar.

Münchener Kommentar zum Handelsgesetzbuch, *Schmidt, Karsten* [ed.], 2nd edition, München 2008; cited: *Author*, in: Münch Komm HGB, sec., mar.

Ringleb, Henrik-Michael/Kremer, Thomas/Lutter, Marcus/v. Werder, Axel, Corporate Governance Kodex, Kodex-Kommentar, 4th edition, München 2010; cited: *Author*, in: Ringleb, DCGK, mar.

Schmidt, Karsten/Lutter, Marcus [eds.], Aktiengesetz, Köln 2007; cited: *Author*, in: Schmidt/Lutter, sec., mar.

Schönke, Adolf/Schröder, Horst [eds.], Strafgesetzbuch, Kommentar, 28th edition, München 2010; cited: *Author*, in: Schönke/Schröder, StGB, sec., mar.

Spindler, Gehard/Stilz, Eberhard, Kommentar zum Aktiengesetz, 2nd edition, München 2010; cited: *Author*, in: Komm AktG, sec., mar.

III. Festschriften

Assmann, Heinz-Dieter, Corporate Governance im Schnittfeld von Gesellschaftsrecht und Kapitalmarktrecht; in: *Ekkenga, Jens/Hadding, Walther/Hammen, Horst* [eds.], Bankrecht und Kapitalmarktrecht in der Entwicklung, Festschrift für Siegfried Kümpel zum 70. Geburtstag, Berlin 2003, p. 1; cited: *Assmann*, FS Kümpel, 1

Bezzenberger, Gerold/Keul, Thomas, Die Aufgaben und Sorgfaltspflichten von Aufsichtsratsmitgliedern - Eine Übersicht -, in: *Grundmann, Stefan/Kirchner, Christian/et. al.* [eds.], Festschrift für Eberhard Schwark zum 70. Geburtstag, 2009, p. 121; cited: *Bezzenberger/Keul*, FS Schwark, 121

Börsig, Clemens/Löbbe, Marc, Die gewandelte Rolle des Aufsichtsrats - 7 Thesen zur Corporate Governance Entwicklung in Deutschland, in: *Krieger, Gerd/Lutter, Marcus/Schmidt, Karsten* [eds.], Festschrift für Michael Hoffmann-Becking zum 70. Geburtstag, 2013, p. 125; cited: *Börsig/Löbbe*, FS Hoffmann-Becking, 125

Bussmann, Kai-D., Sozialisation in Unternehmen durch Compliance, in: *Hellmann, Uwe/Schröder, Christian* [eds.], Festschrift für Hans Achenbach, 2011, p. 57; cited: *Bussmann*, FS Achenbach, 57

Casper, Matthias, Whistleblowing zwischen Denunziantentum und Integralem Baustein von Compliance-Systemen, in: *Hoffmann-Becking, Michael/Hüffer, Uwe/Reichert, Jochem* [eds.], Liber Amicorum für Martin Winter, 2011, p. 77; cited: *Casper*, Libor Amicorum Winter, 77

Cromme, Gerhard, Die Konvergenz der Corporate Governance in ein- und zweigliedringen Board-Systemen, in: *Krieger, Gerd/Lutter, Marcus/Schmidt, Karsten* [eds.] Festschrift für Michael Hoffmann-Becking zum 70. Geburtstag, 2013, p. 283; cited: *Cromme*, FS Hoffmann-Becking, 283

Dreher, Meinrad, Antikorruptionsuntersuchungen durch den Aufsichtsrat - Compliance und Bildung eines Antikorruptionsausschusses, in: *Habersack, Mathias/et. al.* [eds.], Festschrift für Wulf Goette zum 65. Geburtstag, 2011, p. 43; cited: *Dreher*, FS Goette, 43

Dreher, Meinrad, Die Vorstandsverantwortung im Geflecht von Risikomanagement, Compliance und interner Revision, in: *Kindler, Peter* [ed.], Festschrift für Uwe Hüffer zum 70. Geburtstag, 2010, p. 161; cited: *Dreher*, FS Hüffer, 161

Dreher, Meinrad, Direktkontakte des Aufsichtsrats in der Aktiengesellschaft zu dem Vorstand nachgeordneten Mitarbeitern, in: *Habersack, Mathias/et. al.* [eds.], Festschrift für Peter Ulmer zum 70. Geburtstag, 2003, p. 87; cited: *Dreher*, FS Ulmer, 87

Fleischer, Holger, Die "Business Judgment Rule" im Spiegel von Rechtsvergleichung und Rechtsökonomie, in: *Wank, Rolf/Hirte, Heribert/et.al.* [eds.], Festschrift für Herbert Wiedemann zum 70. Geburtstag, München 2002, p. 827; cited: *Fleischer*, FS Wiedemann, 827

Habersack, Mathias, Die Legalitätspflicht des Vorstands der AG, in: *Burgard, Ulrich/Hadding, Walther/Mülbert, Peter O./Nietsch, Michael/Welter, Reinhard*, Festschrift für Uwe H. Schneider zum 70. Geburtstag, 2011, p. 429; cited: *Habersack*, FS Schneider, 429

Hefendehl, Roland, Der Bilanzeid: Erst empört zurückgewiesen, dann bereitwillig aus den USA importiert, in: *Sieber, Ulrich/et. al.* [eds.], Strafrecht und Wirtschaftsstrafrecht, Festschrift für Klaus Tiedemann zum 70. Geburtstag, 2008, p. 1065; cited: *Hefendehl*, FS Tiedemann, 1065

Hopt, Klaus J., Der deutsche Corporate Governance Kodex: Grundlagen und Praxisfragen, in: *Krieger, Gerd/Lutter, Marcus/Schmidt, Karsten* [eds.] Festschrift für Michael Hoffmann-Becking zum 70. Geburtstag, 2013, p. 563; cited: *Hopt*, FS Hoffmann-Becking, 563

Hüffer, Jens, Corporate Governance: Früherkennung nach § 91 Abs 2 AktG – Neue Pflichten des Vorstands zum Risikomanagement?, in: VEW Energie AG [ed.], Recht und Vernunft: Festschrift für Hans-Diether Imhoff, 1998, p. 91; cited: *Hüffer, J.*, FS Imhoff, 91

Hüffer, Uwe, Compliance im Innen- und Außenrecht der Unternehmen, in: *Altmeppen, Holger* [ed.], Festschrift für Günter H. Roth zum 70. Geburtstag, 2011, p. 299; cited: *Hüffer*, FS Roth, 299

Immenga, Ulrich, Compliance als Rechtspflicht nach Aktienrecht und Sarbanes-Oxley-Act, in: *Grundmann, Stefan/Kirchner, Christian/et. al.* [eds.], Festschrift für Eberhard Schwark zum 70. Geburtstag, 2009, p. 199; cited: *Immenga*, FS Schwark, 199

Kindler, Peter, Pflichtverletzung und Schaden bei der Vorstandshaftung wegen unzureichender Compliance, in: *Altmeppen, Holger* [ed.], Festschrift für Günter H. Roth zum 70. Geburtstag, 2011, p. 367; cited: *Kindler*, FS Roth, 367

Kirchner, Christian, Institutional Deficits in the International Financial Markets Crisis Combined Effects of Deficits in Corporate Governance and in Financial Reporting, in: *Grundmann, Stefan/et. al.*[eds.], Festschrift für Klaus J. Hopt zum 70. Geburtstag am 24. August 2010, 2010 volume 2, p. 2095; cited: *Kirchner*, FS Hopt, 2095

Kirchner, Christian, Privatrechtsmethodik: ökonomische und transnationale Ansätze, in: *Grundmann, Stefan/Kloepfer, Michael/Paulus, Christoph G./Schröder, Rainer, Werle, Gerhard* [eds.], Festschrift 200 Jahre Juristische Fakultät der Humboldt-Universität zu Berlin, 2010, p. 937; cited: *Kirchner*; FS HU-Juristische Fakultät, 937

Kort, Michael, Rechtsfragen der Compliance-Organisation von Unternehmen außerhalb spezialgesetzlich geregelter Branchen im deutschen Recht, in: *Altmeppen, Holger* [ed.], Festschrift für Günter H. Roth zum 70. Geburtstag, 2011, p. 407; cited: *Kort*, FS Roth, 407

Kremer, Thomas, Kooperation des Unternehmens mit der Staatsanwaltschaft im Compliance Bereich, in: *Burgard, Ulrich/Hadding, Walther/Mülbert, Peter O./ Nietsch, Michael/Welter, Reinhard* [eds.], Festschrift für Uwe H. Schneider zum 70. Geburtstag, 2011, p. 701; cited: *Kremer*, FS Schneider, 701

Lutter, Marcus, Aufsichtsrat und Sicherung der Legalität im Unternehmen, in: *Kindler, Peter* [ed.], Festschrift für Uwe Hüffer zum 70. Geburtstag, 2010, p. 617; cited: *Lutter*, FS Hüffer, 617

Lutter, Marcus, Konzernphilosophie vs. konzernweite Compliance und konzernweites Risikomanagement, in: *Habersack, Mathias/et. al.* [eds.], Festschrift für Wulf Goette zum 65. Geburtstag, 2011, p. 289; cited: *Lutter*, FS Goette, 289

Marsch-Barner, Reinhard, Zur Information des Aufsichtsrats durch Mitarbeiter des Unternehmens, in: *Grundmann, Stefan/Kirchner, Christian/et. al.* [eds.], Festschrift für Eberhard Schwark zum 70. Geburtstag, 2009, p. 219; cited: *Marsch-Barner*, FS Schwark, 219

Martín, Adán N., Soziale Verantwortung, corporate governance, Selbstregulierung und Unternehmensstrafrecht, in: *Sieber, Ulrich/et. al.* [eds.], Strafrecht und Wirtschaftsstrafrecht, Festschrift für Klaus Tiedemann zum 70. Geburtstag, 2008, p. 485; cited: *Martín*, FS Tiedemann, 485

Painter, Richard W., Christian Kirchner's New Institutional Economics and Jurisdictional Competition in Regulation of Public Companies and Financial Services Firms, in: *Kaal, Wulf A./Schmidt, Matthias/Schwartze, Andreas* [eds.], Festschrift zu Ehren von Christian Kirchner: Recht im ökonomischen Kontext, 2014, p. 1247; cited: *Painter*, FS Kirchner, 1247

Rieder, Markus S., Vom juristischen Gewissen zum Straftäter? Rechtsstellung, Verantwortung und Schutz von Compliance-Beauftragten, in: *Habersack, Mathias/et. al.* [eds.], Festschrift für Wulf Goette zum 65. Geburtstag, 2011, p. 413; cited: *Rieder*, FS Goette, 413

Schünemann, Bernd, Strafrechtliche Sanktionen gegen Wirtschaftsunternehmen?, in: *Sieber, Ulrich/et. al.* [eds.], Strafrecht und Wirtschaftsstrafrecht, Festschrift für Klaus Tiedemann zum 70. Geburtstag, 2008, p. 429; cited: *Schünemann*, FS Tiedemann, 429

Seibert, Ulrich, Corporate Governance: The Next Phase - Die Corporate Governance Debate schreitet weiter zu den Pflichten der Eigentümer und ihrer Helfer, in: *Krieger, Gerd/Lutter, Marcus/Schmidt, Karsten* [eds.] Festschrift für Michael Hoffmann-Becking zum 70. Geburtstag, 2013, p. 1101; cited: *Seibert*, FS Hoffmann-Becking, 1101

Seibert, Ulrich, Die Entstehung des § 91 Abs. 2 AktG im KonTraG - "Risikomanagement" oder "Frühwarnsystem"?, in: *Westermann, Harm Peter/Mock, Klaus* [eds.], Festschrift für Gerold Bezzenberger zum 70. Geburtstag, 2000, p. 427; cited: *Seibert*, FS Bezzenberger, 427

Semler, Johannes, Überlegungen zur Praktikabilität der Organhaftungsvorschriften, in: *Habersack, Mathias/et. al.* [eds.], Festschrift für Wulf Goette zum 65. Geburtstag, 2011, p. 499; cited: *Semler*, FS Goette, 499

Sieber, Ulrich, Compliance-Programme im Unternehmensstrafrecht, ein neues Konzept zur Kontrolle von Wirtschaftskriminalität, in: *Sieber, Ulrich/et. al.* [eds.], Strafrecht und Wirtschaftsstrafrecht, Festschrift für Klaus Tiedemann zum 70. Geburtstag, 2008, p. 449; cited: *Sieber*, FS Tiedemann, 449

Spindler, Gerald, Von der Früherkennung von Risiken zum umfassenden Risikomanagement - zum Wandel des § 91 AktG unter europäischem Einfluss, in: *Kindler, Peter* [ed.], Festschrift für Uwe Hüffer zum 70. Geburtstag, 2010, p. 985; cited: *Spindler*, FS Hüffer, 985

Vetter, Eberhard, Zur Compliance-Verantwortung des Vorstands und zu den Compliance-Aufgaben des Aufsichtsrats, in: *Genzow, F. Christian/Grunewald, Barbara/ Schulte-Nölke Hans* [eds.], Zwischen Vertragsfreiheit und Verbraucherschutz, Festschrift für Friedrich Graf von Westphalen zum 70. Geburtstag, 2010, p. 719; cited: *Vetter*, FS v. Westphalen, 719

Windbichler, Christine, How Assuring are Auditors' Assurances? The External Audit as Corporate Governance Element, in: *Antapassis, Antonios/ et. al.* [eds.], Festschrift für Nokolaos K. Rokas, 2012, p. 1389; cited: *Windbichler*, FS Rokas, 1389

Windbichler, Christine, Sunlight for a Healthy Body Corporate, in: *Grundmann, Stefan/et. al.* [eds.], Festschrift für Klaus J. Hopt zum 70. Geburtstag am 24. August 2010, 2010 volume 1, 1505; cited: *Windbichler*, FS Hopt, 1505

Windbichler, Christine, Zukunft des Gesellschaftsrecht: Orientierungen für die kapitalmarktorinentierte Aktiengesellschaft, in: *Grundmann, Stefan/Kloepfer, Michael/ Paulus, Christoph G./Schörder, Rainer/Werle, Gerhard* [eds.], Festschrift 200 Jahre Juristische Fakultät der Humboldt-Universität zu Berlin, 2010, p. 1079; cited: *Windbichler*, FS HU-Juristische Fakultät, 1079

Winter, Martin, Die Verantwortlichkeit des Aufsichtsrats für "Corporate Compliance", in: *Kindler, Peter* [ed.], Festschrift für Uwe Hüffer zum 70. Geburtstag, 2010, p. 1103; cited: *Winter*, FS Hüffer, 1103

IV. Articles

Abraham, Jens, Whistleblowing - Neue Chance für eine Kurswende!?, ZRP 2012, 11; cited: *Abraham*, ZRP 2012, 11

Achenbach, Hans, Gedanken zur strafrechtlichen Verwantwortlichkeit des Unternehmens, in: *Kempf, Eberhard/Lüderssen, Klaus/Volk, Klaus* [eds.], Unternehmensstrafrecht, 2012, p. 271; cited: *Achenbach*, in: Unternehmensstrafrecht, 271

Adams, Edward S., Bridging the Gap between Ownership and Control, 34 Iowa J. Corp. L. 409 (2009); cited: *Adams*, 34 Iowa J. Corp. L. 409 (2009), p.

Agami, Abdel M., Reporting on Internal Control over Financial Reporting, The CPA Journal 2006, available at: http://www.nysscpa.org/printversions/cpaj/2006/1106/p32.htm visited: February 8, 2011; cited: *Agami*, CPA Journal 2006

Aggarwal, Reena/Williamson, Rohan, Did New Regulations Target the Relevant Corporate Governance Attributes? February 2006, available at: http://ssrn.com/abstract=859264 visited: April 29, 2012; cited: *Aggarwal/Williamson*, 2006

Ahmed, Anwer S./McAnally, Mary L./Rasmussen Stephanie, How costly is the Sarbanes Oxley Act? Evidence on the effects of the act on corporate profitability, September 2009, available at: http://ssrn.com/abstract=1480394 visited: March 16, 2011; cited: *Ahmed/McAnally/Rasmussen*, 2009, p.

Akerlof, George A., The Market for "Lemons": Quality, Uncertainty and the Market Mechanism, 84 Q.J. Econ. 488 (1970); cited: *Akerlof*, 84 Q.J. Econ. 488 (1970)

Albanese, Robert/van Fleet, David D., Rational Behavior in Groups: The Free-Riding Tendency, 10 Acct. Mgmt. Rev. 244 (1985); cited: *Albanese/van Fleet*, 10 Acct. Mgmt. Rev. 244 (1985)

Alexander, Cindy R./Arlen, Jennifer/Cohen, Mark A., Regulating Corporate Criminal Sanctions: Federal Guidelines and the Sentencing of Public Firms, 42 Journal of Law and Economics 393 (1999); cited: *Alexander/Arlen/Cohen*, 42 Journal of Law and Economics 393 (1999), p.

Alexander, Cindy, On the Nature of the Reputational Penalty for Corporate Crime: Evidence, 42 J.L. & Econ. 489 (1999); cited: *Alexander*, 42 J.L. & Econ. 489 (1999)

Alwart, Heiner, Über "Unternehmensstrafrecht", Humboldt Forum Recht 2000, Beitrag 5; cited: *Alwart*, HFR 2000, p.

Amling, Thomas/Bantleon, Ulrich, Interne Revision - Grundlagen und Ansätze zur Beurteilung deren Wirksamkeit, DStR 2008, 1300; cited: *Amling/Bantleon*, DStR 2008, 1300

Amling, Thomas/Bantleon, Ulrich, COSO-Regelwerk 2013 "Internal Control - Integrated Framework" - Neue Anforderungen an die Corporate Governance in Deutschland, WPg 2014, 343; cited: *Amling/Bantleon*, WPg 2014, 343

Annuß, Georg/Pelz, Christian, Amnestieprogramme - Fluch oder Segen? BB 2010, Beilage 4, 14; cited: *Annuß/Pelz*, BB 2010, Beilage 4, 14

Arbeitskreis "Externe und Interne Überwachung der Unternehmung" der Schamlenbach-Gesellschaft für Betriebswirtschaft e. V., Köln, Best Practice für die Interne Revision, DB 2006, 225; cited: *AEIÜU Schmalenbach-Ges.*, DB 2006, 225

Arbeitskreis "Externe und Interne Überwachung der Unternehmung" der Schmalenbach-Gesellschaft für Betriebswirtschaft e. V., Köln, Überwachung der Wirksamkeit des internen Kontrollsystems und des Risikomanagementsystems durch den Prüfungsauschuss - Best Practice, DB 2011, 2101; cited: *AKEIÜ Schmalenbach-Ges.*, DB 2011, 2101

Arbeitskreis "Externe und Interne Überwachung der Unternehmung" der Schmalenbach-Gesellschaft für Betriebswirtschaft e. V. Köln, Compliance: 10 Thesen für die Unternehmenspraxis, DB 2010, 1509; cited: *AKEIÜ Schmalenbach-Ges.*, DB 2010, 1509

Arbeitskreis "Externe Unternehmensrechnung"/ Arbeitskreis "Externe und Interne Überwachung der Unternehmung" der Schamlenbach-Gesellschaft für Betriebswirtschaft e. V., Köln, Anforderungen an die Überwachungsaufgaben von Aufsichtsrat und Prüfungsausschuss nach § 107 Abs. 3 Satz 2 AktG i. d. F. des Bilanzrechtsmodernisierungsgesetzes, DB 2009, 1279; cited: *AKEU/AKEIÜ Schmalenbach-Ges.*, DB 2009, 1279

Arlen, Jennifer, Corporate Criminal Liability: Theory and Evidence, Law & Economics Research Paper Series Working Paper No. 11-25, July 2011, available at: http://ssrn.com/abstract=1890733 visited: December 21, 2011; cited: *Arlen*, 2011a, p.

Arlen, Jennifer, Removing Prosecutors From the Boardroom: Limiting Prosecutorial Discretion to Impose Structural Reforms, in: *Barkow, Anthony, S./Barkow, Rachel E.*[eds.], Prosecutors in the Boardroom, Using Criminal Law to Regulate Corporate Conduct, 2011, p. 62; cited: *Arlen*, in: Prosecutors in the Boardroom, p.

Arlen, Jennifer, The Failure of the Organizational Sentencing Guidelines, Law & Economics Research Paper Series Working Paper No. 11-21, August 2011, available at: http://ssrn.com/abstract=1903975 visited: October 28, 2011; cited: *Arlen*, 2011b, p.

Arlen, Jennifer, The Potentially Perverse Effects of Corporate Criminal Liability, 23 J. Legal Stud. 833 (1994); cited: *Arlen*, 23 J. Legal Stud. 833 (1994), p.

Arlen, Jennifer, The Story of Allis-Chalmers, Caremark, and Stone: Directors' Evolving Duty to Monitor, Law & Economics Research Paper Series Working Paper No. 08-57, November 2008, available at: http://ssrn.com/abstract=1304272 visited: November 19, 2011; cited: *Arlen*, 2008, p.

Arlen, Jennifer/Carney, William, Vicarious Liability for Fraud on Securities Markets: Theory and Evidence, in: *Andersen, Peder/Jensen, Vibeke/Mortensen, Jørgen Birk* [eds.], Governance by Legal and Economic Measures, 1993, p. 147; cited: *Arlen/Carney*, in: Governance by Legal and Economic Measures, p.

Arlen, Jennifer/Kraakman, Reinier, Controlling Corporate Misconduct: An Analysis of Corporate Liability Regimes, 72 N.Y.U.L. Rev. 687 (1997); cited: *Arlen/Kraakman*, 72 N.Y.U.L. Rev. 687 (1997), p.

Arnold, Michael, Verantwortung und Zusammenwirken des Vorstands und Aufsichtsrats bei Compliance-Untersuchungen, ZGR 2014, 76; cited: *Arnold*, ZGR 2014, 76

Ashbaugh-Skaife, Hollis/Collins, Daniel W./Kinney, William R. Jr., The Effect of SOX Internal Control Deficiencies on Firm Risk and Cost of Equity, June 2008, available at: http://ssrn.com/abstract=896760 visited: March 16, 2011; cited: *Ashbaugh-Skaife/Collins/Kinney*, 2008, p.

Ashbaugh-Skaife, Hollis/Collins, Daniel W./Kinney, William R., The Discovery and Reporting of Internal Control Deficiencies Prior to SOX-Mandated Audits, McCombs Research Paper Series No. ACC-02-05, February 2006, available at: http://ssrn.com/abstract=694681 visited: March 16, 2011; cited: *Ashbaugh-Skaife/Collins/Kinney*, 2006

Aviram, Amitai, In Defense of Imperfect Compliance Programs, 32 Fla. St. U. L. Rev. 763 (2005); cited: *Aviram*, 32 Fla. St. U. L. Rev. 763 (2005), p.

Bachmann, Gregor, Annotation of LG München I, decision of December 12, 2013 - 5 HK O 1387/10, ZIP 2014, 579; cited: *Bachmann*, ZIP 2014, 579

Bachmann, Gregor, Compliance - Rechtsgrundlagen und offene Fragen, in: Gesellschaftsrechtliche Vereinigung [ed.], Gesellschaftsrecht in der Diskussion 2007 - Jahrestagung der gesellschaftsrechtlichen Vereinigung (VGR), 2008, p. 65; cited: *Bachmann*, VGR, 2008, 65

Bachmann, Gregor, Die Erklärung zur Unternehmensführung (Corporate Governance Statement), ZIP 2010, 1517; cited: *Bachmann*, ZIP 2010, 1517

Bachmann, Gregor/Prüfer, Geralf, Korruptionsprävention und Corporate Governance, ZRP 2005, 109; cited: *Bachmann/Prüfer*, ZRP 2005, 109

Baer, Miriam H., Governing Corporate Compliance, 50 Boston College L. Rev. 949 (2009); cited: *Baer*, 50 Boston College L. Rev. 949 (2009), p.

Bainbridge, Stephen M., A Critique of the NYSE's Director Independence Listing Standards, UCLA Research Paper No. 02-15 (June 2002), available at: http://ssrn.com/abstract=317121 visited: October 4, 2011; cited: *Bainbridge*, 2002, p.

Bainbridge, Stephen M., *Caremark* and Enterprise Risk Management, 34 J. Corp. L. 967 (2009); cited: *Bainbridge*, 34 J. Corp. L. 967 (2009), p.

Bainbridge, Stephen M., The Creeping Federalization of Corporate Law, University of California, Los Angeles School of Law Research Paper Series Research Paper No. 03-7, Spring 2003, available at: http://ssrn.com/abstract=389403 visited: February 9, 2012; cited: *Bainbridge*, 2003

Bargeron, Leonce/Lehn, Kenneth/Zutter, Chad, Sarbanes Oxley and Corporate Risk-Taking, March 2008, available at: http://ssrn.com/abstract=1104063 visited: April 18, 2012; cited: *Bargeron/Lehn/Zutter*, 2008

Barker, M. Ridgway/Hedin, Randi-Jean G., Ineffective Internal Controls: Issues That Public Companies May Face After Receiving A Negative Report - Part II, in: The Metropolitan Corporate Counsel, November 2004, p. 17; cited: *Barker/Hedin*, in: The Metropolitan Corporate Counsel

Baums, Theodor, Risiko und Risikosteuerung im Aktienrecht, ZGR 2011, 218; cited: *Baums*, ZGR 2011, 218

Bays, Carson, A Note on the Efficiency of Common Law, 1996, available at: http://ssrn.com/abstract=10048 visited: March 1, 2012; cited: *Bays*, 1996

Beale, Sara Sun, Die Entwicklung des US-amerikanischen Rechts der strafrechtlichen Verantwortlichkeit von Unternehmen, ZStW 2014, 27; cited: *Beale*, ZStW 2014, 27

Beale, Sara Sun, The Development and Evolution of the U.S. Law of Corporate Criminal Liability, December 2013, available at: http://ssrn.com/abstract=2375318 visited: April 3, 2015; cited: *Beale*, 2013, p.

Beale, Sara, A Response to the Critics of Corporate Criminal Liability, 46 Am. Crim. L. Rev. 1481 (2009); cited: *Beale*, 46 Am. Crim. L. Rev. 1481 (2009), p.

Beale, Sara/Safwat Adam, What Developments in Western Europe Tell Us about American Critiques of Corporate Criminal Liability, 8 Buffalo Crim. L. Rev. 89 (2005); cited: *Beale/Adam*, 8 Buffalo Crim. L. Rev. 89 (2005), p.

Bebchuk, Lucian A./Cohen, Alma, Firms' Decisions Where to Incorporate, 46 J. L. & Econ. 383 (2003); cited: *Bebchuk/Cohen*, 46 J. L. & Econ. 383 (2003), p.

Bedard, Jean C./Graham, Lynford E./Hoitash, Rani/Hoitash, Udi, Sarbanes-Oxley Section 404 and Internal Controls - A Look at Two Years of Compliance, The CPA Journal 2007, available at: http://www.nysscpa.org/printversions/cpaj/2007/1007/p34.htm visited: February 8, 2011; cited: *Bedard/Graham/Hoitash/Hoitash*, CPA Journal 2007

Bédard, Jean, Sarbanes Oxley Internal Control Requirements and Earnings Quality, August 2006, available at: http://ssrn.com/abstract=926271 visited: April 27, 2012; cited: *Bédard*, 2006

Beecher-Monas, Erica, Corporate Governance in the Wake of Enron: An Examination of the Audit Committee Solution to Corporate Fraud, 55 Admin. L. Rev. 357 (2003); cited: *Beecher-Monas*, 55 Admin. L. Rev. 357 (2003)

Behling, Thorsten, Compliance versus Fernmeldegeheimnis - Wo liegen die Grenzen bei E-Mail-Kontrollen als Antikorruptionsmaßnahme?, BB 2010, 892; cited: *Behling*, BB 2010, 892

Benz, Jochen/Klindt, Thomas, Compliance 2020 - ein Blick in die Zukunft, BB 2010, 2977; cited: *Benz/Klindt*, BB 2010, 2977

Berg, Cai, Korruption in Unternehmen und Risikomanagement nach § 91 Abs. 2 AktG, AG 2007, 271; cited: *Berg*, AG 2007, 271

Berger, Philip G./Li, Feng/Wong, M.H. Franco, The Impact of Sarbanes-Oxley on Cross-listed Companies, September 9, 2011, available at: http://citeseerx.ist.psu.edu/viewdoc/download?doi=10.1.1.232.4756&rep=rep1&type=pdf visited: April 19, 2013; cited: *Berger/Li/Wong*, 2011, p.

Bergmoser, Ulrich/Theusinger, Ingo/Gushurst, Klaus-Peter, Corporate Compliance - Grundlagen und Umsetzung, BB 2008, Beilage 5, 1; cited: *Bergmoser/Theusinger/Gushurst*, BB 2008, Beilage 5, 1

Berkowitz, Daniel/Pistor, Katharina/Richard, Jean-Francois, Economic development, legality, and the transplant effect, 47 European Economic Review 165 (2003); cited: *Berkowitz/Pistor/Richard*, 47 European Economic Review 165 (2003), p.

Berndt, Thomas/Hoppler, Ivo, Whistleblowing - ein integraler Bestandteil effektiver Corporate Governance, BB 2005, 2623; cited: *Berndt/Hoppler*, BB 2005, 2623

Berndt, Thomas/Jeker, Marc, Fraud Detection im Rahmen der Abschlussprüfung, BB 2007, 2615; cited: *Berndt/Jeker*, BB 2007, 2615

Bianconi, Marcelo/Chen, Richard/Yoshino, Joe A., Firm Value, the Sarbanes-Oxley Act and Cross-Listing in the US, Germany and Hong Kong Destinations, November 2010, available at: http://ssrn.com/abstract=1373897 visited: March 16, 2011; cited: *Bianconi/Chen/Yoshino*, 2010, p.

Binder, Jens-Hinrich, Bericht über die Diskussion zu den Referaten Wohlmannstetter und Kort ("Risikomanagement nach dem BilMoG"), ZGR 2010, 489; cited: *Binder*; ZGR 2010, 489

Bixby, Michael B., The Lion Awakens: The Foreign Corrupt Practices Act – 1977 to 2010, 12 San Diego Int'l L. J. 89 (2010); cited: *Bixby*, 12 San Diego Int'l L. J. 89 (2010), p.

Black, Bernard/Cheffins, Brian/Klausner, Michael, Outside Director Liability, 58 Stan. L. Rev. 1055 (2006); cited: *Black/Cheffins/Klausner*, 58 Stan. L. Rev. 1055 (2006), p.

Blasche, Sebastian, Die Mindestanforderungen an ein Risikofrüherkennungs- und Überwachungssystem nach § 91 Abs. 2 AktG, CCZ 2009, 62; cited: *Blasche*, CCZ 2009, 62

Bock, Dennis, Strafrechtliche Aspekte der Compliance-Diskussion – § 130 OWiG als zentrale Norm der Criminal Compliance, ZIS 2009, 68; cited: *Bock*, ZIS 2009, 68

Bosch, Wolfgang/Colbus, Birgit/Harbusch, Antionia, Berücksichtigung von Compliance-Programmen in Kartellbußgeldverfahren, WuW 2009, 740; cited: *Bosch/ Colbus/Harbusch*, WuW 2009, 740

Böttcher, Lars, Compliance: Der IDW PS 980 - Keine Lösung für alle (Haftungs-) Fälle!, NZG 2011, 1054; *Böttcher*, NZG 2011, 1054

Branson, Douglas M. Too Many Bells? Too Many Whistles? Corporate Governance in the Post-Enron, Post-WorldCom Era, 58 S. C. L. Rev. 65 (2006); cited: *Branson*, 58 S. C. L. Rev. 65 (2006), p.

Brown, J. Robert Jr., Corporate Governance, the Securities and Exchange Commission, and the Limits of Disclosure, 57 Cath. U. L. Rev. 45 (2007); cited: *Brown*, 57 Cath. U. L. Rev. 45 (2007), p.

Brown, J. Robert Jr., Criticizing the Critics: Sarbanes-Oxley and Quack Corporate Governance, 90 Marq. L. Rev. 309 (2006); cited: *Brown*, 90 Marq. L. Rev. 309 (2006), p.

Brown, J. Robert Jr., The Irrelevance of State Corporate Law in the Governance of Public Companies, 38 U. Rich. L. Rev. 317 (2004); cited: *Brown*, 38 U. Rich. L. Rev. 317 (2004)

Bryan, Stephen/Lilien, Steven, Characteristics of Firms with Material Weaknesses in Internal Control: An Assessment of Section 404 Sarbanes Oxley, March 2005, available at: http://ssrn.com/abstract=682363 visited: March 16, 2011; cited: *Bryan/Lilien*, 2005

Buderath, Hubertus M./Amling, Thomas, Neue Aspekte der Qualitätssicherung in der Internen Revision: Quality Assurance Review, BB 2005, Beilage 3, 8; cited: *Buderath/Amling*, BB 2005, Beilage 3, 8

Bungartz, Oliver, Effiziente und effektive Interne Kontrollsysteme, in: *Wagenhofer, Alfred* [ed.], Controlling und Corporate Governance-Anforderungen. Konzepte, Maßnahmen, Umsetzungen, 2009, p. 131; cited: *Bungartz*, in: *Wagenhofer*, 2009, p.

Bungartz, Oliver/Strobl, Gregor, Mehrwert durch Interne Kontrollsysteme (IKS), Ergebnisse einer europäischen Studie, ZIR 2012, 138; cited: *Bungartz/Strobl*, ZIR 2012, 138

Bürkle, Jürgen, Corporate Compliance - Pflicht oder Kür für den Vorstand der AG?, BB 2005, 565; cited: *Bürkle*, BB 2005, 565

Bürkle, Jürgen, Corporate Compliance als Standard guter Unternehmensführung des Deutschen Corporate Governance Kodex, BB 2007, 1797; cited: *Bürkle*, BB 2007, 1797

Bürkle, Jürgen, Grenzen der strafrechtlichen Garantenstellung des Compliance-Officers, CCZ 2010, 4; cited: *Bürkle*, CCZ 2010, 4

Bürkle, Jürgen, Weitergabe von Informationen über Fehlverhalten in Unternehmen (Whistleblowing) und Steuerung auftretender Probleme durch ein Compliance-System, DB 2004, 2158; cited: *Bürkle*, DB 2004, 2158

Bushman, Robert M./Smith, Abbie J., Financial accounting information and corporate governance, 32 J. Acct. and Econ. 237 (2001); cited: *Bushman/Smith*, 32 J. Acct. and Econ. 237 (2001), p.

Bussmann, Kai-D., Business Ethics und Wirtschaftsstrafrecht - Zu einer Kriminologie des Managements, 2003 MschrKrim, 89; cited: *Bussmann*, 2003 MschrKrim, 89

Bussmann, Kai-D., Integrität durch nachhaltiges Compliance Management über Risiken, Werte und Unternehmenskultur, CCZ 2016, 50; cited: *Bussmann*, CCZ 2016, 50

Bussmann, Kai-D., The Control Paradox and the Impact of Business Ethics: A Comparison of US and German Companies, 2007 MschrKrim, 260; cited: *Bussmann*, 2007 MschrKrim 260

Bussmann, Kai-D./Matschke, Sebastian, Der Einfluss nationalen Rechts auf Kontroll- und Präventionsmaßnahmen von Unternehmen - ein Vergleich zwischen USA und Deutschland -, wistra 2008, 88; cited: *Bussmann/Matschke*, wistra 2008, 88

Bussmann, Kai-D./Matschke, Sebastian, Die Zukunft der unternehmerischen Haftung bei Compliance-Verstößen, CCZ 2009, 132; cited: *Bussmann/Matschke*, CCZ 2009, 132

Bussmann, Kai-D./Matschke, Sebastian, The impact of the US legislation on company measures of control and prevention, Crime, Law and Social Change 2008, 349; cited: *Bussmann/Matschke*, Crime, Law and Social Change 2008, 349

Bussmann, Kai-D./Salvenmoser, Steffen, Der Wert von Compliance und Unternehmenskultur - Ergebnisse der aktuellen Studie von PricewaterhouseCoopers zur Wirtschaftskriminalität, CCZ 2008, 192; cited: *Bussmann/Salvenmoser*, CCZ 2008, 192

Bussmann, Kai-D./Salvenmoser, Steffen/Jeker, Marc, Compliance ist im Markt, aber noch nicht im Recht – Ergebnisse einer Unternehmensbefragung, CCZ 2016, 235; cited: *Bussmann/Salvenmoser/Jeker*, CCZ 2016, 235

Bussmann, Kai-D./Salvenmoser, Steffen, Internationale Studie zur Wirtschaftskriminalität, NStZ 2006, 203; cited: *Bussmann/Salvenmoser*, NStZ 2006, 203

Büssow, Thomas/Taetzner, Tobias, Sarbanes-Oxley Act Section 404: Internes Kontrollsystem zur Sicherstellung einer effektiven Finanzberichterstattung im Steuerbereich von Unternehmen - Pflicht oder Kür?, BB 2005, 2437; cited: *Büssow/Taetzner*, BB 2005, 2437

Campos Nave, José A./Bonenberger, Saksia, Korruptionsaffären, Corporate Compliance und Sofortmaßnahmen im Krisenfall, BB 2008, 734; cited: *Campos Nave/Bonenberger*, BB 2008, 734

Campos Nave, Jose/Vogel, Henrik, Die erforderlichen Veränderungen von Corporate Compliance-Organisationen im Hinblick auf gestiegene Verantwortlichkeiten des Compliance Officers, BB 2009, 2546; cited: *Campos Nave/Vogel*, BB 2009, 2546

Campos, Roel C., Directors vs. Shareholders?: Remarks of SEC Commissioner, 55 Case W. Res. J. Rev. 527 (2005); cited: *Campos*, 55 Case W. Res. J. Rev. 527 (2005), p.

Carney, William J., The Costs of Being Public After Sarbanes-Oxley: The Irony of "Going Private", 55 Emory L. J. 141 (2006); cited: *Carney*, 55 Emory L. J. 141 (2006), p.

Cassuto, David N., Crime, War & Romanticism: Arthur Andersen and the Nature of Entity Guilt, 13 Va. J. Soc. Pol'y & L., 179 (2005-2006); cited: *Cassuto*, 13 Va. J. Soc. Pol'y & L., 179 (2005-2006), p.

Chandler, William B. III/Strine, Leo E. Jr., The New Federalism of the American Corporate Governance System: Preliminary Reflections of Two Residents of One Small State, 152 U. Pa. L. Rev. 953 (2003); cited: *Chandler/Strine*, 152 U. Pa. L. Rev. 953 (2003), p.

Cheffins, Brain R., Did Corporate Governance "Fail" During the 2008 Stock Market Meltdown? The Case of the S&P 500, July 2009, available at http://ssrn.com/abstract=1396126 visited: November 12, 2012; cited: *Cheffins*, 2009

Cichy, Patrick/Cziupka, Johannes, Compliance-Verantwortung der Geschäftsleiter bei Unternehmenstätigkeit mit Auslandsbezug, BB 2014, 1482; cited: *Cichy/Cziupka*, BB 2014, 1482

Clark, Robert C., Corporate Governance Changes in the Wake of the Sarbanes-Oxley Act: A Morality Tale for Policymakers Too, 22 Ga. St. U. L. Rev. 251 (2005); cited: *Clark*, 22 Ga. St. U. L. Rev. 251 (2005), p.

Coates, John C. IV, The Goals and Promise of the Sarbanes-Oxley Act, 21 J. Econ. Perspectives 91 (2007); cited: *Coates*, 21 J. Econ. Perspectives 91 (2007), p.

Coffee, John C., A Theory of Corporate Scandals: Why the U.S. and Europe Differ, March 2005, available at: http://ssrn.com/abstract=694581 visited: April 7, 2013; cited: *Coffee*, 2005, p.

Coffee, John C., Law and the Market: The Impact of Enforcement, Columbia Law School Working Paper No. 304, April 4, 2007, available at: http://ssrn.com/abstract=967482 visited: April 20, 2013; cited: *Coffee*, 2007

Coffee, John C., Racing Towards the Top?: The Impact of Cross-Listings and Stock Market Competition on International Corporate Governance, 102 Colum. L. Rev. 1757 (2002); cited: *Coffee*, 102 Colum. L. Rev. 1757 (2002), p.

Coffee, John C., Understanding Enron: It's About the Gatekeepers, Stupid, Columbia Law & Economics Working Paper No. 207, July 2002, available at: http://ssrn.com/abstract=325240 visited: March 21, 2012; cited: *Coffee*, 2002, p.

Cohen, Daniel A./Dey, Aiyesha/Lys, Thomas Z., Real and Accrual-based Earnings Management in the Pre- and Post-Sarbanes Oxley Periods, June 2007, http://ssrn.com/abstract=813088 visited: April 23, 2012; cited: *Cohen/Dey/Lys*, 2007

Cohen, Daniel A./Dey, Aiyesha/Lys, Thomas Z., The Sarbanes Oxley Act of 2002: Implications for Compensation Contracts and Managerial Risk-Taking, November 2007, available at: http://ssrn.com/abstract=1027448 visited: March 16, 2011; cited: *Cohen/Dey/Lys*, 2007

Cohen, Daniel A./Dey, Aiyesha/Lys, Thomas Z., Trends in Earnings Management and Informativeness of Earnings Announcements in the Pre-and Post-Sarbanes Oxley Periods, February 2005, available at: http://ssrn.com/abstract=658782 visited: April 23, 2012; cited: *Cohen/Dey/Lys*, 2005

Conac, Pierre-Henri, Director's Duties in Groups of Companies - Legalizing the Interest of the Group at the European Level, ECFR 2013, 194; cited: *Conac*, ECFR 2013, 194

Cooter, Robert, Prices and Sanctions, 84 Colum. L. Rev. 1523 (1984); cited: *Cooter*, 84 Colum. L. Rev. 1523 (1984), p.

Cosenza, Elizabeth, The Holy Grail of Corporate Governance Reform: Independence or Democracy?, 2007 B.Y.U.L. Rev. 1; cited: *Cosenza*, 2007 B.Y.U.L. Rev. 1, p.

Costello, Anna/Wittenberg-Moerman, Regina, The impact of financial reporting quality on debt contracting: Evidence from internal control weakness reports, September 2004, available at: http://ssrn.com/abstract=1455985 visited: March 16, 2011; cited: *Costello/Wittenberg-Moerman*, 2010

Cox, James D., The Role of Empirical Evidence in Evaluating the Wisdom of the Sarbanes-Oxley Act, 40 U.S.F. L. Rev. 823 (2006); cited: *Cox*, 40 U.S.F. L. Rev. 823 (2006), p.

Cunningham, Lawrence A., The Appeal and Limits of Internal Controls to Fight Fraud, Terrorism, and Other Ills, 29 J. Corp. L. 267 (2004); cited: *Cunningham*, 29 J. Corp. L. 267 (2004), p.

Dann, Matthias, Die neue Kronzeugenregelung: ein Störfaktor aus Compliance-Sicht?, CCZ 2010, 30; cited: *Dann*, CCZ 2010, 30

Dann, Matthias/Gastell, Roland, Geheime Mitarbeiterkontrollen: Straf- und arbeitsrechtliche Risiken bei unternehmensinterner Aufklärung, NJW 2008, 2945; cited: *Dann/Gastell*, NJW 2008, 2945

Davies, Paul L./Hopt, Klaus J., Boards in Europe - Accountability and Convergence, ECGI Working Paper Series in Law, Working Paper No. 205/2013, April 2013, available at: http://ssrn.com/abstract_id=2212272 visited: October 12, 2013; cited: *Davies/Hopt*, 2013, p.

De Franco, Gus/Guan, Yuyan/Lu, Hai, The Wealth Changes and Redistribution Effects of Sarbanes-Oxley Internal Control Disclosures, April 2005, available at: http://ssrn.com/abstract=706702 visited: March 15, 2012; cited: *De Franco/Guan/Lu*, 2005, p.

Deiseroth, Dieter/Derleder, Peter, Whistleblower und Denunziantoren, ZRP 2008, 248; cited: *Deiseroth/Derleder*, ZRP 2008, 238

Desai, Hemang/Hogan, Chris E./Wilkins, Michael S., The Reputational Penalty for Aggressive Accounting: Earnings Restatements and Management Turnover, 81 Acct. Rev. 83 (2006); cited: *Desai/Hogan/Wilkins*, 81 Acct. Rev. 83 (2006)

Desio, Paula J., Introduction to Organizational Sentencing and the U.S. Sentencing Commission, 39 Wake Forest L. Rev. 559 (2004); cited: *Desio*, 39 Wake Forest L. Rev. 559 (2004), p.

Deutscher, Jörg, Zur Strafbarkeit des Compliance Officer - Erhöhte Berufsrisiken nach dem Urteil des BGH vom 17.7.2009, WM 2010, 1387; cited: *Deutscher*, WM 2010, 1387

Dhaliwal, Dan/Hogan, Chris/Trezevant, Robert/Wilkins, Michael, Internal Control Disclosures, Monitoring, and the Cost of Debt, 86 Acct. Rev. 1131 (2011); cited: *Dhaliwal/Hogan/Wilkins*, 86 Acct. Rev. 1131 (2011)

Dierks, Kristin/Sandmann, Thomas/Herre, Uwe, Das neue überarbeitete COSO-Rahmenwerk für Interne Kontrollsysteme und die Konsequenzen für die deutsche Unternehmenspraxis, CCZ 2013, 164; cited: *Dierks/Sandmann/Herre*, CCZ 2013, 164

Dodwell, William J., Six Years of the Sarbanes-Oxley Act - Are We Better Off?, The CPA Journal 2008, available at: http://www.nysscpa.org/printversions/cpaj/2008/808/p38.htm visited: February 8, 2011; cited: *Dodwell*, CPA Journal 2008

Dörr, Felix, Die Haftung von Unternehmen nach dem Gesetz über Ordnungswidrigkeiten, in: *Kempf, Eberhard/Lüderssen, Klaus/Volk, Klaus* [eds.], Unternehmensstrafrecht, 2012, p. 24; cited: *Dörr*, in: Unternehmensstrafrecht, 24

Doyle, Jeffrey/Ge, Weili/McVay, Sarah, Determinants of weaknesses in internal control over financial reporting, May 2006, available at: http://ssrn.com/abstract=770465 visited: March 16, 2011; cited: *Doyle/Ge/McVay*, 2006

Dreher, Meinrad, Ausstrahlungen des Aufsichtsrechts auf das Aktienrecht - Unter besonderer Berücksichtigung des Risikomanagement, ZGR 2010, 496; cited: *Dreher*, ZGR 2010, 496

Dreher, Meinrad/Hoffmann, Jens, Die Wirksamkeitsprüfung durch den Prüfungsausschuss nach § 107 Abs. 3 Satz 2 AktG, Internes Kontrollsystem, Risikomanagementsystem und Governancesystem, ZGR 2016, 445; cited: *Dreher/Hoffmann*, ZGR 2016, 445

Driscoll, Dawn-Marie/Hoffman, W. Michael/Murphy, Joseph E., Business Ethics and Compliance: What Management Is Doing and Why, 99 Business and Society Rev. 35 (1998); cited: *Driscoll/Hoffman/Murphy*, 99 Business and Society Rev. 35 (1998), p.

Drygala, Tim/Drygala, Anja, Wer braucht ein Frühwarnsystem? Zur Ausstrahlungswirkung des § 91 Abs. 2 AktG, ZIP 2000, 297; cited: *Drygala/Drygala*, ZIP 2000, 297

Drygala, Tim, Eurpäisches Konzernrecht: Gruppeninteresse und Related Party Transactions, AG 2012, 198; cited: *Drygala*, AG 2013, 198

Dück, Hermann/Eufinger, Alexander/Schultes, Marion, Das Spannungsverhältnis zwischen kartellrechtlicher Kronzeugenregelung und Akteneinsichtsanspruch nach § 406e StPO, EuZW 2012, 418; cited: *Dück/Eufinger/Schultes*, EuZW 2012, 418

Dyck, Alexander/Morse, Adair/Zingales, Luigi, Who Blows the Whistle on Corporate Fraud?, University of Chicago Booth Working Paper No. 08-22, October 2008, available at: http://ssrn.com/abstract=891482 visited: March 16, 2011; cited: *Dyck/Morse/Zingales*, 2008

Easterbrook, Frank H., The Race for the Bottom in Corporate Governance, 95 Va. L. Rev. 685 (2009); cited: *Easterbrook*, 95 Va. L. Rev. 685 (2009), p.

Eggemann, Gerd/Konradt, Thomas, Risikomanagement nach KonTraG aus dem Blickwinkel des Wirtschaftsprüfers, BB 2000, 503; cited: *Eggemann/Konradt*, BB 2000, 503

Eldrige, Susan W./ Kealey, Burch T., SOX Costs: Auditor Attestation under Section 404, June 2005, available at: http://ssrn.com/abstract=743285 visited: March 13, 2012; cited: *Eldrige/Kealey*, 2005, p.

Engel, Ellen/Hayes, Rachel M./Wang, Xue, The Sarbanes-Oxley Act and Firms' Going-Private Decisions, May 2004, available at: http://ssrn.com/abstract=546626 visited: March 16, 2011; cited: *Engel/Hayes/Wang*, 2004

Ernst, Christoph/Seidler, Holger, Der Regierungsentwurf eines Gesetzes zur Modernisierung des Bilanzrechts, ZGR 2008, 631; cited: *Ernst/Seidler*, ZGR 2008, 631

Ernst, Christoph/Seidler, Holger, Kernpunkte des Referentenentwurfs eines Bilanzrechtsmodernisierungsgesetzes, BB 2007, 2557; cited: *Ernst/Seidler*, BB 2007, 2557

Favoccia, Daniela/Richter, Thomas, Rechte, Pflichten und Haftung des Compliance Officers aus zivilrechtlicher Sicht, AG 2010, 137; cited: *Favoccia/Richter*, AG 2010, 137

Fich, Eliezer M./Shivdasani, Anil, Financial Fraud, Director Reputation, and Shareholder Wealth, 2006, available at: http://ssrn.com/abstract=687412 visited: March 2, 2012; cited: *Fich/Shivdasani*, 2006

Files, Rebecca, SEC Enforcement: Does Forthright Disclosure and Cooperation Really Matter?, June 2011, available at: http://ssrn.com/abstract=1640064 visited: November 4, 2011; cited: *Files*, 2011

Fisch, Jill E., The New Federal Regulation of Corporate Governance, 28 Harvard J. Law & Public Policy 39 (2004); cited: *Fisch*, 28 Harvard J. Law & Public Policy 39 (2004)

Fischel, Daniel R./Sykes, Alan O., Corporate Crime, 25 J. Legal Stud. 319 (1996); cited: *Fischel/Sykes*, 25 J. Legal Stud. 319 (1996), p.

Fleischer, Holger, Aktienrechtliche Compliance-Pflichten im Praxistest: Das Siemens/Neubürger-Urteil des LG München I, NZG 2014, 321; cited: *Fleischer*, NZG 2014, 321

Fleischer, Holger, Corporate Compliance im aktienrechtlichen Unternehmensverbund, CCZ 2008, 1; cited: *Fleischer*, CCZ 2008, 1

Fleischer, Holger, Corporate Governance in Europa als Mehrebenensystem - Vielfalt und Verflechtung der Gesetzgeber, Standardsetzer und Verhaltenskodizes, ZGR 2012, 160; cited: *Fleischer*, ZGR 2012, 160

Fleischer, Holger, Das Aktiengesetz von 1965 und das neue Kapitalmarktrecht, ZIP 2006, 451; cited: *Fleischer*, ZIP 2006, 451

Fleischer, Holger, Der deutsche "Bilanzeid" nach § 264 Abs. 2 Satz 3 HGB, ZIP 2007, 97; cited: *Fleischer*, ZIP 2007, 97

Fleischer, Holger, Haftung des herrschenden Unternehmens im faktischen Konzern und untermehmerisches Ermessen (§§ 317II, 93I AktG) - Das UMTS-Urteil des BGH, NZG 2008, 371; cited: *Fleischer*, NZG 2008, 371

Fleischer, Holger, Kartellrechtsverstöße und Vorstandsrecht, BB 2008, 1070; cited: *Fleischer*, BB 2008, 1070

Fleischer, Holger, Legal Transplants im deutschen Aktienrecht, NZG 2004, 1129; cited: *Fleischer*, NZG 2004, 1129

Fleischer, Holger, Legal Transplants in European Company Law - The Case of Fiduciary Duties, ECFR 2005, 378; cited: *Fleischer*, ECFR 2005, 378

Fleischer, Holger, Regresshaftung von Geschäftsleitern wegen Verbandsgeldbußen, DB 2014, 345; cited: *Fleischer*, DB 2014, 345

Fleischer, Holger, Vorstandsverantwortlichkeit und Fehlverhalten von Unternehmensangehörigen - Von der Einzelüberwachung zur Einrichtung einer Compliance-Organisation, AG 2003, 291; cited: *Fleischer*, AG 2003, 291

Fleischer, Holger, Zukunftsfragen der Corporate Governance in Deutschland und Europa: Aufsichtsräte, institutionelle Investoren, *Proxy Advisors* und *Whistleblowers*, ZGR 2011, 155; cited: *Fleischer*, ZGR 2011, 155

Fleischer, Holger, Zur Zukunft der gesellschafts- und kapitalmarktrechtlichen Forschung, ZGR 2007, 500; cited: *Fleischer*, ZGR 2007, 500

Ford, Christie/Hess, David, Can Corporate Monitorships Improve Corporate Compliance?, 34 J. Corp. L. 679 (2009); cited: *Ford/Hess*, 34 J. Corp. L. 679 (2009), p.

Forst, Gerrit, Strafanzeige gegen den Arbeitgeber - Grund zur Kündigung des Arbeitsvertrags?, NJW 2011, 3477; cited: *Forst*, NJW 2011, 3477

Förster, Christian, Europäische Corporate Governance - Tatsächliche Konvergenz der neuen Kodizies?, ZIP 2006, 162; cited: *Förster*, ZIP 2006, 162

Franks, Julian/Mayer, Colin, Ownership and Control of German Corporations, 14 Rev. Financ. Stud. 943 (2001); cited: *Franks/Mayer*, 14 Rev. Financ. Stud. 943 (2001), p.

Garrett, Brandon L., Globalized Corporate Prosecution, 97 Va. L. Rev. 1775 (2011); cited: *Garrett*, 97 Va. L. Rev. 1775 (2011), p.

Garrett, Brandon L., Structural Reform Prosecution, 93 Va. L. Rev. 853 (2007); cited: *Garrett*, 93 Va. L. Rev. 853 (2007), p.

Ge, Weili/McVay, Sarah, The Disclosure of Material Weaknesses in Internal Control after Sarbanes-Oxley Act, 19 Acct. Horizons 137 (2005); cited: *Ge/McVay*, 19 Acct. Horizons 137 (2005), p.

Gelhausen, Friedrich/Wermelt, Andreas, Haftungsrechtliche Bedeutung des IDW EPS 980: Grundsätze ordnungsmäßiger Prüfung von Compliance-Management-Systemen - gleichzeitig: Replik zum Aufsatz von Dr. Markus S. Rieder und Marcus Jerg zum Thema "Anforderungen an die Überprüfung von Compliance-Programmen" (CCZ 2010, 201), CCZ 2010, 208; cited: *Gelhausen/Wermelt*, CCZ 2010, 208

Glaum, Martin/Thomaschewski, Dieter/Weber, Silke, Auswirkungen des Sarbanes-Oxley Acts auf deutsche Unternehmen: Kosten, Nutzen, Folgen für US-Börsennotierungen, in: *von Rosen* [ed.], Studien des Deutschen Aktieninstituts, Issue 33, February 2006; cited: *Glaum/Thomaschewski/Weber*, Studien des Deutschen Aktieninstituts 2006, p.

Goldsmith, Michael/King, Chad W., Policing Corporate Crime: The Dilemma of Internal Compliance Programs, 50 Vand. L. Rev. 1 (1997); cited: *Goldsmith/King*, 50 Vand. L. Rev. 1 (1997), p.

Göpfert, Burkhard/Merten, Frank/Siegrist, Carolin, Mitarbeiter als "Wissensträger" - Ein Beitrag zur aktuellen Compliance-Diskussion, NJW 2008, 1703; cited: *Göpfert/Merten/Siegrist*, NJW 2008, 1703

Görtz, Birthe/Roßkopf, Michael, Kosten von Compliance-Management in Deutschland, Überlegungen zu Risiken, Nutzen und Bewertung, ZRFC 2010, 150; cited: *Görtz/Roßkopf*, ZRFC 2010, 150

Grau, Carsten/Meshulam, Deborah R./Blechschmidt, Vanessa, Der "lange Arm" des US-Foreign Corrupt Practices Act: unerkannte Strafbarkeitsrisiken auch jenseits der eigentlichen Korruptionsdelikte, BB 2010, 652; cited: *Grau/Meshulam/Blechschmidt*, BB 2010, 652

Grechenig, Kristoffel/Gelter, Martin, Divergente Evolution des Rechtsdenkens - Von amerikanischer Rechtsökonomie und deutscher Dogmatik, RabelsZ 72 (2008), 513; cited: *Grechenig/Gelter*, RabelsZ 2008, 513

Greenwald, Bruce C./Stiglitz, Joseph E., Asymmetric Information and the New Theory of the Firm: Financial Constraints and Risk Behavior, Working Paper No. 3359, May 1990, available at: http://ssrn.com/abstract=226660 visited: July 19, 2012; cited: *Greenwald/Stiglitz*, 1990

Griffin, Lisa K., Compelled Cooperation and the New Corporate Criminal Procedure, 82 N.Y.U. L. Rev. 311 (2007); *Griffin*, 82 N.Y.U. L. Rev. 311 (2007), p.

Gros, Marius/Velte, Patrick, Corporate Governance Reporting zum Prüfungsausschuss - Eine empirische Untersuchung im DAX und MDAX für das Geschäftsjahr 2011 unter besonderer Berücksichtigung der Finanzexpertise im Prüfungsausschuss, DStR 2012, 2243; cited: *Gros/Velte*, DStR 2012, 2243

Grossman, Nadelle, Director Compliance with Elusive Fiduciary Duties in a Climate of Corporate Governance Reform, 12 Fordham J. Corp. & Fin. L. 393 (2007); cited: *Grossman*, 12 Fordham J. Corp. & Fin. L. 393 (2007), p.

Grundfest, Joseph A./Bochner, Steven E., Fixing 404, 105 Mich. L. Rev. 1643 (2007); cited: *Grundfest/Bochner*, 105 Mich. L. Rev. 1643 (2007), p.

Gruson, Michael/Kubicek, Matthias, Der Sarbanes-Oxley Act, Corporate Governance und das deutsche Aktienrecht (Teil I), AG 2003, 337; cited: *Gruson/Kubicek*, AG 2003, 337

Gruson, Michael/Kubicek, Matthias, Der Sarbanes-Oxley Act, Corporate Governance und das deutsche Aktienrecht (Teil II), AG 2003, 393; cited: *Gruson/Kubicek*, AG 2003, 393

Grützner, Thomas, Annotation of LG München I, decision of December 12, 2013 - 5 HK O 1387/10, BB 2014, 850; cited: *Grützner*, BB 2014, 850

Gupta, Parveen P., Internal Control - COSO 1992 Control Framework and Management Report on Internal Control: Survey and Analysis of Implementation Practices, June 11, 2009, available at: http://ssrn.com/abstract=1417604 visited: March 16, 2011; cited: *Gupta*, 2009, p.

Gupta, Parveen P./Leech, Tim, Making Sarbanes-Oxley 404 work: Reducing cost, increasing effectiveness, 3 Int. J. Disclosure and Governance 27 (2006); cited: *Gupta/Leech*, 3 Int. J. Disclosure and Governance 27 (2006), p.

Guthrie, Chris/Rachlinski, Jeffrey J./Wistrich, Andrew J., Inside the Judicial Mind, 86 Cornell L. Rev. 777 (2001); cited: *Guthrie/Rachlinski/Wistrich*, 86 Cornell L. Rev. 777 (2001), p.

Hammersley, Jacqueline S./Myers, Linda A./Shakespeare, Catherine, Market Reactions to the Disclosure of Internal Control Weaknesses and to the Characteristics of those Weaknesses under Section 302 of the Sarbanes Oxley Act of 2002, January 2007, available at: http://ssrn.com/abstract=951085 visited: April 19, 2012; cited: *Hammersley/Myers/Shakespeare*, 2007

Hansen, Bowe/Pownall, Grace/Wang, Xue, The Robustness of the Sarbanes Oxley Effect on the U.S. Capital Market, April 2008, available at: http://ssrn.com/abstract=1013392 visited: March 16, 2011; cited: *Hansen/Pownall/Wang*, 2008

Happ, Dominik/Pott, Christiane, Auswirkungen des Sarbanes-Oxley Act Section 404: Kosten und Nutzen für europäische Unternehmen, KoR 2006, 206; cited: *Happ/Pott*, KoR 2007, 666

Hastenrath, Katharina, Auswirkungen des BGH-Urteils zur Garantenstellung des Compliance Officers aus Sicht der Unternehmenspraxis, CCZ 2011, 32; cited: *Hastenrath*, CCZ 2011, 32

Hauschka, Christoph E., Compliance am Beispiel der Korruptionsbekämpfung – Eine Erwiderung aus der Praxis auf Uwe H. Schneiders Vorschläge, ZIP 2004, 877; *Hauschka*, ZIP 2004, 877

Hauschka, Christoph E./Greeve, Gina, Compliance in der Korruptionsprävention - was müssen, was sollen, was können die Unternehmen?, BB 2007, 165; cited: *Hauschka/Greeve*, BB 2007, 165

Hauschka, Christoph, Compliance - Praktische Erfahrungen und Thesen, in: Gesellschaftsrechtliche Vereinigung [ed.], Gesellschaftsrecht in der Diskussion 2007 - Jahrestagung der gesellschaftsrechtlichen Vereinigung (VGR), 2008, p. 51; cited: *Hauschka*, VGR, 2008, 51

Hauschka, Christoph, Compliance, Compliance-Manager, Compliance-Programme: Eine geeignete Reaktion auf gestiegene Haftungsrisiken für Unternehmen und Management?, NJW 2004, 257; cited: *Hauschka*, NJW 2004, 257

Hellwig, Hans-Jürgen, The US Concept of Corporate Governance under the Sarbanes-Oxley Act of 2002 and Its Effects in Europe, ECFR 2007, 417; cited: *Hellwig*, ECFR 2007, 417

Henning, Peter J., The Organizational Guidelines: R.I.P.?, 116 Yale L. J. Pocket Part 312 (2007), available at: http://yalelawjournal.org/images/pdfs/528.pdf visited: November 14, 2011; cited: *Henning*, 116 Yale L. J. Pocket Part 312 (2007), p.

Henselmann, Klaus, Das KonTraG und seine Anforderungen an das Risikomanagement, in: *Götze, Uwe/Henselmann, Klaus/Mikus, Barbara* [eds.], Risikomanagement, 2001, p. 29; cited: *Henselmann*, in: Risikomanagement, p. 29

Herfs, Achim, Weiter im Blindflug - Zur Ad-hoc-Pflicht bei gestreckten Geschehensabläufen aus Sicht der Praxis, Anmerkungen zum Beschluss des BGH vom 23. 4. 2013 - II ZB 7/09 (Geltl/Daimler), DB 2013, 1350; cited: *Herfs*, DB 2013, 1350

Hern, Jeffery D., Delaware Courts' Delicate Response to the Corporate Governance Scandals of 2001 and 2002: Heightening Judicial Scrutiny on Directors of Corporations, 41 Willamette L. Rev. 207 (2005); cited: *Hern*, 41 Willamette L. Rev. 207 (2005), p.

Hess, David/McWhorter, Robert S./Fort, Timothy L., The 2004 Amendments to the Federal Sentencing Guidelines and their Implicit Call for a Symbiotic Integration of Business Ethics, 11 Fordham J. Corp & Fin. L. 725 (2006); cited: *Hess/McWhorter/Fort*, 11 Fordham J. Corp & Fin. L. 725 (2006), p.

Hicks, John R, The Foundations of Welfare Economics, The Economic Journal 49, 696 (1939); cited: *Hicks*, The Economic Journal 49, 696 (1939)

Hindelmeier, Alexandra/Maier, Benjamin, Das Interne Kontrollsystem: Pflichtübung oder Steuerungsinstrument?, Ergebnisse einer aktuellen Studie: Deutsche Unternehmen geben ihrem Internen Kontrollsystem im Durchschnitt nur ein "befriedigend", ZIR 2009, 119; cited: *Hindelmeier/Maier*, ZIR 2009, 119

Hohmann-Dennhardt, Christine, Gesellschaftliche Impulse für eine stärkere Gemeinwohlorientierung von Unternehmen, in: *Kempf, Eberhard/Lüderssen, Klaus/Volk, Klaus* [eds.], Unternehmensstrafrecht, 2012, p. 7; cited: *Hohmann-Dennhardt*, in: Unternehmensstrafrecht, 7

Hoitash, Rani/Hoitash, Udi/Bedard, Jean C., Internal Control Quality and Audit Pricing under the Sarbanes-Oxley Act, January 2007, available at: http://ssrn.com/abstract=960720 visited: March 16, 2011; cited: *Hoitash/Hoitash/Bedard*, 2007

Hoitash, Udi/Hoitash, Rani/Bedard, Jean C., Corporate Governance and Internal Control over Financial Reporting: A Comparison of Regulatory Regimes, November 2008, available at: http://ssrn.com/abstract=954057 visited: March 22, 2012; cited: *Hoitash/Hoitash/Bedard*, 2008

Hommelhoff, Peter, Protection of Minority Shareholders, Investors and Creditors in Corporate Groups: the Strengths and Weaknesses of German Corporate Group Law, EBOR 2001, 61; cited: *Hommelhoff*, EBOR 2001, 61

Hommelhoff, Peter/Mattheus, Daniela, Risikomanagementsystem im Entwurf des BilMoG als Funktionselement der Corporate Governance, BB 2007, 2787; cited: *Hommelhoff/Mattheus*, BB 2007, 2787

Hopson, Mark D./Koehler, Kristin Graham, Effektive ethische Compliance-Programme im Sinne der United States Federal Sentencing Guidelines, CCZ 2008, 208; cited: *Hopson/Koehler*, CCZ 2008, 208

Hopt, Klaus J., Conflict of Interest, Secrecy and Insider Information of Directors, A Comparative Analysis, ECFR 2013, 167; cited: *Hopt*, ECFR 2013, 167

Hopt, Klaus J., Self-dealing and Use of Corporate Opportunity and Information: Regulating Directors' Conflicts of Interest, in: *Hopt, Klaus J./ Teubner, Gunther* [eds.], Corporate Governance and Directors' Liabilities - Legal, Economic and Sociological Analyses on Corporate Social Responsibility, Berlin 1985, p. 285; cited: *Hopt*, in: Corporate Governance and Directors' Liabilities, p.

Hopt, Klaus J., Vergleichende Corporate Governance – Forschung und international Regulierung, ZHR 175 (2011), 444; cited: *Hopt*, ZHR 175 (2011), 444

Hoven, Elisa/ Wimmer, Renate/Schwarz, Thomas/Schumann, Stefan, Der nordrhein-westfälische Entwurf eines Verbandsstrafgesetzes – Kritische Anmerkungen aus Wissenschaft und Praxis, Teil 2, NZWiSt 2014, 201; cited: *Hoven/Wimmer/Schwarz/Schumann*, NZWiSt 2014, 201

Hüffer, Jens/Schneider, Uwe H., Juristen an die Compliance-Front!, ZIP 2010, 55; cited: *Hüffer/Schneider*, ZIP 2010, 55

Hufnagel, Wolfgang/Tönnissen, Stefan, IT-Governance, Interne Revision, CoBiT, BilMoG, ZIR 2010, 110; cited: *Hufnagel/Tönnissen*, ZIR 2010, 110

Hugger, Heiner, Standpunkt, BB 2012, 2125; cited: *Hugger*, BB 2012, 2125

Huth, Mark-Alexander, Grundsätze ordnungsmäßiger Risikoüberwachung, BB 2007, 2167; cited: *Huth*, BB 2007, 2167

Hütten, Christoph/Stromann, Hilke, Umsetzung des Sarbanes-Oxley Act in der Unternehmenspraxis, BB 2003, 2223; cited: *Hütten/Stromann*, BB 2003, 2223

Ide, R. William, Post-Enron Corporate Governance Opportunities: Creating a Culture of Greater Board Collaboration and Oversight, 54 Mercer L. Rev. 829 (2003); cited: *Ide*, 54 Mercer L. Rev. 829 (2003), p.

Iliev, Peter, The Effect of SOX Section 404 Compliance on Audit Fees, Earnings Quality and Stock Prices, August 2009, available at: http://ssrn.com/abstract=983772 visited: April 25, 2012; cited: *Iliev*, 2009, p.

Illing, Diana/Umnuß, Karsten, Die arbeitsrechtliche Stellung des Compliance Managers - insbesondere Weisungsunterworfenheit und Reportingpflichten, CCZ 2009, 1; cited: *Illing/Umnuß*, CCZ 2009, 1

Imberg, Alexander P./Geissl, Katrin E., Dokumentenmanagementrichtlinien und Aufbewahrungspflichten im Hinblick auf die rechtlichen Anforderungen des U.S. Zivilverfahrens, CCZ 2009, 190; cited: *Imberg/Geissl*, CCZ 2009, 190

Itzen, Uta, Richtungswechsel, Bestandsaufnahme, Prävention. Das Gerüst einer erfolgreichen Compliance-Strategie, BB 2008, Beilage 5, 12; cited: *Itzen*, BB 2008, Beilage 5, 12

Jain, Pankaj K./Kim, Jang-Chul/Rezaee, Zabihollah, Trends and Determinants of Market Liquidity in the Pre- and Post-Sarbanes-Oxley Act Periods, September 2006, available at: http://ssrn.com/abstract=488142 visited: May 7, 2012; cited: *Jain/Kim/Rezaee*, 2006

Jensen, Michael C./Meckling, William H., Theory of the Firm: Managerial Behavior, Agency Costs, and Ownership Structure; in: *Wittman* [ed.], Economic Analysis of the Law, 2003, p. 162; cited: *Jensen/Meckling*, Theory of the Firm

Johnson, Lyman P.Q./Sides, Mark A., The Sarbanes-Oxley Act and Fiduciary Duties, 30 Wm. Mitchell L. Rev. 1149 (2004); cited: *Johnson/Sides*, 30 Wm. Mitchell L. Rev. 1149 (2004), p.

Jonas, Gregory/Rosenberg, Alan/Gale, Marc/Hedges, Luke, The Third Year of Section 404 Reporting on Internal Control, May 2007, available at: http://ssrn.com/abstract=985546 visited: March 14, 2012; cited: *Jonas/Rosenberg/Gale/Hedges*, 2007, p.

Jungmann, Carsten, The Effectiveness of Corporate Governance in One-Tier and Two-Tier Board Systems - Evidence from the UK and Germany, ECFR 2006, 426; cited: *Jungmann*, ECFR 2006, 426

Kaal, Wulf A./Lacine, Timothy A., The Effect of Deferred and Non-Prosecution Agreements on Corporate Governance: Evidence from 1993-2013, November 2014, available at: http://ssrn.com/abstract=2486570 visited: May 5, 2015; cited: *Kaal/Lacine*, 2014

Kaal, Wulf A./Painter, Richard W., Initial Reflections on an Evolving Standard: Constraints on Risk Taking by Directors and Officers in Germany and the United States, 40 Seton Hall L. Rev. 1433 (2010); *Kaal/Painter*, 40 Seton Hall L. Rev. 1433 (2010), p.

Kaldor, Nicholas, Welfare Propositions of Economics and Interpersonal Comparisons of Utility, The Economic Journal 49, 549 (1939); cited: *Kaldor*, The Economic Journal 49, 549 (1939)

Karmel, Roberta S., The Securities and Exchange Commission Goes Abroad to Regulate Corporate Governance, 33 Stetson L. Rev. 849 (2004); cited: *Karmel*, 33 Stetson L. Rev. 849 (2004), p.

Karpoff, Jonathan M./Lee, D. Scott/Martin, Gerald S., The Impact of Anti-Bribery Enforcement Actions on Targeted Firms, February 2012, available at: http://ssrn.com/abstract=1573222 visited: June 1, 2012; cited: *Karpoff/Lee/Martin*, 2012

Kersting, Christian, Auswirkungen des Sarbanes-Oxley-Gesetzes in Deutschland: Können deutsche Unternehmen das Gesetz befolgen?, ZIP 2003, 233; cited: *Kersting*, ZIP 2003, 233

Khanna, Vikramaditya S., Corporate Criminal Liability: What Purpose Does It Serve?, 109 Harvard L. Rev. 1477 (1996); cited: *Khanna*, 109 Harvard L. Rev. 1477 (1996), p.

Khanna, Vikramaditya S., Should the Behavior of Top Management Matter?, September 2002, available at: http://ssrn.com/abstract=339940 visited: December 6, 2011; cited: *Khanna*, 2002, p.

Khanna, Vikramaditya/Dickinson, Timothy L., The Corporate Monitor: The New Corporate Czar?, 105 Mich. L. Rev. 1713 (2007); cited: *Khanna/Dickinson*, 105 Mich. L. Rev. 1713 (2007), p.

Kim, Sung Hui, The Banality of Fraud: Re-Situating the Inside Counsel as Gatekeeper, 74 Fordham L. Rev. 983 (2005); cited: *Kim*, 74 Fordham L. Rev. 983 (2005)

Kinney, William R./McDaniel, Linda S., Characteristics of Firms Correcting Previously Reported Quarterly Earnings, 11 J. Acct. and Econ. 71 (1989); cited: *Kinney/McDaniel*, 11 J. Acct. and Econ. 71 (1989), p.

Király, Andrei, Der rechtliche Schutz von Whistleblowern, Lehren aus US-amerikanischen Regelungen, ZRP 2011, 146; cited: *Király*, ZRP 2011, 146

Kirchner, Christian, § 5 Die ökonomische Theorie, in: *Riesenhuber* [ed.], Europäische Methodenlehre - Handbuch für Ausbildung und Praxis, 2nd edition, 2010; cited: *Kirchner*, in: Riesenhuber, sec. 5, mar.

Kirchner, Christian, Comparative Law and Institutional Economics – Legal Transplants in Corporate Governance, in: *Nobel, Peter/Gets, Marina* [eds.], New Frontiers of Law and Economics, 2006, 201; cited: *Kirchner*, in: New Frontiers of Law and Economics 2006, p.

Kirchner, Christian/Koch, Stefan, Norminterpretation und ökonomische Analyse des Rechts, Analyse & Kritik, Zeitschrift für Sozialwissenschaften, 1989, 111; cited: *Kirchner/Koch*, ZfSozW 1989, 111

Kirchner, Christian, Ökonomische Analyse des Rechts: Interdisziplinäre Zusammenarbeit von Ökonomie und Rechtswissenschaft, in: *Assmann, Heinz-Dieter/ Kirchner, Christian/Schanze, Erich*, Ökonomische Analyse des Rechts, 1993, p. 62; cited: *Kirchner*, in: Ökonomische Analyse des Rechts, p.

Kirchner, Christian, Szenarien einer 'feindlichen' Unternehmensübernahme: Alternative rechtliche Regelungen im Anwendungstest, BB 2000, 105; cited: *Kirchner*, BB 2000, 105

Kirchner, Christian, The Difficult Reception of Law and Economics in Germany, 11 International Review of Law and Economics 277 (1991); cited: *Kirchner*, 11 International Review of Law and Economics 277 (1991), p.

Klasen, Evelyn/Schaefer, Sandra, Whistleblower, Zeuge und "Beschuldigter" - Informationsweitergabe im Spannungsfeld grundrechtlicher Positionen, BB 2012, 614; cited: *Klasen/Schaefer*, BB 2012, 641

Klengel, Detlef W./Mückenberger, Ole, Internal Investigations - typische Rechts- und Praxisprobleme unternehmensinterner Ermittlungen, CCZ 2009, 81; cited: *Klengel/Mückenberger*, CCZ 2009, 81

Kless, Thomas, Beherrschung der Unternehmensrisiken: Aufgaben und Prozesse eines Risikomanagements, DStR 1998, 93; cited: *Kless*, DStR 1998, 93

Klindt, Thomas, Nicht-börsliches Compliance-Management als zukünftige Aufgabe der Inhouse-Juristen, NJW 2006, 3399; cited: *Klindt*, NJW 2006, 3399

Klindt, Thomas/Pelz, Christian/Theusinger, Ingo, Compliance im Spiegel der Rechtsprechung, NJW 2010, 2385; cited: *Klindt/Pelz/Theusinger*, NJW 2010, 2385

Koch, Jens, Die Konzernobergesellschaft als Unternehmensinhaber i.S.d. § 130 OWiG?, AG 2009, 564; cited: *Koch*, AG 2009, 564

Koch, Robert, Einführung eines obligatorischen Selbstbehalts in der D&O-Versicherung durch das VorstAG, AG 2009, 637; cited: *Koch*, AG 2009, 637

Kock, Martin, Compliance im Unternehmen - Etisch sei der Mensch, hilfreich und gut!, ZIP 2009, 1406; cited: *Kock*, ZIP 2009, 1406

Köhler, Annette G./Marten, Kai-Uwe/Schlereth, Dieter, Stärkung der Corporate Governance in Deutschland - Umsetzungsstand und Effektivität, DB 2009, 1477; cited: *Köhler/Marten/Schlereth*, DB 2009, 1477

Koniak, Susan P./Cohen, George M./Cramton, Roger C., Legal and Ethical Duties of Lawyers after Sarbanes-Oxley, Boston University School of Law Working Paper No. 04-20, January 2010, available at: http://www.bu.edu/law/faculty/scholarship/workingpapers/2004.html visited: March 24, 2017; cited: *Koniak/Cohen/Cramton*, 2010, p.

Kort, Michael, Lückenhafte Reform des Beschäftigtendatenschutzes - Offene Fragen und mögliche Antworten in Bezug auf die geplanten §§ 32 ff. BDSG, MMR 2011, 294; cited: *Kort*, MMR 2011, 294

Kort, Michael, Risikomanagement nach dem Bilanzrechtsmodernisierungsgesetz, ZGR 2010, 440; cited: *Kort*, ZGR 2010, 440

Kort, Michael, Verhaltensstandardisierung durch Corporate Compliance, NZG 2008, 81; cited: *Kort*, NZG 2008, 81

Kostant, Peter C., From Lapdog to Watchdog: Sarbanes-Oxley Section 307 and a New Role of Corporate Lawyers, 52 N. Y. L. Sch. L. Rev. 535 (2007/2008); cited: *Kostant*, 52 N. Y. L. Sch. L. Rev. 535 (2007/2008), p.

Kottek, Petr, Die Beschlagnahme von Unterlagen aus unternehmensinterenen Compliance-Ermittlungen, CB 2016, 349; cited: *Kottek*, CB 2016, 349

Kraakman, Reinier H., Vicarious and Corporate Civil Liability, in: *Faure, Michael* [ed.], Tort Law and Economics, Encyclopedia of Law and Economics, 2nd edition, 2009, 134; cited: *Kraakman*, in: Encyclopedia of Law and Economics, p.

Kraft, Oliver/Winkler, Klaus, Zur Garantenstellung des Compliance-Officers - Unterlassungsstrafbarkeit durch Organisationsmangel?, CCZ 2009, 29; cited: *Kraft/Winkler*, CCZ 2009, 29

Krawiec, Kimberly D., Cosmetic Compliance and Failure of Negotiated Governance, 81 Wash. U. L. Quarterly 487 (2003); cited: *Krawiec*, 81 Wash. U. L. Quarterly 487 (2003), p.

Krawiec, Kimberly D., Organizational Misconduct: Beyond the Principal-Agent Model, 32 Fla. St. U. L. Rev. 571 (2005); cited: *Krawiec*, 32 Fla. St. U. L. Rev. 571 (2005), p.

Krebs, Peter/Eufinger, Alexander/Jung, Stefanie, Bußgeldminderung durch Compliance- Programme im deutschen Kartellbußbeldverfahren?, CCZ 2011, 213; cited: *Krebs/Eufinger/Jung*, CCZ 2011, 213

Kremer, Thomas/Klahold, Christoph, Compliance-Programme in Industriekonzernen, ZGR 2010, 113; cited: *Kremer/Klahold*, ZGR 2010, 113

Krieger, Steffen/Günther, Jens, Die arbeitsrechtliche Stellung des Compliance Officers - Gestaltung einer Compliance-Organisation unter Berücksichtigung der Vorgaben im BGH-Urteil vom 17.7.2009, NZA 2010, 367; cited: *Krieger/Günther*, NZA 2010, 367

Krishnan, Gopal V./Visvanathan, Gnanakumar, Reporting Internal Control Deficiencies in the Post-Sarbanes-Oxley Era: The Role of Auditors and Corporate Governance, October 2005, available at: http://ssrn.com/abstract=646925 visited: April, 27, 2012; cited: *Krishnan/Visvanathan*, 2005

Krishnan, Jagan/Rama, Dasaratha/Zhang, Yinghong, Costs to Comply With SOX Section 404, August 2007, available at: http://ssrn.com/abstract=1091902 visited: March 16, 2011; cited: *Krishnan/Rama/Zhang*, 2007

Kromschröder, Bernhard/Lück, Wolfgang für den Arbeitskreis „Externe und Interne Überwachung der Unternehmung" der Schmalenbach-Gesellschaft für Betriebswirtschaft e.V., Grundsätze risikoorientierter Unternehmensüberwachung, DB 1998, 1573; cited: *Kromschröder/Lück*, DB 1998, 1573

Kuhl, Karin/Nickel, Johann-Peter, Risikomanagement im Unternehmen - Stellt das KonTraG neue Anforderungen an die Unternehmen?, DB 1999, 133; cited: *Kuhl/Nickel*, DB 1999, 133

Kuntz, Laura R., Lessons To Be Learned From The First Go Around At Compliance With Internal Controls Reporting, in: The Metropolitan Corporate Counsel, May 2005, p. 37; cited: *Kuntz*, in: The Metropolitan Corporate Counsel 2005

Lackhoff, Klaus/Schulz, Martin, Das Unternehmen als Gefahrenquelle? Compliance-Risiken für Unternehmensleiter und Mitarbeiter, CCZ 2010, 81; cited: *Lackhoff/Schulz*, CCZ 2010, 81

Lampert, Thomas, Gestiegenes Unternehmesrisiko Kartellrecht - Risikoreduzierung durch Competition-Compliance-Programm, BB 2002, 2237; cited: *Lampert*, BB 2002, 2237

Lanfermann, Georg/Röhricht, Victoria, Pflichten des Prüfungsausschuss nach dem BilMoG, BB 2009, 887; cited: *Lanfermann/Röhricht*, BB 2009, 887

Langenbucher, Katja, Zentrale Akteure der Corporate Governance: Zusammensetzung des Aufsichtsrats - Zum Vorschlag einer obligatorischen Besetzungserklärung, ZGR 2012, 314; cited: *Langenbucher*, ZGR 2012, 314

Langevoort, Donald C., Cultures of Compliance, 2016, available at: http://ssrn.com/abstract=2840762 visited: April 5, 2017; cited: *Langevoort*, 2016.

Langevoort, Donald C., Internal Controls After Sarbanes-Oxley: Revisiting Corporate Law's "Duty of Care as Responsibility for Systems", 31 J. Corp. L. 949 (2006); cited: *Langevoort*, 31 J. Corp. L. 949 (2006), p.

Langevoort, Donald C., Monitoring: The Behavioral Economics of Corporate Compliance with Law, 2002 Colum. Bus. L. Rev. 71; cited: *Langevoort*, 2002 Colum. Bus. L. Rev. 71, p.

Langevoort, Donald C., On Leaving Corporate Executives "Naked, Homeless and Without Wheels": Corporate Fraud, Equitable Remedies, and the Debate over Entity versus Individual Liability, 42 Wake Forest L. Rev. 627 (2007); cited: *Langevoort*, 42 Wake Forest L. Rev. 627 (2007), p.

Langevoort, Placebo Statutes?: Sarbanes-Oxley and Ethics Code Disclosures, 96 Va. L. Rev. 9 (2010); cited: *Langevoort*, 96 Va. L. Rev. 9 (2010), p.

Langevoort, The Social Construction of Sarbanes-Oxley, 105 Mich. L. Rev. 1817 (2007); cited: *Langevoort*, 105 Mich. L. Rev. 1817 (2007), p.

Laufer, William S., Corporate Liability, Risk Shifting, and the Paradox of Compliance, 52 Vand. L. Rev. 1343 (1999); cited: *Laufer*, 52 Vand. L. Rev. 1343 (1999), p.

Laufer, William S., Social Accountability and Corporate Greenwashing, 43 Journal of Business Ethics 253 (2003); cited: *Laufer*, 43 Journal of Business Ethics 253 (2003), p.

Leary, Elliott/Dooley, Joseph P./Stryker, Nicole, Trends In FCPA Enforcement, in: The Metropolitan Corporate Counsel, May 2007, p. 18; cited: *Leary/Dooley/Stryker*, in: The Metropolitan Corporate Counsel 2007

Leuchten, Alexius, Der gesetzliche Schutz für Whistleblower rückt näher, ZRP 2012, 142; cited: *Leuchten*, ZRP 2012, 142

Li, Xi, An Examination of the Impact of the Sarbanes-Oxley Act on Cross Listed Foreign Private Issuers and the Legal Bonding Hypothesis, March 20, 2011, available at: http://ssrn.com/abstract=952433 visited: April 20, 2013; cited: *Li*, 2011, p.

Liese, Jens, Much Adoe About Nothing? oder: Ist der Vorstand einer Aktiengesellschaft verpflichtet, eine Compliance-Organization zu implementieren?, BB 2008, Beilage 5, 17; cited: *Liese*, BB 2008, Beilage 5, 17

Liese, Jens/Schulz, Martin, Risikomanagement durch Compliance-Audits - Neue Herausforderungen für die Unternehmensorganisation, BB 2011, 1347; cited: *Liese/Schulz*, BB 2011, 1347

Linck, James S./Netter, Jeffry M./Yang, Tina, The Effects and Unintended Consequences of the Sarbanes-Oxley Act on the Supply and Demand for Directors, February 2008, available at: http://ssrn.com/abstract=902665 visited: April 23, 2012; cited: *Linck/Netter/Yang*, 2008

Litvak, Kate, Sarbanes-Oxley and the Cross-Listing Premium, 105 Mich. L. Rev. 1857 (2007); cited: *Litvak*, 105 Mich. L. Rev. 1857 (2007), p.

Litvak, Kate, The Effect of the Sarbanes-Oxley Act on Non-US Companies Cross-Listed in the US, 2007, available at: http://ssrn.com/abstract=876624 visited: July 28, 2010; cited: *Litvak*, 2007, p.

Litvak, Kate, The Long-Term Effect of the Sarbanes-Oxley Act on Cross-Listing Premia, European Financial Management 2008, 875; cited: *Litvak*, European Financial Management 2008, 875

Lorenz, Manuel, Einführung in die rechtlichen Grundlagen des Risikomanagements, in: *Romeike, Frank* [ed.], Rechtliche Grundlagen des Risikomanagements - Haftungs- und Strafvermeidung für Corporate Compliance, 2008; cited: *Lorenz*, in: Grundlagen des Risikomanagements, p.

Lösler, Thomas, Die Mindestanforderungen an Compliance und die weiteren Verhaltens-, Organisations- und Transparenzpflichten nach §§ 31 ff. WpHG (MaComp), WM 2010, 1917; cited: *Lösler*, WM 2010, 1917

Lösler, Thomas, Spannungen zwischen der Effizienz der internen Compliance und möglichen Reporting-Pflichten des Compliance Officers, WM 2007, 676; cited: *Lösler*, WM 2007, 676

Lück, Wolfgang, Der Umgang mit unternehmerischen Risiken durch ein Risikomanagementsystem und durch ein Überwachungssystem - Anforderungen durch das KonTraG und Umsetzung in der betrieblichen Praxis, DB 1998, 1925; cited: *Lück*, DB 1998, 1925

Lück, Wolfgang, Elemente eines Risiko-Managementsystems - Die Notwendigkeit eines Risiko-Managementsystems durch den Entwurf eines Gesetzes zur Kontrolle und Transparenz im Unternehmensbereich (KonTraG) -, DB 1998, 8; cited: *Lück*, DB 1998, 8

Mahnhold, Thilo, "Global Whistle" oder "deutsche Pfeife" - Whistleblowing-Systeme im Jurisdiktionskonflikt, NZA 2008, 737; cited: *Mahnhold*, NZA 2008, 737

Manne, Geoffrey A., The Hydraulic Theory of Disclosure Regulation and Other Costs of Disclosure, 58 Ala. L. Rev. 473 (2007); cited: *Manne*, 58 Ala. L. Rev. 473 (2007), p.

Marks, Stephen G., The Separation of Ownership and Control, in: *Bouckaert, Baudewijn/De Geest, Gerrit* [eds.], Encyclopedia of Law and Economics, Vol. III, The Regulation of Contracts, 2000, p. 962; cited: *Marks*, in: Encyclopedia of Law and Economics, p.

Marosi, András/Massoud, Nadia, "You Can Enter but You Cannot Leave..." - U.S. Securities Markets and Foreign Firms, November 2006, available at: http://ssrn.com/abstract=882152 visited: March 22, 2012; cited: *Marosi/Massoud*, 2006

Marschlich, Annette, Praxis der Compliance-Organization: Geschenke und Einladungen, CCZ 2010, 110; cited: *Marschlich*, CCZ 2010, 110

Marx, Franz Jürgen/Korff, Matthias/Kläne, Sebastian, Die Interne Revision unter dem Einfluss internationaler Prüfungsnormen, ZIR 2009, 47; cited: *Marx/Korff/Kläne*, ZIR 2009, 47

Marxen, Klaus/Taschner, Katharian, Zur Strafbarkeit der Führung schwarzer Kassen, EWiR 2009, 253; cited: *Marxen/Taschner*, EWiR 2009, 253

Maschmann, Frank, Compliance versus Datenschutz, NZA-Beilage 2012, 50; cited: *Maschmann*, NZA-Beilage 2012, 50

McDonnell, Brett H., SOX Appeals, 2004 Mich. St. L. Rev. 505; cited: *McDonnell*, 2004 Mich. St. L. Rev. 505, p.

McGreal, Paul E., Corporate Compliance Survey, 66 Bus. Law. 125 (2010); cited: *McGreal*, 66 Bus. Law. 125 (2010), p.

McKendall, Marie/DeMarr, Beverly/Jones-Rikkers, Cathrine, Ethical Compliance Programs and Corporate Illegality: Testing the Assumptions of the Corporate Sentencing Guidelines, 37 Journal of Bus. Ethics 367 (2002); cited: *Kendall/DeMarr/Jones-Rikkers*, 37 Journal of Bus. Ethics 367 (2002), p.

Meier-Greve, Daniel, Vorstandshaftung wegen mangelhafter Corporate Compliance, BB 2009, 2555; cited: *Meier-Greve*, BB 2009, 2555

Melcher, Winfried/Mattheus, Daniela, Zur Umsetzung der HGB-Modernisierung durch das BilMoG: Neue Offenlegungspflichten zur Corporate Governance, DB 2009, Beilage 5, 77; cited: *Melcher/Mattheus*, DB 2009, Beilage 5, 77

Mengel, Anja/Hagemeister, Volker, Compliance und Arbeitsrecht, BB 2006, 2466; cited: *Mengel/Hagemeister*, BB 2006, 2466

Mengel, Anja/Hagemeister, Volker, Compliance und arbeitsrechtliche Implementierung im Unternehmen, BB 2007, 1386; cited: *Mengel/Hagemeister*, BB 2007, 1386

Merkt, Hanno, Compliance und Risikofrüherkennung in kleinen und mittleren Unternehmen, ZIP 2014, 1705; cited: *Merkt*, ZIP 2014, 1705

Merkt, Hanno, Überprüfung des Compliance-Management-Systems zwischen Wirtschaftsprüfern und Juristen (Teil 1), DB 2014, 2271; cited: *Merkt*, DB 2014, 2271

Merkt, Hanno, Überprüfung des Compliance-Management-Systems zwischen Wirtschaftsprüfern und Juristen (Teil 2), DB 2014, 2331; cited: *Merkt*, DB 2014, 2331

Meyer, Jürgen, Criminal Responsibility of Legal and Collective Entities: Comments on Developments in Germany, in: *Eser, Albin/Heine, Günter/Huber, Barbara* [eds.], Criminal Responsibility of Legal and Collective Entities, 1998, p. 129; cited: *Meyer*, in: Criminal Responsibility, p.

Meyer, Susanne, Compliance-Verantwortlichkeit von Vorstandsmitgliedern - Legalitätsprinzip und Risikomanagement Besprechung des Urteils LG München I vom 10.12.2013 - 5 HK O 1387/10, DB 2014, 1063; cited: *Meyer*, DB 2014, 1063

Möllers, Thomas M.J., Creating Standards in a Global Financial Market - The Sarbanes-Oxley Act and other Activities: What Europeans and Americans could and should learn from each other -, ECFR 2007, 173; cited: *Möllers*, ECFR 2007, 173

Möllers, Thomas M.J., Treuepflichten und Interessenkonflikte bei Vorstands- und Aufsichtsratsmitgliedern, in: *Hommelhoff, Peter/Hopt, Klaus J./v. Werder, Alex* [eds.], Handbuch Corporate Governance - Leitung und Überwachung börsennotierter Unternehmen in der Rechts- und Wirtschaftspraxis, 2nd edition, 2009, p. 423; cited: *Möllers*, Hdb Corporate Governance, 423

Moosmayer, Klaus/Gropp-Stadler, Susanne, Der Diskussionsentwurf des Bundesministeriums der Justiz zur Änderung des §§ 30, 130 OWiG: Ein Zwischenruf, NZWiSt 2012, 241; cited: *Moosmayer/Gropp-Stadler*, NZWiSt 2012, 241

Müller, Stefan/Ergün, Ismail, Das rechnungslegungsbezogene interne Kontrollsystem, Analyse der praktischen Umsetzung am Beispiel von Nicht-Finanzunternehmen, ZRFC 2012, 102; cited: *Müller/Ergün*, ZRFC 2012, 102

Müller-Bonanni, Thomas/Sagan, Adam, Arbeitsrechtliche Aspekte der Compliance, BB 2008, Beilage 5, 28; cited: *Müller-Bonanni/Sagan*, BB 2008, Beilage 5, 28

Murdock, Charles W., Sarbanes Oxley Five Years Later: Hero or Villain, 39 Loy. U. Chi. L. J. 525 (2008); cited: *Murdock*, 39 Loy. U. Chi. L. J. 525 (2008), p.

Murphy, Diana E., The Federal Sentencing Guidelines for Organizations: A Decade of Promoting Compliance and Ethics, 87 Iowa L. Rev. 697 (2002); cited: *Murphy*, 87 Iowa L. Rev. 697 (2002), p.

Murphy, Joseph E., Examining the Legal and Business Risks of Compliance Programs, 13 ETHIKOS 4 (Jan/Feb 2000); cited: *Murphy*, 13 ETHIKOS 4 (2000)

Nell, Mathias, Korruptionsbekämpfung ja - aber richtig! - Reformüberlegungen zur Unternehmenshaftung nach OWiG, ZRP 2008, 149; cited: *Nell*, ZRP 2008, 149

Nelson, Mark W., Ameliorating Conflicts of Interests in Auditing: Effects of Recent Reforms on Auditors and Their Clients, 31 Academy of Management Rev. 30 (2006); cited: *Nelson*, 31 Academy of Management Rev. 30 (2006), p.

Neumann Vu, Stacey, Note, Corporate Criminal Liability: Patchwork Verdicts and the Problem of Locating a Guilty Agent, 104 Colum. L. Rev 459 (2004); cited: *Neumann Vu*, 104 Colum. L. Rev 459 (2004), p.

Nezmeskal-Berggötz, Susanna, Einführung und Inhalte von Ethikrichtlinien in multinationalen Unternehmen, CCZ 2009, 209; cited: *Nezmeskal-Berggötz*, CCZ 2009, 209

Nimwegen, Sebastian, Die Vermeidung und Aufdeckung von Fraud durch den Aufsichtsrat - Verantwortung und mögliche Vergehensweise, ZRFC 2010, 161; cited: *Nimwegen*, ZFRC 2010, 161

Nimwegen, Sebastian/Koelen, Peter, COSO II als Rahmen für die Beschreibung der wesentlichen Merkmale des internen Kontroll- und des Risikomanagementsystems, DB 2010, 2011; cited: *Nimwegen/Koelen*, DB 2010, 2011

Nonnenmacher, Rolf/Pohle, Klaus/v. Werder, Axel, Aktuelle Anforderungen an Prüfungsausschüsse - Leitfaden für Prüfungsausschüsse (Audit Committees) unter Berücksichtigung der 8. EU-Richtlinie, DB 2007, 2412; cited: *Nonnenmacher/Pohle/v. Werder*, DB 2007, 2412

Nonnenmacher, Rolf/Pohle, Klaus/v. Werder, Axel, Aktuelle Anforderungen an Prüfungsausschüsse - Leitfaden für Prüfungsausschüsse (Audit Committees) unter Berücksichtigung der 8. EU-Richtlinie, DB 2007, 2412; cited: *Nonnenmacher/Pohle/v. Werder*, DB 2007, 2412

Nonnenmacher, Rolf/Pohle, Klaus/v. Werder, Axel, Aktuelle Anforderungen an Prüfungsausschüsse - Leitfaden für Prüfungsausschüsse (Audit Committees) unter Berücksichtigung des Bilanzrechtsmodernisierungsgesetzes (BilMoG), DB 2009, 1447; cited: *Nonnenmacher/Pohle/v. Werder*, DB 2009, 1447

O'Brien, Patrick, Reducing SOX Section 404 Compliance Costs - A Top-Down, Risk-Based Approach Part I, The CPA Journal 2006, available at: http://www.nysscpa.org/printversions/cpaj/2006/706/p26.htm visited: February 8, 2011; cited: *O'Brien*, CPA Journal 2006a

O'Brien, Patrick, Reducing SOX Section 404 Compliance Cots Via a Top-Down, Risk-Based Approach Part II, The CPA Journal 2006, available: http://www.nysscpa.org/printversions/cpaj/2006/806/p36.htm visited: February 8, 2011; cited: *O'Brien*, CPA Journal 2006b

Oded, Sharon, Inducing corporate compliance: A compound corporate liability regime, International Review of Law and Economics, June 2011, available at: http://ssrn.com/abstract=1928485 visited: September 21, 2015; cited: *Oded*, 2011

Ogneva, Maria/Subramanyam, K. R./Raghunandan, K., Internal Control Weakness and Cost of Equity: Evidence form SOX Section 404 Disclosures, July 2006, available at: http://ssrn.com/abstract=766104 visited: March 16, 2011; cited: *Ogneva/Subramanyam/Raghunandan*, 2006

Overwetter, Christian, Arbeitnehmerrechte bei Lidl, Aldi & Co., NZA 2008, 609; cited: *Overwetter*, NZA 2008, 609

Painter, Richard W./Kaal, Wulf A., Extraterritorial Application of US Securities Law - Will the US become the Default Jurisdiction for European Securities Litigation?, August 2010, available at: http://ssrn.com/abstract=1664809 visited: November 1, 2011; cited: *Painter/Kaal*, 2010

Pampel, Gunnar, Die Bedeutung von Compliance-Programmen im Kartellordnungswidrigkeitenrecht, BB 2007, 1636; cited: *Pampel*, BB 2007, 1636

Pan, Eric J., Rethinking the Board's Duty to Monitor: A Critical Assessment of the Delaware Doctrine, 38 Fla. St. U. L. Rev. 209 (2011); cited: *Pan*, 38 Fla. St. U. L. Rev. 209 (2011), p.

Pape, Jonas, Zur Wirksamkeit von Corporate Compliance, CCZ 2010, 233; cited: *Pape*, CCZ 2009, 233

Paredes, Troy, A., Blinded by the Light: Information Overload and its Consequences for Securities Regulation, 81 Wash. U. L. Q. 417 (2003); cited: *Paredes*, 81 Wash. U. L. Q. 417 (2003), p.

Parisi, Francesco, Positive, Normative and Functional Schools in Law and Economics, European Journal of Law and Economics, 2004, p. 259, available at http://ssrn.com/abstract=586641 visited: January 12, 2014; cited: *Parisi*, 2004

Pauthner, Jürgen/de Lamboy, Christian, Aufbau unternehmensinterner Kompetenz- und Wissensressourcen für das Compliance Management, Teil 1, CCZ 2011, 106; cited: *Pauthner/de Lamboy*, CCZ 2011, 106

Pauthner, Jürgen/de Lamboy, Christian, Aufbau unternehmensinterner Kompetenz- und Wissensressourcen für das Compliance Management, Teil 2, CCZ 2011, 146; cited: *Pauthner/de Lamboy*, CCZ 2011, 146

Peglau, Jens, Unbeantwortete Fragen der Strafbarkeit von Personenverbänden, ZRP 2001, 406; cited: *Peglau*, ZRP 2001, 406

Pietzke, Rudolf, Die Verantwortung für Risikomanagement und Compliance im mehrköpfigen Vorstand, CCZ 2010, 45; cited: *Pietzke*, CCZ 2010, 45

Posner, Richard A., The Law and Economics Movement, in: *Posner, Richard A./Parisi, Francesco* [eds.], Economic Foundations of Private Law, 2002, p. 3; cited: *Posner*, in: Economic Foundations of Private Law, p.

Powilleit, Simone, Compliance im Unternehmen: Rechtliches Risikomanagement als Wertschöpfungsfaktor, GWR 2010, 28; cited: *Powilleit*, GWR 2010, 28

Prentice, Robert A., Sarbanes-Oxley: The Evidence Regarding the Impact of SOX 404, 29 Cardozo L. Rev. 703 (2007); cited: *Prentice*, 29 Cardozo L. Rev. 703 (2007), p.

Prentice, Robert A., The Inevitability of a Strong SEC, 91 Cornell L. Rev. 775 (2006); cited: *Prentice*, 91 Cornell L. Rev. 775 (2006), p.

Prentice, Robert A./Spence, David B., Sarbanes-Oxley as Quack Corporate Governance: How Wise is the Received Wisdom?, 95 Geo. L. J. 1843, (2007); cited: *Prentice/Spence*, 95 Geo. L. J. 1843, (2007), p.

Preußner, Joachim, Deutscher Governance Kodex und Risikomanagement, NZG 2004, 303; cited: *Preußner*, NZG 2004, 303

Preußner, Joachim, Risikomanagement und Compliance in der aktienrechtlichen Verantwortung des Aufsichtsrats unter Berücksichtigung des Gesetzes zur Modernisierung des Bilanzrechts, NZG 2008, 574; cited: *Preußner*, NZG 2008, 574

Preußner, Joachim/Becker, Florian, Ausgestaltung von Risikomanagementsystemen durch die Geschäftsleitung - Zur Konkretisierung einer haftungsrelevanten Organisationspflicht, NZG 2002, 846; cited: *Preußner/Becker*, NZG 2002, 846

Preußner, Joachim/Pananis, Panos, Risikomanagement und strafrechtliche Verantwortung - Corporate Governance am Beispiel der Kreditwirtschaft, BKR 2004, 347; cited: *Preußner/Pananis*, BKR 2004, 347

Quall, Joel C., Implementing Section 404 - A Practical Approach to the Sarbanes-Oxley Act, The CPA Journal 2004, available at: http://www.nysscpa.org/printversions/cpaj/2004/804/p52.htm visited: February 8, 2011; cited: *Quall*, CPA Journal 2004

Ransiek, Andreas, Strafrecht im Unternehmen und Konzern, ZGR 1999, 613; cited: *Ransiek*, ZGR 1999, 613

Ransiek, Andreas, Überlegungen zur strafrechtlichen Verantwortung des Unternehmensträgers, in: *Kempf, Eberhard/Lüderssen, Klaus/Volk, Klaus* [eds.], Unternehmensstrafrecht, 2012, p. 285; cited: *Ransiek*, Unternehmensstrafrecht, 285

Ransiek, Andreas, Zur strafrechtlichen Verantwortung von Unternehmen, NZWiSt 2012, 45; cited: *Ransiek*, NZWiSt 2012, 45

Rapp, Geoffrey C., Beyond Protection: Invigorating Incentives for Sarbanes-Oxley Corporate and Securities Fraud Whistleblowers, 87 B.U. L. Rev. 91 (2007); cited: *Rapp*, 87 B.U. L. Rev. 91 (2007), p.

Raum, Rolf, Strafrechtliche Pflichten von Compliance-Beauftragten - Zum Urteil des Bundesgerichtshofs vom 17.7.2009 (5 StR 394/08), CCZ 2012, 197; cited: *Raum*, CCZ 2012, 197

Reichert, Joachem/Ott, Nicolas, Non Compliance in der AG - Vorstandspflichten im Zusammenhang mit der Vermeidung, Aufklärung und Sanktionierung von Rechtsverstößen, ZIP 2009, 2173; cited: *Reichert/Ott*, ZIP 2009, 2173

Rettenmaier, Felix/Palm, Lisa, Das Ordnungswidrigkeitenrecht und die Aufsichtspflicht von Unternehmensverantwortlichen, NJOZ 2010, 1414; cited: *Rettenmaier/Palm*, NJOZ 2010, 1414

Reufels, Martin/Deviard, Katja, Die Implementierung von Whistleblower-Hotlines aus US-amerikanischer, europäischer und deutscher Sicht, CCZ 2009, 201; cited: *Reufels/Deviard*, CCZ 2009, 201

Ribstein, Larry E., Market vs. Regulatory Responses to Corporate Fraud: A Critique of the Sarbanes-Oxley Act of 2002, 28 Iowa J. Corp. L. 1 (2002); cited: *Ribstein*, 28 Iowa J. Corp. L. 1 (2002)

Ribstein, Larry E., Sarbanes-Oxley After Three Years, 3 NZ L. Rev. 365 (2005); cited: *Ribstein*, 3 NZ L. Rev. 365 (2005), p.

Ribstein, Larry E., Sarbox: the Road to Nirvana, 2004 Mich. St. L. Rev. 279; cited: *Ribstein*, 2004 Mich. St. L. Rev. 279, p.

Rieble, Volker, Zivilrechtliche Haftung der Compliance-Agenten, CCZ 2010, 1; cited: *Rieble*, CCZ 2010, 1

Rieder, Markus/Jerg, Marcus, Anforderungen an die Überprüfung von Compliance-Programmen - Zugleich kritische Anmerkungen zum Entwurf eines IDW Prüfungsstandards: Grundsätze ordnungsgemäßer Prüfung von Compliance-Management-Systemen (IDW PS 980), CCZ 2010, 201; cited: *Rieder/Jerg*, CCZ 2010, 201

Rodewald, Jörg/Unger, Ulrike, Corporate Compliance - Organisatorische Vorkehrungen zur Vermeidung von Haftungsfällen der Geschäftsleitung, BB 2006, 113; cited: *Rodewald/Unger*, BB 2006, 113

Rodewald, Jörg/Unger, Ulrike, Kommunikation und Krisenmanagement im Gefüge der Corporate Compliance-Organisation, BB 2007, 1629; *Rodewald/Unger*, BB 2007, 1629

Rodrigues, Usha/Stegemoller, Mike, Placebo Ethics: A Study in Securities Disclosure Arbitrage, 96 Va. L. Rev. 1 (2010); cited: *Rodrigues/Stegemoller*, 96 Va. L. Rev. 1 (2010), p.

Romano, Roberta, Does the Sarbanes-Oxley Act have a Future?, 26 Yale J. on Reg. 229 (2009); cited: *Romano*, 26 Yale J. on Reg. 229 (2009), p.

Romano, Roberta, The Sarbanes-Oxley Act and the Making of Quack Corporate Governance, 114 Yale L. J. 1521 (2005); cited: *Romano*, 114 Yale L. J. 1521 (2005), p.

Rosinus, Christian, Grenzen und Ansatzpunkte einer globalen Compliance-Organisation - Inwieweit ist eine globale Uniformität möglich, ZRFG 2008, 260; cited: *Rosinus*, ZRFG 2008, 260

Rostain, Tanina, General Counsel in the Age of Compliance: Preliminary Findings and New Research Questions, 21 Georgetown Journal of Legal Ethics 456 (2008); cited: *Rostain*, 21 Georgetown Journal of Legal Ethics 456 (2008), p.

Roth, Markus, Information und Organisation des Aufsichtsrats, ZGR 2012, 343; cited: *Roth*; ZGR 2012, 343

Roth, Markus, Möglichkeiten vorstandsunabhängiger Information des Aufsichtsrats, AG 2004, 1; cited: *Roth*, AG 2004, 1

Rotsch, Thomas, Criminal Compliance, ZIS 2010, 614; cited: *Rotsch*, ZIS 2010, 614

Roxin, Imme, Im Straf- und Strafprozessrecht geregelte Sanktionen gegen Unternehmen, in: *Kempf, Eberhard/Lüderssen, Klaus/Volk, Klaus* [eds.], Unternehmensstrafrecht, 2012, p. 37; cited: *Roxin*, in: Unternehmensstrafrecht, 37

Rübenstahl, Markus, Zur "regelmäßigen" Garantenstellung des Compliance Officers, NZG 2009, 1341; cited: *Rübenstahl*, NZG 2009, 1341

Rubin, Paul H., Common Law and Statute Law, 11 J. Legal Stud. 205 (1982); cited: *Rubin*, 11 J. Legal Stud. 205 (1982)

Rubin, Paul H., Micro and Macro Legal Efficiency: Supply and Demand, 13 Supreme Court Econ. Rev. 19 (2005); cited: *Rubin*, 13 Supreme Court Econ. Rev. 19 (2005)

Rubin, Paul H., Why is the Common Law Efficient?, 6 J. Legal Stud. 51 (1977); cited: *Rubin*, 6 J. Legal Stud. 51 (1977)

Ruder, David S./Sun, Yuji/Sycz, Arek, The Securities and Exchange Commission's Pre- and Post-Enron Responses to Corporate Financial Fraud: An Analysis and Evaluation, 80 Notre Dame L. Rev. 1103 (2005); cited: *Ruder/Sun/Sycz*, 80 Notre Dame L. Rev. 1103 (2005), p.

Rünnau, Thomas/Schneider, Frédéric, Der Compliance-Beauftragte als strafrechtlicher Garant, Überlegungen zum BGH-Urteil v. 17.7.2009 - 5 StR 294/08, ZIP 2010, 53; cited: *Rünnau/Schneider*, ZIP 2010, 53

Sachs, Michael, Ziele eines Unternehmensstrafrecht und die Frage seiner Vereinbarkeit mit dem Verfassungsrecht, in: *Kempf, Eberhard/Lüderssen, Klaus/Volk, Klaus* [eds.], Unternehmensstrafrecht, 2012, p. 195; cited: *Sachs*, in: Unternehmensstrafrecht, 195

Sahan, Oliver/Berndt, Thomas, Neue Kronzeugenregelung - aktive Beendigung von Korruptionssystemen durch effiziente Compliance-Strukturen alternativlos, BB 2010, 647; cited: *Sahan/Berndt*, BB 2010, 647

Sale, Hillary A., Delaware's Good Faith, 89 Cornell L. Rev. 456 (2004); cited: *Sale*, 89 Cornell L. Rev. 456 (2004), p.

Sale, Hillary A., Monitoring Caremark's Good Faith, 32 Del. J. Corp. L. 719 (2007); cited: *Sale*, 32 Del. J. Corp. L. 719 (2007), p.

Salvenmoser, Steffen/Hauschka, Christoph, Korruption, Datenschutz und Compliance, NJW 2010, 331; cited: *Salvenmoser/Hauschka*, NJW 2010, 331

Satzger, Helmut, "Schwarze Kassen" zwischen Untreue und Korruption - Eine Besprechung des Urteils BGH - 2 StR 587/07 (Siemens-Entscheidung), NStZ 2009, 297; cited: *Satzger*, NStZ 2009, 297

Scalia, Antonin, The Rule of Law as a Law of Rules, 56 U. Chi. L. Rev 1175 (1989); cited: *Scalia*, 56 U. Chi. L. Rev 1175 (1989), p.

Schaefer, Hans/Baumann, Compliance-Organization und Sanktionen bei Verstößen, NJW 2011, 3601; cited: *Schaefer/Baumann*, NJW 2011, 3601

Schäfer, Albrecht, Der Prüfungsausschuss – Arbeitsteilung im Aufsichtsrat, ZGR 2004, 416; cited: *Schäfer*, ZGR 2004, 416

Schemmel, Alexander, Minkoff, Andreas, Die Bedeutung des Wirtschaftsstrafrechts für Compliance Management Systeme und Prüfungen nach dem IDW PS 980, CCZ 2012, 49; cited: *Schemmel/Minkoff*, CCZ 2012, 49

Schmidt, Bernd, Vertrauen ist gut, Compliance ist besser! - Anforderungen an die Datenverarbeitung im Rahmen der Compliance-Überwachung, BB 2009, 1295; cited: *Schmidt*, BB 2009, 1295

Schmidt, Reinhard H./Spindler, Gerald, Path dependence and complementarity in corporate governance, in: *Gordon, Jeffery N./Roe, Mark J.* [eds.], Convergence and Persistence in Corporate Governance, 2004, p. 114; cited: *Schmidt/Spindler*, in: Convergence and Persistence, p.

Schmidt, Reinhard H./Tyrell, Marcel, What constitutes a financial system in general and the German financial system in particular?, Working Paper Series: Accounting & Finance No. 111, July 2003, available at: http://www.econbiz.de/archiv/f/uf/finanzierung/what_constitutes_system.pdf visited: January 2, 2014; cited: *Schmidt/Tyrell*, 2003, p.

Schneider, Hendrik, Das Unternehmen in der Schildkröten-Formation, Der Schutzbereich des Anwaltsprivilegs im deutschen und US-Strafrecht, ZIS 2016, 626; cited: *Schneider, H.*, ZIS 2016, 626

Schneider, Uwe H., Ausländisches Unternehmensstrafrecht und Compliance, CCZ 2008, 18; cited: *Schneider*, CCZ 2008, 18

Schneider, Uwe H., Compliance als Aufgabe der Unternehmensleitung, ZIP 2003, 645; cited: *Schneider*, ZIP 2003, 645

Schneider, Uwe H., Compliance im Konzern, NZG 2009, 1321; cited: *Schneider*, NZG 2009, 1321

Schneider, Uwe H., Investigative Maßnahmen und Informationsweitergabe im konzernfreien Unternehmen und im Konzern, NZG 2010, 1201; cited: *Schneider*, NZG 2010, 1201

Schoberth, Joerg/Servatius, Hand-Gerd/Thees, Alexander, Anforderungen an die Gestaltung von Internen Kontrollsystemen, BB 2006, 2571; cited: *Schoberth/Servatius/Thees*, BB 2006, 2571

Schulz, Mike, Compliance - Internes Whistleblowing, Die Verpflichtung zur Meldung von Fehlverhalten Dritter aus den arbeitsvertraglichen Nebenpflichten, BB 2011, 629; cited: *Schulz*, BB 2011, 629

Schürrle, Thomas/Fleck, Franziska, "Whistleblowing Unlimited" - Der U.S. Dodd-Frank Act und die neuen Regeln der SEC zum Whistleblowing, CCZ 2011, 218; cited: *Schürrle/Fleck*, CCZ 2011, 218

Schürrle, Thomas/Olbers, Lucie, Compliance-Verantwortung in der AG - Praktische Empfehlungen zur Haftungsbegrenzung an Vorstände und Aufsichtsrat, CCZ 2010, 102; cited: *Schürrle/Olbers*, CCZ 2010, 102

Seffer, Adi/Mayer-Wegelin, Clemens, Whistleblowing - Chancen und Risiken von Hinweisgebersystemen für Unternehmen, ITRB 2009, 41; cited: *Seffer/Mayer-Wegelin*, ITRB 2009, 41

Seibert, Ulrich, Das 10-Punkte-Programm 'Unternehmensintegrität und Anlegerschutz', BB 2003, 693; cited: *Seibert*, BB 2003, 693

Seibt, Christoph H., Informationsfluss zwischen Vorstand und Aufsichtsrat (dualistisches Leitungssystem) bzw. innerhalb des Verwaltungsrats (monoistisches Leitungssystem), in: *Hommelhoff, Peter/Hopt, Klaus J. /v. Werder, Axel* [eds.], Handbuch Corporate Governance: Leitung und Überwachung börsennotierter Unternehmen in der Rechts- und Wirtschaftspraxis, 2nd edition, 2009, p. 391; cited: *Seibt*, Hdb Corporate Governance, 391

Seibt, Christoph H./Cziupka, Johannes, 20 Thesen zur Compliance-Verantwortung im System der Organhaftung aus Anlass des Siemens/Neubürger-Urteils LG München I vom 10.12.2013 - 5 HK O 1387/10, DB 2014, 1598; cited: *Seibt/Cziupka*, DB 2014, 1598

Seligman, Joel, The SEC at 70: A Modest revolution in Corporate Governance, 80 Notre Dame L. Rev. 1159 (2005); cited: *Seligman*, 80 Notre Dame L. Rev. 1159 (2005), p.

Shakespeare, Catherine, Sarbanes-Oxley Act of 2002 Five Years On: What Have We Learned?, 3 J. Bus. & Tech. 333 (2008); cited: *Shakespeare*, 3 J. Bus. & Tech. 333 (2008), p.

Shishido, Zenichi, "Enterprise Law" as the Infrastructure of Incentive Mechanism: The Case of Sox and J-Sox, Working Paper Corporate Governance Workshop at Yale Law School on October 29, 2008; cited: *Shishido*, 2008, p.

Smith, Murphy L./Drake, Michael S./Shaub, Michael, Pivotal Change in US Public Policy: How the Sarbanes-Oxley Act Affected Internal Auditing and Its Relationship to External Auditing, September 2009, available at: http://ssrn.com/abstract=1474463 visited: March 16, 2011; cited: *Smith/Drake/Shaub*, 2009

Spießhofer, Birgit, Die neue europäische Richtlinie über die Offenlegung nichtfinanzieller Informationen - Paradigmenwechsel oder Papiertiger?, NZG 2014, 1281; cited: *Spießhofer*, NZG 2014, 1281

Spindler, Gehard, Compliance in der multinationalen Bankengruppe, WM 2008, 905; cited: *Spindler*, WM 2008, 905

Spinelli, Joseph/Moritz, Scott/Perlman, Jay, Using Technology to Develop a Risk-Based Approach to FCPA Compliance, in: *Biegelman, Martin T./Biegelman, Daniel R.*, Foreign Corrupt Practices Act Compliance Guidebook - Protecting Your Organization from Bribery and Corruption, 2010, p. 230-234; cited: *Spinelli/Moritz/Perlman*, in: FCPA Guidebook, p. 230

Srinivansan, Suraj/Piotroski, Joseph D., Regulation and Bonding: The Sarbanes-Oxley Act and the Flow of International Listings, Rock Center Working Paper No. 11, January 2008, available at: http://ssrn.com/abstract=956987 visited: March 16, 2011; cited: *Srinivansan/Piotroski*, 2011, p.

Stadtmann, Georg/Wißmann, Markus, Risikomanagement und Interne Kontrollsysteme im deutsch/amerikanischen Vergleich - Einfluss des Sarbanes-Oxley-Acts, ZRFG 2006, 16; cited: *Stadtmann/Wißmann*, ZRFG 2006, 16

Stamm, Florian, A Comparative Study of Monitoring of Management in German and U.S. Corporations After Sarbanes-Oxley: Where are the German Enrons, WorldComs, and Tycos?, 32 Ga. J. Int'l & Comp. L. 813 (2004); cited: *Stamm*, 32 Ga. J. Int'l & Comp. L. 813 (2004), p.

Stansbury, Jason/Barry, Bruce, Ethics Programs and the Paradox of Control, 2007, available at: http://ssrn.com/abstract=962499 visited: November 14, 2011; cited: *Stansbury/Barry*, 2007, p.

Steele, Myron T., Sarbanes-Oxley: The Delaware Perspective, 52 N.Y.L. Sch. L. Rev. 503 (2007-2008); cited: *Steele*, 52 N.Y.L. Sch. L. Rev. 503 (2007-2008), p.

Steele, Myron T./Verret J. W., Delaware's Guidance: Ensuring Equity for the Modern Witenagemot, 2 Va. L. & Bus. Rev. 189 (2007); cited: *Steele/Verret*, 2 Va. L. & Bus. Rev. 189 (2007), p.

Stefou, Marina, The SOX 404 Procedure; Is it Still so Repelling to Foreign Issuers?, Corporate Ownership & Control, Vol. 6, Issue 1 2008, 147; cited: *Stefou*, Corporate Ownership & Control 2008, p.

Stevelman, Faith, Foreword to Corporate Governance Five Years After Sarbanes-Oxley: Is there Real Change?, 52, N.Y.L. Sch. L. Rev. 475 (2007-2008); cited: *Stevelman*, 52, N.Y.L. Sch. L. Rev. 475 (2007-2008), p.

Stoltenberg, Clyde/Lacey, Kathleen A./George, Barbara C./Cuthbert, Michael, A Comparative Analysis of Post-Sarbanes-Oxley Corporate Governance Developments in the US and European Union: The Impact of Tensions Created by Extraterritorial Application of Section 404, 53 Am. J. Comp. L. 457 (2005); cited: *Stoltenberg/Lacey/George/Cuthbert*, 53 Am. J. Comp. L. 457 (2005), p.

Strieder, Thomas, Erweiterung der Lageberichterstattung nach dem BilMoG, BB 2009, 1002; cited: *Strieder*, BB 2009, 1002

Sünner, Eckart, Rechtliche Grundlagen für Aufsichtsratsprüfungsausschüsse und ihre Aufgabenwahrnehmung auf dem Gebiet der Compliance, CCZ 2008, 56; cited: *Sünner*, CCZ 2008, 56

Swenson, Winthrop M./Clark, Nolan E., The New Federal Sentencing Guidelines: Three Keys to Understanding the Credit for Compliance Programs, 1 Corporate Conduct Quarterly 1 (1991); cited: *Swenson/Clark*, 1 Corporate Conduct Quarterly 1 (1991)

Sybon, Ernst, IKS/BilMoG/COSO/SOX, Entwicklungen eines auf COSO basierenden Modells zur Erfüllung der Vorschriften des Bilanzrechtsmodernisierungsgesetzes hinsichtlich der Mindestanforderungen eines wirksamen internen Kontrollsystems für den Rechnungslegungsprozess, ZIR 2011, 93; cited: *Sybon*, ZIR 2011, 93

Szesny, André-M, Beschlagnahme von Unterlagen beim Ombudsmann? Anmerkungen und Praxishinweise zu LG Bochum, Beschl. v. 16.3.16 – 6 Qs 1/16, CCZ 2017, 25; cited: *Szesny*, CCZ 2017, 25

Talukdar, Ashoke S., The Voice of Reason: The Corporate Compliance Officer and the Regulated Corporate Environment, 6 U.C. Davis Bus. L. J. 45 (2005); cited: *Talukdar*, 6 U.C. Davis Bus. L. J. 45 (2005), p.

Theile, Hans, Unternehmensrichtlinien - Ein Beitrag zur Prävention von Wirtschaftskriminalität?, ZIS 2008, 417; cited: *Theile*, ZIS 2008, 417

Theile, Hans/Petermann, Stefan, Die Sanktionierung von Unternehmen nach dem OWiG, JuS 2011, 496; cited: *Theile/Petermann*, JuS 2011, 496

Theisen, Manuel R., Gesetzliche versus funktionsgerechte Informationsversorgung - Eine Einladung zur interdisziplinären Diskussion, ZGR 2013, 1; cited: *Theisen*, ZGR 2013, 1

Theusinger, Ingo/Liese, Jens, Besteht eine Rechtspflicht zur Dokumentation von Riskioüberwachungssystemen i.S. des § 91 II 1 AktG?, NZG 2008, 289; cited: *Theusinger/Liese*, NZG 2008, 289

Thomas, Stefan, Bericht über die Diskussion zu den Referaten Dreher und Weber-Rey ("Risikomanagement nach dem BilMoG"), ZGR 2010, 591; *Thomas*, ZGR 2010, 591

Thompson, Robert B., Collaborative Corporate Governance: Listing Standards, State Law, and Federal Regulation, 38 Wake Forest L. Rev. 961 (2003); cited: *Thompson*, 38 Wake Forest L. Rev. 961 (2003), p.

Thompson, Robert B., Corporate Governance After Enron, 40 Hous. L. Rev. 99 (2003); cited: *Thompson*, 40 Hous. L. Rev. 99 (2003), p.

Thompson, Robert B./Sale, Hillary A., Securities Fraud as Corporate Governance: Reflections Upon Federalism, 56 Vand. L. Rev. 859 (2003); cited: *Thompson/Sale*, 56 Vand. L. Rev. 859 (2003)

v. Busekist, Konstantin/ Fahrig, Stephan, Whistleblowing und der Schutz von Hinweisgebern, BB 2013, 119; cited: *v. Busekist/Fahrig*, BB 2013, 119 *v. Busekist, Konstantin/Hein, Oliver*, Der IDW PS 980 und die allgemeinen Rechtlichen Mindestanforderungen an ein wirksames Compliance Management System (1) - Grundlagen, Kultur und Ziele, CCZ 2012, 41; cited: *v. Busekist/Hein*, CCZ 2012, 41

v. Busekist, Konstantin/Schlitt, Christian, Der IDW PS 980 und die allgemeinen rechtlichen Mindestanfoderungen an ein wirksames Compliance Management System (2) - Risikoermittlungspflicht, CCZ 2012, 86; cited: *v. Busekist/Schlitt*, CCZ 2012, 86

v. Hulle, Karel/Maul, Silja, Aktionsplan zur Modernisierung des Gesellschaftsrechts und Stärkung der Corporate Governance, ZGR 2004, 484; cited: *v. Hulle/Maul*, ZGR 2004, 484

v. Rosen, Rüdiger, Fehlentwicklungen bei Compliance und Risikomanagement - Zugleich eine Anmerkung zum Regierungsentwurf des BilMoG, AG 2008, 537; cited: *v. Rosen*, AG 2008, 537

v. Rosen, Rüdiger, Zielkonflikt - Unerwünschte Nebenfolgen eines Unternehmensstrafrechts, in: *Kempf, Eberhard/Lüderssen, Klaus/Volk, Klaus* [eds.], Unternehmensstrafrecht, 2012, p. 263; cited: *v. Rosen*, in: Unternehmensstrafrecht, 263

van der Elst, Christoph/van Daelen, Marijn, Risk Management in European and American Corporate Law, Working Paper No. 122/2009, April 2009, available at: http://ssrn.com/abstract=1399647 visited: April 24, 2013; cited: *van der Elst/van Daelen*, 2009, p.

Veasey, E. Norman/Di Guglielmo, Christine T., What Happened in Delaware Corporate Law and Governance From 1992-2004? A Retrospective on Some Key Developments, 153 U. Pa. L. Rev. 1399 (2005); cited: *Veasey/Di Guglielmo*, 153 U. Pa. L. Rev. 1399 (2005), p.

Veasey, Norman E., State-Federal Tension in Corporate Governance and the Professional Responsibilities of Advisors, 28 Iowa J. Corp. L. 441 (2003); cited: *Veasey*, 28 Iowa J. Corp. L. 441 (2003), p.

Velte, Patrick, Direktzugriff des Aufsichtsrats auf die Interne Revision - Ausnahme oder Regelfall?, NZG 2011, 1401; cited: *Velte*, NZG 2011, 1401

Vetter, Eberhard, Der Prüfungsausschuss in der AG nach dem BilMoG - Aufgaben und Zusammensetzung, ZGR 2010, 751; cited: *Vetter*, ZGR 2010, 751

Voet van Vormizeele, Philipp, Kartellrechtliche Compliance-Programme im Rahmen der Bußgeldbemessung *de lege lata* und *de lege ferenda*, CCZ 2009, 41; cited: *Voet v. Vormizeele*, CCZ 2009, 41

Vogel, Florian/Glas, Vera, Datenschutzrechtliche Probleme unternehmensinterner Ermittlungen, DB 2009, 1747; cited: *Vogel/Glas*, DB 2009, 1747

Vogler, Matthias/Gundert, Martin, Einführung von Risikomanagementsystemen - Hinweise zur praktischen Ausgestaltung -, DB 1998, 2377; cited: *Vogler/Gundert*, DB 1998, 2377

Vogt, Volker, Compliance und Investigations - Zehn Fragen aus Sicht der arbeitsrechtlichen Praxis, NJOZ 2009, 4206; cited: *Vogt*, NJOZ 2009, 4206

Voigt, Stefan, Institutionenökonomik, 2002; cited: *Voigt*, 2002

von Zimmermann, Georg, "Whistleblowing" - Anforderungen des Sarbanes-Oxley-Acts, WM 2007, 1060; cited: *von Zimmermann*, WM 2007, 1060

Wackerbarth, Ulrich, Investorvertrauen und Corporate Governance, ZGR 2005, 686; cited: *Wackerbarth*, ZGR 2005, 686

Wade, Cheryl L., Sarbanes-Oxley Five Years Later: Will Criticism of SOX Undermine Its Benefits?, 39 Loy. U. Chi. L. J. 595 (2008); cited: *Wade*, 39 Loy. U. Chi. L. J. 595 (2008), p.

Wagner, Jens, "Internal Investigations" und ihre Verankerung im Recht der AG, CCZ 2009, 8; cited: *Wagner*, CCZ 2009, 8

Wagner, Klaus R./Spemann, Thomas F., Organhaftungs- und Strafbarkeitsrisiken für Aufsichtsräte, NZG 2015, 945; cited: *Wagner/Spemann*, NZG 2015, 945

Waxman, Robert N., A Test of Controls, The CPA Journal 2004, available at: http://www.nysscpa.org/printversions/cpaj/2004/804/p26.htm visited: February 8, 2011; cited: *Waxman*, CPA Journal 2004

Webb, Dan K./Molo Steven F., Some Practical Considerations in Developing Effective Compliance Programs: A Framework for Meeting the Requirements of the Sentencing Guidelines, 71 Wash. U. L. Q. 375 (1993); cited: *Webb/Molo*, 71 Wash. U. L. Q. 375 (1993), p.

Weber, Jürgen/Weißenberger, Barbara/Liekweg, Arnim, Ausgestaltung eines unternehmerischen Chancen- und Risikomanagements nach dem KonTraG, DStR 1999, 1710; cited: *Weber/Weißenberger/Liekweg*, DStR 1999, 1710

Weber, Stefan C./Lentfer, Thies/Köster, Max, Einfluss der Corporate Governance auf die Kapitalkosten eines Unternehmens - Ein institutionenökonomischer Erklärungsansatz, eine Bestandsaufnahme empirischer Studienergebnisse und eine Partialbetrachtung des Corporate Governance Reporting, ZCG 2007, 53; cited: *Weber/Lentfer/Köster*, ZCG 2007, 53

Weber, Stefan/Velte Patrick, Die Bedeutung von Corporate Governance Reports aus Investorensicht - Eine empirische Untersuchung im DAX, DStR 2011, 1141; cited: *Weber/Velte*, DStR 2011, 1141

Weber-Rey, Daniela, Ausstrahlungen des Aufsichtsrechts (insbesondere für Banken und Versicherungen) auf das Aktienrecht - oder die Infiltration von Regelungssätzen?, ZGR 2010, 543; cited: *Weber-Rey*, ZGR 2010, 543

Weber-Rey, Daniela, Effects of the Better Regulation Approach on European Company Law and Corporate Governance, ECFR 2007, 370; cited: *Weber-Rey*, ECFR 2007, 370

Weber-Rey, Daniela, Festung Unternehmen oder System von Schlüsselfunktionen - ein Diskussionsbeitrag zum Thema Risiko, Haftung und Unternehmensstrafrecht, in: *Kempf, Eberhard/Lüderssen, Klaus/Volk, Klaus* [eds.], Unternehmensstrafrecht, 2012, p. 321; cited: *Weber-Rey*, in: Unternehmensstrafrecht, 321

Weber-Rey, Daniela, Gesellschafts- und aufsichtsrechtliche Herausforderungen an die Unternehmensorganisation - Aktuelle Entwicklungen im Bereich Corporate Governance, Compliance und Risikomanagement, AG 2008, 345; cited: *Weber-Rey*, AG 2008, 345

Weinstein, Martin/Meyer, Robert J./ Clark, Jeffrey D., Sharp Increases in Recent FCPA Enforcement, The Harvard Law School Forum on Corporate Governance and Financial Regulation, May 9, 2010, available at: http://blogs.law.harvard.edu/corpgov/2010/05/09/sharp-increases-in-recent-fcpa-enforcement/ visited: March 15, 2011; cited: *Weinstein/Meyer/Clark*, 2010

Weissmann, Andrew, A New Approach to Corporate Criminal Liability, 44 American Criminal Law Review 1319 (2007), available at: http://ssrn.com/abstract=1085400 visited: April 3, 2015; cited: *Weissmann*, 2007, p.

Werner, Rüdiger, Die Enthaftung des Vorstands: Die strafrechtliche Dimension, CCZ 2011, 201; *Werner*, CCZ 2011, 201

Werner, Rüdiger, Die zivilrechtliche Haftung des Vorstands einer AG für gegen die Gesellschaft verhängte Geldbußen gegenüber der Gesellschaft, CCZ 2010, 143; cited: *Werner*, CCZ 2010, 143

Westhausen, Hans-Ulrich, Das COSO-Modell: bisher nur eine Randerscheinung in Deutschland?, Ein 13 Jahre altes IKS-Modell und seine Verbreitung in Deutschland, ZIR 2005, 98; *Westhausen*, ZIR 2005, 98

Wiederholt, Norbert/Walter, Andreas, Compliance - Anforderungen an die Unternehmensorganisation, BB 2011, 968; cited: *Wiederholt/Walter*, BB 2011, 968

Willems, Marion, Der Sarbanes-Oxley-Act - Anforderungen, praktische Umsetzung und Lessons Learned, ZRFC 2007, 79; cited: *Willems*, ZRFC 2007, 79

Wilsing, Hans-Ulrich, Corporate Governance in Deutschland und Europa - Die Rolle der institutionellen Investoren, der Proxy Advisors und die der Aktionäre, ZGR 2012, 291; cited: *Wilsing*, ZGR 2012, 291

Windbichler, Christine, Corporate Governance internationaler Konzerne unter dem Einfluss kapitalmarktrechtlicher Anforderungen, in: *Hommelhoff, Peter/Hopt, Klaus J. /v. Werder, Axel* [eds.], Handbuch Corporate Governance: Leitung und Überwachung börsennotierter Unternehmen in der Rechts- und Wirtschaftspraxis, 2nd edition, 2009, p. 825; cited: *Windbichler*, Hdb Corporate Governance, 825

Windbichler, Christine, Zur Trennung von Geschäftsführung und Kontrolle bei amerikanischen Großgesellschaften. Eine "neue" Entwicklung und europäische Regelungen im Vergleich, ZGR 1985, 50; cited: *Windbichler*, ZGR 1985, 50

Wisskirchen, Gerlind/Jordan, Christopher/Bissels, Alexander, DB 2005, 2190; cited: *Wisskirchen/Jordan/Bissels*, DB 2005, 2190

Wisskirchen, Gerlind/Körber, Anke/Bissels, Alexander, 'Whistleblowing' und 'Ethikhotlines', Probleme des deutschen Arbeits- und Datenschutzrechts, BB 2006, 1567; cited: *Wisskirchen/Körber/Bissels*, BB 2006, 1567

Withus, Karl-Heinz, Neue Anforderungen nach BilMoG zur Beschreibung der wesentlichen Merkmale des Internen Kontroll- und Risikomanagementsystems im Lagebericht kapitatmarktorientierter Unternehmen, KoR 2009, 440; cited: *Withus*, KoR 2009, 440

Withus, Karl-Heinz, Sicherstellung der Compliance durch wirksame Managementsysteme, ZIR 2010, 99; cited: *Withus*, ZIR 2010, 99

Withus, Karl-Heinz, Zur Umsetzung der HGB-Modernisierung durch das BilMoG: Wirksamkeitsüberwachung interner Kontroll- und Risikomanagementsysteme durch Aufsichtsorgane kapitalmarktorientierter Gesellschaften, DB 2009, Beilage 5, 82; cited: *Withus*, DB 2009, Beilage 5, 82

Withus, Karl-Heinz/Hein, Oliver, Prüfung oder Zertifizierung eines Compliance Management Systems - Voraussetzungen und mögliche Rechtsfolgen, CCZ 2011, 125; cited: *Withus/Hein*, CCZ 2011, 125

Wohlers, Wolfgang, Strafzwecke und Sanktionsarten in einem Unternehmensstrafrecht, in: *Kempf, Eberhard/Lüderssen, Klaus/Volk, Klaus* [eds.], Unternehmensstrafrecht, 2012, p. 231; cited: *Wohlers*, in: Unternehmensstrafrecht, 231

Wohlmannstetter, Gottfried, Risikomanagement nach dem BilMoG, ZGR 2010, 472; cited: *Wohlmannstetter*, ZGR 2010, 472

Wolf, Klaus, Der IDW Prüfungsstandard 980 zur ordnungsgemäßen Prüfung von Compliance Management Systemen, DStR 2011, 997; cited: *Wolf*, DStR 2011, 997

Wolf, Klaus, Zur Anforderung eines internen Kontroll- und Risikomanagementsystems im Hinblick auf den (Konzern-) Rechnungslegungsprozess gemäß BilMoG, DStR 2009, 920; cited: *Wolf*, DStR 2009, 920

Wybitul, Tim, Das neue Bundesdatenschutzgesetz: Verschärfte Regeln für Compliance und interne Ermittlungen, BB 2009, 1582; cited: *Wybitul*, BB 2009, 1582

Wybitul, Tim, Schwarze Kassen sind strafbar, BB 2009, 111; cited: *Wybitul*, BB 2009, 111

Wybitul, Tim, Strafbarkeitsrisiken für Compliance-Verantwortliche, BB 2009, 2590; cited: *Wybitul*, BB 2009, 2590

Zhang, Ivy X., Economic Consequences of the Sarbanes-Oxley Act of 2002, February 2007, available at: http://ssrn.com/abstract=961964 visited: April 23, 2012; cited: *Zhang*, 2007, p.

Zhang, Jian/Pany, Kurt Current Research Questions on Internal Control over Financial Reporting Under Sarbanes-Oxley, The CPA Journal 2008, available at: http://www.nysscpa.org/printversions/cpaj/2008/208/p42.htm visited: February 8, 2011; cited: *Zhang/Pany*, CPA Journal 2008

Zhang, Yan/Zhou, Jian/Zhou, Nan, Audit Committee Quality, Auditor Independence, and Internal Control Weaknesses, 2006, available at: http://ssrn.com/abstract=925732 visited: March 16, 2011; cited: *Zhang/Zhou/Zhou*, 2006

Zimmer, Mark/Seebacher, Krikor R., Whistleblowing - Wichtige Erkenntnisquelle oder gefährliches Pflaster?, CCZ 2013, 31; cited: *Zimmer/Seebacher*, CCZ 2013, 31

Zywicki, Todd J., The Rise and Fall of Efficiency in Common Law: A Supply-Side Analysis, Law and Economics Working Paper Series 02-21 December 2003, available at: http://ssrn.com/abstract_id=326740 visited: February 15, 2012; cited: *Zywicki*, 2003

B. Materials

Aguilar, Melissa K., 404 Disclosures Show Dramatic Improvement, Compliance Week, November 27, 2007, available at: http://www.complianceweek.com/index.cfm?printable=1&fuseaction=article.viewArticle&article_ID=3804 visited: March 14, 2012; cited: *Aguilar*, 2007

American Electronics Association (AeA), Sarbanes-Oxley Section 404: The 'Section' of Unintended Consequences and its Impact on Small Business, February 2005, available at: http://www.businesswire.com/portal/binary/com.epicentric.contentmanagement.servlet.ContentDeliveryServlet/services/ir_and_pr/ir_resource_center/editorials/2005/AEA.pdf visited: April 26, 2012; cited: AeA, 2005

American Institute of Certified Public Accountants (AICPA), Management Override of Internal Controls: The Achilles' Heel of Fraud Prevention, The Audit Committee and Oversight of Financial Reporting, 2005, available at: http://www.aicpa.org/forthepublic/auditcommitteeeffectiveness/downloadabledocuments/achilles_heel.pdf visited: April 2, 2012; cited: AICPA, 2005

American Institute of Certified Public Accountants (AICPA), Statement on Auditing Standards No. 1, November 1972; cited: AICPA, SAS 1, §

arc morgan, Sarbanes-Oxley Implementation Costs - What companies are reporting in their SEC Filings, February 2005, available at: http://www.auditnet.org/articles/Sarbanes-Oxley_Implementation_Costs.pdf visited: April 23, 2012; cited: *arc morgan*, 2005, p.

Article 29 Data Protection Working Party, Opinion 1/2006 on the application of EU data protection rules to internal whistleblowing schemes in the fields of accounting, internal accounting controls, auditing matters, fight against bribery, banking and financial crime, 00195/06/EN WP 117, adopted February 1, 2006; cited: *Art. 29 Working Party*, 2006, p.

Association of Certified Fraud Examiners, Report to the Nations on Occupational Fraud and Abuse, 2006, available at: http://www.acfe.com/uploadedFiles/ACFE_Website/Content/documents/2006-rttn.pdf visited: July 18, 2012; cited: ACFE Report 2006, p.

Association of Certified Fraud Examiners, Report to the Nations on Occupational Fraud and Abuse, 2010, available at: http://www.acfe.com/uploadedFiles/ACFE_Website/Content/documents/rttn-2010.pdf visited: April 25, 2011; cited: ACFE Report 2010, p.

Association of Certified Fraud Examiners, Report to the Nations on Occupational Fraud and Abuse, 2012, available at: http://www.acfe.com/uploadedFiles/ACFE_Website/Content/rttn/2012-report-to-nations.pdf visited: May 14, 2012; ACFE Report 2012, p.

Baker & Hostetler LLP, NYSE Enforcement Memos Provide Guidance on Sanctions Determinations and the Benefits of "Extraordinary Cooperation", Executive Alert, October 2005, available at: http://www.bakerlaw.com/files/publicdocs/nyse.pdf visited: October 11, 2011; cited: *Baker & Hostetler*, Executive Alert, p.

Bressac, Annie, The COSO risk framework: A reference for internal control? Transition from COSO I to COSO II, IAS Conference, November 25, 2005, available at: http://ec.europa.eu/dgs/internal_audit/pdf/conference_2005/bressac.pdf visited: November 2, 2011; cited: *Bressac*, 2005, p.

Breuer, Lanny A., Assistant Attorney General Lanny A. Breuer Speaks at the 24th National Conference on the Foreign Corrupt Practices Act, November 16, 2010, available at: http://www.justice.gov/criminal/pr/speeches/2010/crm-speech-101116.html visited: October 12, 2011; cited: *Breuer*, 2010

Bundesanstalt für Finanzdienstleistungsaufsicht, Mindestanforderungen an die Geschäftsorganisation von Versicherungsunternehmen (MaGo), Rundschreiben 2/2017 (VA), January 2017, available at: https://www.bafin.de/SharedDocs/Veroeffentlichungen/DE/Rundschreiben/2017/rs_1702_mago_va.html?nn=8236192 visited: February 13, 2017; cited: BaFin, MaGo, mar.

Bundesanstalt für Finanzdienstleistungsaufsicht, Mindestanforderungen an das Risikomanagement - MaRisk, Rundschreiben 10/2012 (BA), December 2012, available at: https://www.bafin.de/SharedDocs/Veroeffentlichungen/DE/Rundschreiben/rs_1210_marisk_ba.html visited: February 13, 2017; cited: BaFin, MaRisk (BA), mar.

Bundesanstalt für Finanzdienstleistungsaufsicht, Mindestanforderungen an die Compliance-Funktion und die weiteren Verhaltens-, Organisations- und Transparenzpflichten nach §§ 31 ff. WpHG für Wertpapierdienstleistungsunternehmen (MaComp), Rundschreiben 4/2010 (WA), August 2012, available at: http://www.bafin.de/SharedDocs/Veroeffentlichungen/DE/Rundschreiben/rs_1004_wa_macomp.html visited: September 18, 2012; cited: BaFin, MaComp, mar.

Bundesanstalt für Finanzdienstleistungsaufsicht, Circular 3/2009 – Minimum Requirements for Risk Management in Insurance Undertakings, January 2009, available at: http://www.bafin.de/SharedDocs/Veroeffentlichungen/EN/Rundschreiben/rs_0903_va_marisk_en_va.html?nn=2821306 visited: September 9, 2012; cited: BaFin, MaRisk (VA),

Bundeskartellamt, Bekanntmachung Nr. 9/2006 über den Erlass und die Reduktion von Geldbußen in Kartellsachen - Bonusregelung - vom 7. März 2006; cited: Bundeskartellamt, Bonusregelung

Bundeskartellamt, Leitlinien für die Bußgeldzumessung in Kartellordnungswidrigkeitenverfahren, June 25, 2013, available at: http://www.bundeskartellamt.de/wDeutsch/download/pdf/Merkblaetter/Merkblaetter_deutsch/Bekanntmachung-_Bu__geldleitlinien-Juni_2013.pdf visited: November 11, 2013; cited: Bundeskartellamt, Bußgeldzumessung

Bundeskriminalamt, Bundeslagebild, Korruption 2006, available at: http://www.bka.de/nn_193368/SharedDocs/Downloads/DE/Publikationen/JahresberichteUndLagebilder/Korruption/korruptionBundeslagebild2006,templateId=raw,property=publicationFile.pdf/korruptionBundeslagebild2006.pdf visited: March 12, 2013; cited: BKA, Korruptionsbericht 2006, p.

Bundeskriminalamt, Korruption, Bundeslagebild 2011, available at: http://www.bka.de/nn_193368/SharedDocs/Downloads/DE/Publikationen/JahresberichteUndLagebilder/Korruption/korruptionBundeslagebild2011,templateId=raw,property=publicationFile.pdf/korruptionBundeslagebild2011.pdf visited: March 12, 2013; cited: BKA, Korruptionsbericht 2011, p.

Bundeskriminalamt, Korruption, Bundeslagebild 2015, available at: https://www.bka.de/SharedDocs/Downloads/DE/Publikationen/JahresberichteUndLagebilder/Korruption/korruptionBundeslagebild2015.pdf visited: April 6, 2017; cited: BKA, Korruptionsbericht 2015, p.

Bundeskriminalamt, Lagebild Korruption, Bundesrepublik Deutschland 2002, available at: http://www.bka.de/nn_193368/SharedDocs/Downloads/DE/Publikationen/JahresberichteUndLagebilder/Korruption/korruptionBundeslagebild2002,templateId=raw,property=publicationFile.pdf/korruptionBundeslagebild2002.pdf visited: March 12, 2013; cited: BKA, Korruptionsbericht 2002, p.

Bundesverband der Deutschen Industrie e.V., Korruption verhindern – Empfehlungen des BDI, 3rd edition, BDI-Drucksache Nr. 390; cited: BDI, Drs. 390

Bussmann, Kai-D./Krieg, Oliver/Nestler, Claudia/Savenmoser, Steffen/et. al., Compliance und Unternehmenskultur, Zur aktuellen Situation in deutschen Großunternehmen, edited by PricewaterhouseCoopers and Martin-Luther-Universität Halle-Wittenberg, February 2010, available at: http://www.pwc.de/de_DE/de/risiko-management/assets/studie_Compliance-und-Unternehmenskultur.pdf visited: November 9, 2012; cited: *Bussmann*, PwC Study 2010, p.

Bussmann, Kai-D./Nestler, Claudia/Savenmoser, Steffen, Studie zur Wirtschaftskriminalität 2011: Kommissar Zufall deckt am meisten auf, edited by PricewaterhouseCoopers and Martin-Luther-Universität Halle-Wittenberg, October 2011, available at: http://www.pwc.de/de/risiko-management/studie-zur-wirtschaftskriminalitaet-2011-kommissar-zufall-deckt-am-meisten-auf.jhtml visited: November 9, 2012; cited: *Bussmann*, PwC Study 2011

Bussmann, Kai-D./Nestler, Claudia/Salvenmoser, Steffen, Wirtschaftskriminalität und Unternehmenskultur 2013, edited by PricewaterhouseCoopers and Martin-Luther-Universität Halle-Wittenberg, November 2013, available at: http://files.vogel.de/vogelonline/vogelonline/files/5947.pdf visited: April 6, 2017; cited: *Bussmann*, PwC Study 2013, p.

Bussmann, Kai-D./Nestler, Claudia/Salvenmoser, Steffen, Wirtschaftskriminalität in der analogen und digitalen Wirtschaft 2016, edited by PricewaterhouseCoopers and Martin-Luther-Universität Halle-Wittenberg, Februar 2016, available at: http://www.pwc.de/de/risiko-management/assets/studie-wirtschaftskriminalitaet-2016.pdf visited: April 6, 2017; cited: *Bussmann*, PwC Study 2016, p.

Charles River Associates International, Sarbanes-Oxley Section 404 Costs and Implementation Issues: Spring 2006 Survey Update, April 2006, available at: http://www.complianceweek.com/s/documents/cra_survey.pdf visited: April 24, 2012; cited: *Charles River Associates*, 2006, p.

Charles River Associates, Sarbanes-Oxley Section 404 Costs and Remediation of Deficiencies: Estimates from a Sample of Fortune 1000 Companies, April 2005, available at: http://www.sec.gov/spotlight/soxcomp/soxcomp-all-attach.pdf visited: March 15, 2012; cited: *Charles River Associates*, 2005, p.

Committee of Sponsoring Organizations of the Treadway Commission (COSO), Internal Control – Integrated Framework, Mai 2013; cited: COSO I, mar.

Committee of Sponsoring Organizations of the Treadway Commission (COSO), Enterprise Risk Management – Integrated Framework, September 2004; cited: COSO II, p.

Committee of Sponsoring Organizations of the Treadway Commission (COSO), Internal control over Financial Reporting – Guidance for Smaller Public Companies, 2006; cited: COSO Guidance for Smaller Public Companies

Committee of Sponsoring Organizations of the Treadway Commission (COSO), Internal Control – Integrated Framework, Guidance on Monitoring Internal Control Systems, Introduction, January 2009, available at: http://www.coso.org/documents/COSO_Guidance_On_Monitoring_Intro_online1.pdf visited: September 15, 2011; cited: COSO Monitoring Introduction, p.

Committee of Sponsoring Organizations of the Treadway Commission (COSO), Internal Control – Integrated Framework, Guidance on Monitoring Internal Control Systems, January 2009; cited: COSO Monitoring, p.

Committee of Sponsoring Organizations of the Treadway Commission (COSO), COSO'S 2010 Report, Current State of Enterprise Risk Oversight and Market Perceptions of COSO's ERM Framework, December 2010, available at: http://www.coso.org/documents/COSOSurveyReportFULL-Web-R6FINALforWEBPOSTING111710.pdf visited: September 21, 2011; cited: COSO, Report, 2010

Committee of Sponsoring Organizations of the Treadway Commission (COSO), COSO Homepage, available at: http://www.coso.org/ visited: March 23, 2012; cited: COSO Homepage

Committee of Sponsoring Organizations of the Treadway Commission (COSO), Effective Enterprise Risk Oversight, The Role of the Board of Directors, 2009, available at: http://www.coso.org/documents/COSOBoardsERM4pager-FINALRELEASEVERSION82409_001.pdf visited: September 21, 2011; cited: COSO, 2009

Committee of Sponsoring Organizations of the Treadway Commission (COSO), COSO Internal Control-Integrated Framework – Frequently Asked Questions, May 2013, available at: https://www.coso.org/Documents/COSO-FAQs-May-2013-branded.pdf visited: February 17, 2017; cited: COSO, 2013 FAQ, no.

Committee of Sponsoring Organizations of the Treadway Commission (COSO), COSO Internal Control – Integrated Framework – Executive Summary, May 2013, available at: https://www.coso.org/Documents/990025P-Executive-Summary-final-may20.pdf visited: February 17, 2017; cited: COSO I, Executive Summary, p.

Committee on Capital Markets Regulation, Interim Report, November 30, 2006, available at: http://www.capmktsreg.org/pdfs/11.30Committee_Interim_ReportREV2.pdf visited: March 21, 2012; cited: *Committee Capital Markets Reg.*, 2006, p.

Coombes, Paul/Watson, Mark, Three surveys on corporate governance, McKinsey Quarterly 2000, available at: http://ebookbrowse.com/gvcr-mckinsey-coombes-paul-watson-mark-three-surveys-on-corporate-governance-2000-pdf-d95746605 visited: April 23, 2011; cited: *Coombes/Watson*, 2000

Cornerstone Research, Securities Class Action Filings 2009: A Year in Review, available at: http://securities.stanford.edu/clearinghouse_research/2009_YIR/Cornerstone_Research_Filings_2009_YIR.pdf visited: March 20, 2012; cited: *Cornerstone Research*, 2009, p.

Cornerstone Research, Securities Class Action Filings 2012: A Year in Review, available at: https://www.cornerstone.com/Publications/Reports/Securities-Class-Action-Settlements-2012-YIR.pdf visited: April 9, 2017; cited: *Cornerstone Research*, 2012, p.

Cornerstone Research, Securities Class Action Filings 2016: A Year in Review, available at: https://www.cornerstone.com/Publications/Reports/Securities-Class-Action-Filings-2016-YIR visited: April 9, 2017; cited: *Cornerstone Research*, 2016, p.

Council of Europe, Liability of enterprises for offences, Recommendation No. R (88) 18 adapted by the Committee of Ministers of the Council of Europe and explanatory memorandum, October 20, 1998, available at: https://wcd.coe.int/com.instranet.InstraServlet?command=com.instranet.CmdBlobGet&InstranetImage=233230&SecMode=1&DocId=698704&Usage=2 visited: February 2, 2013; cited: *Council of Europe*, R (88) 18, p.

Cutler, Stephen M., Speech by SEC Staff: The Themes of Sarbanes-Oxley as Reflected in Commission's Enforcement Program, September 2004, available at: http://www.sec.gov/news/speech/spch092004smc.htm visited: April 24, 2011; cited: *Cutler*, 2004

Deloitte, Establishing an Internal Audit Function – Meeting the NYSE Listing Requirements for Improved Enterprise Value, 2004; cited: *Deloitte*, Internal Audit, p.

Department of Health and Human Services (HHS), Publication of the OIG Compliance Program Guidance for Hospitals, Fed. Reg. 63 (1998), 8987, available at: https://oig.hhs.gov/authorities/docs/cpghosp.pdf visited: Mai 6, 2015; cited: HHS, Compliance Program Guidance

Department of Justice, Deferred Prosecution Agreement, United States of America v. Monsanto Company, Crim. No. 1:05-cr-00008-ESH-ALL, January 6, 2005, available at: http://www.justice.gov/archive/dag/cftf/chargingdocs/monsantoagreement.pdf visited: February 23, 2011; cited: DOJ, Deferred Prosecution Agreement Monsanto

Department of Justice, Evaluation of Corporate Compliance Programs, Criminal Division, Fraud Section, February 8, 2017, available at: https://www.justice.gov/criminal-fraud/page/file/937501/download visited: June 4, 2017; cited: DOJ, Evaluation of Corporate Compliance Programs

Department of Justice, Federal Prosecution of Corporations, "Holder Memo", June 1999, available at: http://federalevidence.com/pdf/Corp_Prosec/Holder_Memo_6_16_99.pdf visited: November 4, 2011; cited: DOJ, Holder Memo

Department of Justice, Foreign Corrupt Practices Act Review Opinion Procedure Release No. 04-02, July 12, 2004, available at: http://www.justice.gov/criminal/fraud/fcpa/opinion/2004/0402.pdf visited: March 3, 2011; cited: DOJ, Opinion Release 04-02

Department of Justice, Justice Department Revises Charging Guidelines for Prosecuting Corporate Fraud, Press Release, August 28, 2008, available at: http://www.justice.gov/opa/pr/2008/August/08-odag-757.html visited: May 28, 2012; cited: DOJ, Press Release 2008

Department of Justice, Lay Person's Guide to the FCPA, available at: http://www.justice.gov/criminal/fraud/fcpa/docs/lay-persons-guide.pdf visited: February 23, 2011; cited: DOJ, Lay Person's Guide

Department of Justice, Opinion Release 08-02, available at: http://www.justice.gov/criminal/fraud/fcpa/opinion/2008/0802.pdf visited: March 3, 2011; cited: DOJ, Opinion Release 08-02

Department of Justice, Principles of Federal Prosecution of Business Organizations, "Thompson Memo", January 2003, available at: http://www.justice.gov/dag/cftf/corporate_guidelines.htm visited: November 4, 2011; cited: DOJ, Thompson Memo

Department of Justice, Principles of Federal Prosecution of Business Organizations, "McNulty Memo", December 2006, available at: http://www.justice.gov/dag/speeches/2006/mcnulty_memo.pdf visited: May 28, 2012; cited: DOJ, McNulty Memo

Department of Justice/Securities and Exchange Commission, FCPA, A Resource Guide to the U.S. Foreign Corrupt Practices Act, 2012, available at: https://www.sec.gov/spotlight/fcpa/fcpa-resource-guide.pdf visited: April 23, 2017; cited: DOJ/SEC, FCPA Resource Guide

Department of Justice, Selection and Use of Monitors in Deferred Prosecution Agreements and Non-Prosecution Agreements with Corporations, Memorandum March 7, 2008, available at: http://www.justice.gov/dag/morford-useofmonitorsmemo-03072008.pdf visited: March 2, 2011; cited: DOJ, Memo on Monitors

Department of Justice, U.S. Deputy Attorney General Paul J. McNulty Revises Charging Guidelines for Prosecuting Corporate Fraud, Press Release, December 12, 2006, available at: http://www.justice.gov/opa/pr/2006/December/06_odag_828.html visited: May 28, 2012; cited: DOJ, Press Release 2006

Department of Justice, USAM Principles of Federal Prosecution of Business Organizations, "Filip Memo", August 2008, available at: www.justice.gov/opa/documents/corp-charging-guidelines.pdf visited: February 23, 2011; cited: DOJ, USAM, Filip Memo, sec.

Department of Justice, Individual Accountability for Corporate Wrongdoing, "Yates Memo", September 2015, available at: https://www.justice.gov/dag/file/769036/download visited: February 16, 2017; cited: DOJ, Yates Memo.

Detzer, Daniel/Dodig, Nina/Evans, Trevor/Hein, Eckhard/Herr, Hansjörg, The German Financial System, Financialization, Economy, Society and Sustainable Development (FESSUD), Studies in Financial Systems No 3, May 2013, available at: http://www.fessud.eu/wp-content/uploads/PDF/German%20Financial%20System%20-%20Final%2015.05.2013.pdf visited: January 2, 2014; cited: *Detzer/Dodig/Evans/Hein/Herr*, 2013, p.

Deutsche Bank AG, Form 20-F Annual Report, filed March 15, 2011; cited: *Deutsche Bank*, 20-F, p.

Deutscher Bundestag, Experten befürworten ein Korruptionsregister, öffentliche Anhörung des Ausschusses für Wirtschaft und Technologie am 25.02.13, available at: http://www.bundestag.de/dokumente/textarchiv/2013/42359076_kw09_pa_wirtschaft_korruptionsregister/index.html visited: March 1, 2013; cited: Deutscher Bundestag, Hearing February 23, 2013

Donaldson, William H., Testimony Concerning Implementation of the Sarbanes-Oxley Act of 2002 - Before the Senate Committee on Banking, Housing and Urban Affairs, September 9, 2003, available at: http://www.sec.gov/news/testimony/090903tswhd.htm visited: March 20, 2012; cited: *Donaldson*, 2003

Düsseldorfer Kreis, Whistleblowing - Hotlines: Firmeninterne Warnsysteme und Beschäftigungsdatenschutz, Arbeitsbericht der Ad-hoc-Arbeitsgruppe "Beschäftigtendatenschutz", April 2007, available at: https://www.ldi.nrw.de/mainmenu_Datenschutz/submenu_Datenschutzrecht/Inhalt/Personalwesen/Inhalt/6_Whistleblowing-Hotlines/Whistleblowing-Hotlines.pdf visited: October 17, 2012; cited: *Düsseldorfer Kreis*, 2007, p.

Eichenwald, Kurt, Andersen Judge Rules in Favor of Prosecution on Jury Question, New York Times June 14, 2002 available at: http://www.nytimes.com/2002/06/14/business/14CND-AUDIT.html visited: April 6, 2015; cited: *Eichenwald*, NYTimes 2002

Environmental Protection Agency (EPA), Incentives for Self-Policing: Discovery, Disclosure, Correction and Prevention of Violations, Fed. Reg. 65 (2000), 19618, available at: http://www.gpo.gov/fdsys/pkg/FR-2000-04-11/pdf/00-8954.pdf visited: Mai 6, 2015; cited: EPA, Incentives for Self-Policing

Ernst & Young, 404 Perspectives, Issue No. 2 Efficient Testing Strategies for 2006, 2006, available at: http://www.sarbanes-oxley.be/AABS_404Perspectives_Issue2.pdf visited: October 23, 2009; cited: *Ernst & Young*, 2006a, p.

Ernst & Young, 404 Perspectives, Issue No. 3 Case Studies on Testing, 2006, available at: http://www.sarbanes-oxley.be/AABS_404Perspectives_Issue3.pdf visited: October 23, 2009; cited: *Ernst & Young*, 2006b, p.

Ernst & Young, Emerging Trends in Internal Controls - Fourth Survey and Industry Insights, September 2005, available at: http://www.sarbanes-oxley.be/aabs_emerging_trends_survey4.pdf visited: October 23, 2009; cited: *Ernst & Young*, Survey 2005, p.

Ernst & Young, Growing Beyond: a place for integrity, 12th Global Fraud Survey, 2012, available at: http://www.ey.com/Publication/vwLUAssets/Global-Fraud-Survey-a-place-for-integrity-12th-Global-Fraud-Survey/$FILE/EY-12th-GLOBAL-FRAUD-SURVEY.pdf visited: February 4, 2013; cited: *Ernst & Young*, 12th Global Fraud Survey, p.

Ethics Resource Center, 2009 National Business Ethics Survey – Ethics in the Recession, available at: http://www.ethicspoint.com/Upload/Articles/NBES_2009.pdf visited: November 23, 2011; cited: ERC, NBES 2009, p.

Ethics Resource Center's FSGO 20th Anniversary Advisory Group, The Federal Sentencing Guidelines for Organizations at Twenty Years – A Call to Action for More Effective Promotion and Recognition of Effective Compliance and Ethics Programs, Discussion Draft for Public Comment, November 1, 2011, available at: http://www.ethics.org/files/u5/FSGO-Discussion-Draft.pdf visited: November 22, 2011; cited: Ethics Resource Center, 2011, p.

European Commission, Commission Notice on Immunity from fines and reduction of fines in cartel cases, 2006/C 298/ 11, OJEU C 298/17 of December 8, 2006; cited: Commission, 2006/C 298/11

European Commission, Commission Recommendation of 15 February 2005 on the role of non-executive or supervisory directors of listed companies and on the committees of the (supervisory) board, 2005/162/EC, OJEU L 52 of February 2, 2005, p. 51; cited: Commission, 2005/162/EC

European Commission, Communication from the Commission to the Council and the European Parliament on Preventing and Combating Corporate and Financial Malpractice, COM (2004) 611, September 27, 2004; cited: Commission, 2004, p.

European Commission, Communication from the Commission to the Council and the European Parliament, Modernising Company Law and Enhancing Corporate Governance in the European Union - A Plan to Move Forward, COM (2003) 284, May 21, 2003; cited: Commission, Action Plan 2003, p.

European Commission, Communication from the Commission to the European Parliament, the Council, the European Economic and Social Committee and the Committee of the Regions, A renewed EU strategy 2011-14 for Corporate Social Responsibility, COM(2011) 681 final, October 25, 2011; cited: Commission, Strategy for Corporate Social Responsibility

European Commission, Communication From the Commission to the European Parliament, the Council, the European Economic and Social Committee and the Committee of the Regions, Action Plan: European company law and corporate governance – a modern legal framework for more engaged shareholders and sustainable companies, COM(2012) 740 final, Strasbourg, December 12, 2012; cited: Commission, Action Plan 2012

European Commission, Communication to the Commission: Revision of the Internal Control Standards and Underlying Framework – Strengthening Control Effectiveness, SEK2007(1341) dated October 16, 2007; cited: Commission, 2007, p.

European Commission, Green Paper, The EU corporate governance framework, COM (2011) 164, April 5, 2011; cited: Commission, Green Paper, p.

European Commission, Green Paper, The EU corporate governance framework, COM(2011) 164 final, Brussels, April 5, 2011; cited: Commission, Green Paper

European Commission, Guidelines on the method of setting fines imposed pursuant to Article 23(2)(a) of Regulation No 1/2003, 2006/C 210/02, OJEU C 2010/2 of September 1, 2006; cited: Commission, 2006/C 210/02

European Corporate Governance Forum, Statement of the European Corporate Governance Forum on Risk Management and Internal control, Brussels, June 2006, available at: http://ec.europa.eu/internal_market/company/docs/ecgforum/statement_internal_control_en.pdf visited: February 6, 2017; cited: *European Corporate Governance Forum*, Risk Management and Internal Control, 2006

European Insurance and Occupational Pensions Authority (EIOPA), Guidelines on system of governance, EIOPA-BoS-14/253; cited: EIOPA, Guidelines

FCPA Blog, Recent Cases, Foreign Companies Dominate New Top Ten, January 5, 2011, available at: http://www.fcpablog.com/blog/2011/1/5/recent-cases-foreign-companies-dominate-new-top-ten.html?printerFriendly=true visited: March 11, 2011; cited: FCPA Blog, 2011

Federal Ministry of the Interior, Empfehlungen zur Korruptionsprävention in der Bundesverwaltung of February 9, 2012, available at: http://www.bmi.bund.de/SharedDocs/Downloads/DE/Themen/OED_Verwaltung/Korruption_Sponsoring/empfehlungen_zur_richtline_korruptionspraevention_de.pdf;jsessionid=70A3E41DF0CE238A3B05B70CBA9FF314.2_cid373?__blob=publicationFile visited: November 11, 2013; cited: BMI, Empfehlungen zur Korruptionsprävention in der Bundesverwaltung, 2012

Federal Ministry of the Interior, Praktische Hilfestellungen für Antikorruptionsmaßnahmen, July 2013, available at: http://www.bmi.bund.de/SharedDocs/Downloads/DE/Broschueren/2013/praktische-hilfestellungen-antikorruptionsmassnahmen.pdf?__blob=publicationFile visited: November 11, 2013; cited: BMI, Praktische Hilfestellungen für Antikorruptionsmaßnahmen, 2013

Ferrara, Ralph C./Rust, K. Oliver, Practicing Law Institute, Corporate Law and Practice Course Handbook Series, PLI Order No. 28850, Corporate Governance: All You Ever Wanted to Know (or Need to Know) About Corporate Governance, February 16, 2011; cited: *Ferrara/Rust*, PLI Corporate Governance, p.

Financial Executives International, Average 2007 SOX Compliance Cost $1.7 Million, Press Release, April 2008, available at: http://www.financialexecutives.org/KenticoCMS/News---Publications/Press-Room/2008-press-releases/FEI-Survey--Average-2007-SOX-Compliance-Cost-$1-7-.aspx visited: April 20, 2012; cited: FEI, 2008

Financial Executives International, Management Drives Sarbanes-Oxley Compliance costs Down by 23%, But Auditor Fees Virtually Unchanged, Press Release Mai 2007, available at: http://www.financialexecutives.org/KenticoCMS/News---Publications/Press-Room/2007-press-releases/FEI-Survey--Management-Drives-Sarbanes-Oxley-Compl.aspx visited: April 20, 2012; cited: FEI, 2007

Financial Executives International, Sarbanes-Oxley Compliance Costs Exceed Estimates, Press Release, March 2005, available at: http://www2.financialexecutives.org/download/404_pr_3_21_2005.pdf visited: April 22, 2012; cited: FEI, 2005

Financial Executives International, Sarbanes-Oxley Compliance Costs are Dropping, Press Release, April 2006, available at: http://www2.financialexecutives.org/download/SOX_404_%20Survey_PR_4_6_06.pdf visited: April 22, 2012; cited: FEI, 2006

financial executives research foundation, Sarbanes-Oxley Section 404 Implementation - Practices of Leading Companies, May 2005, available at: http://www.grantthornton.com/staticfiles/GTCom/files/services/BusinessAdvisoryServices/Publications/FEI.pdf visited: April 22, 2012; cited: *financial executives research foundation*, 2005, p.

Financial Industry Regulatory Authority, Sanction Guidelines, 2011, available at: http://www.finra.org/web/groups/industry/@ip/@enf/@sg/documents/industry/p011038.pdf visited: October 12, 2011; cited: FINRA Sanction Guidelines, p.

Financial Industry Regulatory Authority/New York Stock Exchange, FINRA to Perform NYSE Regulation's Market Oversight Functions, News Release May 4, 2010, available at: http://www.finra.org/Newsroom/NewsReleases/2010/P121365 visited: October 12, 2011; cited: FINRA/NYSE News Release

Fresenius Medical Care AG & Co. KGaA, Form 20-F Annual Report, filed February 23, 2011; cited: *Fresenius*, 20-F, p.

Frey, Jeremy D., SEC's Seaboard Report Offers Guidance on Internal Investigations, April 2002, available at: http://www.pepperlaw.com/publications_update.aspx?ArticleKey=131 visited: April 19, 2012; cited: *Frey*, 2002

Fried Frank, Client Memorandum: Sarbanes-Oxley Act Expands Corporate Governance and Accounting Requirements for SEC-Registered Non-U.S. Companies, February 2006, available at: http://www.friedfrank.com/siteFiles/ffFiles/060217_corp_gov_non_us.pdf visited: April 29, 2012; cited: *Fried Frank*, 2006, p.

Friedman, Paul T./Smithline, Ruti/Kleine, Angela E., 2010: Another Record-Breaking Year for FCPA Enforcement, Confirming "New Era", Client Alert Morrison/Foerster, January 12, 2011, available at: http://www.mofo.com/files/Uploads/Images/110112-FCPA-Enforcement.pdf visited: March 12, 2011; cited: *Friedman/Smithline/Kleine*, 2011

Friedrich, Matthew, Transcript of Press Conference Announcing Siemens AG and Three Subsidiaries Plead Guilty to Foreign Corrupt Practices Act Violations, Acting Assistant Attorney General at the Department of Justice's Criminal Division, December 15, 2008, available at: http://www.justice.gov/opa/pr/2008/December/08-opa-1112.html visited: March 10, 2011; cited: *Friedrich*, Transcript of DOJ's Press Conference for Siemens

General Accounting Office (GAO), Financial Restatements: Update of Public Company Trends, Market Impacts, and Regulatory Enforcement Activities GAO-06-678, July 2006, available at: http://www.gao.gov/new.items/d06678.pdf visited: February 12, 2010; cited: GAO, 2006, p.

General Accounting Office (GAO), Report to The Congress of the United States: Impact Of Foreign Corrupt Practices Act On U.S. Business, AFMD-81-34, March 4, 1981, available at: http://archive.gao.gov/d46t13/114503.pdf visited: May 14, 2012; cited: GAO, 1981, p.

Gibson Dunn, 2010 Year-End FCPA Update, January 3, 2011, available at: http://www.gibsondunn.com/publications/Documents/2010YearEndFCPAUpdate.pdf visited: March 10, 2011

Gibson Dunn, 2011 Year-End FCPA Update, January 3, 2012, available at: http://www.gibsondunn.com/publications/Documents/2011YearEndFCPAUpdate.pdf visited: May 15, 2012; cited: *Gibson Dunn*, 2012

Goette Wulf, speech on „Reformbedarf bei der Managerhaftung?“, at Forum Finanz- und Wirtschaftsrecht an der Humboldt-Universität zu Berlin, September 29, 2011; cited: *Goette*, 2011

Grothe, Mark, The Errors of Their Ways, Glass Lewis & Co Yellow Card Trend Alert, February 2007, available at: http://www.section404.org/UserFiles/File/Website%20-%20Misc/GlassLewis-Errors%20of%20their%20ways.pdf visited: March 14, 2012; cited: *Grothe*, 2007b, p.

Grothe, Mark, The Materially Weak, Glass Lewis &Co Yellow Card Trend Alert, February 2007, available at: http://www.section404.org/UserFiles/File/research/GlassLewis-Materially.pdf visited: March 14, 2012; cited: *Grothe*, 2007a, p.

IIA/AICPA/ACFE, Managing the Business Risk of Fraud: A Practical Guide, April 2008, available at: http://www.acfe.com/uploadedFiles/ACFE_Website/Content/documents/managing-business-risk.pdf visited: January 4, 2011; cited: IIA/AICPA/ACFE, 2008, p.

Institut der Wirtschaftsprüfer [ed.], IDW Prüfstandard: Abschlussprüfung bei Einsatz von Informationstechnologie (IDW PS 330), effective date September 2002; cited: IDW PS 330, mar.

Institut der Wirtschaftsprüfer [ed.], IDW Prüfstandard: Die Prüfung des Risikofrüherkennungssystems nach § 317 Abs. 4 HGB (IDW PS 340), effective date September, 2000; cited: IDW PS 340, mar.

Institut der Wirtschaftsprüfer [ed.], IDW Prüfstandard: Grundsätze ordnungsmäßiger Prüfung von Compliance Management Systemen (IDW PS 980), effective date March 2011; cited: IDW PS 980, mar.

Institut der Wirtschaftsprüfer [ed.], IDW Prüfstandard: Rechnungslegungs- und Prüfungsgrundsätze für die Abschlussprüfung (IDW PS 201), effective date September 2009; cited: IDW PS 201, mar.

Institut der Wirtschaftsprüfer [ed.], IDW Prüfstandard: Zur Aufdeckung von Unregelmäßigkeiten im Rahmen der Abschlussprüfung (IDW PS 210, effective date September 2010; cited: IDW PS 210, mar.

Institut der Wirtschaftsprüfer [ed.], IDW Prüfstandard: Feststellung und Beurteilung von Fehlerrisiken und Reaktionen des Abschlussprüfers auf die beurteilten Fehlerrisiken (IDW PS 261 n.F.), effective date March 2012; cited: IDW PS 261, mar.

Institute of Internal Auditors, Code of Ethics, available at: https://na.theiia.org:443/standards-guidance/Public%20Documents/2010-06-16_10165_Code_of_Ethics.pdf visited: September 12, 2012; cited: IIA Code of Ethics

Institute of Internal Auditors, Definition of Internal Audit on IIA Homepage, available at: http://www.theiia.org/guidance/standards-and-guidance/ippf/definition-of-internal-auditing/ visited: November 1, 2011; cited: IIA Definition of Internal Audit

Institute of Internal Auditors, International Standards for the Professional Practice of Internal Auditing (Standards), available at: https://na.theiia.org:443/standards-guidance/mandatory-guidance/pages/standards.aspx visited: June, 28, 2012; cited: IIA Standard No.

Institute of Internal Auditors, Sarbanes-Oxley Section 404: A Guide for Management by Internal Controls Practitioners, 2nd edition, January 2008, available at: http://www.theiia.org/download.cfm?file=31866 visited: April 12, 2012; IIA Guide 2008, p.

International Chamber of Commerce, Korruption bekämpfen – Ein ICC-Verhaltenskodex für die Wirtschaft, available at: http://www.icc-deutschland.de/fileadmin/ICC_Dokumente/ICC-Verhaltenskodex_Korruption_final.pdf visited: November 4, 2012; cited: ICC, Code of Conduct

Jahn, Joachim, Schärfere Strafen für Unternehmen, F.A.Z. of August 13, 2012; cited: *Jahn*, F.A.Z. of August 13, 2012

Justizministerium des Landes Nordrhein-Westphalen, Entwurf eines Gesetzes zur Einführung der strafrechtlichen Verantwortlichkeit von Unternehmen und sonstigen Verbänden, available at: https://www.justiz.nrw.de/JM/justizpolitik/jumiko/beschluesse/2013/herbstkonferenz13/zw3/TOP_II_5_Gesetzentwurf.pdf visited: April 2, 2015; cited: *NRW-Justiz*, Gesetzentwurf Unternehmensstrafrecht

Khuzami, Robert, Speech by SEC Staff: Remarks Before the New York City Bar: My First 100 Days as Director of Enforcement, August 5, 2009, available at: http://www.sec.gov/news/speech/2009/spch080509rk.htm visited: May 30, 2012; cited: *Khuzami*, 2009

Kirkpatrick, Grant, The Corporate Governance Lessons from the Financial Crisis - Report of the OECD Steering Group on Corporate Governance, 2009; cited: *Kirkpatrick*, OECD, 2009

Kommission zur Reform des strafrechtlichen Sanktionensystems, Abschlussbericht, March 2000, available at: http://www.bib.uni-mannheim.de/fileadmin/pdf/fachinfo/jura/abschlussber-der-komm-strafreform.pdf visited: February 4, 2013; cited: *Kommission zur Reform des strafrechtlichen Sanktionensystems*, Abschlussbericht, p.

Körner, Constantin, NRW-Justizminister plant Unternehmensstrafrecht: „Deutschlands Inselstatus beenden“, Legal Tribune Online April 9, 2012, available at: http://www.lto.de/persistent/a_id/5965 visited: February 3, 2013; cited: *Körner*, LTO of April 9, 2012

KPMG, Creating Value within Your Organization, Internal Audit's Evolving Role, 2008, available at: http://www.kpmginstitutes.com/404-institute/insights/2008/pdf/creating-value-within-your-organization.pdf visited: November 7, 2011; cited: *KPMG*, 2008

KPMG, Enhancing Business Performance through Governance, Risk, and Compliance, 2011, available at: http://www.kpmg.com/SG/en/IssuesAndInsights/CFOPublications/Documents/EnhancingBusinessPerformancethroughGovernanceRiskandCompliance_Governance.pdf visited: November 7, 2011; cited: *KPMG*, 2011a, p.

KPMG, Global Anti-Bribery and Corruption Survey 2011, available at: http://www.kpmg.com/UK/en/IssuesAndInsights/ArticlesPublications/Documents/PDF/Advisory/23816NSS_Global_ABC_Survey.PDF visited: February 4, 2013; cited: KPMG, 2011, p.

KPMG, Placing a Value on Enterprise Risk Management, 2009, available at: http://www.kpmg.com/PT/pt/IssuesAndInsights/Documents/erm22432PHL.pdf visited: November 7, 2011; cited: *KPMG*, 2009, p.

KPMG, Prüfungsbericht (Kurzfassung), Angemessenheit, Implementierung und Wirksamkeit des Compliance Management Systems zum 30. September 2011, ThyssenKrupp AG Duisburg und Essen, available at: http://www.thyssenkrupp.com/documents/investor/ThyssenKrupp_Pruefungsbericht_2011_09_30.pdf visited: March 8, 2013; cited: *KPMG*, Report IDW PS 980 on ThyssenKrupp, p.

KPMG, The convergence challenge, Global survey into the integration of governance, risk and compliance, February 2010, available at: http://www.kpmginstitutes.com/404-institute/insights/2010/pdf/eiu-survey-convergence-challenge.pdf visited: November 7, 2011; cited: *KPMG*, 2010, p.

KPMG, Turning risk into advantage: A case study, 2011, available at: http://www.kpmginstitutes.com/404-institute/insights/2011/pdf/turning-risk-into-advantage-case-study.pdf visited: November 7, 2011; cited: *KPMG*, 2011b, p.

Krempl, Stefan, Bundesregierung kommt beim Whistleblower-Schutz nicht voran, heise-online, September 1, 2014, available at: http://www.heise.de/newsticker/meldung/Bundesregierung-kommt-beim-Whistleblower-Schutz-nicht-voran-2305694.html visited: March 31, 2015; cited: *Krempl*, heise-online

Kutschaty, Thomas, „Das Unternehmen als Straftäter", Sprechzettel für Herrn Justizminister Thomas Kutschaty anlässlich der Veranstaltung der Juristischen Gesellschaft Ruhr am 22. März 2012 in Bochum, available at: http://www.justiz.nrw.de/JM/Presse/reden/archiv/2012_01_Archiv/12-03-22/index.php visited: February 26, 2013; cited: *Kutschaty*, Das Unternehmen als Straftäter

Laux, Johann, Am Arbeitsplatz verhört, in: Die Zeit, October 9, 2014, available at: http://www.zeit.de/2014/40/wirtschaftskriminalitaet-unternehmen-korruption-untreue-insiderhandel, visited: September 14, 2015; cited: *Laux*, Die Zeit, 2014

Leyendecker, Hans/Ott, Klaus, Verfahren gegen ehemaligen Siemens Chef - Auch Kleinfeld droht Millionenbuße, May 16, 2008, available at: http://www.sueddeutsche.de/wirtschaft/2.220/verfahren-gegen-ehemaligen-siemens-chef-auch-kleinfeld-droht-millionenbusse-1.182499 visited: June 10, 2015; cited: *Leyendecker/Ott*, Süddeutsche Zeitung, 2008

Lord & Benoit, The Lord & Benoit Report: Do the Benefits of 404 Exceed the Cost?, May 2006, available at: http://www.section404.org/pdf/Lord%20&%20Benoit%20Report%20Do%20the%20Benefits%20of%20404%20Exceed%20the%20-Cost.pdf visited: October 6, 2011; cited: *Lord & Benoit*, 2006, p.

Lytton, William B./Swenson, Winthorp M., The Effective Answer to Corporate Misconduct: Public Sector Encouragement of Private Sector Compliance Programs, ACCA Docket 20, no. 10 (2002), p. 42; cited: *Lytton/Swenson*, 2002, p.

McDermott, John V./Smith, Matthew J., SEC Enforcement Actions: Cooperation After the Seaboard Report, May 11, 2007, available at: http://www.hro.com/files/publications/Securitiesconference.pdf visited: October 14, 2011; cited: *McDermott/Smith*, 2007, p.

NACD Blue Ribbon Commission, Risk Governance: Balancing Risk and Reward, Report, 2009, available at: www.wlrk.com/docs/1605831_1.pdf visited: February 6, 2017; cited: *NACD*, 2009

National Commission on Fraudulent Financial Reporting, Report of the National Commission on Fraudulent Financial Reporting, October 1987, available at: http://www.coso.org/publications/ncffr.pdf visited: July 20, 2012; cited: *National Commission on Fraudulent Financial Reporting*, 1987

New York City Bar, Report of the Task Force on the Lawyer's Role in Corporate Governance, November 2006, available at: http://www.abcny.org/pdf/report/CORPORATE_GOVERNANCE06.pdf visited: October 12, 2011; cited: *New York City Bar*, Report 2006, p.

Newman, Bernard H./Oliverio, Mary E., Perceived Flaws in Sarbanes-Oxley Implementation, The CPA Journal 2006, available at: http://www.nysscpa.org/printversions/cpaj/2006/906/p6.htm visited: February 8, 2011; cited: *Newman/Oliverio*, 2006

NRW-Justiz, Vermögensabschöpfung - Straftaten dürfen sich nicht lohnen, available at: http://www.justiz.nrw.de/JM/justizpolitik/schwerpunkte/vermoegensabsch/index.php?print=1 visited: February 26, 2013; cited: *NRW-Justiz*, Vermögensabschöpfung

NYSE Commission on Corporate Governance, Report of the New York Stock Exchange Commission on Corporate Governance, September 23, 2010, available at: http://www.nyse.com/pdfs/CCGReport.pdf visited: September 27, 2011; cited: Report of NYSE Commission on Corporate Governance, p.

NYSE Commission on Corporate Governance, Report of the New York Stock Exchange Commission on Corporate Governance, Overview of Principles and Summary, September 23, 2010, available at: http://www.nyse.com/pdfs/CCG-Overview_of_Principles_and_Summary_of_Conclusions.pdf visited: September 27, 2011; cited: NYSE Commission on Corporate Governance, Overview of Principles and Summary

NYSE Division of Enforcement, NYSE Information Memo No. 05-65, Cooperation, September 14, 2005, available at: http://www.nyse.com/nysenotices/nyse/information-memos/detail?memo_id=05-65 visited: October 12, 2011; cited: NYSE Cooperation Memo, p.

NYSE Division of Enforcement, NYSE Information Memo No. 05-77, Factors Considered by the New York Stock Exchange Division of Enforcement in Determining Sanctions, October 7, 2005, available at: http://www.nyse.com/nysenotices/nyse/information-memos/pdf?memo_id=05-77 visited: October 12, 2011; cited: NYSE Sanctions Memo, p.

NYSE, Accountability Report Sets Higher Bar, in: The Exchange Volume 9 Number 6, June 2002, available at: http://www.nyse.com/pdfs/xnlv 9n06.pdf visited: October 14, 2011; cited: NYSE The Exchange, p.

NYSE, Financial Compliance on NYSE Homepage, available at: http://usequities.nyx.com/regulation/listed-companies-compliance/financial-compliance; visited: September 26, 2011; cited: NYSE Financial Compliance

NYSE, NYSE Completes Formation Of "Commission on Corporate Governance" – Expert Panel To Evaluate Corporate Governance Reform, Proxy Process –, News Release November 12, 2009, available at: http://www.nyse.com/press/1258023407401.html visited: September 27, 2011; cited: NYSE News Release Nov. 12, 2009

NYSE, NYSE Disciplinary Actions on NYSE Homepage, available at: http://usequities.nyx.com/regulation/nyse-disciplinary-action visited: October 24, 2011; cited: NYSE Disciplinary Actions

NYSE, NYSE Forms "Commission on Corporate Governance" to Examine U.S. Corporate Governance – NYSE Brings Together Leading Experts to Create Dialogue on Governance Issues --, News Release September 1, 2009, available at: http://www.nyse.com/press/1251799796551.html visited: September 27, 2011; cited: NYSE News Release Sept. 1, 2009

NYSE, NYSE Listed Company Manual Section 303A Corporate Governance Standards Frequently Asked Questions, January 4, 2010, available at: http://www.nyse.com/pdfs/FINAL_FAQ_NYSE%20Listed%20Company%20Manual%20Section%20303A_updated_1_4_10.pdf visited: September 27, 2011; cited: NYSE-LCM FAQ, p.

NYSE, NYSE Listed Company Manual, available at: http://nysemanual.nyse.com/lcm/ visited: March 2, 2017; cited: NYSE-LCM

NYSE, NYSE Listing Fees on NYSE Homepage, available at: https://usequities.nyx.com/listings/fees visited: April 15, 2013; cited: NYSE Fees

NYSE, Report of the New York Stock Exchange Corporate Accountability and Listing Standards Committee, June 6, 2002, available at: http://usequities.nyx.com/sites/corporate.nyx.com/files/corp_govreport.pdf visited: September 27, 2011; cited: NYSE Report, p.

Office of Management and Budget, Guidelines to Agencies on Governmentwide Debarment and Suspension (Nonprocurement), 2 CFR 180; cited: *Office of Management and Budget*, Guidelines on Nonprocurement, sec.

Office of the United States Attorneys, United States Attorneys' Manual (USAM), available at: http://www.justice.gov/usao/eousa/foia_reading_room/usam/ visited: May 16, 2012; cited: Office of the U.S. Attorneys, USAM

O'Melveny & Myers, Foreign Corrupt Practices Act Handbook, 6th edition 2009, available at: http://www.omm.com/files/upload/OMelvenyMyers_Sixth_Edition_FCPA_Handbook.pdf visited: October 26, 2009; cited: *O'Melveny & Myers*, 2009, p.

Organization for Economic Co-operation and Development (OECD), Good Practice Guidance on Internal Controls, Ethics, and Compliance, Annex II of OECD Recommendation of the Council for Further Combating Bribery of Foreign Public Officials in Internal Business Transactions of November 26, 2009, adopted February 18, 2010; cited: OECD Good Practice Guidance

Organization for Economic Co-operation and Development (OECD), Principles of Corporate Governance, 2004; cited: OECD Corporate Governance

Organization for Economic Co-operation and Development (OECD), Report on the Application of the Convention of Combating Bribery of Foreign Public Officials in International Business Transactions and the 2009 Revised Recommendation on Combating Bribery in International Business Transactions, Germany: Phase 3, March 17, 2011, available at: http://www.oecd.org/investment/briberyininternationalbusiness/anti-briberyconvention/47416623.pdf visited: November 4, 2012; cited: OECD, Report on Germany, p.

Ott, Klaus, Thyssen-Krupp verklagt Ex-Manager auf 100 Millionen Euro, Korruptionsaffäre bei Großkonzern, December 10, 2012, available at: http://www.sueddeutsche.de/wirtschaft/korruptionsaffaere-bei-stahlkonzern-thyssen-verklagt-ex-manager-auf-millionen-euro-1.1546105 visited: March 15, 2013; cited: *Ott*, Süddeutsche.de, 2012

Oversightsystems, The 2005 Oversight Systems Report On Corporate Fraud, available at: http://www.oversightsystems.com/pdf/whitepapers/Oversight_Systems_Survey_on_Fraud.pdf visited: August 23, 2012; cited: *Oversightsystems*, 2005, p.

Oversightsystems, The 2007 Oversight Systems Report On Corporate Fraud, available at: http://www.oversightsystems.com/pdf/whitepapers/Oversight_2007_Fraud_Survey.pdf visited: May 22, 2012; cited: *Oversightsystems*, 2007, p.

Oxley, Michael G., Financial Emergency: The Crisis that Began and Ended the Decade, The 2010-11 Matsui Lecturer at University of California Berkeley School of Law, April 6, 2011, video available at: http://media.law.berkeley.edu/qtmedia/bclbe/20110406_BCLBE.mp4 visited: July 19, 2012; cited: *Oxley*, 2011, at hh:mm:ss

Reilly, David, Restatements Still Bedevil Firms, Wall St. J. February 12, 2007; cited: *Reilly*, 2007

PricewaterhouseCoopers, Corruption crackdown - How the FCPA is changing the way the world does business, July 2009, available at: http://www.pwc.com/us/en/foreign-corrupt-practices-act/publications/assets/pwc-corruption-crackdown-fcpa-2009.pdf visited: March 9, 2011; cited: *PwC*, 2009, p.

PricewaterhouseCoopers, The Use of Spreadsheets: Considerations for Section 404 of the Sarbanes-Oxley Act, July 2004, available at: http://www.auditsoftware.net/community/excel/PwCwpSpreadsheetsSection404Sarbox.pdf visited: April 23, 2011; cited: *PwC*, 2004, p.

PricewaterhouseCoopers/Compliance Week, Broader perspectives; higher performance – State of Compliance: 2011 Study, May 2011, available at: http://www.pwc.com/en_US/us/risk-management/assets/SOC_Exec_Summary-FINAL.pdf visited: December 13, 2011; cited: *PwC/Compliance Week*, 2011, p.

protiviti, 2010 Sarbanes-Oxley Compliance Survey, Where U.S.-Listed Companies Stand: Reviewing Cost, Time, Effort and Processes, June 2010, available at: http://www.protiviti.com/en-US/Documents/Surveys/2010-SOX-Compliance-Survey-Protiviti.pdf visited: December 28, 2010; cited: *protiviti*, 2010, p.

protiviti, 2012 Sarbanes-Oxley Compliance Survey, Where U.S.-Listed Companies Stand: Reviewing Cost, Time, Effort and Processes, May 2012, available at: http://www.protiviti.com/en-US/Documents/Surveys/2012-SOX-Compliance-Survey-Protiviti.pdf visited: July 17, 2012; cited: *protiviti*, 2012, p.

protiviti, Guide to Enterprise Risk Management, Frequently Asked Questions, January 2006, available at: http://www.ucop.edu/riskmgt/erm/documents/protiviti_faqguide.pdf visited: April 13, 2011; cited: *protiviti*, 2006, p.

Public Company Accounting Oversight Board, Release No. 2004-001, Auditing Standard No. 2 – An Audit of Internal Control Over Financial Reporting Performed in Conjunction with an Audit of Financial Statements, March 9, 2004, available at: http://pcaobus.org/Rules/Rulemaking/Docket008/2004-03-09_Release_2004-001-all.pdf visited: October 26, 2009; cited: PCAOB, AS 2, par.

Public Company Accounting Oversight Board, Release No. 2005-009, Policy Statement Regarding Implementation of Auditing Standard No. 2, An Audit of Internal Control Over Financial Reporting Reformed in Conjunction with an Audit of Financial Statements, May 16, 2005, available at: http://pcaobus.org/Rules/Rulemaking/Docket008/2005-05-16_Release_2005-009.pdf visited: March 19, 2012; cited: PCAOB, Release No. 2005-009

Public Company Accounting Oversight Board, Release No. 2005-023, Report on the Initial Implementation of Auditing Standard No. 2, An Audit of Internal Control Over Financial Reporting Performed in Conjunction with an Audit of Financial Statements, November 30, 2005, available at: http://pcaobus.org/Inspections/Documents/2005_11-30_Release_2005-023.pdf visited: March 19, 2012; cited: PCAOB, Release No. 2005-023

Public Company Accounting Oversight Board, Release No. 2007-005A, Auditing Standard No. 5 – An Audit of Internal Control Over Financial Reporting That Is Integrated with An Audit of Financial Statements, June 12, 2007, available at: http://pcaobus.org/Rules/Rulemaking/Docket%20021/2007-06-12_Release_No_2007-005A.pdf visited: April 2, 2011; cited: PCAOB, AS 5, par.

Rauhofer, Judith, Blowing the whistle on Sarbanes-Oxley: Anonymous hotlines and the historical stigma of denunciation in modern Germany, BILETA Annual Conference 2007, available at: http://bileta.ac.uk/content/files/conference%20papers/2007/Blowing%20the%20whistle%20on%20Sarbanes-Oxley%20-%20Anonymous%20hotlines%20and%20the%20historical%20stigma%20of%20denunciation%20in%20modern%20Germany.pdf visited: October 15, 2012; cited: *Rauhofer*, 2007, p.

Reichling, Tilman, Geplante Verschärfung der Verbandsgeldbuße: Deutschlands nächster Schritt zu einem Unternehmensstrafrecht?, Legal Tribune Online May, 22, 2012, available at: http://www.lto.de/persistant/a_id/6239/ visited: August, 31, 2012; cited: *Reichling*, LTO of May 22, 2012

Rosbach, Jens, SPD und Union streiten um ein Whistleblower-Gesetz, Deutschlandfunk – DLF-Magazin, August 21, 2014, available at: http://www.deutschlandfunk.de/schutz-fuer-hinweisgeber-in-firmen-spd-und-union-streiten.862.de.html?dram:article_id=295303 visited: March 31, 2015; cited: *Rosbach*, DLF

SAP AG, Form 20-F Annual Report, filed March 18, 2011; cited: *SAP*, 20-F, p.

Schumacher, Harald/Seiwert, Martin/Bergermann, Melanie/Berke, Jürgen, Große Show, kleines Kaliber, Wirtschaftswoche No. 47 of November 19, 2012, p. 48; cited: *Schumacher/Seiwert/Bergermann/Berke*, Wirtschaftswoche, p. 48

Searcey, Dionne, U.S. Cracks Down on Corporate Bribes, Wall St. J., May 26, 2009; cited: *Searcey*, Wall St. J.

Securities and Exchange Commission, Division of Corporate Finance, Office of the Chief Accountant, Staff Statement on Management's Report on Internal Control Over Financial Reporting, May 16, 2005, available at: http://www.sec.gov/info/accountants/stafficreporting.htm visited: March 27, 2012; cited: SEC, Staff Statement

Securities and Exchange Commission, Division of Corporate Finance, Office of the Chief Accountant, Management's Report on Internal Control Over Financial Reporting and Certification of Disclosure in Exchange Act Periodic Reports Frequently Asked Questions (revised October 6, 2004), available at: http://www.sec.gov/info/accountants/controlfaq1004.htm visited: March 27, 2012; cited: SEC, ICFR-FAQ

Securities and Exchange Commission, In the Matter of Primier Financial Bancorp, Inc., Release No. 52370, August 2005, available at: http://www.sec.gov/litigation/admin/34-52370.pdf visited: May 25, 2012; cited: SEC Release No. 52370

Securities and Exchange Commission, Interpretive Release No. 33-8810, Commission Guidance Regarding Management's Report on Internal Control Over Financial Reporting Under Section 13(a) or 15(d) of the Securities Exchange Act of 1934, available at: http://www.sec.gov/rules/interp/2007/33-8810.pdf visited: March 27, 2012; cited: SEC Release No. 8810

Securities and Exchange Commission, Office of Economic Analysis, Study of the Sarbanes-Oxley Act of 2002 Section 404 Internal Control over Financial Reporting Requirements, September 2009, available at: http://www.sec.gov/news/studies/2009/sox-404_study.pdf visited: April 7, 2011; cited: SEC Study Sec. 404, p.

Securities and Exchange Commission, Office of the Chief Accountant, Study and Recommendations on Section 404(b) of the Sarbanes-Oxley Act of 2002 For Issuers With Public Float Between $75 and $250 Million, April 2011, available at: http://www.sec.gov/news/studies/2011/404bfloat-study.pdf visited: October 6, 2011; cited: SEC Study Sec. 404(b)

Securities and Exchange Commission, Release No. 19986, SEC v. Anthony L. Hurley, Civil Action No. 07cv 022, available at: http://www.sec.gov/litigation/litreleases/2007/lr19986.htm visited: April 19, 2012; cited: SEC Release No. 19986

Securities and Exchange Commission, Release No. 33-8124, Certification of Disclosure in Companies' Quarterly and Annual Reports, August 2002, available at: http://www.sec.gov/rules/final/33-8124.htm visited: February 9, 2011; cited: SEC Release No. 8124

Securities and Exchange Commission, Release No. 33-8177, Disclosure Required by Sections 406 and 407 of the Sarbanes-Oxley Act of 2002, January 2003, available at: http://www.sec.gov/rules/final/33-8177.htm visited: April 30, 2012; cited: SEC Release No. 8177

Securities and Exchange Commission, Release No. 33-8185, Implementation of Standards of Professional Conduct for Attorneys, August 2003, available at: http://www.sec.gov/rules/final/33-8185.htm visited: May 8, 2012; cited: SEC Release No. 8185

Securities and Exchange Commission, Release No. 33-8220, Standards Relating to Listed Company Audit Committees, available at: http://www.sec.gov/rules/final/33-8220.htm visited: October 17, 2011; cited: SEC Release No. 8220

Securities and Exchange Commission, Release No. 33-8238, Management's Report on Internal Control over Financial Reporting and Certification of Disclosure in Exchange Act Periodic Reports, June 2003, available at: http://www.sec.gov/rules/final/33-8238.htm visited: February 4, 2011; cited: SEC Release No. 8238

Securities and Exchange Commission, Release No. 33-8400, Additional Form 8-K Disclosure Requirements and Acceleration of Filing Date, August 2004, available at: http://www.sec.gov/rules/final/33-8400.htm visited: May 8, 2012; cited: SEC Release No. 8400

Securities and Exchange Commission, Release No. 33-8651, In the Matter of Applix, Inc., available at: http://www.sec.gov/litigation/admin/33-8651.pdf visited: April 19, 2012; cited: SEC Release No. 8651

Securities and Exchange Commission, Release No. 33-8762, Proposed Rule, Management's Report on Internal Control Over Financial Reporting, available at: http://www.sec.gov/rules/proposed/2006/33-8762.pdf visited: April 2, 2012; cited: SEC Release No. 8762

Securities and Exchange Commission, Release No. 33-8809, Amendments to Rules Regarding Management's Report on Internal Control Over Financial Reporting, http://www.sec.gov/rules/final/2007/33-8809.pdf visited: March 27, 2012; cited: SEC Release No. 8809

Securities and Exchange Commission, Release No. 33-8829, Definition of the Term Significant Deficiency, available at: http://www.sec.gov/rules/final/2007/33-8829.pdf visited: April 10, 2012; cited: SEC Release No. 8829

Securities and Exchange Commission, Release No. 33-8831, Concept Release on Allowing U.S. Issuers to Prepare Financial Statements in Accordance with International Financial Reporting Standards, August 2007, available at: http://www.sec.gov/rules/concept/2007/33-8831.pdf visited: July 19, 2012; cited: SEC Release No. 8831

Securities and Exchange Commission, Release No. 33-8879, Acceptance From Foreign Private Issuers of Financial Statements Prepared in Accordance with International Financial Reporting Standards Without Reconciliation to U.S. GAAP, March 2008, available at: http://www.sec.gov/rules/final/2007/33-8879.pdf visited: July 19, 2012; cited: SEC Release No. 8879

Securities and Exchange Commission, Release No. 33-8982, Roadmap for the Potential Use of Financial Statements Prepared in Accordance with International Financial Reporting Standards by U.S. Issuers, November 2008, available at: http://www.sec.gov/rules/proposed/2008/33-8982.pdf visited: July 19, 2012; cited: SEC Release No. 8982

Securities and Exchange Commission, Release No. 33-9089, Proxy Disclosure Enhancements, December 2009, available at: http://www.sec.gov/rules/final/2009/33-9089.pdf visited: July 19, 2012; cited: SEC Release No. 9089

Securities and Exchange Commission, Release No. 33-9142, Internal Control Over Financial Reporting in Exchange Act Periodic Reports of Non-Accelerated Filers, available at: http://www.sec.gov/rules/final/2010/33-9142.pdf visited: April 3, 2012; cited: SEC Release No. 9142

Securities and Exchange Commission, Release No. 34-44969, Report of Investigation, available at: http://www.sec.gov/litigation/investreport/34-44969.htm visited: February 28, 2011; cited: SEC Release No. 44969

Securities and Exchange Commission, Release No. 34-44969, Report of Investigation Pursuant to Section 21(a) of the Securities Exchange Act of 1934 and Commission Statement on the Relationship of Cooperation to Agency Enforcement Decisions, available at: http://www.sec.gov/litigation/investreport/34-44969.htm visited: October 14, 2011; cited: SEC Release No. 44969

Securities and Exchange Commission, Release No. 34-44970, In the Matter of Gisela de Leon-Meredith, Respondent, available at: http://www.sec.gov/litigation/admin/34-44970.htm visited: February 28, 2011; cited: SEC Release No. 44970

Securities and Exchange Commission, Release No. 34-48745, Self-Regulatory Organizations; New York Stock Exchange, Inc. and National Association of Securities Dealers, Inc.; Order Approving Proposed Rule Changes (SR-NYSE-2002-33 and SR-NASD-2002-141) and Amendments No. 1 thereto; Order Approving Proposed Rule Changes (SR-NASD-2002-77, SR-NASD-2002-80, SR-NASD-2002-138 and SR-NASD-2002-139) and Amendments No. 1 to SR-NASD-2002-80 and SR-NASD-2002-139; and Notice of Filing and Order Granting Accelerated Approval of Amendment Nos. 2 and 3 to SR-NYSE-2002-33, Amendment Nos. 2, 3, 4 and 5 to SR-NASD-2002-141, Amendment Nos. 2 and 3 to SR-NASD-2002-80, Amendment Nos. 1, 2, and 3 to SR-NASD-2002-138, and Amendment No. 2 to SR-NASD-2002-139, Relating to Corporate Governance, available at: http://www.sec.gov/rules/sro/34-48745.htm visited: October 14, 2011; cited: SEC Release No. 48745

Securities and Exchange Commission, Release No. 34-49675, In the Matter of The Warnaco Group, Inc., available at: http://www.sec.gov/litigation/admin/34-49675.pdf visited: April 19, 2012; cited: SEC Release No. 49675

Securities and Exchange Commission, Release No. 34-56145, Self-Regulatory Organizations; National Association of Securities Dealers, Inc.; Order Approving Proposed Rule Change to Amend the By-Laws of NASD to Implement Governance and Related Changes to Accommodate the Consolidation of the member Firm Regulatory Functions of NASD and NYSE Regulation, Inc., July 2007, available at: http://www.sec.gov/rules/sro/nasd/2007/34-56145.pdf visited: October 12, 2011; cited: SEC Release No. 56145

Securities and Exchange Commission, Release No. 34-57933, In the Matter of Faro Technologies, Respondent, available at: http://www.sec.gov/litigation/admin/2008/34-57933.pdf visited: March 2, 2011; cited: SEC Release No. 55933

Securities and Exchange Commission, Release No. 34-64545, Implementation of the Whistleblower Provisions of Section 21F of the Securities Exchange Act of 1934, May 2011, available at: http://www.sec.gov/rules/final/2011/34-64545.pdf visited: July 18, 2012; cited: SEC Release No. 64545

Securities and Exchange Commission, SEC Adopts Rules to Establish Whistleblower Program, Press Release No. 2011-116, May 2011, available at: http://www.sec.gov/news/press/2011/2011-116.htm visited: July 18, 2012; cited: SEC Release No. 2011-116

Securities and Exchange Commission, SEC Announces Next Steps Relating to International Financial Reporting Standards, Press Release No. 2007-72, April 2007, available at: http://www.sec.gov/news/press/2007/2007-72.htm visited: July 19, 2012; cited: SEC Release No. 2007-72

Securities and Exchange Commission, SEC Approves Enhanced Disclosure About Risk, Compensation and Corporate Governance, Press Release No. 2009-268, December 2009, available at: http://www.sec.gov/news/press/2009/2009-268.htm visited: July 19, 2012; cited: SEC Release No. 2009-268

Securities and Exchange Commission, SEC Charges Halliburton and Two Former Officers for Failure to Disclose a 1998 Change in Accounting Practice, Press Release No. 2004-104, August 2004, available at: http://www.sec.gov/news/press/2004-104.htm visited: May 25, 2012; cited: SEC Release No. 2004-104

Securities and Exchange Commission, SEC Charges Six Former Officers of Putnam Fiduciary Trust Company with Defrauding Clients of $4 Million, Press Release No. 2006-2, January 2006, available at: http://www.sec.gov/news/press/2006-2.htm visited: May 25, 2012; cited: SEC Release No. 2006-2

Securities and Exchange Commission, Statement of the Securities and Exchange Commission Concerning Financial Penalties, January 2006, available at: http://www.sec.gov/news/press/2006-4.htm visited: December 12, 2011; cited: SEC Statement Concerning Financial Penalties

Securities and Exchange Commission, Work Plan for the Consideration of Incorporating International Financial Reporting Standards into the Financial Reporting System for U.S. Issuers, A Comparison of U.S. GAAP and IFRS, November 2011, available at: http://www.sec.gov/spotlight/globalaccountingstandards/ifrs-work-plan-paper-111611-gaap.pdf visited: July 19, 2012; cited: SEC Comparison of U.S. GAAP and IFRS

Securities and Exchange Commission, Xerox Settles SEC Enforcement Action Charging Company with Fraud, Press Release No. 2002-52, April 2002, available at: http://www.sec.gov/news/press/2002-52.txt visited: May 25, 2012; cited: SEC Release No. 2002-52

Siemens Aktiengesellschaft, Form 20-F Annual Report, filed December 2, 2008; cited: *Siemens*, 20-F 2008, p.

Siemens Aktiengesellschaft, Form 20-F Annual Report, filed December 2, 2010; cited: *Siemens*, 20-F 2010, p.

Siemens Aktiengesellschaft, Statement of Siemens Aktiengesellschaft: Investigation and Summary of Findings with respect to the Proceedings in Munich and the US, December 15, 2008, available at: http://www.siemens.com/press/pool/de/events/2008-12-PK/summary-e.pdf visited: March 8, 2011; cited: *Siemens*, Statement 2008, p.

Spiegel Online, Daimler fällt bei US-Börsenaufsicht durch, December 11, 2011, available at: http://www.spiegel.de/wirtschaft/unternehmen/0,1518,803054,00.html visited: March 1, 2017; cited: *Spiegel Online*, Daimler

Spiegel Online, Trittin fordert deutsches Unternehmensstrafrecht, December 18, 2012, available at: http://www.spiegel.de/politik/deutschland/deutsche-bank-trittin-fordert-nach-skandal-unternehmensstrafrecht-a-873657.html visited: February 3, 2013; cited: *Spiegel Online*, December 18, 2012

Staatsanwaltschaft München I, Bußgeldbescheid Siemens – Entwurf –, December 2008, available at: http://www.siemens.com/press/pool/de/events/2008-12-PK/MucStaats.pdf visited: November 2, 2012; cited: Staatsanwaltschaft München I, Bußgeldbescheid Siemens, p.

Steer, John R., Changing Organizational Behavior – The Federal Sentencing Guidelines Experiment Begins to Bear Fruit, unpublished paper presented at the Twenty-Ninth Annual Conference on Value Inquire, Tulsa, Oklahoma, 2001, available at: http://www.ussc.gov/Guidelines/Organizational_Guidelines/Selected_Articles/corpbehavior2.pdf visited: November 14, 2011; cited: *Steer*, 2001, p.

Steinbuch, Anja, Schlüssel zur Kasse, Wirtschaftswoche No. 36 of September 2, 2013, p. 74; cited: *Steinbuch*, Wirtschaftswoche, p. 74

Thiel, Simon, Siemens Names Merck & Co.'s Peter Loescher New Chief (Update 4), in: Bloomberg.com, available at http://www.bloomberg.com/apps/news?pid=newsarchive&sid=agxq4nZkE.lc&refer=germany visited: March 9, 2011; cited: *Thiel*, Bloomberg

ThyssenKrupp AG, Compliance Program on ThyssenKrupp homepage, available at: http://www.thyssenkrupp.com/de/konzern/compliance.html visited: March 8, 2013; cited: ThyssenKrupp, Compliance Program

Transparency International Deutschland, Regelung der Rechtsnachfolge bei Bußgeldverfahren gegen juristische Personen und Personenvereinigungen und zur Anhebung des Bußgeldrahmens für juristische Personen (§§ 30, 130 OWiG), May 25, 2012; cited: Transparency International Deutschland, 2012

Transparency International, Checkliste für „Self-Audits" zur Korruptionsprävention in Unternehmen, 2007, available at: http://www.transparency.de/fileadmin/pdfs/Themen/Wirtschaft/Checkliste_Self-Audits_TID.pdf visited: February 4, 2013; cited: Transparency International, Checkliste

Transparency International, Schäden durch Korruption oder Warum Korruptionsprävention sein muss, available at: http://www.transparency.de/index.php?id=1186&type=98 visited: February 4, 2013; cited: Transparency International, Schäden durch Korruption

Transparency International, Transparency in Corporate Reporting: Assessing the World's Largest Corporations, 2012, available at: http://files.transparency.org/content/download/459/1891/file/2012_TransparencyInCorporateReporting_EN.pdf visited: February 4, 2013; cited: Transparency International, Corporate Reporting

Tüllner, Jörg, Dynamic Risk Management, Ein Leitfaden, edited by PricewaterhouseCoopers, January 2010; cited: *Tüllner*, PwC Guidance 2010, p.

Twardy Jr., Staney A./Wenner, Daniel E., "One Rouge Worker Can Take an Entire Company Down", National Law Journal, July 16, 2009, available at: http://www.law.com/jsp/cc/PubArticleCC.jsp?id=1202432285270 visited: February 23, 2011; cited: *Twardy/Wenner*, 2009

U.S. v. Siemens Aktiengesellschaft, Statement of Offense, filed December 15, 2008, Cr. No. 08-367-RJL, United States District Court for the District of Columbia, available at: http://www.justice.gov/opa/documents/siemens-ag-stmt-offense.pdf visited: March 9, 2011; cited: *U.S. v. Siemens,* Statement of Offense, mar.

USSC, Report of the Ad Hoc Advisory Group on the Organizational Sentencing Guidelines, October 7, 2003, available at: http://www.ussc.gov/Guidelines/Organizational_Guidelines/advgrprpt/AG_FINAL.pdf visited: November 21, 2011; cited: USSC, Ad Hoc Report, p.

USSC, Supplementary Report on Sentencing Guidelines for Organizations, August 30, 1991, available at: http://www.ussc.gov/Guidelines/Organizational_Guidelines/Historical_Development/OrgGL83091.pdf visited: January 28, 2012; cited: USSC, Suppl. Report, p.

Wagner, Stephen/Dittmar, Lee, The Unexpected Benefits of Sarbanes-Oxley, Harvard Bus. Rev. April 2006; cited: *Wagner/Dittmar*, 2006, p.

Westdeutscher Rundfunk, SPD will Unternehmens-Strafrecht, WESTPOL of September 16, 2012, available at: http://www.wdr.de/tv/westpol/sendungsbeitraege/2012/0916/strafrecht.jsp visited: February 3, 2013; cited: *WDR*, WESTPOL of September 16, 2012

Wildhagen, Andreas, Von Aufpassern eingerahmt, Wirtschaftswoche No. 4 of January 21, 2013, p. 52; cited: *Wildhagen*, Wirtschaftswoche, p. 52

Wittig, Petra, speech „Die strafrechtliche Verantwortung des Geschäftsherrn für Straftaten im Unternehmen", at Ludwig Maximilian Universität München, October 13, 2011, available at: http://www.zaar.uni-muenchen.de/download/event/vortrag/2011/vr_111013_wittig_zf.pdf visited: October 30, 2012; cited: *Wittig*, 2011

Wirtschaftsprüferkammer (WPK), Summaries of qualified or supplemented attestations as attachments to the reports on the supervision of annual auditors of the years 2005 to 2015, available at: http://www.wpk.de/oeffentlichkeit/berichte/berufsaufsicht/#c7506 visited: March 17, 2017; cited: *WPK*, Summaries 2005-2015

Zellner, Wendy et. at., The Fall of Enron, Business Week, December 17, 2001; cited: *Zellner*, 2001